Encyclopedia of
Greco-Roman
Mythology

Encyclopedia of
Greco-Roman
Mythology

Mike Dixon-Kennedy

ABC·CLIO

Santa Barbara, California
Denver, Colorado
Oxford, England

Library of Congress Cataloging-in-Publication Data
Dixon-Kennedy, Mike, 1958–
    Encyclopedia of Greco-Roman mythology / Mike Dixon-Kennedy.
        p.   cm.
    Includes bibliographical references and index.
    1. Mythology, Classical—Encyclopedias.   I. Title.
BL715.D56   1998
292.1'3'03—dc21   98-40666
                                                                                                               CIP

ISBN 1-57607-094-8 (hc)
ISBN 1-57607-129-4 (pbk)

04   03   02   01   00   99   98   10   9   8   7   6   5   4   3   2   1

ABC-CLIO, Inc.
130 Cremona Drive, P.O. Box 1911
Santa Barbara, California 93116-1911

Typesetting by Letra Libre

This book is printed on acid-free paper ∞.
Manufactured in the United States of America.

For my father,
who first told me stories
from ancient Greece and Rome

Contents

Preface

Perhaps more words have been written, and over a longer period of time, about the classical Greek and Roman cultures than any other. The time is right, however, for a book that takes the legwork out of finding reliable information about Greek and Roman beliefs. Obviously this volume cannot cover each and every character, event, and place that may be found in the classical Greek and Roman myths and legends. To do so would involve a great many more words, and thus a great many more pages (and volumes). However, this volume does cover all the major players, places, and events and includes many of the lesser known or more obscure so as to enable you—the reader, the student, the like-minded—quick and relatively painless access to the information.

Additionally, so that further independent research might be facilitated with the minimum of fuss, this book has been researched, to a great extent, from the works of the essential classical authors and Robert Graves, with the remainder of the information coming from original personal research. This approach will enable readers to find further information without having to look for obscure publications and to decide on their own course for further research.

The myths and legends of ancient Greece and Rome have been close to my heart from a very early age, when my father, a classical scholar, would tell me the myths as most fathers would tell their children bedtime stories. I grew up with the stories of Heracles and his amazing adventures, of the perils of Odysseus as he spent ten years traveling home from the Trojan War, of Theseus and the Minotaur, of Perseus and Medusa, of Romulus and Remus, and many, many more. This childhood knowledge led to my starting a database of my own research in the mid-1970s, and since then that database has grown until it now contains a mass of information about each and every world culture, from the Aztecs to Zoroastrianism.

The most extensive part of the database covers the classical cultures of Greece and Rome. I attribute this fact to three main factors. First, these cultures have permeated the very essence that is present-day Europe (indeed, if it had not been for the story of Europa, Europe might have had an altogether different name). Second, the teachings of the classical thinkers have, to a large extent, shaped not only Europe but the rest of the world. Third, a large number of texts from the period have survived into the modern day, along with the archaeology to support them. From all this comes a relative ease of research, and it is that ease, the simplicity with which students or researchers can lay their hands on the information, that has led to a plethora of books (good and bad) on the subject.

Love of mythology and legend leads to research of people themselves, and as a result I have been drawn into those personal histories—their cultures, their wars, their laws, their very existences. This further research has, to a small degree, been incorporated within the pages of this volume so that you can, without having to look further afield, get a feeling for the people and their times—and, I hope, a feeling for the reasons why the classical Greeks and Romans revered their deities as no other civilizations have or possibly ever will. I hope that one day I will be asked to write a history of the classical peoples.

I hope you will find this volume of considerable use. It has taken many painstaking years of solitary research. I have not relied on the contributions of anyone other than myself, so only I can take blame for any mistakes that may have found their way into the text. No doubt some exist; after all, it is only human to make mistakes. However, should you wish to bring these mistakes to my attention, or to make any other points or suggestions, I should only be too happy to hear from you. If you address your letters to me in care of the publisher of this book, I will be sure to receive them.

Finally it remains for me to thank those who have helped to bring this volume to light. First and foremost my thanks have to go to my father, for without his storytelling I might never have developed an interest in mythology. Next I have to thank Robert Neville and everyone at ABC-CLIO, whether in Oxford, Denver, or Santa Barbara, for taking the raw text and turning it into the finished product you now hold, along with Jon Howard for his copyediting. Finally my thanks go to the five people most important to me: my wife, Gill, and our four children, Christopher, Charlotte, Thomas, and Rebecca. I thank them for their patience, love, and understanding as I have immersed myself in my passion—and for keeping the house quiet enough for me to work. One should always remember that even though writing is a solitary occupation, it is the writer's partner who endures the true solitude.

Mike Dixon-Kennedy
Lincolnshire, England

How to Use This Book

This book is organized as a straightforward *A*-to-*Z* encyclopedia, accompanied by two appendices. However, to make the encyclopedia as simple as possible to use, a number of conventions have been adopted.

All entries start with a relevant headword. Where these headwords have alternative spellings, they are included. If the variant spellings are widely different, then each variant spelling is given its own, shorter entry directing you to the main entry. Where the variant is simply a matter of the omission or addition of a letter or letters, then those letters affected are enclosed in parentheses within the headword. For example, the entry Asop(h)us gives two versions, Asophus and Asopus, both of which are acceptable.

Where the variation is a different ending, then the most common or proper is given first. For example, the entry Ereb~os, ~us means that the most common or proper is Erebos, the lesser so Erebus. This variation occurs frequently, particularly among the Greek entries, as the *~os* ending is the original, the *~us* ending a Latinization.

Where the addition is *s* for plural, this too is given in parentheses. Where the difference is a complete word, that word is enclosed in parentheses. This usually occurs when an epithet or surname is a part of the full title but is not commonly used: for example, *Argo (Navis)*.

Italic words in headwords, following standard editorial conventions, indicate the title of a book or poem or the name of a ship or that a foreign language is being used. Words appearing in italics as subheadings give the origin of the myth or legend.

Some headwords contain more than one entry; cross-references may thus include the number for a specific entry, for example, Ajax (1).

Citations

Unusually for a book of this nature you will not find citations following the entries. This omission has not been made to hinder your research. Rather it is because the volumes required to facilitate further research would be endlessly repeated for a huge number of entries, as research was done in a minimum of volumes. Those used to research this volume, and thus those needed for further research, are as follows:

Robert Graves, *The Greek Myths* (2 vols.), Penguin Books
Homer, *Odyssey*
Homer, *Iliad*
Virgil, *Aeneid*

All the other information within the book comes from original personal research. However, each and every volume listed within the bibliography contains essential information to some degree or another, and it is my hope that my restricting my own research to these four essential works will stimulate your own original research. The works by Homer and Virgil are available in a large number of translations and from almost as many publishers. Those I used were published by Penguin Books, but that does not mean that you should not use any translation that is easy for you to locate. Excellent modern translations have been done by Robert Fagles, but it is up to you to decide on the version you wish to put your faith in and use to further your own original research.

Spelling and Pronunciation

Greek names present a minor problem in both spelling and pronunciation. As far as possible I have tried to weed out the inconsistencies, but some will undoubtedly have slipped through. The major problem with these names is that they have undergone centuries of Latinization, and as a result we most commonly use a *~us* ending for Greek names when we should be using the *~os* ending. Thus, we most commonly know the deity Cronos as Cronus, Oceanos as Oceanus, and so forth. Following the headword conventions used within the encyclopedia, I have attempted to ensure that all Greek names have their correct ending, with the subsequent Latinized variant as an alternative version.

Pronunciation of all Greek and Roman names is literal. All letters should be sounded, particularly the ending. Thus, Aphrodite should be pronounced not so she rhymes with light, or night but rather as A-(as in *apple*)-fro-*die*-tea. Likewise, Aeneas should be pronounced E-(as in *each*)-*nay*-ass. A little practice and common sense will lead to the correct pronunciation, but I have always maintained that if you know what or whom you are talking about, that is all that matters.

Greece and Greek Civilization

Due to the enormous diversity of Greek myths and legends, it is hard to envisage a proper understanding of European culture as a whole without some understanding of, or at least familiarity with, these stories as well as how Greek civilization evolved and was subsequently absorbed.

The gods and goddesses of Greek culture derive their origins from a number of widely diverse, largely uncivilized earlier cultures; they were amalgamated, absorbed, modified, and assimilated to produce a highly complex yet also highly organized hierarchy among the deities worshipped within an increasingly civilized society. Their evolution into the pantheon of gods inhabiting Mount Olympus is very closely allied to the emergence of this civilization.

The first farming settlers in Greece, prior to 6000 B.C., brought with them many cults, but most importantly they introduced the ambivalent Mother goddess who presided over land and fertility. This goddess was to evolve through various stages, from the self-created Ge to the far gentler Demeter, who was yet capable of displaying the ferocity of her evolutionary partners.

The first Hellenes appear to have started their influx into Greece with the Minyan and Ionian peoples sometime around 2000 B.C. They came from the north and brought with them the art of horsemanship, and their mastery of horses and wheeled vehicles made their conquest of the region remarkably simple. They penetrated far into the south and well into the islands and branched out to Sicily, southern Italy, and Asia Minor. Becoming excellent navigators as they expanded, they were greatly influenced by the flourishing Minoan culture they discovered on Crete. They brought back features of this cult, and it began to have a considerable effect on Greek mainland culture beginning about 1580 B.C.

Calamity then overcame Knossos, which fell c. 1400 B.C., destroyed either by an earthquake or by the second wave of Hellenic invaders—the Achaeans, who founded Mycenae on the mainland, which probably became the center of civilization in the Aegean world. The site of Mycenae even today indicates the former glory and stature of this city of Agamemnon, which was thought to be purely legendary until it was uncovered by Heinrich Schliemann.

The best view of this Mycenaean culture is through the epic works of Homer, the *Odyssey* and the *Iliad*. The Mycenaean dominance of the Greek world was centered around a feuding aristocracy, a feature well illustrated in the stories of the era, particularly that of the siege of Troy.

Following the collapse of Mycenae, the Dorians, who have obscure origins but are ancestors of the classical Greeks, arrived in Greece c. 1100–900 B.C. These settlers sprang from a great many different prehistoric origins, *dorian* being a generic term for settlers of that era, and as a consequence worshipped a wide variety of deities. They practically destroyed the Mycenaean culture, and their wide diversity in origin led to many wars between the ancient city-states. These are believed by some to have given rise to the greatest epic of Greek mythology, the Trojan War. Traditionally this mammoth enterprise took place c. 1184 B.C., but archaeological evidence suggests that it took place some time before and was an attempt by the Achaeans to capture the Black Sea trade route.

Both Troy and Mycenae have been excavated, most notably by the eccentric millionaire Heinrich Schliemann in the nineteenth century. The excavation of two of the most important city-states of preclassical Greece has revealed a great many facts originally thought to be pure legend and has added an early chapter to the history of Greek evolution, that of the Mycenaean culture that flourished from c. 1550 B.C. to 1200 B.C. Troy itself was considered to be legendary before these excavations took place. The excavated sites of Troy and Mycenae can be visited today, those of Mycenae being the more impressive.

The evolution of myths during the period between the arrival of the Dorian settlers and the eighth century B.C. may be viewed as the reflection of events that are now lost to history. They can all be interpreted beyond face value. Many were probably used for purely political purposes. Others probably embodied traditions from earlier periods. The legend of Theseus and the Minotaur, for example, would seem to reflect the memory of the palace at Knossos, which certainly is labyrinthine in construction, the Minotaur itself mirroring the Minoan bull cult.

From the eighth century B.C. Greek civilization was once again ascendant. Of the many city-states of this time, Sparta and Athens grew to prominence, peaking in the sixth century B.C. One hundred years later, during the fifth century B.C., Athens in particular, but Greece as a whole, led the world in philosophical thought and artistic achievement. In 490 B.C. Athens was triumphant in one of the most famous battles ever fought, that of Marathon.

Here the Persians were defeated, and Greece entered a new Golden Age. Athens's period of predominance and prosperity was, however, short-lived, for Sparta and its allies successfully attacked Athens during the Peloponnesian Wars (460–445 B.C. and 431–404 B.C.). The city-states then engaged in a power struggle that ended with the rise of Macedonia under Philip II. His successor, Alexander the Great, one of the most famous leaders known to history, conquered the Persian Empire and carried Greek influence as far as the River Indus. Upon his death in 323 B.C. his generals quarreled, leaving Ptolemy to conquer Egypt and Seleucus to found a dynasty in Asia.

Worship within Greece was important for uniting the small, constantly squabbling city-states. Major shrines to the deities attracted pilgrims from all over the Greek world and became important markets where business could be transacted under the patronage of the gods. However, ethnic barriers still existed, with certain ethnic groups concentrating their worship at particular sanctuaries. The sanctuary of the Ionians was at Delos; the Dorians favored Mount Olympus.

Prayer became an important way of life, but not in the manner that modern minds would consider it, for by prayer the gods could be persuaded to intercede in worldly matters. Much of Greek worship therefore concentrated on propitiating the gods, with offerings, sacrifices, and libations being made to put the gods in a good mood, for results depended on the mood of the particular deity being called upon. When prayers were answered the gods were rewarded with special offerings such as a new statue or a thanksgiving altar or, in exceptional circumstances—for example, where the help received bordered on the miraculous—the establishment of a new sanctuary. Allegiances also shifted between the worshippers, for if one god would not answer their prayers, ancient Greeks saw no harm in shifting faith to another who might be more receptive. For these people there was no promise of a happy afterlife in return for piety, a situation clearly illustrated within the structure of the Greek Underworld. Here a dead spirit would not even be admitted if the worldly body had not been buried with an *obolos* on the tongue, a coin to pay the ferryman Charon to transport the spirit across the River Styx. No coin, no crossing. To their sensibilities, the situation was that clear-cut.

By the fifth century the Greeks had begun to consider even their Olympian gods insufficient, and many turned to philosophy in an attempt to discover a rationale for life. They also turned to increasingly exotic and mystic cults. Those that offered the worshipper hope for immortality or close union with the god, as well as those that emphasized the exclusivity of their votaries through wild, complex, and sometimes extremely libidinous initiation ceremonies, became increasingly popular. Eleusis became one of the most important centers of worship at this time, and the Eleusinian Mysteries, which centered on the worship of Demeter and Persephone, attracted a huge number of followers.

Greek art also developed in distinct stages, with early attempts at statuary dating from before the seventh century B.C. probably being simple wooden carvings. The seventh to the late sixth century B.C. is known as the Archaic period of Greek art. Here the artistic representations were stiff-standing, striding, or seated figures, their poses copied from cultures that had drifted into Greece and settled there.

However, by the fifth and fourth centuries B.C., the classical period, Greek artists, particularly sculptors, had mastered their medium, having lost all the contrived awkwardness of their earlier pieces. The most important sculptor during the fifth century B.C. was probably Phintias, though Polykeitos was possibly just as famous during his own time. In the fourth century B.C. greater naturalism and individuality developed, particularly in the written word but also in the visual arts. Three sculptors of this period remain perhaps the most outstanding of all ancient Greek artisans: Skopas of Paros, Lysippos of Sikyon, and the great artistic genius Praxiteles of Athens.

The last period of Greek artistic development was the Hellenic, a development that was subsequently to inspire the Romans. Figures became even more naturalistic, but they were more attenuated and less pleasing.

Encyclopedia of
Greco-Roman
Mythology

A

Abaris
Greek

A priest of Apollo who lived without the need for food and rode upon a golden arrow that was given to him by the god.

Abas
Greek

1. A son of Celeus, king of Eleusis, and Metaneira; brother of Triptolemus. He mocked the visiting goddess Demeter while she wandered earth in search of her lost daughter, Persephone, for her eagerness in drinking a whole pitcher of barley water. In return Demeter instantly turned him into a lizard, a form in which he, at least, could survive without water.

2. A great warrior and twelfth king of Argos, the grandson of Danaus, the father of the twins Acrisius and Proetus, and the grandfather of Danaë. He was renowned for a sacred shield, which originally belonged to his grandfather and had the power to subdue revolt.

See also: Acrisius; Argos (1); Danaë; Danaus; Proetus

Abdera
Greek

A prosperous trading port within Thrace whose inhabitants, the Abderans, were synonymous with stupidity, even though the philosophers Democritus and Protagoras lived among them. The city was reputedly founded by Heracles in honor of his friend Abderus, who had been eaten by the flesh-eating mares of Diomedes during the eighth labor of Heracles when the great hero left the monstrous horses in his care.

See also: Thrace

Abderus
Greek

Friend of Heracles who during that hero's eighth labor was left in charge of the flesh-eating mares of Diomedes, a savage king of the Bistones in Thrace, while Heracles repelled the attacking Bistones. He was, however, soon eaten by the monstrous horses. Having killed Diomedes, Heracles threw the king's corpse to his own mares and then founded the city of Abdera to honor his lost friend before driving the mares back to Eurystheus.

Aborigine
Roman

According to some early myths the members of this tribe, allegedly of Greek origin, were the founders of Rome, along with the similar Pelasgians.

A~bsyrtus, ~psyrtus
Greek

The son of Aeëtes and half-brother of Medeä. When Jason and Medeä fled Colchis after Jason and the Argonauts had obtained the Golden Fleece, they took Absyrtus with them. Pursued by the furious Aeëtes, Medeä ruthlessly murdered her young half-brother, cutting him into pieces. These she dropped one by one over the side of the boat so that Aeëtes had to stop to collect them for burial, thereby allowing time to escape.

See also: Aeëtes; Jason; Medeä

Abydos
Greek

An ancient city in Phrygia, Asia Minor, northeast of Troy, on the southern shore of the Hellespont (modern Dardanelles) at its narrowest point opposite ancient Sestos; home of the lover Leander. Nightly he swam the channel to visit Hero on the opposite shore where she was a priestess to Aphrodite. One night Hero's signal lamp blew out during a storm, and Leander drowned. In her grief Hero threw herself into the sea.

The settlement lies near the site of an Athenian naval victory over the Spartans in 411 B.C.

See also: Hero; Leander; Phrygia

Ab~yla, ~ila
Greek

The ancient name for Ceuta, the African site of the Pillars of Heracles (Hercules), located at the far northern tip of Morocco and sometimes identified with Mount Acho. It was supposedly a marker, along with Calpe, the opposite of the Pillars of Heracles, of the western boundary of the known world, beyond which lay the legendary Atlantis. The two pillars were supposedly set in place by Heracles during the course of his tenth labor, but according to some versions of the story they were at one time joined; he drove the channel between them, thereby letting the sea flood in to form the Mediterranean.

See also: Calpe

Academia
Greek

The name of a garden-park on the River Cephisus on the west side of Athens where a gymnastic school was first established. It was named after the hero Academus, hence "academy."

Academus
Greek

Hero who revealed the hiding place of their sister, Helen, to the Dioscuri—Castor and Polydeuces—when they invaded Attica in search of her following her abduction by Theseus. They rescued Helen and took Aethra, Theseus's mother, as her slave. Academus maintained a garden on the west side of Athens, called Academia, where Plato met

with his pupils, the association giving rise to the modern usage of the word "academy."

See also: Dioscuri; Helen; Theseus

Acamantides
Greek

An Athenian tribe named for Acamas, son of Theseus and Phaedra.

Acamas
Greek

The son of Theseus and Phaedra, brother of Demophoön, grandson of Aethra, and the eponym of the Athenian tribe Acamantides. He went with Diomedes to Troy to demand the release of Helen prior to the commencement of the Trojan War. There he fell in love with Priam's daughter, Laodice. They were married and had a son, Munitus, who was killed while hunting at Olynthus. According to some sources Acamas was said to have taken part in the capture of Troy through the stratagem of the Wooden Horse.

After the Trojan War he and his brother, Demophoön, rescued their grandmother, Aethra, who had been enslaved to Helen by the Dioscuri when they rescued Helen from Theseus, who had abducted her many years earlier.

See also: Aethra; Demophoön; Phaedra; Theseus

Acarnan
Greek

The son of Alcmaeon who, with his brother, Amphoretus, dedicated the necklace of Harmonia at Delphi. Later he founded the colony of Acarnania, which became the name of an entire region.

See also: Harmonia

Acarnania
Greek

A state in northwest Greece colonized by Acarnan from Argos; its inhabitants had a reputation for barbarous piracy and for skill with the sling. Later the colony gave its name to the entire region through which River Acheron runs today.

Acastus

Greek

Father of Laodameia, the Argonaut son of Pelias, the usurping king of Iolcos and uncle of Jason. He was cut up and boiled by his daughters after Medeä suggested such an operation would rejuvenate the old man. Acastus expelled both Jason and Medeä, who had title to the throne. As king of Iolcos, Acastus purified Peleus, his companion during the hunt for the Calydonian Boar, for involuntary parricide during the confusion of that epic struggle. However, Acastus's wife falsely accused Peleus of trying to seduce her after he had repulsed her advances, and for this Acastus challenged Peleus to a hunting contest; Acastus stole his magic sword and abandoned him on Mount Pelion. Later, having overcome these difficulties, Peleus married Thetis, fathered Achilles, and avenged himself by killing both Acastus and his treacherous wife.

See also: Acastus; Jason; Laodameia; Medeä; Pelias

Acca Larentia

Roman

1. A Roman goddess originally said to have been a rich prostitute who left her property to the Roman people.
2. Wife of the shepherd Faustulus. She succeeded the she-wolf as nurse to the infants Romulus and Remus after Faustulus found them and brought them home.

See also: Remus; Romulus

Acestes

Greco-Roman

The son of the river god Crimisus and the noble Trojan refugee Egesta; founded Segesta in Sicily. It was either to Segesta or Drepanum that Acestes welcomed Aeneas and the Trojan refugees after the Trojan War.

Achaea

1. Greek

An area in ancient (and modern) Greece of the north Peloponnesos, on the southern border of the Gulf of Corinth. The Achaeans were the dominant society during the Mycenaean period and, according to Homer, took part in the siege of Troy. The Achaeans, or Achaei, were an ancient Hellenic race originating from the north and modeled, with their Nordic features, the "Greek god" type of manly beauty, contrasting with the shorter, swarthier eastern Mediterranean type. The Greeks were collectively referred to by Homer as Achaeans.

The Achaean League of 12 cities allied for mutual protection in the fourth century B.C. and became politically important after 251 B.C., when membership was extended to additional cities, including Corinth and later Sparta. However, the League fell to the Romans in 146 B.C., and the region became incorporated within the province of Roman Achaea.

The region has also been identified with the region known as Akkaia, named after the city-state of Akkad in Mesopotamia.

2. Roman

A province that included all of the southern part of Greece, that is, the same area as Greek Achaea, following the Roman conquest of Corinth in 146 B.C.

See also: Corinth; Mycenaean civilization

Achaean League

Greek

A union between 12 cities within the ancient region of Greek Achaea formed during the fourth century B.C. These cities allied for mutual protection and became politically important after 251 B.C., when membership was extended to additional cities, including Corinth and later Sparta, which they had previously managed to defeat. The League fell to the Romans in 146 B.C.

See also: Corinth; Sparta

Achaei

Greek

A term used to refers to the Achaeans; inhabitants of Greek Achaea.

Achates

Greco-Roman

A character from Virgil's *Aeneid*, the faithful friend of Aeneas, usually called *fidus* (Latin: faithful) Achates or faithful friend. His name was absorbed into Roman mythology, as ancient Romans considered Aeneas to be the founder of their state. His name has become a byword for a faithful companion.

Achelous
Greek

The name of a river in Boeotia—modern Aspropotamo. Also the name of the god of the river, the eldest son of Oceanos and Tethys who, like many gods of rivers and seas, could change his form at will. He battled with Heracles for the right to marry Deianeira, a fight that Heracles won. He had a daughter named Callirrhoë who was married to Alcmaeon after Achelous had purified Alcmaeon for the murder of his own mother, Eriphyle.

See also: Heracles; Oceanos; Tethys

Acheron
Greek

One of the five rivers within the Underworld realm of Hades, across which the souls of the dead were ferried by the ghostly ferryman Charon. The other rivers within this realm were the Styx, which is alternatively given as the river across which Charon ferries the dead souls, Phlegethon, Cocytus, and Lethe. The banks of the river were said to be peopled by the shades of the dead.

Acheron is also the name of a modern river in Acarnania (Epirus), which occasionally runs underground. Near its mouth there was a famous Oracle of the Dead, at Ephyra, where mortals could obtain advice from the gods of the Underworld. Today, some of the machinery used by the priests of this oracle can still be seen.

See also: Charon; Hades

Achilles
Greek

The only mortal son of Peleus, king of the Myrmidones at Phthia in Thessaly, and the Nereid Thetis; he grew up to become one of the leading heroes of the Trojan War and the literary hero of Homer's *Iliad*, the ninth-century B.C. epic account of the siege of Troy,

which probably took place four centuries earlier.

When Achilles was first born his mother, Thetis, prepared to make him immortal. Two versions of her attempt exist: The earlier version has her placing the infant on the fire (as Demeter did with the baby Demophoön); the later, better known version has her dipping Achilles into the River Styx, one of the five rivers of the Underworld. According to the earlier version, Peleus caught her in the act and cried out, thus breaking the taboo that forbids mortals to speak to their mermaid wives. Thetis fled back to her undersea world, and Achilles remained a vulnerable mortal. In the latter story Thetis was undisturbed in her task, but the heel by which she held Achilles did not come into contact with the waters of the River Styx; this point alone remained vulnerable, thus giving rise to an adage still used today, the "Achilles' heel."

Achilles was brought up on the slopes of Mount Pelion by the wise centaur Cheiron, who taught him how to catch animals without nets through native cunning and, so it appears, to eat their entrails uncooked. This latter aspect appears to combine Greek ephebic rites and naturistic savagery, setting the tone for the later life of this impatient and violent hero. Having been taught all the skills of the centaur, Achilles returned to his father and was educated by a tutor, Phoenix, and became renowned for his strength, fleetness of foot, and courage. At about this time Patroclus, the son of Menoetius, arrived at Peleus's court, and the pair became inseparable. Later accounts of their friendship commonly hint at a homosexual relationship, although Achilles had numerous other male and female lovers.

Thetis, able to foresee Achilles' future, knew that he was fated to die at Troy and, in an attempt to save his life, sent him into hiding at the court of Lycomedes on the island of Scyros. Here he was dressed as a girl and hidden among Lycomedes' own daughters, one of whom, Deidameia, later bore Achilles a son, Neoptolemus, or Pyrrhos.

However, Odysseus, accompanied by Nestor and Ajax the Greater, came to the island of Scyros to recruit for the Trojan War and uncovered Achilles' disguise by bringing with him a collection of presents for the girls—

ornaments, jewelry, and beautiful clothes but also a shield and spear. Naturally the youthful Achilles picked the latter and was taken off to Troy, along with the tutor Phoenix and friend Patroclus. He was just 15 years old.

Having set out from Aulis, the Greek fleet, en route to Troy, first landed, mistakenly, in Mysia, where Achilles wounded Telephus, the Mysian king and son of Heracles and Auge, in battle. Apparently Achilles was able to inflict this injury only after Telephus had first repelled the Greeks, but Dionysos caused Telephus to stumble over a vine, thereby allowing Achilles to spring upon him. The wound refused to heal; consulting an oracle, Telephus was told that only the inflictor of the wound could cure it. Dressing in rags, Telephus went as a supplicant to Achilles, who was at a loss to understand the meaning of the oracle. At last he came to realize that the true inflictor of the wound was the spear; by scraping some rust from the spear into the wound Telephus recovered. The Greeks now consulted an oracle and were told that they could not take Troy without Telephus, and in return for being cured of his wound Telephus showed the Greeks the route they should follow.

Following the advice of Telephus, the Greek fleet landed on the island of Tenedos, within sight of Troy. Here Achilles killed King Tenes and his father, Cycnus. Finally proceeding from Tenedos, Achilles became the second to land on Trojan soil and soon distinguished himself as the most courageous and formidable warrior among the Greek host. It was through Achilles that Aeneas entered the war. At first Aeneas had remained sublimely neutral, even though he was the son of Priam's cousin, Anchises. But when Achilles raided his herds on Mount Ida, he led his Dardanian forces against the Greeks and distinguished himself in battle. His mother, Aphrodite, frequently helped him and once carried him out of harm's way when he was wounded by Diomedes; Poseidon, although hostile to Troy, also saved him, this time from Achilles.

For the first nine years of the Trojan War the city of Troy remained impregnable to the besieging Greek hordes, so they contented themselves by sacking neighboring cities and islands allied with Troy. In Thebes, in Cilicia, Achilles killed Eëtion, the father of Hector's

wife, Andromache; in the tenth year of the war, during one such raid on Lyrnessus, Achilles carried off the beautiful Briseis to be his concubine and slave. This single event is the main plot within Homer's classic work, *Iliad*. Chryseis, the daughter of the Trojan priest Chryses, had been taken prisoner and assigned to Agamemnon, but when Chryses came to ransom her he was roughly repulsed. In revenge Apollo sent a plague among the Greek armies, and, on Calchas's advice, Agamemnon reluctantly sent Chryseis back.

Agamemnon, commander in chief of the Greek forces, compensated himself by claiming Briseis. In a furious rage Achilles stormed off to his tent and refused to take any part in further fighting, though some accounts attribute this behavior to the fact that Achilles had fallen deeply in love with Priam's daughter, Polyxena, and that his refusal to fight was an attempt to curry favor with Priam. This led to a series of Greek misfortunes that led Agamemnon to offer to return Briseis to Achilles—an offer Achilles firmly but courteously declined—and Patroclus to go into battle wearing his friend Achilles' armor in an attempt to turn the tide. Rather it is the death of Patroclus at the hands of Trojan Prince Hector, aided and abetted by Apollo, that leads Achilles back into battle, and this redresses events back in favor of the Greeks. At one stage Achilles even fought the River Scamander before he avenged the death of Patroclus by killing Hector in single combat. Still mourning the death of Patroclus, Achilles dishonored Hector's body by tying it to the back of his chariot and dragging it around the walls of Troy three times before concealing it in his tent. He then built a huge funeral pyre for Patroclus and slaughtered 12 Trojan youths on it. Eventually Priam, Hector's father and the king of Troy, led by Hermes, made his way to Achilles' tent under cover of darkness, pleading for the return of his son's body. Achilles relented at such an exhibition of love and devotion, and *Iliad* ends with Hector's funeral.

Some accounts vary these last events, saying that Hector was chased three times around the walls of Troy before being killed, and that Achilles, tying the corpse by the ankles, simply dragged it ignominiously back to the Greek lines. Each morning at dawn he would drag the body three times around the tomb of Patroclus, until at last Priam is led by Hermes to ransom his son's body for burial.

The further battles of Achilles are described in other epics and include his fight with Penthesilea, Queen of the Amazons and the daughter of Otrere and Ares. It is said that Penthesilea and Achilles fell in love at the very moment that he killed her, and his grief over her death was ridiculed by Thersites, until Achilles felled him with a single blow. This action angered Diomedes, a kinsman of Thersites, and he flung the body of Penthesilea into the River Scamander, but it was rescued and given an honorable burial, some accounts saying this was performed by Achilles himself.

Achilles next engaged Ethiopian Prince Memnon in single combat while Zeus weighed their fates in the balance. Achilles won the fight, and at the request of Eos, Memnon's mother, Zeus caused birds, called Memnonides, to rise from his funeral pyre in his honor until they fell back onto it as a sacrifice. They were said to visit the hero's tomb on the Hellespont every year. Achilles was also said to have killed Priam's son, Polydorus, and Troilus, whom he lusted after. Finally the prophecy of Thetis came true, and Achilles was killed by a poisoned arrow shot by Paris, aided by Apollo, who in revenge for the killing of Troilus guided the arrow, which struck his vulnerable heel during a battle near the Scaean Gate. His body was recovered by Odysseus and Ajax the Greater, but the pair quarreled over possession of his armor. Homer, in *Odyssey*, says that Odysseus killed Ajax the Greater, whereas Sophocles, in his tragedy *Ajax*, tells that Ajax was sent mad when he offended Athene after the armor had been awarded to Odysseus, slew the sheep of the Greeks (believing them to be his enemies), and finally killed himself by falling on the sword that Hector had given him. Achilles' ashes were buried along with those of his greatest friend, Patroclus, in a barrow by the sea.

The ghost of Achilles demanded the sacrifice of Polyxena, a duty carried out by Neoptolemus to ensure favorable winds for the Greeks' journey home from the war. Some accounts say that this took place at Troy, others that it happened only after they had reached Thrace and were becalmed.

According to some versions, after his death Achilles was transported by Thetis to the White Island in the Black Sea, where he lived with other fallen heroes, married Helen, and spent his time brooding on how he might have revenge over the Trojans. A local legend tells that he once beset a passing merchant and asked him to bring a particular girl to the island, the last descendant of the Trojans. Thinking that Achilles was in love with the girl, the merchant complied, but as he sailed away from the island he looked back and saw the ghostly image of Achilles tearing the unfortunate maiden limb from limb.

Astronomical: The name Achilles has been applied to one of the asteroids.

See also: Aeneas; Agamemnon; Ajax (1); Briseis; Cheiron; Hector; *Iliad;* Lycomedes; Myrmidones; Neoptolemus; Odysseus; Patrocles; Peleus; Phoenix; Telephus; Thetis; Trojan War

Acho

General

Mountain, also called Mount Hacho, at the far northern tip of Morocco that is sometimes identified as being Abyla (or Ceuta), the southernmost of the Pillars of Heracles (Hercules), the northernmost being Calpe, commonly identified with the Rock of Gibraltar.

See also: Calpe

Acippe

Greek

Offspring of Ares, the god of war, though it may simply be a misspelling of Alcippe (daughter of Ares).

Acis

Greek

The son of a river nymph and, according to some accounts, of Faunus, god of the River Acis (Aci) in eastern Sicily. He loved the sea nymph Galatea but had a rival for her love in the Cyclops Polyphemus. Some accounts say that Polyphemus crushed Acis under a huge rock and that Galatea, in order to release him, turned him into the river that carries his name. Other accounts say that Polyphemus simply threw huge boulders at him—they landed in the sea to become the Isole Ciclopi near Acitrezza—and that Acis turned himself into the river in order to escape.

See also: Faunus

Aconite

1. Greek

According to tradition the aconite flower grew where the saliva of Cerberus, guardian dog of Hades, fell.

2. Roman

Flower sacred to Saturn.

Acontius

Greek

A youth of Chios (Ceos) who, during a festival in Delos, fell in love with the Athenian maiden Cydippe. In order to win her he threw her a quince upon which he had scratched the words, "I swear by the sanctuary of Artemis that I will marry Acontius." Cydippe picked up the quince, and, as the ancients always did, read the message aloud, and was compelled by Artemis to keep her vow.

Acrisius

Greek

Son of Abas, the twelfth king of Argos, and the twin brother of Proetus. After much discussion, following the death of their father, the twins agreed to divide their inheritance. Proetus became the ruler of Tiryns, whose massive walls he built with the aid of the Cyclopes. Acrisius, for his part, ruled uneasily in Argos, for an oracle had foretold that he would be killed by a son born to Danaë, his daughter.

In an attempt to circumvent this prophesy, Acrisius imprisoned Danaë in a brazen dungeon or tower, with doors of brass, but all in vain, for while imprisoned she was visited by Zeus in a shower of gold, and she conceived Perseus. Unwilling to kill his daughter and her son, Acrisius set them adrift in a chest that floated to the island of Seriphos, one of the Cyclades. Here it was found by the sailor Dictys, who took mother and child to the king, Polydectes, who received them hospitably.

Many years later Perseus, having slain Medusa and rescued Andromeda, made Dictys king of Seriphos and returned with Danaë and Andromeda to Argos. Immediately fearing for his life as he remembered the prophecy, Acrisius fled to Larissa, but even this was in vain, for Perseus visited the city and, taking part in public games, accidentally killed his grandfather with a discus he had thrown.

See also: Abas (2); Argos (2); Danaë; Proetus

Acrocorinth~os, ~us

Greek

Also: Akrocorinth

The name specifically applied to the acropolis above ancient Corinth where Aphrodite's fertility cult was established, possibly not until as late as the eighth century B.C.

Acropolis

Greek

The name given to the citadel or central upper fortified part of an ancient Greek city. The most famous one is in Athens; situated on a hill about 250 feet high, it was walled before the sixth century B.C. It originally contained the palace of the first kings of the city and a temple of Athene, thus being used for both religious and defensive purposes. After destruction by the Persians, the Acropolis was rebuilt during the fifth century B.C. with the Parthenon—then containing an enormous statue of Athene; the temple of Athene Nike; the Erechtheum—a shrine to a fabled king of Athens; and the Propylaea, or porch.

Actaeon

Greek

The son of Aristaeus and Autonoë, a daughter of Cadmos, the legendary founder of Thebes. He became a skillful hunter after learning the art of hunting from the centaur Cheiron. One day, however, he was unfortunate enough to come across Artemis bathing naked in a spring with her nymphs, and in anger Artemis turned him into a stag. He was torn to pieces by his own fifty hounds on the slopes of Mount Cithaeron.

See also: Aristaeus; Artemis; Autonoë

Actaeus

Greek

The first king of Athens and grandfather of Agraulos.

Actium

Greco-Roman

A town, now called Akri, and a promontory in Acarnania (opposite modern Preveza on the Gulf of Amurakia) in the Ambracian Gulf of the Ionian Sea, the promontory being the site of a temple to Apollo. A naval battle was fought and won by Augustus (Octavian) on 2 September 31 B.C. against Antony and Cleopatra off of the promontory.

Admete

Greek

The daughter of Eurystheus for whom Heracles had to fetch the golden girdle of the Amazon queen Hippolyte as his ninth labor.

See also: Heracles

Admetus

Greek

King of Pherae in Thessaly to whom Pelias promised the hand of his daughter, Alcestis, provided he came to claim her in a chariot drawn by a lion and a boar. Apollo, who was undergoing a banishment on earth at that time, was working as Admetus's cattle drover and helped him to accomplish this task. At the wedding feast Admetus forgot to sacrifice to Artemis, and realizing that Admetus was doomed, Apollo promised him that he need not die on the day decreed by the Fates provided he could find a willing substitute; he arranged this by getting the Fates (Moirae) drunk and making them promise this condition.

When the time came and Hermes summoned Admetus to Tartarus the only willing substitute that could be found was his wife, Alcestis. There two versions of what happened next. The earlier says that Persephone, queen of the Underworld, refused her sacrifice and sent her back. The latter says that on the day of her death Heracles arrived in Pherae and either prevented Hades, who had arrived in person, from carrying her off or, alternatively, went down into the Underworld and so harried Hades that he was compelled to send her back to her husband.

See also: Fates, the; Pelias; Tartarus

Adonis

Greco-Phoenician

The true Phoenician name of this divinity is uncertain. The name we use is that used by the Greek Philo and seems to derive from the Canaanite *adon*, meaning "lord" or "master." The Greeks adopted the fertility cult associated with Adonis, who was killed by a wild boar, an animal that was sacred to the Syrians. His most important temples were at Byblos, where he was the third most important god, and Paphos. In Byblos, the temple of Astarte celebrated the annual death of Adonis, his reappearance on earth being marked by the blooming of the red anemone. The River Adonis, which flowed through Byblos, ran red with blood each year on the festival of his death. The Greeks worshipped him as a god of vegetation and made him the son of an incestuous relationship between Myrrha or Smyrna and her father, Theias, king of Syria, or Cinyras, king of Cyprus—the girl's punishment for refusing to honor Aphrodite. Under the cover of darkness, her nurse helped her to satisfy her craving, but when her father discovered the trick he tried to kill her. The gods rescued her by transforming her into a myrrh tree. In due course the tree gave birth to Adonis, who was brought up by nymphs.

He was such a handsome youth that Aphrodite became infatuated with him, but he was killed while hunting, either by the jealous Hephaistos, Aphrodite's husband, or by a boar (according to the Phoenician legend) on Mount Idalion or Mount Lebanon. This boar may have been sent, for unknown reasons, by Artemis and may have been Ares in animal form. From his spilled blood sprang the anemone. Aphrodite mourned his passing so keenly that the gods called a dispensation on death, but Persephone, having restored him back to life in Hades, had also fallen for his beauty. To resolve the problem Zeus decreed that Adonis should spend half of the year on earth with Aphrodite, the other half with

Persephone in the Underworld. His death and subsequent resurrection were celebrated in the cult of the winter-spring rhythm of nature. In Athens and elsewhere a spring festival was celebrated by women in which small trays, known as Gardens of Adonis, were planted with lettuces, watered until they sprouted, and then left to wither and die. The rite symbolized the transience of the life of vegetation.

A variant of this story says that Adonis was brought up in the Underworld by Persephone, who refused to return him because of his beauty, this alone being the reason for his spending part of the year above earth, part below. The lengths of time are variously given, the most common being half above and half below, but others say that Adonis spent two-thirds of the year with Aphrodite in the land of the living, one-third in the dark realm of the Underworld.

He seems to have been identified with the Egyptian god of the Underworld, Osiris, and is called Tammuz in the Holy Bible (see Ezek. 8:14).

Astronomical: The name Adonis has been applied to one of the asteroids.

See also: Aphrodite; Byblos; Paphos; Persephone

Adrastus
Greek
King of Argos, the son of Talaus. Adrastus fled to Sicyon, where the king bequeathed him the kingdom when Talaus was murdered during a riot by Amphiaraus, his cousin. He and Amphiaraus made their peace when Adrastus offered the hand of his daughter, Eriphyle, to his cousin, and returned to become king of Argos. Both Polyneices of Thebes, who married Adrastus's daughter Argia, and Tydeus of Calydon, who married Argia's sister, Deiphyle, sought refuge at his court, and together with Capaneus, Hippomedon, Parthenopaeus, the son of Meleager and Atalanta, and Amphiaraus, Adrastus led the expedition of the Seven Against Thebes, even though Amphiaraus, a seer, had prophesied death for all the leaders save Adrastus.

His six companions were killed during the campaign, and Adrastus alone escaped and took refuge in Athens. Ten years later he accompanied a second expedition of the sons of the previous champions (the Epigoni)

against Thebes, and this time they won. Polyneices' son Thersander became king of Thebes, but Adrastus's own son, Aegialeos, was killed, and Adrastus died from his grief at Megara.

In Sicyon Adrastus was venerated as a hero and an object of cult worship until the tyrant Cleisthenes, at war with Athens, transferred the cult to Dionysos.

See also: Amphiaraus; Eriphyle; Seven Against Thebes

Aeacides
Greek
Name given to the descendants of Aeacus.

Aeacus
Greek
The son of Zeus and the nymph Aegina. He was born on the island of Oenone (later to be called Aegina), and to populate it he asked Zeus to turn its numerous ants into people, which were called Myrmidones (or Myrmidons), from *myrmex,* or "ant." He was the father of Telamon and Peleus by Endeis and thus the grandfather of Achilles, who led the Myrmidones to Troy. By the Nereid Psamanthe he was the father of Phocus (Seal). Telamon and Peleus killed their half-brother with a discus, so Aeacus expelled them from Aegina.

He helped Apollo and Poseidon build the walls of Troy; another time, when all of Greece was struck by a terrible drought and the Delphic Oracle pronounced that only the prayers of Aeacus could relieve it, he climbed Mount Panhellenion on his island home of Aegina, prayed to Zeus, and was rewarded with success.

So virtuous was his life that after death he became one of the three judges of the Underworld, along with the brothers Minos and Rhadamanthus.

See also: Achilles; Aegina; Minos; Rhadamanthus

Aeaea
Greek
The island home of the enchantress Circe, daughter of Helios and Perse. When the sole surviving ship of Odysseus landed on the

island, the men he sent to explore were turned into swine by Circe; of these men, only Eurylochus returned unaltered to tell Odysseus the news. Hastening to their rescue, Odysseus was given the plant moly by Hermes, and this vanquished Circe's charms. She restored Odysseus's men and then lavishly entertained them for a year.

See also: Circe; Moly; Odysseus

Aedon

Greek

The daughter of Pandareus, wife of Zethus, king of Thebes, and mother by him of Itylus. Aedon was envious of Niobe, the wife of Zethus's brother, Amphion, who had a family of 12, and she resolved to kill Niobe's eldest son. However, she mistakenly killed her own son, Itylus, and her constant lamentation induced Zeus to change her into a nightingale, whose song still mourns for Itylus.

See also: Amphion; Niobe

Aeëtes

Greek

King of Colchis, father of Medeä and her half-brother, Absyrtus. He had been given the Golden Fleece of the ram that carried Phrixus to safety and had hung the fleece on an oak tree in the sacred grove of Ares, where it was guarded by a sleepless dragon (Draco?).

When Jason and the Argonauts arrived in Colchis on their quest, Aeëtes promised that he would give Jason the fleece provided he could yoke together a pair of fire-breathing bulls with brazen feet, the work of Hephaistos, plough the field of Ares, and sow it with the dragon's teeth left over from the time Cadmos sowed them at Thebes. It was the sorceress-princess, Medeä, who enabled Jason to accomplish this terrible feat. She had fallen instantly in love with Jason and promised to help him if he would swear, by all the gods, to marry her and remain faithful. This he did, and she gave him a fire-resistant lotion that enabled him to complete the task. However, Aeëtes then failed to keep his promise, so Medeä charmed the dragon to

sleep while Jason took down the fleece, and they fled together in the *Argo Navis*.

Aeëtes gave chase, but Medeä, who had taken the young Absyrtus with them, killed and cut up the youth and threw the pieces of his body over the side of the ship. Aeëtes stopped to collect these parts of the corpse for burial, and the fugitives thus escaped.

See also: Colchis; Jason; Medeä

Aegaeon

Greek

Another name for Briareus.

Aegean Sea

Greece

That part of the Mediterranean Sea between Greece and Asia Minor, subdivided into the Thracian Sea in the north, the Myrtoan in the west, the Icarian in the east, and the Cretan in the south. It is connected via the Dardanelles (Hellespont) with the Sea of Marmara.

The Aegean Sea is reputedly named after the legendary King Aegeus who, believing that his son, Theseus, had been killed, threw himself into the sea and drowned.

See also: Aegeus; Theseus

Aegeus

Greek

One of the four sons of Pandion. Originally childless, he consulted the Delphic Oracle, which told him that he should not loosen the spout of the wineskin until he returned to Athens. Unsure about the meaning of this ambiguous oracle, Aegeus consulted Pittheus, king of Troizen (Troezen); in response Pittheus made him drunk and gave him his daughter, Aethra, to lie with, and thus Theseus was conceived. Some said that she was visited on the same night by Poseidon and that Theseus was really the son of Poseidon. Aegeus told Aethra, before leaving for Athens, to bring up her son without revealing the identity of his father; he also said that when the boy was big enough he was to move a certain rock, underneath which he would find Aegeus's sandals and sword as a token of paternity.

When Theseus was of age, Aethra showed him the sandals and sword, an heirloom of Cecrops; Theseus, able to lift the rock, recovered the tokens and proceeded to Athens.

Meanwhile, Aegeus had married Medeä, who had fled to Athens for safety from Corinth, and they had borne a son, Medus. When Theseus arrived Medeä recognized him; jealous for her own son, she attempted to poison him. Luckily Aegeus recognized Cecrops's sword in the nick of time and welcomed his son amid great rejoicing. Medeä fled, taking Medus with her, and Theseus scattered other rivals—the fifty sons of Pallas, nephew of Aegeus, who had hoped to succeed him to the throne.

During the Panathenaic Games a son of Minos, Androgeos, won every contest but was slain at the instigation of Aegeus. In revenge Minos invaded Attica, thus originating the annual tribute of youths and maidens to be fed to the Minotaur. Some accounts number these as high as fifty youths and fifty maidens, but the most common number is seven of each. Theseus determined to end this barbaric tribute and sailed as a member of one year's tribute to kill the Minotaur, promising his father that his ship would carry black sails on its return if he had failed, white ones to signify success. However, Theseus, in his joy at overcoming the Minotaur and returning home to his father, forgot this promise, and Aegeus, seeing the black sails and thinking his son had perished, threw himself from the southwest corner of the Acropolis into the sea, which thenceforth bore his name, the Aegean Sea.

See also: Medeä; Minos; Pandion

Aegial~eos, ~eus
Greek

One of the Epigoni, the son of Adrastus, who was killed before the walls of Thebes during the second campaign of the Seven Against Thebes; upon hearing of his death his father, Adrastus, died of grief in Megara.

See also: Seven Against Thebes

Aegina
Greek

1. Greek Aíyna or Aíyina. An island in the Gulf of Aegina about 32 kilometers (20 miles) southwest of Piraeus with an area of 83 square kilometers (32 square miles). It was originally called Oenone but became known as Aegina after the daughter of Asophus, Aegina, gave birth to Aeacus, the son of Zeus, there.

Commercially very active, this island is distinctive for striking the silver tortoises that were to become the first Greek—indeed, European—coinage sometime in the seventh century B.C. The island also provides a fine scenic setting for the temple of Aphaia (built c. 490 B.C.), a goddess who seems to have been connected with Artemis and was the protector of women, having been pursued from Crete by Minos.

The island was conquered and colonized by Athens in the fifth century B.C., and in 1811 remarkable sculptures were recovered from a Doric temple situated in the northeast of the island (restored by Thorwaldsen) and taken to Munich. Between 1828 and 1829, Aegina was the capital of Greece.

2. The daughter of the river god Asophus who, on the island of Oenone, gave birth to Aeacus, her son by Zeus. Thereafter the island became known as Aegina.

See also: Aeacus

Aegis
Greco-Roman

The aegis is usually attributed to Zeus/Jupiter and was said to have been the sacred skin of the goat Amalthea, which suckled the infant Zeus; the skin was worn by him or occasionally borrowed by his daughter, Athene/Minerva. Later the word came to mean a shield, although usually the aegis was worn whereas the shield was carried. The aegis was possessed with the power to protect friends and terrify enemies.

Later Athene/Minerva was said to have her own aegis, which in this case was a shield patterned with a border of snakes; having a central petrifying image of the head of the Gorgon Medusa, it is said to have been given to Athene by Perseus.

See also: Amalthea

Aegisthus
Greek

The son of Thyestes by his daughter, Pelopia. She stole Thyestes' sword during the rape. She then married Thyestes' brother, Atreus, who was visiting Sicyon and thought that Pelopia was the daughter of Threspotus. When Pelopia gave birth to Aegisthus she abandoned him, but Atreus, believing the boy to be his own, took him in and reared him.

When Aegisthus grew up, Atreus sent him to kill Thyestes, but when the latter saw the sword Aegisthus carried, he recognized it as the one Pelopia had stolen, and the secret was discovered. Pelopia killed herself, and Aegisthus killed Atreus, thus restoring Thyestes to the throne of Mycenae.

During the Trojan War, Aegisthus seduced Clytemnestra, the wife of Agamemnon. Clytemnestra conspired with Aegisthus to kill Agamemnon on his return from the campaign, along with his booty from the war, Cassandra. Clytemnestra welcomed her husband regally on his return, but while he was in his bath she entangled him in a net, and after Aegisthus struck him twice she beheaded him with an axe. Clytemnestra then went out to kill Cassandra, who had refused to enter the palace.

Aegisthus lived in constant fear of vengeance and would have killed Electra had Clytemnestra allowed it. Instead he married her to a peasant who was fearful of consummating their union. Orestes meanwhile took refuge with Strophius, king of Phocis, who had married Agamemnon's sister, and here he formed a friendship with Pylades, the son of Strophius, that became proverbial.

For seven years Clytemnestra and Aegisthus ruled Mycenae, Aegisthus being portrayed as a lustful, cruel, but weak man dominated by Clytemnestra. Electra, burning for revenge, sent constant messages to Orestes, and when he and Pylades were of age, they came secretly to the city and, with Electra's help, killed both Aegisthus and Clytemnestra.

See also: Agamemnon; Atreus; Thyestes

Aegyptus
Greek

Eponym of Egypt, which he ruled along with Arabia; his brother, Danaus, ruled Libya. He suggested a mass marriage between his fifty sons and the fifty daughters of Danaus, the Danaides. Danaus fled with his daughters to Argos, but the fifty sons of Aegyptus followed and demanded the girls in marriage. Danaus consented but ordered each of his daughters to kill her respective husband on their wedding night. Forty-nine of the Danaides followed these orders, but Hypermnestra saved her husband, Lynceus.

See also: Danaides; Danaus

Aemilii
Roman

One of the five powerful families that dominated Rome by the end of the fifth century B.C., the others being the Claudii, Cornelii, Manlii, and Valerii. All five families decisively affected the myths and legends of ancient Rome by altering them to suit their own purposes, thus boosting their power and influence.

Aeneas
Greco-Roman

Son of Anchises, the cousin of King Priam of Troy, and Aphrodite; raised by nymphs until he was five years old. The friend of Achates. Unfortunately, Anchises boasted of Aphrodite's love and was struck blind by a thunderbolt from Zeus. His wife is given as Creusa, a daughter of Priam, and the mother by him of Ascanius, though some sources quote Ascanius's mother as being Lavinia, who Aeneas married after he had arrived and settled in Italy.

At the start of the Trojan War he stayed out of the fighting, but when Achilles raided his herds on Mount Ida he led his Dardanian forces into battle and soon distinguished himself. His mother frequently helped him, once carrying him away after he had been wounded by Diomedes. On another occasion, though hostile to Troy, Poseidon saved him from Achilles, whom he had been urged to challenge by Apollo.

At the end of the Trojan War, having been wounded with his mother, Aphrodite, by Diomedes, he carried his blind father through the Dardanian Gate on his back, thereby escaping. The Romans said that he took with him the Palladium, the one stolen by Odysseus only being a replica, and after seven years he reached Italy.

The tradition of Aeneas's arrival in Italy is of unknown origin, though Homer's *Iliad* makes it clear that he escaped the final sack of Troy. One strong Roman tradition that dates from at least as early as the fourth century B.C. (and later recorded by Q. Lutatius Catulus in *Origin of the Roman Nation*) said that Aeneas betrayed Troy to the Greeks out of hatred for Paris and was thus given safe conduct.

According to Virgil's *Aeneid*, Aeneas, helped by his mother, Venus/Aphrodite, rescued the Penates of Troy, leading his son, Ascanius, and carrying Anchises on his back, thereby escaping the destruction, his first stop being on the slopes of Mount Ida.

Along with a small band of Trojan refugees, Aeneas set sail to find a new home. He consulted the Oracle of Apollo at Delos and was told to seek the country of his ancestors. He originally set sail for Crete since it was said that Dardanos, the founder of the Trojan royal house, had originated there, but he altered course for Italy when the Penates said that Dardanos's first home had been there.

He landed at Epirus, now under the rule of Helenus, and was further advised that when he reached Italy he should seek a white sow and 30 piglets and there establish his city. Additionally he was told by Helenus that further counsel could be had from the Sibyl of Cumae.

When he arrived in Sicily he was welcomed at Drepanum by Acestes; while there his aged father, Anchises, died. Aeneas and his men stayed for a year in Drepanum before setting sail again, but due to the hostility of the goddess Hera/Juno they were driven ashore near the city of Carthage, whose queen was Dido.

Dido immediately fell passionately in love with Aeneas, and Aphrodite/Venus persuaded Hera/Juno to agree to their marriage. However, Dido had vowed on the death of her husband, Sychaeus, that she would never take another husband, and her marriage to Aeneas broke this vow. Divine retribution followed, for Zeus/Jupiter now told Aeneas that he must depart, which he planned to do in secret, but Dido uncovered his plan, failed to persuade him to remain, and committed suicide. As Aeneas once again put out to sea the smoke rose from her funeral pyre.

Their first port of call was once again Drepanum, where Aeneas honored his dead father with funeral games. While there Hera/Juno incited some of his female followers to set fire to four of his five ships; undaunted, and leaving some of his retinue behind, Aeneas resumed his journey.

The remainder of Aeneas's story is distinctly Roman.

At length Aeneas succeeded in landing in Italy, even though his pilot, Palinurus, fell asleep at the wheel and was washed overboard. Immediately Aeneas went to Cumae, and here the sibyl told him to arm himself with the Golden Bough from a wood near Lake Avernus. Then she led him down to the Underworld to consult his father's shade. On the way he encountered the spirit of Dido, but she silently turned her back on him. When he consulted Anchises he learned of the future glory of the city he was to found and its ultimate splendor under the great Emperor Augustus.

Having returned to the upper world Aeneas once again reboarded his ship and sailed on to the estuary of the River Tiber. Here the god of the river appeared to him in a dream and told him that the prophecy of Helenus was about to be fulfilled. Forewarned, Aeneas set out the very next day and soon came upon the white sow and her 30 piglets at the site of the city of Alba Longa, a city his son would found some 30 years later.

In neighboring Laurentum (or Latium), the old Aborigine King Latinus had been told by an oracle that Lavinia, his daughter, would marry a foreigner and so agreed to her marriage to Aeneas. However, Juno now incited the Rutulian Prince Turnus of Ardea to claim that since he was of Mycenaean ancestry the oracle obviously referred to him, not to Aeneas. This was not the only opposition to Aeneas's suit, for Latinus's queen, Amata, also objected. When Ascanius accidentally shot a pet stag, nothing could avert war between the rival factions.

Aeneas now sought the aid of the Arcadian Greek King Evander, who ruled the Palatine Hill. Evander told Aeneas of the visit of Heracles/Hercules to the hill and his slaughter of the terrible man-eating Cacus, son of Vulcan, who had stolen the great hero's cattle.

Salamis (c. 480 B.C.). He visited the court of Hieron I, king of Syracuse, twice and died at Gela in Sicily.

He is widely regarded as the founder of Greek tragedy, and by the introduction of a second actor he made true dialogue and action possible. His first poetic victory was gained during dramatic competitions in c. 484 B.C.; having won some 13 first prizes for tragedies, he was then defeated by Sophocles in 468 B.C. It may have been this defeat that induced him to leave Athens and go to Sicily, although his trial before the Areopagus for divulging the secrets of the Eleusinian Mysteries is also given as a reason for his departure. In Sicily he produced a new edition of his extant *The Persians*, which had originally been staged in 472 B.C.

Aeschylus wrote some 90 plays between 499 B.C. and 458 B.C., of which just seven survive. These are: *The Suppliant Women* (performed about 490 B.C.), *The Persians* (472 B.C.), *Seven Against Thebes* (467 B.C.), *Prometheus Bound* (c. 460 B.C.), and the *Oresteia* trilogy (458 B.C.), his last great victory, which comprises the three works *Agamemnon*, *Choephoroe*, and *Eumenides*.

The genius of Aeschylus is quite peculiar in Greek literature, for he has no equal. The grandeur of his theological perceptions, the providential ruling of the world, the inheritance of sin, and the conflict of rude with purer religion sets him apart from great contemporaries like Pindar, as well as successors like Sophocles.

Aesc(u)lap~ios, ~ius
Greco-Roman
Variant of Asclepios.

Aesc(u)lep~ios, ~ius
Greco-Roman
Variant of Asclepios.

Aeson
Greek
The son of Cretheus, founder and king of Iolcos, and Tyro, who had previous twin sons by Poseidon, Pelias and Neleus, these boys

being adopted by Cretheus when Tyro later married him. Aeson's own son was Jason, whose life was saved only because he was smuggled out of Iolcos and entrusted to the care of Cheiron, the centaur.

When Cretheus died, Pelias imprisoned Aeson, the rightful heir to the throne, and expelled Neleus, thus making himself supreme. However, he promised to surrender the throne if Jason would fetch for him the Golden Fleece, a quest Jason successfully completed with the aid of the Argonauts and Medeä. On their return they found that Pelias had forced Aeson to take his own life, though one tradition says that he was renewed to youthful vigor by the witchcraft of Medeä.

All agree, however, that Medeä took terrible revenge on Pelias. She managed to persuade his daughters (with one exception—Alcestis) to cut up their father and boil the pieces in a cauldron, falsely promising them that this action would rejuvenate him. Acastus, son of Pelias, was horrified by the murder and expelled Jason and Medeä.

See also: Cretheus; Jason; Neleus; Pelias; Tyro

Aesop
Greek
Semilegendary Greek fabulist, who, according to Herodotus, lived in the sixth century B.C. He was variously described as a Phrygian slave, some say of Iadmon, a Thracian, and as a slave in Samos. He was granted his freedom, and as a confidant of King Croesus of Lydia he undertook various unlikely missions. The *Fables* are attributed to him, but no evidence of his authorship exists; in all probability they are a compilation from many sources. They are anecdotal stories centered around animal characters to illustrate some moral or satirical point. They were popularized in the first century A.D. by the Roman poet Phaedrus and rewritten in sophisticated verse in 1668 by La Fontaine.

Aethiopia
Greek
Ethiopia to the ancient Greeks, Cepheus and Cassiopeia having been the rulers.

Aethra

Greek

Daughter of Pittheus, king of Troizen (Troezen). Her first lover was Bellerophon, but she was visited by Poseidon the same night she laid with Aegeus, and as a result she bore the great hero of Attica, Theseus, whom she brought up in secret. When he was of age she showed him the sword of Cecrops and the sandals that Aegeus had left as a sign of his paternity; reclaiming them, Theseus proceeded to Athens.

After the death of Hippodameia, Peirithous and Theseus abducted Helen of Sparta (later to become Helen of Troy), and she fell by lot to Theseus. She was hidden by Aethra in the village of Aphidnae, as she was too young to marry. When the Dioscuri—Castor and Polydeuces—came to Attica in search of her, having been told of her whereabouts by Academus, Aethra was taken captive as a servant to Helen, who she followed to Troy. Following the end of the Trojan War she was rescued by her grandsons, Acamas and Demophoön, the sons of Theseus and Phaedra. When Theseus died she committed suicide.

See also: Bellerophon; Pittheus; Theseus

Aetna

Greco-Roman

Ancient name of the active volcano on Sicily now known as Mount Etna. Two historic eruptions occurred in the fifth century B.C.

Aetolia

Greek

A district of ancient Greece on the northwest shore of the Gulf of Corinth. The Aetolian League was a confederation of the cities of Aetolia, which, after the death of Alexander the Great, became the chief rival of Macedonian power, as well as of the Achaean League.

Aetolus

Greek

The son of Endymion. Originally he was king of Elis, but having accidentally killed Apis during a chariot race he was banished across the Gulf of Corinth, where he conquered the country that became known as Aetolia. He had two sons, Pleuron and Calydon, their names being used for cities within Aetolia.

See also: Endymion

Africus

Greek

The southwest sirocco wind, or the personification of that wind as a deity.

Agamedes

Greek

Son of Erginus and brother of Trophonius. The two sons built a treasury for Hyrieus, a king of Boeotia, but included a secret opening through which they entered to steal the riches within. They also built a temple to Apollo at Delphi. As a reward they lived merrily for six days; on the seventh day they died in their sleep.

Agamemnon

Greek

The most famous of all the kings of Mycenae, the son or grandson of Atreus, king of Argos and possibly Mycenae, and the brother of Menelaus. According to legend, Agamemnon was a descendant of Tantalus, son of Zeus and the nymph Pluto, and father of Pelops, Broteas, and Niobe. Homer tells us that his kingdom comprised all of Argolis and many islands. Both brothers married daughters of Tyndareus, king of Sparta, in whose court they had sought refuge from Thyestes. Menelaus married Helen, and Agamemnon married her half-sister, Clytemnestra, having murdered her first husband, Tantalus, and their baby. He had four children of his own by her, though the given names vary. Attic tragedy gives them as Iphigeneia, Electra, Chrysothemis, and Orestes, whereas Homer gives the first two as Iphianassa and Laodice. Some say that Tyndareus helped Agamemnon to expel Thyestes and so regain his father's throne.

When Helen was abducted by Paris, thus signaling the start of the Trojan War, Menelaus called on his brother to raise a Greek force. The first to rally to his cause was Nestor of Pylos, but Agamemnon also needed more distant allies. In the company of Menelaus and Palamedes, he traveled to Ithaca to persuade Odysseus to join their cause. Others who joined the expedition were Ajax the Greater, the son of King Telamon of Salamis, along with his half-brother, Teucer, the best archer in the whole of Greece. They brought 12 ships with them. Ajax the Lesser, the son of Oileus, king of Locris, also rallied, bringing forty ships. Idomeneos, king of Crete, brought one hundred ships and shared command with Agamemnon. He was accompanied by Meriones.

The huge Greek army assembled at Aulis twice, because the first time they set off they mistakenly invaded Mysia and had to return. As they assembled the second time a hare was torn in half by two eagles, a sign, according to the interpretation of the prophet Calchas, that Troy would be taken, but the Greek forces would be opposed by Artemis, the first sign of this being at Aulis, where contrary winds kept the fleet from sailing. This delay is usually attributed to Agamemnon having killed a hart, thereby gaining the ill favor of Artemis.

Calchas announced that Agamemnon should sacrifice his daughter, Iphigeneia, to appease the goddess. This was duly done, and Agamemnon gained his fair wind—but also the undying hatred of his wife. An alternative version to this story says that Iphigeneia was replaced on the altar at the last moment by a stag as the goddess Artemis carried Iphigeneia away to become her priestess in the barbarian country of Tauris, where she was later rescued by her brother, Orestes.

Agamemnon distinguished himself as commander in chief of the Greek forces at Troy, but his career was marred by a plague sent by Apollo because he had seized Chryseis, the daughter of Apollo's priest, Chryses. To appease Apollo, Agamemnon reluctantly sent the girl back, but to compensate for the loss he claimed Briseis, the concubine-slave of Achilles, thereby precipitating the famous quarrel that is the subject of Homer's *Iliad*.

Achilles, angered by Agamemnon's actions, refused to take any further part in the fighting, and the Trojans soon began to gain the upper hand. Some say Achilles' refusal stemmed from his falling in love with Polyxena, a daughter of Priam, and was simply an attempt to curry favor with the father.

With Achilles sulking in his tent and the Trojans now getting the better of the Greeks, Agamemnon was only too pleased to grant a truce so that Menelaus and Paris might settle their quarrel in single combat. But with Paris losing, Aphrodite carried him away, and the battle restarted. Still the Trojans held the upper hand, and in alarm Agamemnon attempted to induce Achilles back into the fray by offering to return Briseis. His offer was refused.

Instead, Patroclus led the Myrmidones while wearing Achilles' armor, and it was his death at the hands of Hector that led Achilles back into the battle. He made his peace with Agamemnon, who at last returned Briseis to him. Now the battle went in the favor of the Greeks once again.

The decisive action of the Trojan War was the stratagem of the Wooden Horse, supposedly implemented by Odysseus. Leaving behind only Sinon and the massive horse, the Greek forces burned their encampment and sailed to the island of Tenedos, from which they returned on Sinon's signal after the horse had been taken inside the city by the unsuspecting and foolish Trojans.

Following the successful completion of the campaign, Agamemnon returned home, accompanied by Cassandra, a Trojan prophetess he claimed as booty. Here he found his wife's vengeance awaiting him. While he had been away she had taken Aegisthus as her lover, and together they planned to murder both him and Cassandra. Greeting her returning husband regally, she trapped him in a net while he was taking a bath, and after Aegisthus had struck him twice she beheaded him with an axe. Then Clytemnestra disposed of Cassandra. Orestes fled to Phocis, from whence he later returned to wreak his vengeance. Electra and Chrysothemis remained under the tyranny of Aegisthus and Clytemnestra.

According to Pausanias, the ancient kings of Mycenae were buried within the walls of the citadels. In 1876 Heinrich Schliemann uncovered the grave circle, including its magnificent golden grave goods. Among these was the famous funerary mask that he hailed as the "face of Agamemnon." The identification has never been substantiated, but it is romantic and unforgettable by its association with the king who was the leader of the most famous and best known of all Greek myths and legends—the Trojan War.

See also: Achilles; Atreus; Briseis; Menelaus; Mycenae

Aganippe

Greek

A fountain at the foot of Mount Helicon in Boeotia that was sacred to the Muses, hence they subsequently were called Aganippides. It was thought to inspire those who drank from it. Another fountain, Hippocrene, also sacred to the Muses, was known as Aganippis.

See also: Muses, the

Aganippides

Greek

Name used to refer to the Muses following their association with the sacred fountain of Aganippe.

Aganippis

Greek

Epithet added to the fountain of Hippocrene because it was sacred to the Muses, who were also known as Aganippides through their association with another fountain, Aganippe.

Agathyrsans

Roman

According to Virgil's *Aeneid,* a tribe living in Thrace.

Agave

Greek

Daughter of Cadmos, legendary founder and king of Thebes, and his wife, Harmonia, daughter of Ares and Aphrodite. She was the sister of Autonoë, Ino, Semele, Polydorus, and Illyrius and the mother of Pentheus. When Pentheus resisted Dionysos he was driven mad and, when caught spying on the orgiastic worship of the god, was torn to pieces by the Maenads, or Bacchae. Among these frenzied worshippers were his own mother, Agave, and her sisters, Autonoë and Ino. Agave bore his head back to Thebes in triumph, believing it to

be that of a lion. When she recovered her senses she fled from Thebes to Illyria. Some said that her murder of Pentheus was Dionysos's revenge on her, for she had spread the rumor that her sister Semele had had a liason with a mortal, meaning Dionysos was not the son of Zeus but of a man.

The legend of Agave is used by Euripides in his play *Bacchae.*

Agenor

Greek

1. Son of Poseidon and king of Phoenicia who, according to common tradition, was the father of Europa and Cadmos by his wife, Telephassa. When Zeus, in the form of a bull, carried off Europa, Agenor sent Cadmos in search of her.

2. The son of the Trojan Antenor and Theano.

Aglaia

Greek

"The Bright One"; the third of the three Charities or Graces. A bestower of beauty and charm.

See also: Graces

Aglauros

Greek

1. The wife of Cecrops.

2. The daughter of Cecrops. The infant Erichthonius was entrusted to her and her sisters.

Agraulos

Greek

The granddaughter of Actaeus, the first king of Athens. She threw herself to her death from the Acropolis because an oracle demanded a self-sacrifice for Athens.

See also: Actaeus

Agrigento

Greek

The site, on the island of Sicily, of two outstanding fifth-century B.C. temples dedicated to Hera and Concord and situated on either side of a scenic ridge.

Aias
Greek

The Greek form of the more common, Latinized Ajax.

Aid~es, ~oneus
Greek

Another name for Hades—the realm, not the god.

Aíyina
Greece

Modern Greek name for the island of Aegina; also Aíyna.

Aíyna
Greece

Alternative modern Greek name for the island of Aegina; also Aíyina.

Ajax
Greek

1. The son of Telamon, king of Salamis. Known as Ajax the Greater or Great Ajax to distinguish him from Ajax the Lesser, he was a courageous fighter who boasted that he did not need the help of the gods and brought 12 ships and his half-brother, Teucer, the best archer in all Greece, to the Trojan War. He was distinguished by his huge shield.

He accompanied Odysseus and Nestor when they went to Scyros to recruit for the Trojan War, the occasion when Achilles was discovered disguised as a girl among the daughters of King Lycomedes. Ajax the Greater was second only to Achilles among Greek heroes of the war.

Sometime during the first nine years of the war, he and his company raided the Thracian Chersonesus, and in Teuthrania he killed King Teuthras and took his daughter, Tecmessa, as booty. During the tenth and final year of the war he and Hector fought in single combat until nightfall. Then, remembering the friend-

ship between their forefathers, they exchanged gifts, Hector giving Ajax the Greater a sword and receiving a purple baldric. When Patroclus was slain by Hector, Ajax joined Menelaus in retrieving the body.

Following the death of Achilles he and Odysseus rescued the body, and Ajax treated Achilles' son, Neoptolemus, as his own. But then he and Odysseus fought for possession of Achilles' fabulous armor, destined by Thetis for the bravest of the Greeks. However, the Trojan prisoners named Odysseus the bravest, and the arms were duly awarded. Homer, in *Odyssey*, says that Odysseus killed him, whereas Sophocles in his tragedy *Ajax* tells that Ajax was sent mad when he offended Athene after the armor had been awarded to Odysseus, slew the sheep of the Greeks (believing them to be his enemies), and finally killed himself by falling on the sword that Hector had given him. A long dispute then ensued over his burial rights in light of what he had done.

Another story, one that conflates Ajax the Greater with his namesake, says that the argument was not over the arms of Achilles but over the Palladium, a statue of Athene, that Odysseus is said to have stolen from within the city of Troy while it was under siege.

From the blood of Ajax the Greater a flower sprang up that bears on its petals the letters "AI"—an exclamation of grief as well as the initial letters of Aias, the Greek form of Ajax. His tomb in Salamis was venerated by the straightforward Dorians who, like Pindar, did not approve of the trickery of Odysseus.

2. The son of Oileus, king of Locris, he took 40 ships to the Trojan War and was referred to as Ajax the Lesser or Little Ajax to distinguish him from Ajax the Greater, so called because he was not the equal of Ajax the Greater. As a soldier he was expert in throwing the spear and second only to Achilles for fleetness of foot; he was portrayed as a charmless, god-defying man.

With the fall of Troy he committed sacrilege against Athene by ravishing Cassandra in the temple of Athene beside the statue of the goddess, then carrying off both the girl and the goddess's image. Cassandra was claimed as booty by Agamemnon, and on his journey home Athene sent a violent storm to drown him. Poseidon, however, saved Ajax the Lesser but was overruled, and so destroyed with his trident the rock upon which Ajax had taken refuge.

Three years after the return of the heroes from the Trojan War a series of bad harvests in Locris were attributed by the Delphic Oracle to the continuing anger of Athene. As expiation she demanded two Locrian maidens every year, the first to be sent being killed by the Trojans. This custom continued into historic times, but by then the girls were simply made, on arrival on Trojan soil, to run the gauntlet from the beach to the temple. If they managed to escape death by beating they spent the rest of their lives in the shrine of Athene, unmarried.

See also: Achilles; Hector; Odysseus; Telamon

Ajax
Greek

Tragic play by Sophocles in which he tells of the fate of Ajax the Greater following his dispute with Odysseus over the armor of Achilles. Sophocles tells that Ajax was sent mad when he offended Athene after the armor had been awarded to Odysseus, slew the sheep of the Greeks (believing them to be his enemies), and finally killed himself by falling on the sword that Hector had given him. A long dispute then ensued over his burial rights in light of what he had done. Homer simply states that Odysseus killed him.

See also: Ajax (1)

Akri
Greco-Roman

The modern name for the town of Actium.

Akrocorinth
Greek

Also: Acrocorinthos

Variant of Acrocorinthos, the acropolis above ancient Corinth that was the site of the fertility cult of Aphrodite.

Alba Longa
Roman

A city of ancient Latium sited near Lake Albano or Alban Lake, about 19 kilometers (12 miles) southeast of Rome. Today it is known as Castel Gandolfo. According to legend it was founded c. 1152 B.C. by Ascanius, the son of Aeneas, 30 years after Aeneas had found the white sow and her 30 piglets on that site, fulfilling the prophecy of Helenus. It was ruled by Ascanius's descendants for nearly three centuries. However, Amulius then usurped the throne of his brother, Numitor, who was exiled. Numitor's daughter, Rhea Silvia, was forced to become a Vestal Virgin, but she was raped by Mars and bore the twins Romulus and Remus. It was the head of the Roman League and the mother city of Rome, as from here Romulus and Remus set out to found the new city.

Destroyed c. 600 B.C., the city was never rebuilt, though the area was appropriated for the villas of the aristocracy.

See also: Aeneas; Ascanius

Alban Lake
Roman

A lake near the site of ancient Alba Longa that was drained by the Romans, according to legend, to ensure the fall of the city of Veientia, this condition being first pronounced by a Veientine soothsayer, then confirmed by the Delphic Oracle.

Alban Mount
Roman

The mount around which, during the twelfth century B.C., the colonies of immigrants into Latium were centered. The towns of Alba Longa, Aricia, Ardea, and Lavinium gradually arose in the vicinity.

Albano, Lake
Roman

Alternative name for Alban Lake.

Alcaeus
Greek

The father of Amphitryon who was the husband of Alcmene.

Alcestis

Greek

The sole daughter of Pelias, king of Iolcos, who was not persuaded by Medeä's ruse that the action of cutting up Pelias and boiling the parts in a cauldron would rejuvenate the aging king; she thus did not participate in her father's murder. She married Admetus, king of Pherae, and gave her life in return for her husband being allowed to live. It was said that she was returned to the land of the living, either because Persephone refused the self-sacrifice, or because Heracles rescued her.

See also: Medeä

Alcides

Greek

A name given to Heracles when considered as the reputed grandson of Alcaeus.

Alcin(i)ous

Greek

The king of the paradisiacal Phaeacia (often identified with Corfu) and the father of Nausicaa. He had given sanctuary to Jason and Medeä when they were being pursued by the angry Colchians. When Odysseus, on his way home from the Trojan War, was found shipwrecked on the shore of the island of Scheria by Nausicaa—the raft he was sailing had been wrecked by Poseidon and his life saved by Leucothea and Athene—he welcomed the marooned hero to his palace, entertained him regally, and then furnished a ship that conveyed Odysseus home to Ithaca in an enchanted sleep. The ship was turned into a rock by Poseidon en route, this rock often being identified with Pondikonisi (Mouse Island) south of the Canoni Peninsula.

See also: Jason; Medeä; Nausicaa; Odysseus

Alcippe

Greek

The daughter of Ares whom Halirrhothius, a son of Poseidon, attempted to rape. Her father killed Halirrhothius and was placed on trial by the other gods. He was, however, acquitted when he gave the full facts behind the murder; the place of the trial became known as the Areopagus.

See also: Halirrhothius

Alcmaeon

Greek

Son of Amphiaraus and Eriphyle, and father of Acarnan and Amphoretus. He slew his own mother, Eriphyle, in revenge for her vanity and deceit toward both his father and himself, having been bribed by Polyneices' son to urge him and his brother, Amphilochus, to lead a second attack against Thebes, just as she had been bribed to force Amphiaraus to accompany the first attack of the Seven Against Thebes.

Driven mad and pursued for his matricide by the Erinnyes, he fled to the king of Psophis, Phlegeus (or Phegeus), who purified him and married Alcmaeon to his daughter, Arsinoë; he gave her, as a wedding gift, the robe and necklace of Harmonia. However, uncured of his madness he was soon forced to flee and was again purified, this time by the river god Achelous, who married Alcmaeon to his daughter, Callirrhoë, who soon demanded the necklace and robe of Harmonia, knowing them to be in his possession. Alcmaeon dared to return to Psophis and obtained the sacred items from Phlegeus on the pretext of taking them to Delphi. Phlegeus uncovered the true reason for Alcmaeon's return and had his sons kill him, before he himself sent the ill-fated treasures to Delphi.

In Euripides' *Alcmaeon* the hero encountered Tiresias's daughter, Manto, and had by her Amphilochus and Tisiphone, who he gave to Creon of Corinth to rear; he later bought daughter Tisiphone back as a slave.

See also: Harmonia; Seven Against Thebes

Alcmaeon

Greek

Play by Euripides in which Alcmaeon encountered Tiresias's daughter, Manto, and had by her Amphilochus and Tisiphone, who he gave to Creon of Corinth to rear; he later bought daughter Tisiphone back as a slave.

Alcmen~e, ~a

Greek

Wife of Amphitryon (Amphitrion), son of Alcaeus. She refused to consummate her marriage until her brothers, who had been killed by the Taphians, had been avenged by her husband. While Amphitryon was away from Thebes fighting the Taphians, Zeus visited her in the form of Amphitryon, telling her of his victory over the Taphians, and lay with her, supposedly halting the sun for a day to extend his night with her. The true Amphitryon returned the following day, and the confusion that followed is the subject of many comedies.

Nine months later the boastful Zeus pronounced that he was about to become the father of a son, who would be called Heracles or "glory of Hera" and become the ruler of the house of Perseus. Jealous Hera made Zeus promise that any son born that day to the house of Perseus would become its king. Having made the promise, Hera then brought on the birth of Eurystheus, a grandson of Perseus, and delayed the birth of Heracles. Eventually Alcmene bore twin sons, Heracles, the son of Zeus, and Iphicles, Amphitryon's son, who was one night younger due to the time difference between conceptions. In fear of Hera, Alcmene exposed Heracles, and in error Hera nursed him, thus conferring immortality upon him. Later he was returned to Alcmene.

When Eurystheus acceded to the throne of the house of Perseus, he was determined to remove the threat of Alcmene, Heracles, and his children and tried to expel them from Greece. In Athens they found protection, and when Eurystheus attacked the city he was resisted by Theseus or his sons, Demophoön, Iolaus, and Hyllus. Following the self-sacrifice of Macaria, Heracles' daughter, as demanded by an oracle, Eurystheus was defeated by either Hyllus or Iolaus and dispatched by Alcmene.

Following Amphitryon's death—and by then living in Boeotia—Alcmene was married to Rhadamanthus, who proved so just a ruler that he later became one of the three judges of the Underworld.

See also: Amphitryon; Heracles; Iphicles

Alcyone

Greek

Also: Halcyone.

1. One of the daughters of Atlas and Pleione. Along with the six sisters—Celone, Electra, Maia, Merope, Sterope, and Taygeta—she was placed in the heavens in the star cluster known as the Pleiades, or "seven sisters," of which she is said to be the leader.

Astronomical: One of the seven stars of the Pleiades cluster in the constellation of Taurus. For a full description see Pleiades.

2. The daughter of Aeolus, god, demigod, or king of the winds. She married Ceyx, the son of the morning star. Conflicting reasons are given for the pair's transformation into birds. Apollodorus says that the gods, enraged with their marital bliss or because they began calling themselves Zeus and Hera, caused the transformation. Ovid, however, tells a different story. Returning from a voyage, Ceyx was shipwrecked and drowned; Alcyone, finding her dead husband's body, threw herself into the sea in her grief. In sympathy the gods changed them both into birds, though here again there is some difference between the birds. All versions agree that Alcyone herself was changed into a kingfisher, and some accounts say that Ceyx was also turned into a kingfisher; others say the male bird was a gannet.

Following the transformation Zeus forbade Aeolus to release the winds and decreed that the seas should remain calm for seven days before and after the winter solstice while Alcyone was hatching her eggs. This has led to modern usage of the phrase "halcyon days."

See also: Aeolus; Ceyx; Pleiades

Alcyoneus

Greek

One of the 24 giant sons of Gaia (Ge) with serpents' tails. Alcyoneus led the brothers' attempt to avenge the imprisonment of their other brothers, the Titans, and attacked Olympus. Among the 24 were Porphyrion, Ephialtes, Mimas, Pallas, Enceladus, and Polybutes. Only following a tremendous battle, both in Olympus and on earth, were the giants defeated by the gods, who were helped by a magic herb of invulnerability that had been found by Heracles (who appears here out of normal chronological order many years before his supposed birth). Heracles always gives the giants the final blow.

See also: Gaia; Titan

Alecto

Greek

One of the Furies or Erinnyes born from the drops of blood that fell on Mother Earth when Uranos was castrated by Cronos. They were described as winged daughters of earth or night, having serpents for hair. Their purpose was to punish unnatural crime, such a parricide. Later they became known euphemistically as the Eumenides or "well-meaning," the name said to have been given them after the acquittal of Orestes. Originally there may have been many sisters of Alecto, but later writers only name two other Furies, Tisiphone and Megaera.

Having serpent hair they are often confused with the three Gorgons: Medusa, Euryale, and Stheno.

See also: Erinnyes; Eumenides; Furies

Aleus

Greek

King of Tegea and father of Auge and, through her seduction by Heracles, grandfather of Telephus.

Alexander

Greek

A name sometimes used to refer to Paris.

Alexander Romance

Greek

Possibly dating from the third century B.C. the *Alexander Romance* is a remarkable work that builds on the travels of Alexander the Great and brings him into contact with many strange beasts. In it he is made the son of the last Pharaoh of Egypt, Nectanebo, and during his travels he meets the Queen of the Amazons and also visits the legendary Queen Candace of Meroe.

He marches through a land of perpetual darkness in search of the Water of Life, a quest in which he is beaten by his cook or his daughter. He explores the depths of the seas in a diving bell and also ascends to the heavens in a basket borne aloft by four eagles. He visits the abodes of the gods as well as the Oracle of King Sesonchosis of Egypt at the extreme eastern limit of the world.

The recurring theme of all these adventures is Alexander the Great's anxiety over learning the date of his death and his attempts to obtain immortality. As a twist he meets with a group of Indian Brahmans, and they request the latter as a boon from him, suggesting that at some stage he had succeeded in his quest. Finally human-headed birds persuade him to give up his futile search, and he dies at Babylon of poison.

Alexander the Great

Greek

King of Macedonia between 356 B.C. and 323 B.C. and the conqueror of the large Persian Empire. The son of King Phillip II of Macedonia and Queen Olympias, Alexander was born in Pella and was educated by the great philosopher Aristotle. Alexander first saw fighting in 340 B.C. at the age of 16, and two years later (338 B.C.) at the battle of Chaeronea he contributed to the victory with a cavalry charge. His father was murdered when Alexander was 20, and the Macedonian throne and army passed into his more than capable hands.

First he secured his northern borders and, in 336 B.C., suppressed an attempted uprising in Greece by capturing Thebes. In 334 B.C. Alexander and his armies crossed the Dardanelles for their campaign against the huge Persian Empire, and at the River Granicus, close to the Dardanelles, he won his first victory. In 333 B.C. he defeated Persia's King Darius at Issus and then set out for Egypt, where he was greeted as Pharaoh, founding the coastal city of Alexandria. Meanwhile, Darius had assembled a half-million men for a final battle, but in 331 B.C. at Arbela on the Tigris, with just 47,000 men, Alexander drove the Persians into retreat.

Following his victory over the Persians he stayed a month in Babylon before marching to

Susa and Persepolis. In 330 B.C. he marched on Ecbatana (now Hamadán, Iran), and soon afterwards he learned that Darius was dead. He founded colonies at Herat and Kandahar in Afghanistan, and in 328 B.C. he reached the plains of Sogdiana. It was here that he married Roxana, the daughter of King Oxyartes. The mighty continent of India now lay before him, and he marched forth to the Indus. Near the River Hydaspes (now Jhelum) he contested one of his fiercest battles ever against the raja Porus. At the River Hyphasis (now Beas) his armies refused to continue, and reluctantly he retreated back along the Indus and along the coast. In 324 B.C. they reached Susa, where Alexander married his second wife, Darius's daughter, and ended his reign as a recluse, dying in Babylon of malarial fever.

In the centuries that followed he became a legendary figure in Greek tradition (said to originate from Alexandria), his exploits being described in every language of the Orient and medieval Europe. The basis of these accounts is the Greek *Alexander Romance* that possibly dates from the third century B.C.

In this extraordinary work, Alexander is made the son of the Pharaoh Nectanebo, the last pharaoh of Egypt. Using as his theme the travels of Alexander beyond the known limits of the world, the author brings Alexander into contact with many weird and savage beasts and equally strange races of men—pygmies, lions with six legs, hairy women with wings, and so on. He meets the Queen of the Amazons and also visits the legendary Queen Candace of Meroe.

He marches through a land of perpetual darkness in search of the Water of Life but is beaten in the quest by his cook or his daughter. He explores the depths of the seas in a diving bell and also ascends to the heavens in a basket borne aloft by four eagles. He visits the abodes of the gods as well as the Oracle of King Sesonchosis of Egypt at the extreme eastern limit of the world.

The recurring theme of all these adventures is Alexander's anxiety over learning the date of his death and his attempts to obtain immortality. As a twist he meets a group of Indian Brahmans, and they request the latter as a boon from him, suggesting that at some stage he had succeeded in his quest. Finally human-headed birds persuaded him to give up his futile search, and he dies at Babylon of poison.

Medieval Greek sources add further details to the image of the seeker of universal knowledge, making him a sage of supreme knowledge. He turned his daughter—the only contender for having beaten him to the Water of Life—into a mermaid, and thereafter all mermaids acknowledge him as their father (or as spiritual brother in some sources). In Macedonia he is thought to rule the whirlwinds, and in modern Greek his name has been conflated into Megalexandros.

Even now, if caught by storms while at sea, sailors may see the mermaids appear. They ask the sailors, "Where is King Alexander the Great?" The correct reply: "Alexander the Great lives and rules and keeps the world at peace." Provided the correct answer is given, the storms will subside and the sailors may sail on in safety.

In medieval romance, Alexander the Great even appears in the Arthurian legends. In one such romance, *Perceforest*, he is made an ancestor of Arthur himself as the result of an affair with Sebille, the Lady of the Lake in his time.

Alipes
Greek
The winged sandals worn by and therefore an attribute of Hermes, whose other attributes were the petasus and the caduceus.

Alma Mater
Roman
A title given to the goddess Ceres.

Aloeus
Greek
The husband of Iphimedeia who adopted her sons by Poseidon, the gigantic Ephialtes and Otus, who thenceforth became known as Aloeidae.

Alo(e)idae
Greek
The gigantic sons, Ephialtes and Otus, of Poseidon by Iphimedeia who later married

Aloeus, hence Aloeidae. At the age of nine the two boys captured and imprisoned Ares for 13 months in a brazen vessel. They then vowed to outrage Hera and Artemis, and in their attempt to reach the heavens they piled Mount Pelion on Mount Ossa. Artemis tricked them into going to Naxos, where they hoped to encounter her, but she disguised herself as a doe and as she leaped between them they accidentally killed each other. Hermes then released Ares, and the spirits of the Aloeidae were committed to Tartarus, where they were tied with vipers back-to-back to a pillar for all time.

See also: Ephialtes; Otus

Alpheus
Greek

The god of the River Alpheus, the principal river of Elis in the Peloponnesos, and the son (like all the river deities) of Oceanos and Tethys. Falling in love with the nymph Arethusa, he pursued her under the sea to the Sicilian island of Ortygia, where she rose as a spring or fountain. It was believed that the waters of the Alpheus in fact flowed through the sea, not mingling with the salt waters, to rise mixed into the waters of the spring Arethusa at Syracuse.

See also: Oceanos; Tethys

Althaea
Greek

The wife of her uncle, Oeneus, king of Calydon, and mother of Deianeira, Gorge, and Meleager. At Meleager's birth the Fates pronounced that he would die when a brand that was then on the fire was consumed. Althaea immediately seized the brand, extinguished it, and then hid it safely away. When Meleager grew up he took part in the Calydonian Boar Hunt and succeeded in slaying the beast that was ravaging the countryside. However, he quarreled with his fellow huntsmen, Althaea's brothers, when he gave away the head of the boar to Atalanta, who, it is said, he loved. During the violent argument Meleager killed his uncles, and in revenge Althaea immediately threw the brand onto the fire to fulfill the prophecy of the Fates. When the brand burned out Meleager died, whereupon Althaea took her own life.

See also: Fates, the; Oeneus

Amalthea
Greek

It is usually said that Amalthea was the goat that nursed the infant Zeus while he was being hidden by Rhea in the Dictaean Cave on Crete from his father, Cronos. As a reward the goat was subsequently placed in the heavens as the constellation Capricorn(us), one of her horns becoming the Cornucopia or "horn of plenty," sometimes called the Horn of Amalthea, her skin becoming the aegis of Zeus.

However, some accounts vary by saying that Amalthea was the name of a nymph into whose care Zeus was placed by Rhea, and that it was she who gave Zeus the she-goat to act as a wet nurse. As a child Zeus was then said to have given Amalthea one of the goat's horns, promising her that it would always be miraculously filled with fruit.

See also: Zeus

Amata
Roman

The wife of Latinus and mother by him of Turnus. When her son met Aeneas in single combat she hanged herself, convinced that her son was dead before he actually died.

See also: Aeneas; Turnus

Amazon
Greek

The Amazons were a race of legendary female warriors living near the Black Sea beyond the River Thermodon in Scythia, at least according to Herodotus. Some said they came from the Caucasus and then settled in Asia Minor.

They were said to keep their men segregated on an island and only mated with them in order to produce children, the male infants either being killed or sent back to be raised with the men, whereas the girls were kept and raised to become warriors. This matriarchal society was certainly believed to have a real existence, and they are usually portrayed in fifth-century B.C. art in Scythian tunics and leggings.

Many heroes fought them, though they knew that if they were defeated they would be enslaved by them. Among the heroes was Bellerophon. One of the 12 labors of Heracles was to capture the girdle of the Amazon Queen Hippolyta (Hippolyte). It was either on this occasion or later that Theseus, who accompanied Heracles, carried off the Amazon Antiope, though another tradition says that he did not carry off Antiope but her sister Hippolyta, and it was she that became the mother, by Theseus, of Hippolytus. In revenge the Amazons attacked Athens but were defeated by Theseus and his army. Some accounts say it was not until after the Amazons had been routed at Athens that Theseus took Hippolyta captive.

When the Amazons came to the aid of Troy during the Trojan War, they were led by the beautiful Penthesilea, the daughter of Otrere and Ares. She was killed by Achilles, and it is said that at the very moment that he plunged his sword into her body they fell in love with each other.

Alexander the Great was said to have conquered the Amazons and to have met their queen, Thalestris, but, according to some versions, she failed to seduce him. The Amazons were also said to have built the original temple of Artemis at Ephesus.

Later accounts of this race of warrior women derived their name from a false etymology of *A-mazon* or "breastless," leading to the popular claim that they cut off one breast, usually their right, to facilitate their use of the bow.

The term *Amazon* has come to depict any tall, strong, fierce, and attractive woman, or a female warrior.

See also: Achilles; Bellerophon; Penthesilea

Ambologera
Greek
Epithet of the goddess Aphrodite meaning "she who postpones old age."

Ambrosia
Greco-Roman
Greek: "immortal." The food of the gods in both Greek and Roman mythology, which is often equated with honey. It was supposed to confer immortal life, and thus the gods kept their immortality by bathing in it, rubbing it into their skin, or simply eating it. Without ambrosia a god became weakened, and any mortal who ate it became strong and immortal. Nectar, the wine of the gods, was drunk with it.

Ammon
Greco-Egyptian
A variant of Amon that appears to have been a slight corruption used by the classical Greeks in an attempt to give the deity a more Greek complexion.

In this form he was identified with Zeus, and Alexander the Great claimed him as his father, therefore being represented on coins wearing the ram's horns that characterized the god. The *Alexander Romance*, however, says that Alexander the Great was the son of the last pharaoh, the wizard Nectanebo, who came to his mother in the depths of night wearing a long robe and the horns of a ram.

The temple of Amon at Siwa Oasis in Libya was the site of the famous Oracle of Ammon. Herodotus tells us that he was told by the priests of Thebes that two priestesses were abducted by the Phoenicians, one being sold in Libya, the other in Greece. These priestesses, the Theban priests said, were the founders of divination in both countries and set up the original oracles there.

Amor
Roman
An alternative name for Cupid, the god of love, and the equivalent of the Greek Eros.

Astronomical: The name Amor has been given to one of the smaller asteroids.

Amphiaraus
Greek
The father of Alcmaeon and Amphilochus, he killed his uncle, Talaus of Argos, drove out Adrastus, and so became king. However, to quiet their quarrel, Amphiaraus married Eriphyle, Adrastus's sister, who was given the authority to arbitrate any future disagreement

between the two cousins. When Adrastus was preparing the expedition of the Seven Against Thebes, Amphiaraus, in his role as seer, prophesied the death of all the leaders save Adrastus himself, and so refused to go. However, Polyneices, whose claim to the throne of Thebes was the reason for the expedition, bribed Eriphyle by giving her the famous necklace of Harmonia, and she arbitrated that Amphiaraus should accompany the expedition. He duly went but made his sons swear to kill Eriphyle in revenge.

The seven leaders—hence the expedition's name, the Seven Against Thebes—were Adrastus, Amphiaraus, Polyneices, Tydeus, Capaneus, Hippomedon, and Parthenopaeus. The death at Nemea of another member of the party, Opheltes, was interpreted as another omen that they were doomed to failure.

In the battle at Thebes, Capaneus was struck by Zeus's lightning while attempting to scale the walls. Hippomedon, Parthenopaeus, and Polyneices were all killed. Melanippus was mortally wounded by Amphiaraus, who was then pursued by Periclymenus. Zeus threw his thunderbolt and caused the ground to open up and swallow Amphiaraus, chariot and all. At his loss Adrastus lost heart, and the expedition was defeated.

However, Amphiaraus reemerged from earth near Oropos in Attica, where he was revered in classical times as a healing and oracular deity. His sanctuary, the Amphiareion, became an important place of pilgrimage, especially for the sick.

See also: Polyneices; Seven Against Thebes

Amphiareion
Greek

The sanctuary of Amphiaraus at Oropos in Attica where he was revered as a healing and oracular deity in classical times. The sanctuary became an important place of pilgrimage, especially for the sick.

Amphilochus
Greek

Son of Amphiaraus, brother of Alcmaeon, and a seer like his father. He joined his brother on the second expedition of the Seven Against Thebes. Following that successful campaign against Thebes he traveled overland to Colophon and joined with the seer Mopsus in founding the city of Mallus, but they killed each other in a fight for its possession.

See also: Seven Against Thebes

Amphion
Greek

Son of Antiope by Zeus and twin brother of Zethus. Antiope was divorced by her husband, Lycus, who then married Dirce, who treated his first wife cruelly. She then married Epopeus of Sicyon. The twins were exposed at birth on Mount Cithaeron, where they were brought up either by a shepherd or cattlemen. In maturity they learned what had happened and returned to Thebes to take their revenge by killing Lycus and Dirce, who was tied to the horns of a bull and her body thrown into a fountain that thenceforth bore her name. They then took possession of Thebes.

Next they fortified the lower part of the city below the Cadmea, Amphion moving his share of the stones by playing so skillfully on the lyre given him by Hermes (increasing the number of strings on the instrument from four to seven) that they moved into place of their own accord. The brothers then jointly ruled the city, Zethus marrying Thebe, eponym of the city, and Amphion marrying Niobe; when Niobe's seven sons and seven daughters were killed by Apollo and Artemis, and she turned by Zeus into a stone on Mount Sipylus, Amphion also died, either by his own hand or that of Apollo.

See also: Antiope; Dirce; Lycus; Thebes; Zethus

Amphitheia
Greek

The wife of Autolycus and mother by him of Anticleia, thus the grandmother of Odysseus.

Amphitrite
Greek

Daughter of Nereus to whom Poseidon turned his attentions after having been told that his first intended wife, Thetis, would bear a son greater than his father. At first

Amphitrite rejected Poseidon's advances and his proposal of marriage, fleeing to Atlas. However, Delphinos pleaded Poseidon's suit so eloquently that Amphitrite changed her mind and allowed Delphinos to bring her back. In gratitude for his help, Poseidon placed Delphinos in the heavens. Through her marriage to Poseidon, Amphitrite became the goddess of the seas, receiving a wreath of roses from the goddess Aphrodite at her wedding.

Her offspring included Triton and, sometimes, the Nereides, though the latter are usually said to be the children of Nereus, her father. Poseidon, however, was a philanderer like his brother, Zeus, and had many other children by mortals and divinities. When he paid court to the nymph Scylla, who was particularly hateful to Amphitrite, it was said that it was Amphitrite who turned her into a monster with six barking heads and 12 feet.

Another of Poseidon's children, by Aethra, was Theseus, who on his way to Crete dived into the sea to retrieve a ring that Minos had thrown overboard to challenge his parentage. While underwater Amphitrite entertained him at her court among the Nereides, welcoming him as a son of Poseidon and giving him the wreath of roses she had received from Aphrodite.

See also: Nereus; Thetis

Amphitr(y)oniades
Greek
A name given to Heracles in recognition of his putative father, Amphitryon.

Amphitr~yon, ~ion
Greek
Grandson of Pelops and son of Alcaeus. He married Alcmene, the daughter of Electryon, king of Tiryns and Mycenae, sending her home to Thebes to await him while Electryon sent Amphitryon to retrieve from Elis some cattle stolen by the Teleboae or Taphioi who lived on the Taphian Islands off Acarnania. The Taphioi or Taphians had also killed Alcmene's brothers. However, upon returning from Elis with the stolen cattle

Amphitryon accidentally killed Electryon (though some say this act was deliberate), and Electryon's brother Sthenelus became king and expelled Amphitryon.

Now Amphitryon returned to Thebes, but his wife refused to consummate their marriage until he had avenged the death of her brothers. First Amphitryon sought the help of King Creon of Thebes, who agreed to give assistance on the condition that Amphitryon first rid Thebes of a vixen sent by Hera to ravage Termessus. This vixen was in fact uncatchable, but Zeus turned it and the hound Amphitryon had sent after it into stone.

Now Amphitryon went to the Taphian Islands, but while he was there avenging the deaths of his wife's brothers the daughter of King Pterelaus of the Teleboae, Comaetho, fell in love with Amphitryon and betrayed her father by plucking out the single golden hair that gave him his immortality. Amphitryon was victorious but executed Comaetho for her treachery.

While away Zeus visited Alcmene in the form of Amphitryon and lay with her, even holding the sun still for a day to extend his night of pleasure. Amphitryon returned the following day, and by their consummation of the marriage Alcmene bore twins, as was usual in such cases, the half-divine Heracles and the mortal Iphicles.

Amphitryon, accompanying Heracles, was killed in battle against the Minyans, and after his death Alcmene married Rhadamanthus.

See also: Alcaeus; Alcmene; Pelops; Thebes

Amphoretus
Greek
Son of Alcmaeon and brother of Acarnan. The two brothers dedicated the necklace of Harmonia at Delphi.

See also: Harmonia

Amulius
Roman
The king who usurped the throne of his brother, Numitor, whom he exiled; also ordered that the Vestal Virgin mother of Romulus and Remus, Rhea Silvia (the daughter of Numitor), be imprisoned and the twins

drowned. However, his instructions to drown the children were ignored, and the babies were left on the riverbank underneath the Ruminalis fig tree. There they were suckled by a she-wolf until found by the shepherd Faustulus, who took them home to his wife, Acca Larentia. Later, when grown up, the twins assassinated Amulius and replaced Numitor on his throne.

See also: Numitor; Remus; Romulus

Amyclae

Greek

One of the most sacred sites in the Peloponnesos, a sanctuary a few miles from Sparta that was consecrated to Hyacinthos.

Amycus

Greek

King of the savage Bebryces on the island of Bebrycos in Bithynia. He was the son of Poseidon and an expert boxer. Amycus contrived to kill all strangers that came to his kingdom by challenging them to a boxing match, but when the Argonauts landed on Bebrycos, his challenge was met by Polydeuces, who killed him.

See also: Bebrycos

Amymone

Greek

One of the fifty daughters of Danaus and thus a Danaid. When she was sent to find water in arid Argolis she began to chase a deer, but when she cast her javelin she disturbed a satyr, who in turn pursued her. Coming to her rescue, Poseidon hurled his trident at the satyr, frightening it away. Having laid with Amymone he removed his trident from the rock into which it had stuck, and the spring of Lerna gushed forth. This spring is alternatively known as Amymone after her.

See also: Danaus

Amythaon

Greek

The father of the seer Melampus and also of Bias.

Anadyomene

Greek

Epithet of Aphrodite as she was said to have risen out of the sea foam (Greek: rising).

Anatolia

The Asiatic part of modern Turkey, often used in ancient writing and legends to describe Asia Minor.

Ancaeus

Greek

1. The son of Lycurgus of Arcadia. He was responsible for killing the Calydonian Boar and accompanied Jason as one of the Argonauts.

2. The son of Poseidon and one of the Argonauts. He took the helm of the *Argo Navis* after the death of Tiphys.

Anchises

Greco-Roman

King of Dardanus on Mount Ida, the descendant of Tros (eponym of Troy), grandson of Ilus, nephew of Laomedon and cousin of Priam. When Zeus grew tired of Aphrodite's mockery of the other gods and goddesses, whom she caused to fall in love with mortals, Zeus caused her to fall in love with Anchises. Appearing to him on Mount Ida in the guise of a beautiful mortal maiden, Aphrodite lay with Anchises, but when he discovered her true identity he was extremely frightened. However, Aphrodite, already knowing she was pregnant from their union, reassured him and promised to get nymphs to raise the boy until he reached the age of five, after which he would be returned to Anchises, who was to say that the boy was the son of a nymph. This boy, his son by Aphrodite, was Aeneas.

When Anchises was drunk he boasted of his union with the goddess, and as a result Zeus struck him with a thunderbolt and left him lame in one leg and blind. However, some say that it was Aphrodite herself, not Zeus, who inflicted these injuries on Anchises. Following the Trojan War he was carried on the back of his son, Aeneas, to safety through the Dardanian Gate; he accompanied his son and the other Trojan refugees as far as Drepanum in Sicily, where he died, although the Arcadians said that Anchises was buried at the foot of Mount Anchision in Arcadia.

In Roman mythology he became the father of Aeneas by Venus.

See also: Aeneas; Tros

Anchision
Greek

An Arcadian mountain at whose foot the Arcadian people said Anchises, the father of Aeneas, was buried.

Ancus Mar~cius, ~tius
Roman

The legendary third successor to Romulus as king, thus the fourth king of Rome, ruling from 640 B.C. to 616 B.C. and succeeding Tullus Hostilius. He was the son of the daughter of Numa Pompilius and regarded as the founding ancestor of the Marcian family. He is spoken of as the first king to bridge the River Tiber and to colonize Ostia; Virgil, unlike other writers, speaks of him as a braggart and a murderer. He was succeeded by Tarquin the Elder.

Ancyra
Turkey

Ancient name, subsequently Angora, of Ankara, the capital of Turkey. It is the site of a temple dedicated by the Galatians to Rome and Augustus that contained the Monumentum Ancyranum (still extant), a marble inscription of the exploits of Augustus, duplicating the bronze tablets ordered to be cut in Rome by the emperor.

Andraemon
Greek

The husband of Gorge and father of Thoas who succeeded Oeneus as the king of Calydon.

Androcl~es, ~us
Roman

Traditionally a legendary Roman slave who ran away from his tyrannical and cruel master into the African desert, where he hid in a cave inhabited by a lion from whose paw he removed a thorn. Later, after being recaptured and brought back to Rome, he was sentenced to face a lion in the arena. There the lion he faced held out his paw to him, recognizing him as his old friend who had removed the thorn, and refused to harm Androcles. Due to this he was freed by Emperor Tiberius, some say along with the lion, which he subsequently took around Rome on a lead. His story was told by Aulus Gellius in the second century A.D.

Androg~eos, ~eus
Greek

The son of King Minos of Crete and wife Pasiphaë. Two versions give the account of his death. In the first he was killed while fighting the Bull of Marathon, which Minos attributed to Athenian treachery. In the second, having won every contest in the Panathenaic Games (or Panathenaea), he was slain at the instigation of Aegeus. In any event, the revenge of Minos remains the same. For the death of his son Minos demanded the yearly tribute of seven youths and seven maidens from Athens to be fed to the Minotaur.

See also: Minos; Minotaur; Pasiphaë

Andromache
Greek

Daughter of Eëtion, king of Thebe in Cilicia, faithful wife of Hector, the eldest son of Priam, and mother by him of Astyanax. After the fall of Troy, when the baby Astyanax was flung to his death from the walls of the city, she was awarded to Neoptolemus, son of Achilles, and bore him three sons. Either after Neoptolemus's death or when he married Hermione, Andromache married Hector's brother, Helenus, who had fled to Epirus. She bore him a son, and her descendants became the rulers of Epirus.

See also: Hector

Andromache
Greek

Tragic play by Euripides first performed c. 426 B.C. In it Hermione, wife of Neoptolemus, seeks revenge on Andromache, her husband's concubine, blaming her for her own childlessness, but she fails in her attempt to murder Andromache and her son. Neoptolemus is murdered by Orestes, one of Hermione's former suitors.

Andromeda

Greek

The beautiful daughter of Cepheus, king of Aethiopia (Ethiopia), and Queen Cassiopeia. When Cassiopeia boasted that Andromeda was more beautiful than the Nereides, and when they had complained of this to Poseidon, that god sent a sea monster, Cetus, to ravage the land. According to the Oracle of Ammon the only way to appease Cetus was to sacrifice Andromeda to it.

Chained naked to a sea cliff, Andromeda was rescued when Perseus, on his way home from slaying Medusa, rode overhead on Pegasus. Learning her plight from Cepheus and Cassiopeia, he offered to rescue Andromeda provided she became his wife. Her parents quickly agreed. Perseus then flew over Cetus on Pegasus and disposed of the monster in one of two ways. Either he simply felled it with his sickle, the same sickle he had used to behead Medusa, or he simply held the head of the Gorgon aloft, and Cetus was turned to stone.

However, Cepheus and Cassiopeia were reluctant to keep their promise to Perseus, saying that Andromeda had already been betrothed to Phineus, her uncle, who, with his followers, arrived at Perseus and Andromeda's wedding and attempted to seize the bride. Perseus overcame them by holding the head of Medusa aloft, and they all turned to stone.

Leaving Cepheus's court, the newly married couple traveled to Seriphos, where they found that Danaë and Dictys had been forced by Polydectes to take refuge in a temple. Once again Perseus used the head of Medusa and turned the king and his court to stone. Now Perseus gave the head to Athene, who placed it in the center of her aegis.

Perseus and Andromeda, in the company of Danaë, then traveled to Argos before proceeding to jointly found Mycenae with her husband. After her death the gods placed her in the sky as the constellation that bears her name, along with husband Perseus, father Cepheus, and mother Cassiopeia, the latter being placed upside down to humiliate her for her boastfulness.

Astronomical: Andromeda is a major constellation of the northern celestial hemisphere that is visible in the autumn. Its main feature is the Andromeda galaxy; the star Andromedae (Alpheratz) forms one corner of the famous Square of Pegasus. The Andromeda galaxy is 2.2 million light-years away and is the most distant object visible to the naked eye, also being the largest member of the Local Group of Galaxies, being about 200,000 light-years across.

The constellation Andromeda lies at approximate celestial coordinates: right ascension 23h to +3h, declination +20° to +50°.

See also: Aegis; Cassiopeia; Perseus

Androphonos

Greek

Literally "man killer," a name used for the goddess Aphrodite and reflecting older aspects of her cult.

Anius

Greek

The son and priest of Apollo in Delos whose three daughters had been dedicated to Dionysos. As a gift Dionysos gave the three girls the power to produce corn, oil, and wine at will, and when the Greek host sailed for Troy, Anius and his daughters were taken along to keep the fleet abundantly supplied with provisions.

Ankara

Turkish

Modern name for Ancyra, the capital of Turkey.

Anna

Roman

According to Varro (d. 27 B.C.), Anna was the sister of Dido, and it was she, not Dido, who killed herself for the love of Aeneas.

See also: Dido

Anna Perenna

Roman

Minor fertility goddess; noted similarity in name to the Hindu goddess Annapurna.

Anosia

Greek

Literally "the unholy," a name used for the goddess Aphrodite and reflecting older aspects of her cult.

Antaeus

Greek

The giant son of Poseidon and Ge, king of a part of Libya. He liked to wrestle with strangers and was always able to win, for contact with his mother, Earth, kept his strength constant. He used the skulls of those he defeated to roof a temple. However, Heracles, returning from his eleventh labor, learned his secret and, lifting him clean off the ground, killed him by crushing him in a bear hug.

Anteia

Greek

Daughter of Iobates, king of Lycia, and the wife of Proetus, king of Tiryns. When Bellerophon fled to the court of Proetus after killing Bellerus, Anteia fell in love with him, but when he refused her advances she falsely accused him to her husband of trying to seduce her. Reluctant to kill his guest, Proetus sent Bellerophon to Anteia's father, Iobates, with a letter requesting that the bearer be put to death.

See also: Iobates; Proetus

Antenor

Greek

The wisest of the Trojans and father of Laocoön. He was sent by Priam to demand that Telamon return Hesione, but the scornful refusal of the Greeks was later stated as one of the causes of the Trojan War. It was Antenor who courteously entertained the envoys Menelaus, Odysseus, and Palamedes just prior to the start of the Trojan War when they came to request the return of Helen, but even though Antenor advised that she should be returned, the Trojans refused.

When the war was going against the Trojans, Priam sent Antenor to sue Agamemnon for peace, but out of hatred for Deiphobus Antenor conspired with the Greek leader as to how the Greeks might secure the Palladium, and for this task it was decided that Odysseus should gain entry to Troy disguised as a filthy runaway slave.

Following the admission of the Trojan Horse into the city it was Antenor who gave the word for the warriors hidden inside to emerge and take the city from within. For helping the Greeks, Antenor, his wife Theano, and all their children were spared from slavery or death and were said to have sailed to the west coast of the Adriatic Sea, founding Venice and Padua.

Anteros

Greek

A personification of the "love returned," that is, the son of Aphrodite and Ares and the brother of Eros. Anteros's altar at Athens was erected by the friends of Timagoras in remembrance of him and his love for a beautiful boy, Meles. Meles had asked Timagoras to jump from the Acropolis to prove his devotion, which he did without hesitation. In remorse, Meles followed his example.

Anticle(i)a

Greek

The daughter of the wily thief Autolycus and mother of Odysseus by either Laertes, king of Ithaca, or Sisyphus, with whom she had earlier lived. She died of grief while Odysseus was away at the siege of Troy, but her shade appeared to Odysseus as he endured the difficulties while returning home after the success of the Trojan War.

See also: Odysseus

Antigone

Greek

The daughter of Oedipus by his own mother, Jocasta, and the sister of Eteocles, Polyneices, and Ismene. When her father went into exile she accompanied the blind man as his guide, later to be joined by Ismene, returning to Thebes only after his death. Later, when her brother, Polyneices, was killed fighting with the Seven Against Thebes, a rebellion aimed at dethroning her brother, Eteocles, she went against the orders of the new king, Creon, and buried Polyneices' body at night, thus complying with the wishes of the gods.

Two versions exist of Antigone's fate after she defied King Creon. In the first, the subject of the tragedy *Antigone* by Sophocles, Creon ordered that she be immured as a punishment, but rather than face burial while alive she hanged herself; Haemon, the son of Creon to whom she was betrothed, committed suicide alongside her. In the second version, Creon turned Antigone over to Haemon for punishment, but he smuggled her away, and she later bore him a son. When Creon refused to forgive them, Haemon killed both himself and Antigone.

See also: Creon; Jocasta; Oedipus

Antigone
Greek

Tragedy by Sophocles that was written c. 411 B.C. In it Antigone buries her dead brother, Polyneices, in defiance of the Theban king, Creon, but in accordance with the wishes of the gods. As punishment Creon imprisons Antigone in a cave, but after receiving warning that he has defied the gods, he goes to the cave, where he finds that Antigone has hanged herself.

See also: Creon

Antiloch(us)
Greek

The gallant son of Nestor who, too young to sail with the original expedition from Aulis, joined his father when old enough. He was killed by Memnon while defending his father. After his death he dwelled with other heroes on the White Island or the Islands of the Blessed.

See also: Memnon

Antin(i)ous
1. Greek

The leader of the unruly mob of potential suitors who besieged Penelope while Odysseus was away fighting in the Trojan War. When Odysseus returned he used the great bow of Eurytus to kill Antinous.

2. Roman

A beautiful Bithynian youth from Claudiopolis who became the favorite of Emperor Hadrian and his companion on all his journeys. He was made a god by Hadrian after his drowning in the River Nile, near Besa, in A.D. 122, perhaps by suicide. Hadrian also founded the city of Antinopolis on the banks of the Nile in his memory.

See also: Odysseus; Penelope

Antiope
Greek

1. A queen of the Amazons who was carried off by Theseus when he accompanied Heracles to their country. According to another tradition, Theseus did not take Antiope but instead took her sister, Hippolyte; by whichever Amazon queen he took Theseus became the father of Hippolytus.

2. The daughter of Nycteus of Thebes, or of the River Asophus. She was of such beauty that she attracted the attentions of Zeus, who made her pregnant, but she had to flee from her father's anger and then married Epopeus, king of Sicyon. Out of shame Nycteus killed himself, but not before making his brother, King Lycus of Thebes, promise to punish her. At Eleutherae Antiope gave birth to twin boys, Amphion and Zethus, who were exposed on Mount Cithaeron and subsequently raised by cattle herders.

Returning to Thebes, Antiope was imprisoned by Lycus and cruelly treated by his wife, Dirce. Some accounts say that Antiope was Lycus's first wife, divorced by him for her infidelity with Zeus, and it was Dirce's jealousy of her that caused her to be treated badly. However, one day Antiope was miraculously freed, and just as Dirce was about to have her tied to the horns of a wild bull, two young men turned up and recognized Antiope as their mother. These youths were Amphion and Zethus, and they inflicted on Dirce the punishment she had planned for their mother, her body being thrown into a fountain that thenceforth carried her name.

Then they killed Lycus and seized the city of Thebes.

Dionysos, who favored Dirce, now drove Antiope mad until she was cured by Phocus, son of Ornytion. Antiope married him, and when they died they were buried together at Tithorea in Phocis.

See also: Amazon; Dirce; Hippolyte; Lycus; Theseus

Aphaia
Greek

A goddess whose purpose, characteristics, and attributes are not clear but to whom a temple was built at Aegina c. 490 B.C.

Apharetidae
Greek

Names used to collectively refer to Idas and Lynceus, as they were the children of Aphareus.

See also: Idas; Lynceus

Aphareus
Greek

The king of Messene and father of Idas and Lynceus, who were hence called Apharetidae.

Aphidnae
Greek

The village in Attica where Theseus hid the maiden Helen in the care of his mother; here she was rescued by the Dioscuri, Castor and Polydeuces, after Academus revealed the hiding place to them.

See also: Dioscuri; Theseus

Aphrodite
Greek

One of the 12 elite Olympian deities, Aphrodite was the goddess of love (especially sensual), feminine beauty, marriage, and fertility and was the patroness of prostitutes. Identified by the Romans with Venus, though Venus's origins were markedly different, as she was originally the patroness of vegetable gardens. It was not until the cult of Aphrodite proper had been introduced into Rome around the end of the third century B.C. from Sicily that Venus took on her attributes and legends. However, the Julian family claimed their descent from her through her grandson, Aeneas. Her cult was of eastern origin, seemingly Anatolian, her counterpart being the orgiastic Astarte/Ashtoreth of Phoenician Syria or Ishtar of Babylon, though it is also thought that she may have derived from a Minoan goddess. The Greeks recognized her oriental nature, and Herodotus states that her oldest shrine was at Ashkelon. In Roman times she was worshipped in Syria in the form of a fish as the Syrian Goddess.

Older aspects of her cult survive in her various names. She was Apostrophia, or "she who turns herself away"; Androphonos, "man killer"; Tymborychos, "gravedigger"; Anosia, "the unholy"; Epitymbidia, "she upon the tombs"; and, above all else, Pasiphaessa, "the far shining queen of the Underworld." The Athenians regarded her as the oldest Moirae— the senior of the Fates, and as goddess of love Aphrodite also collected special epithets, like Kallipygos, or "she of the beautiful buttocks"; Morpho, "the shapely"; and Ambologera, "she who postpones old age."

Her worship in Hellenic Greece was derived from the earlier worship of the Great Goddess of pre-Hellenic times. She was worshipped as a fertility goddess in Paphos, her chief cult center, from where the Phoenicians took her worship to Cythera, the supposed place of her birth (hence her surname, Cytherea). It was not until possibly as late as the eighth century B.C. that her fertility cult was established on the Acrocorinthos (Akrocorinth) above Corinth. There was a similar sanctuary on Mount Eryx in Sicily, the cult being introduced into Rome sometime around the end of the third century B.C. In all these places Aphrodite was served by young girls who emphasized her cult of sacred prostitution, a trait reflected in the myth of the daughters of Cinyras, who became her votaries. In other Greek states her worship focused more on her role as protectress of the city. In Athens during the Arrephoria festival two maidens carried phallic symbols to her shrine, thus demonstrating that she still functioned as a fertility goddess.

According to Hesiod, Aphrodite was born out of sea foam that had been fertilized by drops of blood after Cronos emasculated Uranos. She rose naked from the sea and stepped ashore from a scallop shell near the island of Cythera off the southern Peloponnesos, then passed on to Paphos in Cyprus. She was therefore also sometimes regarded as the goddess of the sea and seafaring. However, Homer makes Aphrodite the daughter of Zeus and Dione. The Greeks explained her name as deriving from *aphros,* or "foam," seemingly concurring with Hesiod in respect of her origin, though this is not a "traditional" Olympian origin, as it would make her more ancient and therefore more essential than Zeus.

When Olympus was attacked by the monstrous Typhon, created by Ge in revenge for the destruction of the giants, Aphrodite fled, with the other gods, to Egypt in the form of a fish, the other deities taking other animal forms.

She loved many gods and legendary mortals and in Homer's *Odyssey* is the wife of the smith god Hephaistos, though in Homer's *Iliad* his wife is said to be Charis. On one occasion Aphrodite was caught in bed with her lover, Ares, by an invisible net that Hephaistos had made. This story, and how Hephaistos exposed the pair to the ridicule of the other gods, is told in a poem known as the "Lay of Demodocos" that was incorporated into the eighth book of Homer's *Odyssey.* One of her children by Ares was Harmonia. Aphrodite also bore sons to Poseidon, bore Priapus to Dionysos, and later stories say that she bore Hermaphroditos to Hermes and Eros to either Hermes, Ares, or Zeus, as well as the deities known as Phobos and Deimos, their most likely father also being the god of war, Ares.

She loved the mortal Adonis, their love being the subject of Shakespeare's play *Venus and Adonis.* She was heartbroken when he was killed, so Zeus decreed that he should be allowed to spend part of each year with Aphrodite on earth, the remainder being spent in the Underworld with Persephone. She also loved, according to one of the Homeric hymns, Anchises, and bore him Aeneas. Aphrodite also helped young lovers and punished those who refused love. She helped Milanion (or Hippomenes) to win the hand of Atalanta by giving him three of the golden apples of the

Hesperides to drop in a footrace against Atalanta. By dropping he caused Atalanta to stop to pick them up, and so won the race. She also endowed life upon a statue made and then loved by Pygmalion after he had prayed to Aphrodite for a wife in its image, the statue being referred to by some as Galatea.

Aphrodite possessed a magic girdle that made the wearer irresistible and desirable, but she was usually depicted nude or partially naked. She had many attributes; among them the swan, the pomegranate, the dove, myrtle, and sparrows were sacred to her. She would periodically renew her virginity in the sea at Paphos, where her cult was at its most intense.

When her daughter by Ares, Harmonia, was given to Cadmos as his wife by Zeus, Aphrodite gave her a fabulous necklace that had been made by Hephaistos and that conferred irresistible loveliness on the wearer. Zeus had originally given this necklace to Europa. From Athene the bride received a magic robe that conferred divine dignity.

Aphrodite is to be considered the main cause of the Trojan War due to her temptation of Paris. The story goes that of all the gods, only Eris was not invited to the wedding of Peleus and Thetis, and in revenge she flung among the guests the golden Apple of Discord, inscribed with the words, "To the fairest." Immediately, Hera, Athene, and Aphrodite all claimed that the apple was rightfully theirs, and to solve the immense problem he faced, Zeus commanded Hermes to lead the three quarreling goddesses to Mount Ida so that Paris could judge the dispute.

Each goddess appeared naked before Paris, but that alone was not enough to satisfy them, for each made Paris a tempting offer. Hera promised him rule in Asia, Athene fame in war. However, Aphrodite promised him the most beautiful women in the world as his wife. Thus Paris judged in favor of Aphrodite, and under her protection he sailed to Sparta where he abducted Helen, the wife of Menelaus, thus starting the Trojan War—and leading to the ultimate destruction of Troy.

During the ten-year war Aphrodite frequently helped her son, Aeneas, who was fighting with the Trojans, and once carried him away when he had been wounded by Diomedes (who even managed to wound the goddess herself, thereby earning her undying hatred). She also carried Paris out of harm's way when he was losing in single combat to Menelaus, precipitating the resumption of all-out fighting.

Her priestess at Sestos was the tragic Hero, who killed herself in grief when her lover, Leander, drowned while swimming across the Hellespont from Abydos on the opposite shore one stormy night to visit her.

Astronomical: The name Aphrodite Terra has been applied to an area of high ground revealed by radar mapping of the planet Venus, which, of course, is associated with her.

See also: Adonis; Aeneas; Hephaistos

Apis

Greek

The son of Phoroneus.

Apollo

Greco-Roman

One of the 12 great Olympian deities whose worship was paramount in shaping the character of Greek civilization. Apollo was the most popular of all Greek gods and presided over many aspects of life. He was the god of prophecy and divine distance, of beneficent power and righteous punishment. He presided over law and made men aware of their guilt, also cleansing them of it. He was god of music, poetry, and dance, archery, pastoral life, and, as Nomios or "the Herdsman," of agriculture, presiding over crops and herbs and protecting flocks from wolves. He also protected animals from disease and was the patron of farmers, poets, and physicians. In later times he also became recognized as the god of light and the sun, as his forename, Phoebus, indicated.

His mythology suggests that he was a comparatively late addition to the Greek pantheon, at one time being regarded as borrowed from Near Eastern mythology. He has no obvious counterpart in the other Indo-European pantheons and apparently is not found in the Linear B texts of Mycenaean Greece. His worship probably derived from two sources: the Dorians, who entered Greece in about 1100 B.C. and reached as far south as Crete, and the Ionians, who lived in the islands and mainland of Anatolia or Asia Minor and acquainted his worship with that of a Hittite divinity worshipped in Lycia and hence called him Lycius (though this name may be connected with the word *lycos* or "wolf"). His name may be cognate with the Hittite god Apulunas or possibly with the Spartan *apella*, "to drive away." It may even be derived, at least in part, as suggested by other titles of the god, from *polios* or "gleaming." Both Lycius and Phoebus seem to be connected with the idea of light and his identity as a sun god.

His Dorian shrine was at Delphi at the southern foot of Mount Parnassus, near the Castalian spring, both mountain and spring being sacred to him. Here he was called the Pythian or Loxias, the Ambiguous. His Ionian shrine was at Delos in the Cyclades, where he was called Lycius and Phoebus, or "Shining," and was more closely associated with his twin sister, Artemis. It was thought he traveled from the shrine at Delphi to spend each winter feasting with the Hyperboreans, with Dionysos reigning in his stead.

The Delian Homeric *Hymn* of c. 700 B.C. says that Apollo and Artemis were twin offspring of Zeus and Leto. However, prior to their birth the jealous Hera made Leto wander from place to place until she gave birth to Artemis under a palm tree at Ortygia and to Apollo under a palm tree on the island of Delos, which until that time had been a floating island but was anchored to the seabed by Poseidon to steady it for Apollo's birth (though some say Zeus accomplished this by thinking of his son). To this day Delos is still considered as being so sacred that no one may be born or allowed to die there, no one may stay there at night, and the sick and parturient are ferried to Ortygia (modern Magali Dili).

When he grew up Apollo left Delos for the Greek mainland to seek a place to establish a sanctuary. He first came to Telphusa in Boeotia, but the nymph who resided there (also called Telphusa) did not want to be bothered with hordes of pilgrims and so sent him off to Crisa, that name as yet unused. There he came to the sanctuary of Mother Earth where he killed the serpent Python, a clear sign of the new Olympian regime replacing that of the old earth-matriarch religion. After this hard struggle he realized that Telphusa had been playing a trick on him, so he returned and threw her over a cliff before establishing a sanctuary there as well. Then he set off and waylaid some sailors by rushing their ship in the form of a dolphin, making them take him back to Crisa, renaming it on his return. The name used before Crisa (named after the dolphin) remains unknown. The first temple to Apollo here was built by the heroes Trophonius and Agamedes.

The Delphic *Hymn,* however, tells a different story. Four days after his birth Apollo called out for a bow and arrows and went in search of his mother's enemy. He sought out the she-dragon Python on Mount Parnassus, traveling from Delos to Delphi on a dolphin, as in the other version of this story, and killed her, taking over the Oracle of Earth at Delphi. Here his priestess, the Pythoness, became the mouthpiece of his oracles, which were imparted in hexameter verse. To purify Apollo Zeus commanded him to visit the Vale of Tempe and to preside over the Pythian Games that were to be held in honor of Python. Another legend makes the dispossessed creature a she-dragon by the name of Delphyne, the "Womblike"—hence Delphi.

Hera, still implacable with her jealousy of Zeus's philandering with Leto, sent the giant Tityus to violate Leto as she came from Delos with Artemis, though some say that it was Artemis who was attacked. This attempt failed when Tityus was killed by the twins' arrows.

When Ge created Typhon to avenge the death of the giants, and Typhon attacked Olympus, Apollo fled to Egypt in the form of a crow, accompanied by the other Olympian deities, who took other animal forms.

Not always subservient to Zeus, Apollo once joined in a conspiracy led by Hera, and in the company of Poseidon he put Zeus in chains, only to see him be freed by Thetis and Briareus. As punishment he was sent with Poseidon as a bondsman to King Laomedon; by playing his lyre and tending the flocks he helped the sea god build the unassailable walls of Troy. On another occasion Apollo, furious that Zeus had killed his son, Asclepios, retaliated by killing the Cyclopes. As punishment Zeus sent Apollo to serve King Admetus of Pherae in Thessaly, where, once again, he tended the flocks. While there he helped Admetus to win the hand of Alcestis and exacted the promise from the Fates that Admetus would be restored to life provided one of his family died in his stead.

Though Apollo remained unmarried, he loved many mortal women, among them Cyrene, the mother of Aristaeus, Coronis, the mother of Asclepios (her infidelity brought her death from Artemis's arrows), Manto, the mother of the seer Mopsus, and Aria, the mother of Miletus. He also seduced the nymph Dryope, and his love for the nymph Marpessa went unrequited, for she preferred his rival, Idas. When he pursued the nymph Daphne she cried out for help and was turned into a laurel bush, which henceforth became sacred to the god. Thereafter Apollo wore a laurel branch or wreath on his head as a symbol of his love and grief. Both he and Posedion sought the love of Hestia, though she swore by Zeus to always remain a virgin.

Apollo may have been the father of Troilus by Hecuba and also loved her daughter by Priam, Cassandra. He bestowed on her the gift of prophecy on the condition that she become his lover. However, when she disappointed him he decreed that she should never be believed. He also displayed a homosexual inclination, as did many gods, with his love for Hyacinthos, a Spartan prince who was in origin an earth deity. When this beautiful youth was killed by the god's jealous rival, Zephyrus, Apollo caused the Hyacinth flower to spring up from his blood. Some versions, however, attribute Hyacinthos's death to a quoit (used in a throwing game) thrown by Apollo himself. He was also said to have loved the boy Kyparissos (cypress), a kind of double of Apollo himself.

Apollo had many and varied characteristics. He was a destroyer, as his arrows indicated, and sudden deaths were attributed to his will. As Apollo Smintheus (mouse god), his archery represents the sending out of his arrows of disease. It was in this guise that he sent plagues among the Greek hordes that were besieging Troy in revenge for the abduction and imprisonment of Chryseis, the daughter of his priest at Troy, Chryses. He also guided the fatal arrow shot by Paris that struck Achilles in his heel, his only vulnerable spot.

In conjunction with his sister, he killed the Niobids, the children of Niobe, in revenge for her having boasted that as she had seven sons and seven daughters (some say six of each) she was superior to Leto, who only had two. Apollo killed the boys (some say he killed only five of the six) and Artemis the girls. Niobe was turned by Zeus or Apollo into a stone on Mount Sipylus from which her tears trickled as a stream. Apollo was also said to have killed Amphion, though some say he took his own life.

Laocoön, a priest of both Apollo and Poseidon at Troy, supported the declaration by Cassandra that the Trojan Horse held warriors, and even went so far as to throw a spear at it, causing a clatter of arms from within. However, due to Laocoön having previously offended Apollo by marrying despite of his vow of celibacy, the warning went unheeded, for Apollo now sent two enormous serpents that crushed both the priest and his two sons to death. This was wrongly interpreted as a punishment for smiting the horse, the gift of the gods, and it was welcomed within the city amid great feasting and revelry.

In direct contrast to his aspect as the destroyer he was also the protector, warding off evil, as his fatherhood of Asclepios affirmed, in which aspect he was given the title Paian or Paieon (healer). He also defended Orestes against the Erinnyes at the Areopagus on the grounds that motherhood is less important than fatherhood, although another tradition said that rather than saving him from his madness in this manner, Apollo advised Orestes that he would be freed from madness if he fetched the statue of Artemis from the Tauric Chersonese. Apollo also protected cattle and flocks, as his compulsory service to both Admetus and Laomedon indicated, an aspect that later writers particularly emphasized. As Apollo Aguieus he was also the god of roads.

As the god of prophecy Apollo could confer that gift to gods and mortals alike, and of all the centers of his worship, Delphi was the most famous. The shrine was possibly established by a pre-Hellenic people who worshipped Mother Earth. This was seized by the invading Hellenes, who killed the oracular serpent, Python, and took over the oracle in the name of their own god, Apollo. However, to placate the original inhabitants they held funeral games in honor of Python, these being the Pythian Games that Zeus commanded Apollo to preside over. The Delphic shrine was supposed to contain the Omphalos, or "navel stone of the world," which fell to this spot when Cronos regurgitated the stone Ge had given him to swallow instead of the baby Zeus. Over this Pythia, Apollo's priestess and regarded as his mystical bride, sat on a tripod, uttering his oracle after becoming intoxicated through chewing laurel leaves. These oracles were then interpreted by his priests.

The remains at Delphi are extensive, and they include the ruins of Apollo's temple (built during the fourth century B.C. to replace one destroyed by an earthquake) and a series of treasuries that contained the gifts of thanks received from city states that consulted the oracle; of these the Athenian treasury is now the best preserved. Also at Delphi is the stadium that would have been the focus of the Pythian Games.

As wounds and diseases were often treated with incantation Apollo also became the god of song and music and was said to have received the lyre from Hermes, its seven strings being associated with the seven Greek vowels. Hermes, when only a few hours old, had gone to Pieria and stolen some of Apollo's oxen, which he drove to Pylos; returning to Cyllene he invented the lyre by stringing a tortoise shell with cowgut. Apollo denounced the thief to Zeus when he discovered who it was, and Zeus ordered the return of the beasts. However, when Apollo heard the lyre he was so delighted that he accepted it in exchange for the oxen, after which he became the firm friend of Hermes, restoring him in the eyes of Zeus. None surpassed him in music, not even Pan or the satyr Marsyas, who found the magical, self-playing flute that Athene had thrown away. Marsyas once challenged Apollo to a musical contest judged by Midas. When Midas ruled in favor of Marsyas, Apollo flayed Marsyas alive and turned Midas's ears into those of an ass. A variant on this story has Midas judging Pan to be the better musician, leading Apollo to curse the king with ass ears. He also gave a lyre to Orpheus, which the latter used to charm Hades into releasing Eurydice.

Apollo was the leader of the Muses, often relocated from Mount Helicon to Mount Parnassus due to this association. In this position he was known as Musagetes. He valued order and moderation in all things and delighted in the foundation of new towns, his oracle always being consulted before any new town was founded. Legend also says that Apollo sent a crow to fetch water in his cup, but the crow dallied, and when questioned by Apollo the crow lied to him. In his anger Apollo decreed that from that time forward crows should be black in color. He then placed the deceitful crow in the sky as the constellation Corvus and, next to him, placed the cup as the constellation Crater, from which the crow is forever forbidden to drink. He is also said to have placed the arrow with which he slew the Cyclopes in revenge for Zeus killing his son, Asclepios, in the heavens as the constellation Sagitta, though some say that this was the arrow Apollo used to shoot the vulture that daily prayed on the liver of Prometheus.

In later writers Apollo was identified with the sun god, the result of Egyptian influences, at which time his sister, Artemis, was identified with the moon. Homer, however, writing in an earlier period, makes Helios the god of the sun a completely distinct god to Apollo; just like Selene, the moon goddess was distinct from Artemis.

Apollo also had a priest named Abaris who lived without food and to whom he had given a golden arrow on which the priest rode.

The worship of Apollo, typical of all that was most radiant in the Greek mind, has no direct counterpart in Roman religion, and it was not until the end of the third century B.C. that the Romans adopted his worship from the Greeks, the date given in the *Sibylline Books* as 431 B.C., although this was not to Rome itself but rather to Cumae. During a famine Rome imported grain from Cumae, and the cult was adopted. This first Cumaean Apollo was more prophetic than the later Roman god and was associated with healing. The later god differed little from his earlier Greek counterpart and was greatly revered by Emperor Augustus. Apollo has the distinction of being the only member of the Greek pantheon to be absorbed into Roman tradition without a name change.

Astronomical: A group of small asteroids with orbits crossing that of earth are named after the first of their kind, which was discovered in 1932, named Apollo, and then lost until 1973. The Apollo asteroids are so small and faint that they are difficult to locate, except when close to earth. Apollo itself is only about 2 kilometers across.

Apollo asteroids can, from time to time, collide with earth. In 1937 the Apollo asteroid Hermes passed 800,000 kilometers (500,000 miles) from earth, the closest observed approach of an asteroid, and it is thought by some that a member of the Apollo group of asteroids collided with earth about 65 million years ago, leading to the extinction of the dinosaurs. For details on the constellations Corvus, Crater, and Sagitta see the relevant entries.

See also: Artemis; Delphi; Hyperborean; Marsyas; Muses, the; Niobe; Pan; Python

Apollo Aguieus
Greek

An aspect of the god Apollo in which he was considered the god of the roads.

Apollodorus
Greek

An Athenian scholar (fl. c. 140 B.C.), he was the author of a work on mythology and one on etymology; best known for his *Chronicle* of Greek history from the time of the fall of Troy.

Apollonius of Rhodes or Apollonius Rhodius
Greek

Greek poet (c. 220–180 B.C.) born in Alexandria; longtime resident of Rhodes, he wrote many works on grammar and the epic *Argonautica*, which tells the story of Jason and the Argonauts, noted more for its learning than its poetic genius.

Apostrophia
Greek

Literally "she who turns herself away," a name given to Aphrodite and recalling the older aspects of her cult.

Apple of Discord
Greek

A golden apple inscribed with the words, "To the fairest" or "For the fairest." It was thrown into the congregation at the marriage of Peleus and Thetis by Eris, who was the only deity not to have been invited to the celebration. Immediately Hera, Athene, and Aphrodite claimed the apple was rightfully theirs, and Zeus, faced with an almost impossible dilemma, commanded Hermes to lead the goddesses to Mount Ida for Paris to judge the dispute. Even though Hera and Athene offered Paris bribes, he decided on Aphrodite, as her bribe was, in his eyes, the best (the most beautiful women in the world as his wife). This decision ultimately led to the Trojan War, his own death, and the destruction of Troy.

See also: Eris; Thetis

Apsyrtus
Greek

See Absyrtus.

Aquarius
Greek

When Ganymede, cupbearer to the gods, died he was transferred to the heavens as the constellation Aquarius.

Astronomical: Literally "the Water Carrier." Recognized from ancient times, Aquarius is part of the zodiac, the sun being within its boundaries between 17 February and 13 March. The constellation is usually seen as a man pouring water from a jar and is located in the watery part of the sky, known to the ancient Babylonians as "the sea."

Straddling both the ecliptic and celestial equators, this constellation lies mostly in the southern celestial hemisphere between approximate right ascensions 23h55m and 21h25m, declination +3° to -26°.

This zodiacal sign has achieved special significance in the mythology of the twentieth century because of the pronouncements of astrologers that the world is shifting out of the 2,000-year-old cycle of the Age of Pisces, the fish, into Aquarius. The exact date of the transition is a matter of great astrological contro-

versy, but the consensus is that it began in 1960 and will be completed sometime in the twenty-fourth century. The Age of Aquarius is predicted to be one of peace and harmony, replacing the era of strife, which, ironically, has marked the dominance of the Christian symbol of the fish.

See also: Ganymede

Aquila
Greek

The eagle that carried the thunderbolts of Zeus in his battle against the Titans. Later the same eagle was said to have carried Ganymede, the son of the king of Troy, to Olympus to serve as cupbearer to the gods. Aquila was transferred to the heavens as the constellation that bears his name, Ganymede as the constellation Aquarius.

Astronomical: Recognized by several ancient peoples as an eagle, the constellation lies across the celestial equator between approximate right ascensions 21h26m and 19h16m, declination −11° to +19°.

See also: Ganymede

Ara
Greek

The altar of the centaur at which Zeus burned incense to celebrate the victory of the gods over the Titans. Afterwards he placed it in the heavens as the constellation that bears its name.

Astronomical: The constellation Ara lies in the southern celestial hemisphere, appearing upside down from the northern hemisphere, with the altar flame "rising" downwards. It lies between approximate right ascensions 18h05m and 17h29m, declination −68° to −45°.

Arab
Modern Greek

In modern Greek folklore Arab is an evil spirit in the form of a black man who lives at the bottom of a well smoking his pipe. This belief has been associated with the ancient custom of sacrificing a Muslim or a Jew at the sinking of a new well.

Ara~chne, ~kne
Greek

A Lydian maiden whose skills in weaving and embroidery were so great that even the nymphs admired them. Basking in this glory she boasted that her work excelled even that of the goddess Athene, who challenged her to a contest. When Athene found that Arachne's work, a tapestry depicting the loves of the gods, was indeed better than her own she furiously destroyed Arachne's work, and the unfortunate girl hanged herself. Athene then turned Arachne into a spider (hence *arachnidae* for the genus of spiders) doomed to weave forever, and turned her weaving, or the rope with which she hanged herself, into a cobweb.

Arcadia
Greek

An ancient mountainous Greek region in the central Peloponnesos that was famous for its bucolic simplicity of life. The Arcadians claimed to be born "before the sun and moon," in other words autochthonous, like the Athenians and other regional Greeks. They were credited with the invention of amoebean singing (singing in turn), and their land became an important literary landscape in the pastoral tradition.

The region also featured prominently in Greek mythology. Pan was originally, and chiefly remained, an Arcadian deity. Hermes was said to have been born in a cavern on Mount Cyllene in Arcadia, and it was there that his worship flourished, often to be found in the company of Pan and the Muses.

Lycaon, a king of Arcadia, once entertained Zeus at a banquet where he offered the great god human flesh to eat in a test of his divinity. Lycaon was killed by lightning or turned into a wolf, the latter event being more likely as ancient Greeks referred to the constellation Boötes as Lycaon.

See also: Boötes

Arcadians
Roman

The name given to legendary Greek settlers who colonized the Palatine Hill, supposedly originating from the Greek region of Arcadia.

Arcas
Greek

The son of Zeus and Callisto who, when Callisto was killed (or transformed into a bear), was brought up by Maia (or Lycaon). He then became the king of the region to which he gave his name, Arcadia, and taught its inhabitants all the arts of civilization. He is represented, with other heroes, on the east pediment of the temple of Zeus at Olympia.

Archemorus
Greek

See Opheltes.

Arctos
Greek

The name given to the image of Callisto after she had been transferred to the heavens by Zeus to save her from being hunted down, at Hera's insistence, by Artemis.

Ardea
Roman

One of the original settlements, in the vicinity of the Alban Mount, of a wave of immigrants who reached Latium c. 1200 B.C., the others being Alba Longa, Aricia, and Lavinium. Ardea was the home of Prince Turnus, who disputed the right to marry Lavinia with Aeneas. It was also the town that Tarquinius was besieging when the people of Collatia, led by Brutus, marched on Rome and persuaded the people to shut the gates against Tarquinius, after which he and his sons fled into exile and Rome became a republic.

Areopagus
Greek

From the Greek *Areios pagus*, "Hill of Ares," the court in Athens formed by Athene, who preferred to settle quarrels peaceably. She held the casting vote and cast it in the instance of the trial of Orestes. Late tradition attributes the name to the trial of Ares who, having been accused of murdering Poseidon's son, Halirrhothius, pleaded that he had saved his daughter, Alcippe, from being violated. Ares was duly acquitted, and the place of the trial became known as the Areopagus. In antiquity the highest judicial court met on this hill, members of the court being known as Areopagites.

Ares

Greek

One of the 12 great Olympian deities; the god of war. Identified with the planet Mars by the Romans, he was originally a divinity of Thracian origin. From there his worship spread through Macedonia to Thebes, Athens, and the cities of the Peloponnesos, especially Sparta. He was, however, not a popular god with the Greeks, unlike his Roman counterpart, Mars, who was second in popularity to Jupiter, as they disliked purposeless war and despised the Thracians for enjoying it. Their attitude toward Ares is reflected in the myths of this god. His name is thought to possibly derive from a root meaning "scream" or the Greek word for "revenge" and has often been used as a synonym for war or battle. He is known in Mycenaean Greece in the Linear B texts, but unlike such personifications as Eris (Strife), his sister, he is fully humanized by the time of Homer, said to be a berserk giant with the voice of 10,000 men. Aeschylus calls him the "gold-changer of corpses."

Although his cult is found in Athens it is otherwise exceedingly rare, found mainly in Scythia and his land of origin, Thrace. In art Ares is often represented as a stalwart figure with a helmet, shield, and spear.

He was the son of Zeus and Hera and brother of Hebe and Hephaistos, although Hephaistos is sometimes regarded as the parthenogenous son of Hera. He was hated by the other gods, with the exception of Eris, Hades, and Aphrodite, as he delighted in battle simply for the sake of it; vindictive and short-tempered, he was also handsome. His love affair with Aphrodite is particularly well known, as is the hilarious instance when the two lovers were trapped together in bed under a net that Hephaistos, Aphrodite's husband and his brother, had engineered. Harmonia was one of their children along with Phobos (Fear) and Deimos (Panic). It is also possible that he was the father, by Aphrodite, of Eros,

though Hermes and Zeus are also considered as likely candidates for this role.

Among his other children were Amazonian Queen Penthesilea by Otrere; Alcippe; Cycnus, who was slain by Heracles; and Oenomaus, to whom he gave some wind-begotten horses and an inescapable spear. Some think that he may have fathered the entire race of the Amazons.

When Ge sent Typhon against Olympus in revenge for the gods' destruction of the giants, he fled to Egypt in the guise of a boar with the other gods, who assumed other animal forms.

Though the god of war he was not always successful in battle. The Aloeidae conquered him and left him imprisoned in a brazen vessel for 13 months until released by Hermes. He was twice vanquished by Athene and forced to return to Olympus when Heracles also defeated him. When he went into battle he was usually accompanied by his sister, Eris, and his sons, Phobos and Deimos. Sometimes he was also associated with two minor war deities, Enyalios and Enyo.

In Sparta prisoners of war were sacrificed in his honor, and at night dogs were offered to Enyalios. At Geronthrae in Laconia women were banned from his grove, though at Tegea women made sacrifices to him. During the Trojan War he sided with the Trojans and afforded the Trojan leader, Hector, personal protection.

Various places were sacred to him, notably the grove in which the Golden Fleece was hung in Colchis, as well as the nearby field that Jason had to plough using two fire-breathing bulls and then sow with the remaining dragon's teeth left by Cadmos at Thebes. These teeth had come from the dragon that guarded the sacred spring of Ares at Thebes. The Stymphalian birds, killed by Heracles in his sixth labor, were also sacred to Ares.

According to later tradition he was once called upon to defend himself before the gods in a trial when he was accused of murdering Halirrhothius, a son of Poseidon. Ares pleaded that he had acted to save his daughter, Alcippe, from being violated and was duly acquitted. The place of his trial became known as the Areopagus or "Hill of Ares."

Astronomical: The name Ares Vallis has been applied to a major channel on the surface of the planet Mars, the planet named after his Roman counterpart. The two moons of this planet are named after his sons, Phobos and Deimos.

See also: Mars

Arethusa
Greek

Though Arethusa is usually regarded as a rural deity, she was supreme in three great cities: Ephesus, Marseilles (to which Ionian Greeks from Asia Minor took her cult between 600 and 500 B.C.), and Syracuse (where she was known as Artemis Arethusa).

Her mythology says that she was a Nereid, a water nymph, with whom the river god Alpheus fell in love. In an attempt to escape him she fled from Greece to Ortygia, near Syracuse on the southern coast of Sicily, where she became a fountain or spring. Alpheus pursued her, and it was believed that the waters of the River Alpheus flowed unmixed through the sea to merge unmingled with her fountain.

Arges
Greek

One of the three one-eyed Cyclopes who were the offspring of Ge and Uranos. The other two were named Brontes and Steropes.

Argia
Greek

The daughter of Adrastus and sister to Deiphyle. She married Polyneices when he sought her father's help to overthrow his brother, Eteocles.

Argo (Navis)
Greek

More commonly known simply as the *Argo*, this was the name of the ship that Jason commissioned the Thespian Argus to build when he undertook the expedition to gain the Golden Fleece. It had 50 oars and in its prow an oracular beam, made from one of the prophetic oaks of Dodona, that was fitted by Athene herself. The crewmembers of the ship were known as the Argonauts and included most of the heroes of the day. After the death of Jason, who died according to some sources peacefully under the prow of the ship, Athene placed it in the heavens as four different constellations.

Astronomical: All four constellations that make up the *Argo Navis* lie in the southern celestial hemisphere. They are: Carina, the Keel, which lies between right ascensions 6h and 11h and declination –50° to –75°; Vela, the Sail, between right ascensions 8h and 11h and declination –40° to –60°; Puppis, the Poop or Stern, between right ascensions 6h and 9h and declination –10° to –50°; and Pyxis, the Ship's Compass between right ascensions 8h and 10h and declination –20° to –40°.

See also: Jason

Argolis
Greek

A region of the eastern Peloponnesos and once the kingdom of Atreus and Agamemnon, who had their capital at Mycenae. The region also contained the city of Argos that later overshadowed Mycenae and became second only to Sparta in political importance. The great temple of Hera, the Heraeum, was built in Argolis between Argos and Mycenae.

Argonautica
Greek

Epic poem by Apollonius of Rhodes (Apollonius Rhodius) that recounts the legend of Jason and the Argonauts. It is widely respected more for its learning than its poetic genius.

Argonauts
Greek

The collective name given to the band of 50 or 60 heroes who accompanied Jason aboard the *Argo Navis* in his quest for the Golden Fleece. Among their number were Acastus, the Dioscuri (Castor and Polydeuces), Heracles, Hylas, Zetes and Calais, Peleus and Telamon, Idas and Lynceus (who acted as lookouts), Admetus, Periclymenus, Augeias, Argus (the builder of the *Argo Navis*), Tiphys or Ancaeus (steersman), Idmon and Mopsus (seers),

Theseus and Pirithous (though not in Apollonius of Rhodes), Amphiaraus, Laertes, Deucalion, Meleager, Asclepios, and Orpheus.

For the story of their voyage and their many adventures, see Jason.

Arg~os, ~us
Greek

1. Ancient city in the east Peloponnesos at the head of the Gulf of Nauplia from which the peninsula of Argolis derived its name. It was given as the possible location, competing with Cnossos in Crete, where Zeus sought out his sister, Hera, in the form of a cuckoo just prior to their marriage. It was at a spring near Argos that Hera bathed each year to renew her virginity, and the city became one of her seats of worship, as did Samos. The worship of Athene also flourished in Argos, later to be joined by the worship of Dionysos, though at first the Argives refused to accepted him as a god. In the Homeric era the name "Argives" was sometimes used instead of "Greeks."

Argos was the kingdom of Diomedes; of Adrastus, who led expeditions against Thebes; of Atreus, who was murdered by his nephew Aegisthus and who had set the flesh of his brother Thyestes' children before their father at a banquet in revenge for the seduction of his wife by Thyestes; and of Orestes, who was also the king of Sparta and Mycenae.

Abas, the grandson of Danaus, was the twelfth king. His twin sons, Acrisius and Proetus, agreed to divide their inheritance, Proetus becoming the ruler of Tiryns, Acrisius (the father of Danaë) of Argos. After Acrisius was accidentally killed by Perseus, Danaë's son by Zeus, at Larissa, Perseus and Proetus exchanged kingdoms, so Proetus now became ruler of Argos, Perseus of Tiryns.

2. The builder of the ship *Argo Navis* for Jason to undertake his quest for the Golden Fleece. Sometimes referred to as Argos, he also became a member of the crew and therefore one of the Argonauts. On his death he was changed into a peacock by the goddess Hera and placed in the heavens as the constellation Pavo, though there is some confusion over this, as Hera transferred the eyes of Argus into the tail of a peacock, and some say that it is this peacock that is represented by the constella-

tion. Argus was later joined in the heavens by four constellations made up from the *Argo Navis* that was placed there by Athene—Carina, the Keel; Vela, the Sail; Puppis, the Poop or Stern; and Pyxis, the Ship's Compass.

Astronomical: The constellation Pavo lies in the southern celestial hemisphere between approximate right ascensions 17h and 21h, declination –50° to –75°.

3. A giant with a hundred eyes, half of which remained open at all times, who was given the task, by Hera, of guarding Io, who Zeus had turned into a heifer to put Hera off the scent of his philandering unsuccessfully. He was killed by Hermes at Zeus's request, and Hera took his hundred eyes and placed them in the tail of her favorite bird, the peacock. This association has led to confusion between this Argus and the other Argus, the builder of the *Argo Navis*, whom Hera placed in the heavens as the constellation Pavo, the peacock, after his death.

4. The faithful dog of Odysseus who recognized his master after he had been away from home for 20 years, ten of them at Troy fighting the Trojan War, ten more experiencing difficulties in returning home to his wife, Penelope, on Ithaca. Argus died of joy immediately after greeting his master home.

See also: Jason; Odysseus; Perseus

Aria
Greek

The mother of Miletus by Apollo.

Ariadne
Greek

In all probability Ariadne was originally a Cretan goddess, her name appearing to mean "all-holy." Later she was adopted into Greek mythology, where she appears as the daughter of Minos, king of Crete, and Pasiphaë, thus being the sister of Glaucus, Androgeos, and Phaedra.

When Theseus, son of Aegeus, voluntarily joined the tribute of Athenian youths that were to be fed to the monstrous Minotaur, Ariadne instantly fell in love with him and contrived to help him kill the beast. She gave him a skein of thread and a sword. By unwinding the thread behind him as he searched for the Minotaur within its labyrinth, he was able, after having killed the monster, to escape its confines. Together Theseus and Ariadne fled to the island of Dia (Naxos), where they were married but where Theseus later abandoned her when he returned to Athens, later marrying her sister, Phaedra, there.

She was found on the island by the god Dionysos, who made her his wife, and when she died he placed the crown he had given her as a wedding gift in the heavens as the constellation Corona Borealis—the Northern Crown.

Astronomical: The constellation Corona Borealis lies in the northern celestial hemisphere between approximate right ascensions 15h and 17h, declination +25° and +40°.

See also: Dionysos; Minos; Minotaur

Aricia

Roman

One of the original settlements in the vicinity of the Alban Mount of the wave of immigrants who reached Latium c. 1200 B.C., the other towns being Alba Longa, Ardea, and Lavinium.

Aries

Greek

1. A little-used variant for the god of war, Ares.

2. The winged ram, sent by Zeus, that rescued Phryxus and Helle, children of the king of Thessaly, from their heartless stepmother. During the flight to Colchis, Helle fell from the back of the animal into the stretch of water that thenceforth became known as the Hellespont (modern Dardanelles). Having safely arrived in Colchis, Phryxus sacrificed the ram and hung its fleece in the sacred grove of Ares, where it turned to gold. There it was guarded by a sleepless dragon (some say Draco) who was put to sleep by Medeä as she helped Jason and the Argonauts complete their quest for this Golden Fleece. In its memory the ram was placed in the heavens as the constellation Aries.

Astronomical: The first sign of the zodiac (March 21 to April 20) and a well known but ill-defined constellation straddling the ecliptic and lying in the northern celestial hemisphere

between approximate right ascensions 1h50m and 3h30m, declination +10° to +30°. Its most distinctive feature is a curve of three stars of decreasing brightness. When the constellation was first defined the sun was in Aries on the first day of spring (approximately March 21), the vernal equinox, and even though this is now in Pisces due to the effect of earth's precession, it is still referred to as the "first point of Aries." The sun is now in Aries from April 19 to May 15.

Arimaspea

Greek

A lost poem by Aristaeus of Proconnesos that describes the Arimaspians or Arimaspi as a one-eyed race who lived in the northern regions of the world.

Arimaspi

Greek

Described in the lost poem *Arimaspea* by Aristaeus of Proconnesos, the Arimaspi (Anglicized as Arimaspians) were a one-eyed race living on the Scythian steppes, neighbors to the Hyperboreans. They constantly fought a group of griffins for the horde of gold they guarded.

Arion

Greek

1. An actual historical figure from the seventh century B.C.; a native of Methymna on Lesbos, he lived at the court of Periander of Corinth in about 625 B.C. He was a lyric poet, virtuoso on the cithara (a more sonorous version of the lyre), and developed the dithyramb (a form a choral song). A curious legend is told of this character.

Having visited Sicily, where he won a musical contest, he boarded a ship to return to Corinth laden with gifts, but while en route the captain and crew decided to murder him for his treasure. Given permission to sing one last song, Arion dedicated the hymn to Apollo and then leaped into the sea. There he was rescued by Delphinos, one of the music-loving dolphins (Apollo's beast) that had gathered to hear his song, who carried him on its back to

Taenarum. From there Arion made his way to Corinth and told Periander of his adventures. Later, when the ship had arrived, the captain and crew swore that Arion had been detained in Sicily, but Periander confronted them with Arion and had them executed by crucifixion. Arion and his lyre were subsequently placed among the stars.

2. A fabulous talking horse, the divine offspring of Poseidon and Demeter conceived when Poseidon, in the form of a stallion, raped his sister, who had taken the form of a mare. It was Arion's speed that saved Adrastus in the expedition of the Seven Against Thebes.

See also: Seven Against Thebes

Aristaeus

Greek

The son of Apollo and the nymph Cyrene; born in Libya, he became the father of Actaeon. On the advice of Cyrene he sacrificed some cattle to the nymphs, and after nine days he found bees swarming in the remains.

He traveled to Thrace, where he fell in love with and pursued Eurydice, the wife of Orpheus. In her flight from his lust she received a fatal snake bite and died. As punishment the nymphs destroyed his bees, and how he raised a new swarm is told in Virgil's fourth *Georgics*. After his death he became a minor deity of healing and was regarded as the inventor of beekeeping and other agricultural pursuits. He also features in the story of Erigone.

Arist(a)eus of Proconnesos

Greek

A historical figure probably dating from the seventh century B.C. who described in a lost poem, the *Arimaspea*, a visit he once made to the northern regions of the world that were inhabited by the one-eyed Arimaspians, the gold-guarding griffins, and the Hyperboreans. Legend held that he was sometimes to be seen in more than one place at a time, which suggests that he may have been a practitioner of the kind of shamanistic out-of-body experiences known to be characteristic of Central Asia. His name was still known as that of a magician in thirteenth-century Byzantium.

Arktoi

Greek

At Brauron all girls between the ages of five and ten would spend a period in the service of Artemis, known as being *arktoi,* "bear virgins" or "bears for Artemis," after which they would take part in a procession at Athens to mark their arrival at maturity.

See also: Artemis

Arrephoria

Greek

Festival held in ancient Athens during which two maidens carried phallic symbols to the shrine of Aphrodite to symbolize her role as a fertility goddess.

Arruns

Roman

The Etruscan ally of Aeneas in his battle with Turnus.

Arsinoë

Greek

The daughter of Phlegeus, king of Psophis, who married Alcmaeon after her father had purified him for the murder of his mother, Eriphyle, for which he was being pursued by the Erinnyes. As a wedding gift, Alcmaeon gave Arsinoë the fabulous necklace and robe of Harmonia. However, the Erinnyes were still in pursuit, and so Alcmaeon was forced to flee and abandon his wife.

See also: Erinnyes

Artemis

Greek

One of the 12 great Olympian deities whom the Romans identified with Diana, although she was also known to them as Cynthia, being said to have been born on Mount Cynthus. The virgin goddess of the chase; the Mistress of the Animals who was worshipped in primitive matriarchal society; protectress of children and young animals; protectress of the hunted and vegetation; goddess of chastity; later, moon goddess. Her worshippers tended to be the ordinary populace.

In reality Artemis is a far more frightening creature. She is just one of many forms of the primitive mother goddess, having special concern for the lives of women, both before and after marriage. Her name is found in the Mycenaean Linear B texts, and she is close to the shadowy Cretan goddesses Britomartis and Dictynna. It is said that Britomartis was a nymph who was pursued for nine months by Minos until she leaped into the sea and was deified by Artemis. Thenceforth they shared the name Dictynna. She may be identified with the *potina theron* of Minoan religion and is often referred to as *potina* (lady) of bears or bulls.

During the classical period she was especially associated with the rites of passage of girls into womanhood. At Brauron all girls between the ages of five and ten would spend a period in her service, known as being *arktoi,* "bear virgins" or "bears for Artemis," after which they would take part in a procession at Athens to mark their arrival at maturity.

At Halae Araphenides in Attica a festival known as the Tauropolia involved the offering of some drops of blood from a man's neck to the presiding goddess, Artemis Tauropolos (the bull goddess Artemis).

She was commonly identified with Eileithyia, the goddess of childbirth, and was known as Locheia and Soödina in this aspect. She was also, on occasions known as Kourotrophos, "Midwife" and "Nurse," further emphasizing her association as a fertility goddess especially concerned with childbirth.

In Tauris (the Tauric Chersonese) her cult was said to involve the sacrifice of all strangers. In this cult Iphigeneia was once her priestess, and it was from Tauris that she and her brother, Orestes, were said to have taken her image to Brauron, whence the goddess was known as Brauronia. This Brauronian Artemis was worshipped in Athens, as well as in Sparta, under the name of Orthia, where she was worshipped in rituals that included the violent flogging of youths at her altar until they sprinkled it with their blood. During Roman times these youths sometimes died from the floggings. A similar claim of human sacrifices in her honor was made for her aspect of Artemis Triklaria at Patras.

She is perhaps closest to the Anatolian Mother Goddess as Artemis Ephesia (Artemis of Ephesus), who was represented with a huge number of pendulous breasts, though these were sometimes identified as bulls' scrotums, and worshipped as an orgiastic goddess. Ephesus in Turkey was her chief cult center, with an immensely wealthy temple first built by Croesus. It was this Artemis that Saint Paul encountered (see Acts 19:1–35).

She is commonly, as Artemis Agrotera, a goddess of the wild; on Delos she was worshipped at an altar of counterclockwise-turning goats' horns. It was at this Ionian shrine that she was most closely associated with her mythological twin brother, Apollo. However, she was worshipped early in Arcadia as a huntress among the nymphs, and this Arcadian Artemis has no connection whatsoever with Apollo, the association being made only by later writers.

In mythology she is Korythalia, "laurel maiden," the twin sister of Apollo, daughter of Zeus and Leto. Hera, jealous of Zeus's continued philandering, caused Leto to wander from place to place until she gave birth to Artemis under a palm tree on the island of Ortygia and to Apollo on the island of Delos. Artemis shares many of Apollo's attributes and carried a bow and arrows that were made for her by Hephaistos. She had the power to send plague and sudden death.

As Leto came with Artemis from Delos to Delphi, the still implacable Hera sent the giant Tityus to violate Leto, though some say that it was Artemis herself that was attacked. The giant was killed by the arrows of the twins.

When the gigantic Aloeidae, Ephialtes and Otus, vowed to outrage Hera and Artemis, they piled Mount Pelion on Mount Ossa in their attack on Olympus. Artemis induced the giants to go to the island of Naxos in the hope of meeting her there, but disguising herself as a doe she leaped between the pair, and they killed each other in error. Now Ge, to avenge the deaths of the giants, brought forth the gigantic monster Typhon and sent him against Olympus. All the gods fled to Egypt in animal form, Artemis assuming that of a cat.

Like Apollo, Artemis remained unmarried, and later writers stressed the fact that she was a maiden goddess and punished any lapses severely. She changed the hunter Actaeon into a stag to be torn to pieces by his own hounds simply because he had chanced upon her bathing naked with the nymphs. Some traditions also attribute the death of the giant Orion to Artemis because of his unchasteness. The nymph Callisto, whom Zeus had seduced, was transformed into a bear and hunted down by the hounds of Artemis. The only mortal to whom she is known to have been kind was Hippolytus, but she abandoned even him as he lay dying.

Artemis was attended by Dryades and Naiades, attendants that were usually represented by girls who performed wild and erotic dances.

She displayed her vengeful nature in the story of Niobe. When the latter boasted that she was superior to Leto, for she had had seven sons and seven daughters, the Niobids (though some sources quote only six boys and six girls), whereas Leto only had two children. In punishment Apollo killed the boys and Artemis the girls, although alternative sources say that Artemis only killed five of the six girls. Either they or Zeus turned Niobe into a rock on Mount Sipylus from which her tears fell as a stream.

Artemis also appears briefly in the story of the Trojan War. When the Greek fleet was beset by contrary winds at Aulis, said to have been caused by Agamemnon killing a hart and thus displeasing Artemis, Calchas advised that only the sacrifice of Iphigeneia, Agamemnon's daughter, would appease the goddess. Reluctantly Agamemnon gave his permission, though some say that Artemis snatched the girl from the altar in the nick of time and substituted a deer for her, bearing Iphigeneia off to Tauris to become her priestess. It was from there that she was later rescued by her brother, Orestes. Following this rescue Artemis pardoned Orestes for the murder of his mother, Clytemnestra, and her lover, Aegisthus, and thus halted the pursuit of the Erinnyes.

When Apollo came to be identified with the sun and known as Phoebus, Artemis came to be associated with the moon, coming to be known as Phoebe. Perhaps this is function of her virgin purity, though it is incompatible with the existence of Selene. Later still she came to be identified, more or less, with Hecate.

Though usually represented as a rural divinity, Artemis was the supreme deity in three great cities: Ephesus in Turkey, which was her main cult center; Massalia (Marseilles), to which Ionian Greeks from Asia Minor took her cult between 600 B.C. and 500 B.C.; and in Syracuse, in southern Sicily, where she was known as Artemis Arethusa. She was often portrayed as a huntress, and as such her chlamys reached only to the knees. She carried a bow, quiver, and arrows and was often accompanied by stags or dogs. When she became associated with Selene she wore a long robe and veil, showed a crescent moon on her forehead, and drove a two-horse chariot.

See also: Apollo; Britomartis; Dictynna; Eileithya; Ephesus; Iphigeneia

Artemis Agrotera
Greek

An aspect of Artemis in which she is described as the goddess of the wild.

Artemis Arethusa
Greek

The name by which Arethusa was known in Syracuse, Sicily.

Artemis Ephesia
Greek

"Artemis of Ephesus." The aspect of Artemis where she is perhaps closest to the Anatolian Mother Goddess and in which she was represented with a huge number of pendulous breasts, though these were sometimes identified as bulls' scrotums, and worshipped as an orgiastic goddess. Ephesus in Turkey was her chief cult center, with an immensely wealthy temple first built by Croesus. It was this Artemis that Saint Paul encountered (see Acts 19:1–35).

Artemis Tauropolos
Greek

At Halae Araphenides in Attica a festival known as the Tauropolia involved the offering of some drops of blood from a man's neck to the presiding goddess, Artemis Tauropolos (the bull goddess Artemis).

Artemis Triklaria
Greek
An aspect of Artemis worshipped at Patras, where it is claimed human sacrifices were carried out in her honor.

Ascalaphus
Greek
Freed from the Underworld by Heracles when that hero also freed Theseus during his twelfth (and final) labor, he was, according to some, turned into an owl by Demeter for revealing that he had seen Persephone eat while in the Underworld.

Ascanius
Greco-Roman
The son of Aeneas who was led away from the doomed city of Troy at the end of the Trojan War by his father, who carried his grandfather, Anchises. However, as some sources give Ascanius's mother as Lavinia, he might have been born after his father had arrived in Italy and therefore could not have been at Troy. Thirty years after Aeneas's arrival in Italy he was to found the city of Alba Longa (c. 1152 B.C.) on the site where Aeneas had come across a white sow and her 30 piglets, as foretold in the prophecy of Helenus. The city was ruled by his descendants for some 300 years.

His significance to the Romans is that they called him Iulus; the Julian clan, including Julius Caesar, claimed descent from Aeneas and Aphrodite (Venus) through him.

See also: Aeneas

Asclap~ios, ~ius
Greco-Roman
Variant of Asclepios.

Asclepiadae
Greco-Roman
A priestly cast, the supposed descendants of Asclepios, in which the knowledge of medicine as a sacred secret was transmitted from father to son.

Asclep~ios, ~ius
Greek
Also: Aesculapius, Asclepius, Aesclepius, Asculepius, Aesculepius, Asclapius, Aesclapius, Asculapius

A god of medicine whose name, it appears, may be related to the word *ascalaphos,* "a lizard." He was commonly identified early in the form of or, later, accompanied by a snake, and when his cult was introduced into Athens the poet Sophocles acted as host to the god while his temple was being built. That is to say, Sophocles looked after the sacred snake. Originating from Trikka in Thessaly, Asclepios became the patron deity of three famous healing sanctuaries: Epidaurus, Pergamum, and Cos. On account of the belief that the god prescribed cures in dreams, it was customary for the sick to sleep in his temples or in the "health centers" that were associated with them. The remains of these centers are extensive at Epidaurus and Pergamum and include, in each case, a fine theater.

According to some traditions, he was the son of Apollo and the nymph Coronis raised by the wise centaur Cheiron, who taught him the arts of healing. In other traditions, Homer included, he was not a god but rather a native of Epidaurus, which was the center of his worship, the "blameless physician" and father of Machaon and Podalirius, the physicians to the Greek army at Troy. These sons became the founding fathers of medicine. Serpents were sacred to him, as shown by his symbol, a *caduceus* with two serpents entwined around it, and cocks were sacrificed in his honor. His supposed descendants were called the Asclepiadae, a priestly caste where father transmitted to son the knowledge of medicine as a sacred secret.

In the tradition where Asclepios was divine he acted as the physician to the Argonauts and once restored a man to life—usually Hippolytus. Thus he cheated Hades and was struck down by a thunderbolt from Zeus; because Hades was so worried about this power, he persuaded Zeus to place him in the heavens out of the way, where he formed the constellation Ophiuchus. Furious, his father, Apollo, killed the Cyclopes in revenge and was duly punished by being made to serve the mortal Admetus for a year.

Asclepios was the father of Panaceia and a daughter named Hygeia, from whom the modern English word *hygiene* has derived. Asclepios was usually depicted in art wearing a long cloak but bare-chested and carrying his snake-entwined staff. He was one of the elements, along with Zeus, Hades, and Osiris, who was combined into the new, and for a short time successful, god Serapis by Ptolemy I in an attempt to unite Greeks and Egyptians in common worship. Despite his death, Asclepios was regarded as divine, and his role as a savior god made him a particularly dangerous rival to Christianity.

His cult was introduced to Rome c. 293 B.C. in order to cure a pestilence on the order of the prophetic *Sibylline Books,* and his name became corrupted to Aesculapius.

Astronomical: See Ophiuchus.

See also: Cheiron; Jason

Asculap~ios, ~ius
Greco-Roman
Variant of Asclepios.

Asculep~ios, ~ius
Greco-Roman
Variant of Asclepios.

Asellus Australis
Greek
The Southern Ass ridden by Silenus in the company of Dionysos, who rode the Northern Ass, Asellus Borealis, in their battle with the Titans.

Astronomical: Asellus Australis, lying within the constellation Cancer exactly on the ecliptic at approximate celestial coordinates right ascension 8h45m, declination +18°, is a 4Σ17 magnitude gK0 star at 217 light-years distance.

See also: Silenus

Asellus Borealis
Greek
The Northern Ass ridden by Dionysos in the company of Silenus, who rode the Southern

Ass, Asellus Australis, in their battle with the Titans.

Astronomical: Asellus Borealis, lying within the constellation Cancer at approximate celestial coordinates right ascension 8h45m, declination +22°, is a 4.73 magnitude type A0 star at 233 light-years distance.

Ashkelon
Greek
Site of the oldest shrine to Aphrodite according to Herodotus.

Asia
Greek
Daughter of Oceanos and Tethys; the mother of Atlas, Prometheus, and Epimetheus by Iapetus. She was sometimes identified as Clymene.

Asia Minor
In ancient times referred to as Anatolia, this was the westernmost part of Asia and comprised the great peninsula that makes up most of modern Turkey. It is bordered by the Black Sea on the north, the Mediterranean Sea on the south, and the Aegean Sea on the west. The waterway made up of the Bosphorus, the Sea of Marmara, and the Dardanelles (ancient name Hellespont) divides the region from Europe. Within the boundaries of Asia Minor were the Aeolian Islands (the Lipari Islands).

Asop(h)us
Greek
The god of the River Asophus, of which there were two on mainland Greece, one in Sicyonia and one in Boeotia. The god was, like all of the river gods, the son of Oceanos and Tethys. He married Merope, the daughter of Ladon, and became the father of Evadne, Euboea, and Aegina, the latter name also being an island with another River Asophus in antiquity.

Aspropotamo
Greek
The modern name for the River Achelous in Boeotia.

Asteria

Greek

The Thracian wife of Perseus; mother of Hecate.

Asterion

Greek

A greyhound whose name means "starry" who, along with Chara (beloved), was a hunting dog used by Boötes in his pursuit of the bear Callisto.

Astronomical: An ill-defined constellation by the name of Canes Venatici—"the Hunting Dogs"—represents both Asterion and Chara, although only the latter has a star named after it, designated alpha Canes Venatici. The constellation is found in the northern celestial hemisphere between approximate right ascensions 12h and 14h, declination between +30° and +50°.

Asterope

Greek

One of the Pleiades, the daughters of Atlas, who is also known as Sterope.

Astronomical: See Pleiades.

Astraea

Greek

The Greek goddess of justice who is usually depicted carrying scales and wearing a crown of stars. The daughter of Zeus and Themis, she fled to the skies to become the constellation Virgo when men began forging weapons of war.

Astronomical: The well known constellation of Virgo forms one of the constellations of the zodiac as the ecliptic runs through it. Virgo straddles the celestial equator between approximate right ascensions 12h and 1h, declination between +15° and –20°. The Egyptians identified the constellation with the goddess Isis. However, the connection to Astraea is usually considered the more important, as next to her in the sky is the constellation Libra—"the Scales"—which Astraea, as the goddess of justice, was commonly depicted holding. The name Astraea has also been applied to one of the asteroids.

Astraeus

Greek

One of the second-generation Titans who fathered the four beneficent winds by the goddess of the dawn, Eos. Boreas (north), Zephyrus (west), Notus (south), and Eurus (east) all lived on the floating island of Aeolia, from where Aeolus controlled their release. Astraeus was also the father, by Eos, of Hesperus, the evening star and, some say, of all the other stars as well.

See also: Titan (2)

Astyanax

Greek

The son of Hector and Andromache who was hurled from the walls of Troy by the Greeks to destroy the Trojan royal line, fearful that he might one day avenge his parents. He makes a memorable appearance in Homer's *Iliad* when, as a baby, he was frightened by the nodding plume on his father's helmet.

Atalanta

Greek

1. The huntress-daughter of Iasus of Arcadia and Clymene, Atalanta was exposed at birth by her father, who wanted a son, and suckled by a she-bear sent by the goddess Artemis, with whom she would become significantly connected. Atalanta was raised by hunters who taught her their arts, and when she grew to adulthood she attempted to join the expedition of the Argonauts, but Jason refused to allow her to board the *Argo Navis*. She did, however, join in the Calydonian Boar Hunt, where Meleager fell in love with her and gave her the head of the boar he had slain, though Atalanta herself scored the first hit. She also killed two among the party that tried to ravish her.

In due course her father, Iasus, learned that she was still alive, and the pair reconciled. Iasus wanted her to marry, but she wanted to preserve her virgin freedom as a huntress, even killing two centaurs who attempted to rape her. To elude her father's wishes she devised a test: She would marry the man who won a footrace against her—but would kill those she beat. The fleetest of all mortals, she felt confident she would never have to marry. Many suitors failed and were executed by Atalanta.

She was finally beaten by either Milanion, an Arcadian, or Hippomenes, a Boeotian, the former being normally accepted as the vanquisher. This young man prayed to Aphrodite for help in the race, and she gave him three of the golden apples of the Hesperides. As they raced he dropped the apples one by one; enchanted by their beauty, Atalanta stopped to pick up each one, thus losing the race. The couple married and had a son, whom they named Parthenopaeus. Some sources have Meleager, the young man who fell in love with Atalanta during the Calydonian Boar Hunt, as the father of Parthenopaeus, but his usual parentage is Atalanta and Milanion.

Ovid says that Milanion (Melanion) forgot to thank Aphrodite for her help and lay with his wife in a shrine dedicated to Zeus. For this transgression she turned them both into lions, for the ancient Greeks believed that lions mated only with leopards, not with other lions. Alternative sources say that it was not Aphrodite who transformed the pair, or that they laid together in a shrine of Zeus; instead it was a shrine sacred to the goddess Cybele, and she transformed the couple.

See also: Artemis; Atalanta (2); Hippomenes; Meleager; Milanion

2. Said to be the daughter of Schoeneus (Schoineus) of Boeotia, but she has been frequently confused with, and thus connected to, the Arcadian huntress of the same name, Atalanta. This Atalanta was said to have married Hippomenes, but due to the confusion the same stories are told as being appropriate to both Atalantas.

Atana potina
Greek

Possibly a specialized form of the mother goddess mentioned in the Mycenaean Linear B texts; identified with Athene.

Ate
Greek

The goddess of infatuation and the surrender of moral principles, the personification of the "moral blindness" that pitches men into disaster. She was mythologized as the daughter of Zeus or Eris, and her concept is central to the understanding of ancient Greek religion.

She was thrown out of Olympus by Zeus, who was angered at her mischief, and so lives among mortal men and women. However, when she descends on a mortal to destroy him, her externality does not absolve that person from bearing full responsibility for any actions committed while under her influence. Ate is the essential key to the concept of the Greek tragic hero, who destroys himself by forces he unleashes yet is powerless to control. In Homer's *Iliad* it is "wild Ate" whom Agamemnon blames for his anger at Achilles, not himself.

Athamas
Greek

The son of Aeolus; king of Orchomenus in Boeotia. By his first wife, Nephele, whom he married at Hera's command, Athamas became the father of Phrixus and Helle, but he secretly loved Ino, the daughter of Cadmos and Harmonia, and took her as his second wife; she bore him two sons, Learchus and Melicertes. In her jealousy Ino plotted the deaths of Phrixus and Helle.

She roasted the corn seed so that the crops failed, and when Athamas sent to Delphi to find out how to appease the gods, Ino bribed the returning messengers to say that the god had ordered the sacrifice of Phrixus. Just as Athamas was about to carry out the sacrifice he thought had been ordered by the god, Hermes sent a winged ram that carried Phrixus and Helle away on its back. Helle fell off on the journey into the stretch of water that was thenceforth known as the Hellespont, but Phrixus reached the safety of Colchis, where he sacrificed the ram to Zeus and gave the fleece to Aeëtes, who hung it in a grove sacred to Hermes, and there the fleece turned to gold. This Golden Fleece later became the object of the quest undertaken by Jason and the Argonauts.

Meanwhile, Zeus had sent the infant Dionysos, born from the ashes of Ino's sister, Semele, to be brought up by Athamas and Ino. In her anger Hera drove the couple mad, and

Athamas shot Learchus thinking him to be a deer (or a lion cub), and Ino jumped with Melicertes into the Saronic Gulf. Both were transformed into sea deities, with Ino becoming Leucothea and Melicertes becoming Palaemon, though some accounts call Palaemon a hero rather than a deity.

Athamas was forced into exile and fled to Thessaly, where he took Themisto as his third wife. However, Euripides places this marriage at home. Also in Euripides' account, Ino meanwhile had become a bacchant on Mount Parnassus, and it was from there that Athamas brought her home. Themisto planned to kill Ino's children but was tricked by the nurse into killing her own. Athamas and Ino were then both sent mad, killing their own children as before.

In his old age Athamas was nearly sacrificed as a scapegoat by the people of Achaea in Thessaly, but Phrixus's son, Cytissorus, rescued him (Heracles, according to Sophocles in his lost *Athamas Crowned*). After that Athamas returned to Orchomenus and was given sanctuary by King Andreus until his death.

See also: Aeolus; Ino; Jason

Athamas Crowned
Greek

Lost work by Sophocles that tells the story of Athamas and how in old age he was saved by Heracles from being sacrificed as a scapegoat by the Achaeans in Thessaly. After that Athamas returned to Orchomenus and was given sanctuary by King Andreus until his death.

Athen~e, ~a
Greek

One of the 12 great Olympian deities and one of the most popular. Athene was the virgin goddess of war, industry, arts, and crafts. She is the embodiment of wisdom, protectress (and eponym) of Athens and other cities, and identified by the Romans with Minerva. Her name is pre-Hellenic, being referred to in the Mycenaean Linear B texts as Atana potina, probably a specialized form of the mother goddess. When the Achaeans entered pre-Hellenic Greece they brought a young warrior goddess who bore the titles Core or Kore (girl), Parthenos (virgin), and Pallas (maiden), the last seeming to be the most common. It is perhaps related to *pallax* (cf. modern Greek *pallikari*, meaning "a young brave"), thus meaning "maiden" or "female brave." Another common yet unexplained title is Tritogeneia, perhaps being derived from her supposed birth on the shores of a lake named Triton.

Circa 1700 B.C. she was identified with a much older, pre-Hellenic "Palace Goddess" who was worshipped in Crete. This goddess was one aspect of the Great Goddess who was revered not for motherhood but for feminine intuition. Thus the complex Pallas Athene was not only the patroness of women's arts, such as weaving, protectress of agriculture, and inventor of plough, rake, and ox-yoke but also a formidable warrior and a wise, able tactician. Yet she was an urban, civilized goddess, which accounted for her popularity among the people.

The centers of her cult were Attica and Athens, her chief cult center, where she was worshipped as Polias (of the city), Poliouchos (protector of the city), Parthenos (virgin), and Promachos (defender). Her temple on the Athenian Acropolis is dedicated to "Athene Parthenos," the Parthenon. It was erected between 447 B.C. and 438 B.C. under Pericles' administration, the work of the architect Iktinos, and housed the giant Chryselephantine statue of Athene sculpted by Phidias or his school. Other pre-Hellenic acropolises were sacred to Athene, and her worship flourished in Sparta, Corinth, Argos, and Thebes. At Athens the Panathenaic festival, during which the statue of Athene was decked in new robes, was celebrated every four years beginning in 566 B.C. She is also frequently identified with Nike, and it is possible that this might have been her surname.

In Homer she is regularly given the epithet *glaukopis*, often translated as "gray-eyed" but possibly meaning "owl-faced," alluding to her sacred bird, with which she is sometimes depicted. She is always portrayed in art wearing armor, including a shield, her aegis, with *gorgoneion* and edged with the Gorgon's snaky locks. Sometimes the aegis is shown as a goatskin edged with the snake's hair of the Gorgon in which she is draped, though she occasionally borrowed the goatskin aegis, usually accepted as being that of Zeus. Due to these associations she also sometimes has the epithet *gorgopis*, "gorgon-faced." The olive was sacred to her, and the snake was another attribute. Legends of her birth reveal how the heretofore patriarchal Hellenes made theirs a matriarchal society.

In mythology she was said to be the daughter of Zeus and his first wife, the Oceanid Metis, whom Zeus swallowed after an oracle foretold that the child she carried was a girl (Athene) but that if she had another child it would be a son who would overthrow him, as Zeus had his father. Later, while walking by Lake Triton he suffered an agonizing headache. Hermes, realizing the cause, persuaded Hephaistos (Prometheus, according to some) to split open Zeus's skull. From the opening Athene sprang, full-grown and armed.

When Ge created the monstrous Typhon to exact her revenge on Olympus for the destruction of the giants, Athene—single-handedly destroying two of the most violent, Enceladus and Pallas—fled to Egypt, the other gods taking animal forms. She alone remained undaunted and persuaded Zeus to attack Typhon; Zeus eventually prevailed with his thunderbolts and buried Typhon under Mount Etna, which still breathes fire. During the war against the Titans Athene hurled the dragon Draco into the sky, where it became wrapped around the northern celestial pole and formed the constellation Draco.

She plays a leading part in Homer's *Odyssey*, often in disguise, as the adviser of the cunning Odysseus, whose craftiness was due to her wisdom. She is also an important figure in Homer's *Iliad*, where she is shown fighting on the side of the Greeks. In one notable scene she restrains Achilles from venting his anger on Agamemnon, tugging his hair.

Her association with Athens began with a contest between her and Poseidon for possession of the land during the reign of Cecrops, who awarded it to the goddess, for her gift of an olive tree was judged the better. Hephaistos attempted to rape Athene but failed, his semen spilling onto the Acropolis and producing the child Erichthonius. Yet she is associated with Hephaistos thanks to her patronage of crafts-

men, and as such she is afforded the title Hephaistia. When Poseidon and Athene again contested earthly possession, this time over Troezen, Zeus judged that they should share it equally.

As the goddess of war she proved herself on one occasion to be superior to Ares, the god of war, another indicator of the dominant matriarchal nature of the Hellenes.

Athene was responsible for the creation of the hideous Gorgons—Medusa, Stheno, and Euryale, originally the beautiful daughters of Phorcys and Ceto. Living in Libya, Medusa lay with Poseidon in one of the temples of Athene, and the enraged goddess changed Medusa's appearance to that of a winged monster with brazen claws and serpents for hair, so hideous that she turned to stone all who gazed at her.

Eager to help Perseus vanquish her enemy Medusa, Athene provided him with a polished shield that enabled him to see Medusa only as a reflection. She then petitioned the other gods for their help. Hermes provided him with a sickle and told him how to obtain winged sandals, a magic bag in which to carry Medusa's head, and Hades' helmet of invisibility. After Perseus killed Medusa Athene invented flute-playing from the sound of the wailing Stheno and Euryale. When Perseus gave her the head of the Gorgon she placed it as the central, petrifying image of her aegis, in this case meaning her shield.

She helped many major heroes in completing their tasks. She advised Bellerophon to catch the winged horse Pegasus, and gave him a golden bridle, which he flung over the horse's head when he captured it; astride this flying steed he easily shot the Chimaera. She also helped Jason and the Argonauts in their quest for the Golden Fleece by personally building an oracular beam into the prow of their ship, the *Argo Navis*. The hero she helped most, however, seems to be Heracles.

During his sixth labor, freeing the marshy lake of Stymphalia in Arcadia of the man-eating Stymphalian birds, Athene helped Heracles flush the birds into the air so that the hero could shoot them. Athene also helped Heracles during his twelfth labor when, with the additional help of Hermes, she guided the great hero down to Tartarus, where he obtained Hades' permission to carry away

Cerberus. Having then taken part in the Trojan War, Athene led Heracles to Phlegra, where he helped the gods in their fight against the giants (chronologically this event occurred before the great hero's birth).

She advised Cadmos to sow the teeth of the dragon he had slain; immediately sprang up the Sparti, or "Sown Men," who were fully armed and fought with each other until only five survived. These five were the ancestors of Thebes, and with their help Cadmos built the Cadmea. At Cadmos's wedding to Harmonia, which the gods attended, Athene gave the bride a magic robe that conferred divine dignity.

She was, however, less kind to other mortals. When Tiresias accidentally came across her while she was bathing, she instantly struck him blind, although by way of consolation she bestowed on him the power to foretell the future. During the campaign of the Seven Against Thebes, Tydeus, wounded by Melanippus, might have been saved by Athene with an elixir given to her by Zeus. However, Amphiaraus persuaded him to drink the brains of the dead Melanippus, which so disgusted Athene that she left him to die.

Athene was challenged to a weaving contest by the unfortunate Arachne, whose work— clearly better than that of Athene—was torn up by the angry goddess. Arachne hanged herself, and Athene turned her into a spider; she also transformed either Arachne's hanging rope or her weaving into a cobweb.

Yet Athene was helpful to Orestes when, pursued by the Erinnyes, he reached Athens and embraced the image of Athene in her temple on the Acropolis. She then summoned the Areopagus, the court she established, as she preferred to settle quarrels peaceably, where Apollo defended him against the Erinnyes on the grounds that motherhood is less important than fatherhood. Here her casting vote acquitted him finally of any guilt for the murder of his mother, Clytemnestra. The furious Erinnyes were then pacified by Athene, who persuaded them to accept a grotto in Athens where they would be offered sacrifices, libations, and first fruits. Thenceforth they were known by the euphemistic title of Eumenides, the "well-meaning."

When Athene attended the wedding of Peleus and Thetis with all the other gods (save Eris), she was one of three goddesses (with Hera and Aphrodite) who vied for ownership of the golden Apple of Discord that the vengeful Eris threw into the gathered congregation. Zeus decreed that to solve the problem Hermes should lead the three goddesses to Mount Ida for Paris to judge the dispute.

There the goddesses tried to bribe Paris. Athene offered him fame in war, Hera rule in Asia; Aphrodite offered him as his wife the most beautiful of all women, Helen, and so Paris awarded her ownership of the apple. This ultimately led to the Trojan War, in which Athene actively sided with the besieging Greeks.

The stratagem of the Wooden Horse was just one instance where the goddess was involved. The horse was built under her supervision by Epeius (after a plan devised by Odysseus, whose conscience Athene appears to have been) and bore an inscription dedicating it to the goddess. When the armor of Achilles was awarded to Odysseus (her favorite, it seems) she was offended by Ajax the Greater, and in revenge she sent him mad. When the city fell to the stratagem of the fake horse Cassandra fled to her sanctuary within the city; also, Menelaus failed to sacrifice to her, and so it took him eight years to reach home. She also requested that Zeus command the release of Odysseus by Calypso, who taught the hero how to make a raft on which he could sail home.

However, after Odysseus was 18 days at sea Poseidon wrecked the raft, and only with the help of Athene and Leucothea did Odysseus land on the island of Scheria. From there he finally made it home to Ithaca, where Athene disguised him as a beggar.

The name Pallas features in her mythology in a number of ways. First, it was one of her most common titles. She also killed a giant called Pallas, flaying him to use his skin as the Palladium, a shield. According to Apollodorus, however, who seems to be trying to tidy up this tradition, she also had a friend named Pallas (daughter of Triton), whom she killed in an accident. Athene then made a wooden statue of Pallas and wrapped it in her aegis. This Palladium was worshipped in the citadel at

Troy and was one of the most important prizes that the Greeks seized from the captured city. In Homer's *Iliad* it was this Palladium that Helenus said must be removed from the city before it could be taken; it was duly stolen by Odysseus.

Athene Nike
Greek

An aspect of Athene to whom there is a temple on the Athenian Acropolis.

Athene Parthenos
Greek

An aspect of Athene, whose temple on the Athenian Acropolis is dedicated to "Athene Parthenos," hence the Parthenon. It was erected between 447 B.C. and 438 B.C. under Pericles' administration, the work of the architect Iktinos, and housed the giant Chryselephantine statue of Athene sculpted by Phidias or his school.

Athens
Greek

The capital of modern Greece and of the ancient Greek district of Attica, an area ruled by separate kings until about 900 B.C. Named after the goddess Athene, it is most famous for its Acropolis, which is topped by the temple of Athene Parthenos—the Parthenon, a name that refers to the priestesses of Athene, who lived in a chamber of the temple (built by fifth-century B.C. architect Iktinos). Its friezes display sculptural representations of various subjects, including the Panathenaic Procession that wound its way to the Acropolis. In 394 B.C. the Erechtheion was completed to replace the old temple of Athene built on the site where Poseidon and Athene contested for patronage of the city. The Athenian Acropolis has been inhabited from at least the fifth millenium B.C. but was abandoned by the people to become a sanctuary to the gods after 510 B.C. The whole complex is entered through a grand processional gate, the Propylaia.

The Eleusinian Festival in honor of Demeter and Persephone was probably fully established in Athens by Pesistratus at the end of the sixth century B.C., probably about the time when the cult of Dionysos was introduced. The festivals of the Panathenaea and the Dionysia were both introduced, also by Pesistratus, at about this time. There was an annual procession from Eleusis, about 12 miles distant, to Athens, and those who spoke Greek could be initiated into the final rite of the mysteries. The Thesmaphoria celebrating the foundation of laws was also held in Demeter's honor, in Athens as well as in other parts of Greece.

The city itself has had a stormy history, with the Romans, Byzantines, Franks, and Turks all making additions and alterations. Originally it was connected to its main seaport of Piraeus by parallel walls, which enable the city to remain in contact with the port during sieges. The temple of Hephaistos (the Theseum) is virtually complete. The temple of Athene Nike (the Victorious) perches in the southwest corner of the Acropolis. The theater of Dionysos was rebuilt in stone during the fourth century B.C. below the wall. After c. 900 B.C. the monarchial system in Athens and elsewhere was supplanted by an aristocracy; later an immature struggle for democracy led to tyranny before a democratic constitution was established in the sixth century B.C.

The leading role taken by Athens in the war against Persia consolidated its supremacy in fifth-century B.C. Greece, and in this period the arts and sciences flowered. During the next century Athens was weakened by her resistance to Spartan imperialism, but prosperity returned, and once again the arts and sciences flourished. However, in the third and second centuries B.C. the impact of Athens markedly diminished as the power of Rome grew. In 146 B.C. Athens became part of the Roman Empire and existed as a quiet university town.

In legend Athene was said to have formed the court known as the Areopagus in Athens, and it was there that the famous trial of Orestes was held.

Atlantiades
Greek

A title given to Hermes as it was said that his mother was Maia, a daughter of Atlas and an embodiment of the Great Goddess.

Atlantis

Greek

The legend of the lost island of Atlantis is known from Plato's dialogues *Timaeus* and *Critias*, which he claimed to have derived from the writings of Sodon, who in turn got his information from the Egyptians. Many scholars remain skeptical as to whether Atlantis ever existed and believe that Plato invented the entire tale as an elaborate allegory. Not surprisingly, Atlantis is not mentioned in any other ancient source.

The lost island, or continent, was circular in shape, larger than Asia and Libya combined and the seat of an empire that dominated parts of Europe and Africa. The island was divided by concentric bands of water, with a palace of the king on the central island. Plato placed it beyond the Pillars of Hercules in the Atlantic Ocean, thus beyond the limits of the known world at the time. Although the Atlantic Ocean is probably named after it, the topography and structure of the ocean floor rule out the possibility that it ever existed there. Its powerful and virtuous inhabitants having become degenerate, they were conquered by the Athenians, and the island was swallowed up by the ocean in a day and a night.

The circumstantial evidence of Plato's description has induced many commentators to seek a factual basis. For centuries people were convinced that the New World, discovered by Columbus, was Atlantis. In 1882 Ignatius Donelly published a book arguing that Atlantis had existed and was identical with the Garden of Eden, the origin of all mythology, the alphabet, and more, with its destruction being equivalent to the biblical story of the world flood. However, in Greek mythology this is associated with Deucalion (the Greek Noah whose story seems to derive from the much earlier Sumerian tale of Ziusudra, the son of Prometheus and Clymene) and has no connection whatsoever with Atlantis.

Other interpretations range from the wild reports of lost cities glimpsed on the floor of the Atlantic Ocean (Charles Berlitz) to the dominant theory that the story recalls, in a much amplified form, the destruction of Thera (Santorini) in c. 1450 B.C. by a huge volcanic eruption, far in excess of that of Krakatoa, which caused the abandonment of the Minoan town there and the inundation of the northern coast of Crete. Some even say that the ensuing earthquakes and tidal waves brought about the collapse of the entire Minoan Empire.

A more recent theory relies heavily on the reported topography of Atlantis and identifies the lost island with a marshy region on the lower Guadalquivir River in Spain.

However, Atlantis also has an occult significance, mainly as a result of the writings of W. Scott-Elliot, whose book, *The Story of Atlantis*, alleged that by clairvoyance he had been able to contact the spirits of the Atlanteans, who stated they had been destroyed because of their addiction to black magic. Through such mediumistic contact the name of one of the high priests of Atlantis has been given as Helio-Arconaphus. In addition, some occultists maintain that both Merlin and Igraine originally came from Atlantis.

Atlas

Greek

1. A second-generation Titan, the son of Iapetus and Clymene; brother of Prometheus and Epimetheus and father of the Pleiades, Hyades, and Hesperides by Aethra, a daughter of Oceanos. His name means "much enduring," and his task—a punishment, according to Hesiod, for leading the Titans who revolted against the gods—was to hold the sky upon his shoulders. Atlas was situated in North Africa and identified with Mount Atlas. This task is also found in Hittite mythology, where Upelluri is the giant yoked with the labor. According to Homer he was a marine being who supported the pillars that divided Heaven and Earth. This view is enhanced by the legend that he gave shelter to Amphitrite, who had fled to him to escape the advances and proposals of Poseidon.

Atlas also guarded the Gardens of the Hesperides. When Heracles was sent to fetch the Golden Apples of the Hesperides he asked Atlas to fetch them for him while he held up the sky for awhile. Relieved of his burden, Atlas attempted to trick Heracles into permanently taking over his labor by offering to deliver the apples to Eurystheus himself. Heracles agreed but asked Atlas to momentarily take back the sky while he adjusted his position, but as soon as the sky was back on Atlas's shoulders, Heracles snatched the apples and ran off as fast as he could.

According to Ovid, Atlas, growing weary of his task, asked Perseus to turn him into stone using the head of Medusa.

Astronomical: The name Atlas has been given to a crater located in the upper western quadrant of the surface of the moon next to that known as Hercules.

2. According to Ovid, the mountain into which Perseus turned Atlas using the severed head of Medusa; also the mountain in North Africa with which Atlas is now identified. It was also the home of the three Graeae, sisters of the Gorgons, and the location of the Gardens of the Hesperides in which Hera had planted the tree that grew the Golden Apples. This garden was guarded by Atlas, the Hesperides, and the dragon Ladon, the apples becoming known as the Golden Apples of the Hesperides, which were the object of Heracles' eleventh labor.

See also: Graeae; Heracles; Pleiades

Atreus

Greek

The king of Argos; son of Pelops and Hippodameia, brother of Thyestes, and half-brother to Chrysippus. Chrysippus was abducted and introduced into pederasty by Laius, the king of Thebes. Fearing that Pelops preferred Chrysippus over her own sons, Hippodameia tried to persuade Atreus and Thyestes to kill Chrysippus. When they demurred she herself stabbed Chrysippus with the sword of Laius while the two men lay in bed together, thus setting in motion the ancestral curse on the house of Pelops that lasted for three generations. The two brothers, in a mixture of guilt and confusion, fled and became the joint kings of Midea. Atreus married Aerope and had two sons, Agamemnon and Menelaus, though in Hesiod they are his grandsons, the sons of Pleisthenes, Atreus's son by his first wife, who were reared by Atreus.

Atreus had promised to sacrifice his first lamb to Artemis, but when a lamb was born with a Golden Fleece, he hid the precious fleece away in a chest. Aerope, who Thyestes had seduced, stole it and gave it to her lover. When the Mycenaeans were told by an oracle following the death of King Eurystheus to choose one of the kings of Midea as their ruler, Thyestes suggested they pick whomever could produce a Golden Fleece. Naturally Thyestes won the throne, but Atreus, knowing he had been tricked, suggested a second test. He proposed that the kingdom should go to whichever king could cause the sun to run backwards. Atreus won, possibly by arrangement with Zeus, and became king of Mycenae; he banished Thyestes, who first tricked Atreus into killing his son, Pleisthenes, though some accounts say this was in self-defense, Pleisthenes being sent to kill Atreus by Thyestes.

Atreus then invited his brother to a banquet, pretending a proposed reconciliation by promising half the kingdom. At that banquet Atreus served Thyestes with a stew made from the flesh of Thyestes' children, just as his grandfather, Tantalus, had served Pelops to the gods. After the meal Thyestes was shown the heads and hands of his dead children. Angered by the horrible murder the gods sent a famine against Mycenae. An oracle told Atreus to bring Thyestes back to Mycenae, and Atreus, visiting Sicyon in search of his brother, met and married his third wife, Pelopia, daughter of Thyestes, thinking her to be the daughter of King Thesprotus. When Pelopia gave birth to a son, Aegisthus—actually the son of her father, Thyestes—his mother exposed the child at birth, but Atreus, thinking the child to be his own, took him in and raised him.

His sons Agamemnon and Menelaus were sent to Delphi to discover the whereabouts of Thyestes and by chance met him there and brought him back to Mycenae, where he was imprisoned. Aegisthus, just seven years old, went to kill him, but Thyestes recognized the sword as his own. Pelopia then revealed her true identity before taking her own life. Aegisthus refused to kill Thyestes and instead bloodied the sword and told Atreus that Thyestes was dead. When Atreus went to offer sacrifice in thanks, Aegisthus killed him.

See also: Aegisthus; Pelops; Thyestes

Atropos

Greek

The eldest of the three Fates and the most decisive. She was the one who insisted that the destiny her sisters had shaped out for a man must be carried through, and she was considered to cut the thread of human life with her shears.

Attica

Greek

A wedge-shaped district of ancient Greece; Athens, named after the goddess Athene, was its capital. Bounded on two sides by the Aegean Sea, to the west by Megaris, and to the north by Boeotia, it is now a department of central Greece, and Athens has become the national capital.

According to legend, King Cecrops divided the region into 12 colonies that were united by Theseus under the administrative control of Athens c. 700 B.C. It was also the region invaded in one legend by the Dioscuri (Castor and Polydeuces), who were searching for their sister, Helen, who had been abducted by Theseus. Her hiding place with Theseus's mother, Aethra, was revealed to the Dioscuri by Academus.

Part of the region was the island of Salamis off the southwest coast near the port of Piraeus of which Telamon was a legendary king.

See also: Cecrops

At~tis, ~ys

Greco-Roman

A early Phrygian god whose periodic death and resurrection symbolized the end of winter and the return of spring. A youthful shepherd, semidivine, and a beloved attendant of the mother goddess Cybele (some versions make Attis her son), who made him promise chastity and drove him mad when he broke this vow. As a result she caused him to castrate himself under a fir tree so that no other might have him; or, according to Pausanias, he was killed by a boar like Adonis. Yet another version puts his self-mutilation down to the harassment of an overtly affectionate monster. During the spring festival his death was mourned for two days in the spring, when his spirit passed into a pine tree and violets sprang up from his blood, his recovery then celebrated.

His cult became especially popular under the Roman Empire after it was introduced in 205 B.C. In this cult his priests, the Galli, castrated themselves and sought him in the woods during an annual ritual.

Auge

Greek

The daughter of Aleus, king of Tegea. She was seduced by Heracles and became the mother of Telephus, king of Mysia, by him.

Augean Stables

Greek

The stable buildings in which Augeias (Augeas), king of Elis, kept a herd of 3,000 cattle. They had never been cleaned when Heracles was set the task, as his fifth labor, to clean them in a day. This he did by diverting the Rivers Alpheus and Peneius through the building.

Aug~e(i)as, ~ias

Greek

The king of Elis who, accompanying Jason as one of the Argonauts, took part in the quest for the Golden Fleece. However, his main claim to fame is the appalling filth in which he kept his herd of 3,000 cattle in their stables. Thus Heracles was set the enormous task of cleaning them in a single day as the fifth of his 12 Great Labors. He accomplished the task by diverting the Rivers Alpheus and Peneius through the buildings; although Heracles had cleaned thus the stables, Augeias refused to pay the agreed price—one-tenth of the herd. Heracles then made war on him and the Molionidae, defeated them, and made Phyleus, Augeias's son, king, though one tradition says that Augeias was spared.

See also: Heracles

Augustus

Roman

Great Emperor of the Roman Empire (63 B.C.–14 A.D.). The dead Anchises revealed to his son, Aeneas, the future glory of the city he was to found and its ultimate splendor under Augustus. On the Palatine Hill, Venus presented Aeneas with armor made by Vulcan, which included a shield that depicted the future history of Rome, including Augustus's great victory at the Battle of Actium.

The son of Gaius Octavius, senator and praetor, and Atia, Julis Caesar's niece. He became Gaius Julius Caesar Octavianus through adoption by Caesar in his will (44 B.C.), later receiving the name Augustus (sacred, venerable) in recognition of his services and position (27 B.C.). By way of the naval victory of Actium he became the sole ruler of the Roman world.

Emperor Augustus appears in the New Testament of the Holy Bible in what must be one of the best-known passages: "And it came to pass in those days, that there went out a decree from Caesar Augustus, that all the world should be taxed" (see Luke 2:1).

Aulis

Greek

Ancient Greek town on the Boeotian coast, the Euripus, where the Greek fleet assembled prior to setting sail for Troy at the beginning of the Trojan War. Their first departure ended in the fleet making a false landing in Mysia, the land of Telephus. Having regrouped at Aulis, the fleet was delayed by unfavorable winds, as Agamemnon had vexed Artemis by the killing of a hart. Calchas foretold that only the sacrifice of Iphigeneia, Agamemnon's daughter, would appease the goddess, and Agamemnon reluctantly gave permission. Some say that just as the knife was about to fall Iphigeneia was snatched from the altar by Artemis and carried off to Tauris, where she became her priestess. Finally the fleet set sail for Troy.

Aulus Vibenna

Romano-Etruscan

The brother of Cales Vibenna possibly identified with Olus and whose head was uncovered when the foundations for the Capitoline temple were being dug. This Olus, and by association, Aulus Vibenna, was said to have been a local king.

Auriga

Greek

Astronomical: "The Charioteer." Recognized since early times and displaying many fine objects, this constellation is usually identified with Erichthonius, the legendary fourth king of Athens whose lameness inspired him to invent the chariot. Alternatively, it is sometimes thought of as Poseidon rising from the sea in his chariot, though Auriga is often shown as a herdsman holding a goat, with two kids nearby.

The constellation lies in the northern celestial hemisphere between approximate right ascensions 7h30m and 4h45m, declination +28° to +56°. Its 1st magnitude alpha star (A Aur) is named Capella, the She-Goat star, said to honor Amalthea, the goat that suckled Zeus.

See also: Erichthonius

Aurora

Roman

The Roman goddess of the dawn, equivalent to the Greek Eos.

Auster

Roman

The Roman name for the southwest sirocco wind, equivalent to the Greek Notus.

Autolycus

Greek

The son of Hermes and the mortal Chione who received from his father the gift of being able to make anything he touched become invisible. He was an accomplished thief (Hermes was the god of thieves) and trickster, and using the gift from his father he committed numerous crimes against Sisyphus, stealing a large part of his herds. Sisyphus then marked the hooves of the remaining cattle and thereby caught the thief. He also excelled in swearing and was the father of Polymele, the mother of Jason.

He married Amphitheia by whom he became the father of Anticleia, who married Laertes; thus Autolycus became the grandfather of Odysseus, who he named and who inherited his grandfather's cunning ways. While visiting Autolycus Odysseus received a wound in his thigh from being gored by a boar. It is also said that Autolycus taught Heracles how to wrestle.

Automedon
Greek
A charioteer and comrade of Achilles. Eventually his name, like that of Jehu, referred to any charioteer.

Autonoë
Greek
The daughter of Cadmos and Harmonia and sister to Ino, Semele, Agave, Polydorus, and Illyrius. A bacchant, Autonoë, along with sisters Ino and Agave, was involved in the killing of Pentheus, Agave's son, who resisted the worship of Dionysos, as depicted in *Bacchae* by Euripides.

Aventine Hill
Roman
The southernmost of the hills on which Rome is built. When the city was first founded a legend says that Romulus and Remus could not agree which of them should give his name to the new city, so they consulted the auguries. Romulus stood on the Palatine Hill while Remus stood on the Aventine. Soon Remus saw six vultures, but no sooner had this been reported than Romulus saw 12. Each was acclaimed king by the augur, but a fight ensued and Remus was killed. The Aventine Hill is close to the River Tiber, outside the pomerium, and was associated with the plebians.

See also: Rome

Avernus, Lake
Roman
The lake in Campania, Italy (modern Lago di Averno, near Naples), nearby where Aeneas was told to arm himself with the Golden Bough by the Sibyl of Cumae before she led him to the Underworld to consult his dead father, Anchises. The ancients regarded it as the entrance to the infernal regions on account of the noxious fumes it once exhaled.

B

Bacch~ae, ~antes

Greco-Roman

Also: Maenads, Thyiads

Name used to refer to the female votaries of the god of wine, Dionysos, that is taken from his alternative name, Bacchus, the name by which the god was later absorbed into the Roman pantheon. The male followers of the god were known as Bacchoi.

Bacchae

Greek

Play by Euripides depicting how Pentheus, king of Thebes, resisted the cult of Dionysos and as a result was torn to pieces by the Bacchae, who spotted him spying on their celebrations. Among those that killed the hapless king were his own mother, Agave, and her two sisters, who believed him to be a wild beast come to kill them.

Bacchanal

Greco-Roman

Technically *bacchanal* is used to refer to topics relating to or about Bacchus. However, as a noun, the word can also be applied to the worshippers of Bacchus irrespective of gender, or to the priest who would conduct the frenzied worship.

Bacchanalia

Greco-Roman

The orgiastic rites of the god of wine, Dionysos or Bacchus. During these rites his followers would whip themselves into an intoxicated frenzy when they believed themselves to be at one with the god. The cult was particularly popular with women and was indicative that among the recently civilized Greeks there was a longing for a far more instinctive and impulsive life.

In his play *Bacchae*, Euripides relates the legend of Pentheus, the king of Thebes who in resisting the spread of the Dionysos cult spied on the Bacchae. However, he was spotted, and the Bacchae—in their drunken frenzy mistaking him for a wild beast come to kill them—tore him to pieces. Among the Bacchae were Agave, the hapless king's mother, and her two sisters.

See also: Agave; Pentheus

Bacchoi

Greco-Roman

The name given to male worshippers of the god of wine, Dionysos, later known as Bacchus. His female followers were known as Bacchae, Bacchantes, Maenads, or Thyiads.

Bacchus

Greco-Roman

Also: Liber(a)

A name for the god of wine, Dionysos. While the name Bacchus is usually considered Roman in origin, it was used first by the ancient Greeks and later absorbed into the Roman pantheon. His male votaries were known as Bacchoi; female worshippers were variously known as Bacchae, Bacchantes, Maenads, or Thyiads.

Bassareus

Greek

An epithet of Dionysos used almost exclusively in Thrace. It derives from the Bassaris, a fox skin worn by the god and his worshippers.

Bassarid

Greek

Female votary of Dionysos, the male variant being Bassaroi. The term was almost exclusively used in the region of Mount Pangaeum in Thrace; elsewhere the worshippers of Dionysos/Bacchus were known as Bacchae, Bacchantes, Maenads, Thyiads, and Bacchoi.

Both male and female votaries in this region of Thrace reveled in human sacrifice and, in a delirium of drunken cannibalism, devoured each other. In one famous incident, Orpheus scorned them for their worship of Dionysos, preferring to give his praise to Apollo. In a fit of pique Dionysos drove his votaries into a wild frenzy and made them tear Orpheus to pieces. Whether or not they consumed the carcass is not clear, but by displaying dual characteristics of human sacrifice followed by cannibalism the two groups instantiate the tension of favorable and unfavorable attitudes toward human sacrifice.

See also: Orpheus

Bassaris

Greek

A fox skin said to have been worn by the god Dionysos. This attribute of the god is to be found only in Thrace, where the fox skin was also said to have been worn by the Bacchae or Maenads, the god's worshippers.

Bathos

Greek

Reputed sight of one of the battles between the Olympian deities and the 24 giants with serpents' tails, the sons of Ge, intent on taking their revenge for the imprisonment of their brothers, the Titans. The stories surrounding this epic struggle have been used to explain the volcanic fires at both Bathos and Cumae, the huge bones found at Trapezus, and the volcanic nature of Etna, supposed burial place of Enceladus, and Nisyrus, the final resting place for Polybutes.

See also: Enceladus; Polybutes

Battus

Greek

The nickname given to Aristoteles due to his stammer. A descendant of Euphemus, one of the Argonauts, he created Thera with a clod of Libyan soil given to him by Triton. Wanting to rid himself of his terrible stammer, Aristoteles visited the Delphic Oracle and was told that a cure could be had if he were to found a colony in Libya. For seven years he ignored what seemed an impossible condition, but during that time Thera suffered a terrible drought. Finally, mindful of the oracle, he set off on his mission, first founding a colony on the island of Platea. However, the drought on Thera persisted, so he and his colonists moved to the Libyan mainland, first settling near Aziris but finally deciding on Cyrene. Still afflicted by his stammer, Battus was cured when he met a lion in the Libyan desert and screamed in terror.

Battus's descendants, as kings of Cyrene, were alternatively called Arcesilaus and Battus, all of who have some historicity attached to them. Arcesilaus IV was honored in two odes by Pindar.

Baubo

Greek

The wife of Dysaules of Eleusis and mother of Iacchus, an honorific title afforded the god Dionysos. Baubo is perhaps most famous for an incident at Eleusis when the grief-stricken Demeter visited while searching for her daughter, Persephone. Realizing that the goddess needed nourishment, Baubo offered her some soup. Too grief-stricken to even contemplate the food, Demeter politely refused. However, Baubo then lifted her skirts and displayed her pudenda in an attempt to cheer up the grieving goddess and make her laugh.

The trick worked, and Demeter drank the soup offered to her. The story of Baubo is almost identical to that told of Iambe. Baubo's crude trick has a historical analogue in the vulgar abuse that was traditionally hurled at the participants in the procession along the Sacred Way to Eleusis, from Athens.

See also: Demeter; Eleusis; Persephone

Baucis

Greek

The aged wife of Philemon. The couple was uniquely hospitable to Zeus and Hermes when they visited their region of Phrygia. In return the gods saved them from a river inundation, gave them a shrine in which to serve, and, upon their deaths, turned them both into trees.

Bebrycos

Greek

The island realm of Amycus, son of Poseidon. A renowned boxer, he had the habit of challenging all strangers to a boxing contest and, having never been beaten, killed many who strayed onto his island. His bullying reign came to an end when the Argonauts landed on the island and put forward Polydeuces as their champion; he killed the bully.

See also: Polydeuces

Begoe

Romano-Etruscan

Also: Vegoia

Thought by some to be the derivative of Egeria, this nymph was said to have advised the king of Clusium, Arruns Veltumnus.

See also: Egeria

Bellatrix

Greek

The name of an Amazon warrior.

Astronomical: The gamma star of the constellation Orion (ß Ori) is named after this warrior-maiden. Of magnitude 1.63, spectral type B2III, it is 303 light-years away. It may be located at approximate celestial coordinates right ascension 5h20m, declination +8°.

Bellerophon(tes)

Greek

Son of King Glaucus of Ephyra (Corinth) and grandson of Sisyphus; some sources name him as a son of Poseidon. It would appear as if Bellerophon was not his original name but rather a nickname earned after he had accidentally killed Bellerus, an act for which he fled to Proetus, king of Tiryns, to seek purification. However, Anteia (also called Stheneboea), the wife of Proetus, fell in love with the young man, and when he repulsed her advances she treacherously accused him of trying to seduce her.

Reluctant to kill a guest, Proetus sent Bellerophon to Iobates, his father-in-law and the king of Lycia, carrying with him a letter requesting that the bearer be put to death. The letter said to have been carried by Bellerophon is the earliest reference in Greek literature to writing. Iobates likewise shrank from killing a guest and decided that he would let fate take a hand by sending Bellerophon to kill the Chimaera, a fire-breathing monster with a lion's head, goat's body, and serpent's tail, said to be the offspring of Echidne and Typhon; at that time, the Chimaera was ravaging the countryside of Lycia.

Seeking advice from the gods, Bellerophon succeeded in trapping the winged horse Pegasus beside the fountain of Pirene on the Acropolis at Athens. Harnessing the wondrous steed with a golden bridle given to him by the goddess Athene, Bellerophon flew above the Chimaera and shot it in the mouth with an arrow tipped with lead. This leaden point melted in the beast's mouth and burned out its insides.

Next Iobates sent Bellerophon to fight the Solymi, which he did with equal success, and then against the Amazons. Again Bellerophon succeeded. Iobates then set up an ambush for Bellerophon by his own soldiers, but when they too were soundly defeated Iobates finally realized that he was not up against only Bellerophon but the gods as well. Producing the letter sent to him by Proetus, Iobates finally learned the truth and gave Bellerophon half his kingdom and the hand of his daughter, Philonoë.

The fate of Anteia, the cause of Bellerophon's troubles, is somewhat confused. Some accounts say that she took her own life, whereas others, including Euripides, say that she was taken for a ride on Pegasus and that Bellerophon pushed her off from a great height.

Later tradition records that Bellerophon, greatly bolstered by his resounding successes and realizing that he had been aided by the gods, presumptuously tried to ride up to Heaven upon Pegasus, thinking he must himself have a godly status. Zeus sent a gadfly to sting Pegasus, who reared and threw his rider to earth. Mortally wounded—some accounts say lame, others blind—Bellerophon drifted sadly across the Plains of Wandering until he died. Pegasus continued his upward flight and safely reached the godly confines of Olympus.

See also: Proetus

Bellerus

Greek

The character, about whom nothing else is known, that the son of Glaucus, king of Corinth, accidentally killed, thus earning the nickname Bellerophon.

Bellona

Roman

The goddess of war. Possibly the sister, wife, or daughter of Mars, she may have been, in origin, an Asian goddess of war who was worshipped in Cappadocia and Phrygia, her adoption into the Roman pantheon being made under the patronage of the dictator Sulla.

Belus

Greek

One of the countless sons of Poseidon and father of Aegyptus, Danaus, and Cepheus. Through confusion with the Phoenician god Baal, Belus was reputed by some to have been the founder of Babylon.

Bendis

Greek

Goddess of Thracian origin associated with the moon and with hunting.

Bias

Greek

The brother of Melampus.

Biton

Greek

Brother of Cleobis; both were sons of a priestess of the goddess Hera at Argos. Once, in an act of filial devotion, they dragged their mother's chariot to the temple. In return she prayed that Hera should grant them the best boon possible for mortals; both died while they slept within the confines of the temple.

See also: Argos

Boeotia

Greek

An ancient country of central Greece, formed in the seventh century B.C.; its inhabitants were renowned for their slow-wittedness. Now a department in central Greece, on the north shore of the Gulf of Corinth, its capital is Levádhia. The Boeotian League of ancient Greek cities was dominated by the Boetian city of Thebes, founded in legend by Cadmos, until the league was disbanded sometime after 479 B.C. In more recent times, during the nineteenth century, the site of Thebes was excavated by Heinrich Schliemann, who uncovered the Treasure of the Minyas.

The region has many legends attached to it. Thebes, the most powerful city within the country, was said to have been founded by Cadmos, whereas the country itself was said to have been the home and hunting ground of the giant Orion.

On its coast lies the port of Aulis, where the Greek fleet was becalmed en route for the Trojan War and where Iphigeneia was offered in sacrifice to the goddess Artemis by her father, Agamemnon, the Greek commander. Within its boundaries lies Mount Helicon, sacred to the Muses, upon which rose the fountains of Aganippe and Hippocrene.

See also: Thebes

Bona Dea

Roman

An oracular goddess who would reveal her oracles only to women.

Boötes

Greek

The son of Zeus and Callisto and the reputed inventor of the plough; translated, his name means "ox driver" or "herdsman." The ancient Greeks sometimes identified the constellation of Boötes with Callisto's son, Arcas, or Arctophylax. Confusion exists over the actual identity of the person said to be represented by the constellation, as some also sought to connect it with a wolf named Lycaon, an association many think answers the question whether Zeus killed Lycaon or turned him into a wolf.

Astronomical: A large constellation of the northern celestial hemisphere that contains the star Arcturus, the fourth brightest in the night sky. It is located within the night sky at approximate celestial coordinates right ascension 13h00m to 16h00m, declination +10° to +55°.

See also: Lycaon

Boreas

Greek

The north wind; son of the Titan Astraeus by Eos, goddess of dawn, and brother to the other kindly winds—Notus (south), Eurus (east), and Zephyrus (west), as well as the evening star, Hesperus. Boreas was kept, along with his three brother-winds, in a cave on the floating island of Aeolia. They were released by the god of the winds, Aeolus, either when he felt like it or when the gods so requested. He was considered to be more beneficent than his brother Zephyrus, though on an equal footing with both Eurus and Notus.

He carried off the nymph Oreithyia, daughter of Erechtheus, while she played on the banks of the Ilissus in Athens. They had four children: two daughters, Chione and Cleopatra (the wife of Phineus); and two sons, Zetes and Calais, who took part in the expedition of the Argonauts and distinguished themselves as the heroes who chased away the ravenous Harpies from the dinner table of the blind Phineus, their brother-in-law.

Although not a popular deity, Boreas was particularly worshipped in Athens and was always well disposed toward the city and its inhabitants. During the fifth century B.C. the Athenians attributed the destruction of the fleet of the Persian Xerxes to Boreas.

Bosp(h)orus

Greek

The strait of water joining the Black Sea to the Mediterranean. It was so named, literally translated as "Ox-Ford," because it was said that Io had crossed it while still in the form of a heifer.

This particular stretch of water, which cuts off the Thracian Peninsula of Turkey, including Istanbul, from the remainder of the country, also features in the story of Jason and the Argonauts. At the entrance to the waterway were said to be the perilous Symplegades, rocks that clashed together to crush any vessel that tried to slip between them. Upon the advice of Phineus, Jason released a dove between the so-called Clashing Rocks, which came together, clipping the fleeing bird's tail feathers. As the rocks recoiled Jason urged his oarsmen on and, with a helping push from Athene, the *Argo Navis* passed safely through. From that time forward the rocks remained fixed. Some sources move the location of these events away from the Bosphorus to the opposite end of the Sea of Marmara, saying that the Symplegades were located at the entrance to the Hellespont instead.

See also: Io

Branchidae

Greek

The site of an oracle of Apollo to the south of Miletus that contains important relics of Ionian sculpture. Today the site is on the western seaboard of Asiatic Turkey.

Brauron

Greek

A major shrine in Attica to the goddess Artemis, Brauron was particularly frequented by pregnant women. The worship of Artemis at Brauron was said to have been initiated by Iphigeneia and her brother, Orestes. Iphigeneia, the daughter of Agamemnon, had once been a priestess to Artemis at Tauris until rescued by Orestes. When they left Tauris they took with them the image of Artemis, which they brought to Brauron, hence the goddess becoming known as Brauronia. This Brauronian Artemis was not worshipped solely at Brauron but in Athens as well and especially in Sparta, where youths were scourged at her altar until they sprinkled it with their blood.

One particular feature of the sanctuary at Brauron was the presence of girls aged between five and ten known as *arktoi*—"bear virgins" or "bears for Artemis." Each would spend a period in the service of the goddess before taking part in a procession at Athens to mark their arrival at maturity.

Extensive remains still exist at Brauron, dating back to the Mycenaean period, and include the tomb of Iphigeneia. The most impressive remains today are those of a Doric temple complex dating from c. 420 B.C., complete with the quarters that would have been occupied by the *arktoi*.

See also: Artemis

Brennus

Roman

A Gaul who was said to have been besieging Rome at the time when Camillus, returned from exile, attacked the Gauls from the rear, decimated their forces, and thus saved Rome from almost certain destruction.

Briareus

Greek

Also: Aegaeon

One of the Hecatoncheires or Centimani, the 100-handed, 50-headed giant sons of Ge and Uranos, the other two being Cottus and Gyas or Gyges. They were in turn the brothers of the one-eyed Cyclopes and the 12 Titans. When Hera, in cahoots with Poseidon and Apollo, succeeded in leading a conspiracy against Zeus and put him in chains, Briareus and Thetis freed the great god.

His variant name of Aegaeon suggests that he was a god of the Aegean Sea, a supposition supported by the fact that he is sometimes regarded as the son or son-in-law of Poseidon. This watery association is further supported by the fact that he was said to have awarded the Isthmus to Poseidon during his dispute with Helios, giving the latter the Acrocorinthos.

Having once appeared to help Zeus, he later appears to have taken part in a rebellion against all of Olympus. Foretold by an oracle that the roasted viscera of a monstrous bull that lived in the River Styx would enable whoever ate them to overthrow Zeus and rule in his stead, Briareus caught the beast and was about to roast the viscera as he had been instructed when a kite flew down, snatched the entrails, and took them to Zeus.

With the giant's revolt finally put down, Zeus punished those who had plotted against him, Briareus being confined beneath Mount Etna in Sicily along with some of the other giants. He is considered to be venting his anger at his continued imprisonment, along with the other confined giants, each time Etna erupts.

See also: Cyclopes; Etna; Hecatoncheires

Briseis

Greek

The daughter of Brises, a priest from Lyrnessus. She was carried off by Achilles during the Trojan War to be his concubine and later was the object of a notorious quarrel between Achilles and Agamemnon. *Iliad* in fact opens with this quarrel. Agamemnon had been assigned Chryseis, the daughter of the Trojan priest Chryses, as his concubine. However, when Chryses came to ransom her he was roughly repulsed. In revenge, Apollo sent a plague to afflict the Greek hordes until finally, on Calchas's advice, Agamemnon returned Chryseis to her father.

To recompense himself for his loss, Agamemnon took Briseis, an act that led Achilles to sulk in his tent and resolutely refuse any further part in the Trojan War. Some sources, however, attribute this behavior to the simple fact that Achilles had fallen in love with Polyxena, the daughter of Priam, king of Troy, and was, by refusing to participate further in the war, simply trying to curry favor with Polyxena's father.

With Achilles no longer fighting with the Greeks, the Trojans soon began to get the upper hand. Alarmed, Agamemnon offered to return Briseis, an offer that Achilles politely but firmly refused. Instead, Patroclus, Achilles' inseparable companion, donned the great warrior's armor and attempted to turn the tide back in favor of the Greeks. He failed, being killed by Hector. It was this that led Achilles to rejoin the battle, and Agamemnon finally to return Briseis.

See also: Achilles

Brises

Greek

A priest from Lyrnessus whose daughter, Briseis, was taken captive by Achilles, who made her his favorite concubine while the Greek forces were laying siege to Troy.

Britomartis
Greek

Also: Dictynna

A goddess of Cretan origin identified with Aphaia, whose temple is on Aegina. She was relentlessly pursued by Minos for nine months before leaping into the sea, there to be rescued by the goddess Artemis, who deified her and gave her the epithet Dictynna, which she herself shares. The epithet Dictynna, which is sometimes used as a variant name, is certainly Cretan in origin, possibly being connected with Mount Dicte on Crete, though it is also said that she derived the name from having fallen into a fisherman's net (*diktys*) after falling off a cliff in her flight from Minos, or because she was once caught in a hunting net, or that she actually invented these nets.

See also: Dictynna

Brom~ios, ~ius
Greek

An alternative name for the god of fertility and wine, Dionysos or Bacchus, used by his votaries, who referred to him as Bromios "the Boisterous."

Brontes
Greek

One of the one-eyed Cyclopes, sons of Ge and Uranos. His brothers were Steropes and Arges, along with the three Hecatoncheires, or Centimani, named Cottus, Briareus (or Aegaeon), and Gyas (or Gyges), and the 12 Titans.

See also: Cyclopes

Broteas
Greek

One of the children of Agamemnon, along with Pelops and Niobe. Broteas could trace his line of descent back to Zeus and the nymph Pluto, as legend said that Agamemnon was the son of Tantalus and thus the grandson of Zeus and Pluto.

Brutus
Greco-Romano-British

The legendary founder of the British people and the great-grandson of the Trojan Aeneas. Exiled from Italy for accidentally killing his father, Silvius, he traveled to Greece, where he found a group of Trojan exiles who had been enslaved by the Greek King Pandrasus. Brutus challenged the king and defeated him. Claiming the hand of the king's reluctant daughter, Ignoge, he compelled Pandrasus not only to release his Trojan slaves but also to supply them with ships, provisions, and bullion to leave the country.

Traveling west he landed on an island beyond the Pillars of Heracles (Hercules) where he found another group of Trojan exiles led by Corineus. They joined forces and finally landed in Britain at Totnes, in Devon. There they were attacked by and defeated a group of giants. Brutus established his capital, Troia Nova or Troynovant, on the banks of the River Thames, and it was there that Brutus was subsequently buried. His capital has now become known as London.

See also: Aeneas

Brutus, Lucius Junius
Roman

In the company of the sons of Tarquinius Superbus, Lucius Junius Brutus traveled to the Delphic Oracle, where the sons of Tarquinius Superbus asked which one of them would succeed their father. The oracle replied that it would be the first of them that kissed their mother; pretending to stumble, Brutus fell and kissed the earth, thus immediately alienating himself from the Tarquins. Returning to Rome he witnessed the suicide of Lucretia, who had been raped by Sextus, the son of Tarquinius Superbus, who had told her story to her father, Spurius Lucretius Tricipitinus, and husband, Lucius Tarquinius Collatinus, before stabbing herself to death in front of their eyes and those of Brutus and Publius Valerius Poplicola.

Brutus then led the people of Collatia, the city from which Lucretia's husband originated, against Rome, roused the city, and persuaded its people to shut the gates against

Tarquinius Superbus, who was absent besieging Ardea. Realizing that their reign was at an end, Tarquinius Superbus and his sons fled into exile.

Having freed itself of the monarchy, Rome became in 500 B.C. a republic governed by consuls, Brutus being the most renowned during this early period. Three abortive attempts were made to restore the hated monarchy. In the first of these, Brutus's own sons were implicated, so he had them executed. Finally Brutus was killed in single combat with Arruns Tarquinius.

Busiris

Greek

One of the numerous sons of Poseidon who became the king of either Libya or Egypt, the latter being the more likely as Busiris was the Greek name for the Egyptian Delta city of Djedu, an early cult center for the Egyptian deity Osiris. He had the habit of sacrificing all foreign visitors to his land to Zeus until Heracles visited and the tables were turned.

Butes

Greek

A priest of Pallas Athene and the son of the king of Athens, Pandion.

See also: Pandion

Byblis

Greek

A nymph who became infatuated with her brother, Caunus, until she was finally changed into a fountain.

Bybl~os, ~us

Greco-Romano-Phoenician

Ancient Phoenician city (modern Jebeil) 32 kilometers (20 miles) north of Beirut, Lebanon. Known to the Assyrians and Babylonians as Gubla, it first became known as Byblos during the Roman period, when the city boasted an amphitheater, baths, and a temple dedicated to an unknown male god. It is, however, perhaps best known as the center for the worship of Adonis, the god of vegetation whose annual death and resurrection reflects the passing of the seasons.

See also: Adonis

Byzantium

Greek

Ancient Greek city located on the northern shore of the Thracian Bosphorus. Founded as a colony of the Greek city Megara on the Corinthian Isthmus about 667 B.C., it was recolonized in 628 B.C. This settlement was wiped out by the Persians of Darius I but subsequently recaptured and recolonized with a mixed force from Sparta and Athens by Puasanias of Sparta following the battle of Plataea in 479 B.C.; its sovereignty was disputed by both Sparta and Athens throughout the fifth century B.C. Philip of Macedon laid siege to the city in 340 B.C., but it was preserved by a miraculous flash of light that revealed the approaching army, a miracle still used on Turkish coins.

The city continued to prosper, and it resisted the Thracian Gauls until it fell to the Roman Emperor Septimus Severus, who razed the city and then rebuilt it in 196 A.D. Emperor Constantine made it his capital in 330 A.D., renaming the city Constantinople. In 1453 the city fell to the Muslims and gradually extended the use of its Turkish name, Istanbul (Stamboul).

C

Cabiri

Greek

Originating in Phrygia, these fertility deities, usually described as twins though their number does vary, were worshipped in Thebes and Athens, to which the phallic hermas (cairns) were said to have been brought as part of their cult, but especially on the northern Aegean islands of Samothrace, Lemnos, and Imbros. The Samothracians put their number at four, christening them Axieros, Axiokersos, Axiokersa, and Cadmilus. They played an important role in the Samothracian mysteries, being identified with the Olympian deities—Demeter, Persephone, Hades, and Hermes.

Often referred to simply as the "Great Gods," their names appear related to the Semitic root *kbr,* which simply means "great," and they may represent the Phrygian version of the twin agricultural deities known elsewhere among the Indo-European peoples, such as the Vedic Ashvins. As twin deities they were often identified with the Dioscuri, in which guise they were regarded as helpers of distressed sailors, appearing to them in the form of Saint Elmo's fire.

Their parentage greatly varied. On Lemnos they were said to be the children of Hephaistos and were regarded as smiths. Elsewhere they were said to have been sons of Uranos, who assisted the birth of Zeus, or of Proteus and thus guardians of sailors, or even of Zeus and the Muse Calliope.

See also: Dioscuri

Cacus

1. Romano-Etruscan

Later to become identified with Caeculus, the legendary ancestor of the powerful Caecilii family of the Roman republic, this exceptionally beautiful youth, singer, and seer was killed by Hercules.

2. Greco-Roman

Originating in Greek mythology, Cacus was later absorbed into Roman culture. He was described as a half-human demigod, a maneating ogre, the son of Hephaistos and Medusa; the Romans made him the son of Vulcan, a direct parallel, but left his mother nameless. He was said to have lived in a cave on the Palatine Hill, though some sources make this the Aventine Hill, from where he terrorized the Arcadians.

During the tenth labor of Heracles that great hero drove the cattle he had taken from Geryon through Italy, encountering, on the Palatine Hill, Cacus, who attempted to make off with the oxen. Heracles clubbed him to death, a story subsequently told to Aeneas by King Evander, who some sources say used Cacus as a slave.

See also: Medusa

Cadme(i)a

Greek

The citadel of Thebes said to have been built by Cadmos with the aid of the five Sparti or "Sown Men" who survived their battle with each other. These five—Echion, Udaeus, Chthonius, Hyperenor, and Pelorus—became revered as the ancestors of Thebes. The fortifications below the Cadmea were built at a later date by Amphion and Zethus, the latter marrying Thebe, who gave her name to the city.

See also: Sparti

Cadm~os, ~us

Greek

The legendary founder of Thebes in Boeotia. According to common tradition, he was the son of Agenor (son of Poseidon and king of Phoenicia) and Telephassa. When his sister, Europa, was carried off by Zeus, who appeared to her in the form of a bull, Agenor sent his sons, Cadmos among them, to search for her.

Having no success, the sons returned without their sister, but Cadmos decided to consult the Delphic Oracle. There he was advised to relinquish his fruitless search and instead follow a cow until she sank down with fatigue and there found a city. This he did, following the cow from Phocis to Boeotia, where she sank down to rest; he decided to found his city there.

Sacrificing to Athene, he sent his men to fetch water from a spring that was sacred to Ares, not knowing that it was guarded by a dragon. This beast killed most of his men, but Cadmos prevailed and, upon the advice of Athene, sowed the teeth from the slain dragon. Immediately fully armed men, the Sparti or "Sown Men" sprang up from the teeth and began to menace Cadmos, who threw stones into their midst. Thinking that his neighbor was hitting him, each started to fight one another until only five remained. These five—Echion, Udaeus, Chthonius, Hyperenor, and Pelorus—helped Cadmos to build the Cadmea, the citadel of the city that was subsequently to become known as Thebes after Zethus had married Thebe and so became revered as ancestors of the city and its people.

To atone for killing the dragon, Cadmos became a slave to Ares for eight years before Zeus gave him Harmonia, the daughter of Ares and Aphrodite, to be his wife. All the Olympian deities attended their wedding, the first time the gods had attended the wedding of a mere mortal, and several fabulous gifts were given to the bride. From Aphrodite came the famous necklace that had been made by Hephaistos, which Zeus had originally given to Europa and which bestowed irresistible loveliness on its wearer. From Athene she received a magic robe woven by the Graces that conferred divine dignity.

Cadmos was said to have introduced the alphabet and writing to Thebes from Phoenicia. The children of Cadmos and Harmonia were Autonoë, Ino, Semele (the mother of Dionysos), Agave, Polydorus, and later Illyrius. In his old age Cadmos relin-

quished his throne to his grandson, Pentheus, the son of Agave and Echion, but he was murdered attempting to resist the cult of Dionysos. Following the murder Cadmos and Harmonia left Thebes and went to Illyria; later, in the form of serpents, they were received in the Islands of the Blessed.

See also: Boeotia; Sparti

Caduceus
Greco-Roman

The winged staff carried by Hermes as an attribute along with his winged hat, the petasus, and winged sandals, the alipes. The staff was originally represented as being adorned with white ribbons, but these later became serpents due to Hermes' association as the herald of Hades, the intimator of death who gently laid the golden rod on the eyes of the dying. When Hermes was absorbed into the Roman pantheon as Mercury, the caduceus remained as a serpent-entwined rod.

Though normally associated with Hermes or Mercury, the caduceus was also carried by Asclepios, the god of medicine, and has found its way into modern symbology as the emblem of many medical associations and organizations.

See also: Asclepios; Hermes

Caeles Vibenna
Romano-Etruscan

Brother of Aulus Vibenna with whom he attacked Cacus. Said to have given his name to the Caelian Hill in Rome, he was once rescued from a period of enforced captivity by his faithful companion, Mastarna.

Caeneus
Greek

Born as the nymph Caenis, she was raped by Poseidon, who, as was customary after such enjoyment by the gods, granted a boon. Caenis asked to be turned into a man to avoid being raped again. Poseidon consented, making him invulnerable at the same time. So Caeneus was created.

Having taken part in the hunt for the Calydonian Boar in the company of the

Argonauts, Caeneus became the king of the Lapithae, demanding worship as a god. At Zeus's instigation a great battle ensued between the Lapithae and the centaurs, who, unable to overcome Caeneus, bludgeoned him into the ground and buried him under a mass of felled trees, a scene depicted on a bronze plaque at Olympia. His soul was released in the form of a bird, after which his body regained its female form.

Caere

Romano-Etruscan

A great metal-working center some 15 miles northwest of Rome. One of the most Hellenized of all the Etruscan cities, Caere had a large Phoenician population and controlled several dependant ports. Other important Etruscan cities within the vicinity were Tarquinii, Vulci, and Veii.

Calais

Greek

The brother of Zetes, winged twin sons of Boreas and Oreithya. They accompanied the expedition of Jason and the Argonauts and, upon reaching the island of Bebrycos, drove off the rapacious Harpies that had been plaguing the blind King Phineus, husband of their sister, Cleopatra, before releasing Cleopatra's sons from imprisonment by their father, who falsely suspected they rather than the Harpies had been plaguing him.

See also: Zetes

Calchas

Greek

Treacherous Trojan seer; the father of Cressida and originating from either Mycenae or Megara. Fated to die when he met a better diviner than himself, he assisted the Greek forces in the run up to and during the Trojan War. Prior to the Greek fleet assembling at Aulis he foretold that Troy could not be taken without the aid of Achilles (then age nine), the son of Peleus (king of the Myrmidones and Phthia in Thessaly) and the Nereid Thetis.

Then, with the fleet becalmed at Aulis, Calchas advised that the only way to gain favorable winds was to sacrifice Iphigeneia, the daughter of the Greek commander-in-chief, Agamemnon, to the goddess Artemis to appease her for the killing of a hart. Agamemnon reluctantly consented, but the goddess carried the hapless maiden away to serve as her priestess in Tauris.

In the tenth year of the Trojan War there occurred the famous incident between Achilles and Agamemnon, the latter having taken Chryseis, the daughter of the Trojan priest Chryses, as his concubine. Apollo sent a plague among the Greek hordes, and on Calchas's advice Chryseis was returned to her father.

Agamemnon now took Briseis, the concubine of Achilles, to recompense himself, and as a result Achilles refused to take any further part in the battle, turning the tide firmly in favor of the besieged city.

With many Greek heroes dead, Calchas said they must fetch the bow and arrows of Heracles then owned by Philoctetes, who had been left on the island of Lemnos because of the stench from a festering snake bite. Odysseus and Diomedes sailed to the island to persuade him to join their cause.

Next, Calchas advised the Greeks that they would gain final victory over Troy only if they were to capture Helenus, for only he knew the secret oracles that protected the city. He also participated in the plot that led to the death of Palamedes. Following the fall of Troy, Calchas, like Amphilochus, made his way overland to Colophon. There he contended in a contest of prophecy with Mopsus, a son of Apollo and Manto, and was beaten when Mopsus correctly stated the number of figs on a fig tree. Having been surpassed, he died of grief, as was fated, and was buried at Notium. Calchas and Mopsus are venerated as the joint founders of several cities including Perge, Selge, and Sillyum.

See also: Cressida; Trojan War; Troy

Calipe

Greek

A misspelling of Calpe, one of the Pillars of Heracles (Hercules), that appears in some early source texts.

Calliope
Greco-Roman

One of the nine daughters of Zeus and Mnemosyne who were collectively known as the Muses. She was the eldest daughter and therefore the leading Muse—the Muse of eloquence, lyre-playing, and heroic or epic poetry. She is represented in art with a tablet and stylus, sometimes with a roll of paper or even a book. She had two daughters by Apollo and was the mother of Orpheus. Once Greek culture had been absorbed by the Romans, the Muses were said to have been the nine daughters of Jupiter.

See also: Muses, the

Callir(r)hoë
Greek

1. The daughter of the river god Achelous who married Alcmaeon after her father had purified him. She demanded the necklace and robe of Harmonia from her husband, but he had already given them to Arsinoë, the daughter of Phlegeus to whom he was already married. Alcmaeon returned to Arsinoë and almost succeeded in getting the wondrous artifacts back, but Phlegeus discovered the true reason behind the request and ordered his sons to kill Alcmaeon.

2. A daughter of Oceanos and the mother of Geryon.

3. A daughter of the River Scamander; the wife of Tros and mother by him of Ilus, Assaracus, Ganymede, and Cleopatra.

See also: Alcmaeon; Arsinoë

Callisto
Greek

The daughter of Lycaon; a nymph, she was one of Artemis's huntresses and, like that goddess, sworn to chastity. She was seduced and raped by Zeus, with some sources saying that Zeus appeared to her in the guise of Artemis, and the unfortunate maiden was then transformed into a bear. Here the sources again differ. Some say that the transformation was made by Zeus in order to deceive his wife, Hera, whereas others say that it was carried out by Artemis in anger when Callisto's pregnancy became apparent.

As a bear she was hunted down and shot, and here again there is some confusion among varying accounts. Some say that Hera, discovering the attempt made by her deceitful husband to hide his lust for the maiden, contrived to have Artemis kill the bear that was Callisto, whereas others say she was hunted down and shot by her son by Zeus, Arcas (sometimes called Boötes), when she wandered into the sanctuary of Zeus Lycaeus.

Having been shot she was set in the heavens, some saying that she became Arctos, others that she became the constellation Ursa Major (Great Bear), her son becoming either Ursa Minor (Little Bear) or Arctophylax.

Hera now made the sea gods promise never to let her rival enter their realm, and so in the northern hemisphere the constellation Ursa Major never sets.

Astronomical: See the relevant entries for the constellations Boötes, Ursa Major, and Ursa Minor. The name Callisto has been given to the second largest of the four Galilean satellites of the planet Jupiter. With a diameter of 4,800 kilometers (300 miles) and orbiting every 16.7 days at a distance of 1.9 million kilometers (1.2 million miles) from the planet, its surface is covered with large craters. The moon lies fifth closest to the surface of the planet between the orbits of Ganymede and Leda.

See also: Arcas; Lycaon

Calpe
Greco-Roman

The ancient name for Gibraltar, the European of the Pillars of Heracles (Hercules), the other being Abyla, or Ceuta, in North Africa. These pillars were supposedly markers of the western boundary of the known world, beyond which lay the legendary Atlantis.

See also: Abyla

Calydon
Greek

Town in Aetolia, north of the western stretch of the Gulf of Corinth. Situated in the mountains, it is most famous as the location of the epic struggle best known as the hunt for the Calydonian Boar, which was sent by Artemis to ravage Calydon, as its King Oeneus had forgotten to include the goddess in his annual offering of the first fruits to the gods.

Calydonian Boar
Greek
A huge boar that was sent to ravage Calydon by the goddess Artemis as Oeneus, king of Calydon, had omitted the goddess in his annual offering of first fruits to the gods. Oeneus pleaded with the Greek cities to send their greatest heroes to rid him of the monstrous beast, offering its hide as the prize to the hero who managed to kill it. Many cities replied by sending their heroes, and among those who took part in the hunt were Peleus, Amphiaraus, Meleager, and Atalanta. Meleager was the successful contestant in the hunt and, having been presented with the hide, promptly gave it to Atalanta, with whom he was in love. His uncles, the sons of Thestius, quarreled with Meleager over his gift of the hide to Atalanta, and this ultimately led to the heroes' deaths.

See also: Atalanta; Meleager; Oeneus

Calypso
Greek
The nymph daughter of Atlas who lived on the island of Ortygia or Ogygia. Having fallen in love with Odysseus after he was washed ashore following a shipwreck while returning home to Ithaca at the end of Trojan War (having previously been held captive by Circe), she kept him there for seven or eight years, offering him ageless immortality as part of the bargain. Finally, Zeus sent Hermes to command that Odysseus be released. To help Odysseus return home, Calypso showed him how to make a raft on which he set sail from her island home. Apart from her role in the story of Odysseus as related in Homer's *Odyssey*, Calypso is not referred to in any other context.

See also: Circe; Odysseus

Camenae
Roman
Generic term used to refer to water nymphs.

Camilla
Roman
The Amazonian daughter of King Metabus of Privernum, king of the Volscii, who to preserve his daughter tied her to a javelin, dedicated her to Diana, and threw her across the River Amisenus. She was allied to Turnus during his great battle with Aeneas and was killed by Arruns.

Camillus, Murcus Furius
Roman
Historical figure who in 396 B.C. was appointed dictator—sole governor of Rome—for the duration of the Romans' war against Veii, the Etruscan city that commanded the River Tiber at Fidenae. Having captured a soothsayer from the Etruscan city, the Romans were told that the only way to take the city was to drain Alban Lake, a fact confirmed by the Delphic Oracle. Camillus ordered it drained and then had his men tunnel under the city to a point below a temple sacred to Juno.

Above them they heard the king of the beleaguered city preparing to sacrifice to Juno, stating that whosoever should make the sacrifice would triumph in their war. At that point the Romans burst through, made the sacrifice, and took the city. Watching from a high tower as his troops stormed the city, Camillus wept. The figure of Juno from the temple in Veii was then taken to Rome, and spoils from the city were sent to be dedicated to Apollo at Delphi. Camillus, however, was charged with retaining some of the spoils for himself and was forced into exile.

This story has obvious parallels with the story of the sacking of Troy, in which gaining secret entry into the city after receiving information from one of the city's seers is a common factor. Many years later, in a story that is a complete fabrication, Camillus was said to have returned from exile while Rome was besieged by the Gauls under Brennus and, attacking them from the rear, decimated their forces. The fact is the Gauls successfully sacked Rome and later left unharmed. It is practically certain that they captured the Capitoline Hill, said to have been saved by the cackling of Juno's sacred geese, as well as the rest of the city, but this would have been an unacceptable fact to later generations, so a more suitable and fitting conclusion was thus invented—in the process restoring the name of the exiled Camillus.

See also: Capitoline Hill

Canc~er, ~ri
Greco-Roman
While Heracles was fighting the Hydra, the goddess Hera, who hated Heracles, sent a crab to bite the great hero and thereby distract him. Heracles simply crushed the insignificant creature, and for its loyal service Hera placed it in the heavens, where it formed the constellation Cancer. Later this constellation also was referred to as the Gate of Men, through which the souls descended from Heaven into newborn babies.

Astronomical: This famous but inconspicuous constellation lies in the northern celestial hemisphere, straddling the ecliptic between approximate right ascensions 9h15m and 7h55m, declination from +7° to +33°. It forms the fourth sign of the Zodiac (June 22–July 23), and the sun is today in Cancer from July 7 to August 11. The constellation contains the stars Asellus Australis (d Cnc) and Asellus Borealis (G Cnc), they being the Southern Ass and Northern Ass that were ridden by Dionysos and Silenus in their battle with the Titans.

See also: Hydra

Candace
Greek
A queen of Meroe who was visited by a disguised Alexander the Great. Candace, however, recognized him, for she had had his portrait drawn in secret. Originally it was her intention to kill Alexander, for he had executed King Porus of India, to whom she was related, but she relented when she discovered that he had actually saved her son, Candaules, from the Bebryces. Another of her sons, called Kargos, appears in later versions of the *Alexander Romance,* his name seeming to be a form of the modern Greek shadow-puppet hero Karagiozis.

Canes Venatici
Greek
Astronomical: "The Hunting Dogs." Though not defined until the seventeenth century by the Polish astronomer Johannes Hevelius, this constellation represents Asterion (Starry) and Chara (Beloved), the dogs or hounds that are held on leash by Boötes pursuing the bear. Lying in the northern celestial hemisphere between approximate right ascensions 14h05m and 12h05m, declination from +28° to +53°, the constellation seems to reflect some more ancient naming of the stars within its boundaries. A single star, the Beta star (ß CVn), is said to represent both hounds.

Canis Major
Greco-Egyptian
Astronomical: "The Great Dog." One of the hunting dogs of Orion along with Canis Minor (the Small Dog). Sirius (the Dog Star), brightest in the sky, was carefully observed by the ancient Egyptians because around the date it rose at dawn the Nile would flood the surrounding countryside. The constellation Canis Major lies in the southern celestial hemisphere between approximate right ascensions 7h25m and 6h10m, declination from –12° to –34°.

Canis Minor
Greco-Egyptian
Astronomical: "The Small Dog." The companion of Canis Major (the Great Dog) and one of the hunting dogs of Orion. Placed in the sky for his loyal and faithful service, he drinks from the Milky Way, once thought to be a river. Whereas the Greeks called the whole group Procyon, the Egyptians referred to him as Anubis, the jackal-headed god. The alpha star of the group, a CMi, is known as Procyon and was particularly important to the Egyptians. Meaning "rising before the dog," it heralded the arrival of Sirius the Dog Star and thus the forthcoming inundation of the Nile.

Canis Minor is a small and badly defined constellation lying in the northern celestial hemisphere between approximate right ascensions 7h05m and 8h10m, declination from 0° (on the celestial equator) to +13°.

Canopus

Greek

The helmsman of Menelaus who, on the return from Troy at the end of the Trojan War, died in Egypt where a coastal town near Alexandria was named after him.

Astronomical: The primary or alpha star of the constellation Carina (α Car) is named after Menelaus's helmsman. The second brightest star in the night sky, it is of magnitude –0.73, spectral type FOIb. Lying some 196 light-years from earth, it may be found at approximate celestial coordinates right ascension 6h20m, declination –53°.

See also: Menelaus

Capaneus

Greek

Husband of Evadne (the daughter of Iphis), father of Sthenelus, and one of the Seven Against Thebes, his compatriots being named as Adrastus, Amphiaraus, Polyneices, Tydeus, Hippomedon, and Parthenopaeus. The attackers were soon repelled, Capaneus being struck by a bolt of lightning from Zeus as he scaled the walls. When his body was given funeral rites, his wife, Evadne, threw herself onto the pyre and perished.

See also: Seven Against Thebes

Capella

Greek

Astronomical: Lying within the constellation Auriga, this star, the alpha, or primary, star of that grouping (α Aur), honors the she-goat that suckled the infant Zeus and may therefore be identified with Amalthea. Lying at approximate celestial coordinates right ascension 5h15m, declination +46°, the star is actually a spectroscopic binary, the primary being a G8III, slightly variable star at about 0.08 magnitude some 46 light-years from earth. Its companion is of type F. The pair makes up the sixth brightest star in the night sky.

Capitoline Hill

Roman

One of the seven hills of Rome. It was on this hill that Romulus, having become king of Rome, made a sanctuary where any fugitive might take refuge and so increase the population of the new settlement. This, however, led to a serious imbalance within the population—the men far outnumbered the women—so at the time of the annual festival in honor of Consus, when Sabine visitors had flocked to Rome, Romulus ordered that all the Sabine women should be seized.

Titus Tatius, king of the Sabines, then led his army against Rome and was circling the Capitoline Hill when Tarpeia, the daughter of the Roman garrison commander, looked down on the Sabine enemies and was impressed by the gold ornaments they wore. She secretly sent a message to Titus Tatius suggesting that in return for all the gold worn by the Sabines on their left arms she would let them into the citadel by night. This she did, but when the time came for payment the Sabines hurled their gold shields at her and killed her.

The Capitoline Hill was later saved when the city was under siege from Brennus the Gaul, so it is said, by the cackling of the geese sacred to Juno. So far as it is known, this is a complete fabrication, for the Gauls successfully sacked all of Rome, including the Capitoline Hill.

See also: Rome; Sabine

Cappadocia

Roman

Ancient region of Asia Minor, the boundaries of which differed greatly at various times. A Roman province from 17 A.D., it was here that Bellona, the Roman goddess of war, was worshipped.

Capricorn(us)

Greco-Roman

There are two legends surrounding Capricorn, the first being Greek and relating an earthly event, the second being Roman after Greek culture had been absorbed. Legend says that the god Pan, to escape the giant Typhon, leaped into the River Nile and, midleap, his head, still above the waters of the river, became that of a goat while his hindquarters became the rear part of a fish. In this way the Sea Goat or Capricorn was created, later to be placed in the heavens as the constellation of the same name.

When their culture absorbed the complexities of Greek culture Romans added that the constellation Capricorn was a Gate of Men, through which the souls of the dead passed on their way to Heaven. This should be compared with Cancer, the Gate of Men through which souls were said to pass in the opposite direction.

Astronomical: The tenth sign of the Zodiac, Capricorn is a badly defined constellation lying in the southern celestial hemisphere straddling the ecliptic between approximate right ascensions 20h and 22h, declination from –9° to –30°.

See also: Pan

Capys
Greek

The father of Anchises.

Carina
Greek

Astronomical: "The Keel." One of the four constellations said to have been formed when Athene placed the *Argo Navis,* the ship of Jason and the Argonauts built by Argos, in the heavens. The other three constellations that make up the remaining parts of the vessel are Vela, the Sail; Puppis, the Poop or Stern; and Pyxis, the Ship's Compass. The constellation lies in the southern celestial hemisphere, easily spotted near Canopus, the second brightest star in the night sky, between approximate right ascensions 6h05m and 11h10m, declination from –52° to –76°.

See also: Argo (Navis)

Carmentia
Roman

Said to have been the mother of Evander; a goddess of water, childbirth, and prophecy, she is sometimes credited with having taught the Romans how to write.

Carna
Roman

A goddess of physical fitness.

Carthage
Greco-Romano-Phoenician

Ancient Phoenician port in northern Africa, 16 kilometers (10 miles) north of modern Tunis, Tunisia, lying on a peninsula in the Bay of Tunis. Said to have been founded in c. 814 B.C. by Phoenician emigrants under the leadership of the legendary Princess Dido. It developed extensive commercial interests throughout the Mediterranean, including trade with the Tin Islands, believed by some to be identifiable with Cornwall but more likely to have been southwest Spain.

After the capture of Tyre by the Babylonians in the sixth century B.C., Carthage became the natural leader of the Phoenician colonies in northern Africa and Spain. A prolonged struggle, mainly centered in Sicily, now ensued between Carthage and the Greeks, the former occupying most of the eastern side of the island, the latter the western. About 540 B.C. the Carthaginian forces defeated a Greek attempt to land in Corsice, whereas in 480 B.C. a Carthaginian attempt to conquer the whole of Sicily was put down by Greek forces at Himera. The city itself finally fell to the Romans in 146 B.C. at the end of the Third Punic War (149–146 B.C.).

Prior to its destruction, and subsequent recolonization by the Romans c. 45 B.C., the city had a population of approximately 700,000, governed by the constitution of an aristocratic republic having two chief magistrates who were elected annually and a senate of 300 life members. Its religion was typically Phoenician, including worship of the great sun god Baal-Hammon, the moon goddess Tanit, and the Tyrian Melkarth. Human sacrifices were not unknown.

Following recolonization of the city, it was rebuilt under the auspices of Augustus c. 29 B.C. and rose to be the wealthy and important capital of the African province. Captured by the Vandals in 439, it was reduced to little more than a pirate stronghold. From 533 it formed a part of the Byzantine Empire until it was finally destroyed by the Arabs in 698.

See also: Dido

Cassandra
Greek

Daughter of Priam (king of Troy) and Hecuba. Having fallen in love with Cassandra, Apollo taught her the art of prophecy, but when she continued to refuse his advances he ordained that her prophecies, including the foretelling of the fall of Troy, should not be believed. However, it would appear as if this order from Apollo was not made until after some of her prophecies had been believed, and acted upon, for she foretold that Paris would one day bring about the fall of Troy, and for this reason he was exposed at birth.

During the Trojan War Cassandra made several important prophecies, but none were believed. When the Wooden Horse was found outside the walls of the city, Cassandra declared that it hid Greek warriors, a statement supported by Laocoön, but both were disbelieved, even though Laocoön flung a spear at the horse and caused a clatter of arms from within.

When Troy finally fell to the Greek hordes, Cassandra was raped by Ajax the Lesser at the altar in the temple to Athene, after which she was taken as part of Agamemnon's booty. Upon their return to Mycenae, Cassandra refused to enter the city with her master because, in a visionary trance, she had been horrified to smell the ancient shedding of blood and the curse of Thyestes. Following the murder of Agamemnon by Clytemnestra and her weak-willed lover, Aegisthus, Cassandra suffered the same fate.

See also: Agamemnon; Hecuba; Laocoön; Priam

Cassiope(ia)

Greek

Wife of Cepheus (king of Aethiopia) and mother of the beautiful Andromeda. Rashly boasting that either she or her daughter was more beautiful than the Nereides, she incurred the displeasure of Poseidon, who demanded that Andromeda be chained to a sea cliff as a sacrifice to Cetus, a terrible sea monster. Some sources vary this by saying that Cetus was originally sent by Poseidon to ravage the countryside and that the Oracle of Ammon said that only the sacrifice of Andromeda could save the land.

While Andromeda was chained naked to the sea cliff, Perseus flew overhead on the winged-horse Pegasus, having successfully defeated and beheaded the Gorgon Medusa.

Learning of the reasons behind Andromeda's plight, Perseus promptly offered to rescue the maiden on the proviso that she should become his wife. Her parents were only too happy to comply; flying over the monstrous Cetus, Perseus exposed the head of Medusa and turned the monster to stone. After their daughter was rescued, Cepheus and Cassiopeia now reneged on their agreement, for they said that Andromeda was already betrothed to another. Perseus, however, was not put off, and the wedding went ahead, only to be interrupted by Andromeda's betrothed and his followers, who attempted to carry off the bride. Perseus once again exposed the head of Medusa, and the interlopers were all turned to stone.

Following her death Cassiopeia was placed in the heavens by Poseidon, hanging upside down in a chair for half the time as final and eternal punishment for her boasting.

Astronomical: An easily recognized constellation within the northern celestial hemisphere, shaped like an "M" or "W" depending on one's viewing aspect, it lies between approximate right ascensions 22h55m and 3h10m, declination from +46° to +77°. The constellation remains circumpolar as far south as latitude 50°N.

See also: Andromeda; Cepheus

Castalia

Greek

The spring on Mount Parnassus, near Delphi, that is sacred to Apollo and the Muses.

Castalides

Greek

Name applied to the Muses through their association with Castalia, the sacred spring on Mount Parnassus.

Castor

Greco-Roman

One of the Dioscuri, a heroic son of Zeus with his twin, Polydeuces (Pollux to the Romans), yet not in reality the son of Zeus. He was the offspring of Tyndareus, king of Sparta, by his daughter, Leda, who was almost simultaneously impregnated by Zeus and accordingly bore the mortal Castor at the same time as the immortal Polydeuces. It would appear as if this elaborate myth was an attempt to rationalize the primitive institution of a sacred king reigning as a lay king. He and his brother were either full or half-brothers to Helen and Clytemnestra.

Demigods who were particularly beneficent to sailors who invoked them to gain favorable winds, the pair was inseparable. A renowned fighter, Castor taught the young Heracles how to fight. When their sister, Helen, was abducted by Theseus they raided Attica and, discovering the whereabouts of Helen from Academus, they rescued her, taking Aethra, Theseus's mother, with them to act as Helen's slave. Later they joined Jason and the Argonauts on their quest for the Golden Fleece.

It was on this epic voyage that Polydeuces outboxed and killed Amycus, but then the twins went up against Idas and Lynceus, a fight that cost the mortal Castor his life. Heartbroken, Polydeuces prayed that, even though immortal, he should not be allowed to live one day longer than his brother. Zeus, in mercy, at first let them live on alternate days until he later placed them in the heavens as the constellation Gemini, the Heavenly Twins.

The Dioscuri were particularly worshipped in Sparta and later among the Romans, having a temple dedicated to them in Rome. Castor is one of the few Greek gods or heroes whose name was retained after Greek religion was absorbed into the Roman culture.

Astronomical: The third sign of the Zodiac (May 22–June 21), the constellation Gemini lies in the northern celestial hemisphere between approximate right ascensions 6h00m and 8h00m, declination from +10° to +35°. The primary or alpha star (a Gem) is designated Castor. A close double (separation 2″) of magnitudes 1.97 and 2.95, the stars have spectral types A1V and A5 respectively. Each is a spectroscopic binary. A third binary, 9th magnitude, 73″ away completes a system of six stars at a distance of 46 light-years. This system may be found at approximate celestial coordinates right ascension 7h40m, declination +32°.

See also: Dioscuri

Catulus, Q. Lutatius
Roman
A historical person, consul in 102 B.C., who in his *Origin of the Roman Nation* recorded a much earlier tradition that said that Aeneas had betrayed Troy to the Greeks out of hatred for Paris and was, as a result of his help, later given safe conduct away from the fallen city.

Cecrops
Greek
The chthonic, mythical first king of Attica, the gift of Athene, and founder of Athens who, being earth-born, had the hindquarters of a snake. He had three daughters, Aglauros (sparkling water), Herse (dew) and Pandrosos (all-dewy) who acted as the nurses of Cecrops's successor, Erichthonius, who was also chthonic.

During his reign a spring and an olive tree suddenly appeared on the Acropolis and, upon consulting the Delphic Oracle, Cecrops was told that Athens must choose as patron one of the deities whose respective symbols these were (Athene and Poseidon). Cecrops acted as the arbiter in the ensuing contest between the gods for the patronage of Athens, the role in which he and Pandrosos are portrayed on the west pediment of the Parthenon.

A simple election was held, the women voting for Athene and the men for Poseidon. As the women far outnumbered the men, Athene easily won the contest, but the women were punished for their choice by being deprived of the right to vote in Athens thereafter.

Cecrops also acknowledged Zeus as the supreme god and successfully brought 12 other Greek cities under the control of Athens. He was also said to have introduced the institution of monogamous marriage to the city, a fact that strengthens the political position of Athenian women as shown in the story of the choosing of Athene as the patron deity. He also instituted religious worship without blood sacrifice.

Cela(e)no
Greek
One of the three Harpies or Harpyiae.

Celeus

Greek

King of Eleusis who received the goddess Demeter hospitably during her grief-stricken wanderings on earth in search of her daughter, Persephone. In return Demeter taught Celeus and his son, Triptolemus, the art of agriculture, but his other son, Abas, she turned into a lizard for ridiculing her. The goddess further attempted to make Celeus's other son, Demophoön, immortal, but she fumbled the operation and he died. In return for her kindness, Celeus became the first priest of Demeter at Eleusis and was said by some to have instigated the Eleusinian Mysteries.

See also: Demeter; Eleusis

Centaur

Greek

Mythical creature that is half-man, half-horse. Said to live on Mount Pelion in Thessaly, a region famous for hunting the bull on horseback, and other mountainous regions, centaurs were, in the main, wild and lawless. One notable exception to this general rule was Cheiron, the mentor of Heracles.

Due to their sensual nature they were sometimes associated with both Dionysos and Eros, the former making a gift of a potent wine to the centaur Pholus. Early art portrayed centaurs as having the head, arms, torso, and forelegs of a man and the hindquarters of a horse, but later the forelegs also became those of a horse. Homer referred to them as Pheres— "beasts." The word *centaur* is, in fact, a general designation for many sorts of composite creatures, the horse-men normally referred to as centaurs strictly being Hippocentaurs.

One explanation of their origin has offered that they were the result of a misunderstanding by the Greeks of their first encounter with mounted warriors from the east. However, this seems highly unlikely, as horses and horsemanship were well known among the ancient Greeks; therefore the image of the centaur must surely derive from the repertoire of Near Eastern man-beast combinations that are common figures on sixth century B.C. pottery. The centaurs or wild man-beasts of legend were then given the iconography of these creatures.

Mythology places the origin of the centaurs with Ixion's attempted rape of Hera. She substituted a cloud in her form, which later gave birth to Kentauros, which can be etymologized as "prick-air." This character, sometimes called Centauros, then mated with the mares of Magnesium on the slopes of Mount Pelion to produce the horse-centaurs known throughout Greek myth. Arming themselves with clubs or branches torn from trees, centaurs were brutal and wild. An interesting opposition to this general concept of the centaurs is brought about through Cheiron, a teacher of medicine, mentor of Heracles, Achilles, and Jason, and immortal.

Centaurs had an altar, known as Ara, at which Zeus burned incense to celebrate his victory over the Titans. Featuring in many fights against Greek heroes, notably Heracles, their most famous battle was against the Lapithae, another Thessalanian race. The centaurs had been invited to the wedding feast of Peirithous, king of the Lapithae, and Hippodameia. There a drunken centaur tried to carry off the bride, and a ferocious battle ensued in which Theseus, a guest at the wedding, took part.

The centaur Nessus once tried to carry off Deianeira, the wife of Heracles. Heracles shot him; dying, the centaur gave Deianeira his blood-stained tunic as a charm that would reclaim an unfaithful husband. This tunic would become the eventual cause of Heracles' death.

Astronomical: There are two constellations that are said to have been centaurs. One is aptly named Centaurus, lying in the southern celestial hemisphere between approximate right ascensions 11h00m and 15h00m, declination from –30° to –63°. The other is Sagittarius, also in the southern celestial hemisphere between approximate right ascensions 17h30m and 20h30m, declination from –10° to –50°. Both are said to represent Cheiron.

See also: Cheiron

Centaur~os, ~us

Greek

Alternative spelling of Kentauros, the result of the union between Ixion and the cloud in the form of Hera, whom he thought he was raping. This hero, said by some to have a serpent's hindquarters, then mated with the mares of Magnesium on the slopes of Mount Pelion, the result being the centaurs. This spelling of his name has been applied to one of the two centaur constellations in the night sky.

Centimani

Greek

Alternative collective name for the 100-handed, 50-headed sons of Ge and Uranos who are more commonly referred to as the Hecatoncheires. They were Cottus, Briareus (also called Aegaeon), and Gyas (or Gyges).

Cephalonia

Greek

Greek Kefallinía, an island off the west coast of Greece in the Ionian Sea; said to have been named after Cephalos.

Cephal~os, ~us

Greek

A son of Herse, the daughter of Cecrops, by Hermes. Married to Procris, a daughter of Erechtheus, he was beloved by Eos, goddess of the dawn, who took him to her home in the east. Procris became jealous of her husband's infidelity and hid in the bushes to spy on him while he was out hunting. There she heard him call out the name of Aura and became very agitated, not realizing that Aura was the name of the breeze he called upon to cool his limbs. Her angry movements within the bushes caused Cephalos to think that a wild beast was readying to spring upon him and, throwing his spear into the bushes, he killed his jealous wife.

An alternative version of these events is told. Eos, having fallen in love with Cephalos and having her advances refused, revealed to him that Procris was easily seduced by gold. To prove this point Eos changed Cephalos's appearance and gave him a gold crown to offer to Procris provided she would sleep with the offerer. Procris readily complied. Afterwards she fled in shame to Crete, where she was seduced by Minos. Later she returned to Athens in the guise of a youth with hound, named Laelaps, and spear, gifts from Artemis that never missed their mark. Cephalos so coveted these that husband and wife were reconciled. However, Procris still suspected Cephalos of loving Eos and so spied upon him while he was hunting; during one such occasion Cephalos accidentally killed his wife with the spear of Artemis.

For the involuntary murder of his wife Cephalos was banished. Traveling to the kingdom of Amphitryon, he was asked to rid the country of an uncatchable vixen by using Laelaps, his inescapable hound. As the vixen could not be caught and Laelaps would never have given up the chase, Zeus solved the impasse by turning both animals to stone. Cephalos then joined Amphitryon's expedition against the Taphians, finally settling in their country, where he gave his name to the island of Cephalonia.

See also: Amphitryon; Eos; Laelaps

Cepheus

Greek

1. Son of Aleus the king of Tegea in Arcadia. He accompanied Jason as one of the Argonauts on the quest for the Golden Fleece and had 20 sons. All but three of these were killed, along with Cepheus himself, when they helped Heracles in his fight against Hippocoön. His sister, Auge, became the mother of Telephus by Heracles.

2. King of Aethiopia, husband of Cassiopeia, and father of Andromeda. Following his wife's impudent boast to the Nereides, he jointly promised the hand of his daughter to Perseus should he rescue her from Cetus, then attempted to back out of the deal. Following his death he was placed in the heavens as the constellation that bears his name, along with his wife, daughter, and son-in-law.

Astronomical: A constellation of the northern celestial hemisphere between approximate right ascensions 8h05m and 20h00m, declination from +52° to +90°. Like the constellation Draco it covers almost 180° and wraps itself around the northern celestial pole.

See also: Aleus; Andromeda; Cassiopeia; Jason

Cerberus

Greek

The three-headed dog, said by some to be another of the monstrous offspring of

Echidne and Typhon, brother of the Chimaera, the Hydra, and the Sphinx, that guarded the entrance to the Underworld, the realm of Hades, though Hesiod maintained that Cerberus had 50 heads. His three heads were said to represent the past, the present, and the future. He was also said by some to have had a serpent for a tail. As it was his job to actively discourage those who tried to leave the Underworld—by tearing them to pieces—he sat forever facing inwards or downwards, his serpent's tail welcoming newcomers.

To complete his eleventh labor, Heracles entered the Underworld through a cave at Taenarum in Laconia to bring back Cerberus. Guided by Athene and Hermes, Heracles crossed the River Styx and freed his friends Theseus and Ascalaphus before obtaining Hades' permission to carry away Cerberus, provided he could do so without use of any weapon. Heracles seized Cerberus by the throat and dragged the monstrous animal back to Eurystheus, who was so afraid at the sight of it that he made Heracles return it to Tartarus immediately.

Visitors to Hades were supposed to take honey cakes (possibly baklava) to placate the dog as they entered, for he had a spiteful tendency to bite newcomers. Where his saliva fell the aconite, later to become sacred to the Roman god Saturn, was said to have grown.

See also: Chimaera; Echidne; Hydra; Sphinx; Typhon

Cercopes
Greco-Roman

The two dwarfish ruffians (some say more) who lived in Lydia and robbed and killed passers-by. They were finally defeated by Heracles while he was a slave of Queen Omphale. Tying their feet to a pole, Heracles carried them off slung over his shoulders. From their position the Cercopes were given a good view of the hero's hairy bottom, and they made such ludicrous jokes about it that Heracles in his amusement relented and set them free. They were finally turned into either stone or monkeys by Zeus.

The Romans embellished this story by saying that the Pithecussae, the Monkey Islands off Naples, were named after them, seeming to suggest that their transformation into monkeys was the more popular fate to have befallen them.

Cercyon
Greek

A son of either Poseidon or Hephaistos. Living near Eleusis, he challenged all travelers to a wrestling match and then killed them. He was finally overcome and killed by Theseus.

Ceres
Roman

The patron goddess of Sicily, goddess of growing vegetation and agriculture whom the Romans later came to identify with Demeter, giving her many of the same attributes. In this later cult she was worshipped as the goddess of earth and corn.

Astronomical: Name applied to a large asteroid, approximately 1,000 kilometers in diameter, discovered in 1800 by Guiseppe Piazzi and catalogued as 1Ceres.

See also: Demeter

Ceryneian Hind
Greek

A fabulous creature having brazen hooves and golden antlers, the latter often causing it to be mistakenly called a stag. Heracles was set the task of capturing it as the third of his Great Labors, a task he accomplished after tirelessly pursuing it for a year. He shot it with an arrow that pinned its forelegs together without loss of blood, then carried it back to Eurystheus over his shoulders.

Ceto
Greek

A sea goddess, wife of the sea god Phorcys and mother by him of Stheno and Euryale, the immortal Gorgons, and their sister, Medusa, the only mortal Gorgon, once beautiful but turned into a hideous monster by Athene for having laid with Poseidon in one of the temples sacred to the goddess.

See also: Gorgon; Phorcys

Cetus
Greek

The sea monster sent by Poseidon to ravage Aethiopia after Cassiopeia had boasted that either she or her daughter, Andromeda, was more beautiful than the Nereides. The oracle of Ammon said that only the sacrifice of Andromeda to Cetus could save the land, and so the hapless princess was chained naked to a sea cliff. There Perseus spotted her; having struck a deal with Andromeda's parents for her hand if he saved her, he flew over Cetus riding on the winged horse Pegasus. Using the severed head of the Gorgon Medusa he turned Cetus to stone.

Cetus is identified with Tiamat, the serpent of ancient Assyrian and Babylonian mythology.

Astronomical: An extremely large constellation lying across the celestial equator between approximate right ascensions 23h50m and 3h20m, declination from –25° to +10°. It is sometimes confused with the constellation Hydra due to the connection made between Cetus and the serpent Tiamat.

See also: Andromeda; Cassiopeia

Ceuta
Greco-Roman

The African of the Pillars of Heracles (Hercules), ancient name Abyla, situated at the very northern tip of Morocco and sometimes identified with Mount Acho. The European of the Pillars of Heracles was Calpe, and beyond these—the markers of the western boundary of the known world—was supposed to lie the fabled lost city of Atlantis.

See also: Calpe

Ceyx
Greek

Husband of Alcyone. Perishing in a shipwreck, his wife threw herself into the sea upon finding his body. In pity for the unfortunate couple the gods turned them into a pair of birds, usually identified as kingfishers, said to breed during the "halcyon days" of the winter solstice when Aeolus forbids the winds to blow.

See also: Alcyone

Chaos
Greek

In Greek cosmology, the infinite and empty space that existed before the creation that also came to be associated with Tartarus, the lowest and most infernal region of the Underworld. Out of Chaos sprang Ge, "the Earth," who gave birth to Uranos, thus starting the creation.

Chara
Greek

"Beloved"; a greyhound who was held on leash, along with Asterion (Starry) by Boötes in pursuit of the she-bear Callisto.

Astronomical: The name applied to the secondary, or beta, star of the constellation Canes Venatici (ß CVn), which lies next to the constellation Boötes in the northern celestial hemisphere. This particular star may be found at approximate celestial coordinates right ascension 12h35m, declination +42°. However, this star, type dG0, magnitude 4.32, 30 light-years away, is also sometimes referred to as Asterion, though this is usually the alpha or primary star that was renamed by Sir Edmund Halley in honor of King Charles II of England.

Charis
Greek

The wife of Hephaistos according to *Iliad*, a role normally taken by Aphrodite. Originally she had been the sole personification of Grace until later replaced by the three Graces or Charites.

Charites
Greek

The three goddesses of charm and beauty; daughters of Zeus who are also known as the Graces. They were Euphrosyne (representing joy), Aglaia (the radiance of beauty), and Thalia (the flowering of beauty). They lived on Mount Olympus with the Muses, with whom they were especially friendly. The Romans equated them with their Gratiae.

Charon

Greek

The surly ferryman of the Underworld; son of Erebos who ferried the souls of the dead across the River Styx, though some accounts say he crossed the River Acheron instead. Payment to Charon was made in the form of a bronze coin, an *obolos,* that was placed under the tongue of the corpse during the burial service. Without this coin he would refuse to ferry them across the river, leaving their soul in permanent limbo.

In modern Greek folklore he has become Charos or Charontas, the spirit of death himself, riding on his black charger across the plains and the mountains, scooping up heroes and maidens alike and setting them on his saddlebow. Great heroes, such as Digenis Akritas, wrestle with him for mastery of death itself.

Astronomical: The sole satellite of the planet Pluto.

See also: Erebos; Styx

Charybdis

Greek

A daughter of Poseidon and Ge who stole the cattle of Heracles and was hurled by Zeus into the sea, where she created a whirlpool. Said to lie in a narrow channel, later identified with the Strait of Messina (where there is no such whirlpool) opposite the cave of Scylla, she swallowed up many ships. Both Jason and Odysseus managed to negotiate her menace, the latter losing his ship but managing to escape by clinging to a tree in the cliff's face until the sucking subsided.

Chim(a)era

Greek

A fabulous fire-breathing monster that had the head of a lion, the body of a goat, and the tail of a serpent or dragon. The son of Typhon (Typhoeus) and Echidne; brother of Cerberus, the Hydra, and the Sphinx. Living on Mount Chimaera in the Taurus, he seems to be a representation or personification of the volcanic fires that still burn near the summit. It has been said that the form of the Chimaera was an allegory of the volcanic mountain on which it was said to live, with fire at its peak, lions and goats roaming its slopes, and snakes at its base.

The Chimaera was killed by Bellerophon while it was ravaging the countryside of Lycia. Riding above the monstrous beast on the back of Pegasus, Bellerophon shot a lead-tipped arrow into his mouth. The lead melted and burned away his insides.

See also: Cerberus; Echidne; Hydra; Sphinx

Ch(e)iron

Greek

The wisest of all the centaurs and completely opposite to their ilk, who were wild and uncivilized. Not of the same breed as the other centaurs, the offspring of Ixion and a cloud, Cheiron was the son of Cronos and Philyra; hence called Philyrides, he lived on the slopes of Mount Pelion. Taught by the twins Apollo and Artemis, he was skilled in medicine, music, prophecy, hunting, and gymnastics and taught many heroes, such as Jason, Achilles, Peleus, Asclepios, Actaeon, Castor and Polydeuces, and Heracles. He helped Peleus to escape from the wild centaurs and taught him how to win the hand of the Nereid Thetis. His death was accidentally caused by Heracles, who shot him during his struggle with the centaurs in Arcadia. Being immortal Cheiron was unable to die despite the pain he suffered until he relinquished his immortality to Prometheus. After his death Zeus placed his image in the heavens as either Sagittarius or Centaurus.

Astronomical: The name Chiron has been given to an asteroid discovered in 1977 (1977UB) that lies in an orbit between Saturn and Uranus. For details of the constellations Centaurus and Sagittarius see the relevant entries.

See also: Ixion; Prometheus

Chione

Greek

1. The daughter of Oreithyia and Boreas and mother of Poseidon of Eumolpus; hence called Chionides.

2. The mortal mother of Autolycus by Hermes; killed by Artemis.

See also: Autolycus

Chloris

Greek

1. The goddess of spring.

2. The only daughter of Niobe, hence a Niobid, who was not killed.

3. The mother of Nestor.

See also: Niobe

Chrysaor

Greek

The warrior son of Medusa fathered on her by Poseidon; he was born, fully grown, along with the winged horse Pegasus, from the body of the Gorgon after she had been beheaded by Perseus. Chrysaor became the father, by the Oceanid Callirrhoë, of Geryon, the three-headed giant whose cattle had to be stolen by Heracles as one of his Great Labors.

See also: Medusa

Chryseis

Greek

Daughter of the Trojan priest Chryses. She was taken by the Greek commander in chief, Agamemnon, as his concubine during the siege of Troy. When her father came to ransom her he was rudely repulsed by Agamemnon, so Apollo sent a plague among the Greeks. Seeking the advice of Calchas, Agamemnon returned Chryseis to her father but took Briseis as recompense, an act that led to the famous quarrel between Agamemnon and Achilles that almost turned the course of the Trojan War back in favor of Troy.

See also: Agamemnon

Chryses

Greek

A priest of Apollo Smintheus at Troy and father of Chryseis. When his daughter had been seized by the Greek commander Agamemnon during the course of the Trojan War, his prayers propitiated Apollo to spread a pestilence among the Greek forces until the girl was returned.

Chrysippus

Greek

Son of Pelops and half-brother of Atreus and Thyestes. Loved by Laius, who raped him, that act being the probable cause of the ancestral curse on the house of Laius, which features in the events of the *Oedipus* saga. He was murdered by his half-brothers at the instigation of their mother to prevent him from inheriting the throne, after which they had to flee their home.

See also: Atreus; Thyestes

Chrysothemis

Greek

The daughter of Agamemnon and Clytemnestra. She featured as the gentle foil to the tough Electra, her sister, in Sophocles' play *Electra*.

Chthonic gods

Greek

Gods born of earth. Being so conceived, chthonic deities are usually closely linked with the ideas of death and regeneration. The sinister figures of the Erinnyes and the Keres are also thought of as spirits of earth. In direct contrast to the chthonic deities were those of Olympus, gods who were conceived and lived in the rarified heights of Heaven.

Chthonius

Greek

One of the five Sparti, or "Sown Men," who survived their infighting and went on to help Cadmos to build the Cadmea, the citadel of the city that was later to become known as Thebes. The other four to survive were Echion, Udaeus, Hyperenor, and Pelorus.

See also: Sparti

Cicones

Greek

Islands visited by Odysseus and his men following their departure from Troy at the end of the Trojan War and where Odysseus received several jars of a sweet and particularly potent wine.

Cilix

Greek

King of Cilicia who was helped in his fight against the Lycians by Sarpedon.

Cim(m)erii

Greek

A mythical people who dwelled on the boundary of the Western Ocean. It was in their land that Odysseus, on the advice of Circe, sought the advice of the dead seer Teiresias. Preparing a libation of blood he summoned the spirits of the dead. First to appear was Elpenor, one of his crew who died when he fell from the roof of Circe's palace in a drunken stupor. Later came Teiresias, who gave him prophetic advice before Anticleia, his mother, appeared before him. In some Latinized texts the Cimerii are referred to as Cimmerians.

See also: Circe; Odysseus

Cimmerians

Greek

Alternative reference for Cimerii found in some Latinized source texts.

Cinyras

Greek

Son of Apollo and king of Cyprus, possibly being born in Cilicia, and husband of the daughter of Pygmalion. He was said to have founded the cult of the Paphian Aphrodite, which practiced sacred prostitution. This has led to an alternative tradition that says that Cinyras had a daughter, possibly by another wife, named Myrrha or Smyrna. Aphrodite made the girl fall in love with her father as punishment for her mother having boasted of the girl's beauty. Under cover of darkness, Myrrha's nurse helped the helpless maiden sleep with her father, the result of their illicit union being Adonis. When Cinyras discovered what had happened he committed suicide.

See also: Pygmalion

Circe

Greek

The enchantress daughter of Helios and Perse, sister of King Aeëtes, and mother of Comus who lived on the island of Aeaea, identified by some with Malta. She had the power to turn men into animals, on one occasion turning Picus, who rejected her love, into a woodpecker. When Glaucus came to her to obtain a magic potion to make Scylla love him, she instead gave him one that turned her into a monster. She also purified Jason and Medeä of murder, but she is best known for her association with Odysseus.

Having lost all but one of his ships on his eventful journey home after the end of the Trojan War, Odysseus landed on Aeaea and sent his men to explore. All but one, Eurylochus, were turned into swine by Circe. When Odysseus set off to rescue his men, he was given the plant moly by Hermes as a charm against the sorcery of Circe. She relinquished to Odysseus, restored his men to their original form, and then lavishly entertained them for a whole year. At the end of the year she advised Odysseus to seek the advice of the dead seer Teiresias, whom he would have to propitiate in the land of the Cimerii. Having done that, Odysseus returned to Aeaea to gain further help from her. She now advised him on how he might circumvent the Sirens and the monstrous Scylla and Charybdis, and so return home.

One tradition says that Circe had a son by Odysseus, Telegonus. While this son was searching for his father he landed on Ithaca and began to plunder for food. When opposed by his father and Telemachus, neither party recognizing the other, Telegonus unwittingly killed his father. He then took Telemachus and Penelope back to Aeaea with him and there married Penelope while Telemachus married Circe.

Appearing in both *Odyssey* of Homer and the *Argonautica* of Apollonius Rhodius, Circe also appeared in the medieval legends of King Arthur, in which she is said to have brought the Romans to England.

See also: Aeëtes; Comus; Odysseus

Ciris

Greek

The bird into which Scylla, daughter of King Nisus of Megara, was turned after she killed her father; his soul, in the form of an eagle, pounced on her. Other traditions say that Scylla was changed into a fish named Ciris when she was drowned by Minos, who had been horrified by her parricide. She is not to be confused, though often is, with another named Scylla, the daughter of Phorcys who was turned into a monster with six heads.

See also: Minos; Scylla

Cithaeron
Greek

The lofty mountain, named after a king of Plataea, which lies at its foot, that separates Attica from Boeotia and that is sacred to the Muses and Dionysos. When just 18 years old Heracles set out to rid the area of a savage lion that was ravaging the herds of both Amphitryon and his neighbor Thespius, the latter acting as Heracles' host for the 50 days of the hunt. Finally Heracles killed the lion with a wild olive club and made himself a garment from the pelt with the head as a helmet, though some say that it was the skin of the Nemaean Lion that he wore. As a reward, Thespius gave Heracles his 50 daughters. Cithaeron was also the location of many episodes connected with Thebes, including the exposure of the infant Oedipus. It was also where both Pentheus and Actaeon were killed.

Claudii
Roman

One of the five powerful families that dominated the early Roman republic, probably toward the end of the fifth century B.C. The other families were the Aemilii, Cornelii, Manlii, and Valerii. Each family decisively affected the Roman myths and legends in attempts to make theirs the most prominent family.

Cleobis
Greek

Son of a priestess of Hera at Argos; brother of Biton. In a display of filial devotion the brothers once dragged their mother's chariot to the temple, where she prayed to Hera that they should be granted the best boon for mortals. Hera granted it by allowing them to die while asleep within the confines of her temple,

though some say that they simply expired from the sheer exhaustion of dragging their mother's chariot to the temple.

See also: Biton

Cleonaean Lion
Greek

An alternative name for the lion dispatched by Heracles as his first Great Labor; better known as the Nemaean Lion. The name derives from the fact that Nemea lay close to Cleonae, both being troubled by this monstrous creature, another of the offspring of Typhon and Echidne.

Clio
Greco-Roman

One of the nine Muses, being that of epic poetry, which she was said to have invented, prophecy, and history. In art she was represented with a roll of paper, a chest of books, or with musical instruments. She was the mother of Orpheus and Hyacinthos.

See also: Muses, the

Cloelia
Roman

One of the hostages taken by Porsenna when he agreed to a truce with Rome. She requested that she and her fellow hostages should be allowed to go for a swim, but once the guards' backs were turned she swam back to Rome with her companions. Porsenna was so impressed by Cloelia's daring and cunning that he allowed all the hostages to remain at liberty.

Clotho
Greek

One of the three Fates or Moirae, associate of Lachesis and Atropos, and the one who spun the thread or web of life, thus controlling men's lives. After Tantalus had killed Pelops to feed the gods at a banquet, a crime for which he was duly punished, Zeus ordered Hermes to boil the limbs in a cauldron. Clotho took Pelops from the cauldron and restored him to life.

See also: Fates, the

Clusium

Roman

The home of Lars Porsenna, a city that rose toward the end of the sixth century B.C. and controlled the route through central Italy.

Clymene

Greek

1. A nymph, the daughter of Oceanos and Tethys, wife of Iapetus, and mother of Atlas and Prometheus.

2. The wife of Merops, king of Aethiopia, and mother of Phaëthon by Helios.

See also: Atlas; Iapetus; Prometheus

Clyt(a)emnestra

Greek

Daughter of Tyndareus and Leda, half-sister to Helen and the Dioscuri, Castor and Polydeuces. Hesiod referred to her and Helen as the *lipesanores,* the "husband-deserters." She was forcibly married by Agamemnon after he had killed her first husband and became the mother by him of Iphigeneia, Orestes, and Electra.

While Agamemnon was away for the ten years of the Trojan War, Clytemnestra was seduced by Aegisthus, though she was the stronger of the two in character, and the weak-willed Aegisthus may have actually been seduced by Clytemnestra. Together they plotted to murder Agamemnon on his return from Troy, a resolve strengthened when Clytemnestra heard of Agamemnon's sacrifice of Iphigeneia at Aulis.

On Agamemnon's return, Clytemnestra welcomed him regally; later, while he was in his bath, she entangled him in a net, and after Aegisthus had struck him twice Clytemnestra beheaded him. She then went out to kill Cassandra, the daughter of Priam who had fallen to Agamemnon as booty upon the fall of Troy. Cassandra had refused to enter the city when, in a visionary trance, she was horrified to smell the ancient shedding of blood and the curse of Thyestes.

Clytemnestra now seized power of Mycenae, and she and Aegisthus ruled for many years, Aegisthus living in constant fear of vengeance. He wanted to kill Electra, but Clytemnestra refused. Instead he married her to a peasant who was fearful of consummating their union. Orestes had been smuggled out of the city and took refuge with Strophius, king of Phocis. There he planned his revenge, and when he and Pylades, the son of Strophius, had come of age they returned to Mycenae and, with Electra's help, killed both Clytemnestra and Aegisthus.

These events are recounted in Aeschylus's great trilogy the *Oresteia,* which begins at the point when Agamemnon returned to Mycenae with Cassandra.

See also: Aegisthus; Agamemnon

Clytie

Greek

A nymph who was loved and then jilted by Helios. Revealing their secret to her next lover, Helios began to hate her, so she transformed into a heliotrope, thus following his course across the sky with her gaze, day after day, forever.

See also: Helios

Cnidos

Greek

Greek colony in Caria, Asia Minor, where the statue of Aphrodite by Praxiteles was once displayed. A fine statue of Demeter, dating from c. 330 B.C., was found at Cnidos and is today in the British Museum.

Cnossos

Greek

Variant of Knossos, the important archaeological site on the island of Crete; this site contains the remains of the magnificent, unfortified, and labyrinthine so-called Palace of Minos.

Cocal~os, ~us

Greek

King of Sicily. He welcomed Daedalus after he fled to his realm from Cumae, where he landed after flying away from Crete on wings he made himself, a flight that led to the death of his son, Icarus. When Minos came in pursuit of the craftsman, Cocalos's daughters delayed

Minos to enable their father and Daedalus to kill him.

See also: Daedalus

Cocles, Publius Horatius

Roman

Hero who protected the Pons Sublicus, the wooden bridge over the River Tiber that gave direct access to the heart of Rome, against the attacking hordes under the leadership of Lars Porsenna. Holding the attackers at bay while the bridge was demolished, Publius Horatius Cocles had the help of Spurius Lartius and Titius Herminus for a while. As the bridge was set to fall, Cocles ordered his helpers back to safety while single-handedly holding the enemy at bay until the bridge finally collapsed. Then, with a prayer to Father Tiber, he leaped fully armed into the raging river and swam to safety beneath a cloud of Etruscan missiles. Though denied easy entry to Rome in this manner, Lars Porsenna still laid siege to it.

The story of Publius Horatius Cocles is dramatically related in the immensely popular *Lays of Ancient Rome* by Thomas Babington Macaulay, published in 1842.

Cocytus

Greek

The "River of Wailing"; one of the five rivers in the Underworld realm of Hades. The other rivers encountered in this realm were the Styx, Phlegethon, Acheron, and Lethe. There is an actual River Cocytus in Epirus that flows for a portion of its course underground, and was thus said to lead directly to the Underworld.

Codrus

Greek

Mythical king of Athens who, in order to save his country from invading Dorians, disguised himself in Dorian costume and penetrated the enemy camp, killing their leaders and so routing them. This story seems to have later been used by the Romans when Scaevola was said to have disguised himself and crept into the camp of Lars Porsenna who was, at that time, laying siege to Rome. This is further supported by Dionysus of Halicarnassus, who said that Scaevola's surname was Cordus, an obvious derivation of Codrus.

Coeus

Greek

One of the offspring of Uranos and Ge, and thus a Titan.

Colchis

Greek

Ancient country to the south of the Caucasus at the eastern end of the Euxine, or Black, Sea. Dominated by Persia, Greece, and Rome, it was, during the sixth century A.D., disputed by Byzantium and Persia. Today the region forms a part of the independent Russian state of Georgia. It was most famous in Greek tradition as the destination of Aries, the winged ram sent by Zeus who carried away Phrixus and Helle from their cruel and heartless stepmother. Helle fell off en route, but Phrixus reached Colchis, where Aeëtes, king of Colchis and father of the sorceress Medeä, sacrificed the ram and hung its fleece on an oak tree in a grove that was sacred to Ares, whereupon it turned to gold; it was protected by a sleepless dragon, possibly Draco.

Jason and the Argonauts sailed to Colchis aboard the ship *Argo Navis* to carry away the Golden Fleece, and after overcoming many perils they arrived at Phasis. They successfully accomplished their quest with the help of Medeä.

See also: Aeëtes; Helle; Jason; Phrixus

Collatia

Roman

The home city of Lucius Tarquinius Collatinus. When Lucretia was raped, the people of Collatia marched against Rome under the leadership of Brutus, roused the city, and persuaded its inhabitants to bar the city gates against Tarquinius, who was absent laying siege to Ardea. Tarquinius and his sons, better known simply as the Tarquins, fled into exile, and Rome became a republic governed by consuls.

See also: Lucretia

Collatinus, Lucius Tarquinius

Roman

Husband of Lucretia. When she was raped by Sextus, the son of Tarquinius Superbus, his people from the city Collatia marched against Rome, forced the Tarquins (Tarquinius Priscus and Tarquinius Superbus) into exile, and so made Rome a republic.

See also: Lucretia; Sextus

Colon~os, ~us

Greek

A hill in Athens, Attica, where Oedipus, exiled from Thebes, found refuge in a grove sacred to the Eumenides. There, while under the protection of Theseus, Oedipus died and was received by the gods. Near the garden of Academia, it was the birthplace of Sophocles and has a temple dedicated to Poseidon.

See also: Oedipus

Comus

1. Greek

A son of Circe.

2. Roman

A relatively modern god of mirth.

Concord

Greek

The goddess of harmony (known as Concordia to the Romans) to whom a temple was built c. 430 B.C. at Agrigento, Sicily.

Concordia

Roman

The Roman equivalent of the Greek Concord, the goddess of concord who had a temple near the Forum.

Consentes, Di

Roman

The Di Consentes were the 12 principle Roman deities, derived via the Etruscans from the 12 ancient Greek gods of Olympus. Their statues, six male and six female, stood in the Forum.

Consus

Roman

"The Storer"; an ancient nature and agriculture deity worshipped by the early Romans. Practically nothing survives of his ancient mythology. It seems that rather than having a complex mythology, such as would have been current with the Greek deities of the same period, the early Romans were more concerned with practical ritual observances rather than with any religious speculation. Later Consus came to be identified with Poseidon.

The annual harvest festival in Rome was dedicated to Consus, and at one of these festivals, while Sabine visitors had flocked to Rome, Romulus ordered the seizure of the Sabine women in an attempt to equalize the population of Rome in which men far outnumbered women.

See also: Poseidon; Sabine

Cordus

Roman

Surname of Scaevola according to Dionysus of Halicarnassus. Due to a startling similarity of stories, it would appear as if Cordus is a simple derivation of Codrus, a mythical king of Athens.

Core

Greek

Also: Kore

"The Maiden"; a title sometimes applied to Persephone, the daughter of Demeter, though some say that this was Persephone's original name. However, the Achaeans brought with them a young warrior goddess who bore the titles Core, Parthenos, and Pallas, meaning "maiden," "virgin," and "girl." About 1700 B.C. she became identified with an older pre-Hellenic "Palace Goddess" worshipped in Crete; later still she became identified with Athene. It would therefore appear as if Core, when applied to Persephone, was a preservation of this earlier, pre-Hellenic deity all but absorbed into the character of Athene.

See also: Persephone

Corineus

Greco-Romano-British

A giant, the leader of a group of Trojan exiles, renowned as a soldier and giant-killer, who teamed with Brutus and his refugees, sailed to Britain, and received the land of Cornwall, naming it after himself.

Corinth(~os, ~us)

Greco-Roman

Greek Kórinthos. A port in the northeast Peloponnesos, at the southwestern tip of the isthmus that connects the Peloponnesos to the mainland, this rocky isthmus became known as the Isthmus of Corinth. It is today dissected by the Corinth Canal, the 6.5-kilometer (4-mile) waterway that opened in 1893. The ancient city-state of Corinth lies some 7 kilometers (4.5 miles) southwest.

Already a place of commercial importance by the ninth century B.C., Corinth joined the Peloponnesian League at the end of the sixth century B.C. and took a prominent part in the Persian and Peloponnesian Wars. Traditionally a rival of Athens and an ally of Sparta, it did, however, join with Athens, Thebes, and Argos against Sparta during the Corinthian War (395–387 B.C.). In the mid-third century B.C. it was a leading member of the Achaean League. Destroyed by the Romans in 146 B.C. and rebuilt by Julius Caeser in 44 B.C., it was made the capital of the Roman province of Achaea by the Emperor Augustus. St. Paul visited Corinth in 51 A.D. and addressed two of his epistles to its churches, complaining of the licentious ways of the inhabitants. After many changes of ownership the city became a part of independent Greece in 1822.

The chief distinction of the ruins of Corinth is the temple of Apollo, built during the sixth century B.C., of which seven Doric columns still remain. One of the oldest in Greece, it sits high above the town towers named the Akrocorinth, the acropolis of Corinth, which was dedicated to Aphrodite and where her temple once stood, her cult possibly being established at Corinth some time during the eighth century B.C. This acropolis is also the site of Pirene, one of the fountains said to have been created by a stamp of one of Pegasus's hooves. It was beside this fountain that Bellerophon was said to have captured Pegasus prior to killing the Chimaera.

The quadrennial Isthmian Games were held on the Corinthian isthmus in honor of Poseidon; horse and chariot races were held in his honor, for he was said to have both invented the horse and subsequently taught man how to bridle and tame horses.

See also: Akrocorinth

Coriolanus, Cnaeus Marcius

Roman

Originally simply known as Cnaeus Marcius, he received his cognomen after capturing the town of Corioli (Monte Giove) from the Volscii in 493 B.C. Later this legendary Roman hero was charged with tyrannously opposing the plebians and refusing to give them grain, even though they were starving. Banished from Rome, he returned leading an army of Volscii against the city in 491 B.C. He spared Rome after his wife, Volumnia, and his mother, Veturia, pleaded with him, though some accounts make Volumnia his mother and name his wife as Vergilia. As a result he was killed by the Volscii. This story forms the basis of the play *Coriolanus* by William Shakespeare.

Cornelii

Roman

One of the powerful families that dominated the newly founded Roman republic. The others were the Aemilii, Claudii, Manlii, and Valerii. Each family attempted to increase its status by altering the myths and legends of the time to its own advantage; they left many different versions of what are essentially the same stories.

Cornucopia

Greco-Roman

Meaning "horn of plenty," the cornucopia is essentially a Greek icon, though the symbology of the horn that could unceasingly nourish remained in the later Roman tradition. The horn was said to have been created from one of the horns of the she-goat Amalthea that had suckled the infant Zeus in the Dictaean Cave on Crete, where his mother, Rhea, had hidden him away from Cronos, tended by the Curetes, Rhea's priests, who clashed their weapons together to drown the cries of the baby Zeus. In recognition of the faithful service given to him in his infancy, Zeus transferred Amalthea to the heavens on her death and turned one of her horns into the Cornucopia, which had the power to refill itself with food and drink forever more.

See also: Amalthea

Corona Australis

Greek

Astronomical: The "Southern Crown"; to the ancient Greeks this constellation was said to represent the laurel wreath worn by the champions of Greek games. Located in the southern celestial hemisphere, it may be found between approximate right ascensions 17h55m and 19h15m, declination from –37° to –46°.

Corona Borealis

Greek

Astronomical: The "Northern Crown"; being the crown of Ariadne, daughter of Minos, it was placed in the heavens by either Dionysos after he had found her abandoned on the island of Naxos and married her, or by sympathetic goddesses after Theseus had left her. Located in the northern celestial hemisphere, this beautiful semicircle of stars may be found between approximate right ascensions 15h15m and 16h25m, declination from +27° to +40°.

Coronis

Greek

A nymph; the daughter of Phlegyas. Loved and won by Apollo, who made her pregnant, she was unfaithful to the god and made love to the mortal Ischys. This news was brought to Apollo by a crow the god left behind to watch over her during pregnancy. Apollo already knew of Coronis's infidelity, cursed the crow for not pecking out Ischys's eyes, and turned it from white to black. Artemis then killed both Coronis and Ischys with her arrows in sympathy for her brother, but in remorse she rescued Coronis's body from the funeral pyre and bade Hermes to cut the baby, who was still alive,

from her womb. This baby was to become the healer god Asclepios.

An alternative story is told in Epidaurus, where it was said Coronis gave birth to her son, Asclepios, and exposed him on Mount Myrtion, where he was suckled by goats.

See also: Asclepios

Corvus

Greek

Two stories revolve around Corvus, both referring to a crow and thus possibly being different renditions of the same tale. In the first, Apollo sent a crow to fetch water for him in his cup, Crater. The crow dawdled and when questioned by Apollo lied to him. In his anger Apollo placed the crow in the sky as the constellation Corvus and next to him placed the cup as the constellation Crater, from which the crow is forever forbidden to drink. In the other story, the crow was placed in the heavens for telling tales; since that time all crows have been black rather than white.

Both stories echo a part of the story of the crow left by Apollo to guard the pregnant Coronis. The first seems to suggest that the crow was not diligent, a factor within the Coronis story, the second that the crow had its color changed from white to black, again a feature of the story of Coronis.

Astronomical: The constellation Corvus is located in the southern celestial hemisphere between approximate right ascensions 11h50m and 12h55m, declination from –12° to –25°.

See also: Coronis

Corybantes

Greek

Generic name applied to priests of Rhea in Phrygia who were noted for their rhythmical dances to drums and cymbals. They appear to have originated as the attendants of the Asiatic mother goddess Cybele, whose cult later became merged with that of Rhea.

Cos

Greek

One of the islands of the Sporades off Caria in Asia Minor. Famous in classical times as one of the main cult centers of Asclepios, the remains of the Asclepieion are there on three terraces and include temples and a medical school. Hippocrates was born there c. 460 B.C.

Cottus

Greek

One of the Hecatoncheires, the 100-handed, 50-headed, giant sons of Ge and Uranos.

Crater

Greek

The cup in which the crow Corvus was sent to fetch water for Apollo. The crow delayed and when questioned by the god lied to him. In anger Apollo placed the crow in the heavens as the constellation Corvus, placing the cup next to him as the constellation Crater, from which the crow is forever forbidden to drink. The constellation Crater has been seen as a cup or goblet in the folklore of many countries and traditions.

Astronomical: A constellation of the southern celestial hemisphere that lies next to that of Corvus, between approximate right ascensions 10h50m and 11h50m, declination from –6° to –25°.

Creon

Greek

1. King of Thebes, husband of Eurydice, father of Haemon and Menoeceus, brother of Jocasta/Epicaste, and uncle of Oedipus. After the latter had defeated the Sphinx and unwittingly married his own mother, Creon exiled him at Oedipus's own request and acted as regent for Oedipus's two sons, Eteocles and Polyneices, until they quarreled and Polyneices was exiled as well. In the war of the Seven Against Thebes, Menoeceus was killed and Creon refused burial to Polyneices as a traitor. Antigone, Polyneices' sister and lover of Haemon, buried her brother, so Creon had her buried alive in a cave, where she hanged herself. Haemon then took his own life, and Eurydice, Creon's wife, hanged herself. Creon remained king of Thebes until Lycus invaded the city, killed him, and usurped the throne.

2. King of Corinth and father of Glauce, also called Creusa. He raised Alcmaeon's children, Amphilochus and Tisiphone, but his wife sold Tisiphone into slavery, her unwitting purchaser being none other than her own father, Alcmaeon. He also gave shelter to Jason and Medeä after they fled Iolcos. However, Jason fell in love with Glauce and deserted Medeä. Medeä reacted by sending the young bride a garment that burned her to death, set fire to the palace, and killed Creon as well.

See also: Seven Against Thebes

Cressida

Greek

A daughter of the Trojan priest Calchas who features mainly in medieval legends of the Trojan War, which tell of her love affair with the Trojan warrior Troilus, one of the sons of the king of Troy, Priam. Her uncle, Pandarus, acted as a go-between for the lovers, but finally she deserted Troilus for the Greek soldier Diomedes.

See also: Troilus

Cretan Bull

Greek

A magnificent white bull that was given to Minos by Poseidon for sacrifice in recognition of Minos's position as the sole ruler of Crete. Minos was so delighted by the magnificent creature that he substituted an inferior beast for the sacrifice. Later the bull ran savage and ravaged the island until it was captured single-handedly by Heracles as the seventh of his Great Labors. Heracles took it back to Eurystheus, who set it free again. It roamed through Greece to Marathon, where it was captured by Theseus, who took it to Athens to be sacrificed to Athene.

Additional traditions state that, as Minos had substituted an inferior beast for the sacrifice, Poseidon punished him by making his wife, Pasiphaë, fall in love with the bull. She had Daedalus construct a wooden cow in which she could lie to mate with the bull, the result of their union being the terrible Minotaur.

See also: Minos; Minotaur; Pasiphaë

Cretan Labyrinth

Greek

The labyrinth built for King Minos by Daedalus to hold the Minotaur, into which a yearly tribute of Athenian youths and maidens was sent to be devoured by the beast. On one occasion Theseus, son of Aegeus, joined the tribute and, having gained help from Minos's daughter, Ariadne, entered the labyrinth, slew the Minotaur, and then fled the island along with Ariadne.

See also: Daedalus

Crete

Greek

The largest island that comes under the administrative rule of Greece in the eastern Mediterranean, lying south-southeast of the Greek mainland. Of great historical importance, the island has many connections with classical Greek mythology.

The palace at Knossos, unearthed by Sir Arthur Evans, the excavations starting in 1899, is said to be that of the tyrannical King Minos. This magnificent, unfortified, and labyrinthine palace points to an elegant and highly artistic pre-Hellenic civilization. Archaeological evidence such as this seems to indicate that a highly advanced, pre-Hellenic culture, with many affinities with that of Egypt, existed on Crete between 2500 B.C. and 1400 B.C. A maritime, commercial culture whose sea power made fortification unnecessary, it spread its influence to mainland Greece, where it became known as the Mycenaean culture. Possibly at this time Crete actually exercised some form of suzerainty over the mainland.

Early Cretans probably worshiped a mother goddess served by priestesses, and having many connections with wild beasts, particularly bulls, they worshiped huntress goddesses such as Dictynna and Britomartis. One of the Cretans' favorite sports appears to have been bullfighting, a fact that lends special significance to many of the Greek myths associated with the island, particularly that of the Minotaur contained within its labyrinth, for these seem to have some historical foundation. It was also the island to which Poseidon sent the magnificent Cretan Bull, and that which the infant Zeus was said to have been raised in secret, suckled by the she-goat Amalthea in the Dictaean Cave. Such an important myth illustrates the continuing influence that Crete would appear to have had during the Hellenic period.

See also: Knossos; Minos

Cretheus

Greek

Founder and king of Iolcos, husband of Tyro and father by her of Aeson. Tyro, prior to her marriage to Cretheus, bore twin boys, Pelias and Neleus, by Poseidon, but she exposed them and they were raised by a horse herd. When she married Cretheus he adopted the children. When Cretheus died, Pelias imprisoned Aeson, expelled Neleus, and usurped the throne.

Creusa

Greek

1. Daughter of Creon, the king of Corinth; also known as Glauce. When her father gave shelter to Jason and Medeä, Jason fell in love with her and deserted Medeä. The sorceress retaliated by giving Creusa a poisoned gown that caught fire when the young bride put it on, burned her to death, set fire to the palace, and killed Creon as well.

2. Daughter of Erechtheus and wife of Xuthus of Aeolia. Her son, Ion, was claimed as the result of a brief union with Apollo, thus enabling the Ionians, who included the Athenians, to claim divine descent. Not wishing to be outdone, Euripides also made her the mother of Dorus and thus gave the other main race of Greeks, the Dorians, a similar claim to divine descent.

3. One of the daughters of Priam, king of Troy, and wife of Aeneas.

See also: Aeneas; Ion; Jason; Priam

Crocus

Greek

A youth who fell in love with another named Smilax and was turned into a saffron plant.

Croesus

Greek

A historical king of Lydia (c. 560–545 B.C.) who passed into legend. Said to be the richest of all men, he was also extremely pious; he sent many dedications to Delphi and funded the temple of Artemis at Ephesus. On one occasion he was said to have tested the Delphic Oracle by asking it to reveal what he was doing at a particular time. It answered, correctly, that he was boiling a tortoise and a hare in a cauldron. Thenceforth he placed his absolute confidence in the oracle.

Legend says that he was once visited by Solon and told him that he was the happiest of men. Solon replied that no man should be called happy until he was dead. Prior to making war on Persia, Croesus consulted the Delphic Oracle, which said that if he did go to war he would destroy a great Empire. He did—his own. Defeating him, the Persians seated him on a funeral pyre to be burned alive, but Croesus prayed to Zeus, who sent a shower of rain at just the right moment to extinguish the fire, thus saving his life. He was then transported to the land of the Hyperboreans, where he lived out the rest of his days.

Herodotus and Plutarch vary these last events by saying that rather than Zeus intervening, Croesus told the Persian king of his conversation with Solon and, so impressed was the king with this wisdom, that he spared Croesus's life.

See also: Ephesus

Crommyum
Greek

Region of ancient Greece that was, at one time, ravaged by a wild sow. Like many other terrors of that time, the sow was killed by Theseus.

See also: Theseus

Cron~os, ~us
Greek

Also: Kron~os, ~us

The youngest of the Titans, the son of Uranos and Ge, husband of Rhea, and father of Demeter, Hera, Hades, Hestia, Poseidon, and Zeus, equated by the Romans with Saturn. He deposed Uranus as the ruler of the universe by castrating him using a flint sickle his own father had given him. Drops of blood

from this wound fell onto Mother Earth, and she bore as a result the three Erinnyes or Eumenides, the Furies Alecto, Tisiphone, and Megaera. From drops of blood that fell into the sea, Aphrodite was born.

For a brief moment while Cronos seized power, the Cyclopes enjoyed freedom, being released by the Titans, but he soon sent them back to Tartarus, along with the giants known as the Hecatoncheires. Having married his sister, Rhea, and mindful of the curse of Uranos and Ge that he would also be deposed by one of his own children, he swallowed each in turn as they were born. Tiring of this, Rhea substituted a stone for the baby Zeus, who was, according to Minoan tradition, raised in the Dictaean Cave on Crete, suckled by the she-goat Amalthea while the Curetes clashed their weapons together to mask the sound of the baby's cries.

When Zeus came of age he consulted Metis (some sources say they married), the daughter of Oceanos, and with Rhea's help gave Cronos a potion that made him first disgorge the stone that had been substituted for him at his birth followed by his other children—Hestia, Demeter, Hera, Hades, and Poseidon. They joined forces with Zeus in a battle against their father and the other Titans, who were led by Atlas.

This war, known as the Titanomachia, waged for ten years in Thessaly until finally Ge promised Zeus victory if he would release the Cyclopes and the Hecatoncheires from Tartarus, which he did. In return the Cyclopes gave Zeus a thunderbolt, Hades a helmet of darkness, and Poseidon a trident. With the aid of these weapons the three brothers overcame Cronos while the Hecatoncheires stoned the other Titans. Thus defeated, they were consigned either to Tartarus or to an island in the west, where they were guarded by the Hecatoncheires. Atlas was punished for leading the Titans by being made to carry the sky on his shoulders, but the Titanesses were spared, even though they had taken part in the battle. Thus the prophecy of Uranos and Ge came to fruition, and Zeus superseded his father as the supreme ruler of the universe.

See also: Aphrodite; Erinnyes; Metis; Saturn

Cumae

Greco-Roman

Port near Naples, Italy. The site of the earliest Greek colony in Italy, it was settled from Chalcis c. 750 B.C. It became a great colonizing power in its own right and featured in some notable legends. Having escaped from Minos, Daedalus was supposed to have landed at Cumae before having to flee again from the pursuing king. It is, however, best known as the location of the sibyl whose counsel was sought by Aeneas. She told him to arm himself with the Golden Bough from a wood near Lake Avernus, then led him down into the Underworld to consult with his father's spirit.

See also: Aeneas; Sibyl

Cupid

Roman

Also: Amor

God of love, the son of Venus who corresponded to the Greek Eros. Usually depicted as a beautiful, naked, winged boy carrying a bow and arrows, which he used to make gods and mortals alike either fall in love with each other or refute that advances of another. The youngest and most mischievous of the gods, he played many wanton tricks on mortals and immortals and was an attendant figure in much Roman love poetry and sculpture.

See also: Eros

Curetes

Greek

Priests of Rhea who attended the infant Zeus according to Minoan tradition. While the baby was being suckled by the she-goat Amalthea, they clashed their weapons, or cymbals, together to mask the sound of the baby's cries. Their name, cognate with *kouros,* "youth," specifically identifies them as attendants on the baby Zeus. They are closely allied to the Corybantes who attended the Asiatic mother goddess Cybele, whose cult was merged with that of Zeus's mother, Rhea.

Curiatii

Roman

Collective name for three brothers from Alba Longa who fought and lost a battle to the Horatii.

Curium

Greek

Near to this town on Cyprus lies a sanctuary to Apollo, one of the major sanctuaries on the island. Apollo's cult was practiced here from around the eighth century B.C. to the fourth century A.D. Most of the visible remains today date from the first century A.D. The site has great archaeological importance, as the total layout gives a clear impression of the ways in which ritual and secular needs were combined within a single sanctuary complex.

Curtius, Mettius

Roman

Sabine champion who led his people against Romulus following the rape of the Sabine women. Overconfident, he foundered on his horse in the swamps on the site of what was later to become the Forum. Some commentators say that it was from this incident that the Lacus Curtius in the Forum derived its name.

See also: Sabine

Cybe~le, ~be

Greco-Roman

Ancient Phrygian mother goddess and goddess of caves whose cult centered on Pessinus in Phrygia and at Mount Dindymus in Mysia, where the origins of its rites were attributed to the Argonauts. She was depicted wearing a mural crown as protectress of her people and, as a goddess of wild places, rides in a chariot drawn by lions. Her youthful consort was Attis and her acolytes, the Corybantes, and, in Roman times, the self-mutilating Galli. Her cult was eventually merged with that of Rhea or, in some places, Demeter, though in Piraeus, for example, she was worshipped under her own name along with Attis. She was said to have been married to Gordius, king of Phrygia, and was considered by some as the mother of Midas. Her cult spread to as far as Rome, possibly being taken there by the Trojan refugees who traveled with Aeneas.

Cyclades
Greek

Greek Kikládhes, a roughly circular group of about two hundred islands in the south Aegean Sea lying between Greece and Turkey. A department of modern Greece, it has its capital at Hermoúplois on Síros. Among the group is Delos, the island supposed to have been raised by Poseidon and then anchored to the seabed by Zeus. It became an important center for the worship of Apollo. Also within the group is Naxos, the island on which Theseus was said to have abandoned Ariadne and where she was later found and married by Dionysos. It became the center of worship of Dionysos.

Cyclop(e)s
Greek

Although the Cyclopes are usually described as the children of Uranos and Ge, their purpose differs. Hesiod describes them as Titans, whereas Homer says they were one-eyed giant shepherds living on Sicily, their leader being named as Polyphemus. Later tradition said they were the helpers of Hephaistos living either on, or actually within, Mount Etna.

The three original Cyclopes, the one-eyed giant sons of Uranos and Ge, are usually named as Brontes (Thunderer), Sterope (Lightener), and Arges (Bright), the brothers of the three Hecatoncheires or Centimani and the 12 original Titans. Rebelling against their father, they were imprisoned in Tartarus by Uranos but released for a short while by the Titans when Cronos deposed his father. However, they were soon reimprisoned along with their brothers, the Hecatoncheires.

During the ten-year war known as the Titanomachia, the Cyclopes remained in their Underworld prison but were finally released after Ge had promised Zeus victory in his epic struggle to become supreme on the condition that he did just that. They presented Zeus with his thunderbolt, Hades with his helmet of darkness, and Poseidon with his trident. With

the aid of these fabulous weapons Zeus and his brothers won their battle.

Great builders, the Cyclopes were said to have built the massive walls of Tiryns and, later, of Mycenae, these walls of unhewn stone being today referred to as Cyclopean. Later tradition added to the number of Cyclopes, making them a numerous tribe of savage pastoralists who lived without laws, feeding on dairy produce except when human flesh should chance their way. Most famous of these "other" Cyclopes was Polyphemus, a son of Poseidon who lived in a cave on the west coast of Sicily. Odysseus and his companions took refuge in his cave, and when Polyphemus entered with his flocks they found themselves trapped, two of Odysseus's companions being devoured by the giant. By the following evening only Odysseus and six of his companions remained, so they got Polyphemus drunk with a sweet and extremely potent wine before putting out his single eye. The next morning they escaped by clinging to the bellies of Polyphemus's sheep and so made it safely to their ship, but thereafter they had to contend with the vengeful hostility of Poseidon.

A further tradition concerns the fateful love of Polyphemus for the nymph Galatea and his disposal of his rival for her attentions, Acis. In these later traditions these giant one-eyed beings are usually referred to as Cyclops, Polyphemus often being referred to simply as "the cyclops."

See also: Hecatoncheires; Titanomachia

Cycnus
Greek

1. The father of Tenes, king of Tenedos. He was killed, along with his son, by Achilles when the Greek forces landed on the island, in sight of Troy, on their way to the Trojan War.

2. A son of Ares who was killed in combat by Heracles. Apollodorus tells his story twice, each time giving him a different mother, each giving a different account of his life. In the first he and his mother are separated by Ares, whereas in the second he is killed by Heracles.

3. King of the Ligurians and a friend of Phaëthon. When Phaëthon was killed he

mourned his friend's death unrelentingly until he was transformed into a swan and transferred to the heavens as the constellation Cygnus.

4. One of the numerous sons of Poseidon; king of Colonae. He fought on the side of Troy during the Trojan War but was killed by Achilles, after which he was transformed into a swan.

See also: Achilles; Tenes

Cygnus

Greek

Astronomical: "The Swan." Several legends tell how this constellation came into being. One says that it is the swan, really Zeus in disguise, that wooed Leda. Another says it was Cycnus, transferred to the heavens upon being changed into a swan after mourning the death of his friend Phaëthon. The constellation is located in the northern celestial hemisphere between approximate right ascensions 19h05m and 22h00m, declination from +27° to +62°.

Cyllar~os, ~us

Greek

The horse owned by Castor that was possibly named in memory of a handsome centaur killed at the marriage feast of Peirithous during the famous battle between the centaurs and the Lapithae.

See also: Castor; Dioscuri

Cyllene

Greek

Lofty peak in Arcadia; a cavern said, in the *Hymn of Hermes* (c. 600 B.C.), to have been the birthplace of the messenger god Hermes—hence Cyllenius.

Cyllenius

Greek

Name sometimes used to refer to Hermes due to his connection with Mount Cyllene in Arcadia.

Cynthia

Greek

Name sometimes used to refer to Artemis, as she was said to have been born on the slopes of Mount Cynthus.

Cynthus

Greek

A mountain on Delos where Leto was said to have borne the twins Apollo and Artemis. While Artemis is sometimes referred to as Cynthia due to this association, Apollo is more simply known as Cynthus.

Cyprus

Greek

Large Mediterranean island that is known, through archaeological evidence, to have sheltered Neolithic peoples from at least the fourth millenium B.C. It was later colonized successively by Phoenicians, Greeks, Egyptians, Persians, and Romans.

According to Hesiod, it was the island near to which Aphrodite was born from the sea that had been fertilized with blood dripping from the wound inflicted on Uranos by Cronos. She was said to have traveled straight to Paphos on the island, one of the most important centers of her cult; there she was worshipped as a fertility goddess, and from there the Phoenicians took her worship to Cythera.

Cyrene

Greek

The daughter of Hypseus, king of the Lapithae, and one of those athletic maidens of Greek mythology who was much more given to hunting and outdoor pursuits. Apollo fell in love with her after he had witnessed her prowess wrestling a lion on Mount Pelion. On the advice of Cheiron, Apollo lay with her and then carried her off to Libya, where the city of Cyrene was named after her. This northern African port was colonized from Crete c. 630 B.C. and later became subject to Egypt and then to Rome. It was there that she gave birth to Aristaeus, the child born out of her union with Apollo.

See also: Aristaeus; Cheiron

Cythera

Greek

An island off Laconia in the southeastern Peloponnesos that was colonized by Phrygians. Some accounts say that near this island Aphrodite rose from the sea, though an alternative version says that the goddess rose near the island of Cyprus, and that her cult was brought to Cythera from Paphos on that island. The island was sacred to Aphrodite, who was thence surnamed Cytherea.

See also: Aphrodite

Cytherea

Greek

Surname applied to the goddess Aphrodite after the island of Cythera, which was sacred to her.

D

Dactyli

Greek

Mythical early inhabitants of Mount Ida in Phrygia said to have discovered iron and the art of working it with fire. Some sources refer to them as a group of *daemones,* possibly due to their mastery of iron, and associated them with Cybele, the Phrygian Mother Goddess, and later with Rhea and one of Cybele's Greek analogs, Adrasteia. In addition to being masters of iron, they were considered masters of sorcery and amulets as well as the inventors of certain musical genres.

Later tradition transposed them from Phrygia to Crete, saying that they instead lived on the Cretan Mount Ida, identifying them further with the Curetes, the priests of Rhea said to have guarded the infant Zeus. Their name means "fingers," and this later tradition said that they were named from the marks made when their mother, Rhea, in this tradition, pressed her fingers into the earth while in labor. Their names were given as Heracles, Epimedes, Idas, Paeonius, and Iasus.

Daedal~os, ~us

Greek

Also: Daidal~os, ~us

The inventor of sculpture and other engineering and mechanical arts, the son of Eupalamus and a descendant of Erechtheus. His name is a masculine word form that means "idol" or "carved image." When his apprentice-nephew, Talos or Perdix, invented the chisel, saw, and compasses and boded to be a better artist than Daedalus himself, he threw him headlong from Athene's temple on the Acropolis at Athens. Athene changed Perdix into a partridge, and Daedalus was banished by the Areopagus. He fled to Crete. It

is interesting to note that Daedalus's sister was also named Perdix.

Arriving in Crete, he was first commissioned by Minos to build a wooden cow inside of which his wife, Pasiphaë, could lie to mate with the Cretan Bull. He is, however, most famous for his next commission, the building of the Cretan Labyrinth in which the Minotaur, the result of Pasiphaë's union with the Cretan Bull, would be imprisoned. This he built, according to Pliny, by modeling it on the so-called Egyptian Labyrinth, the temple of Amenehet III.

Homer says that he built a dance floor for Ariadne, Minos's daughter, in the form of a maze, an allegory on the labyrinth itself, for the dance now becomes the story of the hero Theseus as he threads his way into the winding passages of the maze to kill the Minotaur, aided by the ball of thread given to him by Ariadne. Theseus was also, in Homer at least, said to have received instructions from Daedalus himself as to how to penetrate the labyrinth.

Minos now imprisoned Daedalus and his son, Icarus, in the labyrinth he had constructed. Daedalus thus constructed father-son sets of wings out of feathers set into a wax base, and using these they escaped from Crete, having been released from the labyrinth by Pasiphaë. Icarus, however, flew too close to the sun, the wax on his wings melted, and he plunged to his death.

Daedalus made it to safety, first seeking sanctuary at Cumae before traveling on to Sicily. Minos tracked him down by asking each king he met to thread a snail's shell. When Cocalos (whose name means "shell"), king of Sicily, managed to do this, Minos knew that Daedalus had been that way, but Minos was then murdered by Cocalos with the aid of his daughters, some accounts saying the deed was done while the Cretan king lay in a ceremonial bath and either boiling water was poured over him or molten metal was poured down the bath taps. Finally Daedalus went to Sardinia, where his track is lost.

Discoveries such as the excavation of the great labyrinthine palace at Knossos on Crete give legends such as these special significance, for they would seem to suggest that they have at least some foundation in history.

See also: Icarus; Knossos; Minos; Perdix; Talos

Daemon
Greek

A term used to refer to a spirit or divinity when the speaker is not certain which particular deity is at work. However, the word is most commonly used in its plural form to refer to groups or collections of superhuman beings who are rarely referred to individually, such as the Dactyli, Curetes, and nymphs.

Many *daemones* restricted themselves to particular habitats, such as the sea nymphs, the Nereides.

Later, neoplatonic philosophy provided the *daemones* with an important role as mediators between men and gods, the next step being provided by Christianity, which declared that all pagan gods were *daemones,* thus giving the word all the connotations of the modern word *demon.* They dwelled in rivers and groves as of old, as well as statues and pagan temples. Thus the destruction of pagan works of art and buildings was said to be to extirpate the demons that dwelled in them.

See also: Curetes; Dactyli

Daidal~os, ~us
Greek

Alternative form of the great engineer and architect Daedalus.

Damocles
Greco-Roman

A historical figure who lived in the fourth century B.C., residing at the court of Dionysius I, the tyrannical ruler of Syracuse, Sicily, possibly at the same time as Damon and Phintias. Legend says that Damocles once flattered Dionysius I, extolling his happiness, his wealth, and his power. As a result Damocles was invited by Dionysius I to attend a banquet with a sword suspended by a single hair, or very fine thread, hanging over his head. Damocles thus came to realize that those things he had praised were ephemeral and did not bring true happiness but rather illustrated the insecurity of the rich and powerful. This episode has passed into modern usage: Impending disaster is referred to as the "sword of Damocles."

Damon
Greco-Roman

A historical figure, a courtier of Dionysius I of Syracuse, Sicily, possibly residing in the palace of the tyrannical ruler at the same time as Damocles. His friend, Phintias, plotted against Dionysius I and, having been caught and tried, was sentenced to death. Phintias needed time to settle his affairs, so Damon stood bail for him under the threat of being executed in Phintias's stead should the latter fail to return within the allotted time. Phintias did return. Dionysius I was so impressed with the friendship the two displayed that he reprieved Phintias and, thereafter, sought to be admitted to their special bond of friendship.

Danaë
Greek

Daughter of Acrisius (king of Argos). When an oracle foretold that Acrisius would be killed by his grandson, the frightened king locked his daughter in a bronze or brazen tower or dungeon, possibly one of the beehive tombs of Mycenaean Greece, which were lined with bronze plates. However, Zeus still visited Danaë in the form of a shower of gold, and she later gave birth to the hero Perseus. Not wanting to kill his daughter and her child, Acrisius set them adrift in a wooden chest. Finally they washed ashore on the island of Seriphos, where they were found by Dictys, who took them to the king, Polydectes, who welcomed them warmly. Later, when Perseus had come of age, Polydectes sent the young hero to kill Medusa as a ruse to get him out of the way, as he had fallen in love with Danaë and planned to marry her.

Having successfully beheaded the Gorgon and rescued Andromeda from the sea monster Cetus, Perseus returned to Seriphos to find that Danaë and Dictys had fled from Polydectes' palace and had sought refuge in a temple. Furious, Perseus confronted Polydectes and, exposing the head of Medusa, turned the king and all his followers to stone. Perseus then installed Dictys as the new king of Seriphos and returned to Argos with his mother. Mindful of the original oracle, Acrisius fled to Larissa—but in vain, for while visiting Larissa Perseus took part in some public games and accidentally killed his grandfather with a discus.

See also: Acrisius; Perseus

Danai
Greek
A term that was used only by Homer as a generic term to refer to the Greek race.

Danaid(e)s
Greek
The collective name for the 50 daughters of Danaus, son of Belus and king of Libya, by ten different wives. His brother, Aegyptus, had 50 sons and suggested a mass marriage between his sons and the Danaides. Danaus fled, taking his daughters with him to Argos, where he was elected king in place of Gelanor. However, the 50 sons of Aegyptus followed and asked for the hands of the daughters in marriage. Reluctantly Danaus agreed but gave each daughter a weapon, instructing each to kill her new husband on their wedding night. All complied except one, Hypermnestra, who spared her husband, Lynceus, who killed Danaus and went on to become king of Argos. Danaus then remarried them by offering them as prizes in a footrace. Following their deaths the 49 Danaides who had complied with Danaus's orders were condemned to Hades, where they were to eternally carry water in sieves or to fill bottomless vessels.

In origin they appear to be water nymphs, celebrating the introduction of irrigation to the arid region of Argos, a function that is explicit in the myth of Amymone, one of the Danaides. They were also said to have brought the Mysteries of Demeter from Egypt and to have instituted her festival, the Thesmaphoria. The story of the Danaides is used as the central theme of Aeschylus's play *The Suppliants*.

See also: Aegyptus

Danaoi
Greek
Although this term was originally coined to refer to the family descended from Danaë, later, better-known legends made them the descendants of Danaus, and therefore included the Danaides. Homer employed the term more generally, whereas other authors used the term to specifically refer to the Greek troops at the siege of Troy. They seem to be part of the dynasty of Mycenaean Midea and Tiryns and were the subjects of saga deriving from early or mid-Mycenaean times.

Danaus
Greek
The eponym of the Danaoi, at least according to later tradition; son of Belus, king of Libya and later Argos, and brother of Aegyptus, the eponym of Egypt. His family also included his nephew, Phoenix, eponym of the Phoenicians, and displays a mythological treatment of early Mediterranean ethnography and history.

Danaus fathered 50 daughters, the Danaides, by ten wives; his brother, Aegyptus, wanted to wed them to his 50 sons. Danaus fled with his daughters to Argos, where he was elected king in place of Gelanor. However, the 50 sons of Aegyptus followed and demanded the hands of his daughters in marriage. Danaus reluctantly agreed, but he armed each of his daughters and instructed them to kill their new husbands on their wedding night. All but Hypermnestra complied. Danaus then organized a footrace, offering his forty-nine "obedient" daughters as prizes. Finally Lynceus, Hypermnestra's husband—and the only of Aegyptus's sons not to have been killed by the Danaides—killed Danaus and became king of Argos.

See also: Aegyptus

Daphne

Greek

A nymph, the daughter of the river god Peneus in Thessaly or Arcadia. She had two lovers. The first, Leucippus, son of King Oenomaus of Elis, dressed as a girl so that he could go hunting with Daphne and other nymphs. On one such day, however, the nymphs decided to strip to have a swim. Discovering Leucippus's secret, they killed him.

Her other, more famous lover was Apollo, who chased after the girl. Unable to escape, Daphne prayed to the gods to rescue her. Ge responded by turning her into a laurel bush. Thereafter, Apollo wore a laurel branch on his head as a symbol of his love and grief, and the bush became sacred to him. A suburb of Antioch is called Daphne, where this event is alleged to have happened; it is the former location of a famous temple to Apollo.

A variant on this story says that the chase took place in the Vale of Tempe, a myth that probably refers to the capture of Tempe by the Hellenes where the goddess Daphoene was worshipped by votaries, often incorrectly referred to as Maenads, chewed laurel leaves, and thus became intoxicated. After the Hellenes arrived, only the Pythoness of Apollo was permitted to chew laurel.

See also: Leucippus

Daphnis

Greek

A Sicilian demigod, the son of Hermes and an unnamed nymph. Exposed at birth, he was raised by Sicilian shepherds and became a great exponent of the syrinx, which Pan taught him to play. With such great skill he became a minstrel to Apollo. He was also regarded as the inventor of bucolic poetry.

Daphnis pledged his love to a jealous nymph, either Nomeia or Echenais, but he was seduced either by a Sicilian princess or by the nymph Chimaera (not the fire-breathing monster). His lover blinded him for his unfaithfulness, and Daphnis took his own life. To commemorate his son, Hermes caused a fountain, known as Daphnis, to rise at Syracuse.

See also: Hermes

Dardanelles

Greek

Strait of water that separates, along with the Sea of Marmara and the Bosphorus, Asiatic Turkey from the remainder of the country. Its ancient name was the Hellespont, named in honor of Helle, who fell from the back of the winged ram Aries that was carrying her and her brother, Phrixus, away from their cruel stepmother to Colchis.

Dardania

Greek

Town that once stood in the vicinity of Troy, supposedly founded by Dardanos. By the time of Homer, when the sixth city of Troy would have been standing, it was absorbed into the city along with Tros and Ilium. Legend says that the town was built by Dardanos on a piece of land given to him by Teucer.

See also: Tros

Dardan~os, ~us

Greco-Roman

Son of Zeus and Electra (a daughter of Atlas and thus one of the Pleiades) and brother to Iasion. Regarded as the primal ancestor of Troy, he founded and gave his name to Dardania, a town built on land given to him by Teucer, son of the River Scamander, when he arrived in the region from Samothrace. Along with Tros and Ilium, this town was later absorbed into the city that became known as Troy. He built a citadel that later became the citadel of Troy, introduced the cults of the Samothracian gods and of Cybele, and brought the Palladium, the statue of Athene, from Arcadia.

See also: Palladium; Pleiades

Daul~ia, ~is

Greek

An ancient town in Phocis that was the home of Tereus and the setting for the story of Philomela and Procne, who are hence called Daulias.

Daulias

Greek

Name applied to Philomela and Procne, which is derived from Daulia, the town in Phocis where their story is set.

Daunia

Greek

Region in Italy to which Diomedes traveled after the Trojan War, there marrying Euippe, the daughter of Daunus, the king and eponym of the region.

Daun~os, ~us

Greek

King and eponym of Daunia, Italy, whose daughter, Euippe, married Diomedes after he left Argos, he having returned from the Trojan War to discover his wife's infidelity.

Deian~eira, ~ara

Greek

Daughter of Oeneus, king of Calydon and Pleuron. She married Heracles after he defeated her other suitor, the mighty river god Achelous, son of Oceanos and Tethys. Their son was named Hyllus. In a famous incident, Deianeira was being carried across the fast-flowing River Evenus by the centaur Nessus when the centaur made off with her, fully meaning to violate her. Heracles shot Nessus through the breast with one of his poisoned arrows and, as the centaur lay dying, gave Deianeira some of his blood to be used as a charm to reclaim a faithless husband, though some accounts say she was given Nessus's blood-stained tunic.

Later, when Deianeira suspected Heracles was about to abandon her for Iole, the daughter of Eurytus who had been sent to her by Heracles, she sent to him a shirt dipped in Nessus's blood, or the blood-stained tunic, not knowing that the blood had been poisoned by Heracles' arrow, which had caused the death of Nessus. When Heracles put the shirt or tunic on, it burned into his flesh. In excruciating agony Heracles tried to tear the garment from his back, but it simply tore great chunks of his flesh away.

Commanding his son, Hyllus, to build a funeral pyre for him on Mount Oeta, Heracles immolated himself. Deianeira, grief-stricken by what she had unintentionally done, hanged herself. This tragic climax to the career of Heracles was dramatized by Sophocles in *Women of Trachis* or *Trachiniae*. In this work the ill-fated attempt by Deianeira to keep her husband's fidelity is touchingly represented.

See also: Heracles; Oeneus

Deidameia

Greek

Daughter of Lycomedes (king of Scyros) and mother of Neoptolemus, sometimes called Pyrrhos, by Achilles when the latter was hiding disguised as a girl at the court of her father, a ruse devised by Thetis meant to prevent Achilles from going to Troy.

See also: Achilles; Lycomedes

Deimos

Greco-Roman

One of the two horsemen (with companion Phobos) of Ares (Roman Mars); his name means "panic" or "terror."

Astronomical: The outer satellite of the planet Mars that was discovered in 1877, along with Phobos, by Asaph Hall. Irregular in shape, Deimos has a maximum dimension of approximately 13 kilometers (8 miles) and orbits at an average distance of 23,500 kilometers (14,690 miles) from the planet.

Deiphobus

Greek

One of the 50 sons of Priam and one of the 19 born to him by Hecuba, his second wife. Brother to Hector, Paris, Polites, Cassandra, and Helenus, Deiphobus quarreled with the latter for the possession of Helen, who was at this late stage of the Trojan War homesick for Sparta. Deiphobus forcibly married her, and Helenus fled to Mount Ida, where he either freely joined the Greek forces or was captured by Odysseus. Deiphobus was killed by Agamemnon and Menelaus when Troy finally fell to the stratagem of the Wooden Horse.

See also: Hecuba; Priam

Deiphyle

Greek

Daughter of Adrastus (king of Argos), sister of Argia, whom Adrastus married, and wife of Tydeus, the son of Oeneus of Calydon.

Delia

Greek

The quinquennial festival held on Delos in honor of Apollo.

Delos

Greek

One of the smallest of the Cyclades, a roughly circular group of islands in the southern Aegean Sea. Legend says that the island was raised from the seabed by Poseidon and then anchored to the bottom by Zeus; it was considered the birthplace of Apollo and, according to some sources, also of his twin sister, Artemis, though she is usually regarded as having been born on the nearby island of Ortygia.

The island became one of the most important centers of worship of Apollo, who was also known there as Lycius and Phoebus. The oracle of Apollo on Delos was said to have been consulted by Aeneas as he led his band of Trojan refugees to a new home following the end of the Trojan War. The rulers of Delos became treasurers of the Delian League between 478 B.C. and 454 B.C. The ruins on the island are particularly impressive, a vast ruined classical city with a most impressive theater and an underground system of drains and reservoirs. The sanctuary of Apollo, temple of Apollo, temple of Artemis, and the sacred way with the dried-up sacred lake and "lion terrace" cover an even greater area than does the residential area, illustrating the special religious importance of Delos. Mosaics found within the temple of Dionysos are particularly noteworthy.

See also: Aeneas; Cyclades

Delphi

Greco-Roman

Ancient Greek city situated in a rocky valley north of the Gulf of Corinth near the spring Castalia on the southern slope of Mount Parnassus. Delphi became famous as the site of the Delphic Oracle, the Oracle of Apollo that was situated in his temple. In the same temple stood the Omphalos, a conical stone said to stand at the center of earth, though some accounts say that this was the stone first swallowed and subsequently regurgitated by Cronos, the stone being substituted by Rhea for the baby Zeus.

After the sixth century B.C. Delphi became one of the richest sanctuaries of the Greek world. It was plundered by both Sulla and Nero, the latter removing more than 500 bronze statues but scarcely making an impact on the overall appearance of the temple complexes. It is still the most magnificent of all the Greek sites, though time, looters, and Christians have removed all the treasures that were unequaled during their time.

Delphic Oracle

Greco-Roman

The oracle of Apollo and his Dorian sanctuary, at Delphi on the southern slope of Mount Parnassus, where the god was also known as the Pythian or Loxias—"the Ambiguous." Legend gives us several variations on the origins of the Delphic Oracle, the second most important sanctuary to the ancient Greeks after Olympus.

Originally said to be the Oracle of Ge, or the Oracle of Earth, it was guarded by the she-dragon Python. Shortly after his birth, Apollo came to Delphi from Delos, killed the Python, and took over the oracle; the priestess, known as the Pythoness, thereafter became the mouthpiece of his oracles, which were imparted in hexameter verse in his temple. In this same temple was the Omphalos, the navel stone of earth that was supposed to mark its center.

Two different stories tell of its origin. One says that it was the stone swallowed and then regurgitated by Cronos who had been given it by Rhea in place of the infant Zeus. The other says that Zeus sent two eagles to fly from the two horizons, east and west, and placed this conical-stone where they met to mark the center of earth.

Apollo having slain the Python and taken over the oracle, Zeus commanded Apollo to visit the Vale of Tempe for purification and there to found and preside over the Pythian Games that were to be held in Python's honor. Returning to Delphi, Apollo was joined by his sister, Artemis, and their mother, Leto. Hera, still implacable over Zeus's philandering, sent the giant Tityus to violate either Leto or Artemis, but Apollo, sensing the danger, killed the giant with his arrows. The establishment of the oracle at Delphi firmly placed Apollo in the role of god of prophecy.

The original oracle appears to have been founded by pre-Hellenic people who worshipped an ambivalent mother goddess, later to be equated with Ge. When the Hellenes invaded the area and seized the site, they slew the Python, the oracular serpent, and took over the oracles in the name of Apollo; but with respect for ancient customs and the original inhabitants of the region they founded and held the Pythian Games in honor of the oracular serpent.

Within the temple of Apollo was a chasm that was supposed to give out intoxicating fumes, possibly a sulphurous fissure within the volcanic infrastructure of the region. Over this the Pythoness or Pythia sat on a tripod, maintaining an intoxicated state by chewing laurel, uttering the wisdom of the god in hexameter verse. Regarded as the mystical bride of the god, her utterances were interpreted by the oracular priests before being passed onto the questioner.

Further cults had smaller sanctuaries at Delphi, thus adding to the status and wealth of the Delphic Oracle. Among them was that of Dionysos, whose votaries were known at Delphi as Thyiads, who regularly held orgiastic Dyonisiac festivals there, his sepulchre being placed very near to the tripod of the Pythia, whereas his temple, a theater, was built at the highest point of the sacred precinct.

Many legends abound where heroes consulted the Delphic Oracle. Famous among these is the sending of Heracles to labor for 12 years for King Eurystheus, king of Argos, the Pythia being the first person to actually refer to this great hero as Heracles. Cadmos consulted the oracle, and this led him to found the city that was later to be called Thebes. Oedipus learned there that he would kill his father and then marry his own mother. Further traditions stemming from consultations of the Delphic Oracle are found in Roman legends. The Tarquins consulted it to discover which of them would succeed their father, Tarquinius Superbus. The oracle also confirmed to Camillus the information that Veii would only fall after the Alban Lake had been drained. This turned out to be true; following the fall of Veii, booty was sent to the Delphic Oracle.

By the second century A.D. the oracles were given in prose. Both Sulla and Nero plundered the site, the latter taking around 500 bronze statues from the site without adversely affecting its appearance. The last utterance of the oracle was to the emperor Julian: "Tell ye the kings the carven hall is fallen in decay. / Apollo hath no chapel left, no prophesying bay, no talking spring. / The stream is dry that hath much to say."

Shortly afterwards, c. 390 A.D., the oracle was closed down by the Roman Emperor Theodosius. Today the site is still magnificent, though the treasures once held there can only be wondered at, for they have been successively looted (some are preserved in a site museum).

See also: Apollo; Artemis; Ge; Python

Delphin~os, ~us
Greek
1. A dolphin who so eloquently pleaded the suit of Poseidon to Amphitrite and her father, Nereus, that Amphitrite consented to marry the god. In gratitude Poseidon transferred Delphinos to the heavens to form the constellation that bears his name. However, some confusion exists here, for this constellation is also said to represent Delphinos.

Astronomical: A small but exquisite group of stars that lies in the northern celestial hemisphere between approximate right ascensions 20h10m and 21h10m, declination from +3° to +21°.

2. A dolphin who saved the life of the poet-minstrel Arion when he leaped overboard from a ship to escape the attentions of ruffian sailors who were threatening his life. The dolphin carried Arion ashore before the ship arrived and, when it did, the crew was arrested and executed. In return for the dolphin's service to Arion, the gods placed his image in

the sky as the constellation that bears his name.

Astronomical: See Delphinos (1) above.

See also: Amphitrite; Arion

Demeter

Greek

One of the 12 Olympian deities whose Roman counterpart was Ceres, Demeter probably originated as a Minyan goddess, brought along when the Minyans entered Greece c. 2000 B.C. Revered as an earth goddess, it is thought she was also made the mate of their sky god, a character who would seem to have later developed into Poseidon or possibly even Zeus, though the former is the more likely as both Minyan deities were said to have been able to assume the shape of a horse, an attribute that carried forward into Greek legend. The Minyan goddess, merged with the Great Goddess of pre-Hellenic matriarchal society, gave rise to Demeter, specifically goddess of agriculture, nutrition, and crops and fruit, especially corn, but also goddess of human health and fertility.

Her combination with Ceres in Roman religion was mainly due to the influence of the Greek colony of Cumae. As Ceres she presided solely over the growth of cereals and other foodstuffs and was given a male counterpart, Cerus.

According to common ancient interpretation her name means "Earth Mother," and her various titles, such as Karpophoros (fruit-bearing), further emphasize her role. She was also worshipped in specific aspects as Demeter Erinys at Onkeion, and Black Demeter, at Phigaleia, the latter goddess being depicted with a horse's head, for Demeter was said to have fled to Phigaleia following her rape by Poseidon.

Legend makes her the daughter of Cronos and Rhea, sister to Hestia, Hades, Zeus, Poseidon, and Hera. She was raped by her brother, Zeus, and became the mother by him of Persephone, also called Kore or Core, "the maiden," herself an aspect of the goddess. Hades sought permission from Zeus to marry the girl and, receiving neither approval nor refusal, carried her off while she was gathering flowers, some sources placing the abduction at Enna, others firmly at Eleusis. Grief-stricken, Demeter wandered earth in search of her daughter, and it is these wanderings that give rise to most of the legends surrounding Demeter. During them she was raped by Poseidon, who assumed the form of a stallion, for Demeter was then in the guise of a mare, the result of this union being the horse Arion and the nymph Despoena.

At the wedding of Harmonia and Cadmos she united with Iasion, Harmonia's brother, in a ploughed field; as a result she bore the sons Plutus (Wealth) and Plilomelus (the Inventor), who some say later became the constellation Boötes.

Unable to locate Persephone, Demeter wandered far and wide, participating at one point in the banquet prepared for the gods by Tantalus at which a stew made from his son, Pelops, was served. Only Demeter, in her grief, did not notice what she was eating and consumed Pelops's shoulder. After Tantalus had been suitably punished by Zeus and Pelops restored to life, Demeter made him a new shoulder from ivory in recompense, this ivory shoulder becoming a birthmark of sorts for his descendants.

Still Demeter could not locate her daughter until, on the tenth day of her wanderings, which appear to have taken her to almost every corner of the Greek world, Helios told her of what Hades had done. Refusing to return to Olympus, Demeter came instead to Eleusis, where she sat down by the well Callichoron and wept copiously. Here she was found by Celeus, king of Eleusis, who brought her into his home. There Metaneira, Celeus's wife, gave her a drink of *kykeon,* a type of barley water, which she at first refused to drink, but Iambe finally induced her to smile with her lewd antics, and Demeter thirstily downed the drink. However, Abas, one of Celeus's sons, derided the goddess for the avidity with which she had drunk. In retaliation Demeter changed Abas into a lizard, a form in which he, at least, could survive without water, though she still did not reveal to her host and his family her true identity.

Demeter remained with Celeus and his family, becoming the nurse of the baby Demophoön, whom she attempted to make immortal by placing him on the fire. However,

Metaneira discovered her and cried out in alarm. Now Demeter revealed her identity and demanded the foundation of the Eleusinia, in honor of Demophoön.

Even when the temple to Demeter was finished at Eleusis, her daughter had not been returned to her. In her anger Demeter forbade anything to grow on earth, and finally Zeus said that Persephone could return from the Underworld provided she had not eaten anything while there and sent Hermes to escort the maiden back to earth. Unfortunately Hades had given Persephone a pomegranate from which she had eaten but a single seed. As a result Zeus decreed that for a third of the year, some sources say six months, Persephone would dwell in the Underworld; the remainder of the year would be spent with her mother on earth. Before leaving Eleusis, Demeter taught Triptolemus, another of Celeus's sons, all the arts of agriculture and lent him her dragon chariot, which Triptolemus used to travel over all earth, teaching people how to grow and harvest crops wherever he went. This myth originates in the most primitive rites of the seasons, of seedtime and harvest, during an age when only women practiced the arts of agriculture.

Her time spent with Hades was taken to represent the winter, when foliage would die and nothing would grow; her time on earth with Demeter was the growing season. In addition to the Eleusinia the other major festival to Demeter, celebrated in and around Athens, was the women's festival of the Thesmaphoria.

In art Demeter is usually depicted as a mature women with a kindly expression, bountiful and gentle. She is usually represented with a garland of corn or a ribbon, holding a scepter, corn ears, or a poppy, sometimes a torch and basket. On occasions she is shown riding in a chariot pulled by horses or dragons; others depict her walking or enthroned.

Pigs were her sacred animal. Though she was not a popular subject in Greek art, a fine statue of Demeter dating from c. 330 B.C. was found at Cnidos in Asia Minor and is today in the British Museum.

See also: Ceres; Eleusis; Pelops; Persephone; Tantalus

Demodoc~os, ~us
Greek

The writer of a short ballad known as the "Lay of Demodocos" that was incorporated into the eighth book of Homer's *Odyssey*. It tells the humorous story of the occasion when Hephaistos trapped his philandering wife, Aphrodite, in bed with Ares by using an almost invisible net he had made, then displaying the couple to the ridicule of the other gods.

Demo(r)gorgon
Greek

There is only one reference to the Demogorgon in just one source text, the *Thebaid* of Statius. The line ("the dread name of Demogorgon") gives no description of what the Demogorgon might have been, but it is now generally assumed that it was a simple mistake for Demiorgos, "creator god," a mysterious and terrible infernal deity who resolved Chaos into order.

Demopho(ö)n
Greek

1. The son of Celeus and Metaneira whom Demeter attempted to make immortal by immolating him on the fire in return for her hosts' hospitality. Metaneira disturbed her in the process, her scream breaking the spell, and Demophoön died. Demeter then demanded the establishment of the Eleusinia in honor of the boy, a festival that later was combined with the Eleusinian Mysteries.

2. Son of Theseus and Phaedra, though some say his mother was Antiope; brother of Acamas and step-brother of Hippolytus. Following the Trojan War, Demophoön and Acamas rescued their grandmother, Aethra, who had been given as a slave to Helen by the Dioscuri when the divine twins rescued Helen from the village to which Theseus had abducted her. Demophoön then visited Thrace, where Phyllis, the daughter of the king, fell in love with him. Demophoön, however, left her and returned to Athens; she killed herself in despair and was transformed into a tree.

See also: Acamas; Aethra; Demeter; Dioscuri

Despoena

Greek

A nymph, the daughter of Demeter, sister of the horse Arion, the offspring sired on Demeter by Poseidon when the former had disguised herself as a mare and Poseidon assumed the form of a stallion.

Deucalion

Greek

The Greek Noah whose story seems to derive from the much earlier Sumerian tale of Ziusudra. The son of Prometheus and Clymene, he married Pyrrha, the daughter of Epimetheus (Prometheus's brother) and Pandora. When Zeus grew tired of the impiety of mankind he decided to cover the face of earth with a deluge. Forewarned of the coming Flood (a legend common to all Near Eastern peoples and awkwardly displaced to the high and mountainous region of central Greece), Deucalion constructed a vessel in which to ride out the storm. After nine days the waters subsided and the boat came to rest on the slopes of Mount Parnassus.

Wondering how earth would be repopulated, they consulted the Oracle of Themis. Deucalion and Pyrrha were told to throw the bones of their mother over their shoulders. At first unsure what this meant, Pyrrha deciphered that it was Mother Earth that was meant, and they cast stones over their shoulders at Opous. Those thrown by Deucalion became men, those thrown by Pyrrha became women. These new people were the Leleges.

See also: Pandora; Prometheus

Diana

Roman

Ancient Italian moon goddess of Etruscan origin, the virgin huntress and patroness of domestic animals. Initially a woodland goddess, she was rapidly assimilated with Artemis. The daughter of Jupiter and twin of Apollo, she had strong associations as a fertility deity and was invoked by women to aid both conception and childbirth. The lower classes and slaves regarded Diana as their protectress. In art she is usually portrayed as a huntress with bow and arrows accompanied by hunting dogs.

See also: Artemis

Diana of the Ephesians

Roman

An aspect of the goddess Diana who was worshipped as a deity in her own right at Ephesus in Asia Minor. Originally deriving from an early Greek earth goddess, she later became merged with the Roman goddess Diana, yet she always retained a quite separate identity in Ephesus. Her temple was considered one of the wonders of the ancient world.

See also: Ephesus

Dictaean Cave

Greek

Also: Dikt~aean, ~aion Cave

Cave on Dicte, a mountain in the east of the island of Crete, where according to Minoan tradition the baby Zeus was hidden from Cronos by his mother, Rhea. There he was tended by the she-goat Amalthea while the Curetes, priests of Rhea, clattered their weapons or shields together to drown out the baby's cries.

In 1900 this cave, on the Lasithi Plateau near Tzermiádon, was explored by archaeologists who were possibly the first people to enter for almost 2,000 years. Inside they found votive offerings to Zeus that may date from the second millenium B.C., thus indicating that it was an important place of pilgrimage from middle Minoan times.

See also: Amalthea

Dicte

Greek

Mountain lying on the eastern end of the island of Crete, the location of the Dictaean Cave where the infant Zeus was supposedly reared; hence called Dictaeus.

Dictynna

Greek

Also: Diktynna

Ancient virgin-huntress worshipped on Crete who may simply have been an aspect of

Britomartis, though one of the legends surrounding Minos says that as he pursued the nymph Britomartis she leaped into the sea to escape him, whereupon she was deified by Artemis and given the name Dictynna. She was later assimilated into the character of Artemis, who was given the epithet Dictynna, even though the Minos story seems to suggest that her memory was kept alive as a separate deity. It is possible that Britomartis leaped into the sea somewhere near Diktynna on the northern coast of Crete, for this is the site of an important temple, and the similarity in name seems more than mere coincidence.

See also: Britomartis

Dictys

Greek

The sailor who found Danaë and Perseus, who had been cast adrift in a chest by Acrisius, after they washed up on Seriphos. He took them to the king, Polydectes, but later had to flee to the temple with Danaë after Polydectes had sent Perseus off to slay Medusa, a ruse to enable him to take Danaë as his wife. When Perseus returned and discovered the situation he killed Polydectes and his entire court by exposing the head of Medusa, then made Dictys king of Seriphos.

See also: Danaë; Perseus

Dido

Greco-Romano-Phoenician

Legendary Phoenician princess; the daughter of a Tyrian king who fled to Africa after the death of her husband, Sychaeus, and there reputedly founded the city of Carthage. Phoenician legend says that she committed suicide to avoid marrying a local prince or king of Libya, but later Roman tradition says otherwise; Virgil adapted her story to make her a contemporary of Aeneas.

Having left Troy at the end of the Trojan War, Aeneas arrived in Carthage. There Dido fell passionately in love with Aeneas, and Venus, the mother of Aeneas, persuaded Juno to allow them to marry. As Dido and Aeneas had already lain together in a cave, Dido regarded them already married, thus breaking a vow she made on the death of Sychaeus that

she would never remarry. Divine retribution followed, for Jupiter told Aeneas he must depart. Planning to leave in secret, his plan was discovered; failing to persuade Aeneas to stay, Dido took her own life. As Aeneas put out to sea the smoke was already rising from her funeral pyre.

The two did meet on one other occasion, when Aeneas was being led down to the Underworld to consult his dead father, Anchises. Dido would have nothing to do with him and silently turned her back.

See also: Aeneas

Didyma

Greek

Located in modern Turkey, Didyma boasted one of the most important oracular shrines of Apollo in the eastern part of the ancient Greek world, the equivalent of Delphi in the west. Today the temple of Apollo is still most impressive, having the tallest columns in the Greek world.

Dikt~aean, ~aion Cave

Greek

Variant of Dictaean Cave.

Diktynna

Greek

Possibly a variant of Dictynna, or the place after which that deity is named. Diktynna lies near the northernmost tip of Crete, Diktynaion, on the western end of the island, and is the site of a now thoroughly ruined, though very important, temple.

Diodorus the Sicilian

Greco-Roman

Being among the chief sources of Etruscan myths and legends, the writings of this historical person (who flourished in the first century B.C.) join those of Livy, Virgil, and Dionysus of Halicarnassus. Born in Agyrium, Sicily (hence his name, which is more correctly Diodorus Siculus), he traveled to Asia and Europe and lived in Rome, where for 30 years he collected the information for his immense *Bibliotheke*

Historike, a history of the world in 40 books from the creation to the Gallic Wars of Caesar. Of this work the first five books remain intact, the next five are lost, the next ten survive complete, and the remainder survive only in fragmentary form.

Diomed(es)

Greek

1. Savage king of the Bistones in Thrace; son of Ares and Cyrene, he kept mares that he fed on human flesh, they being the goal of Heracles' eighth labor. After Heracles had repelled the attacking Bistones, he returned to where he had left the mares in the charge of Abderus to find that his friend had been eaten by them. Heracles then fed Diomedes to his own horses, after which they never ate human flesh again.

2. Son of Tydeus (king of Argos) and Deiphyle (the daughter of Adrastus); husband of Aegialeia. Taking part in the expedition of the Epigoni against Thebes, he played an important role in Homer's *Iliad*, featuring in a great many of the notable events of the Trojan War.

Arriving from the Peloponnesos with 80 ships, he brought with him two fellow Epigoni: Sthenelus (son of Euryalus) and Capaneus the Argonaut. During the ten-year siege Diomedes wounded Aeneas but saw his quarry rescued by Aphrodite; he is also credited with having wounded the goddess as well as Ares. He then fought Glaucus, a Lycian prince who was second in command to Sarpedon, but when they remembered the friendship that had existed between their forefathers they gave up the fight and exchanged gifts.

In the company of Odysseus, Diomedes made a night raid on the Trojan lines. After killing the spy Dolon he killed Rhesus the Thracian and drove away his snow-white horse, for an oracle had warned that if they drank the water of the River Scamander and ate the grass of the Trojan Plain Troy would not fall. When Achilles killed Thersites, a kinsman of Diomedes, for mocking his remorse at killing Penthesilea, Diomedes threw the body of the slain Amazon queen into the River Scamander. He then accompanied Odysseus to Lemnos to fetch Philoctetes, who had been left there after Calchas had advised the Greeks that they required the bow and arrows of Heracles

if they were ever to take Troy, and these were owned by Philoctetes. He then went with Odysseus and Phoenix to Scyros to let Neoptolemus join them. He was also said to have accompanied Odysseus in disguise into Troy to steal the Palladium, though some sources say Odysseus did this single-handedly.

After the end of the Trojan War, Diomedes returned home briefly. Finding that his wife, Aegialeia, had been unfaithful, he left for Aetolia to help his grandfather, Oeneus, and later settled in Daunia in Italy, where he married Euippe, the daughter of the king, Daunus. He was buried on one of the islands that have since been known as Diomedans, his companions being turned into gentle birds.

The belief that many Greek survivors of the Trojan War settled in Italy was probably current well before 300 B.C. Others said to have emigrated were Epeius, Philoctetes, and Odysseus, though the most notable as far as the Romans were concerned was Aeneas.

See also: Aeneas; Bistones; Epigoni; Odysseus; Trojan War

Dione

Greek

The consort of Zeus who was introduced into Greece c. 1200 B.C. by the invading Achaeans. Her worship was not widespread and did not penetrate as far south as Zeus's shrine at Dodona in Epirus, where the oracular rustling of oak leaves was interpreted as the voice of the god. Here Zeus found other wives, and Dione remained a little-referenced deity, though Homer makes her the mother of Aphrodite by Zeus.

Astronomical: One of the satellites of Saturn, being the sixth closest to the planet of the eleven named between the orbits of Tethys and Rhea. Having a diameter of approximately 1,120 kilometers (700 miles), it lies at an average distance of 378,000 kilometers (236,250 miles) from the surface of the planet.

See also: Dodona

Dionysia

Greek

Name applied to festivals celebrated in ancient Greece, especially in Athens, in honor of the god Dionysos. These included the lesser Dionysia in December, which was chiefly a rural festival, and the greater Dionysia, which was celebrated at the end of March, when new plays were performed. Dionysiac festivals were, however, celebrated elsewhere in Greece, particularly in Corinth, Delphi, and Sicyon. The festival in Athens, founded by Pesistratus at about the same time as the Panathenaic Games, remained the most important.

Dionys(i)us I

Greek

Historical character living from 431 B.C. to 367 B.C. His tyrannical rule over his native city, Syracuse, ended in his making himself absolute ruler in 405 B.C.

After ferociously suppressing several revolts and having conquered some of the Greek colonies of Sicily, he started a running war with Carthage in 398 B.C. Successful at first, he suffered a series of setbacks until he took advantage of a plague within the Carthaginian fleet and gained a complete victory. In 392 B.C. the Carthaginians renewed hostilities but where soon defeated, after which Dionysius turned his attentions to lower Italy, capturing Rhegium in 387 B.C. From this time he exercised great influence over the Greek cities of lower Italy while his fleets swept the Adriatic and Tyrrhenian Seas. In 383 B.C. and again in 368 B.C. he renewed his war against Carthage, wishing to drive the Carthaginian settlers out of Sicily, but he died the following year. He was succeeded by his son, Dionysius II.

In legend Dionysus I is connected with Damocles and Damon and Phintias.

See also: Damocles; Damon; Phintias

Dionys~os, ~us

Greek

God of wine, vegetation, and the life-force and of ecstasy and anomie. Also called Bacchus by both the Greeks and Romans when his rites were less savage, the Romans additionally referred to him as Liber and added a female counterpart, Libera. Dionysos was not, at least in Homer's time, one of the aristocratic Olympian deities but rather a deity worshipped by humble folk.

An extremely unclassical deity, he was probably brought into Greece from Thrace sometime during the eighth century B.C. by nomadic travelers. However, it is possible that Dionysos should really be regarded as one of the oldest Greek deities, for a single Linear B tablet from Pylos refers to di-wo-nu-so-jo, the genitive form of his name in Mycenaean Greek. The cult, which quickly spread through Macedonia and Thessaly to Boeotia, Delphi, Athens, and beyond, was characterized by a mystic frenzy when, intoxicated with wine, the votaries believed themselves to be at one with the god, who was sometimes called Bromius, "the Boisterous." Male votaries were known as Bacchoi, whereas female votaries were given several titles: generally Bacchae, Bacchantes, or Maenads; in Delphi and Athens they were Thyiads.

The immense popularity of the cult of Dionysos, especially among women, seems to indicate that among the recently civilized Greeks there was still a longing for a more impulsive, less-disciplined life valuing enthusiasm in favor of prudence. This led certain wise statesmen during the sixth century B.C. to introduce the cult among the other state religions, and Dyonisiac festivals were established at many of the great cultural centers of the time, especially at Corinth, Delphi, Sicyon, and Athens. At Delphi, where Dionysos has his tomb—thus placing him in the same vein as Heracles, who started life as a mortal before his apotheosis—the sepulcher of Dionysos was placed in close proximity to the tripod of the Pythia, and a temple, actually a theater, was built in his name at the highest point of the sacred precinct. From here the Thyiads climbed the "Bad Stair" up Mount Parnassos to celebrate their orgiastic rites. They wore fawn skins and crowns of ivy, brandished *thyrsoi* (the thyrsus was a staff carried by some during bacchic rites), and chanted "Euoi." They worked themselves into a state of ecstasy by dancing in torchlight to the music of kettledrums and flutes. In this state they were believed to be able to tear living creatures apart with their hands, suckle animals, and charm snakes. During the winter months, while Apollo was said to be away in the land of the Hyperboreans, Dionysos reigned supreme at Delphi.

In Athens the Dionysia was founded by Pesistratus at about the time he instigated the Panathenaic Games; a theater was built in the name of Dionysos, where worshippers performed the first primitive dramas. These plays were also performed at the other festival to Dionysos established in Athens, the Lenaea. They developed into the form of drama known today as tragedy, Dionysos often being celebrated in tragic choruses. At Eleusis, Dionysos was sometimes identified, as Bacchus, with the Iacchus of the Eleusinian Mysteries. His role as a god of life and rebirth makes him an ideal participant.

In the fifth century B.C., following the completion of the Parthenon, the new god replaced Hestia as one of the Olympian deities, thus giving the gods a clear majority over the goddesses, indicating a society that was becoming increasingly patriarchal. Legend says that Dionysos was the son of Semele (the daughter of the king of Thebes) and Zeus, who visited the girl in the guise of a mortal. When six months pregnant Semele was visited by the jealous Hera, disguised as an old woman, and she persuaded Semele to ask her mysterious lover to appear to her in his true form. Unwillingly Zeus consented to this request, and Semele was consumed by the fire of his thunderbolt. The unborn Dionysos was removed from the corpse and the fetus sewn up in Zeus's thigh, to be born three months later. An alternative, Orphic version makes him the child of Zeus and Persephone, who coupled in the form of snakes.

Dionysos had a traumatic start to his life. He was first entrusted to Athamas and Ino of Boeotia, who raised him, disguised as a girl, in the women's quarters. Hera, however, was not deceived and punished Athamas by sending him mad so that he killed his own son. Hermes then took Dionysos to Mount Nysa, where the nymphs raised him, feeding him with honey, and where he was said to have invented wine. Zeus later placed the images of these nymphs in the heavens as the Hyades for their faithful service.

Grown to manhood, Dionysos was not safe, for Hera, still jealous of her husband's philandering, ordered the Titans to seize him, tear him into little pieces, and boil them in a cauldron. During his battle with the Titans, who may not be the Titans of classical mythology but rather a race of pre-men, Dionysos was said to have ridden the ass Assellus Borealis while Silenus rode Assellus Australis. Both became constellations. His grandmother, Rhea, restored him to life, and Zeus, in an attempt to hide him from Hera, turned him into a ram. However, Hera saw through the disguise, sent him mad, and condemned him to wander earth forever. This portion of the life of Dionysos is later in conception, belonging rather to Orphic religious belief.

Wandering over the face of earth Dionysos was not alone, for he was accompanied by his libidinous tutor, Silenus, and an assorted company of satyrs, centaurs, Priapi, Sileni, nymphs, Pans, and Maenads. He traveled through Egypt, where he established the Oracle of Ammon, Syria, and Asia as far as India—where the Pillars of Dionysos were a landmark for the legendary Alexander the Great, overcoming military opposition and teaching the art of making wine, founding numerous cities, and laying down laws. He returned to Europe through Phrygia, where he encountered King Midas (giving that fated king the power to turn everything he touched into gold), and entered Thrace.

He was particularly vicious toward any who opposed the introduction of his rites to their city, a feature of his mythology that may reflect some genuine historical resistance to the spread of his cult—or at least acknowledge that the frenzied worship so typical of his worship was difficult to contain within the bounds of civic society.

Having entered Thrace, his worship was opposed by Lycurgus, king of the Edones; sent mad by Rhea, he mutilated his own son and was sent blind, later cutting off his own leg, mistaking it for a tree. His people, the Edones, sentenced him to be torn to death between two horses.

Passing through Thrace, Dionysos worship entered Boeotia. In Thebes it was again resisted, this time by King Pentheus. A similar fate awaited this king: He was spotted while spying on the Maenads, who tore him to pieces, thinking he was a wild beast. Among the Maenads who killed Pentheus were Agave, his mother, and her two sisters. This legend forms the basis of *Bacchae* by Euripides, which still remains the single fullest source of the rites of Dionysos. His female votaries were said to race across the mountains in an ecstatic, drunken frenzy, seizing small wild animals, which they tore apart before eating their raw flesh. In this way the Maenads sacramentally incorporated the power of the god himself, whom they addressed as Axia Taure, "glorious bull." The Maenads dressed in fawn skins and carried *thyrsoi,* vine branches topped with a fir cone and wreathed in ivy, a common attribute of Dionysos himself. In this play, a true masterpiece of Greek prose, Dionysos also demonstrates his power as the god of fruitful and miraculous transformation. Not only does he cause the ground to flow with milk and honey, possibly a reference to early Greek liquor, but he also appears in the form of a bull, hence Axia Taure, and breaks open the prison in which his votaries are held.

At Argos the daughters of Proteus were driven mad and, thinking themselves to be cows, ran naked through the countryside, tearing children to pieces and eating their flesh. This story is strikingly similar to that at Orchomenus, in which the three daughters of the king declined to dance with Dionysos who changed himself, in quick succession, into a lion, a bull, and a panther. The terror-stricken girls were never the same again.

Dionysos also visited the islands of the Adriatic. At Icaria he hired a ship to take him to Naxos, but the sailors, Tyrrhenian pirates, steered toward Asia intending to sell Dionysos into slavery. The god, however, turned himself into a lion and the oars of the vessel into serpents. Ivy grew around the ship and the sound of flutes was heard. The terrified pirates immediately leaped overboard and were turned into dolphins. Dionysos sailed on to Naxos or Dia and there discovered Ariadne, who had been deserted by Theseus. He married her at once. The island, one of the Cyclades, became an important center of his worship.

His worship at Argos was first refused, but since he had maddened the women the people admitted he was a god. Thus established as a god worshipped throughout the known world, Dionysos was then elevated to the rank of an Olympian deity, displacing Hestia.

Having been enthroned in Olympus, Dionysos descended to the realm of Hades to bring Semele, his mother, back from the Underworld. Descending through Lake Lerna, Dionysos asked the way from Prosymnus, who asked for sexual favors upon his return. Dionysos having reached the Underworld, Hades demanded a gift in return for the release of Semele, so Dionysos gave him one of his favorite plants, the myrtle, which thereafter became associated with mourning. Returning from the Underworld, Dionysos found that Prosymnus had died, so he planted a phallic stick on his tomb. Returning to Olympus, his mother, Semele, thereafter became known as Thyone.

Dionysos even features, albeit briefly, in the stories surrounding the Trojan War. The Greek fleet was provisioned by the three daughters of Anius, upon whom Dionysos had bestowed the power to produce corn, oil, and wine at will. Obviously supporting the Greek forces against Troy, Dionysos caused Telephus, king of Mysia, to stumble over a vine when he was in danger of defeating Achilles, thus turning the tide of that particular battle in Achilles' favor, allowing the great hero to wound Telephus.

He had several notable children, among them Deianeira by Althaea.

Dionysos was worshipped as the god of the vital and intoxicating powers of nature, the god of wine, and also as a law-giver due to his associations with early civilization. He was also the god of tragic art, himself being represented as a young, handsome, athletic (though later somewhat effeminate) youth, sometimes depicted with horns and a crown of serpents, accompanied by a wild crowd of satyrs and Maenads, the latter in an orgiastic frenzy of wine and mystic exaltation. He carried cymbals, swords, and serpents, or the thyrsus, a rod wreathed in ivy and crowned with a fir cone, as well as the *kantharos,* a two-handled cup. Though men did become votaries of the god, his worship appealed most strongly to women, and many would spend entire nights in his worship, dancing and tearing wild animals to pieces. His sacred plants were the ivy, laurel, and asphodel; his animals the dolphin, serpent, tiger, lynx, panther, goat, and ass. Sacrifices to him usually consisted of a goat or an ass. Charming as a youth, Dionysos became the god of extremity and excess, especially sexual.

The myths surrounding Dionysos seem to be evidence of initial opposition to the use of wine for ritual purposes due to the frenzy it engendered. Wine was not invented by the Greeks but was probably first imported by them from Crete, where viniculture had probably spread from Mount Nysa in Libya. The original drink of the ancient Greeks was probably a kind of beer flavored with ivy and honey and as such can be partially equated with Ambrosia, the drink of the Olympian gods. The use of wine spread from Thrace to Athens and other civilized cities and appears to have followed the course of Dionysos's wanderings, the spread of viniculture to India even being represented in the stories.

See also: Agave; Bacchus; Eleusis; Hestia; Midas; Silenus

Dionysus of Halicarnassus

Greco-Roman

Greek critic, historian, and rhetorician whose fragmentary works, along with those of Diodorus the Sicilian, Livy, and Virgil, are among the only remaining sources of Etruscan mythology. Flourishing in the first century B.C., he lived and worked in Rome from c. 30 B.C. His major work, in Greek, was *Romaike Archaeologia*, a history of Rome down to 264 B.C., a veritable mine of information about the constitution, religion, history, laws, and private lives of the ancient Romans. Out of its 20 volumes only the first nine survive complete.

Diosc~uri, ~ouroi

Greco-Roman

Generic term applied to the Heavenly Twins, Castor and Polydeuces (Pollux to the Romans), the twin sons of Zeus and Leda and the brothers of Helen and Clytemnestra. As was common in traditions of that era, Polydeuces was said to have been fathered by Zeus and was thus immortal; Castor, the mortal child, was fathered by Tyndareus, Leda's husband, the conceptions occurring almost simultaneously.

They were especially important deities in Sparta, where many things, including the kings, went in pairs. Here they were also known as the Anakes and were worshipped in the form of a wooden structure in the shape of a capital *H*. Also regarded as the protectors of sailors—to whom they appeared in the form of St. Elmo's fire, for Poseidon gave them power over wind and wave—they have close links with other, earlier Indo-European deities, such as the Ashvins of Vedic and Hindu mythology.

They were regarded as the inventors of the war dance and the patrons of bards, also presiding over the Spartan Games. In art each was usually represented mounted on a magnificent white steed while armed with a spear and wearing an egg-shaped helmet—they were said to have been born from an egg—crowned with a star.

Classical mythology makes them the sons of Leda, Polydeuces and his sister, Helen, being fathered by Zeus, Castor and the other sister, Clytemnestra, by her husband Tyndareus. Thus the latter pair was mortal, although Helen also appears in her mythology as a mortal being. They were notable athletes, Castor a rider and Polydeuces a boxer, the latter's prowess displayed during the voyage with the Argonauts, when he fought and defeated Amycus. They also took part in the epic hunt for the Calydonian Boar. They went to Attica after Theseus had carried off their sister, Helen, and rescued her after her hiding place had been revealed to them by Academus. They themselves, however, carried off the Leucippides, Phoebe and Hilaeira, the daughters of Leucippus (the brother of Tyndareus and king of Messenia). They were pursued by their cousins, Idas and Lynceus, sons of Aphareus, to whom the girls were already betrothed. Lynceus (lynx-eyed) spotted the twins hiding within a hollow oak on Mount Taygetus with his preternatural sight. Idas killed Castor with a spear and Polydeuces killed Lynceus. Idas then hurled a tombstone at Polydeuces, but Zeus intervened and killed Idas with one of his thunderbolts.

Such was the love Polydeuces felt for his brother that he pleaded with Zeus to restore him. Zeus compromised, allowing each to live on alternate days; finally the pair was translated to the heavens as the constellation Gemini.

Astronomical: For details of the constellation Gemini see the relevant entry.

See also: Castor; Helen; Pollux; Polydeuces

Dirce

Greek

The wife of King Lycus of Thebes and a loyal Maenad, a votary of Dionysos. Amphion and Zethus had her dragged to her death behind her bull for her cruelty to their mother, Antiope. At the spot where her death occurred Dionysos caused a spring to rise. In historical times the spring named after her was located either on Mount Cithaeron or in Thebes. A slightly different version says that Amphion and Zethus tied Dirce to the horns of a wild bull, her dead body finally being thrown into a fountain in Thebes that thenceforth bore her name.

See also: Amphion; Antiope; Zethus

Dis (Pater)

Roman

The richest of all the Roman gods; the god of death and the Underworld who was equated with the Greek Hades. He was also known as Orcus, even by the euphemism Pluto, which appears to have been adopted from the Greeks, as this title means "the wealth," a reference to his possession of all the rich metals and gems of earth.

Dithyrambus

Greek

A choral song dedicated to Dionysos that is sung by his votaries in their orgiastic, drunken frenzy.

Dius Fidius

Roman

An ancient god of contracts who has been equated with Mitra but is usually presented as an aspect of Jupiter, especially in later tradition.

Diva Angerona

Roman

A goddess whose festival was celebrated at the winter solstice, the shortest day of the year, and who has been equated, by some authorities, with the Vedic goddess Aditi.

Dodona

Greek

Mountainous location in Epirus of the earliest oracle of Zeus and where that god was sometimes depicted wearing a wreath of oak leaves. The oracle of Zeus interpreted the rustling of the sacred oak leaves as the voice of the god. An oak tree still stands on the site, where the remains of the sanctuary and an impressive theater can be seen.

Dolon

Greek

A Trojan spy who, dressed in a wolf skin, entered the Greek camp under cover of darkness but was captured by Diomedes and Odysseus. They forced him to reveal the strength and disposition of the Trojan forces, then killed him.

Donn

Romano-Celtic

A form of Dis Pater, lord of the hunt and god of the Underworld and all the earth's riches. He would appear to be a direct adaptation to Roman sensibilities of the purely Celtic Donn, god of the dead who welcomes the spirits of the dead to his island.

Dorian

Greek

The Dorians were an ancient Greek race that entered Greece c. 1100 B.C., bringing with them the worship of Apollo, their influence stretching as far south as Crete. They claimed to have originated in Doris, a small area in central Greece from which they take their name, though their name may have come from Dorus, the son of Hellen.

Doris

Greek

1. The daughter of Oceanos and Thetis; mother of the 50 Nereides by Nereus, whom some sources make her brother, others the son of Pontus and Ge.

2. A small area in central Greece from which the Dorian race, who conquered the Peloponnesos, claimed they originated.

See also: Nereides

Dorus
Greek

The son of Hellen and, according to some sources, the mythical ancestor and eponym of the Dorian race. Other sources say this race originated in and took its name from Doris, a small area in central Greece.

Dougga
Roman

Also: Thugga

The best preserved Roman city in Tunisia in northern Africa. The temple of the Capitoline Triad was erected on the capitol during the second century A.D. The ruins of the temple of Juno Caelestis, and those dedicated to Concord, Liber, and Saturn, are also reasonably well preserved.

Draco
Greek

1. The sleepless dragon that guarded the Golden Fleece in the sacred grove of Ares in Colchis. Jason put it to sleep with a potion Medeä gave him to enable the Argonauts to complete their quest. Some say it is this dragon that was subsequently placed in the heavens to form the constellation Draco.

2. A dragon Athene fought during the Titanomachia, the war between the Olympian deities and the Titans. Athene hurled it into the sky, where it became wrapped around the northern celestial pole, thus forming the constellation that bears its name.

Astronomical: One of the largest and most ill-defined of the constellations lying in the northern celestial hemisphere, almost wrapping itself for 180° around the northern celestial pole. The constellation lies between approximate right ascensions 9h10m and 21h00m, declination from +48° to +86°.

See also: Jason; Medeä

Drepanum
Greco-Roman

Town in Sicily where Acestes welcomed Aeneas on his journey from Troy after the end of the Trojan War. It was here that his father, Anchises, died, after which Aeneas and his men stayed for a year before setting sail again. They returned after they had left Carthage, on this occasion staging funeral games in honor of Anchises before leaving once again for Italy.

Dryad
Greek

A specific category of nymph who lived in woodlands; Dryades were the guardian spirits of trees, being particularly protective of oaks. In art they were depicted with crowns of leaves, sometimes carrying axes. Why this latter attribute should be given to guardians of trees is unclear.

Dryope
Greek

A nymph, the daughter of either Eurytus of Oechalia or of King Dryops. Having being seduced and raped by Apollo, she was carried away by the Hamadryads and transformed into a lotus tree.

Dryops
Greek

One of the possible fathers of Dryope, the nymph who was seduced by Apollo and then transformed into a lotus tree. The other possible father is Eurytus of Oechalia.

E

Echemus
Greek

The king of Tegea who killed Hyllus in single combat.

Echidn~e, ~a
Greek

Half-snake, half-woman, usually described as the daughter of Ge and Tartarus. The wife of Typhon, she became the mother by him of the monstrous Chimaera, Hydra, Cerberus, Ladon, and Orthros. In later tradition she also became the mother of the Nemaean Lion, the Sphinx, and the Sow of Crommyum. She was finally killed by Argus of the hundred eyes.

See also: Cerberus; Chimaera; Hydra; Ladon; Orthros; Sphinx; Typhon

Echion
Greek

1. The son of Hermes who took part in the hunt for the Calydonian Boar and joined the expedition of the Argonauts, acting as their herald.

2. One of the five Sparti who remained alive after their infighting and went on, with the survivors—Udaeus, Chthonius, Hyperenor, Pelorus—to help Cadmos build the Cadmea, thereby becoming revered as ancestors of Thebes. Married to Agave, Echion was the father of Pentheus, who became king of Thebes.

See also: Sparti

Echo
Greek

An oread or mountain nymph from Mount Helicon whose incessant chattering distracted the attention of Hera while Zeus amused himself with the nymphs. When Hera uncovered the ruse she took away Echo's ability to use her voice, except to repeat what another had said. Echo then fell in love with Narcissus, a beautiful youth who repulsed her advances; unable to declare her love for him, she pined away until only her voice remained.

Edones
Greek

Ancient Thracian race whose king, Lycurgus, opposed the worship of Dionysos. Sent mad by Rhea, he mutilated his own son, for which he was blinded; later he cut off his own leg, thinking it a tree. His people further punished him by having him pulled apart between two horses.

See also: Lycurgus

Eëtion
Greek

King of Thebes in Cilicia; the father of Andromache, who married Hector. He was killed by Achilles when his city was raided by that hero.

See also: Achilles; Hector

Egeria
Roman

Possibly deriving from the Etruscan Begoe or Vegoia, this goddess or nymph, who became the consort of Numa Pompilius, was credited with prophetic foresight. Her cult appears to have been brought to Rome from Aricia, a hypothesis strengthened by the fact that Ovid says Egeria went to Aricia to mourn after the death of Numa Pompilius.

Eileithyian Cave

Greek

Cave on Crete, approximately 5 kilometers (3 miles) east of the capital, Iráklion, where Hera was said to have given birth to Eileithyia. Archaeological evidence indicates that the cave has been used as a holy place since Neolithic times.

Eil(e)ithy(i)a

Greek

Goddess of childbirth; the daughter of Hera supposedly born in the Eileithyian Cave on Crete.

Elatus

Greek

One of the mythical Lapithae and father of Caeneus.

Electra

Greek

1. Daughter of Agamemnon and Clytemnestra who was married to a peasant afraid to consummate their union after Clytemnestra and Aegisthus had murdered Agamemnon on his return from the Trojan War. She smuggled her young brother, Orestes, out of Mycenae but, burning for revenge, plotted with Orestes the murder of her mother and her lover. Electra secretly tended the tomb of her father until, upon the return of Orestes (in the company of Pylades, whom she later married), she exacted revenge by helping her brother kill their mother, Clytemnestra, and Aegisthus, who was by that time her stepfather. Her story is told in surviving plays by the three great Attic tragedians, two simply entitled *Electra* (Sophocles and Euripides), the other being *The Libation Bearers* (the second play of Aeschylus's trilogy).

2. A daughter of Oceanos and the mother of Iris and the Harpies.

3. A Pleiad, one of the seven daughters of Atlas and mother of Dardanos by Zeus. She was later, with her six sisters, transformed into a star grouping known as the Pleiades within the constellation Taurus.

Astronomical: See Pleiades.

See also: Aegisthus; Agamemnon; Pleiades

Electryon

Greek

King of Mycenae; the son of Perseus and Andromeda and father of Alcmene, who married Amphitryon.

See also: Alcmene

Eleus(in)ian Mysteries

Greek

The collective name of the various ceremonies celebrated in the temple of Demeter at Eleusis in honor of Demeter, Persephone, and Dionysos. During these ceremonies worshippers were said to have seen visions within the darkened confines of the temple, which was supposedly connected to the Underworld.

See also: Demeter

Eleusis

Greek

Religious and cultural center in Attica that is second in importance only to Athens. Today the complex ruins indicate the splendor and importance of Eleusis, the site of one of Greece's most remarkable cults. It was here, in the darkened temple of Demeter, that the Eleusinian Mysteries were celebrated in honor of Demeter, her daughter, Persephone, and Dionysos. It is said that the rites were instigated by King Celeus upon the order of Demeter, with worshippers witnessing strange visions within the temple, itself connected to the Underworld. An annual procession took place from Eleusis to Athens, where Eleusinian-style festivals were established by the tyrant Pesistratus in the sixth century B.C.

See also: Celeus; Demeter

Elis

Greek

Ancient Greek kingdom in the northwest Peloponnesos, south of Arcadia, that was ruled by King Augeias, the owner of the largest herd of cattle in the world. It was housed in the Augean Stables, which Heracles had to clean in a day as the sixth of his Great Labors.

See also: Augeias

Elpenor

Greek

The youngest of Odysseus's crewmen who, while sleeping on the roof or window ledge of Circe's palace on Aeaea, had fallen to his death, some accounts saying because he was drunk. When Odysseus later visited the Underworld to consult the spirit of his father, Elpenor angrily reproached Odysseus for not giving him a proper funeral. Odysseus returned to Aeaea to do this.

See also: Circe; Odysseus

Elys~ian, ~ium

Greek

Usually depicted as the Elysian Fields or Elysian Plain, this paradisiacal land, situated near the River Oceanos and sometimes called the Islands of the Blessed, was the place where souls who found favor with the gods—or with the three judges of the Underworld, Aeacus, Rhadamanthus, and Minos—were sent to live a life of ideal happiness. Although this land was said to be near the Underworld, it formed no part of the realm of Hades. It was a blessed place, with neither cold nor snow nor strong winds, where it never rained and the chosen ones lived in eternal sunshine, a direct contrast to the miserable gloom that surrounded the unfortunate souls committed for all eternity to the realm of Hades.

Usually this paradisiacal land was said to be ruled over by Cronos along with Rhadamanthus. Homer placed it far to the west; later Greek geographers stated simply that it lay beyond the Pillars of Heracles (Hercules). Pausanias identifies it with the White Isle (Leuce) in the Black Sea, where Achilles, Patroclus, the two Ajaxes, Antilochus, and Helen lived on after death. Eventually it came to be identified with the Canary Isles and Madeira.

See also: Aeacus; Minos; Rhadamanthus

Empusae

Greek

Horrible demons, the daughters of Hecate, with the haunches of asses and wearing brazen slippers. These dreadful beings had the ability to change their form at will to that of a bitch, a cow, or a beautiful maiden. In the latter guise they were most dreadful, for they would lie with men and sap their strength until they died. The origin of the Empusae may lie in Palestine, where the daughters of Lilith, the Lilim, displayed similar characteristics.

See also: Hecate

Enceladus

Greek

One of the 24 giants with serpent's tails—the sons of Ge who sought to avenge the imprisonment of their brothers, the Titans, by attacking Olympus. Led by Alcyoneus, others in this revolt were Porphyrion, Ephialtes, Mimas, Pallas, and Polybutes. After a terrible struggle the gods finally were victorious, but only after Heracles—who appears here before his apotheosis, indicating the late origin of the myth—gave the gods a magical herb of invulnerability. Heracles himself always deals the final blow to each giant.

In punishment Enceladus was buried beneath Mount Etna, which some used to explain the volcanic nature of that mountain, for when Enceladus stirred, Etna erupted.

Astronomical: One of the satellites of Saturn lying fourth closest to the planet between the orbits of Mimas and Tethys.

See also: Alcyoneus; Etna

Endymion

Greek

A beautiful youth, sometimes described as the king of Elis or as a shepherd, with whom Selene, the moon goddess, became enamored. Spotting him asleep in a cave on Mount Latmus in Caria, Selene came down and kissed him. Later he returned to the cave, where he fell into a dreamless, eternal sleep, some saying so he might retain his youthful beauty, others so Selene might keep him in perpetuity. Another variant says that he was granted eternal sleep as a favorable alternative to death for his attempted rape of Hera.

By his mortal wife he had four sons, one of them being Aetolus, who later invaded the land now called Aetolia; Selene reputedly bore him 50 daughters. His tomb and sanctuary may be visited outside Heracleia.

Astronomical: The name applied to an impact crater located in the upper western quadrant of the surface of the moon, slightly above and to the west of those known as Hercules and Atlas.

See also: Selene

Enipeus
Greek
The river god who was beloved by Tyro.

Enna
Greco-Roman
Site in Sicily that was, according to Latin poets commenting on Greek tradition, the site of Persephone's abduction by Hades.

Eos
Greek
Goddess of the dawn, daughter of Hyperion and Theia, and sister to Helios (Sun) and Selene (Moon). The Romans equated Eos with Aurora. She drove her chariot across the sky to announce the approach of her brother, Helios; as Hemera (Day) she accompanied him across the sky, becoming Hespera (Evening) upon her arrival in the west. She was the mother of the evening star, Hesperus, and the four winds, Boreas, Zephyrus, Eurus, and Notus, by Astraeus (though some sources say simply that all the stars and winds were their children with the exception of Eurus, the east wind). She was cursed by Aphrodite for having an affair with Ares, whom Aphrodite herself loved. This was just one of many hopeless love affairs entered into by Eos, her most famous being that with Tithones, who fathered Memnon and Emathion by her, though she also trysted Orion and Cephalos. She asked Zeus to bestow immortality upon Tithones but forgot to also ask for eternal youth for him; he subsequently became the oldest man in Olympus, shrinking away until he finally became a cicada. Some say that she was actually married to Tithones, her constant infidelity accounting for the blush of dawn.

See also: Helios; Selene; Tithones

Epaphus
Greek
The son of Zeus and Io who reigned over Egypt and was rumored to be Apis, the sacred bull of the ancient Egyptians.

Epeius
Greek
The cowardly son of Panopeus who, under the supervision of Athene, built the Wooden Horse, carving upon it an inscription dedicating it to the goddess. After the end of the Trojan War he was said to have been among the Greek survivors who emigrated to Italy.

See also: Wooden Horse

Ephesia
Greek
Epithet applied to Artemis at Ephesus, where she was worshipped as an orgiastic goddess, an aspect of an earlier mother goddess originating in Asia Minor.

See also: Artemis

Ephesus
Greek
Magnificent Ionian city on the coast of Asia Minor at the mouth of the River Cayster that became the principal city of the Ionian Greeks. In the sixth century B.C. it came under the control of the Lydian King Croesus. It was destroyed by Goths in 262 A.D. Excavation of the site has revealed much of the earlier splendor of Ephesus and includes the slight remains of the temples to the Artemis Ephesia, whose worship was focused here; Saint Paul was said to have encountered Artemis in this aspect (see Acts 19:1–35).

See also: Artemis; Croesus

Ephialtes
Greek
There are two similar stories surrounding the character of Ephialtes, each giving him different parentage. The earlier of these makes him the brother of Otus and one of the giants, Aloeidae, the sons of Iphimedeia by Poseidon but named after Aloeus, whom their mother

later married. At the age of nine the pair captured and immured Ares. With the god of war out of harm's way they decided, for reasons not explained, to outrage both Hera and Artemis, and to reach the lofty heights of Mount Olympus they piled Mount Pelion atop Mount Ossa. Artemis, however, tricked the giants into going to Naxos, where they thought they would meet the goddess. Disguised as a doe, Artemis leaped between them and they killed each other. Hermes now released Ares; the spirits of the Aloeidae were condemned to Tartarus, where they were tied back-to-back to a pillar with vipers.

A later, post-Homeric tale makes Ephialtes one of the 24 giant sons of Ge with serpents' tales who revolted against the Olympian deities to avenge the imprisonment of their brothers, the Titans. In this version the battles, collectively known as the Titanomachia, were led by Alcyoneus, some of his brothers being named as Enceladus, Porphyrion, Mimas, Pallas, and Polybutes. They were soundly defeated by the Olympians, who had the help of Heracles, though chronologically this was before his apotheosis.

See also: Aloeus; Artemis; Tartarus

Epicaste
Greek

The Homeric name for Jocasta, the mother of Oedipus.

Epidaurus
Greek

Town in Argos that was the center of the cult of Asclepios. A fourth-century B.C. theater, the center of the god's worship there, is still preserved.

See also: Asclepios

Epigoni
Greek

Generic name applied to the descendants of the original Seven Against Thebes when Adrastus assembled them to make a second attack on Thebes ten years after the first one had failed, shortly before the start of the Trojan War. The Epigoni are named as Aegialeos, son of Adrastus; Diomedes, son of Tydeus; Sthenelus, son of Capaneus; Alcmaeon and Amphilochus, sons of Amphiaraus; Polydorus, son of Hippomedon; Euryalus, son of Mecistus; Promachos, or Tlesimenes, son of Parthenopaeus; Thersander, son of Polyneices; and Eteocles. Alcmaeon, at first unwilling to join the Epigoni but persuaded by Eriphyle, who had been bribed by Thersander with the robe of Harmonia, led the expedition after the Delphic Oracle foretold he would lead them to victory. Their first battle was at Glisas near Thebes. Seeing the strength of the advancing Epigoni, the Thebans deserted their city, which was taken without force and then razed. Thersander became the king of the new city of Thebes subsequently built on the site.

See also: Seven Against Thebes

Epimetheus
Greek

"Afterthought"; son of Iapetus and brother of Prometheus ("Forethought") and Atlas. Although his mother's identity remains unclear, it seems likely to have been the nymph Clymene, who was the mother of Atlas by Iapetus. Unlike Atlas, Epimetheus and Prometheus supported Zeus and the Olympian gods during the Titanomachia. He married Pandora, the first woman made by Hephaistos at the order of Zeus to punish mankind following the theft of fire from Heaven by Prometheus. At their wedding she opened the box from which all the ills that plague mankind escaped. Their daughter was Pyrrha, who became the wife of Deucalion.

Epirus
Greco-Roman

Region of ancient Greece north of Acarnania, partly in modern-day Albania. The important sanctuary and oracle of Zeus at Dodona lies within the region. Following Aeneas's escape from Troy he put in at Epirus to seek the counsel of Helenus, who ruled the area. Helenus advised Aeneas that upon reaching Italy he should seek a sow and 30 piglets and there establish his city.

See also: Aeneas

Equuleus

Greek

The colt of the winged horse Pegasus of which very little is known. His mother remains unknown, but he was placed in the heavens as the constellation that bears his name. Although noted by Hipparchus, it seems likely that Equuleus was simply contrived to fill the space in the night sky between Pegasus and Delphinos.

Astronomical: A small, irregular constellation of the northern celestial hemisphere lying directly next to Pegasus between approximate right ascensions 20h50m and 21h20m, declination from +3° to +14°.

See also: Pegasus

Erato

Greco-Roman

One of the nine Muses, the daughters of Zeus and Mnemosyne, being the Muse of love, mime, and erotic or love poetry. In art she is sometimes depicted carrying a lyre.

See also: Muses, the

Ereb~os, ~us

Greek

God of darkness; the son of Chaos who fathered Aether and Hemera on his sister, Night; some sources also make the Fates their offspring. Later tradition made Erebos a place of darkness approximately halfway between Earth and the Underworld, a place of limbo.

Erechtheus

Greek

King of Athens; the son of Pandion and Zeuxippe and grandson of Erichthonius, whom he succeeded. The brother of Procne and Philomela, he was the father by Praxithea of three or four sons, including Cecrops, and seven daughters: Protogonia, Pandora (not the one who became the wife of Epimetheus), Procris, Chthonia, Oreithyia, Otionia, and Creusa. His mythical origins are perhaps an attempt to tidy up the legendary chronology of Athens, which contains the similarly named Erichthonius and two named Cecrops.

The Erectheum on the Acropolis at Athens is named after him. Here he was worshipped along with Athene Polias. He is perhaps a form of Poseidon with whom Athene disputed the possession of Attica.

Legend says that when Eumolpus, king of Eleusis and a son of Poseidon, led the Eleusinians against Athens, an oracle told Erechtheus to sacrifice his daughter, Otionia. This he did, whereupon his two eldest daughters, Protogonia and Pandora, sacrificed themselves. Erechtheus killed Eumolpus in battle. In revenge Poseidon struck Earth with his trident; Earth opened up and swallowed Erechtheus.

See also: Acropolis

Erichthonius

Greek

1. *Also:* Erichtheus

The son of Hephaistos who was born after the latter's semen spilled during his attempted rape of Athene on the Acropolis at Athens. Athene concealed the infant in a box, which she entrusted to the care of Cecrops's daughters, Pandrosos, Herse, and sometimes Aglauros. She forbade the girls to open the box, but curiosity overcame them, and upon opening the box they saw the infant, who had a serpent's tail. Horrified by the sight, they went mad and leaped to their deaths from the north wall of the Acropolis. The infant Erichthonius was then brought up in the temple of Athene and later succeeded Cecrops as king of Athens, founding during his reign the Panathenaean Games. He was, in turn, succeeded by Pandion.

2. A variant sometimes used for Erechtheus.

Eridanus

Greek

A deified river, into which Phaëthon fell to his death. As amber was said to have been found in or near the river, it later became identified as the River Po. Homer called it the River of Oceanos, saying that it encircled a flat earth.

Astronomical: Recognized by many cultures as a river, the faint, winding constellation Eridanus is located in the southern celestial hemisphere between approximate right ascensions 1h25m and 5h10m, declination from 0° to -57°.

See also: Oceanos; Phaëthon

Erigone

Greek

"Spring-born"; the daughter of Icarius, being led to his grave by her father's dog, Maera. In her grief she hanged herself from the tree over the grave, after which a plague or drought ravaged Attica. Upon the instructions of Apollo, Aristaeus instituted a festival in which dolls were hung from the branches of trees. Her mythology is a clear reflection of the importance of the seasons, especially of spring, which heralded the start of the new growing year. According to Ovid, Dionysos was Erigone's lover.

See also: Aristaeus

Erinnyes

Greek

Also: Eumenides, Furies

The three-winged, serpent-haired daughters—Alecto, Megaera, and Tisiphone—who were born of the earth when drops of blood fell from Uranos after he was castrated by Cronos. Usually depicted as hideous black hags with eyes oozing pus, the three named Erinnyes appear to be of later origin, for their number was, in earlier sources, indeterminate. They lived in the Underworld, from where they ventured forth to punish unnatural crime. They pursued Alcmaeon after he had murdered his mother, Eriphyle; possibly they are best known for their pursuit of Orestes following his murder of Clytemnestra.

Driving him mad, they hounded him relentlessly until he finally came to Athens, where he embraced the image of Athene in her temple on the Acropolis. The goddess then summoned the Areopagus to judge his case, Apollo defending him along the lines that fatherhood was more important than motherhood. Orestes was acquitted of his matricide on the casting vote of Athene, a triumph that illustrated the importance of the patriarchal society within ancient Greece.

Furious, the Erinnyes were pacified by Athene, who made them guardians of civic order in Athens and persuaded them to accept a grotto in the city below the Areopagus where they would be offered sacrifices, libations, and first fruits. Thus pacified, the Erinnyes became known thenceforth as the Eumenides, "Well-Meaning Ones" or "Kindly Ones." They had cult centers elsewhere in Greece, usually in connection with the Graces, and had the usual association of chthonic spirits with the fertility of earth.

See also: Areopagus

Eriphyle

Greek

Sister of Adrastus, wife of the seer Amphiaraus, and mother by him of Alcmaeon. She was bribed by Polyneices with the famous necklace of Harmonia to persuade Amphiaraus to join the expedition of the Seven Against Thebes, even though he had already foretold that all the leaders save Adrastus would die, a prophecy that came true. Some ten years later she was once again bribed, this time by Thersander, the son of Polyneices, who gave her the magic robe of Harmonia provided she would persuade her son, Alcmaeon, to become one of the Epigoni. She did, and Alcmaeon went on the second, successful expedition against Thebes. Upon his return he killed Eriphyle for her vanity and deceit of him and his father.

See also: Adrastus; Alcmaeon; Harmonia; Seven Against Thebes

Eris

Greek

The spirit of discord who was the only immortal not to be invited to the wedding of Thetis and Peleus. She turned up at the marriage ceremony nevertheless and threw among the guests an apple, known as the Apple of Discord, which was inscribed "to the fairest." Ownership of the apple was disputed by Hera, Athene, and Aphrodite. To settle the argument, Zeus ordered Paris, prince of Troy and the son of Priam, to decide which goddess should be granted ownership. Each tried to bribe Paris, and he finally awarded the apple to Aphrodite, for she had promised him the fairest woman in the world, Helen, the wife of Menelaus. It was this single action that was said to lead to the Trojan War and the almost complete annihilation of the Trojan people.

According to Hesiod this "wicked fairy" was the mother of a number of other rather unpleasant creatures, including Ate, and the personifications of Labor, Forgetfulness, Famine, Strife, Murderous Quarrelling, and others.

See also: Peleus; Thetis; Trojan War

Eros
Greek

The boy god of love who was identified by the Romans with Cupid or Amor. Initially a personification of cosmic harmony, being a son of Chaos, and born at the same time as Ge and Tartarus, he was later depicted as a beautiful and playful youth with bow and arrows, the servant of his mother, by this time Aphrodite by Ares, Hermes, or Zeus, though some sources name his mother as Iris or Ilithyia. The main legend concerning Eros is his love for the mortal Psyche, a personification of the soul. Psyche was only visited by Eros at night and was allowed to see her lover only reflected in a mirror. Determined to find out who her lover was, Psyche contrived to see him without the aid of a mirror, but after she did so Eros left her. Eventually the two were reunited and Eros married her, making him one of the few gods to chose and marry a mortal wife.

Though normally shown with golden wings, holding a torch, and carrying his bow and arrows, with which he could wound gods and mortals alike, he was also sometimes shown blindfolded or riding a lion or dolphin. In a few classical sculptures he is shown with a hoop or at some other game, a reflection of his youthfulness.

Eros received cult status as a god at various locations. The early conception of Eros as the personification of the principle of attraction lay at the root of much pre-Socratic cosmology. He later came to represent the erotic bond of man and boy rather than that of man and woman, the province of his mother.

His transformation as a "literary" god in romantic narrative is not found in the pre-Hellenic period. Here the handsome winged youth degenerates into a winged putto. The story of Eros and Psyche, the best known concerning Eros and the major source of his mythology, is unknown prior to Apuleius, a writer from the third century A.D.

Astronomical: The name applied to an asteroid discovered in 1898, being 22 million kilometers (14 million miles) from the earth at its nearest point. Eros was the first asteroid discovered to be in orbit within that of Mars. It is elongated, measuring about 36 by 12 kilometers (22 by 7 miles), rotates about its shortest axis once every 5.3 hours, and orbits the sun every 1.8 years.

See also: Aphrodite; Psyche

Erymanthian Boar
Greek

A huge boar that lived on the slopes of Mount Erymanthus, hence its name. Heracles was sent to capture it alive as the fourth of his Great Labors after the boar had come off the mountain to ravage Psophis. Heracles accomplished his task by running the boar into a snowdrift, where he bound it with chains and carried it back to Eurystheus.

Erysichthon
Greek

Son of Triopas; a Thessalanian who cut down a grove of trees that was sacred to Demeter, even though he was warned of the consequences. He was punished by the goddess, who gave him a perpetual, insatiable hunger. Having already devoured all his possessions, his daughter, Mestra, sold herself as a slave to buy him food. As she had the power to change shape at will, Mestra used this ploy time and time again, but nothing could satisfy her father's hunger. Finally Erysichthon devoured himself.

See also: Demeter

Eryx
Greek

Mount in the west of Sicily. On its slopes there was a sanctuary to the cult of Aphrodite as a fertility goddess, served by young girls.

Esus

Romano-Celtic

A deity who has been connected to a lost myth involving the cutting down of trees and to totem animals of three cranes and a bull. An altar to the god shows a man cutting down a tree. Humans were possibly sacrificed to the god, who may have numbered among the chief three gods of Gaul during the Roman period.

Eteocles

Greek

Son of Oedipus and Jocasta and brother of Antigone, Ismene, and Polyneices. He and his brother were cursed by their father when they refused to give him sanctuary after he had blinded himself. Eteocles subsequently broke his oath to rule Thebes jointly with his brother, banished Polyneices, and assumed absolute control. Polyneices then assembled the expedition known as the Seven Against Thebes, but both brothers were killed.

See also: Oedipus; Seven Against Thebes

Ethiopia

Greek

Country in northeastern Africa that was called Aethiopia in antiquity. Legend made it the realm of Cepheus and Cassiopeia and the scene of Perseus's rescue of a princess, Andromeda, from the sea monster Cetus.

Etna

Greek

Active volcano in Sicily under which, so legend tells us, the giant Briareus was confined along with other giants, including Enceladus and Typhon, for their part in the Titanomachia. The activity of this volcano was thenceforth attributed to the anger of the giants imprisoned beneath it.

Etruscan

Roman

A highly cultivated civilization of central Italy that was famous for divining and passed along many of its religious beliefs to the Romans, who readily absorbed them into their own mythology.

Euippe

Greek

1. The daughter of the centaur Cheiron. When she fell pregnant to Aeolus, the son of Hellen, she was changed into a horse. Their child was Melanippe.

2. Daughter of Daunus, king and eponym of Daunia, Italy. She married Diomedes, who settled there after emigrating from Greece following the Trojan War.

See also: Cheiron

Eumaeus

Greek

The swineherd of Odysseus and his father, Laertes, on Ithaca. When Odysseus returned from the Trojan War in the disguise of a beggar, Eumaeus welcomed him hospitably and took him to his hut. Within the hut Odysseus first revealed his identity to his own son, Telemachus.

See also: Odysseus

Eumenides

Greek

"Well-Meaning Ones" or "Kindly Ones"; euphemism given to the Erinnyes or Furies. They were given this name by Athene after Orestes, whom they had been pursuing and tormenting for the murder of his mother, Clytemnestra, was absolved of the crime by the Areopagus in Athens. In addition, Athene gave them a grove below the Areopagus where they would receive sacrifices, libations, and first fruits.

See also: Erinnyes

Eumolpus

Greek

A son of Poseidon and Chione, the daughter of Boreas and Oreithyia. As a newborn Eumolpus was thrown into the sea by Chione to conceal her shame, but he was rescued by Poseidon, his father, and taken to Ethiopia, where he was raised by a king who eventually gave him a daughter as wife.

Eumolpus, however, assaulted his sister-in-law and was duly banished to Thrace, where he lived at the court of King Tegyrius. He was banished again after his son, who remains unnamed, plotted against the Thracian king. This time Eumolpus came to Eleusis, where he was welcomed by Celeus; they cofounded the Eleusinian Mysteries, and Eumolpus became the first priest of the mysteries of Demeter and Persephone, his descendants subsequently becoming the hereditary priests of the Eleusinian Mysteries. While in Eleusis Eumolpus purified Heracles of his murder of the centaurs and initiated him into the mysteries of Demeter. Traveling back to Thrace (some sources say he stayed in Eleusis), Eumolpus became king, and when the Eleusinians were attacking Athens he led an army to help them (though sources saying he remained in Eleusis say he led the Eleusinian forces). He was killed in single combat by Erechtheus.

See also: Boreas; Chione; Eleusis; Oreithyia

Eunomus
Greek

An Aetolian boy who was accidentally killed by Heracles at a feast three years after the hero had first arrived in Aetolia and married Deianeira.

Euphemus
Greek

A son of Poseidon who had the ability to walk on water. He was the deputy helmsman aboard the *Argo Navis* and thus one of the Argonauts. When that great expedition was stranded in Libya he was given a clod of earth by Triton, but he subsequently lost it overboard during a shipwreck and it washed up on the island of Thera. A variant story says that he threw it overboard following a vision telling him to do so and it magically became the island of Thera.

Euphorbus
Greek

Son of Panthous who wounded Patroclus when the latter had attempted to lead the Greek forces against Troy in the place of Achilles, who was sulking in his tent following the seizure of his concubine, Briseis, by Agamemnon. He was subsequently killed by Menelaus.

See also: Menelaus; Patrocles

Euphrosyne
Greek

One of the three Graces or Charites.

Euripides
Greek

Greek dramatist (c. 480 or 484–406 B.C.) whose plays deal with ordinary people and social issues rather than the more grandiose themes employed by his contemporaries. He wrote more than 80 plays, of which just 18 survive, including *Alcestis* (438 B.C.), *Medeä* (431 B.C.), *Andromache* (426 B.C.), *Trojan Women* (415 B.C.), *Electra* (417 B.C.), *Iphigeneia in Tauris* (413 B.C.), *Iphigeneia in Aulis* (405 B.C.), and *Bacchae* (405 B.C.).

His influence on later drama was probably far greater than that of the two great tragedians, Aeschylus and Sophocles. As a realist he was bitterly attacked for his unorthodox "impiety" and the sympathy he felt for the despised, such as slaves, beggars, and women. Toward the end of his life he entered a period of voluntary exile when he left Athens for Macedonia, dying at the court of King Archelaus.

Europa
Greek

Daughter of Agenor (king of Tyre or Sidon in Phoenicia) and Telephassa; sister of Cadmos and the eponym of Europe. As Europa played on the seashore with her maidens, Zeus appeared in the form of a beautiful white bull. She playfully climbed onto his back, at which point Zeus suddenly plunged into the sea and carried her off to the island of Crete. There she bore Zeus three sons: Minos, Rhadamanthus, and Sarpedon. Zeus made for her the bronze giant Talos (though some say this giant was made by Hephaistos at Zeus's bidding) and gave her the dog Laelaps and the famous necklace of Harmonia.

She next married Asterion, and they had a daughter named Crete. In Crete she was worshipped as Helliotis. Europa seems to be another form of the ancient mother goddess, though this time with a certain Cretan coloring.

Astronomical: The fourth largest moon of Jupiter, having a diameter of 3,100 kilometers (1,900 miles). Orbiting 671,000 kilometers (417,000 miles) above the surface of the planet every 3.55 days, it lies between the orbits of Io and Ganymede. Covered in ice, the moon is criss-crossed by thousands of thin cracks.

See also: Cadmos; Minos; Rhadamanthus; Sarpedon; Talos

Eurus
Greco-Roman
The god of, the personification of, or simply the actual east or southeast wind. The son of Astraeus and Eos and brother of Hesperus, the evening star, and the three other winds, Boreas (north), Zephyrus (west), and Notus (south). He and his brothers were kept in a cave on the floating island of Aeolia, where he was released as commanded by the gods or at the will of Aeolus. Some sources say that Eurus was not the offspring of Astraeus and Eos, though they neglect to name his parents.

See also: Aeolus; Boreas; Notus; Zephyrus

Euryale
Greek
An immortal Gorgon; one of the three snake-haired sisters, daughters of Phorcys and Ceto, who lived in Libya and whose look turned the beholder to stone. Her sisters were Stheno, also immortal, and Medusa, the only mortal. After Perseus killed Medusa, Euryale and Stheno chased after him, but aided by Hades' helmet of invisibility he evaded them.

See also: Gorgon; Medusa; Stheno

Euryalus
Greek
One of the Epigoni who accompanied Jason as one of the Argonauts on the quest for the Golden Fleece. He later accompanied Diomedes and Sthenelus, two fellow Epigoni, to the Trojan War.

See also: Epigoni

Eurycleia
Greek
The nurse of Odysseus; apart from Argus, Odysseus's faithful hound, Eurycleia was the only person to recognize Odysseus when he returned to Ithaca after the Trojan War in the disguise of a beggar.

See also: Odysseus

Eur~ydice, ~idice
Greek
1. A Thracian nymph, a dryad, who married the semidivine singer and lyre-player Orpheus. Following her death from a snake bite, though some sources say her death was caused by Aristaeus, Orpheus braved the journey to the Underworld and, using his talents for singing and playing the lyre, charmed Hades into releasing her. Hades set but one condition: that Orpheus should not look back at her before they emerged from the Underworld. However, as they neared the exit Orpheus began to wonder if Eurydice was really following him; unable to contain himself, he looked back and lost Eurydice forever.

2. Wife of King Creon of Thebes and mother by him of Haemon, the tragic lover of Antigone who hanged himself after his betrothed had been interred and had killed herself.

See also: Orpheus

Eurylochus
Greek
The only one of Odysseus's sailors not initially turned into a swine by Circe when they landed on her island of Aeaea. He took the news of his companions' fate to Odysseus, who, protected by the plant moly, forced Circe to restore them to human form.

See also: Circe; Odysseus

Eurynome
Greek
Sea goddess who was the mother of the Graces or Charites by Zeus. She also helped to care for the infant Hephaistos, along with Thetis, in a grotto beneath the sea after Hera had thrown the weak, lame infant from Olympus.

Eurystheus

Greco-Roman

Son of Sthenelus and Nicippe, the daughter of Pelops, king of Mycenae, Argos, or Tiryns. When Heracles murdered his wife and children in a bout of madness, the Delphic Oracle commanded him to labor for 12 years under Eurystheus, doing whatever that king bid without question, after which time immortality would be conferred upon him. Eurystheus set Heracles, who was accompanied and aided by Iolaus, 12 enormous tasks, which were:

1. To bring back the skin of the Nemaean or Cleonaean Lion. When Heracles returned wearing the skin as his armor, Eurystheus became so terrified that he took to hiding in a brazen urn whenever Heracles approached.

2. To kill the Hydra.

3. To capture the Ceryneian Hind.

4. To capture alive the Erymanthian Boar. Following the completion of this task there was a pause in the sequence when Heracles left to join the expedition of Jason and the Argonauts.

5. To clean the Augean Stables in a single day.

6. To kill the Stymphalian Birds.

7. To capture the Cretan Bull. Eurystheus released the bull after Heracles brought it back to him. It roamed through Greece to Marathon, where it became known as the Marathonian Bull. There it was captured by Theseus, who took it back to Athens for sacrifice to Athene.

8. To capture the man-eating mares of Diomedes. Eurystheus subsequently released these creatures on the slopes of Mount Olympus, where they were eaten by wild beasts.

9. To fetch the golden girdle of the Amazon Queen Hippolyte for Admete, the daughter of Eurystheus.

10. To fetch the oxen of Geryon without demanding them or paying for them. When Heracles delivered the oxen, Eurystheus sacrificed them to Hera.

11. To fetch the Golden Apples of the Hesperides. Eurystheus, in a rare display of generosity, made a gift of these fabulous apples to Heracles, who dedicated them to Athene, and she returned them to their rightful place.

12. To bring back the three-headed dog Cerberus that guarded the entrance to the Underworld. When Heracles brought the animal back to show him, Eurystheus was so afraid that he made the hero immediately return the beast to its proper home.

Eurystheus went on to attempt to rid Greece of Alcmene and all the children of Heracles. They fled to Athens, and when Eurystheus attacked that city he was resisted by Theseus (or his son, Demophoön), Iolaus, and Hyllus. An oracle demanded the sacrifice of one of Heracles' children to save the city, so Macaria killed herself. Eurystheus was then defeated by either Iolaus or Hyllus and was killed by Alcmene. Although Eurystheus belongs firmly to Greek tradition, his name followed that of Heracles, with whom he is inexorably connected, into later Roman tradition.

See also: Iolaus; Jason; Theseus

Eurytion

Greek

Son of Ares and herdsman to Geryon, protecting the latter's cattle in the company of the two-headed dog Orthros. When Heracles came to steal the cattle as his tenth labor, both Eurytion and Orthros were felled by that great hero's club.

See also: Geryon

Eurytus

Greek

King of Oechalia and father of Iole; a great archer and friend of Heracles, he taught him his skills with bow and arrows. He owned a great bow that could be fired only by himself or Heracles. He offered his daughter, Iole, to whomever could surpass him in an archery contest. Heracles accomplished this feat, but Eurytus would not surrender his daughter, for Heracles had previously murdered his own wife and children. Later his country was invaded from Trachis by an army led by Heracles, who was determined to take Iole as fair-won maiden. Heracles killed Eurytus and all his family and sent Iole to be looked after by his wife, Deianeira, an event that would eventually lead to Heracles' death.

See also: Deianeira; Iole

Euterpe

Greco-Roman

One of the nine daughters of Zeus and Mnemosyne who were collectively known as the Muses. Euterpe was the patron of flautists, being represented in art with a flute, and was the Muse of lyric poetry.

See also: Musae

Evadne

Greek

Daughter of Iphis, wife of Capaneus, and mother of Sthenelus. When her son received his funeral rites following the failed expedition of the Seven Against Thebes, Evadne threw herself onto the flaming pyre and perished.

See also: Seven Against Thebes

Evander

Greco-Roman

A minor Arcadian deity who is often associated with Pan, an association that led the Romans to sometimes identify him with Faunus. Legend names his father as Hermes and his mother as the nymph Carmentia, or Themis. Roman tradition said that he led a group of Arcadians to Italy and founded Rome many years before Aeneas and his Trojan refugees landed. Evander and his followers settled on the Palatine Hill, which, so this early tradition said, was named after Pallenteum, the Arcadian city from which they had set out. Many years later, when Aeneas and his followers landed, they were said to have consulted Evander, who told them of Hercules' visit to the Palatine Hill and his slaughter of Cacus, the terrible man-eating ogre and the son of Vulcan, who had attempted to steal the cattle of Geryon, which Hercules was driving through Italy. Evander further promised to support Aeneas against Turnus, with his son, Pallas, joining the Trojan forces.

See also: Aeneas; Faunus; Pan

Evenus

Greek

Father of Marpessa. When his daughter was abducted by Idas, Evenus drowned himself in the river that thenceforth carried his name.

F

Fates

Greco-Roman

The name by which the Moirae (Moerae) are better known, though to the Romans they were the Parcae. These three goddess-spirits where said to have been the children of Uranos and Ge, though later tradition made them the offspring of Erebos and Night. They applied the decrees of individual destiny and were named as follows: Clotho, who spun the thread of life and was therefore the Fate who decided birth; Lachesis, who represented the element of chance, spun out the course of life, and measured the thread spun by Clotho, thus becoming the Fate of life itself; and Atropos, the eldest, the inevitable Fate, who cut the thread with her shears and therefore determined the length of any life and became the Fate of death.

As a combined force they appear in a great number of the classical traditions, notably that concerning Meleager, who they declared would die when a brand laying in a fire when he was born was consumed. His mother, Althaea, immediately seized the brand and hid it away. However, when Meleager grew up he took part in the hunt for the Calydonian Boar, killed it, and gave its head to Atalanta. He quarreled with Althaea's brothers over this gift—and killed them. His mother then threw the brand back onto the fire, and the prophecy of the Fates was fulfilled.

Usually depicted in art as elderly and dressed in white robes, the Fates, it has been suggested, originally represented phases of the moon. With the help of Hermes they were the supposed inventors of the alphabet. Although they attracted widespread cult following, only Clotho and Atropos were worshipped at Delphi.

See also: Atropos; Clotho; Lachesis; Meleager

Faun

Roman

One of any number of rural deities that were represented with horns, pointed ears, and the tail of a goat. Later they were also depicted as having goats' legs to bring their image into closer alignment with the satyrs, with whom they had always been associated. Their apparent leader was the god Faunus.

Faunus

Roman

Rural god of fertility and prophecy, Faunus was also regarded as a law-giver. The grandson of Saturn or Mars, father of Latinus by the nymph Marica, he was the leader of the Fauns, being portrayed with the same characteristics of goats' ears, horns, tail, and legs. He was directly identified with the Greek Pan and was sometimes identified as Evander, though he was said to have welcomed Evander and his Arcadians to Italy. Worshipped by shepherds and farmers, he was said to have been able to adopt the form of a wolf known as Lupercus, though some believe that Lupercus more correctly relates to the she-wolf that raised the twins Romulus and Remus.

Legend says that he was once trapped by Numa Pompilius, who, with the aid of Picus, mixed wine and honey in their own drinking water. Having caught Faunus, they persuaded him to tell them all his secrets, including a charm against thunderstorms.

As a god of fertility Faunus was approached by sterile women who desired children. The priests celebrated his rites naked so that their sexual identity was clear, for it was alleged that Faunus once mistakenly tried to make love to Hercules while he was dressed as a woman. He appears to have had a female associate, Fauna, whose rites were exclusively reserved for women and were said to have been excessively lewd.

See also: Pan

Faustulus

Roman

Shepherd who discovered the twins Romulus and Remus being tended by a she-wolf and took them home to his wife, Acca Larentia. This connection has led Faunus to sometimes be considered as the she-wolf Lupercus.

See also: Acca Larentia; Remus; Romulus

Februus

Roman

The eponym of the last month of the Roman calendar, February. A god of purification, he appears to have been adapted from an ancient Etruscan god of the dead. In Rome, February was celebrated as the month of the dead.

Flamen

Roman

A sacrificial priest in ancient Rome. Originally there were three *flamens* for every deity, but later 12 more were added. His post was held for life, being terminated only if he committed some misdemeanor or when his wife, who assisted in his duties, died.

Flood, the

Greek

Common among most world traditions is a legend concerning a mighty deluge that covered the face of the earth. Greek tradition says that Zeus, tired of the impiety of mankind (though some sources add man's infernal racket), decided to destroy man with a great flood. However, Prometheus warned his son, Deucalion, who constructed a vessel in which he and his wife, Pyrrha, the daughter of Epimetheus, could ride out the storm.

After nine days the water subsided and the vessel came to rest on the slopes of Mount Parnassus. Wondering how they might repopulate the earth, Deucalion and Pyrrha prayed at the shrine of Themis, who appeared to them and commanded them to throw the bones of

their mother behind them. Unsure what this meant at first, it was Pyrrha who came to understand she meant the rocks of Mother Earth. Rocks flung by Deucalion became men, whereas those thrown by Pyrrha became women.

See also: Deucalion

Flora

Roman

Personification and goddess of flowers, budding fruits, youth, and spring. Depicted as garlanded with flowers, she was honored as a fertility goddess at the bawdy Floralia, a festival in her honor held toward the end of May.

Floralia

Roman

Bawdy fertility festival held toward the end of May in honor of Flora.

Fornax

Roman

Goddess of baking in the oven. Though there is a constellation in the southern night sky, it is a fairly recent depiction and has no connection to this goddess.

Fortuna

Roman

Goddess of chance and good fortune who has her Greek equivalent in Tyche. Worshipped originally as a fertility goddess, Fortuna adopted her role as the goddess of luck only after the absorption of the Greek pantheon. Usually thought of as the first-born daughter of Jupiter, she was propitiated by those wanting to increase their share of luck and thus bring increased prosperity to themselves or family.

See also: Tyche

Fortunate Isles

Greek

The name for Elysium sometimes used by later writers and geographers who located this paradisiacal abode of the blessed dead—

where neither snow nor rain fell and the winds never blew—beyond the Pillars of Heracles, thereby eventually identifying it with the Canary Isles and Madeira.

See also: Elysium

Fortunatorum Insulae

Roman

Literally "the Islands of the Blessed/Fortunate," the original name of Elysium in Roman tradition, which later changed back to the Greek name.

Furies

Greek

The name by which the Erinnyes are possibly best known. Euphemistically referred to as the Eumenides, the Furies were three hideous and terrible goddesses of vengeance—Alecto, Megaera, Tisiphone—who were sent from Tartarus to avenge wrong, punish crime, and torment those who had committed social crimes. Often depicted as snake-haired, they are sometimes confused with the Gorgons.

See also: Erinnyes

G

Gabii
Roman

An extinct city near Rome where the infants Romulus and Remus were traditionally raised. The city features also in a legend concerning Tarquinius Sextus, who asked his father, Tarquinius Superbus, how Gabii might be taken. Tarquinius Superbus silently decapitated the tallest poppies in his garden. Taking the hint, Tarquinius Sextus executed the Gabian leaders, and his father then took the city.

See also: Remus; Romulus

Ga~ea, ~ia
Greek

Variant form of Ge.

Gaia Caecilia
Roman

An alternative name for Tanaquil.

Galatea
Greek

1. Sea nymph, the daughter of Nereus and Doris. She was loved by Acis and the centaur Polyphemus, whom she shunned on account of his ugliness. In jealousy Polyphemus killed Acis by crushing him under a huge rock; he was released by Galatea, who turned him into a river. Some of the rocks thrown by Polyphemus landed in the sea, where they became the Isole Ciclopi off Acireale in Sicily, thus giving us a location for the incident.

2. The statue made by Pygmalion with which he fell in love. He named the woman Galatea after the statue was brought to life by Aphrodite in answer to his prayers.

See also: Polyphemus; Pygmalion

Galinthias
Greek

Daughter of Proetus of Thebes and a friend of Alcmene.

Ganymede
Greek

The most beautiful of all mortal youths; raped on Mount Ida in Phrygia, he was carried away by the gods to be cupbearer to Zeus in place of Hebe. Homeric tradition makes him the son of King Tros and Callirrhoë, though his father is also sometimes named as Laomedon. Later tradition said that Ganymede was carried off by an eagle, possibly Aquila, or by Zeus himself in the guise of an eagle, after which his father was sent a pair of white horses, or a golden vine, as compensation. When Ganymede died he was placed in the heavens as the constellation Aquarius for his faithful service. To the Romans Ganymede was known as Catamitus, a name that has given us *catamite* and hints of the frequent homosexual tendencies of the classical gods.

Astronomical: For the constellation Aquarius see the relevant entry. Ganymede is the largest moon of the planet Jupiter and the largest satellite within the solar system at 5,300 kilometers (3,300 miles) in diameter, making it larger than the planet Mercury. It orbits the planet once every 7.2 days at an average distance of 1.1 million kilometers (700,000 miles) from the surface of the planet, its own surface being a mixture of cratered and grooved terrain. Ganymede is the fourth most distant satellite of Jupiter, lying between the orbits of Europa and Callisto.

Ge
Greek

Also: Ga~ea, ~ia

The personification of Earth, the Mother

Goddess, patroness of marriage; she was less actively worshipped than goddesses of later origin, having been ousted by the gods and goddesses of Olympus by the time of the classical Greeks. When she was worshipped during classical times she was seen as the giver of dreams and presided over growing plants and children. She was identified as Tellus by the Romans.

Born out of Chaos, the limitless emptiness that existed before creation, along with Tartarus and Eros, Ge gave birth to Pontus (the Sea) and Uranos (the Heavens), who became her consort. Ge remains one of the most prolific of all the classical goddesses. Having given virgin birth to Pontus and Uranos, she went on, usually by Uranos, to become the mother of the Hecatoncheires: Cottus, Briareus (also called Aegaeon), and Gyas, or Gyges; the one-eyed Cyclopes—Brontes, Steropes, and Arges; and the 12 Titans, though here they are not so easy to name, for different sources give different names. The most frequently mentioned Titans are Cronos, Oceanos, Hyperion, Iapetus, Themis, Rhea, Tethys, and Mnemosyne.

After Uranos had thrown the rebellious Cyclopes into Tartarus, Ge persuaded the Titans, with the exception of Oceanos, to rebel. She gave Cronos, the youngest, a flint sickle that he used to castrate Uranos. Blood from the wound fell onto Mother Earth (Ge), and she gave birth to the three Erinnyes (Alecto, Tisiphone, and Megaera) as well as the Meliae. Some sources say that this was also the means by which she conceived the Gigantes. Drops that fell into the sea conceived Aphrodite. In some legends she is also the mother of Typhoeus, Tityus, Arion, and Echidne by Tartarus and Antaeus by Poseidon. She helped the Horae to nurse Aristaeus and was responsible, in some accounts, for the death of Orion. She had oracular powers, as is common with earth goddesses in other traditions; her oracle at Delphi, given to her by Python, later became the Delphic Oracle of Apollo.

See also: Cyclopes; Erinnyes; Hecatoncheires; Tellus; Titan

Gemini
Greco-Roman
Although the Heavenly Twins, Castor and Polydeuces (Pollux to the Romans), were never called Gemini in the legends, the constellation that carries their name has been identified with them since classical times.

Astronomical: A constellation of the northern celestial hemisphere lying between approximate right ascensions 5h58m and 8h05m, declination from +10° to +35°. The stars Castor and Pollux are the prominent members of this star grouping.

See also: castor; Polydeuces

Geryon(es)
Greek
A powerful monster with three bodies and three heads, the son of Chrysaor and Callirrhoë who lived on the island of Erytheia, its exact location being subject to numerous theories. Some have placed it beyond the farthest ocean, whereas others have sought to identify it with Gades, an island off of Cadiz. He had a herd of cattle guarded by Orthros, the two-headed dog that was one of the monstrous offspring of Typhon and Echidne, and the herdsman Eurytion. This herd became the subject of Heracles' tenth labor. Having felled both Orthros and Eurytion with his club, Heracles turned his attention to Geryon, whom he overcame.

Giant
Greek
The giants were huge humanoid beings abound throughout classical Greek mythology, but those most commonly referred to are the Titans, the Cyclopes, and the Hecatoncheires. At the instigation of their mother, Ge, the giants made war on Olympus. They are variously named, but their king is usually called Porphyrion. Others were Alcyoneus, who was killed by Heracles during the great battle, the Titanomachia, many years before that hero's apotheosis; Enceladus was killed by Athene; Mimas was blasted by Zeus's thunderbolt; Ephialtes was blinded by Apollo and Heracles; Hippolytus was killed by Hermes, who was wearing Hades' cap of invisibility; Agrius and Thoas were killed by the Fates using bronze clubs. Apollodorus said that Athene flung the island of Sicily on Enceladus, trapping him below Mount Etna, which still vents his anger, and that Poseidon threw a

fragment of Cos onto Polybutes, forming the island of Nisyrus.

Later traditions added a great number of giants to the classical legends, some of whom were ambivalent, others decidedly nasty. All exhibit superhuman attributes, and many have connections with chthonic principles, particularly volcanoes.

See also: Cyclopes; Hecatoncheires; Titan

Gigantes
Greek

An alternative term for the Titans, the offspring of Ge and Uranos who took part in the Titanomachia against the gods of Olympus. They were giant beings, having serpents' tails, and were variously disposed of during their battle with the Olympian gods, who had the help of Heracles.

Glauce
Greek

Daughter of Creon (king of Corinth); also known as Creusa. When Jason deserted Medeä in her favor the scorned sorceress sent her a poisoned garment that set her body afire when she put it on and that burned down the palace, killing her father and his retinue.

See also: Jason; Medeä

Glaucus
Greek

1. King of Ephyra, or Corinth, son of Sisyphus and Merope, and father of Bellerophon, though most sources say that his wife, Eurynome, bore Bellerophon to Poseidon and that Glaucus simply raised him as his own. He was eaten by his own horses when he lost a chariot race to Iolaus, a race run because he had scorned the power of Aphrodite. His spirit was said to haunt the Isthmus of Corinth for many generations.

2. The grandson of Bellerophon, thus the great-grandson of Glaucus, who at the Trojan War commanded the Lycian forces in association with Sarpedon. During the fray he discovered that Diomedes' father, Oeneus, had once entertained Bellerophon and thus refused to fight him. Instead he exchanged his golden armor for the bronze armor of Diomedes, and

the two restored the friendship of their ancestors. When he was killed by Ajax the Greater his body was brought back to Lycia on the winds by Apollo.

3. Son of Minos and Pasiphaë and brother of Androgeos, Ariadne, and Phaedra. As a boy Glaucus was drowned when he fell into a cask of honey, his body either being discovered by the seer Polyeidus or by the Curetes, who said he would be revived by whoever found the best analogy for a cow belonging to Minos that changed its color from red to white to black. Polyeidus made the comparison to a blackberry. However, unable to revive the boy, Polyeidus was now entombed with the body of Glaucus, and there a serpent revealed to the seer an herb that restored the boy, after which both Glaucus and Polyeidus were released, Polyeidus teaching Glaucus the art of divination.

4. A deity of the sea whose name means "sea-green." Originally a mortal fisherman, he was transformed into a merman when he ate a magic herb. He fell in love with Scylla, but Circe turned Scylla into a sea monster out of jealousy, for she loved Glaucus. A friendly patron of sailors with powers of prophecy, a common attribute of sea gods, he shared an oracle with the Nereides on Delos.

See also: Ajax (1); Bellerophon; Minos

God
Greek

The conventional translation of the Greek *theos,* applied to all the Olympian deities, gods who represented a sort of aristocracy of creation. They were not unlike men in their behavior or passions; in fact many were greatly more immoral than classical sensibilities would seem to permit. But they were infinitely more powerful and beautiful than man (as can be seen, for example, by studying the art portraying Apollo). Most importantly, gods were immortal, thus placing them firmly above mankind. Between them came two other "races"—the *daemones* and the heroes, many of whom were apotheosized.

Golden age
Greco-Roman

A mythical period that was, in classical times, believed to have been the original state of the

world. It was the first and best time, one of innocence when mankind lived in peace and harmony with itself and with nature, an idyll of
happiness and prosperity. Greek legend states
that men lived under Cronos's rule free from
care and enjoyed eternal youth and a life of ease,
not needing to work, for the land produced fruit
spontaneously. When their days on earth came
to an end they died without pain, as if falling
asleep. This mythical paradise disappeared with
the coming of the Olympian order, but men continued to live a similar life after death in the paradisiacal Elysium, where Cronos still reigns.
Later the term came to be used to describe the
flourishing years of any civilization or culture.

See also: Cronos

Golden Bough, the
Greco-Roman

A bough taken from a wood near Lake
Avernus that the Sibyl of Cumae told Aeneas
to arm himself with before descending into the
Underworld to consult the spirit of his dead
father.

See also: Aeneas

Golden Fleece, the
Greek

The fleece of the winged ram Aries, or
Chrysmallus, which Zeus sent to Thebes to substitute for Phrixus when his father, Athamas,
was preparing to sacrifice him at the instigation
of his stepmother, Ino. The ram flew off with
Phrixus and his sister, Helle, on its back, bound
for Colchis, but Helle fell off en route into the
Hellespont. Arriving in Colchis, Phrixus sacrificed the ram to Poseidon, and either he or
Aeëtes, king of Colchis, hung the fleece on an
oak tree in a grove sacred to Ares, where it was
guarded by a sleepless dragon. Later Jason and
the Argonauts mounted an expedition to bring
it back to Greece, which they accomplished with
a little help from Medeä.

See also: Colchis; Helle; Jason; Medeä; Phrixus

Gordian Knot, the
Greek

The mythical knot tied by Gordius, king of
Phrygia, that was to be unraveled only by the

future conqueror of Asia. According to tradition, Alexander the Great cut it open with his
sword in 334 B.C.

See also: Alexander the Great

Gordius
Greek

King of Phrygia and father of Midas. Originally a peasant, he became king after an oracle had told the people of Phrygia that their
new king would arrive riding in a simple
wagon. When Gordius arrived in just such a
manner they proclaimed him king. In gratitude he dedicated his cart to Zeus in the acropolis of Gordium, fastening the pole to the yoke
with a curious knot of bark. An oracle decreed
that whoever should untie the knot would
conquer and rule Asia. According to tradition,
the Gordian Knot was cut open by Alexander
the Great with his sword in 334 B.C.

See also: Midas

Gorge
Greek

Daughter of Althaea and sister of Deianeira.
Wife of Andraemon and mother of Theos, she
and her sister retained their human form when
Artemis changed their other sisters into birds.

Gorgon
Greek

Originally the Gorgons were the three beautiful daughters of the sea deities Phorcys and
Ceto; sisters of the Graeae. The three Gorgons
were named Stheno, Euryale, and Medusa,
who lived in Libya; the first two were immortal, whereas Medusa was vulnerable. Medusa
was seduced by Poseidon and lay with him in
a temple dedicated to Athene. Furious, Athene
transformed Medusa and her sisters into the
Gorgons, hideous beings with golden wings
and brazen claws, vast, grinning mouths with
tusks, and serpents for hair. So ghastly was
their appearance that their looks turned men
to stone, an attribute that is central to the story
of Perseus slaying Medusa. From her body
sprung, fully grown, the winged horse
Pegasus and the warrior Chrysaor, the result
of her union with Poseidon. Stheno and

Euryale pursued Perseus, but he was wearing Hades' helmet of invisibility and escaped to the south. Perseus subsequently used the petrifying power of Medusa's severed head to turn Atlas into the mountain that bears his name, then to turn the sea monster Cetus into stone to save Andromeda.

The hideous, grinning masks of the Gorgons, known as *gorgoneia,* were commonly used as a charm to ward off evil spirits. The origin of the Gorgons is hard to accurately ascertain. They have been interpreted as spirits of the sun, of thunder, of the winds, and of many other powerful forces of nature. Their iconography, like so many of the other monsters of Greek mythology, derives from Near Eastern art.

See also: Ceto; Chrysaor; Euryale; Medusa; Pegasus; Perseus; Phorcys; Stheno

Gorgoneia
Greek

The hideous, grinning masks of the Gorgons that were employed as charms to ward off evil spirits. Athene was said to have had such an image in the center of her Aegis, though this is also said to have been the head of Medusa herself. One such image on the south face of the Acropolis in Athens was said, by medieval travelers, to be able to foretell the embarkation of invading fleets from the far south. Another famous image is found on the temple of Artemis on Corfu.

See also: Aegis

Gort~yn, ~ys
Greco-Roman

Important archaeological site at Aghii Déka in the Messara Plain to the south of the island of Crete. It was on the banks of the river here, so Greek tradition states, that Zeus seduced Europa after he carried her to Crete on his back in the form of a beautiful white bull. Historically speaking the town rose to prominence only at the end of the Minoan period, soon becoming an important city-state. There is a pre-Roman temple to Apollo Pythios at Gortyn, but all that remains today is the altar and sundry bits of broken columns.

See also: Europa

Graces
Greek

The three daughters of Aphrodite, or Hera, by Zeus, or of Aegle by Helios; also known, in Greek, as the Charites. Named Aglaia, Thalia, and Euphrosyne, they had a cult most notably at Orchomenus, where they were worshipped in the form of three meteorites. However, they attain their greatest significance in association with the Muses. Whereas the latter provide the raw material for the arts and sciences, the Graces provide the inspiration. They were the personification of grace and beauty, bestowers of intellectual pleasure who perhaps originated as fertility deities.

See also: Aglaia; Euphrosyne; Thalia

Graeae
Greek

Two, perhaps three, ancient women, the daughters of the sea deities Phorcys and Ceto and thus the sisters of the Gorgons. They lived in the farthest west (one story naming their home as Mount Atlas, but this does not fit the normal chronology of events), where the sun never shone and had but one eye and one tooth between the three of them. Perseus visited them when he was sent to kill Medusa and, by stealing their eye and tooth, made them divulge what he needed to know to overcome their sister. An alternative story says that they guarded the road to where the Gorgons lived and that Perseus, by stealing their eye and throwing it into Lake Triton, was able to sneak past them unchallenged and unannounced.

See also: Gorgon; Perseus; Triton, Lake

Griff~in, ~en, ~on
Greek

Also: Gryphon

A mythical beast having a lion's body and the wings of an eagle. It is known in all Near Eastern artistic traditions. Sometimes variants of the animal's structure are given: a serpent's head, scorpion's tail, bird's feet, and the like. The gold of the Arimaspi was said to have been guarded by Griffins, according to

Aristaeus. Unusually, even though wide-spread throughout neighboring cultures, Griffins have no actual mythology within Greek tradition. Later writers, such as Aristeas, incorporated them into their rendition of earlier stories, such writers often making them the watchdogs of Apollo and Dionysos.

Gryphon
Greek

Variant of Griffin.

Gy~as, ~es, ~ges
Greek

One of the Hecatoncheires or Centimani, the 100-handed, 50-headed giant sons of Uranos and Ge. His two brothers are named Cottus and Briareus, who is also known as Aegaeon. They were brothers of the Cyclopes and Titans. Gyas and his brothers were imprisoned by their father in Tartarus, along with the Cyclopes and Titans, and this imprisonment led Ge to arm Cronos so that he might emasculate his father and usurp his position.

See also: Hecatoncheires

H

Hacho

Greek

Mountain, also called Mount Acho, at the northern tip of Morocco that is sometimes identified as being Abyla, or Ceuta, the southern of the Pillars of Heracles, the northern being Calpe, the modern Gibraltar.

See also: Abyla; Calpe

Hades

Greek

Also: Aides, Aidoneus

Son of Cronos and Rhea; brother of Poseidon, Zeus, Demeter, Hestia, and Hera; one of the 12 great Olympian deities. His name means "the Unseen," a direct contrast to his brother, Zeus, who was originally seen to represent the brightness of day. He was swallowed at birth by his father, along with his brothers and sisters—all except Zeus, who was hidden away by his mother and, when grown to manhood, forced his father, whom he usurped, to disgorge the children. They banded together against Cronos, whom they successfully dethroned with the aid of weapons provided by the Cyclopes.

Zeus, Poseidon, and Hades then divided the government by lot. To Zeus fell the sky, to Poseidon the sea, and to Hades the Underworld, a region that has also become simply referred to as Hades, though it is actually three regions. Thus, *Hades* should always be used to refer to the god.

The god Hades, who in origin was probably a very early pre-Hellenic deity, was the severe and pitiless god of the Underworld and of death, though he was not essentially evil; he presided over the trial and punishment of the wicked. The Greeks usually referred to Hades by a euphemistic title, Plouton or Pluto being the most popular variants. This title, meaning "the Wealth," referred either to Hades' possession of all the precious metals and gems found on earth or, some have suggested, to the fact that he gathered all living things into his realm after they died. He was also known as Clymenos, "the Illustrious One," Eubuleus, "the Giver of Good Advice," or Aides or Aidoneus. The Romans adopted the name Pluto, referring to him also as Dis Pater or Orcus.

His attributes included a staff with which he drove the spirits of the dead, or beckoned the dying to his realm, and a fabulous helmet that conferred invisibility on the wearer. The Cyclopes gave him the helmet, which he later lent to Perseus when that hero was given the task of killing the Gorgon Medusa. Hades asked Zeus for permission to marry Persephone, the daughter of Demeter; neither refused nor given clear consent, he simply abducted her while she was gathering flowers, some sources placing the scene of abduction at Enna in Sicily. Demeter searched endlessly for her daughter, forbidding anything to grow on earth while she looked. Finally Zeus intervened and told Demeter that Persephone might return from the Underworld on the single proviso that she had not eaten anything while in that realm. Persephone had, unfortunately, eaten the seed from a pomegranate; thus she was allowed to return for only part of each year, being Hades' queen during the other part. This story clearly reflects an early attempt to rationalize the sequence of the seasons, for while Persephone is in Hades' realm the earth lies dormant (winter), blossoming forth when she returns.

Hades was not always faithful to his queen. He once pursued the nymph Minthe, who was turned into a mint plant by Persephone during the chase. Hades had more success with another nymph, Leuce, but she was afterwards transformed into the white poplar tree.

The Underworld realm of Hades was divided into three regions through which five rivers ran, the entrance to this eternal world being guarded by the three-headed dog Cerberus. To reach the Underworld the dead, usually accompanied by Hermes, first had to be ferried across the River Styx by the ghostly ferryman Charon, who demanded payment for the journey. Payment was a coin, an *obolos*, which was placed on the tongue of the corpse during the earthly burial service. Having crossed the Styx the spirits of the dead had to propitiate Cerberus, the usual offering being honey cakes.

Once in the Underworld proper, the spirits of the dead had to cross four additional rivers, the Acheron (River of Woe), some sources saying Charon ferried them; Phlegethon (River of Flames); Cocytus (River of Wailing); and finally Lethe (River of Forgetfulness). The first three rivers are connected with the actual funeral rites and their associated emotions. However, all spirits were said to drink from the Lethe, upon which they immediately forgot their past life. Unable to recall any events from past lives, the spirits were brought before the three judges of the Underworld.

These judges—Minos, Rhadamanthus, and Aeacus—ruled on how each individual had spent life on earth; according to their judgment, one of three regions awaited the spirit for all eternity. The good were sent to Elysium, or the "Fortunate Isles," where rain and snow never fell and which can be best equated with Heaven. This realm, though considered a part of the Underworld, actually fell outside of Hades' domain and was ruled by Cronos. The average were sent to the Asphodel Fields, an indifferent area that is best equated as the region directly ruled by Hades. The wicked were sent to Tartarus, the deepest region of the Underworld. To this lowest region many characters from Greek myth were dispatched after death, sometimes simply for eternal punishment. The Titans, Cyclopes, and Hecatoncheires were originally imprisoned there by Cronos, though later, after Cronos had been dethroned, only the Titans remained, guarded by the Hecatoncheires. Sisyphus was condemned to eternally roll a huge stone to the top of a hill, where it immediately rolled down again.

Also occupying this region of Hades' domain was the infernal Hecate, the three-bodied, three-headed goddess who presided over witchcraft and the black arts. Worshipped where three roads met, she had once helped Demeter in her search for Persephone, later becoming the companion of Persephone during the time she spent in the Underworld.

Also occupying Tartarus were the three-winged, snake-haired Erinnyes, or Furies, dispatched from this region to punish unnatural crimes and harry those who committed them. They later became known euphemistically as the Eumenides when Athene pacified them following the acquittal of Orestes.

Seldom figuring in art, usually being represented as a mature, bearded man, sometimes carrying a scepter or key, Hades had no temples, though he did receive cult in Elea. However, religious acts were sometimes carried out in his name. Black animals, usually bulls, were sacrificed to him, notably at Syracuse, Sicily, where black bulls were offered near the site Hades reportedly abducted Persephone. The complex structure of Hades' realm, which by metonymy also came to be called Hades, illustrated the combination of the contradictory ideas that the ancient Greeks had regarding life after death. In the very broadest terms, the deities Persephone and Hecate can be seen to represent the pre-Hellenic hopes of a true afterlife, whereas Hades personifies the Hellenic fear of the finality and totality of death. By the fifth century B.C. the god Hades was becoming the realm over which he had reigned, his position being usurped under the influence of Eleusinian myth by Pluto or, more accurately, Pluton, the name by which he entered Roman tradition.

See also: Acheron; Cerberus; Charon; Cocytus; Cyclopes; Elysium; Erinnyes; Hecate; Lethe; Phlegethon; Pluto; Styx; Tartarus

Haemon

Greek

Son of Creon (king of Thebes). According to Apollodorus, Haemon numbered among the Theban youths killed by the Sphinx for failing to answer the riddle she set. However, Haemon is usually regarded as the lover of Antigone—and therefore alive after Oedipus's victory over the Sphinx. Creon had Antigone immured in a cave, where she hanged herself;

the grief-stricken Haemon, upon finding her body, took his own life.

See also: Sphinx

Halcyone

Greek

A little-used variant of Alcyone.

Halirrhothius

Greek

A son of Poseidon who was, according to late tradition, murdered by Ares. However, Ares pleaded that he had been saving his daughter, Alcippe, from being violated by Halirrhothius and thus was acquitted of murder. The place of Ares' trial became known as the Areopagus.

See also: Areopagus

Hamadryad

Greek

A class of tree nymphs who lived and died with the trees they inhabited.

Harmonia

Greek

Daughter of Ares and Aphrodite. Her wedding to Cadmos was attended by the Olympian deities. Here she was given, by Aphrodite, a fabulous necklace made by Hephaistos that conferred irresistible loveliness on the wearer—but proved fatal to all who wore it. She also received a robe from Athene that conferred divine dignity on the wearer. Her children by Cadmos were the four sisters Ino, Autonoë, Semele, and Agave, as well as Polydorus and later Illyrius. Following the tragic deaths of all their daughters, Cadmos and Harmonia left Thebes for Illyria, where they were turned into snakes by Ares, in which forms they were welcomed to the Islands of the Blessed.

See also: Cadmos

Harpy

Greek

The Harpies were winged female demons, the daughters of Thaumas and Electra; they were the sisters of Iris. In origin they appear to be spirits of the wind. Hesiod identified just two Harpies, Aello and Acypete, but later sources added a third, Celaeno. Usually depicted in art as winged women to differentiate them from similar bird-bodied women such as the Sirens, the Harpies had the head and breasts of a woman and the claws of a vulture. Associated with sudden death, whirlwinds, and storms, they represent the feminine principle in its destructive form. The Harpies were said to have been the mothers, by Zephyrus, of Xanthus and Balius, the talking horses of Achilles, as well as mothers of the horses ridden by the Dioscuri.

Foul beasts, the Harpies are possibly best known through their appearance in the legend of the blind King Phineus. Every time the king sat down to eat they rapaciously descended onto his table, snatching his food and fouling the table. They were driven away by the sons of Boreas when the Argonauts landed on his island.

See also: Boreas; Phineus

Hebe

Greek

Goddess of youth; the daughter of Hera who was engendered parthenogenetically when Hera ate a lettuce (a traditional anaphrodisiacal plant), though some sources say she was the daughter of Hera and Zeus. Eternally young, Hebe became the cupbearer to the gods of Olympus before being replaced by Ganymede. At first married to Ares, she had limited powers to bestow eternal youth. She later married Heracles after he had been deified and had, at last, been accepted by Hera. Hebe was called Juventas by the Romans.

See also: Ganymede; Juventas

Hecabe

Greek

Little-used variant of Hecuba.

Hecale

Greek

A pitifully poor old women who nevertheless entertained Theseus with all the hospitality she could muster while the latter was involved in the hunt for the Marathonian Bull.

Hecate
Greek

An extremely powerful ancient goddess whose origins lie in Asia Minor, possibly Thrace. A mysterious deity, depicted as a triple goddess with three bodies and three heads, she was honored in Heaven, on Earth, and in the Underworld and was held in esteem and awe by all the Olympian deities, including Zeus. Her triple aspect led to her being seen as a deity ruling over Heaven as Semele, over Earth as Artemis, and in Hades as the companion of Persephone. Originally a moon goddess, hence her assimilation with Semele and Artemis, Hecate was the patron of rich men, sailors, and flocks, the bestower of the wealth and blessings of daily life. She later came to be regarded, by the Hellenes in particular, as a dread divinity of the Underworld; she resided in its deepest region, Tartarus, keeping company with the dead and presiding over witchcraft and the black arts. She became the patroness of witches and sorceresses and protectress of graveyards and crossroads, especially those between three roads.

Some sources say that she was the daughter of Perses and Asteria, whereas others give her a more divine status, saying that her parentage was Zeus and Hera and that it was her theft of Hera's cosmetics that led to her being banished from Olympus. She helped Demeter search for Persephone, and when Persephone was found to be in the Underworld she descended to become her companion.

Hecate was characteristically worshipped at gateways or the junction of three roads, where dogs, which were sacred to her, were offered in sacrifice. To the pre-Hellenic people she represented the hope of an afterlife. The Hellenes were a little more clear-cut and simply regarded her as a dreadful, primeval witch.

See also: Hades; Tartarus

Hecatoncheires
Greek

The collective name given to Cottus, Briareus, who is also known as Aegaeon, and Gyas or Gyges, the three giant sons of Uranos and Ge who had 100 hands and 50 heads sometimes known as the Centimani. They were the brothers of the Cyclopes and the 12 Titans. Following the Titanomachia, the Hecatoncheires guarded the Titans, who had been consigned to dwell in Tartarus for all eternity.

Hector
Greek

The greatest of the Trojan heroes during the Trojan War; the eldest son of Priam and Hecuba, brother of Paris, Helenus, Deiphobus, and Cassandra; husband of Andromache and father of Astyanax. During the siege of Troy he was afforded the personal protection of Ares, and in one memorable scene in Homer's *Iliad* he fought a day-long battle with Ajax the Greater until, at nightfall, they exchanged gifts, Hector giving Ajax a sword, receiving in return a purple baldric (a sash or belt worn over the right shoulder to the left hip for carrying a sword). Having killed Patroclus, Hector was chased three times around the walls of Troy before he was killed by Achilles.

Killed, he was stripped of his armor by Achilles who, tying Hector's ankles together, simply dragged the body back to the Greek lines. Some sources vary this, saying that Achilles now dishonored Hector's body by dragging it three times around the walls of Troy by the purple baldric given to him by Ajax. He was then dragged back to Achilles' tent, each day to be dragged three times around the tomb of Patroclus. Finally Priam persuaded Achilles to return his son's body so that it could be afforded the proper funeral rites. The death of Hector led the Amazons to enter the Trojan War on the side of Troy, but their queen, Penthesilea, was killed by Achilles.

See also: Achilles; Ajax (1); Andromache; Priam; Trojan War

Hecub~a, ~e
Greek

The second wife of Priam, king of Troy, she came from an area near the River Sangarius on the southern coast of the Black Sea. She had a total of 19 children by Priam, including the most famous of Priam's 50 sons and daughters: Cassandra, Creusa, Deiphobus, Hector, Helenus, Laodice, Paris, Polites, Polydorus, Polyxena, and Troilus, though the last may have been her son by Apollo rather than Priam. Before the birth of Paris, Hecuba dreamed that she had borne a blazing firebrand. Interpreting this dream as foretelling that this son would bring some calamity to Troy, she exposed him on the slopes of Mount Ida, where he was found and raised by a shepherd.

Following the fall of Troy, during which she had witnessed the death of most of her family, she was given to Odysseus and traveled with him as far as the Thracian Chersonese, where Hecuba discovered that the king of Thrace, Polymester, had murdered her son, Polydorus. In her fury she blinded Polymester and killed all his children, whereupon she was punished by being transformed into a bitch called Maera; following her death, she was buried nearby at a place thenceforth known as Cynossema—"Dog's Grave." Some sources, however, place her canine transformation immediately after the death of Priam and say that she had already taken this form when she blinded Polymester by scratching his eyes out. She was then stoned by the citizens of Polymester's city, with a stone lodging in her throat, after which she was able only to bark. The revenge she exacted on Polymester later led to her being revered as the personification of motherly love and courage.

Another version of this late story says that Polydorus, along with a large quantity of gold, was entrusted to Polymester by Priam shortly before the fall of Troy. When the city had fallen, Polymester killed Polydorus for the gold and cast his body into the sea. There it was found by Hecuba, who swore revenge, later managing to kill Polymester and his children. She then turned herself into the bitch Maera to evade the angry Thracians.

See also: Priam

Helen(~a, ~e)

Greek

The most beautiful woman of her time, the daughter of Tyndareus, king of Sparta, and Leda, Helen was said to have been born from the same egg as the twin deities Castor and Polydeuces (the Dioscuri); she may have been the daughter of Zeus rather than Tyndareus. Her half-sister was Clytemnestra. Although worshipped as a goddess of womanhood at Sparta, throughout the rest of Greece she was considered as a legendary mortal, not a goddess.

It was Helen's remarkable beauty that led to her troubles. While still quite young she was seized by Theseus and Peirithous; falling by lot to Theseus, she was carried off to Attica, where she was placed in the care of Aethra, Theseus's mother, in the village of Aphidnae. She was later rescued by her brothers, the Dioscuri, when they invaded Attica with an army and were told the whereabouts of Helen by Academus. They took the young girl back to Sparta, along with Aethra, who was to act as her servant.

Helen was now courted by innumerable suitors including Idomeneos and Odysseus, though the latter was really more interested in Helen's cousin, Penelope. Odysseus wisely advised Tyndareus to make all her suitors swear allegiance to her final choice. In the end Helen chose Menelaus, brother of Agamemnon, by whom she became the mother of Hermione.

The wisdom of Odysseus's advice to Tyndareus became apparent after Helen had been seized and carried away to Troy, along with a large quantity of gold, by Paris with the help of Aphrodite, to whom he had awarded the Apple of Discord. Her earlier suitors had to honor their oath, leading to the saying that Helen's face "launched a thousand ships" (the Greek fleet that assembled at Aulis before sailing for Troy was immense).

It has been said that Helen was a willing partner in her elopement with Paris, as much in love with him as he with her. However, she was treated with hostility in Troy, being regarded as the cause of the war, and became increasingly lonely. It therefore does not seem surprising that she is credited with helping the Greeks during the final stages of the epic struggle, refusing at one stage to give Odysseus away when he entered the city in disguise, actually providing him with much useful information and confessing that she longed to return to Sparta. One legend contradicts this helpful attitude by saying that Helen tried to trick the occupants of the Wooden Horse by addressing each of the concealed warriors in the voice of his own wife. Odysseus, however, managed to make them refrain from answering, and so they remained undiscover by the Trojans. After Paris was killed, Helen was forcibly married by Deiphobus after he and his brother, Helenus, had fought over her. Helenus fled to Mount Ida, where he was either captured by the Greeks and forced to help them or simply offered advice of his own volition.

With the fall of Troy Helen was exonerated, and she and Menelaus reunited. The traditional version of their reconciliation says that Menelaus was about to transfix her on his sword when, overcome by her beauty, he dropped the sword and took her in his arms. On the way home they stopped at the mouth of the River Nile, where Helen was said to have been taught the secrets of healing herbs. An alternative version, Egyptian in origin, says that the real Helen was spirited away to Egypt prior to Paris abducting her "phantom," which lived at Troy during the war.

The remainder of her life remains undocumented, but several different versions of her death do exist. In the play *Orestes* by Euripides she was translated just as Orestes was about to murder her. A Rhodian legend says that she was driven out of Sparta by the sons of Menelaus and took refuge with Polyxo, the widow of Tlepolemus. However, Polyxo had her maids dress up as Erinnyes and hang Helen from a tree, after which she was worshipped as a goddess. A tradition from the south of Italy placed her on the Islands of the Blessed or the White Island, where she lived an eternal life with other Trojan heroes, marrying Achilles. However, the traditional version was that both Menelaus and Helen died peacefully at Sparta and were buried at Therapnae, becoming the guardians of the city. Their shrine, the Menelaion, may be visited today southeast of Sparta.

See also: Aethra; Agamemnon; Castor; Clytemnestra; Leda; Menelaus; Paris; Polydeuces; Theseus; Tyndareus

Helenus

Greco-Roman

A Trojan seer, a son of Priam and Hecuba. He quarreled with his brother, Deiphobus, over Helen following the death of Paris. When Deiphobus forcibly married Helen, Helenus fled to Mount Ida. There he either voluntarily offered his services to the Greek forces or was captured by Odysseus. He advised the Greek forces that they would capture Troy only if the Palladium could be secured, if Pelops's bones were brought to the battlefield, if Neoptolemus came to join the Greek forces, and if Philoctetes could be persuaded to come to Troy, bringing with him the bow and arrows of Heracles, which he owned.

Following the fall of Troy, Helenus was taken by Neoptolemus on his ship as far as Epirus, where he founded the city of Buthrotum. Neoptolemus also gave him his concubine, Andromache, the widow of Hector, to be his wife. Virgil added to the Trojan traditions by saying that Aeneas stopped in Epirus on his way from Troy, and it was Helenus that prophesied, to him, the foundation of Rome, saying that when Aeneas landed in Italy he should seek out a white sow and 30 piglets and there found his city. He also added that further counsel could be had from the Sibyl of Cumae.

See also: Helen; Priam

Heliades

Greek

The daughters of Helios and sisters of Phaethōn who wept at his death and were transformed into poplar trees. They were sometimes mistakenly identified with the Hyades.

See also: Hyades

Helicaon

Greek

Husband of Laodice, the unfortunate sister of Cassandra who, following the fall of Troy, was swallowed up by the earth, thus being saved from falling into Greek hands.

Helicon

Greek

A lofty mountain in Boeotia that was sacred to Apollo and the home of the Muses, hence Heliconiades and Heliconides. The special haunt of the Muses was the grove of the River Termessus or Permessus that was situated below the sacred spring Hippocrene, which sprung from the earth at the strike of Pegasus's hoof. The sacred spring/fountain Aganippe was also to be found on Mount Helicon.

See also: Apollo; Muses, the

Hel~ios, ~ius

Greek

Ancient god and personification of the sun, the all-seeing god of light who daily rides his golden chariot across the sky. The son of Hyperion and Theia, brother to Eos and Selene, Helios married Persë or Perseis, the mother of Aeëtes, Circe, and Pasiphaë; Neaera; Rhode, the mother of seven sons and one daughter; Gaea; Iphinoë; and Clymene, the mother of Phaethön.

When Zeus, Poseidon, and Hades decided who should rule the three regions of Heaven, Earth, and the Underworld, Helios was absent. To make amends for this omission Zeus awarded Helios the newly arisen island of Rhodes, of which he became patron and where his worship especially flourished. The bronze Colossus of Rhodes was a huge statue of the god. His wife Rhode was the eponym of this island, which, appropriately, claims to receive more hours of sunshine than any other in the Mediterranean. One of Helios's seven sons by Rhode had three sons of his own. These grandsons of Helios were named Lindos, Ialysos, and Camiros, after whom the three major cities of Rhodes were named.

His all-seeing aspect was clearly illustrated when he reported such incidents as the rape and subsequent abduction of Persephone as well as Aphrodite's faithlessness. He, however, failed to notice the theft of his own cattle by the companions of Odysseus. Helios was the father of the Graces by Aegle and successfully seduced Leucothea by disguising himself as her mother. When her father buried her alive as punishment, Helios transformed her into the frankincense bush. Clytie, who was in love with Helios and had revealed the seduction out of jealousy, was turned into a heliotrope.

Helios was frequently confused with Apollo in his guise of Phoebus, but his attributes are purely spiritual, whereas Helios was a tangible deity, the charioteer driving the four winged horses that pulled his chariot from east to west, ferried back to the east at night by Oceanos. His sacred animal was the cock; his sacrifices included white horses, rams, and honey.

The Roman equivalent of Helios was Sol, who had a shrine on the Quirinal Hill, and was later equated with Sol Invictus—"the Invincible"—a special protector of the emperors.

See also: Apollo; Hyperion

Helle

Greek

Daughter of Athamas and Nephele; sister of Phrixus. When she and her brother were being mistreated by their stepmother, Ino, Phrixus about to be sacrificed at Ino's insistence, Zeus sent a winged ram, Aries, to substitute for Phrixus. It flew off with the two children on its back, bound for Colchis. Helle, however, fell into the sea and was drowned—or, some say, became a bride of Poseidon. The stretch of water into which she fell became known as the Hellespont, the modern Dardanelles. Phrixus completed the journey, sacrificed the ram Aries, and hung the fleece in a grove sacred to the god Ares. There it turned to gold, this Golden Fleece subsequently becoming the object of the quest undertaken by Jason and the Argonauts.

See also: Athamas; Jason; Nephele; Phrixus

Hellen

Greek

Grandson of Prometheus, son of Deucalion and Pyrrha, and eponym and mythical ancestor of the Hellenes. The king of Phthia in Thessaly, Hellen was the father of Dorus, Aeolus, and Xuthus.

See also: Deucalion; Prometheus

Hellenes

Greek

Named after the mythical Hellen, son of Deucalion and Pyrrha, the Hellenes or Greeks were an Indo-European people who entered Greece from the north in three main waves, the first, of Minyans and Ionians, beginning c.

2000 B.C. Their mastery of horses and wheeled vehicles made conquest of the indigenous peoples extremely easy.

Penetrating far to the south, the Hellenes soon became excellent navigators, traveling to Sicily, southern Italy, Asia Minor, and throughout the Greek islands. Landing on Crete, they became much influenced by the Minoan culture they found there; they brought it to the mainland, and it began to have a considerable effect after c. 1580 B.C.

However, about 1400 B.C. the Minoan civilization fell, either through invasion or earthquake, and the second wave of Hellenes, the Achaeans, rose to prominence. They remained the prominent force within the Greek world until about 1100 B.C., when Mycenae, the center of civilization during this time, fell, and the third wave, the Dorians, named after Hellen's son, Dorus, entered Greece.

Hellespont
Greek

The ancient name of the Dardanelles, the 50-mile strait that connects the Aegean Sea with the Sea of Marmara. It was named after the legendary Helle, who fell into this stretch of water from the back of the winged ram Aries, which was carrying her and her brother, Phrixus, from Thebes to Colchis.

At its narrowest point, on opposing banks, lay the settlements of Abydos, in Phrygia, and Sestos. Nightly Leander swam from Abydos to visit the priestess Hero in Sestos, but one stormy night Leander drowned and Hero threw herself into the sea.

See also: Helle; Hero; Leander

Hephaest~os, ~us
Greek

Variant of Hephaistos.

Hephaist~os, ~us
Greek

Also: Hephaest~os, ~us

One of the 12 great Olympian deities, Hephaistos—identified by the Romans with Vulcan—possibly originated as a pre-Hellenic fire god near the Mount Olympus of Lycia in Asia Minor, where gaseous vapors, seeping through fissures in the ground, ignited. The Lycians migrated to Lemnos, where they became known as Pelasgians, taking with them their mysterious fire god, and they once again found fire issuing from the ground. This fire became the symbol of their god, who had now become known as Hephaistos. From there the cult spread to Athens, c. 600 B.C., where he achieved great status. His Olympian status appears to reflect the importance of the smith in Bronze Age society, where weapons and tools were held to have magical properties. He was, like other smith gods, represented as lame.

Legend says that he was the brother of Ares and Hebe, the son of Zeus and Hera, though some held that he was the parthenogenous son of Hera alone, springing from that goddess in the same way as his fire springs from earth. Born lame and weak, he was so disliked by his mother that she threw him from Olympus into the sea. There he was cared for in a grotto under the sea by the sea goddesses Thetis and Eurynome. After nine years Hera welcomed him back to Olympus, where he set up his smithy. However, he was once again flung from Olympus, this time by Zeus after he had taken Hera's side. He took a whole day to fall, finally landing at nightfall on the island of Lemnos. Later writers say that it was this second fall from Olympus that was the cause of his lameness, the impact permanently dislocating his hip.

Hephaistos once again returned to Olympus and acted as a mediator between Zeus and Hera, and even though he was the constant butt of the gods' jokes he made each of their palaces. He also made robot tables for the gods that went wherever the gods wanted them, Zeus's throne and scepter, Agamemnon's scepter, the gold and silver dogs of Alcinous, the magnificent armor of Achilles as ordered by Thetis, the necklace of Harmonia, the fire-breathing bulls of Aeëtes with brazen feet, the bow and arrows of Artemis, the golden dog of Rhea, which had been set to guard the cradle of the infant Zeus, and the first woman, Pandora. He also made a golden throne for Hera, but when she sat on it she was bound fast. Hephaistos then left Olympus and refused to return until Dionysos made him drunk and brought him back to release Hera. This story is obviously of later origin due to the appearance of Dionysos.

Later accounts place his workshop well away from Olympus, saying it lay on Sicily, where he was helped by the Cyclopes, either under Mount Etna or Mount Stromboli, where he forged the thunderbolts of Zeus and weapons for the other Olympian deities. His favorite spots on earth were Lemnos and volcanic islands such as Lipara, Hiera, Imbros, and Sicily. An annual festival, the Hephaistia, was held in Athens at which three men carrying torches competed in a race.

Homer says that Hephaistos was married to Aphrodite and fathered Eros by her, but she was constantly unfaithful to him. On one humorous occasion Hephaistos trapped Aphrodite and Ares in bed together under an almost invisible net he had made, then displayed the couple to the ridicule of the other gods and goddesses. *Iliad,* however, says that his wife was Charis; other sources name his wife as Aglaea (Aglaia), the youngest of the Graces.

While Hephaistos walked on the shore of Lake Triton with Zeus and Hermes, Zeus complained of a severe headache. Persuaded by Hermes to cleft open Zeus's skull, Hephaistos released the cause of discomfort, for Athene sprung from the wound, fully grown and fully armed. Hephaistos's lust for Athene and attempted rape of her on the Acropolis at Athens led to the birth of Erichthonius.

Hephaistos, god of fire and patron of smiths, was not a popular subject in Greek art, though he is usually portrayed as a vigorous, bearded man carrying a hammer or similar instrument, normally situated near an anvil and wearing an oval cape or chiton. His lameness does not appear to have been portrayed, but then, given the emphasis on perfection of Greek artisans, this does not surprise greatly. The Theseum, a magnificent temple overlooking the agora in Athens, built in 449 B.C. as the first monument in Perikles' Athenian rebuilding program, was dedicated to him and Athene. It is the best preserved of all Greek temples and was built in the metalworkers' quarter of the city.

See also: Aphrodite; Charis; Erichthonius; Pandora; Vulcan

Her~a, ~e

Greek

One of the 12 elite Olympian deities; daughter of Cronos and Rhea; sister of Poseidon, Zeus, Hades, Demeter, and Hestia. Identified by the Romans as Juno, Hera was worshipped as queen of the heavens and goddess of power and riches, the patroness of marriage and of women in general. In cult she was often worshipped in her aspect of Hera Teleia—"the Fulfilled"—a reflection of her most important role, that of goddess of marriage, the fulfillment of womanhood. She reluctantly became the second wife of her brother, Zeus, who sought her out at either Knossos or Argos in the form of a cuckoo, their wedding night being spent on Samos. As a wedding gift from her new husband, Hera received the tree with the golden apples that was later to be guarded by the Hesperides. A virgin goddess, she annually renewed her virginity by bathing in a spring near Argos, even though her virginity was compromised on several occasions. As she was, properly speaking, the only married goddess among the Olympians, some sources named the Ilithyiae as her daughters, though in classical times she was often equated with Eileithyia, the goddess of birth.

Though Hera was not a popular subject in classical art, several of the earliest Greek temples were dedicated to her, notably those at Olympia, Perachora, Samos, and above all Argos, where she was worshipped as patroness of the city. She also received cult in Athens. It was at Argos that she was said to have vied with Poseidon for mastery of the land. The river gods of the region decreed in favor of Hera, a decision that made Poseidon exact his revenge by drying up the springs that fed the rivers. The ruins of the Heraeum at Argos are extensive, and excavation has shown that the cult of Hera was well established by the eighth century B.C. Dating from about the same period are the remains of a temple and precinct at Samos, where Hera was once again considered patroness. At Olympia her worship vied with that of Zeus. A magnificent (though thoroughly ruined) temple of Hera can be visited at Agrigento (ancient Acragas) in southwest Sicily.

Hera's origin has sometimes been explained as lying with a Mycenaean palace goddess, but her name has not been found in the Linear B texts. Others say that she is a remembrance of a pre-Olympian goddess of Mother Earth, her tempestuous marriage to Zeus marking her absorption into the Indo-European system in which the male sky god is dominant. Cows were often sacrificed to her, leading to her being awarded the epithet Boöpis, or "cow-faced," though some have sought to connect this with the fact that she always seemed disagreeable, and would thus have carried a surly look. She may also have been later awarded the surname Argiva, as there is a temple to Hera Argiva in Italy that was built c. 460 B.C., though this is probably simply an epithet added to indicate the region from which the cult was brought to Italy.

When Typhon made his assault on Olympus, Hera fled to Egypt, along with the other gods and goddesses, Hera taking the form of a white cow. This story once again reflects the association of cows to Hera. The messengers of Hera were the four winds, which she entrusted to Aeolus since Zeus was likely to forget his duties and allow them to blow the earth and sea away. She, like Zeus, had the power to bestow the art of prophecy.

At one stage she conspired with Apollo and Poseidon to lead the Olympians against Zeus. Zeus having been put in chains, he was freed by Thetis and Briareus. Hera was then punished when Zeus bound anvils to her ankles and hung her out of Heaven by her wrists.

Several attempts were made on her virtue, notably by the giant Porphyrion; by Ixion, who was condemned to be bound to a fiery wheel revolving unceasingly through Tartarus; and by Endymion. However, Hera is best remembered for the persecution of Zeus's lovers—Leto, Io, Semele, and the daughters of Proteus—and for her general unkindly demeanor toward gods and heroes alike. When Leto was due to give birth to Apollo and Artemis, the twin children of Zeus, Hera made Leto wander from place to place until she gave birth to Artemis under a palm tree on Ortygia and Apollo on Delos. She then sent the giant Ityus to violate Leto as she was approaching Delphi with Artemis, but Tityus was killed by the arrows of Apollo and Artemis.

When Semele was pregnant six months with Dionysos, Hera disguised herself as an old woman and persuaded Semele to ask her mysterious lover, Zeus, to appear to her in his true form. Zeus reluctantly consented, and Semele was consumed by the fire from his thunderbolt. The unborn infant was sewn up in Zeus's thigh to be born three months later, but this did not stop Hera's hostility. When the child had been entrusted to Athamas and Ino of Boeotia, Hera sent Athamas mad so that he killed his own son. Still Hera continued to hound Dionysos. Once he grew to manhood Hera sent him mad so that he wandered through the world.

She was the mother of Ares, Hebe, and Hephaistos, the first two by Zeus, and Hephaistos parthenogenetically. So disgusted was she with Hephaistos that she flung him from Olympus. She blinded the seer Tiresias when he settled an argument between Zeus and herself over which of the sexes gained the more pleasure from sexual intercourse. His reply that a woman enjoyed it nine times as much as a man angered Hera.

She did, however, support Jason and the Argonauts in their quest for the Golden Fleece. She and Athene also supported the Greeks, particularly Achilles, against Troy after Paris had awarded the Apple of Discord to Aphrodite in favor of herself and Athene even though she had offered Paris rule in Asia. At one stage she helped the Greeks by persuading Zeus to lie with her on Mount Gargarus while Posedion egged on the Greeks.

Her hostility reached new bounds, however, with regard to the hero who bears her name, Heracles. When Zeus boasted that he was about to become the father of a son who would be called Heracles, or "Glory of Hera," and who would be the ruler of the house of Perseus, Hera exacted from him a promise that any son born that day to the house of Perseus should be king. Having made Zeus promise, Hera brought on the birth of Eurystheus, a grandson of Perseus, and delayed Alcmene's labor, so that Heracles and his twin brother Iphicles (though one day younger through the complex conception of Heracles) were born later. Alcmene was greatly afraid of the retribution Hera might take on her, so she exposed Heracles. However, Hera saw the infant and nursed him in error, thus conferring on him his eventual right to immortality. Hera now returned the infant Heracles to Alcmene.

When the great hero reached manhood, Hera sent him mad so that he killed his own children and two of Iphicles'. Having been restored to sanity he sought purification and then went to consult the Delphic Oracle, and there the Pythia called him Heracles for the first time. She advised him to go to Tiryns and serve King Eurystheus for 12 years, doing whatever he asked without question. At the end of that time his due immortality would be conferred on him.

Hera continued to harry Heracles throughout these 12 years. During his second labor, which was to kill the Hydra, one of the monstrous offspring of Typhon and Echidne, Hera (who had raised the Hydra) sent a huge crab to hinder Heracles, but he simply crushed it. Hera placed its image in the heavens.

During his ninth labor, which was to fetch for Admete the golden girdle of Hippolyte, Hera roused the Amazons so that they attacked Heracles, but he easily fought them off, killing their leaders and completing his allotted task.

When Heracles and Telamon sailed from Troy, having sacked the city, Hera raised a terrible storm that shipwrecked Heracles on Cos, where faced more perils. However, after Heracles died and had ascended to Olympus, he and Hera were finally reconciled to the extent that Heracles married her daughter, Hebe.

Hera was usually depicted as a fully clothed and imposing, matronlike woman whose attributes were a diadem, veil, and scepter. She has close associations with the cow, which was often sacrificed to her, a possible reflection of her origin as an earth goddess. Also sacred to her was the cuckoo and, later, the peacock. She transferred the eyes of Argus to the tail of the peacock after Argus had been slain by Hermes. She also changed Argos, the builder of the *Argo Navis,* into a peacock before translating him to the heavens as the constellation Pavo, his ship joining him there as four other constellations.

See also: Aeolus; Dionysos; Heracles; Ixion; Semele

Hera~cles, ~kles

Greco-Roman

The most famous of all the Greek heroes; he is probably better known by the Roman form of his name, Hercules. At one time thought to be of Dorian origin, Heracles, it is now clear, belongs firmly within the Mycenaean period. He is the remarkable formulation *heros theos* (hero god), a semidivine mortal destined for apotheosis.

Legend says that Heracles was the son of Alcmene and Zeus, conceived when Zeus took the form of Alcmene's husband, Amphitryon, while he was away doing battle with the Taphians to avenge the death of Alcmene's brothers, for Alcmene refused to consummate their union until she had been avenged. Zeus visited Alcmene in Amphitryon's form and told her that he had been victorious. Her actual husband returned the following day, and Alcmene's surprise and delight at his sexual prowess led to her conception of twins, a concept common throughout classical Greek legend, indeed throughout Indo-European mythologies.

Nine months later Zeus boasted that he was about to become the father of a child who would one day rule the house of Perseus. Hera, continually jealous of her husband's philandering ways, decided to thwart him. She first extracted a promise from Zeus that any son born that day into the house of Perseus would become king. She then dispatched the goddess of childbirth, Eileithyia, to delay Alcmene's labor while she brought on the birth of Eurystheus, the son of Sthenelus, king of Tiryns, and also of Zeus's line through Perseus. This child grew up to become the king of Tiryns and Mycenae.

Alcmene was in agonizing pain because of the delayed labor she was experiencing. To relieve her, Galanthis, her servant, rushed in and distracted Eleithyia, thereby allowing the birth to take place. Alcmene bore the semidivine Heracles and the wholly human Iphicles; Eileithyia turned Galanthis into a weasel. Fearing Hera, Alcmene exposed Heracles, but he was found and nursed, in error, by Hera, thus conferring on him the right to immortality. Returned to Alcmene, Heracles prospered and soon proved his prowess when Hera sent two snakes to attack the infant in his cradle. Heracles simply grasped one in each hand and squeezed the life out of them.

The young Heracles was taught how to drive a chariot by Amphitryon, fighting by

Castor, how to sing and play the lyre by Eumolpus, wrestling by Autolycus, and archery by the king of Oechalia, Eurytus. Even though the Greeks normally scorned the bow and arrow as the weapon of a coward, they became Heracles' characteristic weapon. His lyre lessons continued under Linus, but when Linus one day censured Heracles these lessons came to an abrupt halt (Heracles killed his teacher with his own lyre). Amphitryon sent Heracles away to herd cattle.

Soon after his eighteenth birthday Heracles visited the court of King Thespius of Thespiae, where he was asked to rid the land of a lion that had been terrorizing Mount Cithaeron. Heracles agreed on the condition that he was, on the 50 successive nights of the chase, to sleep with Thespius's 50 daughters. One refused and was condemned to remain a virgin forever, becoming a priestess in Heracles' temple. Heracles killed the lion with a club of wild olive, another of his well-known attributes. Some sources, notably Apollodorus, say that it was the skin of this lion that Heracles wore as his armor, the head becoming his helmet, but this is more usually said to have been the pelt and head of the Nemaean Lion.

Leaving Thespiae, Heracles now championed Thebes, marrying in the process Megara, the eldest daughter of King Creon of Thebes, Iphicles marrying her youngest sister. When Orchomenus, the Minyan king, sent his heralds to collect a tribute from Thebes, Heracles mutilated the heralds and then led an army against Orchomenus, a campaign that he won but during which Amphitryon was killed. Heracles then made Orchomenus a tributary to Thebes. When he returned from this war, however, he found that Creon's throne had been usurped by Lycus, whom he killed. Hera then sent him mad so that he killed his own children and two of Iphicles'; some sources say he killed his wife, Megara, as well.

After he left Thebes, Heracles' sanity was restored to him, and following purification he sought the advice of the Delphic Oracle. There the Pythia, who was the first to call him Heracles, advised him to travel to the court of King Eurystheus, King of Tiryns and Mycenae, and Argos, at least according to some. There Heracles was to serve him, doing whatever he bid without question for 12 years. If he com-

pleted this period of service immortality would be conferred upon him, as was his right. Reluctantly Heracles set out for Tiryns. His nephew, Iolaus, the eldest son of Iphicles, accompanied him as his charioteer and faithful companion.

This period of Heracles' life forms the most famous part of his saga. Though all sources say that Eurystheus set Heracles 12 immense tasks or labors, some add the additional fact that originally there were only ten, but Eurystheus disallowed two after they had been completed, so Heracles had to perform 12 in all. These, the 12 Great Labors of Heracles, form the basis of innumerable works of art and contain some of the most notable fiends, beasts, and monsters of classical mythology. The most notable representations of Heracles' labors are the series of metopes from the temple of Zeus at Olympia and those from the temple of Hephaistos at Athens. The order of the labors had become canonical by the sixth century B.C., but they are known from both art and literature that dates from the eighth century B.C. They very neatly carry Heracles from his center in the Argolid to all four quarters of the known world:

1. To kill and bring back the skin of the Nemaean Lion, or Cleonaean Lion, the son of Typhon, or Orthros, and Echidne, which lived in a cave on a hill at Nemea near Cleonae. This cave was still shown to travelers during the eighteenth century. As the lion's pelt was impenetrable to any weapon, Heracles fought it bare-handed, strangled it, skinned it with its own claws, and thereafter wore its pelt as his armor. Eurystheus was so terrified by the amazing power Heracles possessed that he now took refuge in a brazen urn whenever the great hero approached. The Nemaean Lion itself was transferred to the heavens as the constellation Leo.

2. To kill the Hydra of Lerna, a huge serpent, another of the monstrous offspring of Typhon and Echidne (though raised by Hera), which had a doglike body and seven, or nine, snaky heads, one of them immortal. It lived at the sevenfold source of the River Amymone and haunted the malarial marshes of Lerna. Some commentators make it a representation of the noxious air to be found in those marshes. Heracles found that every time he cut off one

of the heads, two grew from the stump. He was also harried by a huge crab, sent by Hera, which kept nipping at his toe. Crushing the crab, which subsequently became the constellation Cancer, Heracles called on his nephew, Iolaus, to cauterize each stump with a firebrand when he cut the head off. Finally, with all the heads removed in this manner, and having buried the immortal head underneath a huge rock, Heracles overcame the great beast. He then dipped his arrows in the Hydra's gall to make them even more deadly. However, when Eurystheus learned of Iolaus's help, he discounted the labor, so another had to be added to the cycle.

3. To capture alive, without causing blood loss, the Ceryneian Hind, a deer with brazen hooves and golden horns that was sacred to the goddess Artemis. Heracles pursued it tirelessly for a whole year before he caught it while crossing the River Ladon by firing an arrow that pinned the forelegs together without any loss of blood. He then brought it back to show Eurystheus, carrying it across his shoulders.

4. To capture the Erymantian Boar, a savage creature that lived on Mount Erymanthus in Arcadia and had come down to ravage Psophis. En route to kill this beast, Heracles was entertained by the centaur Pholus, who owned a cask of wine given to him by Dionysos. When this was opened other centaurs came and attempted to steal the divine drink. While Heracles was driving them away, Pholus accidentally poisoned himself on one of Heracles' arrows. Additionally, Heracles accidentally wounded his old friend, the centaur Cheiron. Unable to die due to his immortality, Cheiron longed to be released from his agony, a release that mercifully he gained when he gave up his immortality to Prometheus. Heracles managed to capture the boar alive by driving it into a snowdrift and binding it in chains. He then carried it back to Eurystheus. Some sources say that Eurystheus was so afraid that he hid in a sunken oil jar until Heracles had taken it away again, though this would have been extremely difficult, for Eurystheus was normally considered to have taken to hiding in a brazen urn whenever Heracles approached following his successful completion of the first labor.

At this point there was a break in the 12 labors as Heracles heard of the expedition being mounted by Jason and rushed off, along with Hylas, to become one of the Argonauts. At one stage the Argonauts put into Mysia. There Hylas, while fetching water, was abducted by the Naiades, leaving nothing but an empty pitcher. Heracles left the *Argo Navis* for a while in a vain search for him. Heracles, however, returned to Eurystheus's court on the successful completion of the quest, and the labors recommenced.

5. To clean, in one day, the Augean Stables, the cattle sheds of King Augeias of Elis, who had more sheep and cattle than any other man on earth. The stables had not been cleaned for so long that they were now clogged with dung. Having first agreed to the fee with Augeias—he would receive one-tenth of the cattle as payment for the heinous job, a bargain witnessed by Phyleus, Augeias's son—Heracles cleaned them in the allotted single day by diverting the River Alpheus through them. Augeias refused to pay him when he discovered that Heracles had been acting on the instructions of Eurystheus; Phyleus's loyalty to the contract led to his banishment. Subsequently, when Eurystheus heard that Heracles had intended to receive payment for the labor set him, he discounted the labor and added another, bringing the total to 12.

6. To kill the man-eating Stymphalian Birds sacred to Ares. With bronze beaks and claws and razor-sharp feathers, which they fired at pursuers, they haunted Lake Stymphalus or Lake Stymphalia in Arcadia. Heracles, with the help of Athene, hid in the rushes and, startling them with a rattle so that they flew into the air, shot them with his arrows. Some said that rather than being killed they simply flew off to the island of Aretius in the Black Sea, where they were later discovered by the Argonauts. This would, however, upset the chronology of the saga, for the expedition of the Argonauts is traditionally said to have taken place between the fourth and fifth labors.

7. To capture the Cretan Bull, a gift to Minos from Poseidon, the father of the Minotaur. It was Heracles' first task set outside of the Peloponnesos, taking him south to the island of Crete. Heracles politely turned down the offers of help he received from Minos and single-

handedly captured the bull and brought it back to Tiryns, where Eurystheus set it free again. It then wandered through Greece, settling in and terrorizing the area around Marathon, whereupon it became known as the Marathonian Bull. It was later captured by Theseus, who took it to Athens for sacrifice to Athene.

8. To capture the man-eating mares of Diomedes, a task that was to take Heracles to Thrace. There the king of the Bistones, Diomedes, kept the four mares, which fed on human flesh. On his way to Thrace Heracles descended into the Underworld and persuaded Hades to return Alcestis to Admetus. Arriving in Thrace, Heracles, along with a few companions, drove the mares down to the sea, where they were left in the charge of Abderus while Heracles returned to repel the Bistones. However, Abderus was soon eaten by the horses, whereupon Heracles cured them of their man-eating trait by killing Diomedes and feeding him to them. He then returned to Tiryns with the mares before releasing them on Mount Olympus, where they were killed by wild beasts.

9. To fetch for Admete, the daughter of Eurystheus, the girdle of Hippolyte, a gift to the Amazon queen from Ares. Heracles was accompanied on this expedition, which took him to the land of the Amazons—who were said to live to the northeast on the southern shore of the Black Sea—by Telamon and Theseus. Hippolyte agreed to give Heracles her girdle, but Hera roused the Amazon warriors, who attacked them, and in the ensuing fray Hippolyte was killed along with many other Amazon leaders. It was on this expedition that Theseus abducted Antiope. On their return to Tiryns the party stopped at Troy, which was at that time being ravaged by a monster sent by Poseidon, as Laomedon, king of Troy, had refused to pay Poseidon and Apollo for building the city walls. The monster could only be appeased by the sacrifice of Hesione, Laomedon's daughter, but Heracles killed it, thereby rescuing Hesione. Laomedon refused to reward Heracles with the white horses he had received from Zeus in exchange for Ganymede, thus storing up more trouble for himself later on.

10. To fetch, without making either demand or payment, the cattle of the three-bodied,

three-headed King Geryon, who lived far to the west on the island of Erytheia. There the herd was guarded by the herdsman Eurytion, a son of Ares, and his two-headed dog, Orthros, another of the monstrous offspring of Typhon and Echidne. To reach the land of Geryon, Heracles was lent a golden bowl or vessel by Helios, the loan being made as a mark of Helios's respect after Heracles had shot at him when he shone too brightly. Having reached his objective, Heracles killed Eurytion and Orthros with his wild olive club and made off with the cattle. When Geryon chased him, Heracles killed him as well. He returned the golden vessel to Helios when he first landed at Tartessus in Spain.

To mark his achievement, Heracles erected two pillars, Calpe and Abyla, at the western end of the Mediterranean. The Pillars of Heracles are said to lie on either side of the Strait of Gibraltar, though some sources say that they were originally joined, Heracles parting them to allow the waters of the Atlantic Ocean to mingle with those of the Mediterranean Sea. Another, more suspect story says that Heracles actually formed the Mediterranean when he parted the isthmus, which enclosed the bowl that was to be filled with water from the Atlantic. Heracles now traveled back to Tiryns, following the northern coastline of the Mediterranean. Near Marseilles he was attacked by the Ligurians but beat them off with huge stones, which still lie scattered on the plain around Marseilles. He then traveled down Italy, where, according to a later, Roman tradition he fought with and dispatched the giant Cacus, who lived in a cave near the future site of Rome. One of the cattle escaped from his care near Rhegium and fled to western Sicily, where it was commandeered by King Eryx. Heracles followed it, fought and killed Eryx, and then made his way back to Eurystheus.

11. To fetch the golden apples of the Hesperides, which grew on a tree that Hera had received from Ge at her wedding, and which she had planted in a garden on the slopes of Mount Atlas. There the tree was guarded by the Hesperides and the dragon Ladon, yet another of the offspring of Typhon and Echidne. As the actual location of the garden was not easy to find, Nereus, or Proteus,

was consulted, but he, as was the way of sea gods, forced Heracles to wrestle him before he would divulge the necessary information. During the course of this contest Nereus, or Proteus, changed his form many times, but Heracles resolutely held on, and finally the sea god gave him what he required. The Hesperides were to be found in a land beyond the River Oceanus. To travel there Heracles followed a somewhat curious route that initially led him to the Caucasus, where he released the Titan Prometheus from his bonds; some say Heracles took further advice from Prometheus. The arrow Heracles used to shoot the vulture that was eternally feeding on Prometheus's liver was placed in the heavens as the constellation Sagitta. The route then took him to the northern African coast. In the course of his journey Heracles had several adventures. He was very nearly sacrificed in Egypt by King Busiris, but Heracles killed him at the eleventh hour and so managed to escape. He then went on to wrestle the giant Antaeus, a contest that he won by lifting Antaeus from the ground.

Some sources say that the release of Prometheus, his eleventh-hour escape from Busiris, and his fight with Antaeus happened during his return to Tiryns after he had completed this eleventh labor. At the very edge of the world he found Atlas performing his eternal task—holding up the sky. Heracles persuaded the giant to fetch the apples for him while he held up the sky in his place. Atlas was only too happy to oblige, for he saw an opportunity to be rid of the task forever. When he returned he suggested that he should take the apples to Eurystheus for Heracles, but Heracles saw through the ruse and, pretending to agree, had Atlas once more take the sky while he adjusted his position. With Atlas once again burdened, Heracles snatched the apples and hurried back to Tiryns, leaving the hapless Atlas at his eternal task. Eurystheus made a gift of the apples to Heracles, who dedicated them to Athene. She then returned them to their rightful place.

12. To fetch Cerberus, the three-headed watchdog of the Underworld. In preparation for this, the most difficult of his labors, Heracles had himself initiated into the Eleusinian Mysteries by Eumolpus or Mu-

saeus. Then, guided by Hermes and Athene, he descended into the Underworld from Taenarum in Laconia, where after having freed Theseus and killed one of Hades' cattle he persuaded Hades to let him "borrow" Cerberus on the proviso that he could capture the terrible beast without using any weapon. Heracles did so by simply grabbing Cerberus by the throat. When Heracles returned to Tiryns, Eurystheus was, as usual, so terrified that he ordered Heracles to immediately return the hound. Having done so, Heracles was freed from his obligation to Eurystheus, the last labor having been completed.

Upon leaving Tiryns, Heracles returned to Thebes and gave his wife, Megara, to his nephew, Iolaus. Heracles then heard that his friend Eurytus, king of Oechalia, was offering his daughter, Iole, as the prize in an archery contest to any man who could surpass him and his sons. Heracles won it with ease, but Eurytus refused the prize because Heracles had killed his own children, a position supported by all of Eurytus's children. Heracles stole his cattle instead. Iphitus, Eurytus's brother, invited Heracles to join the search for the cattle, not knowing that it was Heracles who had stolen them. When Iphitus became suspicious Heracles killed him by throwing him from a rooftop, a crime for which he was afflicted by a strange disease. He was purified by Deiphobus at Amyclae, but still the illness would not leave him, so he went to consult the Delphic Oracle. However, the Pythia refused to speak to him, so Heracles stole the tripod upon which the Pythia sat and fought Apollo for it. Their fight was broken up by Zeus with one of his thunderbolts. The Pythia now informed Heracles that to expiate his crime he must sell himself into slavery and give the price he received to the sons of Iphitus.

Heracles complied and was sold by Hermes to become the slave to Omphale, widow of Tmolus and the queen of Lydia. According to some, he swapped his clothes with the queen for the period of his enslavement, which varies between one and three years. While serving her he captured Cercopes, killed a snake that was terrorizing the lands around the River Sangarius, and killed the aggressive farmer Syleus, who forced strangers to work in his vineyard. Some authorities consider that

Heracles is, in his guise as the killer of the snake of Sangarius, depicted in the constellation Ophiuchus, though this is more usually associated with Asclepios.

Having served his years with Omphale, Heracles set out to avenge himself on those who had previously insulted him. Raising an army, and accompanied by Telamon, he marched against Troy. There he killed Laomedon and seized Hesione, giving her to Telamon, by whom she became the mother of Teucer. She did, however, secure the release of her brother, Podarces, by making a gift to Heracles, after which Podarces took the new name Priam.

Leaving Troy, Heracles' ships were driven by foul winds—sent by the ever-hostile Hera—to Cos. There Heracles captured the city of Meropes, after which the gods sent Athene to bring him to Phlegra to help them in their war against the giants, which was fought on two fronts—on Earth and in Olympus. With his help—Heracles discovered a magic herb of invulnerability and always struck the final blow—they won this war, a remarkable achievement for Heracles, who was, after all, yet a mere mortal. He now raised another army, this time against Augeias, but was surprisingly defeated, due mainly to the participation of the Molionidae, the twin warrior-sons of Actor, who fought on the side of Augeias. Heracles later shot them with his poisoned arrows at Cleonae, and a second expedition mounted against Augeias was successful, though some sources say that Heracles spared Augeias.

Having destroyed Augeias, his sons, and his allies Heracles established the Olympic Games in celebration, fetching from the source of the River Danube the wild olive tree, its leaves to crown the victor. He then went on to destroy Pylos, which had fought on the side of Elis, killing Neleus and his sons, including Periclymenus (who had disguised himself as an eagle), but sparing Nestor. Heracles then attacked Hippocoön of Sparta with the help of Cepheus and his 20 sons. Having killed Hippocoön and all his sons, he restored Tyndareus to the throne of Sparta. He then seduced Auge, daughter of Aleus, king of Tegea, and she became the mother of Telephus. In the battle with Sparta, Cepheus and his sons were killed, but victory was ensured when Heracles killed Hippocoön.

After four years in Arcadia, Heracles traveled to Aetolia, and there fell in love with Deianeira, the daughter of Oeneus, king of Calydon and Pleuron. He fought with Achelous, the mighty river god son of Oceanos and Tethys, her other suitor, and won the right to her hand. He then sent Iolaus as the leader of his sons by the daughters of Thespius to settle in Sardinia. Three years later, at a banquet, he accidentally killed Oeneus's cupbearer, Eunomus, and took his wife and their son Hyllus into voluntary exile.

While they were crossing the River Evenus the centaur Nessus, who was carrying Deianeira on his back, tried to run off with her. Heracles shot him through the breast with one of his poisoned arrows, and as Nessus lay dying the centaur gave Deianeira some of his poisoned blood, saying that it would act as a charm if Heracles should ever be unfaithful to her.

Traveling north Heracles did battle with Cycnus before he left Deianeira in Trachis while he went back to take Iole from Eurytus. Heracles killed Eurytus and all his family and sent Iole to Deianeira in Trachis while he visited Caenum in Euboea to prepare a thanksgiving to Zeus, sending Lichas to Deianeira to fetch a white robe to wear at the ceremony. Fearful that she might lose Heracles to Iole, Deianeira smeared some of Nessus's blood onto the shirt. It proved deadly, for when Heracles put on the shirt it burned away his flesh. Trying to remove the shirt simply tore great chunks of his skin away with it. Dying an agonizingly slow death, Heracles threw Lichas into the sea and then returned to Trachis. When Deianeira realized what she had unwittingly done, she hanged herself. Heracles then took his son, Hyllus, to Mount Oeta and there, having made him promise to marry Iole, instructed him to build a funeral pyre. However, when he had climbed onto it, nobody could be persuaded to light it until Philoctetes agreed to do so. Heracles gave Philoctetes his bow and arrows in grateful thanks. The fire engulfed Heracles and he ascended to Olympus, thunderbolts from Zeus demolishing the pyre. Deified at last as was his right, and finally reconciled with Hera, Heracles married her daughter, Hebe.

Eurystheus was now determined to expel Heracles' children from Greece. They found sanctuary in Athens, but Eurystheus attacked the city. He was, however, resisted by Theseus (or by his son, Demophoön), Iolaus, and Hyllus. An oracle foretold that Eurystheus would be defeated only if one of Heracles' children should be sacrificed. Macaria, his daughter, willingly took her own life. Eurystheus was then duly defeated by either Iolaus or Hyllus, his mortal wound being inflicted by Alcmene.

The Heracleian cult was widespread in Greece, and, unlike other heroes, for obvious reasons, he has no single tomb. Rather he had a special type of *heroön* that consisted of a quadrilateral stone base supporting four pillars, one at each corner, the front one surmounted by a pediment, the space between them unroofed. This feature was especially common at Sicyon. He had but a few festivals and received none of the cult status of the Olympian deities. After his apotheosis, Heracles was identified with the gods Melqart of Tyre and Sandan of Tarsus, as both of these cults involved the ritual burning of images on a funeral pyre. Images of Heracles are to be found as far east as Persia, but he remains, without doubt, a character, whether mortal or god, of Greek derivation who later was absorbed almost unaltered into the Roman tradition, that tradition adding just minute detail to his already complex and complete life.

See also: Abderus; Alcmene; Amphitryon; Augeias; Cheiron; Deianeira; Eurystheus; Geryon; Hyllus; Iolaus; Iole; Jason; Megara; Minos; Pholus; Theseus

Heracles, Pillars of
Greco-Roman

Two rocks, identified with Abyla and Calpe, on either side of the Strait of Gibraltar that were supposedly set up as markers of the western limit of the known world by Heracles during the course of his tenth labor. One dubious story says that the two rocks were originally connected, forming an isthmus that cut across the entrance of the Mediterranean Sea joining Africa to Europe. Heracles was said to have split them apart to form the pillars named in his honor, thus allowing the waters

of the Atlantic Ocean to mingle with those of the Mediterranean. An even more suspect story says that it was this division of the isthmus that formed the Mediterranean itself.

See also: Abyla; Calpe; Ceuta

Heracles, 12 Great Labors of
Greco-Roman

The 12 Great Labors undertaken by Heracles for Eurystheus. The order in which the labors was undertaken sometimes varies, though the labors themselves remain constant. For a full description of the 12 labors see the entry for Heracles.

See also: Eurystheus

Heracl(e)idae
Greek

Collective name for the children of Heracles. They and their grandmother, Alcmene, where expelled from Tiryns and all other regions of Greece by Eurystheus, though they managed to find refuge in Athens (some say Marathon). Eurystheus attacked and was resisted by Theseus (or his son, Demophoön), Iolaus, and Hyllus. An oracle demanded the sacrifice of one of Heracles' children in order to secure the safety of Athens. Macaria, Heracles' daughter, committed suicide, and Eurystheus was duly defeated, being finally dispatched by Alcmene.

Nonetheless, the Heracleidae were driven out of the Peloponnesos and consulted the Delphic Oracle, which gave them the obscure instruction to try again at the third harvest. Literal translation of this prophesy failed, for three years later Hyllus attempted to return to the Peloponnesos. He was killed, and the remaining Heracleidae retreated to Doris. The oracle was finally understood by the great-grandsons—they were the third harvest. This time when they invaded the Peloponnesos they were successful, killing Tisamenus, Orestes' successor. Argos fell to Temenus, Messenia to Cresphontes, and Laconia to the sons of Aristodemus. They gave Elis away and left the Arcadians their own land untouched.

This legend clearly derives from the conquest of the Achaeans by later invaders, though the so-called Dorian Invasion is now seen as a gradual seepage rather than a full-blown invasion. This succession of a new order to replace the Mycenaeans was known to the Greeks as the return of the Heracleidae.

Herce

Romano-Etruscan

The name given to Heracles by the Etruscans, with whom he was a most popular deity, the god of merchants and patron of military raids. He was also, somewhat curiously, considered as a chthonic fertility and water god.

Hercules

Roman

The name by which Heracles was known to the Romans. Known as "the Unconquerable," Hercules became the patron of merchants and soldiers. Although the origins of the Roman cult of Hercules may be Phoenician, they certainly exhibit later Etruscan influence (Hercules was known as Herce to the Etruscans). Although it seems likely that the Etruscans introduced the Greek rites for his worship, Roman tradition attributed their introduction to Romulus.

Astronomical: A large constellation lying in the northern celestial hemisphere between approximate right ascensions 16h00m and 18h55m, declination from +5° to +52°. The Babylonians identified the constellation with Gilgamesh, the demigod-hero who overthrew the powers of chaos at the beginning of the world. The Phoenicians recognized it as the sea god Melkarth. The name Hercules has also been applied to an impact crater located in the upper western quadrant of the surface of the moon next to that known as Atlas.

Hercules, Pillars of

Roman

The Roman name for the Pillars of Heracles.

Hercules, 12 Great Labors of

Roman

See Heracles.

Hermaphrodit~os, ~us

Greek

A son of Hermes and Aphrodite who was raised by the nymphs on Mount Ida in Phrygia. While bathing in a spring near Halicarnassus in Caria, the nymph Sal(a)macis fell in love with him. She enfolded him in her arms and prayed to the gods that they should never be parted, a prayer that was answered when their two bodies merged to form a being, half-male and half-female, hence *hermaphrodite*. Since then, all men who have bathed in the spring of Sal(a)macis have shared Hermaphroditos's curse.

Statues showing women's breasts and male genitalia were carved in Greece from at least the fourth century B.C.

Hermes

Greek

Identified by the Romans with Mercurius, Hermes has his origins in a pre-Hellenic deity who dwelled in the cairns, or *herma*, that were set up by shepherds as landmarks in wild countryside. His most common representation in antiquity was as a plain pillar with protruding male genitals, sometimes with a bearded head on top, which stood at street corners and doorways. He is thus a protector against wild animals and a guide to travelers, a delimiter of space, and, in that sense, an intermediary between separate or conflicting parties. He was also identified with a similar deity worshipped in Minoan Crete, a son, or lover, of the Great Goddess and by association a fertility god.

Classical legend, having absorbed the earlier traits of this god, made Hermes the son of Zeus and the Pleiad Maia, herself an embodiment of the Great Goddess, a daughter of Atlas and goddess of midwives, whence Hermes' name Atlantiades. Said to have been born in a cave on Mount Cyllene in Arcadia, from which he was also sometimes called Cyllenius, Hermes grew to manhood with amazing speed. When just a few hours old Hermes went to Pieria and there stole some of the oxen of Apollo. He drove these to Pylos, dragging them backwards to fool any pursuer by the reversed hoof prints, before returning to Cyllene, where he invented the lyre by stringing cowgut across a tortoise shell covered with an ox hide. Apollo, upon discovering the identity of the cattle thief, denounced him to Zeus, who ordered Hermes to return the oxen to their rightful owner. This he did, but when Apollo heard the lyre he was so delighted that he exchanged the stolen cattle for ownership of the instrument. The two became firm friends, and Apollo led Hermes back to be reconciled with Zeus. He was unusual in Olympus, being one of the few characters ever to find favor with Hera, who was usually hostile to one and all.

Hermes was given supreme power over animals by Zeus and was thus invoked as a protector of flocks against wild animals. He was additionally appointed by Zeus to his best-known post, that of herald or messenger to the gods, by which he became patron of travelers. He was also made herald to Hades as Psychopompus, the god who guided the spirits of the dead through the Underworld to stand before the three eternal judges Minos, Rhadamanthus, and Aeacus. As herald Hermes came to be regarded as the god of eloquence, and it was in this role that St. Paul was mistaken for Hermes in Lystra in Asia Minor (see Acts 14:9–12). As heralds also promoted peace and commerce, Hermes also became looked upon as the god of peaceable trade.

However, his early trait of a thief also featured in his character, for Hermes was also god of prudence and cunning, even theft itself. He was also considered a fertility god, and as god of luck he presided over games of dice and other matters of chance. He also presided over dreams, believed by many to be messages delivered by Hermes from the gods, and it became customary to make the last libation to him before going to sleep. Many inventions other than the lyre were attributed to Hermes. In association with the Fates he was said to have devised the Greek alphabet. Alone he was ascribed with the invention of weights and measures, the game of knuckle-bones, the musical scale, astronomy, olive cultivation, boxing, and gymnastics. All these inventions are clearly pre-Hellenic and were later taken over by the Hellenic god Apollo. The story of Hermes' theft of Apollo's oxen, and the subsequent trade-off between the two gods may illustrate the manner in which the Hellenes took over these arts in the name of Apollo, though he shared a patronage of music with Apollo and was later attributed with the invention of the pipes, the instrument favored by his son, Pan.

Hermes features in many well-known, classical stories such as the persuasion of Hephaistos to cleave open the skull of Zeus to release the fully grown Athene; the release of Ares after his imprisonment by the Aloeidae; the delivery of Pandora to Epimetheus; the rescue of Dionysos, whom he escorted to Mount Nysa; the punishment of Ixion; the gift of a lyre to Amphion, the music moving the stones of the Cadmea into place of their own accord; the selling of Heracles to Omphale; the judgment of Paris; the provision of the sickle with which Perseus beheaded Medusa; the giving of the magical plant moly to Odysseus to counter the powers of Circe; the boiling of the limbs of Pelops; the guiding of Heracles into the Underworld to capture Cerberus as his twelfth labor; the return of Protesilaus to Laodameia for just three hours, after which she died; and the leading of Priam to Achilles during the Trojan War to ransom the body of Hector. He is, perhaps, best known for the slaying of Argus, the 100-eyed giant who was sent by Hera to watch over Io.

Hermes became the lover of Aphrodite, Hecate, and Persephone as well as a number of nymphs and several mortals. Several children are attributed to Hermes, notably Echion, the herald to the Argonauts; Autolycus the thief, his son by Chione; Pan by Penelope, whom he visited disguised as a goat; Myrtilus by Clytie, the charioteer of Oenomaus; Cephalos by Herse; Hermaphroditos by Aphrodite; and Daphnis. Later sources say that Hermes, Ares, or Zeus fathered Eros on Aphrodite.

Worship of Hermes flourished in Arcadia, where he was found in the company of the Arcadian deity Pan as well as the Muses, who presided over many of the arts Hermes reportedly invented. Worship spread to Athens, where Hermes became one of the most loved of all the Olympian deities.

In classical art Hermes was usually portrayed as a clean-shaven, youthful or athletic figure wearing the *petasus,* a wide-brimmed traveling hat that was, in later times, adorned with wings, and the *alipes,* his winged sandals.

He also carried a *kerykeion*, or *caduceus*, the winged herald's staff, its white ribbons later becoming mistaken for serpents due to his association with Hades. Early artistic representations tended to show Hermes as a bearded man of mature years wearing a long tunic. Sacred to Hermes were the tortoise, the palm tree, the number four, and some kinds of fish. Sacrifices to him usually took the form of incense, honey, cakes, pigs, lambs, and kids.

Astronomical: The name Hermes has been applied to one of the asteroids.

See also: Aphrodite; Maia; Mercury; Pan; Pleiades

Herminus, Titius
Roman

One of the two Roman warriors who responded to the plea of Publius Horatius Cocles to hold off Porsenna's troops while the Pons Sublicius, the last bridge across the River Tiber, was demolished. His corespondent was Spurius Lartius, the pair of them being sent back to safety moments before the bridge collapsed.

Hermione
Greek

Daughter of Menelaus and Helen, wife of Orestes (the son of Agamemnon, her uncle, and his wife, Clytemnestra). Hermione was claimed by Neoptolemus when she and her father came to Sparta, but Tyndareus, her grandfather, had already betrothed her to Orestes, who either killed his rival or had him killed.

See also: Helen; Menelaus; Orestes

Hero
Greek

Priestess of Aphrodite at Sestos on the European shore of the Hellespont. She was in love with Leander, a youth who lived in Abydos, a settlement on the other side of the channel. Every night Leander swam the short stretch of water that separated them, guided by a lantern hung out by Hero. One stormy night the lamp blew out and Leander drowned. In her grief Hero threw herself into the sea.

See also: Leander

Herodotus
Greek

Greek historian (c. 484–424 B.C.) born at Halicarnassus, a Greek colony on the coast of Asia Minor. He traveled widely in Asia Minor, the Aegean Islands, Greece, Macedonia, Thrace, the coasts of the Black Sea, Persia, Tyre, Egypt, and Cyrene before settling in 443 B.C. at Thurii, a colony founded by Athens on the Tarentine Gulf, southern Italy, where he had previously spent some four years. During his travels he collected historical, geographical, ethnographical, mythological, and archaeological material for his nine-book history of the world, which recorded not only the wars fought by Greece but also the reasons behind them. The first four books record the conquest of the Greek colonies in Asia Minor by Croesus as well as the histories of Lydia, Persia, Egypt, and Babylon. The final five books record the history of the two great Persian Wars (500–479 B.C.). Called "the father of history" by Cicero, Herodotus was the first historian to apply critical evaluation to his material.

See also: Helicon

Herse
Greek

Daughter of Cecrops who was loved by Hermes, by whom she became the mother of Cephalos. It was to Herse and her sisters that the infant Erichthonius was entrusted.

See also: Cecrops; Erichthonius

Hesiod(us)
Greek

Greek didactic poet, flourishing c. 700 B.C., who was born the son of a sea captain in Ascra, at the foot of Mount Helicon. One of the earliest Greek poets, he seems to have lived a little after the time of Homer and is best known for two works, *Works and Days* and *Theogony*.

Works and Days tells of country life and is generally considered to consist of two originally distinct poems, one exalting honest labor while denouncing unjust and corrupt judges, the second relating to the work of a farmer, giving advice on what days may be considered lucky or unlucky. The combination of these two poems gives an invaluable picture of an eighth-century B.C. Greek village community.

Theogony gives an account of the origin of the world out of Chaos and the origin and history of the gods. It remains one of the most valuable tools to the comparative mythologist.

Hesione
Greek

Daughter of Laomedon who was rescued from a sea monster sent by Poseidon to ravage Troy in revenge for Laomedon refusing to pay him for the work he had done during the construction of the city walls. Her rescuer was Heracles, who had been promised the white horses given to her father by Zeus in exchange for Ganymede as a reward. Once Hesione had been saved, Laomedon refused the reward.

Later, following the successful completion of Heracles' ninth labor, Heracles and Telamon attacked Troy, sacked the city, killed Laomedon and all his sons, save Podarces, who was ransomed by Hesione, then changed his name to Priam. Hesione was given to Telamon and bore him the son Teucer. A few years later, Priam sent Antenor to demand that Telamon should return Hesione to her home, a request that was scornfully refused. Some have suggested this was one of the causes of the Trojan War.

Hesperides
Greek

A number of nymphs, their actual number and parentage being variously given—though their name means "Daughters of Evening" and they are usually considered as the daughters of Atlas and Hesperis—who guarded a tree, upon which golden apples grew, given to Hera by Ge on her wedding to Zeus. They were helped in their task by Ladon, a 100-headed serpent or dragon, one of the monstrous offspring of Typhon and Echidne. The garden in which the tree had been planted, and which they watched over, was said by some to be located on the slopes of Mount Atlas or on the Islands of the Blessed.

Heracles was required, as his penultimate labor, to bring the golden apples that grew on the tree back to Eurystheus. He sailed to the garden in a golden vessel on loan from Helios. Once there he tricked Atlas into retrieving the apples for him before making off with them. Eurystheus gave the apples to Heracles, but he dedicated them to Athene, and she returned them to their rightful place. She did, however, give three of the apples to Aphrodite, for that goddess was said to have given these to either Milanion or Hippomenes to enable a race against Atalanta to be won.

See also: Atalanta; Ladon

Hesperis
Greek

The female form of Hesperus, the evening star, the dual-gender offspring of Astraeus and Eos and sister-brother to the four winds. In this form the evening star was said to have been the mother of the Hesperides by Atlas. Possibly at one stage there were two evening stars, Hesperis and Hesperus, but records of the Greek traditions neither confirm nor deny this.

See also: Astraeus; Eos

Hesperus
Greek

The male aspect of the evening star who in its female form, Hesperis, was said to have been the mother of the Hesperides by Atlas. The offspring of Astraeus and Eos, brother-sister to the four winds, Boreas (north), Zephyrus (west), Notus (south), and Eurus (east). Eurus is sometimes not included in this list and is given different parentage. Called Vesper by the Romans, Hesperus later became identified with Phosphorus (Latin: "Lucifer"), the bringer of light, the morning star.

See also: Astraeus; Boreas; Eos; Eurus; Notus; Vesper; Zephyrus

Hest(i)a
Greek

One of the 12 elite Olympian deities; the eldest daughter of Cronos and Rhea; the first to be swallowed, and subsequently disgorged, by her father. Goddess of the hearth, supremely important when fire was so difficult to rekindle, and patroness of the household, she was important in cult, mainly private, but has little mythology, remaining a peculiarly domestic goddess. Later, sometime prior to the fifth century B.C., she was replaced in the Olympian hierarchy by Dionysos, a move that secured a majority of gods over goddesses and seems to reflect a society that was becoming increasingly patriarchal.

Legend says that she scorned the attentions of Apollo and Poseidon and remained unmarried, having sworn to remain a virgin. The eldest sister of Zeus, who installed her in Olympus, where she was revered as the oldest Olympian goddess, Hestia presided over all sacrifices, the first part of any sacrifice to the gods being offered to her. By extension of her patronage of the home, she was credited with the idea of building houses; Hestia also came to preside over the civic hearth in every city and town where a perpetual flame burned in her honor, her sanctuary becoming a place of refuge for those seeking asylum. This practice was later adopted by the Romans, who knew her as Vesta.

Her cultic origins remain unclear, though she does appear to be an aspect of the eastern Mediterranean earth-goddess cult, possibly brought to Greece by the invading Achaeans, though her roots may be Mycenaean, for they worshipped a primitive goddess who displays many of the characteristics of the later Hestia.

Astronomical: The name Hestia has been applied to an asteroid with an orbit that is highly inclined to the ecliptic, taking its aphelion almost to the orbit of Saturn, at perihelion being well within the orbit of Jupiter.

See also: Dionysos; Vesta

Hiera
Greek
A volcanic island that was, along with Lemnos, Lipara, Imbros, and Sicily, one of Hephaistos's favorite spots on earth.

Hippocoön
Greek
Brother of Tyndareus, whom he drove out of Sparta, usurping the throne. He fought against Heracles with Neleus, but Heracles stormed

Sparta, killed Hippocoön and all his sons, and restored Tyndareus to the throne.

See also: Tyndareus

Hippocrates
Greek
A physician of Cos (c. 460–367 B.C.) and the founder of rational medicine who by the third century was receiving cult at the sanctuary of Asclepios. Little is actually known of Hippocrates other than he taught his science for money. His cult status stems from the belief that he was taught medicine by Asclepios himself.

See also: Asclepios

Hippocrene
Greek
A sacred spring on Mount Helicon that was created by the fabulous winged horse Pegasus with a stamp of his hoof, its name actually meaning "fountain of the horse." It was a favorite place of the Muses, to whom it was sacred and who used to dance alongside its waters. It lies some way above the well-known Grove of the Muses on Mount Helicon.

See also: Muses, the

Hippodameia
Greek
1. Daughter of Oenomaus who was offered by her father as the prize in a chariot race, a race organized by Oenomaus after an oracle had foretold that he would be killed by his son-in-law. Oenomaus was fairly sure that he would win the race, for his chariot, driven by Myrtilus, was hauled by wind-begotten horse, the gift of his father, Ares. The fate for the losers was death by Oenomaus's spear, also a gift from Ares. Many young men tried, and died, for their efforts. Finally Pelops arrived in Pisa in Elis and vowed to win the hand of Hippodameia. He already owned a winged chariot, the gift of Poseidon, but to make doubly sure of success he also bribed Myrtilus, the son of Hermes, with a promise of half the kingdom to remove the linchpin from the chariot of Oenomaus and substitute it for one made of wax. During the race the wax linchpin broke,

Oenomaus was thrown out of his chariot and killed, and Pelops married Hippodameia.

2. Wife of Peirithous, king of the Lapiths, whose wedding was interrupted when a drunken centaur tried to carry her off. Theseus, who was a guest at the celebrations, joined the Lapithae in the famous battle against the centaurs.

See also: Lapithae; Oenomaus; Pelops

Hippogryph
Greek

A fabulous, mythical beast—half-horse, half-gryphon—that appears to have solar connections with the winged horses that pulled Apollo's chariot.

Hippolyt~e, ~a
Greek

Queen of the Amazons and sister of Antiope whose golden girdle, a gift from Ares, was the object of Heracles' ninth labor. She agreed to give Heracles and his companions, Theseus and Telamon, the girdle, but Hera aroused the Amazon warriors, and in the ensuing fray Hippolyte and many other Amazon leaders were killed. Her sister, Antiope, was taken by Theseus, though some sources say that it was Hippolyte who became Theseus's wife, and bore him the son Hippolytus.

See also: Theseus

Hippolytus
Greek

The son of Theseus by either Hippolyte or her sister, Antiope, who was raised in Troezen. When Theseus subsequently married Phaedra she fell in love with her stepson, who repulsed her advances as he was a votary of Artemis and sworn to hunting and chastity. Phaedra killed herself but left a letter falsely accusing Hippolytus. Theseus prayed to Poseidon that Hippolytus might die that very day, and the god sent a monster that so terrified the horses drawing Hippolytus's chariot along the seashore that he was thrown out and dragged to his death. Artemis later persuaded Asclepios to restore him to life when his innocence was finally proven.

Hippolytus had cult in Troezen, where girls about to marry dedicated a lock of their hair to him. The Troezenians held that after his death he became the charioteer constellation, Auriga.

See also: Theseus

Hippomedon
Greek

One of the Seven Against Thebes. His companions on the fated expedition were Adrastus, Amphiaraus, Polyneices, Tydeus, Capaneus, and Parthenopaeus. Of these seven, only Adrastus survived.

See also: Seven Against Thebes

Hippomenes
Greek

Son of Megareus, he married the Boeotian Atalanta. Some commentators have sought to make Hippomenes simply another name for Milanion, the hero who ran a race against Atalanta during which he threw down three of the golden apples of the Hesperides. Atalanta stopped to pick these up, and so Milanion won the race.

See also: Atalanta

Hippothous
Greek

The grandson of Cercyon and father of Aepytus, king of Arcadia.

Homer
Greek

One of the main sources for the Greek deities, Homer flourished in the eighth century B.C. Although more than one person may have had a hand in the composition of the writings attributed to him, his work draws on a vast repertoire of oral tradition that stretched for centuries before his time. Homer is attributed with *Iliad* and *Odyssey*, two distinct but complimentary epics, the first telling the story of the fall of Troy, the second the wandering of Odysseus back to Ithaca after the end of the Trojan War.

Nothing is confirmed about Homer. Indeed, many scholars think there never was any

"Homer" or that two or more poets may have been involved in the works attributed to him. Traditionally, Homer seems to have been Ionian, living directly across from mainland Greece. Four city-states claim to have been his birthplace: the mainland's Smyrna, Colophon, and Ephesus and the island of Chios. Tradition also said he was blind, but this seems to have little or no foundation.

Homer's lifetime appears to coincide rather neatly with the introduction of writing into the Greek world, and he may have used this new technique to commit his verses, perhaps dictating them to others. His *Iliad* appears to date from around the second half of the eighth century B.C.; *Odyssey* seems to fall around 700 B.C., half a millenium after the date Troy was thought to have fallen, that is, c. 1200 B.C.

If the works attributed to Homer are indeed the product of one man, then he surely is one of the most individual and supreme literary geniuses of all time. They remain essential reference works for any student of classical mythology and, artistically speaking, are the most influential literary works in the world.

See also: Odysseus; Trojan War

Horae
Greco-Roman

Minor goddesses representing the seasons and the order of nature. Originating in Greek tradition, they were the children of Zeus and Themis and were named Eunomia (Good Order), Dike (Justice) and Eirene (Peace). Later they became the daughters of Helios and Selene. Some commentators have said that the siring of the Horae by Zeus on Themis indicates that the invading Hellenes took over control of the calendar and introduced their own system.

Horatii
Roman

Collective name for three brothers, Roman champions who fought the three Alban Curatii to determine the outcome of the war between Rome and Alba Longa. Only one, Horatius (though they all seem to have been called Horatius), survived. When he returned home he found his sister, who was engaged to one of the Curatii, mourning her loss; he immediately killed her as a traitress. He was arrested but later acquitted, having undergone the purifying ritual of walking veiled beneath a beam.

Horatius
Roman

The name of the single surviving Horatii, three Roman champions—all of whom appear to have been called Horatius—who fought the Curatii to determine the war between Rome and Alba Longa.

"Hundred-Handers"
Greek

The literal translation from the Greek of the Hecatoncheires or Centimani, the 100-handed, 50-headed giant sons of Uranos and Ge: Briareus, or Aegaeon, Cottus, and Gyas, or Gyges.

Hyacinth~os, ~us
Greek

In origin an ancient chthonic deity, Hyacinthos in legend was a beautiful prince of Sparta, the son of Amyclas who was loved by Thamyris, Apollo, and Zephyrus. He was killed out of jealousy by Zephyrus or accidentally by a quoit or discus thrown by Apollo, some sources saying the quoit was blown astray by Zephyrus. From his blood Apollo caused the Hyacinth flower to spring up. Hyacinthos had cult status at Amyclae, where an annual festival was held in his honor.

Hyades
Greek

Varying in number from two to seven, the Hyades were the daughters of Oceanos and Aethra or of Atlas and Pleione, the latter alternative making them the sisters of the Pleiades. Often referred to as the nurses of Zeus at Dodona or of Dionysos on Mount Nysa, their name implies they were rain nymphs. When their brother, Hyas, was killed by a wild boar they died of grief and were translated to the heavens, where they became the star grouping that bears their name (though some sources say they became stars after Zeus placed them in the heavens for caring for Dionysos). The setting of these stars in mid-November signaled an end to the seafaring season and for the ploughing to begin. They were sometimes confused, notably by the poet Claudian, with the sisters of Phaethön, the Heliades.

Astronomical: A star cluster within the constellation Taurus that lies within the northern celestial hemisphere at approximate celestial coordinates right ascension 4h20m, declination +18°. The cluster is more than 6° in diameter and 130 light-years distant.

See also: Pleiades

Hyas
Greek

The brother of the Hyades who was killed by a wild boar. Mourning his loss, the Hyades were transferred to the heavens by Zeus to ease their grief.

Hydra
Greek

A serpent—one of the multitude of monstrous offspring of Typhon and Echidne—with a doglike body and seven, or nine, heads, one of them immortal. Raised by Hera, it lived at the sevenfold source of the River Amymone and haunted the neighboring swampy marshes of Lerna. It was dispatched by Heracles with the help of Iolaus as the second of his 12 labors. However, Heracles' task was not an easy one, for as soon as a head was lopped off two more grew in its place. To overcome this Heracles had Iolaus cauterize each stump with a firebrand as soon as the head was lopped off. He buried the immortal head of the Hydra under a huge boulder and poisoned his arrows by dipping them in the Hydra's gall. Some commentators have sought to make Hydra a personification of the malarial miasmas of this marshy region or of the noxious gases it emits.

Astronomical: The largest and worst defined constellation, winding across more than a quarter of the night sky. It may be located, straddling the celestial equator, between approximate right ascensions 8h10m and 15h00m, declination from +7° to -35°.

Hygeia
Greek

The goddess of health who was either the wife or daughter of Asclepios. In art she was represented as dressed in a long robe, feeding a serpent from a cup. Her name has given us the word *hygiene.*

Hylas
Greek

The son of Theodamus who, after Heracles had killed his father, became the squire and lover of Heracles, accompanying him when he joined the *Argo Navis* at the start of the quest for the Golden Fleece. When the Argonauts put into Mysia, Hylas went in search of fresh water. On this search some water nymphs fell in love with Hylas and, drawing him down into their waters, left nothing but an empty pitcher to indicate he had been that way. When Hylas failed to return to the *Argo Navis,* Heracles searched for him and was left behind when the ship sailed. The search for Hylas became an annual rite in Mysia.

See also: Heracles; Jason

Hyllus
Greek

The son of Heracles and Deianeira who built the funeral pyre on which his father immolated himself, having first been made to promise that he would marry Iole. When Eurystheus determined to drive Alcmene and the Heracleidae from Greece, Hyllus, Iolaus, and Theseus led the Athenian forces against him, a battle that they won, either he or Iolaus actually defeating Eurystheus before Alcmene finally dispatched him. He later led the Heracleidae against Mycenae but was killed in the battle by Echemus, king of Tegea.

Apollonius differs from this traditional view by making Hyllus the son of Heracles by a Phaeacian nymph, saying that he later became the eponym of the Hylleis of northern Illyria.

See also: Heracles; Iole

Hymen
Greek

Patron god of marriage, being the son either of Apollo and a Muse or of Dionysos and

Aphrodite; the personification of the wedding feast and of *hymenaioi,* hymns sung at wedding celebrations. In art he was represented as a youth carrying a bridal torch and veil.

Hyperborean
Greek

One of a legendary race said to live in a land of sunshine and plenty beyond the reach of the north wind—and hence beyond the northernmost point of the known world. Apollo was thought to spend his three-months winter absence from Delphi with the Hyperboreans. They also feature in the story of Perseus, who was said to have visited them in his search for Medusa, some versions saying they actually lived with the Hyperboreans in a land far to the west rather than the north.

Herodotus placed them beyond the Issedones, the one-eyed Arimaspians, and the gold-guarding Griffins, in Central Asia. Aristeas of Proconnesos is thought to have described a visit to the land of the Hyperboreans in his lost poem *Arimaspea.* The word Hyperborean is a corruption of two Greek words, *hyper* meaning "beyond," and the name of the north wind (Boreas).

See also: Arimaspi

Hyperenor
Greek

One of the five Sparti, the "Sown Men" who sprang from the dragon's teeth sown by Cadmos. With his four compatriots—Echion, Udaeus, Chthonius, and Pelorus—Hyperenor helped to build the Cadmea and became revered as one of the ancestors of Thebes.

See also: Sparti

Hyperion
Greek

A son of Uranos and Ge, thus one of the Titans and brother of Cronos, Oceanos, Iapetus, Rhea, Themis, Tethys, and Mnemosyne. The father of Helios (Sun), Selene (Moon), and Eos (Dawn) by Theia, he was said to drive his chariot daily across the sky, returning to the east each night by the River Oceanos. Due to this similarity with the mythology of his son, Helios, he was often said to have been the original sun god, his position possibly being usurped later by his son.

Astronomical: The ninth-closest satellite of Saturn, between the orbits of Titan and Iapetus.

Hyperm(n)estra
Greek

One of the Danaides, the daughters of Danaus, king of Argos. When she and her 49 sisters married the 50 sons of Aegyptus, Hypermnestra was the only one not to carry out her father's instructions to kill her new husband on their wedding night. Her sisters were condemned for their actions to Tartarus for eternity, carrying water in sieves or bottomless vessels.

See also: Danaus

Hypn~os, ~us
Greek

The god of sleep.

Hypseus
Greek

The father of Cyrene, one of the beloved of Apollo.

Hypsipyle
Greek

Queen of Lemnos who set her father, Thoas, adrift in a chest to save him from being killed with the other men of Lemnos when the women of the island decided to rid themselves of men. However, by the time Jason and the Argonauts arrived on Lemnos the women had begun to regret their actions and welcomed the men with open arms. Hypsipyle herself married Jason and bore him twin sons, one of whom appears to be named Euneus.

Later, when the women of Lemnos discovered how she had saved Thoas, they sold her into slavery. She was bought by King Lycurgus of Nemea to act as the nurse to his son, Opheltes. However, she caused the death of her charge by ignoring an oracle that said the child must not be placed on the ground until he could walk. She put Opheltes down to show the Seven Against Thebes where they might find water, and he was bitten by a snake. At Opheltes' grave the Nemaean Games were instigated. She was imprisoned, but she was later released by Dionysos.

See also: Jason; Opheltes; Thoas

I

Iacchus

Greek

A god invented from the initiates' ceremonial cry "Iacche!" in the Eleusinian Mysteries. He was often associated with Dionysos, especially in later tradition, when Dionysos had also become known as Bacchus.

See also: Bacchus; Dionysos

Iambe

Greek

The daughter of Pan and the nymph Echo and a servant to Celeus, king of Eleusis, and Metaneira. When Demeter came to Eleusis during her fruitless search for Persephone, Iambe made the goddess a drink of *kykeon*, a mixture of water, barley, and honey. Demeter despondently refused the drink, so Iambe, whose name is the feminine form of *iambos*, meaning "lampoon," exposed her pudenda and made bawdy jokes until Demeter was forced to smile and accept the drink. The role of Iambe in this legend tracks that of Baubo.

It has been suggested that Iambe forms the mythological explanation of the custom for bystanders to shout abuse at those taking part in the procession along the Sacred Way from Athens to Eleusis. Her direct bawdiness to Demeter is a reflection of the dirty language often associated with rites like the Eleusinian Mysteries.

See also: Demeter; Echo; Pan

Iamus

Greek

The son of Evadne, a daughter of Poseidon, by Apollo. Afraid to expose her pregnancy, Evadne gave birth to Iamus in the woods, where the infant was nourished by snakes with honey as he lay among the violets. Little else is known except that in later life Iamus became a prophet.

Iapetus

Greek

A son of Uranos and Ge, thus a Titan and the brother of Cronos, Oceanos, Hyperion, Rhea, Themis, Tethys, and Mnemosyne; father of Atlas, Prometheus, and Epimetheus by Clymene. The grandfather of Deucalion, the Greek Noah, Iapetus is regarded as the progenitor of mankind through his son, Prometheus.

Astronomical: One of the satellites of Saturn, having a diameter of 1,440 kilometers (900 miles), that lies at an average distance of 3,561,000 kilometers (2,225,625 miles) from the planet. It is tenth closest to the planet, lying between the orbits of Hyperion and Phoebe.

See also: Deucalion; Titan

Ias~ion, ~ius, ~us

Greek

The son of Zeus and Electra, a daughter of Atlas. Coming from Samothrace he traveled to Thebes for the wedding of his sister, Harmonia, to Cadmos. There Demeter fell for him and lay with him in a thrice-ploughed field, her son by this union being named Plutus or Pluton, "Wealth," a chthonic title. Iasion never knew his son, for Zeus killed him for his presumptive behavior with one of his thunderbolts.

Diodorus Siculus names Iasion as the originator of the Mysteries of Samothrace, a god in his own right, and then the husband of Cybele. He is yet another example of a young consort god associated with a fertility goddess.

See also: Cadmos; Harmonia

Icaria
Greek

The island that was named after Icarus when his body was washed up there following his unsuccessful attempt to fly from Crete to the mainland on wings made by his father, Daedalus. Heracles was said to have found the body and buried it. It was also the island where Dionysos hired a ship to take him to Naxos, but the crew, Tyrrhenian pirates, set sail for Asia, fully intending to sell Dionysos into slavery.

See also: Daedalus

Icarius
Greek

1. An Athenian, the father of Erigone who was taught the art of viniculture after he had hospitably received Dionysos. He was killed by shepherds who believed that the effects of drinking wine meant they had been poisoned. Erigone was led to his grave by his dog, Maera, and in despair she hanged herself from the tree over the grave. In revenge Dionysos drove the Athenian maidens mad. An oracle disclosed that this was punishment for the murder of Icarius, so the Athenians instituted an autumn festival to Icarius and Erigone, which involved hanging idols from the lower limbs of trees and swinging from the upper branches.

2. King of Sparta and father of Penelope. After Odysseus had won the right to marry Penelope in a footrace, Icarius tried to persuade his daughter to remain with him. Odysseus told her she could do as she pleased, and, veiling her face to hide her blushes, she went with Odysseus.

See also: Erigone; Odysseus; Penelope

Icar~os, ~us
Greek

Also: Ikar~os, ~us

The son of Daedalus who, along with his father, famously attempted to fly from Crete, where he and Daedalus had been imprisoned by Minos, on wings made of wax and feathers. Although warned by his father, who had made the wings, Icarus flew too close to the sun, the wax melted, and he fell into the

Icarian Sea and drowned. His body was washed up on an island that was named Icaria after him; the body was said to have been discovered and buried by Heracles. Daedalus, however, flew on to Cumae in Italy.

Astronomical: The name given to an Apollo asteroid 1.5 kilometers (1 mile) in diameter discovered in 1949. It orbits the sun every 409 days at a distance of between 2.0 and 0.19 astronomical units. It is the only known asteroid, appropriately enough, to approach the sun closer than the planet Mercury.

See also: Daedalus

Ichor
Greek

The ethereal fluid that flows like blood through the veins of the gods.

Ida, Mount
Greek

1. Mountain in southern Phrygia, near Troy, upon which Paris was exposed, found and raised by a shepherd, and lived with the nymph Oenone until he deserted her for Helen following his judgment, made on this mountain, of which goddess should be awarded the Apple of Discord. It was also the scene of the rape of Ganymede and the place from which Zeus supposedly watched the progress of the Trojan War.

2. The ancient name for Mount Psiloriti, the main mountain of Crete. Some sources say the infant Zeus was hidden from his father in the Idaean Cave there and nursed by the she-goat Amalthea.

Idaea
Greek

A nymph who bore Teucer to Scamander of Crete following his emigration to Phrygia.

Idaean Cave
Greek

A cave located high upon Mount Psiloritis on Crete, a mountain that was in ancient times known as Mount Ida. Some commentators say that Rhea brought the newly born Zeus to this cave when Cronos sought to swallow him, though others opt for the Diktean Cave above the Lasithi Plateau. The cave became a major place of pilgrimage for the classical Greek world.

Idas

Greek

Twin brother of Lynceus (together the sons of Aphareus, king of Messenia) and cousins of the Dioscuri, though his father was, in reality, Poseidon. The twins took part in the hunt for the Calydonian Boar as well as the expedition of the Argonauts aboard the *Argo Navis*. Idas fell in love with Marpessa, the daughter of Evenus, whom Apollo loved, and stole her away in his chariot, a gift from his father, Poseidon. Evenus drowned himself in the river that then took his name. Apollo and Idas fought for Marpessa, but Zeus intervened, commanding that Marpessa should make up her own mind. She chose Idas.

Idas and his devoted brother, Lynceus, had been betrothed to the daughters of Leucippus but were killed when they fought their cousins, the Dioscuri, who had abducted the maidens.

See also: Dioscuri; Lynceus

Idomen~eos, ~eus

Greek

The grandson of Minos (son of Deucalion) who was said, in the company of Meriones, to have taken a fleet of 80 or 100 ships from Crete to the Trojan War, where he shared command with Agamemnon. On his subsequent return from the war he found his throne had been usurped by Leucus, who had also taken his wife, an echo of the fate that awaited his cocommander, Agamemnon. Idomeneos exiled himself and made a new home in southern Italy. A variant story says that Idomeneos, caught in a tempest on the way home, swore to sacrifice to Poseidon the first creature he encountered on his return to Crete after the ten years of the Trojan War. However, this turned out to be his son, and his sacrifice of his kin so angered the gods that they punished Crete with a plague.

Idomeneos was banished from Crete and settled in Calabria in Italy.

See also: Agamemnon; Minos; Trojan War

Ikar~os, ~us

Greek

A variant of Icarus, the son of Daedalus.

Iliad

Greek

The famous Greek epic poem in 24 books attributed to Homer, probably written sometime before 700 B.C. Its title derives from Ilion, another name for Troy. The subject of the work is the wrath of Achilles, an incident that occurred during the tenth year of the Trojan War, when Agamemnon seized Briareus, leading Achilles to refuse to take any further part in the war. This led to the death of his close companion, Patroclus, the reentry of Achilles, and the death of Hector. The work, a masterpiece of Greek literature, graphically portrays many of the tragic battle scenes.

Ilithyia

Greek

Varaint of Eileithyia, the goddess of childbirth.

Ilithyiae

Greek

The daughters of Hera who in *Iliad* and other early poems are represented as midwives who help women in childbirth. Later works, including *Odyssey*, represent a single goddess in this role, Eileithyia, though this goddess is sometimes named as a more direct, and simple variant: Ilithyia.

Illyrius

Greek

Son of Cadmos and Harmonia; brother to Autonoë, Ino, Semele, Agave, and Polydorus. He appears to be a late addition to the lineage of Cadmos and Harmonia and is the mythical eponym of Illyria, his addition possibly being to give increased status to the region.

See also: Cadmos; Harmonia

Ilus

Greek

Son of Tros, father of Laomedon, grandfather of Priam, and founder of Ilion or Troy. Later, the noble Roman Julian family claimed him as their ancestor.

See also: Laomedon; Priam; Tros; Troy

Imbros

Greek

Volcanic island that along with Lemnos, Lipara, Hiera, and Sicily numbered among the favorite spots on earth of Hephaistos.

Inachus

Greek

Son of Oceanos and Tethys, the first king of Argos, and father of Io, he gave his name to a river.

Indiges

Roman

A term used to refer to the deified powers of the dead.

Inferi

Roman

A collective name given to the gods of the Underworld, though sometimes the term was used to refer to all the dead, gods and mortals alike.

Ino

Greek

Daughter of Cadmos and Harmonia; sister of Autonoë, Semele, Agave, Polydorus, and Illyrius. She married Athamas of Boeotia and acted as the nurse to her nephew, Dionysos. She was, however, jealous of Athamas's children by his first wife and tried to have Athamas sacrifice his son, Phrixus. He was saved, along with his sister, Helle, by Aries, the winged ram sent by Zeus that carried Phrixus safely to Colchis. Helle, however, fell off en route into the stretch of water that thereafter became known as the Hellespont. The ram's fleece turned to gold after the ram had been sacrificed and later became the object of the quest of Jason and the Argonauts.

Ino was a votary of Dionysos and, in one famous incident along with Agave and Autonoë, killed Agave's son, Pentheus. Hera drove Athamas and Ino mad. Grabbing her son, Melicertes, Ino leaped into the sea off the isthmus of Corinth. Melicertes was washed ashore and buried by Sisyphus. Thereafter he became known as Palaemon and was honored in the Isthmian Games. Ino herself became the sea goddess Leucothea. She and Palaemon were helpers to sailors in time of distress and are notable for their help of Odysseus.

See also: Athamas; Dionysos; Cadmos; Harmonia

Io

Greek

Beautiful daughter of the Argive river named Inachus. Zeus fell in love with her, which led to Io's banishment after an oracle had warned Inachus that if she remained Argos would be hit by a thunderbolt. Following her banishment, Io was turned into a white heifer, either by Zeus to conceal her from his ever-jealous wife or by Hera herself, who then made Zeus give her the animal as a gift. Hera set the 100-eyed Argos to watch over Io, but Zeus dispatched Hermes to kill Argos. Hermes charmed Argos to sleep before cutting off his head, an act that earned him the epithet Argeiphontes. As a mark of respect Hera set Argus's eyes into the tail of her sacred bird, the peacock, and then sent a gadfly to torment the unfortunate Io. This fly's stinging caused Io to wander all over the world, through Dodona, swimming the Ionian Sea (said to be named after her), across the Bosphorus, and even to the Caucasus, where she came upon the chained Prometheus. She finally found her way to Egypt, where on the banks of the Nile her human form was restored and where Zeus visited her and fathered Epaphus on her. After the child had been born, Hera had the Curetes abduct him and take him to Syria, where he was raised by the queen of Byblos.

Io was often identified by the Greeks with the Egyptian goddess Isis. The daughters of Danaus traced their descent from her.

Astronomical: The third largest moon of the planet Jupiter, 3,600 kilometers (2,240 miles) in diameter, orbiting once every 1.77 days at a mean distance of 413,000 kilometers (257,000 miles) and lying between the orbits of Amalthea and Europa. It is the most volcanically active body in the solar system, covered by hundreds of vents that erupt not lava but sulfur, giving Io an orange-colored surface.

See also: Argos; Danaus

Iobates

Greek

King of Lycia and father of Anteia; his son-in-law, Proetus, sent to him Bellerophon, who carried a letter that requested that the bearer should be put to death after Anteia had falsely accused Bellerophon of trying to seduce her. Iobates did not, like Proetus, want to kill a guest in his home, so instead he sent Bellerophon to slay the fire-breathing Chimaera. When Bellerophon returned, having successfully dispatched the beast, Iobates sent him against the Amazons. Again he succeeded, so Iobates now set up an ambush by his own men. Bellerophon again proved victorious, so Iobates determined to discover the truth. Upon doing so he made amends and gave Bellerophon half his kingdom and the hand of his daughter to make amends.

See also: Belerophon; Chimaera

Iolaus

Greek

Eldest son of Iphicles who accompanied his uncle, Heracles, on his 12 labors, acting as his companion and charioteer. During the second labor—to kill the multiheaded Hydra—Iolaus seared the stumps as Heracles cut off the heads, thereby preventing two new heads from growing in place. Following the completion of all 12 labors, Heracles and Iolaus returned to Thebes, where Heracles gave him Megara, his wife. When Eurystheus determined to expel the Heracleidae from Greece, Iolaus was among those who defended Athens against the king. It was either Iolaus or Hyllus who defeated Eurystheus before Alcmene finally dispatched him.

Finally, after Heracles had won the right to marry Deianeira, Iolaus was sent to settle in Sardinia, where he was regarded as the first colonist, to rule over the sons of Heracles by the daughters of Thespius.

See also: Heracles; Iphicles

Iolc~os, ~us

Greek

Realm founded by Cretheus, later the kingdom of Aeson. This was the homeland of Jason, where he and his Argonauts set sail to search for the Golden Fleece, a quest instigated by Pelias, Jason's uncle, who had usurped the throne.

See also: Golden Fleece; Jason

Iole

Greek

Daughter of Eurytus, king of Oechalia, who was won by Heracles in an archery contest set up by her father to select a husband. Eurytus refused Heracles his prize, as the great hero had killed his previous wife during a bout of madness. Iole was, however, seized by Heracles after he had killed Eurytus and all his sons; he then sent her to be cared for by his wife, Deianeira. This act led Deianeira to suspect unfaithfulness in Heracles, and she sent him the shirt or robe steeped in the blood of Nessus. This garment, when put on, burned into Heracles' flesh and was the cause of his immolation on a funeral pyre.

See also: Deianeira; Heracles

Ion

Greek

Son of Creusa (the daughter of Erechtheus) and Xuthus; brother of Achaeus and Dorus. Some sources made him the son of Apollo by Creusa. In this version, the child was taken to Delphi by Hermes in order to hide Creusa's infidelity, and there the boy was raised as a temple servitor. When Xuthus and Creusa later visited Delphi to consult the oracle about their childlessness, Apollo told Xuthus that the first person he would meet upon leaving the temple would be his son. Xuthus immediately assumed that Ion, who was the first person he met on leaving the temple, was a bastard son of his own. Creusa planned to sacrifice him, but just in time she learned from the Pythia that Ion was her true son. She went on to have two more sons by Xuthus, Dorus and Achaeus, all three of her children becoming the eponyms for different regions and peoples. Ion became the eponym of the Ionian people and peninsula. However, this version did not ideally suit the traditional genealogy, so an alternative version exists in an attempt to fit Ion neatly into a more traditional viewpoint.

In this version, Xuthus left Athens for the northern Peloponnesos, taking Ion with him, Ion becoming the king of this region. He later came to Athens to help lead the war against Eleusis, and at the conclusion of that war he founded the Apolline festival of the Beodromia. He then politically organized Attica and established Athenian primacy among the Ionians.

See also: Creusa; Dorus

Ionia
Greek

The coastal strip of Asia Minor that was settled by the Ionian Greeks; the eponym was Ion, the son of Creusa by either Apollo or Xuthus.

Iphicles
Greek

1. The son of Amphitryon and Alcmene and half-brother to his twin, Heracles, the semidivine son of Alcmene and Zeus who was one night older. He married the youngest daughter of Creon, king of Thebes, when Heracles married Megara. However, two of his children were killed by Heracles when Hera sent him mad. His eldest son, Iolaus, later became Heracles' faithful companion and charioteer during the 12 Great Labors imposed on Heracles by Eurystheus.

2. One of the Argonauts who accompanied Jason on his quest. Some, however, say that this was Iphicles, as Heracles, the half-brother of Iphicles, was also an Argonaut.

See also: Heracles; Jason

Iphigen(e)ia
Greek

The eldest daughter of Agamemnon and Clytemnestra; sister of Electra, Chryso-

themis, and Orestes. When the Greek fleet was becalmed at Aulis prior to sailing to the Trojan War, she was offered as a sacrifice to Artemis by her father. Artemis saved her, replacing a hart for the maiden, and carried her off to become her priestess at Tauris, where she became the ministrant of a rite that involved the human sacrifice of all visitors to the land. Some versions of this story say that Agamemnon carried out the sacrifice and that Iphigeneia was not saved.

Later, Orestes and Pylades came to Tauris to secure the statue of Artemis. There they were seized by the natives and prepared for sacrifice. They were saved by Iphigeneia, who fled with them to Brauron, taking along the statue of Artemis, and introduced her cult to Brauron, where she was known as Brauronia, the cult spreading to Athens and Sparta. At Eleusis they were reunited with Electra and returned to Mycenae, their home city, where Orestes killed Aegisthus's son and became king.

Iphigeneia seems so closely linked to Artemis that she appears to be a surrogate of the goddess herself. She received cult status in Tauris (the Crimea), as well as in some other Greek cities.

See also: Agamemnon; Artemis; Orestes

Iphimed(e)ia
Greek

Wife of Aloeus and mother of the Aloeidae, the giants Ephialtes and Otus, by Poseidon, their generic name coming from Aloeus, whom Iphimedeia later married.

See also: Ephialtes; Otus

Iphis
Greek

Father of Evadne, who became the wife of Capaneus.

Iphitus
Greek

Only son of Eurytus who did not support his father's view that Heracles, although he had fairly won the right to marry Iole in an archery contest, should not be awarded the prize, as Heracles had murdered his previous wife and children. Heracles retaliated and stole Eurytus's cattle. Iphitus invited Heracles to help search for them, but later, when he became suspicious of Heracles, he was thrown from a rooftop and killed. Heracles was then ordered to be sold into slavery, the money he received to be paid to the family of Iphitus.

See also: Heracles

Irene

Greek

Called Pax by the Romans, Irene was the goddess and personification of peace. Worshipped in Athens she was, at least according to Homer, one of the Horae, the daughters of Zeus and Themis.

Iris

Greek

The personification of the rainbow, the guise in which she acts as a messenger to Zeus, bringing his message down to earth. Though she appears in Homer's *Iliad* as a general servant to the gods, personal messenger of Zeus, and bodyguard to Hera, she is not even mentioned in the slightly later *Odyssey*. Iris was depicted as a gold-winged, swift-footed maiden wearing *talaria*, the winged sandals more commonly seen as an attribute of Hermes. Later she wore brightly colored robes and features prominently in the myth of Ceyx and Halcyone.

Islands of the Blessed

Greco-Roman

Fabled islands of the Western Ocean, becoming the abode of the gods' favorites after death or of those who had led particularly virtuous and worthwhile lives. The islands were part of the Greek and Roman traditions, but especially in Greek mythology, being the islands in which the Hesperides, aided by the watchful dragon Ladon, were guardians of a garden in which the golden apples of the goddess Hera grew. The islands may be directly equated with Elysium.

Ismene

Greek

Daughter of Oedipus by his own mother, Jocasta, and sister to Eteocles, Polyneices, and Antigone. She followed Oedipus and Antigone into exile, possibly catching up with them at Colonos in Attica, where Oedipus had found refuge in a grove sacred to the Eumenides and was protected by Theseus.

See also: Oedipus

Issa

Greek

Daughter of Macareus, she was one of those loved by Apollo.

See also: Apollo

Isthmian Games

Greek

Quadrennial games held to honor Poseidon on the isthmus of Corinth, land that was awarded to Poseidon by Zeus in an ownership dispute with Athene.

Ithaca

Greek

The small island home of Odysseus and Penelope (Greek Itháki) to the west of Greece in the Ionian Sea off Epirus adjoining Cephallenia. Some consider that the neighboring, slightly larger island of Levkás or Santa Maura is more likely to have been Odysseus's kingdom.

See also: Odysseus

Itys

Greek

The son of Tereus and Procne.

Ixion

Greek

Son of Phleygas and king of the Lapithae, a mythical race said to inhabit the mountainous regions of Thessaly. He is renowned in Greek tradition as the first murderer. When his father-in-law, Eïoneus, came to try and collect the bride price due to him, which Ixion had refused to pay, Ixion threw Eïoneus into a pit of fire. His son by his earthly wife was Peirithous. No man on earth would purify him of this crime, so Zeus invited him to Olympus. However, no sooner had he arrived than he tried to rape Hera, but she deceived him with a cloud in her form, Nephele. He mated with this phantom, the union leading to the birth of Centauros, who went on to mate with the mares on Mount Pelion to produce the race called Centaurs. As punishment for his attempted rape of Hera, Ixion was condemned to Tartarus, where he was chained to a fiery wheel that would roll eternally through the Underworld. A slight variant of his punishment says that he was chained to a fiery wheel by Hermes, the wheel constantly revolving in the sky rather than through the Underworld.

See also: Hera; Tartarus

Iynx

Greek

The daughter of Pan and Echo. Portrayed as a witch, she once cast an erotic spell on Zeus for which Hera turned her into a wryneck, which was used in binding magic. It was stretched in a wheel and spun around at speed, or it could be substituted by a wheel that spun on a string and duplicated the whistling cry of a bird. Her name endures in the modern word *jinx*.

See also: Pan

J

Janus

Roman

One of the few uniquely Roman gods, who was looked upon as the creator of the world. Being the god of doorways, passages, and buildings in general and of the beginnings and endings of days, months, and years, and the guardian of the gateway Patulicus (the Opener) and Clusivius (the Closer), he became associated particularly with peace and war. Portrayed with two faces, one looking backwards, one looking forwards, his temple was closed during times of peace, an event that occurred for only the third time when Octavian Augustus finally came to power.

Janus, after whom the month of January is named, is sometimes described as an early king of Latium who welcomed Saturnus after Jupiter had expelled him from Crete. Janus was the father of Tiberinus by Camise, his son drowning in the river that thereafter carried his name—the River Tiber.

The origin of Janus is somewhat confused by his later mythology. He may have been an early sun god, his aspect as the god of beginnings indicating that he presided over the creation of the world. Additionally, his two faces, though he may once have had four, are indicative of the chaos out of which order finally came, for having too many faces would make him confused. Janus took precedence over all the gods, even Jupiter, the sun, the moon, and all the heavenly bodies. His cult seems to have been initiated by Romulus and was supremely important to the ancient Romans.

Astronomical: One of the satellites of the planet Saturn lying second closest to the planet.

Jason

Greek

Son of Aeson, the rightful king of Iolcos, whose throne was usurped by his half-brother, Pelias, brother of Neleus and the son of Poseidon and Tyro. As an infant Jason was smuggled out of Iolcos and entrusted to the care of the centaur Cheiron, who raised him on the slopes of Mount Pelion. Meanwhile, Pelias had been warned by an oracle to beware of a man who would come to Iolcos wearing only one sandal.

As a young man Jason returned to Iolcos to demand his kingdom. On his way, Jason met an old woman who was attempting to cross a fast-flowing river. He carried her across but in the process lost a sandal in the mud. The old woman was Hera in disguise, and for this help Hera was Jason's supporter thereafter. Pelias recognized him as the man the oracle had warned him about and, eager to be rid of this nuisance, promised to relinquish the throne on the condition that Jason fetched for him the fleece of the winged ram Aries, which had carried Phrixus to safety from Thebes to Colchis. The fleece was to be found hanging from an oak tree in a grove sacred to Ares where it had turned to gold and was guarded, night and day, by a sleepless dragon, possibly Draco.

Jason welcomed the quest with open arms and immediately commissioned Argus, the Thespian, to build him a 50-oar ship, the *Argo Navis*, in which he could undertake the expedition. When the ship was nearing completion, Athene herself fitted an oracular beam into the prow. As news of the enterprise spread, many heroes of the day hurried to join Jason. His crew, which became known as the Argonauts, included the Dioscuri (Castor and Polydeuces), Heracles and his squire, Hylas, Theseus, and Orpheus.

Their voyage was filled with many adventures. They landed on the island of Lemnos, where the man-hungry women had them stay, Jason marrying their queen. Leaving Lemnos, they slipped through the Hellespont and came to Mysia. There Hylas, the squire of Heracles, went ashore to search for fresh water, but the Naiades of the spring he came to stole him away, leaving nothing behind save an empty pitcher. Heracles went in search of him, and the *Argo Navis* sailed on without him.

On the island of Bebrycos the Argonauts were met by the king, Amycus, a son of Poseidon who sought to kill all visitors by challenging them to a boxing match. Polydeuces undertook to represent the Argonauts and promptly dispatched the bully. Reaching Thrace they encountered the Harpies, who were preying on the table of the blind Phineus. The Argonauts freed him of the attentions of the Harpies, and in gratitude the prophet advised Jason on how he might navigate the Bosphorus. At its entrance lay the perilous floating islands, the Symplegades, which clashed together and crushed any vessel that attempted to pass between. Jason, however, followed the advice of Phineus and released a dove that flew between the islands. They clashed together, nipping the birds' tail feathers, and as they recoiled the *Argo Navis* safely slipped between them. From that time on, the islands remained fixed. Finally the Argonauts reached the River Phasis and Colchis, their goal.

When Aeëtes heard of the purpose of their visit he promised Jason that he would give him the Golden Fleece if he could yoke two fire-breathing bulls with brazen feet, the work of Hephaistos, plough the field of Ares with them, and sow it with the dragon's teeth that had been left over by Cadmos at Thebes. Jason agreed but was helped by Medeä, the sorceress-daughter of Aeëtes, who had fallen in love with Jason and made him swear by all the gods that in return for her help he would marry her and remain faithful. She gave him a fire-resistant lotion and, protected by that, he completed the task.

However, Aeëtes failed to keep his end of the bargain, so Medeä charmed the sleepless dragon, and while it slept Jason and the Argonauts removed the Golden Fleece from its resting place and made off in the *Argo Navis*, Medeä bringing along her half-brother, Apsyrtus. The furious Aeëtes gave chase; to delay him, Medeä ruthlessly murdered Apsyrtus, cut him into small pieces, and dropped these over the side of the boat. Aeëtes stopped to pick them up so that Apsyrtus could be given a decent burial, and the Argonauts escaped with their prize.

The return journey of the *Argo Navis* is given in various accounts, but the routes taken are all unfeasible. Greek knowledge of geography at that time would have been very limited. Tradition does say that they visited the island home of Circe and that she purified Jason and Medeä of the murder of Apsyrtus.

Returning to Iolcos, Jason found that Pelias had forced Aeson to take his own life, though one tradition does say that Medeä successfully rejuvenated him. All sources, however, agree that Medeä exacted a terrible revenge on Pelias. She persuaded his daughters, with the exception of Alcestis, to cut up their father and boil him in a cauldron, falsely promising that this would rejuvenate him, just as it had Pelias. Horrified by this murder, Acastus, Pelias's son, expelled Jason and Medeä, who made their way to Corinth.

There they lived happily for many years, some say ten, during which time Jason joined the hunt for the Calydonian Boar, until Jason deserted Medeä for Glauce, also called Creusa, the daughter of Creon. Medeä retaliated by sending the young bride a poisoned garment that consumed her in flames, set fire to the palace, and killed Creon as well. She then, according to some, also killed her own children by Jason.

Medeä fled Corinth in a chariot drawn by winged serpents and took refuge in Athens with Aegeus, who married her. She left on Theseus's arrival and, after wandering for many years, finally became immortal. Jason either took his own life or returned to Iolcos, where he became king but was killed when the poop of the decaying *Argo Navis*, which had been beached as a memento of the great expedition, fell on him.

See also: Aeëtes; Aeson; Apsyrtus; Argonauts; Cheiron; Dioscuri; Draco; Golden Fleece; Heracles; Iolcos; Medeä; Pelias

Jocasta

Greek

Daughter of Menoeceus and wife of Laius, king of Thebes. Known as Epicaste in the works of Homer, Jocasta became the mother, and subsequently the wife, of Oedipus. As an oracle had said that she should have no son by Laius, she exposed Oedipus on Mount Cithaeron, but he survived, returned to Thebes, defeated the Sphinx, murdered his father, and married his mother, unaware of her identity, or she of his. They had four children: Eteocles, Polyneices, Antigone, and Ismene. According to one tradition, Jocasta committed suicide when she learned the true identity of her husband; another says that she survived long enough to commit suicide over the bodies of her sons, who had been killed in the war of the Seven Against Thebes.

See also: Oedipus

Jove

Roman

An alternative name for Jupiter.

Juno

Roman

Principal Roman goddess who was identified with the Greek Hera. Her marriage to her brother, Jupiter—thus making her the queen of Heaven—symbolized her association with marriage, a ceremony she watched over; she was concerned with all aspects of women's lives. Depicted as a statuesque, matronly figure who was especially worshipped by women, Juno was also goddess of light and childbirth, being known as Lucina in this aspect.

In the Roman tradition applied to the Trojan Aeneas, she was always hostile to him, at one stage forcing his ships ashore at Carthage, though she was persuaded by Venus, Aeneas's Roman mother, to allow Aeneas to marry Queen Dido. Leaving Carthage on the instructions of Jupiter, Aeneas arrived at Drepanum, where Juno led some of his followers' wives to set fire to four of his five ships. Having arrived in Italy, Juno incited the Rutulian Prince Turnus of Ardea to claim that he should marry Lavinia, daughter of Latinus, rather than Aeneas. This led to war between the factions, much to Juno's annoyance.

In order to pacify his wife, Jupiter agreed that Trojans and Latins should unite to form a single nation, thus signaling Aeneas's eventual victory. Aeneas having won, then marrying Lavinia, Jupiter—once again to appease his wife—decreed that the Trojans should forget their native tongue and customs and adopt Italian manners and language.

Though Juno had great cultic status in Rome, she was perhaps outshone by Vesta. However, she was especially beloved, as tradition stated that in 390 B.C. her sacred geese cackled to warn of the impending attack on the Capitoline Hill by Gauls. She became revered as the protector of the city.

Astronomical: The name Juno has been applied to one of the larger asteroids.

See also: Aeneas; Hera; Venus

Juno Sororia

Roman

An aspect of Juno in which she is regarded as the guardian goddess of pubescent girls.

Jupiter

Roman

Also: Jove

Primitive Italian deity who later became the principal Roman god, identified with the Greek Zeus; the son of Saturn who married his sister, Juno. God of the sky, the sun, the moon, and all the heavenly bodies, Jupiter was originally an agricultural deity but later developed to become the protector of Rome and the Roman Empire. His very name is etymologically associated with the Greek Zeus, and several of the latter's adventures were ascribed to him, inasmuch as the Roman gods were permitted adventures.

The natural forces of the sky became his attributes. He dispensed thunder and lightning, taking on various forms, including Lucetius, the bringer of light, Fulgur, the god of lightning and thunderbolts, and Jupiter Elicius, the god of rain. Jupiter had three special thunderbolts at his disposal. Two of these would be used simply as warnings. The third, however, which was only to be hurled earthwards after a conference among all the gods, was the ultimate weapon of destruction. Jupiter watched over battles and decided the outcome.

His altar on the Aventine Hill was where the chief magistrates of the city made sacrifice to him, his smaller altars being used to solemnize oaths. In this way he came to reflect man's honesty. His priest, however, was subject to Jupiter's somewhat touchy character and had to abide by certain, rather strange rules. He was forbidden to ride a horse, have his hair cut by a slave, or even tie it in a decorative knot. He could not spend more than three days away from home, sleep in a bed if its legs had not been smeared with clay, or allow anyone else to sleep in his own bed. He always had to wear a pointed cap and was not allowed to touch nor even mention female goats. His wife was likewise restricted. She could not climb a ladder any higher than the third rung and on some days was even prohibited from combing her hair.

Jupiter Optimus Maximus stood paramount in his temple on the Capitoline Hill, his face smeared with red paint as it had once been with the blood of Rome's enemies. Magnificent games were held in his honor as the patron of Rome and the Roman Empire.

Astronomical: The fifth planet of the solar system and the largest, having an equatorial diameter of 142,800 kilometers (88,700 miles). The mass of Jupiter is more than twice that of all the other planets combined, 318 times that of earth. It takes 11.86 years to orbit the sun at a mean distance of 778 million kilometers (484 million miles) and has at least 16 moons. Largely composed of hydrogen and helium liquefied by the pressure of its interior, and probably having a rocky core larger than the earth, Jupiter is most noted for the Great Red Spot, a turbulent storm of rising gas that is approximately 14,000 kilometers (8,500 miles) wide and some 30,000 kilometers (20,000 miles) long. Its satellites, in order from the planet, include Amalthea, Io, Europa, Ganymede, Leda, Himalia, Lysithea, Elara, Ananke, Carme, Pasiphaë, and Sinope.

See also: Saturn; Zeus

Jupiter Elicius
Roman
One of the forms taken by the principal Roman god Jupiter. In this guise he was regarded specifically as the god of rain.

Juturna
Roman
The daughter of King Daunus of Ardea and sister to Turnus, whom she helped in his fight with Aeneas. When she was finally compelled to abandon all hope of saving Turnus, she sank weeping into the spring at Lanuvium. There Jupiter seduced her and turned her into a water nymph.

See also: Aeneas

Juventas
Roman
The counterpart of Hebe.

K

Keres

Greek

Black, winged demons, the daughters, like the Fates, of Night. They are the source of diseases and most of the other evils that afflict mankind, including old age, death, and blight. They can therefore be assimilated as the ills that escaped from the box carried by Pandora. Keres were kept at bay by chewing buckthorn, smearing pitch on doorways, and similar expedients and had to be placated once a year at the festival of the Anthesteria in Athens.

Homer gives the Keres a more literary interpretation by making them spirits who control the destiny of the heroes and descend on them as they die to tear at their flesh and drink their blood. In this role they were often associated with the Fates, even receiving cult status alongside them. Plato likened them to the Harpies, who are hard to distinguish in art, as both are seen as harbingers of death whose task was to carry off the souls of the departed.

See also: Fates, the; Pandora

Knossos

Greek

The principal city of Minoan Crete, situated approximately 6 kilometers (4 miles) southeast of present-day Iráklion. The archaeological site, excavated by Sir Arthur Evans between 1899 and 1935, dates from about 2000 B.C. and includes a palace throne room and a labyrinth, the legendary home of the Minotaur. The excavation of the site pushed back the understanding of European prehistory by several millennia. Today, with a few exceptions, visible remains on the site date from about 1700 B.C., the so-called New Palace, built after some disaster, possibly an earthquake, though the west wall is marked by the fire of its own final destruction.

The predominance of a bull cult on Crete is displayed through wall paintings and objects that lend some credence to the legend of Theseus and the Minotaur. Games or rituals that involved maidens and youths, the latter leaping over the backs of bulls, are depicted in murals. The complex ruins also include various shrines, notably one to a snake goddess. The site was finally destroyed c. 1400 B.C.

See also: Minotaur; Theseus

Kore

Greek

Meaning "maiden," this title, also spelled Core, was applied to Persephone, the daughter of Demeter.

Kron~os, ~us

Greek

Variant of Cronos, the father of Zeus, who overthrew him.

L

Labdacus

Greek

King of Thebes, grandson of Cadmos, son of Polydorus, and father of Laius.

Labyrinth, the

Greek

The mazelike prison that was built by Daedalus on the order of Minos at Knossos, Crete, as the prison-home of the monstrous Minotaur. It had but one entrance and was composed of many winding alleys with dead ends. Theseus penetrated it, killed the Minotaur, and then safely escaped from its confines by following thread that he had unwound behind him.

The word *labyrinth* derives from the Cretan word *labrys*, a double-headed axe that was an important religious symbol in Minoan Crete. This connection suggests that the labyrinth may have originated as a complex shrine to the Minoan bull cult at Knossos.

The labyrinth was portrayed on many coins from Knossos, and over the years many have sought to find its remains. Some have simply identified it with the complex, labyrinthine layout of the Palace of Minos itself. During the Middle Ages it became identified with a complex system of caves in the hills near Gortyn, an opinion that held sway until the early nineteenth century, when these proved to be the remains of an old quarry.

See also: Minos; Minotaur

Lacedaemon

Greek

Another name for Sparta, the capital of Laconia.

Lachesis

Greek

One of the three Fates who with her spindle spun out the thread of human life, therefore representing the fate of life itself.

See also: Fates, the

Laconia

Greek

Ancient region in southwestern Greece, now a department. The ancient capital, Sparta, also known as Lacedaemon, is still the administrative center.

Lacus Curtius

Roman

Site in the Forum at Rome that was said to have derived its name from Mettius Curtius, the Sabine champion whose horse foundered in the swamps on the site of the later Forum.

See also: Sabine

Ladon

Greek

A dragon, one of the many monstrous offspring of Typhon and Echidne. Along with the Hesperides, Ladon guarded the garden in which the golden apples grew on the tree planted by Hera, a gift she had received from Ge at her wedding to Zeus. He was killed by Atlas when the latter undertook to steal the apples for Heracles on the eleventh of his 12 labors.

Laelaps

Greek

The swift-footed, unerring hound that Procris gave to Cephalos; also the name of the storm wind.

Laertes

Greek

King of Ithaca, husband of Anticleia, and father of Odysseus, though some sources say that Odysseus's father was really Sisyphus. He was one of the Argonauts who accompanied Jason on his quest, and also took part in the hunt for the Calydonian Boar. Even though a king, Laertes was said to till his own fields.

See also: Odysseus

Laestrygones

Greek

A giant, mythical cannibal race whose king, Lamus, ruled over Telepylos. They feature only in the tradition surrounding the wanderings of Odysseus as he attempted to make his way home after the end of the Trojan War. When Odysseus and his men put into Telepylos, one of his men was eaten, so Odysseus and his compatriots fled in their ships. However, the giants harpooned all Odysseus's ships, except the one in which he was fleeing, and ate all the occupants of those ships.

See also: Odysseus

Laius

Greek

King of Thebes, great-grandson of Cadmos, grandson of Polydorus, and son of Labdacus. He was raised at the court of Pelops and there fell in love with Chrysippus, Pelop's son. He subsequently carried him off to Thebes. There he married Jocasta but learned from the Delphic Oracle that he would be killed by his own son. As a result, when Oedipus was born, she exposed the child on Mount Cithaeron, his feet tied together and pierced by a nail. There the child was found by a shepherd and taken to Polybus, king of Corinth, who named him Oedipus because of his swollen feet, and raised him as his own.

Later, when Thebes was plagued by the Sphinx, who strangled all who could not answer her riddle, punishment for the abduction of Chrysippus, Laius was on his way to consult the Delphic Oracle when he came across Oedipus, traveling in the opposite direction. Neither would give way and, in the resulting quarrel, Oedipus fulfilled the prophesy and killed his own father, unaware of his identity.

See also: Cadmos; Jocasta; Oedipus

Lamia

Greek

Daughter of Beleus and beloved by Zeus, she later became one of the Empusae. She became the eponym of a class of monster in the form of a woman that was bestial, usually with serpentine and unmatched legs (for example, one leg could be of bronze while the other might be that of a goat or ass). The Lamiae were dirty, gluttonous, and slovenly and like Gello and the Strigles, they were believed to strangle young children.

Distinct from this class of Lamiae is the pair found in the *Golden Ass* by Apuleius. This pair would tear open a sleeping man's breast and take away his heart. In later belief she was simply named as a bogeywoman whose name was invoked to frighten children.

Lamus

Greek

A Theban youth who failed in his attempt to answer the riddle posed by the Sphinx. As a result he was strangled and thrown from the walls of the city by the monster.

See also: Sphinx

Laocoön

Greek

Son of Antenor; a Trojan priest to both Apollo and Poseidon who married, even though he had taken vows of celibacy, and thus secured the later wrath of Apollo and Poseidon. His warnings about the dangers concealed within the Wooden Horse went unheeded, even after he threw a spear at the horse to show, through the resulting echo, that the horse was not empty. Cassandra supported him in this warning, but she too was ignored, as she always was.

After the horse had been dragged within the walls of Troy, Poseidon or Apollo sent two sea serpents that strangled or crushed Laocoön and his two sons.

See also: Wooden Horse

Laodam(e)ia

Greek

Daughter of Acastus and wife of Protesilaus (the uncle of Philoctetes and the first man to jump ashore at Troy, even though he knew from an oracle that it meant certain death). Grief-stricken, Laodameia beseeched the gods to let her husband return for just three hours. They had pity for her, and Hermes led Protesilaus back from the Underworld to her. When he died for the second time, she died with him.

See also: Acastus

Laodice

Greek

1. Daughter of Priam and Hecuba, sister to Cassandra and Paris, and wife of Helicaon. When Cassandra was dragged away by Ajax the Lesser at the end of the Trojan War and claimed as booty by Agamemnon, the ground opened up and swallowed Laodice, thus saving her from a similar fate.

2. The name given by Homer to Electra, the daughter of Agamemnon.

See also: Ajax (2); Hecuba; Priam

Laomedon

Greek

Son of Ilus, grandson of Tros, father of Ganymede and Hesione, and founder of Ilion, or Troy. Zeus assigned Apollo and Poseidon to Laomedon to build the walls around Troy, thus making them impregnable to human force. Laomedon refused them their payment and threatened to sell them into slavery. In revenge Poseidon sent a sea monster that could be placated only by the sacrifice of Hesione. She was exposed naked to be devoured by the great beast, but Heracles killed the monster and so saved her. Once again Laomedon refused to give the specified reward—the white horses he had received from Zeus in exchange for his son Ganymede. Heracles, however, later returned with Telamon and Theseus, possibly on his way back from gaining the girdle of Hippolyte as one of his Great Labors. They sacked the city, Hesione being taken captive and awarded to Telamon; Laomedon and all his sons, except Podarces, were killed.

See also: Ganymede; Troy

Lapithae

Greek

Mythical race inhabiting Thessaly and ruled over by Peirithous, a son of Ixion and therefore a half-brother to the centaurs. They were, according to Diodorus, descended from their eponym, Lapithes, who was a brother of Centauros, thus cementing the relationship between the two Thessalanian tribes, though they always remained traditional enemies. During the wedding feast of Peirithous and Hippodameia, the centaurs attempted to carry off the bride and a company of other ladies. They were chased by the Lapithae and other guests at the wedding, Theseus among them, and soundly beaten. Peirithous was later said to have driven his people out of Thessaly to Doris. From there the Lapithae were expelled by the Dorian King Aegimus with the help of Heracles and an army of Arcadians.

See also: Centaur; Theseus

Lar

Roman

A short, squat fertility deity with curly hair; a personification of the phallus, he was invoked by men at the time of their marriage.

Lara

Roman

The daughter of Tiber who not only refused to help Jupiter seduce Juturna but actually warned both Juno and Juturna of Jupiter's intentions. In revenge Jupiter tore out her tongue so that she could no longer betray, then banished her to the Underworld, where she was placed in the care of Mercurius. He seduced her, the result being the *lares*.

Larentia

Roman

A shortened, popularized version of Acca Larentia.

Lares

Roman

The sons of Mercurius by the nymph Lara, born to her after she had been banished to the Underworld, her tongue having been torn out for betraying the extramarital intentions of Jupiter. Once considered as gods of cultivated land, they were worshipped by each household at crossroads where the boundaries of fields met. They were regarded as divine ancestors who watched benignly over each household, and as such their worship, in which they were stylized as figurines, moved into the house to join that of the Penates, gods of the threshold. They eventually came under Roman state control when they were regarded as spirits of the community.

Larissa

Greek

City to which Acrisius, mindful of the oracle that foretold his death at the hands of his son, fled when Perseus returned to Argos with Danaë. However, Perseus later visited Larissa and, taking part in public games, accidentally killed Acrisius with a discus.

See also: Perseus

Lartius, Spurius

Roman

One of the codefendants of the Pons Sublicus, along with Publius Horatius Cocles and Titius Herminus, against the attacking hordes under the leadership of Lars Porsenna. He and Titius Herminus were sent back to safety by Publius Horatius Cocles shortly before the bridge was demolished.

Larvae

Roman

Malignant spirits of the dead.

Latinus

1. Greek

The son of Odysseus and Circe who with his brother, Agrius, ruled the Tyrrhenians in the far-off "sacred isles," a possible reference to the Islands of the Blessed.

2. Roman

Old aboriginal king of Laurentum, or Latium, and husband of Amata who some described as the son of Faunus and the nymph Marica, others as the son of Hercules. At first an ally of Aeneas, he later became an enemy. He had been told by an oracle that his daughter, Lavinia, would marry a foreigner. He agreed to the marriage between Aeneas and Lavinia, but Juno incited the Rutulian Prince Turnus of Ardea, who claimed Mycenaean ancestry, and thus the right to marry Lavinia. As Amata opposed Aeneas, Latinus switched his viewpoint. Aeneas conquered Turnus and married Lavinia, though both Latinus and Amata now opposed him.

See also: Aeneas

Latium

Roman

Historic district in central Italy south of the Apennines and east of the Tiber. Inhabited by the Latini, Latium was bordered on the northwest by Etruria, on the southeast by Campania, and on the west by the Tyrrhenian Sea. Latium is regarded as extremely important in the foundation of the Roman state, as Lavinia, daughter of Latinus, the king of Latium, married Aeneas, who is regarded as the founder of the state. Augustus made Latium and Campania the first of the 11 administrative divisions of Italy, the latter name prevailing after 292 A.D.

See also: Aeneas

Latmus

Greek

The mountain in Caria where Selene wooed Endymion.

Latona

Roman

The Roman name applied to Leto.

Laverna

Roman

Goddess who protects thieves and frauds.

Lavinia

Roman

Daughter of Latinus, king of Latium, though some sources make her the daughter of Evander. Sometimes said to be the wife of Hercules, she is more often the wife of Aeneas, her hand being fought over by Aeneas and his great rival, Turnus, the Rutulian prince of Ardea. Aeneas subsequently built the city of Lavinium in her honor.

See also: Aeneas; Turnus

Lavinium

Roman

City legendarily founded by Aeneas in honor of his wife, Lavinia, at the spot where he had first landed in Italy. Traditionally founded c. 1200 B.C., temples to the honor of Venus, Vesta, and the Trojan Penates were established in the city.

See also: Aeneas

Leander

Greek

The tragic lover of Hero, whom he visited each night by swimming from his home in Abydos, across the treacherous waters of the Hellespont, guided by a light in Hero's window, to Sestos, where Hero was a priestess to Aphrodite. One particularly stormy night the lantern blew out and Leander drowned. Hero, in her grief, threw herself into the sea.

See also: Abydos; Hero; Sestos

Leda

Greek

Daughter of Thestius (king of Aeolia), wife of Tyndareus (king of Sparta), and mother of Helen, Polydeuces, Castor, and Clytemnestra, as well as three other obscure and unnamed children. Traditionally Leda was visited by Zeus, who took the form of a beautiful swan, after which she laid an egg that hatched Helen, Castor, and Polydeuces. Clytemnestra was her daughter by her mortal husband, Tyndareus. Another tradition says that although three children hatched from one egg, only Helen and Polydeuces were the children of Zeus, Castor being conceived on the same night but fathered by Tyndareus. Yet another says that only Helen was Zeus's offspring, the version favored by Homer.

Astronomical: One of the satellites of Jupiter lying sixth closest to the planet between the orbits of Callisto and Himalia. Discovered in 1974, Leda has an approximate diameter of just 10 kilometers (6.2 miles).

See also: Dioscuri; Helen; Tyndareus

Lemnos

Greek

Volcanic island of the Aegean Sea to which the Lycians emigrated, after which they became known as Pelasgians. There they established their cult to Hephaistos, the island being regarded as one of that god's favorite spots on earth. It was to the island of Lemnos that Hephaistos was said to have made his way after having been flung out of Olympus the second time. Philoctetes was left on the island on the way to Troy on the advice of Odysseus after a wound he had received had begun to fester. It was also the island on which Jason and the Argonauts spent a considerable amount of time with the man-starved women en route to Colchis.

See also: Jason

Lemures

Roman

The ghosts of the dead, including the benign *lares* and the malign *larvae*.

Leo

Greek

The name applied to the Nemaean Lion that was slain by Heracles as the first of his labors and whose pelt was subsequently worn as Heracles' armor.

Astronomical: Possibly the longest-known of all the heavenly constellations, Leo was recognized as a lion not only by the ancient Greeks but also by the Persians, Turks, Syrians, Hebrews, Assyrians, and Bablyonians. This constellation, the fifth of the 12 signs of the Zodiac (July 24–August 23) lies mostly in the northern celestial hemisphere between approximate right ascensions 9h20m and 11h50m, declination from -5° to +34°.

See also: Heracles

Lepcis Magna
Roman
Perhaps the best preserved of the Roman cities with the exception of Pompeii. The most notable temple remains are those of the temple of Rome and Augustus.

Lepus
Greek
"The Hare"; the favorite quarry of the hunter Orion, which, after Orion was placed in the night sky, joined him.

Astronomical: A constellation of the southern celestial hemisphere lying just below Orion between approximate right ascensions 4h55m and 6h10m, declination from –11° to –28°.

See also: Orion

Lerna
Greek
Marshy area adjoining the sevenfold source of the River Amymone that was inhabited and plagued by the multiheaded Hydra. Heracles traveled to Lerna during the course of his 12 labors to dispose of the Hydra.

See also: Heracles; Hydra

Lethe
Greek
The River of Forgetfulness, also called Oblivion, one of the five rivers that flowed through the Underworld. It was the last river across which Hermes guided the newly dead before they were brought before the three judges of the Underworld, Minos, Aeacus, and Rhadamanthus. All had to drink the water of the river and, upon doing so, forgot their life on earth, though simply crossing it was also said to have had the same effect. Some have suggested that they drank the water after their judgment, as it would have been unwise to have the newly dead forget what they were about to be judged on. Personified, Lethe was considered to be the daughter of Eris.

A spring having the name Lethe ran close by the Oracle of Trophonius at Lebadeia. Visitors to the oracle drank the water of the spring to forget their past, then from another, which would enable them to remember the advice they had received from the oracle.

See also: Eris; Underworld

Leto
Greek
Also: Latona

An ancient goddess originating in Asia Minor known to the Etruscans as Letun. Patroness of the fruitful earth, lady of the beasts and plants, she had cultic status especially in Lycia and at Ortygia, near Ephesus.

Legend makes Leto the daughter of the Titans Coeus and Phoebe and the mother, by Zeus, of the twins Apollo and Artemis. Before the birth of the twins, Hera—once again jealous of her husbands continual philandering—caused Leto to wander aimlessly. She finally gave birth to Artemis under a palm tree on Ortygia and to Apollo beside a palm on Delos, though some say that Delos was originally called Ortygia, so the twins were born on the same island. Hera was still not satisfied, and as Leto came to Delphi with her daughter, Artemis, the goddess sent the giant Tityus to violate her. He was dispatched by Apollo and Artemis. Leto then fled to Lycia, where she was prevented from drinking at a well called Melite, in revenge turning the local peasants into frogs.

See also: Apollo; Artemis; Coeus; Phoebe

Leuce
Greek
1. A nymph who was seduced by Hades and was afterwards turned into the white poplar tree.

2. The "White Island" in the Black Sea to which Achilles, Helen, and other heroes were transported after their deaths. It is possibly the site where the nymph Leuce was transformed into the white poplar tree following her rape by Hades.

Leucippides
Greek
The generic name of Phoebe and Hilaeira, the twin daughters of Leucippus, king of Mes-

senia, who were betrothed to the giants Idas and Lynceus, abducted by the Dioscuri, and rescued by their fiancés, a battle that cost Castor his life.

Leucippus

Greek

1. Son of Oenomaus, he fell in love with Daphne. Disguising himself as a woman, he joined her retinue of nymphs. Apollo advised Daphne and her nymphs to bathe naked, and when they stripped they discovered Leucippus and tore him to pieces.

2. King of Messenia and father of Phoebe and Hilaeira, hence Leucippides, whom he betrothed to Idas and Lynceus.

See also: Dioscuri

Leucothea

Greek

Sea goddess who was formerly Ino, her form being altered when she leaped into the sea. Leucothea was benevolent to sailors in distress and once, aided by Athene, helped Odysseus, after he had been shipwrecked by Poseidon, to the island of Scheria, home of Nausicaa.

See also: Ino; Odysseus

Liber (Pater)

Roman

An ancient Roman god of wine and fruitfulness who made the ground fertile. He was initially identified with the Greek Dionysos, later with the Roman Bacchus, who eventually replaced him.

Libera

Roman

The female counterpart of Liber.

Libertas

Roman

A contrived Roman goddess of political freedom and constitutional government. She was significantly given a temple by Tiberius Sempronius Gracchus in 238 B.C. and later appears in statues wearing the Phrygian cap of liberty. She has no mythology.

Libitina

Roman

An ancient Italian goddess whose original associations were with voluptuous and libidinous pleasures. Later she became identified as the goddess of death, funerals, and undertakers, possibly replacing Proserpina in this role. Money was offered to Libitina in a sacred grove whenever someone died, a grove that also contained the registrar of deaths and the offices of undertakers.

Lichas

Greek

Servant or companion of Heracles who was sent by Heracles to fetch from his wife a white shirt, or robe, to wear at a celebration. Deianeira, fearing that Heracles might leave her for Iole, smeared the shirt with the poisoned blood of Nessus, falsely believing that it would maintain Heracles' love for her. Lichas returned with this shirt, which burned into Heracles' flesh when it was put on. In agony, Heracles flung Lichas into the sea.

See also: Deianeira; Heracles

Lindos

Greek

The most attractively sited temple of Greece is that of Athene at Lindos, where it dominates a cliff-top Acropolis.

Linus

Greek

1. A musician and poet, the son of Apollo, and, usually, one of the Muses, he taught the lyre to Thamyris, Orpheus, and Heracles. He is the personification of a dirge that was sung to mourn the dying vegetation at harvest time. His name is taken from the refrain *al linon*, "alas." He was killed by his father, Apollo, who was jealous of his skill with the lyre, though the Thebans said he once censured Heracles, and it was he who killed him with his own lyre.

2. The son of Apollo and Psamanthe, according to an Argive story. Ashamed of her pregnancy, Psamanthe exposed the newborn, who was raised by shepherds but later torn to pieces by her father's dogs. Her grief revealed her predicament to her father, who sentenced her to death. In revenge Apollo visited Argos with a plague that raged until the Argives propitiated both Linus and Psamanthe with dirges called *linoi*. There is great similarity between this Linus and the other Linus, who is thought of as the personification of a dirge.

See also: Heracles; Orpheus

Lipara
Greek

A volcanic island that, along with Lemnos, Hiera, Imbros, and Sicily, numbered among the favorite places on earth of Hephaistos.

Lipari Islands
Greek

Also known as the Aeolian islands, this group of islands in the Tyrrhenian Sea includes Lipara, one of the favorite spots on earth of Hephaistos. They also include the floating island of Aeolia, where Aeolus was said to keep the four winds in a cave to be released either when Aeolus felt like it or when the gods commanded it.

See also: Aeolus; Hephaistos

Lityerses
Greek

A Phrygian harvest song that became personified as the son of Midas, who forced passersby to work in his fields before beheading them at the end of the day. According to a late development of the legend, Lityerses once did this to Daphnis, and Heracles then punished him with a dose of his own medicine. The song that became known as *Lityerses* was said to have been invented by him.

See also: Heracles

Livy
Roman

Roman historian, properly Titus Livius (59 B.C.–17 A.D.), who was born in Padua to a noble and wealthy family; his works remain one of the major sources of Roman myth and legend. He settled in Rome c. 29 B.C. and was admitted to the court of Augustus. His history of Rome from its foundation to the death of Nero Claudius Drusus (9 B.C.) comprises 142 books; of those, numbers 11–20 and 46–142 have been lost.

Locris
Greek

Ancient kingdom of which Oileus, the father of Ajax the Lesser, was king.

Lotophagi
Greek

Name given to a people who lived on the Libyan coast in a state of enervating dreaminess through eating the fruit of the lotus plant. They were visited by Odysseus and their companions after the end of the Trojan War, his companions who also ate the fruit becoming known as the Lotus-Eaters, the literal translation of *Lotophagi*.

Lotus-Eaters
Greek

The name given to the companions of Odysseus who, while visiting the Lotophagi on the Libyan coast, ate the fruit of the lotus plant and so entered the same state of enervating dreaminess in which the Lotophagi lived. They led a life of perfect, empty-headed contentment and immediately lost all desire to return home. "Lotus-Eater" is the literal translation of *Lotophagi*.

Loxias
Greek

"The Ambiguous"; a name given to Apollo at his Dorian shrine at Delphi near the spring Castalia on Mount Parnassus, where he was also known as the Pythian.

Lua
Roman

The goddess wife of Saturnus who was, according to Livy, invoked to destroy enemy arms.

Lucifer

Greek

Also: Phosphorus

"Bringer of Light"; the name given to the planet Venus when seen in the morning sky before sunrise. Given a masculine personification in myth, the name was equally applied to Artemis, as it was to her brother, Apollo.

Lucina

Roman

An epithet that was chiefly applied to Juno but also sometimes to Diana, in which role she was regarded as the goddess of childbirth, bringing children into the light.

See also: Juno

Lucre~tia, ~ce

Roman

The beautiful and pure wife of Lucius Tarquinius Collatinus who was raped by Sextus, the son of the Etruscan king of Rome, Tarquinius Superbus. She reported the outrage to her father, Spurius Lucretius Tricipitinus, and her husband and made them swear to avenge her. She then stabbed herself to death before them and in the presence of Publius Valerius Poplicola and Lucius Junius Brutus. The latter of these witnesses led the populace in rebellion against the ruling Etruscans. This led to the expulsion of the Tarquins, an end to kingship in Rome, and the establishment of the Roman republic.

See also: Sextus

Luna

Roman

Goddess of the moon, the Roman counterpart to the Greek Selene.

Lupercal

Roman

A cave on the Palatine Hill in ancient Rome that was sacred to Lupercus, or to Faunus in the guise of a wolf deity, and as such has important connections with the story of Romulus and Remus. The Lupercalia festival centered around the sacred cave.

See also: Remus; Romulus

Lupercalia

Roman

A popular festival of unknown origin that was celebrated on 15 February when two teams of aristocratic youths, known as the Lupercii, sacrificed goats and a dog in the Lupercal Cave on the Palatine Hill. They then feasted before donning the skins of the sacrificial goats to race down the hill, whipping anyone in range with goatskin thongs. This was believed to promote fertility.

The festival probably predates the legend of Romulus and Remus, for on one occasion Remus was captured by brigands the twins had been attacking and was taken to Amulius. This abduction of Remus was said to have taken place during the Lupercalia.

See also: Remus; Romulus

Lupercus

Roman

Possibly the name given to the she-wolf who suckled the twins Romulus and Remus, possibly an alias for Faunus in the guise of a wolf deity. A cave on the Palatine Hill in ancient Rome, the Lupercal Cave, was sacred to Lupercus and was the site of the immensely popular annual Lupercalia festival.

Lupus

Greek

Traditional name given to the wolf-form that Lycaon adopted after Zeus transformed him for the crime of serving human flesh as a banquet for the gods. However, the name Boötes was also used to refer to Lycaon in the form of a wolf.

Astronomical: A constellation of the southern celestial hemisphere located between approximate right ascensions 14h15m and 16h00m, declination from –39° to –65°.

Lycaon

Greek

A king of Arcadia, son of Pelasgus, father of Callisto, and founder of the city of Lycosura on Mount Lycaeum who established a rite of child sacrifice. Some versions of the story say that it was his own son, Arcas, who was sacrificed. Lycaon then threw a banquet for the gods at which the flesh of the sacrificed child was served. However, Zeus would not eat, thus refusing Lycaon's sacrifice, and in his anger turned the king into a wolf, along with all his other sons, save Nyctinus, or killed them with his thunderbolt. The former fate is the more likely as the ancient Greeks referred to the constellation Boötes as Lycaon, a wolf.

The story marks the outrage that ended the community of men and gods, finally separating the two races. Following this first sacrifice, at every subsequent sacrifice to the Lycaean Zeus, a man would turn into a wolf for a period of eight or nine years. If during that period the wolf refrained from eating human flesh, the original human form would be restored. It was also said that any creature that entered the sanctuary of the Lycaean Zeus would lose its shadow. In the case of a man this was tantamount to becoming a werewolf, and offenders were immediately stoned to death.

See also: Callisto

Lycia
Greek

Ancient region of Asia Minor on the southern seaboard of modern Turkey. Legend says that the kingdom was once ruled by Iobates, to whom Bellerophon was sent by Proetus and who sent Bellerophon out against the Chimaera, which was ravaging the country. Ancient peoples from Lycia emigrated to Lemnos, where they became known as the Pelasgians, and brought one stem of the worship of Apollo into Greece, associating him with an ancient Hittite deity named Lycius, a name adapted to Apollo on Delos. Hephaistos is thought to have originated from the region.

See also: Bellerophon; Chimaera; Iobates

Lycius
Greek

Originally an ancient Hittite deity worshipped in Lycia, Lycius became one of the names applied to Apollo at his Ionian shrine on Delos, where he was also known as Phoebus. It is possible that Lycius is one of the origins of Apollo, though he also appears to have Dorian aspects.

See also: Apollo

Lycomedes
Greek

King of the Dolopians on the island of Scyros. His daughter, Deidameia, became the mother of Neoptolemus, also called Pyrrhos, by Achilles when the latter was sent there by his mother, Thetis, in the guise of a girl so that he would not have to go to the Trojan War where he was destined to die. Lycomedes is also infamous as the murderer of Theseus, who had taken refuge on Scyros after he fled from Athens.

See also: Achilles; Neoptolemus

Lycurgus
Greek

King of the Edones who opposed the worship of Dionysos and drove the god and his Maenads out with an oxgoad. Like Pentheus, Lycurgus was sent mad, either by Dionysos or Rhea; while chopping down grapevines in the belief that they were poisonous, he mistook his own leg for a vine and cut that off as well. He then killed and mutilated his son, Dryasa (Oak Tree), under the same delusion, and for this his people, the Edones, punished him. His end has several versions. He was either fed to man-eating horses on Mount Pangaeum, torn to pieces between two horses, eaten by panthers to whom he had been thrown by Dionysos, or simply took his own life.

See also: Dionysos

Lycus
Greek

1. The son of Pandion who was expelled by his brother, Aegeus, and took refuge in Lycia, a country to which he gave his name.

2. King of Thebes who either inherited the kingdom from his brother, Nycteus, or won it in battle. He then made war on Sicyon and brought back Antiope, his first wife by whom he became the father of Amphion and Zethus. He later divorced her in favor of Dirce. When his sons, who had been raised by cattle drovers on Mount Cithaeron, grew up, they returned to Thebes, killed Lycus and Dirce, and took possession of the city.

3. A descendant of Lycus who usurped the throne of Thebes after the death of Creon.

While Heracles was at Thespiae the hero's family resided at Thebes, but Lycus persecuted them. Heracles returned and killed the king in revenge for this treatment of his family.

See also: Aegeus; Dirce; Heracles; Pandion

Lydia

Greek

An ancient kingdom and (seventh–sixth century B.C.) empire of the central-western coast of Asia Minor. It was here that Heracles spent his time as a slave to Queen Omphale, dressed as a female and doing female tasks, while she wore his cloak of lion's skin.

See also: Heracles

Lynceus

Greek

1. Son of Amphiaraus and devoted twin brother of Idas. Lynceus was noted for his keen sight, and the inseparable twins took part in the hunt for the Calydonian Boar as well as the expedition of Jason and the Argonauts. They were betrothed to the Leucippides, the daughters of Leucippus, whom the Dioscuri abducted. Their attempted rescue of the girls led to their deaths.

2. One of the 50 sons of Aegyptus who was fortunate enough to marry Hypermnestra, the only one of the 50 Danaides who did not carry out her father's instruction to kill her new husband on their wedding night. He later succeeded Danaus as the king of Argos.

See also: Danaides; Dioscuri; Idas; Jason

Lyra

Greek

Traditionally the name given to the lyre of Orpheus, musician to the Argonauts and husband of Eurydice. With it he charmed Hades into releasing his wife back to him after her death. After his own death it was translated to the heavens to commemorate the beautiful music it had produced at the hands of Orpheus.

Astronomical: Lying in the northern celestial hemisphere, the constellation Lyra contains the brilliant star Vega, the third-brightest star in the night sky. Relatively small, the constellation lies between approximate right ascensions 18h10m and 19h30m, declination from +25° to +48°.

See also: Orpheus

Lystra

Greek

Place in Asia Minor where Saint Paul was mistaken for Hermes (see Acts 14:6–21).

M

Macareus

Greek

The son of Aeolus who had an incestuous relationship with his sister, Canace. Their daughter, Issa, was one of those beloved by Apollo.

See also: Aeolus (2)

Macaria

Greek

Daughter of Heracles, thus one of the Heracleidae, who committed suicide after an oracle demanded the sacrifice of one of Heracles' children if Athens, in which the Heracleidae had sought sanctuary, was to be saved from the attack mounted by Eurystheus. Following the self-sacrifice of Macaria, Eurystheus was defeated by either Iolaus or Hyllus and finally dispatched by Alcmene.

See also: Heracles

Macedonia

Greek

Mountainous Balkan country north of ancient Greece that was divided from Thessaly by a mountain range, the range's eastern end being the location of Mount Olympus. Today, Macedonia is divided between Greece and the independent state of Macedonia, which formed a part of Yugoslavia. Under Philip II and his son, Alexander the Great, Macedonia dominated Greece in the fourth century B.C. In 146 B.C. it became a Roman province, and when the Roman Empire was divided it was assigned to the eastern half.

See also: Alexander the Great

Machaereus

Greek

"Knife Man"; an ancestor of Branchus and the founder of the Oracle of Apollo at Didyma, he became infamous as the murderer of Neoptolemus.

See also: Neoptolemus

Machaon

Greek

Son of Asclepios, brother of Podalirius, and father of Nicomachus and Gorgasus, who were also considered as healing heroes. He and his brother were suitors for the hand of Helen, and both led a fleet to Troy. There, either Machaon or his brother cured the archer Philoctetes of the festering wound that had originally meant his desertion en route to the Trojan War. Machaon met his death at Troy at the hands of either Eurypylus or Penthesilea and was buried at Messedia.

See also: Asclepios; Helen

Maenad

Greek

Name given to a female votary or votaries of the god of wine, Dionysos, who dressed in the skins of wild animals and carried *thyrsoi*, vine branches entwined with ivy and tipped with a pine cone. Maenads assembled in the mountains and, in the orgiastic frenzy induced through drinking wine, they rampaged over the hills, catching wild animals, which they then tore to pieces and ate raw. Various other names were applied to the worshippers of Dionysos, including Bacchoi (male votaries), and Bacchae, Bacchantes, or Thyiads, the latter being specifically restricted to usage in Athens and Delphi. Their rites persisted into historical times, but the introduction of their cult appears to have been widely resisted, as witnessed in the many legends that surround the Maenads and the worship of Dionysos.

See also: Dionysos

Maera

Greek

The name given to the bitch that Hecuba reportedly transformed herself into to evade the angry Thracian people after she had avenged the murder of her son, Polydorus, by killing Polymester and his two sons.

See also: Hecuba

Maia

1. Greek

Daughter of Atlas and the Oceanid Pleione; the eldest and most beautiful of the Pleiades. She was said to have been the mother of Hermes by Zeus, bearing him on Mount Cyllene in Arcadia. As his mother was a daughter of Atlas and an embodiment of the Great Goddess, Hermes also became known as Atlantiades. Later she brought on Arcas, the son of Callisto, after his mother had been killed by Hera or had been turned into a bear.

2. Roman

Ancient agricultural and fertility goddess associated with Vulcan and also, by confusion with Maia, with Mercurius. Sacrifices were made to her to ensure the fertility of crops.

See also: Pleiades

Mamercus

Roman

Legendary founder of the great Aemilian family of ancient Rome. He claimed he was the son of Numa Pompilius, though some claimed he may have been the son of the great Greek philosopher Pythagoras.

Manes, di

Roman

Generic name for the deified spirits of departed ancestors, revered as lesser deities, who were believed to linger either in or near their tomb, there requiring frequent feeding. As they were thought to grow dangerous if neglected, they were provided with a meal at the original funeral and were fed annually thereafter at the Parentalia festival. They were sometimes, incorrectly, identified with the gods of the Underworld.

Manto

Greek

The daughter of Teiresias and mother, by Apollo, of the seer Mopsus.

See also: Teiresias

Marathon(ian) Bull

Greek

The white bull that was originally given to Minos by Poseidon to confirm Minos's supreme rule over Crete. Minos substituted a lesser bull for this magnificent animal in the required sacrifice. Later, Heracles came to Crete and captured the bull as his seventh labor. He took it back to Eurystheus, who released it, whereupon it wandered through Greece before settling in the region of Marathon. It was subsequently recaptured by Theseus, who took it back to Athens as a sacrifice to Athene.

See also: Minos

Marica

Roman

A nymph; the wife of Faunus and mother of Latinus.

Marpessa

Greek

Daughter of the river god Euneus who was loved by Apollo but carried away by Idas in the winged chariot Poseidon had given him. Apollo gave chase and fought Idas for Marpessa until Zeus intervened, saying that Marpessa must be allowed to choose for herself. She chose Idas.

See also: Idas

Mars

Roman

The Roman god of war. He has Sabine origins, the month of March is named for him, and he is the equivalent of the Greek Ares. Originally an agricultural deity, important to the prosperity of the city of Rome, Mars developed into the god of war when Rome expanded its empire, being vital to the success of the Roman campaigns. He became one of the three protector-deities of Rome, along with Jupiter and Quirinius, and in popularity was second only to Jupiter.

Tradition makes Mars the son of Juno, his father having the remarkable guise of a flower. He seduced the Vestal Virgin daughter of Numitor, Rhea Silvia, while she was asleep (and thus unaware of her violation). She bore twin sons, whom she exposed. They were cared for and suckled by a she-wolf before being found and cared for by a shepherd and his wife. These sons of Mars were Romulus and Remus, who were later led by a flock of geese to the site where they founded a new city—Rome.

At first Mars lived in the woods and hills and kept a watchful eye over farming. He remained a pastoral deity for many years, only much later developing into the god of war with a temple sacred to him in Rome. Here sacrifices were made to ensure victory, after which he expected his share in the booty. Occasionally Mars would appear on the battlefield in the guise of a humble infantryman. His popularity grew with the expansion of the Roman Empire, for he was considered a key component in the continued Roman successes. As the empire expanded, temples to Mars became more widespread. He was a particular patron of the horse, a patronage reflected in horseraces that were held on the Campius Martius, the field of Mars, in March and October, dates that marked the beginnings and endings of the military and agricultural years. The winners of these races were given the ultimate reward—they were sacrificed to Mars. The October celebration was also a fertility festival at which Mars was worshipped in the guise of Silvanus, his earth god aspect. It was at this site that the Roman infantry paraded and where there once stood the earliest-known altar to Mars. Each year the army would assemble at another of Mars's temples, on the Appian Way, and from there parade through the city.

Mars was closely associated with Bellona, goddess of war, who was possibly his wife or his sister. The first Roman emperor, Augustus, was particularly fond of and devoted to Mars, considering him his personal protector. Augustus built him many temples, most of which were outside city walls, where they would do most good to the land, a memory of his earlier agricultural aspects. Augustus particularly worshipped Mars in the guise of Mars Ultor, "the Avenger," for he was seen as avenging the assassination of Augustus's adoptive father, Julius Caesar. In art he was often depicted simply as an armed warrior or naked, bearing arms. The wolf and woodpecker were his sacred animals.

Astronomical: The fourth planet of the solar system, lying at an average distance of 228 million kilometers (141.5 million miles) from the sun, being approximately half the size of earth and having an equatorial diameter of 6,794 kilometers (4,247 miles). The planet has a distinctive reddish color that was said to have reminded the ancients of blood, so they named it after their god of war. The largest known volcanic mountain, Olympus Mons, is located on the surface of Mars, which has two satellites, Phobos and Deimos, named after the horsemen of Ares, the Greek god of war.

See also: Remus; Romulus; Sabine

Marsyas
Greek
A satyr from Phrygia who picked up the double-reeded pipe, or *aulos*, which had been discarded by Athene as it forced the player to grimace. This, however, did not bother Marsyas, whose facial characteristics made it simple for him to play. He challenged Apollo to a musical contest that was judged by Tmolus, with contributions by King Midas, a contest that was won by Apollo. As punishment for Marsyas's presumption, Apollo suspended him in a pine tree and flayed him alive, his blood forming the River Marsyas.

Mastarna
Romano-Etruscan
A famous Etruscan hero; the great friend of Vibenna whom the Romans later equated with Servius Tullius.

Matralia
Roman
The festival of Mater Matuta, which was celebrated on 11 April and involved a servant

woman being forced into the temple sanctuary, then forcibly ejected. For the duration of the celebrations, women treated their sisters' children as if they were their own. The actual purpose of the festival remains unclear, but it may have associations with the driving-out of winter by spring, thus marking the start of the growing season.

Medeä
Greek

The sorceress-daughter of Aeëtes, king of Colchis, thus the granddaughter of Helios, sister to Circe, another sorceress, and the priestess of Hecate. Nothing is known of her before her involvement with Jason and the Argonauts. She immediately fell in love with Jason when he arrived in Colchis and helped him against her father.

When Jason first arrived, Aeëtes said that he would only give up the Golden Fleece if Jason could yoke a fire-breathing bull with brazen hooves, the work of Hephaistos, plough the field of Ares with the bulls, and then sow the dragon's teeth that were left over by Cadmos. Medeä supplied a fireproof ointment that enabled Jason to complete the allotted task. Aeëtes failed to keep his promise, so Medeä charmed to sleep the sleepless dragon that guarded the grove in which the Golden Fleece hung, thereby enabling the Argonauts to steal it.

Medeä then fled with Jason, taking with her Apsyrtus, her half-brother. When her father gave chase she ruthlessly murdered Apsyrtus and, cutting him into small pieces, dropped his body over the side of the fleeing ship. Aeëtes stopped to collect the remains for burial, enabling the Argonauts to safely escape. On the island of Aeaea, Jason and Medeä were purified of this murder by Circe. They then made their way to Crete, where Medeä devised a method to dispose of the menacing bronze giant named Talos.

Returning to Iolcos, Jason's home city, they found Aeson a tired, old man, though some sources say he had been forced to take his own life by Pelias. Jason persuaded Medeä to rejuvenate him. This she did by draining Aeson's blood and filling his veins with a magical potion. She then proposed to rejuvenate Pelias, demonstrating a second method to his doubting daughters by cutting up an old sheep and boiling the pieces in a cauldron. From the brew she pulled out a newborn lamb. Pelias's daughters, with the exception of Alcestis, were convinced. They cut up Pelias, but this time the magic did not work. Jason and Medeä were expelled from Iolcos by Acastus, Pelias's son, and traveled to Corinth.

They lived happily as normal citizens until Jason fell in love with Glauce, also called Creusa, the daughter of King Creon. He divorced Medeä, but she, realizing that her position as a resident alien was now in jeopardy, retaliated by sending the young bride a poisoned robe that set her body on fire when she dressed in it. The resulting blaze destroyed the palace and killed Creon. Medeä then killed her children by Jason and fled Corinth in a winged chariot sent by her grandfather, Helios, going now to Athens.

There she married Aegeus and became the mother of Medus. However, Medeä tried to get rid of her stepson, Theseus, the son of Aegeus and Aethra, by sending him out against the Marathonian Bull. When Theseus returned unharmed, Aegeus expelled both Medeä and Medus. They fled back to Colchis but stopped en route at Absoros to put an end to a plague of snakes by confining them in the tomb of Apsyrtus. Having arrived in Colchis, she proposed to cure a crop failure by human sacrifice. Perses, then king, suggested Medus as the victim, but Medeä retaliated by killing Perses. Nothing more is heard of Medeä after this, though some say she became an immortal.

Medeä received cult in Thessaly and Corinth, her children also being revered in the latter city.

See also: Aeëtes; Aegeus; Aeson; Apsyrtus; Circe; Creon; Hecate; Jason; Pelias; Talos; Theseus

Medus
Greek

The son of Medeä and Aegeus, he fled with his mother from Athens after the safe return of Theseus, whom Medeä had sent out against the Marathonian Bull. He traveled with her to Colchis, but after it was suggested by Perses that he should be the sacrifice to cure a crop failure, nothing more is heard of him.

Medusa
Greek

Daughter of the sea deities Phorcys and Ceto, sister to the Graeae and sister to Stheno and Euryale, Medusa was the only mortal Gorgon. She and her sisters had once been beautiful, but Medusa lay with Poseidon in one of the temples sacred to Athene, and in revenge Athene altered their appearance, turning them into winged monsters with brazen claws and serpent hair, so hideous that a single glance had the power to petrify human flesh to stone. She and her sisters were said to live in Libya, though some sources place the Gorgons in the land of the Hyperboreans.

Perseus came to their homeland, wherever it actually might have been, on the orders of Polydectes to behead Medusa. Aided in his quest by Athene, who some say ordered the death of Medusa, her hostility toward the Gorgon unabated, Perseus was armed with a polished shield, the gift of Athene, a sickle provided by Hermes, Hades' helmet of invisibility, a pair of winged sandals, and a special bag in which he was to place Medusa's head.

Confronting the hideous beast, Perseus used the shield to avoid looking directly at Medusa, her reflection not being deadly. He then successfully beheaded the Gorgon with Hermes' sickle and concealed the power of the head in the special leather bag. As he did so, Perseus was amazed to see the winged horse Pegasus and the warrior Chrysaor spring fully grown from her body. These fabulous beings were the children of Poseidon, begotten on Medusa when she lay with the great sea god in the temple of Athene.

Fleeing, Perseus was chased by Stheno and Euryale but escaped to the south by wearing Hades' helmet of invisibility, though some sources say he escaped on Pegasus, who certainly features later in the story of Perseus.

Even though Medusa now lay dead, her head still had the power to turn all who looked upon it into stone. Perseus was said to have used its power on a number of occasions. He turned Atlas into the mountain named after him; then he used it on the sea monster Cetus,

who was about to kill Princess Andromeda, who was being offered in sacrifice by Cepheus and Cassiopeia. When these two refused Perseus his reward, the hand of Andromeda, he again unleashed the terrible power of Medusa's head and turned Andromeda's suitor, and all his retinue, to stone. A similar fate awaited Polydectes when Perseus returned to Seriphos. Having completed his quest, Perseus gave Medusa's head to Athene, who placed its petrifying image in the center of her aegis, the head's snaky locks forming its border.

See also: Aegis; Ceto; Chrysaor; Euryale; Graeae; Pegasus; Perseus; Phorcys; Stheno

Megaera
Greek

One of the Erinnyes or Furies, the snake-haired, winged daughters of Mother Earth who were born when drops of blood from the wound inflicted on Uranos by Cronos fell on her. Her sisters were Alecto and Tisiphone, though the three sisters were named only in the works of later writers. Megaera is sometimes confused with Medusa through the single similarity that both had serpentine hair.

See also: Alecto; Erinnyes; Tisiphone

Megapenthes
Greek

Son of Proetus (king of Tiryns) and cousin of Perseus (king of Argos), with whom he exchanged his kingdom.

Meg~ara, ~era
Greek

Eldest daughter of Creon, king of Thebes, who was given to Heracles as a reward for his helping the city and who became the mother of several children by the great hero. Her youngest sister married Heracles' half-brother, Iphicles. She was later given to Heracles' nephew, Iolaus, but some versions of the story of Heracles said that upon his later return to Thebes the tyrannical king attempted to kill Megara and her children. Heracles killed the tyrant but was then driven mad by Hera, and as a result he killed Megara and their children.

See also: Creon; Heracles

Melampus

Greek

"Black Foot"; son of Amythaon and brother of Bias who gained his name after his mother laid him in the shade as a baby but left his feet in the sun. He gained the power to understand the languages of birds and animals after he had rescued the offspring of a dead snake while staying with the king of Messenia, for while he slept the snakes licked his ears and gave him the power.

He helped Bias to steal the cattle of King Phylacus, which Bias gave to Neleus as the price of marrying his daughter. Melampus, however, was caught and thrown into prison. There he overheard two woodworms discussing the imminent collapse of the roof to his cell, so Melampus asked to be moved to another one, foretelling the collapse. When this did indeed occur, and Melampus thus proved his foresight, the king asked Melampus to cure his son of impotence. Discovering that this was caused by the boy having seen his father brandishing a bloody gelding knife, Melampus traced the knife, and an infusion of rust from its blade was used to cure the boy.

Melampus's best-known task was to cure the daughters of Proteus of Argos of their madness, which caused them to think they were cows and roam the countryside killing people. Melampus demanded payment for himself and Bias—shares in the kingdom—and having gained that promise he prepared a potion that cured the girls. This herbal potion was then thrown into a river that thenceforth smelled foul. Melampus and his brother married Lysippe and Iphianassa, two of Proteus's daughters, Melampus finally succeeding Proteus as king, at which point his career as a seer came to an end. He was the first person to introduce the cult of Dionysos into Greece, his descendants forming the next Argive dynasty.

See also: Amythaon; Bias; Proteus

Melanion

Greek

"The Black One"; a chaste hermit who lived in the mountains, far away from civilization, and spent his time hunting. He appears in just one tradition, where he ends up as the husband of Atalanta, though he also appears in this role as Hippomenes.

See also: Atalanta; Hippomenes

Melanippe

Greek

"Black Horse"; the daughter of Aeolus (son of Hellen) and Hippe or Euippe (daughter of Cheiron). During the period her father was in exile for murder, Melanippe bore twin sons to Poseidon, Aeolus and Boeotus, whom she hid in an ox stall to be suckled by the beasts there. Upon his return her father decreed that these monstrous children should be burned, also blinding and imprisoning Melanippe. The children, however, survived and were reared by herdsmen. They were subsequently adopted by Theano, wife of Metapontus, king of Icaria, but when she had twins of her own the two pairs fought, Aeolus and Boeotus killing their half-brothers. Theano committed suicide and the two boys rescued their mother, whereupon she recovered her sight.

Some later, unreliable sources say that Melanippe was the daughter of Cheiron and that she was changed by the gods into an equine constellation.

See also: Aeolus; Boeotus; Cheiron

Melanippus

Greek

One of the original Seven Against Thebes. Having originally wounded Tydeus, Melanippus was killed in the fight, Tydeus later being persuaded by Amphiaraus, who bore him a grudge, to drink his brains.

See also: Seven Against Thebes

Meleager

Greek

Son of Oeneus and Althaea of Calydon. When he was just seven days old the Fates decreed that he should die when a brand, then on the fire, was finally consumed by the flames. Althaea immediately seized it and hid it away. Saved, Meleager later sailed with the Argonauts before returning to Calydon, where he married Cleopatra, the daughter of Idas and Marpessa.

Artemis later sent a boar to ravage the countryside around Calydon as punishment for Oeneus forgetting to include her in the sacrifice of first fruits. Numerous heroes took part in the hunt for the Calydonian Boar, but Meleager finally succeeded in killing it, skinned it, and gave the skin or head to Atalanta. This enraged his uncles, the sons of Thestius, who snatched it back from her, so Meleager killed them. Homer's *Iliad* varies this, saying that Meleager killed them in a war against the Curetes. Althaea, in her anger, returned the magic brand to the fire, and Meleager died of a wasting sickness as it was consumed. His mother then killed herself. Meleager did, however, appear to survive long enough to have had a son, Parthenopaeus by Atalanta. Meleager's sisters mourned him so bitterly that Artemis finally turned them, with the exception of Gorge and Deianeira, into guinea fowl, hence Meleagrides.

See also: Althaea; Argonauts; Atalanta

Meli(ad)ae
Greek
Nymphs of the manna ash tree who were born from the blood of the severed genitalia of Uranos. Having a warlike tendency, they were said to have invented bronze, or at least to have shown how it might be employed in making weapons, the shafts of spears commonly being made from ash, the trees they were said to inhabit.

See also: Uranos

Melicertes
Greek
Son of Athamas and Ino of Boeotia. Melicertes was carried by his mother when she leaped into the sea. His body was then carried ashore by a dolphin to the Corinthian isthmus. There it was found and given funeral rites by his uncle, Sisyphus, king of Corinth. These rites were the origin of the Isthmian Games. Melicertes was then given the new name, Palaemon, his tomb being the oldest sacred spot in the Isthmian sanctuary.

See also: Athamas; Ino

Melissa
Greek
The nymph who discovered honey.

Melpomene
Greco-Roman
One of the nine Muses and mother of the Sirens, her specific role being patroness of tragic poetry. She is often depicted wearing, or holding, a tragic mask as well as Heracles' club.

See also: Muses, the

Memnon
Greek
The son of Eos and Tithones (the half-brother of Priam) who was regarded as the handsome, black-skinned ruler of an eastern kingdom, possibly Persia or Ethiopia, from there bringing his forces to the aid of Troy during the Trojan War. He killed several famous Greeks during the war, including Antilochus, the gallant son of Nextor, but was himself killed by Achilles. Eos, his mother, persuaded Zeus to honor her son by causing birds, called Memnonides, to rise from his funeral pyre and fight above it until they fell back into the flames as a sacrifice. They were said to visit the hero's tomb on the Hellespont every year to sprinkle water, known as the "tears of Eos," on the tomb.

Many great monuments, known as Memnonia, were supposed to have been erected by the Greeks in Memnon's honor, though the most famous of these, the Colossus of Memnon, erected near the Egyptian city of Thebes, was in fact a statue of the pharaoh Amenophis, or Amenhotep III. It was famous because it "sang" at dawn when the sun's heat caused cracks in the statue to expand. Queen Zenobia repaired the statue when she invaded Egypt in 270 A.D., after which it sang no more.

Memnonia
Greek
The collective name for the many monuments said to have been erected in honor of Memnon. They usually took the form of columns and represented Memnon in a cult emphasizing immortality. The most famous example is the

Colossus of Memnon near Egyptian Thebes. This, however, had nothing to do with Memnon, being in fact a huge statue of a pharaoh, Amenophis or Amenhotep III.

Memnonides
Greek

Birds that Zeus caused to rise, at the request of Eos, from the funeral pyre of Memnon. They fought above the fire until they fell back onto it as a sacrifice. They were said to visit the hero's tomb on the Hellespont near Troy each year to sprinkle it with water, which became known as the "tears of Eos."

Menelaus
Greek

Son of Atreus and Aerope and younger brother of Agamemnon, the two being collectively referred to as the Atridae, the sons of Atreus. As youths the two brothers took refuge with King Tyndareus of Sparta. There, from all the suitors for her hand, Helen, Tyndareus's beautiful daughter, chose Menelaus, who first extracted a promise from all her other suitors that should her life ever be in danger they would join arms in her service. Agamemnon forcibly married Helen's sister, Clytemnestra.

When the Dioscuri were immortalized, Menelaus succeeded Tyndareus as the king of Sparta, the city to which he welcomed Paris, unaware he had come to abduct Helen. When he did so—some saying that Helen had fallen in love with Paris as much as he with her—Menelaus called on all those who had vied for her hand to honor their oath and come to her aid.

Led by Agamemnon, the Greek fleet assembled at Aulis, but Agamemnon considered that even though their fleet was undoubtedly strong, they needed further support. As a result Agamemnon, Menelaus, and Palamedes went to Ithaca to persuade Odysseus to join them. Having sailed from Aulis, the fleet, having made one error en route, landed at Tenedos in sight of Troy. It was probably from there that Menelaus, Odysseus, and Palamedes went as envoys to Priam to request the return of Helen. They were greeted courteously in Troy by Antenor, who advised his fellow Trojans that Helen should be returned, but the Trojans remained obdurate. So the Trojan War started.

While Achilles sulked in his tent and the war appeared to be going against the Greeks, Menelaus and Paris agreed to settle the dispute in single combat. However, just as Paris was about to lose, Aphrodite carried him away and the fighting recommenced, Patroclus now returning to the fray wearing the armor of Achilles, who still stubbornly refused to take part. When Patroclus was killed by Hector, Menelaus, who had recently killed Euphorbus, and Ajax the Greater recovered his body.

Following the fall of Troy after the stratagem of the Wooden Horse proved successful, Menelaus and Odysseus killed and mutilated Deiphobus, who had forcibly married Helen following the demise of Paris. Menelaus then prepared to execute Helen but was once more overcome by her beauty and led her safely back to the Greek ships, taking along Hermione as part of his booty. However, before leaving to return home, Menelaus forgot to sacrifice to Athene, so his return journey took eight years, and it was only after wrestling with Proetus that he finally managed to navigate back to Sparta. There he married Hermione to Neoptolemus.

See also: Aerope; Agamemnon; Atreus; Helen; Paris; Trojan War

Menetheus
Greek

Rebellious Athenian who led the uprising against Theseus when Theseus returned from his imprisonment in Tartarus. Theseus fled to Scyros and Menetheus succeeded him as king, though the sons of Theseus were afterwards restored to the throne.

Menoeceus
Greek

1. Father of Jocasta who was directly descended from the original Sparti, the "Sown Men" who helped Cadmos establish the city. Hence he was also one of the Sparti, for the name applied to descendants as well. Following Oedipus's marriage to his mother, Jocasta, the blind seer Teiresias stated that only

the voluntary sacrifice of one of the Sparti would free Thebes of the plague ravaging the city. Menoeceus threw himself from the walls to his death.

2. Son of Creon, king of Thebes, who, following a prophesy by Teiresias, took his own life. He has frequently been confused with Menoeceus, but the two characters are quite distinct, even if their fates are remarkably similar.

See also: Creon; Sparti

Mentor

Greek

"Adviser"; the right-hand man to Odysseus who managed that great hero's affairs in Ithaca while he was away at the Trojan War. On one occasion Athene assumed the identity of Mentor to give advice to the young Telemachus, or to reconcile the feud between Odysseus and the kinsmen of the suitors of Penelope that Odysseus had killed on his return from Troy.

See also: Odysseus

Mercur~ius, ~y

Roman

God of eloquence, skill, trading, and thieving and messenger to the gods who was early identified with the Greek Hermes, whose role he echoes. Legend made him the son of Maia, a popular deity, though lacking real prestige. Augustus was the only emperor to show any real interest in him. His temple on the Aventine Hill, built c. 495 B.C., was a gathering place for tradesmen and merchants of all kinds, their gatherings holding special significance during the month of May, when the temple had been founded (May was the month sacred to his mother, Maia). His festival was celebrated on May 15.

Romans seemed to enjoy forming special associations based loosely on the worship of Mercurius, where businessmen would meet, coming together for mutual pleasure but never adverse to doing a little business at the same time. As such the worshippers of Mercurius, businessmen in general, were never considered quite gentlemen. Mercurius gradually absorbed the attributes of Hermes and was often depicted as wearing winged sandals (*talaria*) and carrying a winged staff that was entwined with serpents, a *caduceus*.

Astronomical: The smallest and innermost of the planets in the solar system, named after the Roman messenger of the gods because of its relatively swift motion across the sky. The planet lies at an average distance of 58 million kilometers (36 million miles) from the sun and has no satellites. It is approximately one-third the size of earth, having an equatorial diameter of 4,880 kilometers (3,032 miles).

Meriones

Greek

Simply referred to as the companion of Idomeneos when the latter joined the Greek fleet prior to sailing to Troy.

Mermaid

Greek

In ancient Greek mythology, mermaids appear under the name of Nereides, who have many of the characteristics normally associated with these fabulous sea dwellers. They attract men and will marry them yet will disappear at once if the man attempts to talk to them. Ancient Greek mermaids do not have the characteristic fishy attributes of later European mermaids and are thus fully human in form. They do, however, like other sea deities, have the ability to alter their shape at will. Usually benevolent, and having mermen as their male counterparts, mermaids could be destructive and were sometimes, in this role, identified with Sirens.

Mermaids persist into modern Greek folklore, where they are known as Gorgones, regarded as the sisters or daughters of Alexander the Great.

See also: Nereides

Merman

Greek

The male counterpart of the mermaid who, in ancient Greek tradition, was usually the son of a sea deity, such as Triton, the son of Poseidon and Amphitrite. While mermaids were usually equated with the Nereides, mermen could be identified with the conch shell–wielding Tritons.

Merope

Greek

One of the seven daughters of Atlas and Pleione, thus one of the Pleiades. She married the mortal Sisyphus and became the mother of Glaucus. Subsequently, when she and her sisters were transferred to the heavens, she became the dimmest of the group, as she had married a mere mortal, unlike her sisters, who all married gods.

See also: Pleiades; Sisyphus

Messina, Strait of

Greek

The narrow channel of water that separates Sicily from the toe of Italy. Legend said that this treacherous stretch of water contained the whirlpool Charybdis on one side, opposite the cave inhabited by the monstrous Scylla.

Mestra

Greek

The daughter of Erysichthon.

Metaneira

Greek

Wife of Celeus (king of Eleusis) and mother of Abas, Demophoön, and Triptolemus. When Demeter came to Eleusis during her fruitless search for Persephone, Metaneira employed her as the nurse to the infant Demophoön, not knowing the true identity of the goddess. When Demeter attempted to make Demophoön immortal by immolating him, Metaneira disturbed the goddess, who had to make her identity known. Abas derided the goddess for the way in which she consumed a drink in one gulp and was rewarded by being turned into a lizard. Triptolemus, however, fared better, for he was taught the arts of agriculture, which he took to all four corners of the world.

See also: Abas; Celeus; Demeter; Persephone

Metis

Greek

The supreme spirit of mild wisdom, the daughter of Oceanos and Tethys who advised Zeus on how he might make his father, Cronos, disgorge his brothers and sisters. Zeus subsequently married her, but when she became pregnant an oracle predicted that the child would be a girl but that any son born to Metis would depose Zeus, as he had his own father. As a result Zeus swallowed Metis. The oracle was proved correct when, while walking on the shore of Lake Triton, Zeus suffered an agonizing headache. Hermes persuaded Hephaistos, or some say Prometheus, to cleave open Zeus's skull, and the fully grown, fully armed Athene, his daughter by Metis, sprang from the wound.

Mezentius

Roman

The arrogant, blasphemous, and brutal king of Caere who, exiled from his own city, allied with Turnus against Aeneas, but Aeneas killed him. A variant says that Mezentius, having been defeated in single combat by Ascanius, changed his allegiance and thenceforth fought with Aeneas.

See also: Aeneas; Turnus

Midas

Greek

The name of several historical and one legendary king of Phrygia. The natural or adopted son of Gordius, Midas succeeded him as king of Phrygia. Having rescued Silenus from some peasants who had chained him up, he was offered a reward, the offer being made either by Silenus himself or by his master, Dionysos. Midas famously requested that he should have the power to turn everything he touched to gold. However, when his food and wine, all his family and servants, and even his furniture had been turned to gold, Midas realized his mistake and begged Dionysos to rid him of the accursed gift. Dionysos advised him to bathe at the source of the River Pactolus, near Mount Tmolus, which has ever since carried gold. The curse was removed and everything that had been turned into gold was restored to its original form.

Later Midas was involved in the musical contest between Marsyas and Apollo. The judge, Tmolus, asked Midas for his opinion.

Midas voted for Marsyas, and Apollo, angered by this response, made Midas's head sprout asses' ears. Thenceforth Midas wore a tall Phrygian cap to conceal his shame yet could not help but reveal his secret to his barber, who, unable to keep the secret to himself, whispered it to the reeds in the river, or alternatively to a hole in the ground. Either the reeds then began to whisper the secret among themselves, eternally, "King Midas has asses' ears," or a reed grew from the hole, and that started to spread the secret.

See also: Apollo; Dionysos; Marsyas; Silenus

Milanion

Greek

Variant spelling of Melanion.

Miletus

Greek

The son of Apollo by Aria. He fled with Sarpedon from Minos to Asia Minor, where he founded the kingdom that bore his name.

Mimas

Greek

One of the 24 Gigantes, the huge sons of Ge who tried to avenge the imprisonment of their brothers, the Titans, by attacking Olympus. Led by Alcyoneus and including Porphyrion, Ephialtes, Pallas, Enceladus, and Polybutes, the giants were finally defeated by the gods of Olympus with the help of Heracles, who provided them with a magical herb of invulnerability and always lowered the final blow.

Astronomical: One of the satellites of Saturn lying third closest to the planet between the orbits of Janus and Enceladus.

Minerva

Roman

Goddess of education and business who later developed into the goddess of war. Closely related to the Greek Athene, Minerva owes her origins to a warlike primal goddess of the Etruscans, a goddess of battle, death, and sexuality. Later development of Minerva shows her shedding many of her savage aspects. She became patroness of cultural development, the arts and sciences, industry, and particularly domestic skills. She was also regarded, in a somewhat higher form, to be the patroness of heroes who undertook spiritual or magical tasks. Her sacred animal was the owl, an attribute directly absorbed from the Greek cult of Athene. She was honored at the Quinquatria festival, which was originally held on 19 March.

See also: Athene

Minoan civilization

Greek

A Bronze Age civilization, c. 2600–1250 B.C., that was named by Sir Arthur Evans after the legendary king of Crete, King Minos. It was a remarkable civilization, the first true civilized society within Europe. Neolithic people appear to have first reached Crete c. 6000 B.C. and established their main settlement at Knossos, near modern Iráklion, otherwise living in caves and refuges. However, c. 2600 B.C. many of these smaller settlements moved down from the mountains to the coastal regions, a move that was essential for future developments. Some 600 years after the first founding moves had taken place, Minoan culture had become firmly established, its skill and artistry best illustrated by the magnificent palace complexes that were built; these were destroyed by some natural catastrophe that seems to have struck Crete c. 1700 B.C.

However, so secure was the Minoan civilization by that time that they simply picked up where they had left off, this time constructing on the same sites palaces that were even larger and more elaborate than their predecessors. The most impressive of these buildings were those at Knossos and Phaistos, remarkable ruins today. Their construction denotes the rise of architecture to the fore of Minoan artistic expression. Some were on several stories with theatrical touches such as the characteristic inverted pillar with a wider top than base. Walls were lined with the finest materials and decorated with frescoes that remain a familiar trademark of the Minoans. Even today the ruins are extraordinary, if somewhat baffling, as they appear to have served more than simply as houses for the ruling classes.

The palaces, around which Minoan civilization is clearly centered, were the focal point of state and religious life. It was within their confines, or within specially constructed arenas, that the famous bull-leaping ceremonies took place. Religious life within the Minoan society centered around the omnipresent bull, but the leading divinity appears to have been a goddess, the Mistress of the Animals who reflects the earthly and pastoral origins of the Minoans. The second wave of Minoan society, which had risen from the remains of that destroyed c. 1700 B.C., collapsed suddenly c. 1450 B.C., though Knossos seems to have struggled on for 70 years or so.

There are many theories surrounding the sudden collapse of such a highly organized society. Original theory placed the blame firmly on an invasion by the Achaean Greeks (also know as Mycenaeans) from the mainland, for they certainly made wide-ranging expeditions, and it is possible they could have easily stormed the undefended Minoan society, which felt so secure on its island home. A later theory blamed the eruption of the volcanic island of Santorini, itself a Minoan colony. Current theory suggests that the eruption, which would have caused havoc over a wide area of the Mediterranean, occurred about 50 years before the collapse of the Minoan society and that the fall of Minoan civilization was indeed caused by invaders.

The central importance of Crete, and of the Minoans, is reflected in the myths that center around the island. It was the home of Minos, Rhadamanthus, and the Minotaur. It was to Crete that Rhea turned when looking for somewhere to secrete the infant Zeus. Hephaistos even supplied the island with a giant bronze guard, Talos, who survived until the arrival of Jason and Medeä. There is little doubt that without the rise of the Minoan civilization Greek tradition would be sadly the poorer.

See also: Knossos; Minos; Talos

Minos

Greek

King of Crete, son of Zeus and Europa, brother of Rhadamanthus and Sarpedon, husband of Pasiphaë, and father by her of Glaucus, Androgeos, Ariadne, and Phaedra. His life, like that of Sarpedon, seems to have lasted for several generations, giving rise to some very famous incidents.

Claiming sole rule over the island of Crete, Minos beseeched Poseidon to send him a bull from the sea, which he would then sacrifice to the god and thereby prove the legitimacy of his claim. Poseidon duly sent the bull and Minos was awarded the kingdom, building his palace at Knossos, but seeing the beauty of the bull Minos kept it, sacrificing another, lesser animal in its place. To punish him, Poseidon made his wife fall in love with the bull. To allow her to mate with the animal, Minos employed Daedalus to construct a wooden cow. This he did, the result of the union between Pasiphaë and the Cretan Bull being the monstrous Minotaur. After it had run wild on the island the Cretan Bull was captured by Heracles and taken to the mainland. There it once again ran wild until it was caught by Theseus, by which time it had become known as the Marathonian Bull; Theseus took it to Athens for sacrifice to Athene.

Minos was not always faithful to his wife. He chased Britomartis until she threw herself into the sea to escape him, whereupon she was deified by Artemis and became the goddess Dictynna. Angry at his philandering ways, Pasiphaë cast a spell on him that caused his body to produce snakes and scorpions, which killed his mistresses. He was cured of this curse by Procris, another of his lovers, who received his infallible spear and unbeatable hound, Laelaps, as payment.

Minos was regarded by the Greeks as having been the ruler of a vast sea empire that encompassed all of Greece. He was apparently considered so important that it was said that he had a face-to-face audience with Zeus every nine years. While besieging Nisa, the port of Megara, Scylla, the daughter of Nisus, king of Megara, fell in love with Minos. She cut off the lock of hair on which her father's life depended and let Minos into the city. Minos, however, was so offended by her parricide that he left her, and she swam after his ship until her father's soul, changed into a sea eagle, pounced on her, and she was turned into the bird Ciris. Others say that Minos drowned the treacherous maiden and she was turned into the fish Ciris. Minos made war on Athens after his son, Androgeos, had been killed at the instigation of Aegeus. Having defeated the city, Minos imposed an annual tribute of seven maids and seven youths who were to be fed to the Minotaur. Theseus traveled with what was to be the last of these shipments and, with the help of Ariadne, successfully killed the Minotaur.

Shortly afterwards, Daedalus and his son, Icarus, who had been imprisoned by Minos, escaped on wings made of feathers and wax. Minos pursued Daedalus to Sicily and was killed there by the daughters of King Cocalos, in whose house Daedalus was hiding. The soldiers who had accompanied Minos then founded the city of Heraclea Minoa, which contained the tomb of Minos, but this was destroyed by Theron when he founded the new city of Acragas.

The laws Minos passed on Crete were regarded as so exemplary in their justice that after his death Minos joined Aeacus and his brother, Rhadamanthus, in the Underworld as one of the judges who considered the past lives of the newly dead, deciding the region each should be sent to.

See also: Ariadne; Britomartis; Daedalus; Minotaur; Pasiphaë; Rhadamanthus; Sarpedon; Thebes

Minotaur
Greek

The monstrous offspring of the union between the Cretan Bull and Pasiphaë, wife of Minos, who had lain with the animal inside a wooden cow built for her by Daedalus. So horrified was Minos with the appearance of the creature, usually depicted as having a bull's head and a man's body, that he commanded the master engineer Daedalus to construct the Cretan Labyrinth to contain it. Having defeated Athens, Minos extracted from that city an annual tribute of seven youths and seven maidens who were fed to the monster. However, this came to an end when Theseus, the son of Aegeus, made himself a member of the tribute and, with the help of Minos's daughter, Ariadne, killed the Minotaur and escaped from its labyrinthine prison, fleeing from the island with his conspirator.

The Minotaur appears to represent some distorted memory of the importance of the bull in Minoan religion, where numerous frescoes and statuettes attest to the bizarre, and potentially lethal, ceremony of bull-leaping. The tribute from Athens also seems to echo some memory of the supremacy of Crete, the death of the Minotaur possibly also echoing the collapse of the Minoan civilization.

See also: Daedalus; Pasiphaë; Theseus

Minthe
Greek

A nymph who was pursued by Hades and changed by Persephone into the plant that still carries her name—mint.

Minyan
Greek

The Minyans were one of the invading civilizations that entered Greece, along with the Ionians, c. 2000 B.C. It was their mastery of horses and wheeled vehicles that enabled them to quickly suppress any resistance. They brought with them Poseidon, who was often referred to as the "Earth-shaker," a deity who reflected the thundering of horses' hooves. Possibly at this time he was a sky god, later becoming a marine deity to reflect the later mastery of the sea by the Minyans when the Achaeans entered the country c. 1450 B.C. and replaced Poseidon with their own sky god, Zeus. The Minyans also brought with them the eternal Earth Goddess, the mate of the sky god. Her worship merged with that of the pre-Hellenic Great Goddess and so developed into Demeter. Their name appears to be derived from Minyas, the king of Orchomenus.

Minyas
Greek

Eponym of the Minyan people, king of Orchomenus and father of Leucippe, Arsippe, and Alcathoe. These girls resisted the introduction of the worship of Dionysos, even mocking it, preferring instead to sit at home weaving while their fellow women were out on the mountainside worshipping the god. One night they heard mysterious music and their stools were surrounded by a strange growth of ivy. They went mad, tore Leucippe's son to pieces, and joined the other revelers in the mountains.

Mithras
Roman

The form by which the ancient Iranian deity Mitra was introduced into the Roman Empire in 68 B.C.; this form was worshipped throughout the empire, with temples reaching as far north as Britain. By c. 250 A.D. the cult rivaled Christianity in its strength. A favorite of the Roman legionaries, Mithras was a god of the sun, justice, contract, and war who was worshipped by only men, and in secret. His cult developed a savage ritual of bloody baptism, or Taurobolium, in which the votary sits in a trench over which a bull is sacrificed, thus bathing the man below in blood.

Mnemosyne
Greek

"Memory"; the daughter of Uranos and Ge and mother of the Muses by Zeus.

See also: Muses, the

Mo~era, ~ira
Greek

The name of the original single Fate to whom even Zeus had to yield. Later tradition named three Fates who then became known as the Moirae (Moerae) after the original single deity.

Mo~erae, ~irae
Greek

The Fates: Clotho, the spinner; Lachesis, the allotter; and Atropos, the inflexible. They were the daughters of Zeus and Themis who spun the thread of life, determined its course, and cut it when its end was due. They were a later development of Moera or Moira, the single Fate to whom even Zeus had to yield.

See also: Atropos; Clotho; Lachesis

Molionidae
Greek

The twin sons of Actor or Poseidon, and Molione who were later conceived of as Siamese twins. They featured prominently in Homer's *Iliad,* in which they were killed by Heracles during his war with Augeias and buried at Cleonae.

Moly
Greek

The magical plant given to Odysseus by Hermes that allowed Odysseus to overcome the sorcery of Circe and so restore his companions to human form after Circe had turned them into swine. One description of the plant seems to equate it with garlic, with milky white flowers like those of a violet, grassy leaves, and a black root.

See also: Circe; Heracles

Momus
Greek

The personification of sarcasm and mockery, the daughter of Night. Though expelled from Olympus for his continual mockery and criticism of the gods, Momus did suggest to Zeus a plan to relieve some of the weight of the human race, saying that Zeus should marry Thetis to a mortal, as this would result in a war that would significantly reduce the numbers of mortals. The marriage did, in fact, eventually lead to the Trojan War.

See also: Thetis; Trojan War

Moneta
Roman

An aspect of Juno, usually Juno Moneta, as the protectress of money.

Mopsus
Greek

1. A seer of unknown origin who sailed with Jason and the Argonauts but was killed by a snake in Libya.

2. The son of Apollo and Manto (daughter of Teiresias) who made himself the ruler of Caria. Inheriting his powers of prophecy from both sides of his parentage, Mopsus lived in Colophon, where he was challenged to a prophecy contest by Calchas, which he won, and after which Calchas died of grief. Mopsus

was revered as the founder of the Oracle of Apollo at Claros, as well as the founder of many cities of Cilicia, including Aspendus, Phaselis, and Mopsuestia. He and Amphilochus, who had come to Colophon with Calchas, founded the city of Mallus, also in Cilicia, but killed each other in a fight for its possession.

See also: Amphilochus; Calchas; Jason

Mormo

Greek

A female demon somewhat like Lamia or Gello. She was particularly malevolent toward naughty children, whose nurses would scold them with a warning that unless they behaved Mormo would get them.

See also: Lamia

Moros

Greek

The supreme power, Doom or Destiny, the son of Night, whom even the gods of Olympus obeyed. Though seldom personified in the myths, being conceived as shadowy and invisible, his presence as a force is pervasive and omnipotent. From him all power stems, and with him lies the sole power to remove gods from their station.

Morpheus

Greek

The son of Hypsos, god of sleep, and thus the god of dreams who was responsible for sending the human form into the dreams of men. His brothers, Ikelos and Phantasos, had responsibility for sending objects and monsters into these dreams. The Roman directly equated him is the son of Somnus, making him one of the few Greek deities to retain his name in Roman religion.

Mors

Roman

The personification of death who was known as Thanatos by the Greeks.

Mulciber

Roman

A name sometimes given to Vulcan.

Musae

Greek

The Muses, also known as Musagetes, the daughters of Zeus and Mnemosyne who were born at Pieria near Mount Olympus. Their worship as goddesses presiding over the arts and sciences spread into Boeotia, where they were said to dwell on Mount Helicon with its sacred fountains of Aganippe and Hippocrene, the latter springing forth after a hoof-strike from Pegasus, who was a favorite of theirs. Mount Parnassus, with its sacred spring of Castalia, was also a center of their worship. Libations of milk or water were offered to them. Originally there were just three Muses, but later tradition names nine: Clio, the muse of history; Euterpe, the muse of lyric poetry; Thalia, the muse of comedy; Melpomene, the muse of tragedy; Terpsichore, the muse of dance and song; Erato, the muse of erotic or love poetry and mime; Polyhymnia, the muse of the sublime hymn; Calliope, the muse of eloquence and epic poetry; and Urania, the muse of astronomy.

Few myths relate to the Musae, for they were primarily considered as literary deities, called upon by musicians and poets to supply the matter for their work. They did, however, blind the Thracian bard Thamyris, who boasted of his song, and inflicted the same condition upon Demodocos, though they did give him the skill of the minstrel by way of compensation. They sang at the weddings of mortals to gods and were once challenged to a singing contest by the Sirens. The Musae won and plucked out the Sirens' feathers. Their only malevolent act appears to have been the teaching of the riddle to the Sphinx, who then killed any who could not answer it.

See also: Calliope; Clio; Erato; Euterpe; Melpomene; Polyhymnia; Sphinx; Terpsichore; Thalia; Urania

Musagetes

Greek

One of the names applied to the Musae, or Muses.

Muses, the

Greek

The nine Musae, the daughters of Zeus and Mnemosyne who presided over and reflected on the arts and sciences.

Mycenae

Greek

City of ancient Greece that in legend was founded by Perseus and Andromeda, its kings including Orestes, who was also king of Sparta and Argos, and, most famously, Agamemnon. The city lay in the northeast Peloponnesos in the Plain of Argos approximately 11 kilometers (6 miles) north of modern Argos. Dating from the third millenium B.C., Mycenae became the center of the Mycenaean civilization (c. 1580–1120 B.C.). The Mycenaeans entered Greece from the north, bringing with them advanced techniques, especially in agriculture and metallurgy. The city they founded at Mycenae controlled the route from the Peloponnesos to Corinth, being strategically positioned to command the Argive Plain.

Trade developed with Crete, which also helped to develop their own culture, and by 1600 B.C. they were the dominant force in the Aegean. After 1200 B.C. the city began to decline with the Dorian invasion; it was finally destroyed in the fifth century B.C. but was repaired in the third century B.C. Archaeological excavations of what had, until then, been regarded as a purely legendary city were begun in 1876 by the eccentric Heinrich Schliemann, who uncovered such notable remains as the Treasury of Atreus, also known as the tomb of Agamemnon, the lion gate that led to the city, beehive tombs, the city walls, and many golden ornaments and weapons.

Legend says that Perseus and Andromeda founded the city of Mycenae, which had its mighty fortifications built by the Cyclopes. Following the death of Eurystheus, Mycenae was seized by Atreus, though he was opposed by Thyestes, who was immediately banished. Thyestes later had Atreus killed by Aegisthus and thereby finally came to power.

Mycenae is perhaps best known, though, as the home of Agamemnon and his wife, Clytemnestra. While Agamemnon was away leading the Greek forces at Troy, Clytemnestra took Aegisthus as her lover, and upon the return of her husband she murdered him and his concubine, Cassandra. She then seized power and ruled with her consort, Aegisthus, a weak-willed partner who did anything she asked. However, Agamemnon's children, led by Orestes, later exacted their revenge by returning to the city, killing both Aegisthus and Clytemnestra.

Today the ruins are among the most impressive ancient sites in Greece, yet had it not been for the trust put in the writings of Homer by Schliemann, the city may have remained unearthed, a legend waiting to be discovered.

See also: Agamemnon; Andromeda; Orestes; Perseus

Mycenaean civilization

Greek

Civilization that emerged on the Greek mainland c. 1600 B.C., which was centered around the city of Mycenae. In c. 1450 B.C. the Mycenaeans invaded Crete and adopted many aspects of the earlier Minoan civilization. They began to build palaces within their citadels, but they did not employ the labyrinthine designs favored by the Minoans. Instead they adopted a style that had existed for about 500 years. It was based on a central hall, a vestibule, and a courtyard in front, a style that later inspired Greek temple architects.

Mycenaean civilization borrowed extensively from Minoan religion, equating the two pantheons. The Minoan snake goddess appeared again at Mycenae, but she had now acquired a warlike aspect and had become known as Athene. The Minoan nature goddess, Mistress of the Animals, became Demeter.

Mycenaean people employed a primitive form of Greek known as Linear B. Through the translation of these early writings knowledge of the Mycenaean pantheon has been gained, also demonstrating the ancestry of the later, classical deities. The Linear B texts discovered at Mycenae and other Mycenaean cities mention Zeus, Poseidon, Hera, Athene, Artemis, Apollo, Dionysos, Ares as Enyalios, and Demeter. Two of these, Zeus and Poseidon, are obviously Mycenaean in origination and concept, for they play no part in Minoan religion.

Myrmidones

Greek

A warlike people who inhabited the southern borders of Thessaly. They accompanied Achilles, the son of their king, Peleus, and the Nereid Thetis from Phthiotis, or Phthia, to Troy to participate on the side of the Greeks in the Trojan War, and thus became instrumental in the Greek success. At one stage, while Achilles sulked in his tent following the famous argument with Agamemnon, the Myrmidones were led into battle by Patroclus, not meeting with the success they would have if commanded by Achilles.

See also: Achilles; Peleus; Trojan War

Myrtilus

Greek

Son of Hermes and charioteer of Oenomaus who was bribed by Pelops with the promise of half the kingdom if he replaced a linchpin in Oenomaus's chariot axle with one made of wax. It broke as Pelops raced Oenomaus, the latter being thrown from his chariot and killed. Pelops then married Oenomaus's daughter, Hippodameia, but killed Myrtilus to keep the secret safe. As he died, Myrtilus cursed the descendants of Pelops, his image being placed in the heavens as the Charioteer by Hermes.

See also: Pelops

Mysia

Greek

Ancient kingdom, today a part of Asiatic Turkey, that was visited by the Argonauts en route for Colchis. There Hylas, the squire of Heracles, went in search of fresh water; he was stolen away by water nymphs who fell in love with him. Heracles searched for him and found nothing but an empty pitcher; he was left behind when the *Argo Navis* sailed.

See also: Heracles; Hylas

N

Naiad(e)s

Greek

Fresh water–nymphs who preside over springs, rivers, and lakes. Their cult was widespread throughout Greece, where it was believed that mortals could gain inspiration from springs watched over by particular Naiades. They feature in many of the ancient traditions, for example, as the lovers of Hylas, the squire of Heracles, whom they pulled down beneath the water when the Argonauts landed in Mysia, leaving nothing behind for Heracles to find save an empty pitcher.

Narcissus

Greek

The handsome son of the River Cephisus and Liriope who was loved by the nymph Echo. Teiresias prophesied that he would have a long life if he "never knew himself." However, having spurned the love of Echo, who pined away and died, leaving just her voice, Narcissus was condemned by Nemesis to fall in love with his own reflection in a pool. Narcissus now pined away himself, thus fulfilling the prophecy made by Teiresias. The flower that bears his name sprang from the earth where he died.

See also: Echo

Nauplius

Greek

King of Euboea who, eager to avenge the death of his son, Palamedes, lit misleading beacons that led many ships returning from Troy to their doom on the dangerous promontory of Caphareus.

Nausi~caa, ~kaa

Greek

Daughter of Alcinous, king of Phaeacia. She found the shipwrecked and naked Odysseus on her father's island realm of Scheria and took him to the palace, where her parents received him courteously and helped him make his way back to Ithaca.

See also: Odysseus

Naxos

Greek

An island in the Aegean Sea, the largest of the Cyclades group. It was first colonized by the Ionians, became a tributary of Athens in 470 B.C., and was held by the Ottoman Turks between 1566 and 1830, after which it became a part of independent Greece. The island was a center for the worship of Dionysos, for it was on this island that Dionysos found and married Ariadne, deserted there by Theseus.

See also: Dionysos

Necessitas

Roman

Known as Ananke by the Greeks, Necessitas was the irresistible goddess who posted the decrees of Fate using brass nails.

Nectar

Greek

The drink of the gods that accompanied ambrosia, their food.

Neleus

Greek

The son of Poseidon by Tyro, brother of Pelias, and king of Pylos. The two boys were exposed at birth by their mother but were found and reared by horse herders. Returning to the city of their birth after they grew up, Pelias usurped the throne and drove Neleus out of Iolcos. He came to Pylos, with Melampus and Bias, where he was made king. His daughter, Pero, married Bias, the brother of Melampus; his 12 sons included Nestor, the oldest and wisest of the Greeks at Troy. He was killed by Heracles in revenge for Neleus giving help to Augeias, though Homer knows nothing of this, and was succeeded by Nestor, the only member of his family not slain by Heracles.

See also: Heracles; Nestor; Pelias

Nem(a)ea

Greek

City of ancient Argolis where a temple to Zeus once stood and where the Nemaean Games where held in Zeus's honor, the biennial games being established in 573 B.C. The valley in which the city was located was also the scene of the first of Heracles' Great Labors, the killing of the Nemaean Lion.

Nem(a)ean Games

Greek

Biennial games held in the vicinity of the ancient Argolid city of Nemaea. Founded in 573 B.C., the games were held in the honor of Zeus, to whom they were rededicated by Heracles after he had successfully killed the Nemaean Lion.

Nem(a)ean Lion

Greek

The name given to a beast, the monstrous offspring of Typhon and Echidne, that terrorized the Argolid Valley in which the city of Nemaea was located. As the valley was also in the vicinity of Cleonae, the lion is sometimes referred to as the Cleonaean Lion. The killing and skinning of this great lion was the first of the 12 labors that Eurystheus set Heracles. As the skin of the lion was impenetrable to any weapon, Heracles simply caught it and squeezed the life out of it before rededicating the Nemaean Games to the honor of Zeus. He then skinned the lion with one of its own claws, turning the pelt into his cape, said to be the source of Heracles' immense strength. However, anyone else who wore it would have power over Heracles, as was the case with Queen Omphale.

Astronomical: The constellation Leo is said to represent the Nemaean Lion.

See also: Heracles; Omphale

Nemesis

Greek

The daughter of Oceanos and Night and goddess of divine retribution whose specialty was the punishment of hubris, arrogant self-confidence. Nemesis, whose name derives from *nemo*, "to apportion," represents the resentment felt by men at evil deeds as well as undeserved good fortune and the hoped-for downfall of the victim. Originating solely as a deity who decided whether an individual should be happy or sad—but chastising those who were overtly lucky—she later came to be regarded solely as a goddess who devised and handed out punishment.

Though not popular, as her role would suggest, Nemesis did have a shrine at Rhamnus in Attica. She was frequently depicted carrying a wheel identified as signifying the solar year, the sacred king fated either to rise to the height of fortune or die according to its seasons.

Neoptolemus

Greek

The son of Achilles by Deidameia (one of the daughters of Lycomedes, king of Scyros) who was born to the great hero while he was disguised as a girl hiding among Lycomedes' daughters to save him from battle in the Trojan War after a prophecy had foretold of his death. Neoptolemus was also known as Pyrrhos, or Pyrrhus, after Achilles' female name, Pyrrha. Following the prophesied death of Achilles, Odysseus, Phoenix, and Diomedes came to Scyros to persuade Lycomedes to allow Neoptolemus to join the Greek cause against Troy, bringing for the youth his father's armor. This story is a little incredible: Considering that Neoptolemus would have been but a baby when Achilles went to Troy, the war there lasting for ten years, Neoptolemus would have been no older than ten when he went to fight against Troy. Regardless of his age, Neoptolemus traveled to Troy and was one of the warriors secreted within the hollow belly of the Wooden Horse.

With Troy taken, Neoptolemus cornered Priam, Hecuba, and their son, Polites, before an alter sacred to Zeus. There Neoptolemus slaughtered Polites and, when Priam tried to intervene, killed him as well. He also murdered the Trojan infant Prince Astyanax. He was awarded, as his share of the booty, Hector's widow, Andromache, by whom some said he had three sons. Seeking to leave Troy, the Greek ships were once again becalmed, just as they had been en route at Aulis. Achilles' ghost demanded the sacrifice of Polyxena to ensure favorable winds, a sacrifice carried out by Neoptolemus. Returning with Menelaus to Sparta, Neoptolemus married Hermione.

Leaving Sparta, Neoptolemus, in the company of Andromache and Helenus, abandoned his kingdom in Thessaly and traveled to and settled in Epirus, part of which he gave to Helenus, who married Andromache. He was killed by Orestes, to whom Hermione had originally been betrothed by Tyndareus. An alternative to this version of his death says that he visited Delphi, where he was murdered by Machaereus after Neoptolemus had objected to the custom of the priests receiving all the sacrificial meat. He was buried in the temple of Apollo at Delphi, where he received divine honors.

See also: Achilles; Deidameia

Nephele
Greek

The phantom cloud in the form of Hera—created by the goddess or Zeus—that Ixion mated with. Nephele became the mother of Centauros and thus the ancestor of the centaurs.

See also: Ixion

Neptun~e, ~us
Roman

Originally associated with freshwater, Neptune increasingly became identified with the Greek Poseidon, and therefore as the god of the sea, though he retained many of his earlier, fresh-water aspects. His female counterpart was Salacia, goddess of spring water, which testifies to his origins, as did his festival, which was held in July when fresh water was most scarce. Offerings were made to Neptune to assuage any water shortage, but he remained a pale deity when compared to Poseidon for the simple reason that the Romans were not a seafaring nation. Neptune was often depicted riding a dolphin and carrying a trident.

Astronomical: Discovered in 1846, Neptune is one of the gas giant planets of the solar system lying an average distance of 4,496 million kilometers (2,793 million miles) from the sun. It is approximately four times the size of the earth, with an equatorial diameter of roughly 49,800 kilometers (30,940 miles); it has two known satellites, possibly more, and a very faint ring system.

See also: Poseidon

Nereid(e)s
Greek

The fifty or more sea or freshwater nymph daughters of the sea god Nereus and the Oceanid Doris. The chief of the Nereides was Thetis, the mother of Achilles, though others are named from time to time in the works of Homer and Hesiod. Female spirits without any malice for mankind, Nereides were associated solely with the Mediterranean, unlike the Oceanides. As sea nymphs they were protected by Poseidon, who vented his wrath against Cassiopeia when she boasted that she, or her daughter, Andromeda, were more beautiful than the Nereides.

The Neraïda, an alternative name-form, continue into modern Greek folklore, the nymphs of upland country and woodland who can catch a man unawares at midday and send him mad or dumb.

Astronomical: The name Nereid has been given to one of the two known satellites of the planet Neptune. It lies very distant from the planet, well outside the orbit of the other known moon, Triton.

See also: Achilles; Thetis

Nereus

Greek

A sea deity; the son of Pontus and Ge and father of the 50 or more Nereides, nymphs of the Mediterranean, by the Oceanid Doris. He was the father of Amphitrite, who married Poseidon after his suit had been eloquently pleaded by Delphinos. He has sometimes been confused with Proteus, who shares the ability to alter shape at will.

See also: Amphitrite

Nessus

Greek

The centaur charged with carrying people across the River Evenus. While carrying Deianeira, Heracles' wife, Nessus attempted to make off with her, fully intending to violate her, but was shot by Heracles through the breast. Dying, Nessus told Deianeira to take some of his blood, falsely claiming that it would act as a charm to restore the love of a faithless husband. Deianeira later suspected that Heracles was about to desert her for Iole, so she sent him a shirt rubbed with some of Nessus's blood, unaware that the blood was also poisonous because the centaur had been killed by one of Heracles' poisoned arrows. When Heracles put the shirt on, it burned his flesh away; trying to remove the shirt just made matters worse, as great chunks of flesh tore away. Nessus thus had his revenge on Heracles.

See also: Deianeira; Heracles; Iole

Nestor

Greek

One of the 12 sons of Neleus; he succeeded as king of Pylos in Messenia after his father and brothers were killed by Heracles. In his youth he was involved in several battles against Elis, and it appears that it was this that saved him from being killed by Heracles, for Neleus and Nestor's brothers fought on the side of Elis against Heracles. He remained king of Pylos for three generations, defeated the Arcadians and the Eleans, and participated in the famous fight between the Lapithae and the centaurs as well as the voyage of the *Argo* as one of the Argonauts. He was already an old man when the Trojan War, to which he took 90 ships, started. There he was considered among the wisest counselors, if somewhat loquacious. His son, Antilochus, was killed by Memnon after he had joined his father at Troy, being too young to sail at the start of the war.

Nestor accompanied Odysseus and Ajax the Greater to Scyros to recruit for the Greek forces and was thus present when Achilles was discovered, disguised as a girl, hiding in the court of Lycomedes. He returned to Pylos after the Trojan War ended, and on one occasion he entertained Telemachus while the latter was looking for his father, Odysseus.

See also: Heracles; Neleus; Trojan War

Night

Greek

Nox, the daughter of Chaos and sister of Erebos (Darkness), Ge (Earth), Eros, and Tartarus. She was the mother of Aether and Day by her brother, Erebos, but she parthenogenetically produced Momus, Thanatos (Death), Hypnos (Sleep), the Moirae, and Nemesis.

Nike

Greek

Goddess of victory and the daughter of Pallas. She is frequently closely associated with the patron goddess of Athens, Athene, and her temple, to Athene Nike, built c. 427 B.C., standing on the Acropolis at Athens within sight of the Parthenon. The association between Nike and Athene may be that Nike was one of the surnames applied to Athene, as there is also a temple extant to Athene Pallas, Pallas being the father of Nike. It would therefore appear that, though Nike may have originally been a completely separate deity, she later became absorbed by Athene, becoming simply an aspect of that goddess. Nike was depicted as a winged being, often in the company of Zeus or Athene.

See also: 3

Ninus

Greek

Mythical king of Babylon, or Assyria, and husband of Semiramis, who succeeded him. He is the subject of a now fragmentary early Hellenic romance about his love for Semiramis in which he, the great conqueror, is treated as a lovesick youth. This work is one of the earliest known Greek novels.

Niobe
Greek

Daughter of Tantalus, sister of Pelops and Broteas, and wife of Amphion, king of Thebes. She made contemptuous remarks about the fact that Leto had had a mere two children, Apollo and Artemis, while she had had 12, the Niobids, though some say there were 14, seven boys and seven girls. In revenge for Niobe's remarks, Apollo killed the male Niobids and Artemis killed the female Niobids, though some sources say that one of the girls was spared. Niobe died of grief and was turned to stone by Zeus on Mount Sipylus, her tears emerging as the streams that trickle from it. There, the snow-capped crag that is identified with Niobe appears to cry when the sun strikes and melts the snow.

See also: Amphion; Apollo; Artemis; Leto; Tantalus

Niobids
Greek

The collective name of the 12, or 14, children of Niobe and Amphion, six, or seven, being of either gender. When Niobe boasted herself superior to Leto on account of the number of children she had had, compared to Leto's two, Apollo and Artemis, Apollo killed the male Niobids, and Artemis the females, though some say one girl was spared.

Nisus
Greek

1. King of Megara whose daughter, Scylla, fell in love with King Minos, who was attacking the city. She treacherously cut off the purple lock of hair on which her father's life depended and then opened the city gates to enable Minos to take the city. However, Minos was so disgusted by Scylla's parricide that he would have nothing to do with the girl, and as he sailed away she swam after his ship. Nisus

was transformed into an osprey or sea eagle that swooped down onto the girl, who was changed into the bird Ciris. A variant says that Minos simply drowned the girl by making her a figurehead on his ship and that she transformed into the fish Ciris.

2. A warrior from Troy who gave his life for that of an Argonaut, Euryalus.

See also: Minos

Nisyrus
Greek

Volcanic mountain under which Polybutes was said to have been buried after the epic struggle between the Gigantes and the gods of Olympus and whose continued rage was said to be exhibited when the mountain erupted.

Nod~ens, ~ons
Romano-Celtic

A god connected with water and healing who was occasionally equated with Neptune, making him a sea deity as well as a deity of fresh water. He had a sanctuary at Lydney, Gloucestershire, England, where his totem animal appears to have been the dog.

Nom~ios, ~ius
Greek

"The Pasturer"; a title given to gods, such as Apollo, Hermes, and Pan, who protected valuable pasture land.

Notus
Greek

Son of Astraeus and Eos, the personification of the south or southwest wind, called Auster by the Romans. His brothers were all the stars, Hesperus, and the three other winds, Zephyrus (west), Boreas (north) and Eurus (east), though some sources say that Eurus was not the offspring of Astraeus and Eos. All four winds were kept in a cave on the floating island of Aeolia, where they were released on the command of the gods or when Aeolus felt like it.

See also: Aeolus; Boreas; Eurus; Zephyrus

Nox

Greek

Night, the daughter of Chaos and sister of Erebos (Darkness), Ge (Earth), Eros, and Tartarus. She was the mother of Aether and Day by her brother, Erebos, but parthenogenetically produced Momus, Thanatos (Death), Hypnos (Sleep), the Moirae, and Nemesis.

Numa Pompilius

Roman

The successor to Romulus as king of Rome who was traditionally invited to become ruler by contemporaries impressed by his remarkable piety. He taught the Romans their sacred rituals and instructed them in all aspects of the worship of their gods, establishing at the same time the various ranks of the priesthood. He entrusted the sacred hearth of Vesta to the Vestal Virgins so that the sacred flame might guard the city. He invented a calendar, though its form has been lost, and gave Rome its sacred shields and the god Janus as the symbol of war and peace.

According to one story, possibly of Etruscan extraction, Numa Pompilius was married to the goddess Egeria, who suggested all these innovations to him. However, others say that Numa Pompilius simply said that they were suggested to him by Egeria so as to make the concepts easier to accept. Numa Pompilius later came to be regarded as a disciple of Pythagoras, but this conjunction was scorned by later writers.

See also: Romulus

Numicius

Roman

The river beside which Aeneas, in his old age, was said to have met Anna, the sister of Dido. Having been purified for his life on earth in the river's waters, Aeneas was finally received into the company of the gods.

See also: Aeneas

Numina

Roman

Generic name applied to the spirits of creatures and plants and, in men, of the breath, the spirit of the body that upon death became reincarnated in plants. They are a more general spirit than the more personal manes.

Numitor

Roman

Brother of Amulius, who exiled him from Alba Longa. His daughter, Rhea Silvia, was forced to become a Vestal Virgin, but one night she was raped by Mars while she slept and thereby became the mother of the twins Romulus and Remus. When they grew up the twins were accused of raiding the lands of the exiled Numitor, but when they were brought before him their identities were revealed. They then killed Amulius and restored Numitor to the throne.

See also: Remus; Rhea Silvia; Romulus

Nymph(ae)

Greco-Roman

Minor female deity, a guardian spirit of nature. There are many different classes of nymphs common throughout the Greek and Roman traditions, though the Greeks more highly developed their characters and the individual habitats each class was said to inhabit. Although generally conceived of as benevolent, their seductive charm was to be feared, for like Pan they had the power to drive men mad or dumb, especially around midday.

The various classes and habitats of Greek nymphs were:

Oreades: mountains
Dryades, Hamadryades, and Meliae: trees
Naiades: fresh water, the daughters of Nereus
Nereides: the Mediterranean
Napaeae: glens
Oceanides: the ocean

Other groups of nymphs did not have specific habitats. These include the Hesperides, the guardians of the golden apples of Hera; and the Hyades and Pleiades, the daughters of Atlas. Nymphs appear in many if not quite all of the Greek myths. They were scarcer in later Roman tradition, the most notable nymph of

Roman mythology being Marica, the wife of Faunus and mother of Latinus.

See also: Pleiades

Nysa
Greek

Mountain in Libya to which the infant Dionysos was taken by Hermes to be cared for by the nymphs who lived there after Hera had punished Athamas and Ino, who were originally entrusted with the infant. They fed the child honey. Dionysos was said to have first invented wine while living with the nymphs on Mount Nysa, a story that appears to reflect the origin of viniculture, which then spread, along with the cult of Dionysos, to Greece and beyond.

O

Oceanid(es)

Greek

Name given to any one of the daughters of Oceanos and Tethys, the sisters being considered nymphs who specifically inhabited the Western Ocean, unlike the Nereides, who dwelled in the Mediterranean.

Oceanos

Greek

A Titan, the son of Uranos and Ge, brother of Cronos, Hyperion, Iapetus, Rhea, Themis, Tethys, and Mnemosyne. When Ge persuaded his brothers to rise up against Uranos, Oceanos was the only male Titan to refuse. He married his sister, Tethys, and by her became the father of Metis, Zeus's first wife, whom he swallowed; all the rivers and their gods; and more than 3,000 daughters, the Oceanides. The ancient Greeks, as with most ancient civilizations, perceived the world to be flat and encircled by a river flowing from the Underworld, its banks inhabited by the spirits of the dead. Oceanos was seen as the personification of this river, across which lay the Garden of the Hesperides, the entrance to the Underworld, and the home of the Gorgons. Helios (Sun) was ferried back to his starting point in the east every night by Oceanos.

See also: Metis; Tethys

Ocresia

Roman

According to one tradition, possibly Etruscan in origin, the mother of Servius Tullius, whom she conceived from the household fire from which the penis of Vulcan rose.

On several consecutive days Tarchetius, the tyrannical king of Alba Longa, saw a vision of a penis rising from the flames of the household hearth. Consulting the Oracle of Tethys, he was told that should a virgin offer herself to the apparition, she would bear a splendid son. So impressed was Tarchetius with this prospect that he ordered his daughter to unite with the mysterious penis. However, feeling insulted, she ordered Ocresia, her servant, to take her place. Tarchetius imprisoned the two, but Vesta prevented him from having them executed.

Ocresia bore twins, which Tarchetius gave to Teratius, ordering him to kill them, but Teratius exposed them on the river bank, where they were fed by a wolf and birds whose strange behavior attracted the attention of a cowherd. Discovering the baby boys the cowherd immediately adopted them as his own. When they reached manhood they returned to Alba Longa and assassinated Tarchetius.

See also: Vulcan

Odysseus

Greek

Called Ulysses by the Romans, Odysseus was the main character in Homer's *Odyssey* and also appeared in Homer's *Iliad* as one of the top Greek leaders at the siege of Troy, noted for his courage and ingenuity.

He was the son of Laertes, king of Ithaca (though some say his father was really Sisyphus), and Anticleia, the daughter of Autolycus, from whom he inherited his wily, sometimes downright dishonest ways. In his youth Odysseus proved his prowess as a great hunter and once received a severe thigh wound from a wild boar while hunting with his uncles, the sons of his grandfather, Autolycus.

Odysseus married Penelope, daughter of Icarius, winning the right to marry her in a footrace. Her father tried to persuade her to stay with him, and Odysseus simply told her that she could do as she pleased. She veiled her face to hide her blushes and followed her new husband to Ithaca, where Odysseus succeeded his father. However, shortly after the birth of a son, Telemachus, the heroes of Greece were summoned to the Trojan War. To avoid having to serve—an oracle had warned him not to go—Odysseus feigned madness by sowing his land with salt and ploughing it in with an ox and ass before the plough. His ruse was exposed by Palamedes, who placed the infant Telemachus in the furrow before him. Whereas a madman would have ploughed the child into the ground, Odysseus acted like any sane father and rescued him. Having thus been forced to join the Greek forces, he later unmasked the youthful Achilles, who was hiding on Scyros disguised as a girl among the daughters of King Lycomedes, by leaving a shield and spear among gifts for the maidens.

His part in the Trojan War remains fairly inconspicuous until the death of Achilles, though he recommended deserting Philoctetes on Lemnos after that hero had suffered a festering and highly offensive wound. He also accompanied envoys Menelaus and Palamedes in an attempt to persuade Priam to return Helen and thereby avoid war; the mission failed. Odysseus also exacted a cruel revenge on Palamedes for uncovering his ruse and tricking him into joining the Greek forces. Odysseus bribed one of Palamedes' servants to hide a letter written in the name of Priam under Palamedes' bed. He then accused Palamedes of treason; his tent was searched, the letter was found, and Palamedes was stoned to death. Diomedes and Odysseus then made a night raid on the Trojan lines, killed the spy Dolon, and drove off the snow-white horses of Rhesus (they also killed him).

Following the death of Achilles, Odysseus disputed Ajax the Greater for the right to possess the arms of the fallen hero. The adjudicators of the dispute overheard some captive Trojan girls extolling the virtues of Odysseus above Ajax and so awarded the armor to Odysseus. This so enraged Ajax that he went mad, offended Athene, killed the Greek sheep, thinking them to be his enemy, and then killed himself. Homer's simpler variant says that

Odysseus killed Ajax in their quarrel and thereby won the right to Achilles' arms.

Later Odysseus was instrumental in the capture of Helenus, the Trojan seer who fled Troy when Deiphobus forcibly married Helen. He revealed to Odysseus and the Greek forces how Troy might be taken; Odysseus was instrumental in achieving some of these stratagems, including bringing Philoctetes from Lemnos to join the Greek forces and stealing the Palladium, being aided by Diomedes in both tasks. He also went with Diomedes and Phoenix to persuade Lycomedes to allow Neoptolemus to join their forces, giving the lad the armor of his father, Achilles. His most important role, however, was reportedly devising the stratagem of the Wooden Horse, possibly with help from Athene; he was among the Greeks secreted within the gift and hauled into Troy by the unsuspecting Trojans. Having taken the city, Odysseus and Menelaus killed and mutilated Deiphobus. Hecuba, the widow of Priam, fell to Odysseus, and he took her to the Thracian Chersonesus, where she avenged the death of one of her sons, Polydorus. With the war finally over, the most famous part of Odysseus's life began.

His ten-year return journey to Ithaca is the sole subject of Homer's epic *Odyssey,* in which the hero recounts the first nine years of his travels and troubles to his Phaeacian hosts. Soon after leaving Troy, and having visited the Cicones, where Odysseus was given several jars of a potent, sweet wine, his ship was blown off course, and he and his companions were carried to the land of the Lotophagi, the Lotus-Eaters. From there they were driven to the land of the fierce Laestrygones; having escaped, they were imprisoned by Polyphemus, the one-eyed son of Poseidon, on Sicily. They managed to escape from his custody by telling the giant that Odysseus's name was "Nobody," put out his single eye, and then clung to the bellies of his sheep when he let them out of their cave.

They next arrived at the island home of Aeolus, who gave Odysseus a bag containing the winds needed to get home. However, thinking the bag to contain treasure, Odysseus's men opened it and let out all the winds, causing further storms. Next they were washed ashore on Aeaea, the island home of the sorceress Circe, who turned his men into swine. Armed with the plant moly, given to him by Hermes, Odysseus persuaded Circe to restore his men, then became Circe's lover for a year. Then, on Circe's advice, he sailed to the River Oceanos, where he summoned up the shades of the dead, and consulted the shade of the prophet Teiresias, who told him that he and his men would arrive home safely only if they did not harm the cattle of Helios on the island of Thrinacia. Odysseus saw several of the other dead heroes in the Underworld, as well as the great sinners Tityus, Tantalus, and Sisyphus.

Sailing away, Odysseus once again visited Circe, who advised him how he might successfully negotiate the perils of the Sirens and Scylla and Charybdis. He followed the advice but was marooned on Thrinacia. There his crew slaughtered and ate some of Helios's cattle, becoming shipwrecked after they set sail yet again. Odysseus alone survived and was washed up on Ogygia, the home of Calypso, who made him her lover and wanted to make him immortal so that he would remain with her forever. However, after eight years, Zeus sent Hermes to recall him, and Odysseus built a ship or raft and sailed on. Close to Phaeacia, he was again wrecked by Poseidon, who was still angry at him for having blinded Polyphemus, his son. He was saved from drowning by Leucothea, who appeared in the form of a seagull. Washed up on the shore of Phaeacia, he was discovered, naked, by Nausicaa, who took him to her father, King Alcinous, to whom Odysseus related the story of his travels. Alcinous then arranged for Odysseus's transport back to Ithaca in an enchanted sleep. Upon arriving he was deposited close to the Cave of the Nymphs on Ithaca as the Phaeacian ship turned to travel back. Poseidon's last act of vengeance against Odysseus was to turn this ship into stone.

On Ithaca, Penelope had, for a number of years, been besieged by suitors, led by Antinous, who were now living in the palace, waiting for her to make up her mind which to marry. Odysseus, disguised as an old man or beggar by Athene and visiting the hut of his faithful swineherd, Eumaeus, he was reunited with his son, Telemachus. Together they planned the downfall of Penelope's suitors,

their first task being to hide all their weapons. Going to the palace, Odysseus was immediately recognized by his aging hound, Argus, who in his delight promptly expired. He was then bathed by Eurycleia, his old nurse, who recognized him from the scar on his thigh. Odysseus, however, kept his identity a secret from Penelope.

Telemachus then persuaded his mother to tell her suitors that she would marry whoever could bend Odysseus's great bow, which had once belonged to Eurytus, and shoot an arrow through a line of ten axe heads. Odysseus took part in the contest, despite the derision of the other suitors, and was the only one up to the challenge. At this point Telemachus and other supporters rushed in, and with their help Odysseus dispatched all of the suitors before revealing his identity. Reunited with his wife, Odysseus then went to visit Laertes, but the kinsmen of the slain suitors rose up against him and battle ensued. Peace was restored only after Athene, disguised as Mentor, intervened.

At this point *Odyssey* ends. A later epic, *Telegony*, by the sixth-century B.C. poet Eugammon of Cyrene, tells of Odysseus's further wanderings, during which he met Telegonus, his son by Circe, in battle after the latter came to Ithaca to search out his father. Telegonus was ignorant of whom he was fighting and killed Odysseus. He married Penelope; Telemachus married Circe.

See also: Achilles; Aeolus; Ajax (1); Anticleia; Calypso; Circe; Ithaca; Laertes; Penelope; Polyphemus; Telemachus; Trojan War; Wooden Horse

Odyssey
Greek

Greek epic poem written in 24 books that is attributed to Homer, probably dating before 700 B.C. It describes the return of Odysseus from the siege of Troy, the vengeance of Poseidon, and encounters between Odysseus and such characters as Circe, Aeolus, Polyphemus, Scylla, and Charybdis. On his return to Ithaca, his home, after ten years of wandering, he finds his wife, Penelope, besieged by suitors. He dispatches the suitors, and husband and wife are reunited.

See also: Homer; Odysseus

Oebalus

Greek

King of Sparta and father of Icarius, Hippocoön, and Tyndareus.

Oedipus

Greek

The son of Jocasta and Laius, king of Thebes, through whom he could claim direct descent from Cadmos, the founder of Thebes, via Polydorus and Labdacus. His mother exposed him as a newborn on the slopes of Mount Cithaeron, his feet tied together and pierced by a nail, after Laius had been told by the Delphic Oracle that he would be killed by his own son. The child was found by a shepherd of Polybus, king of Corinth, to whom the child was taken; the king raised him as his own, naming the boy Oedipus after his swollen feet.

Grown to manhood, Oedipus traveled to Delphi to consult the oracle, being told that he was destined to kill his own father and marry his mother. As he had always thought Polybus was his father, he immediately vowed never to return to Corinth and set off toward Thebes. On the road he met Laius coming to Delphi, but neither would give way. In the resulting quarrel, Oedipus killed Laius, thus fulfilling the first part of the prophecy.

Arriving in Thebes, Oedipus correctly answered the riddle of the Sphinx, who had been plaguing the city. He was rewarded by being made king, taking Jocasta as his wife; neither mother nor son knew of their connection. The original prophecy was now fully realized. They had four children: Eteocles, Polyneices, Antigone, and Ismene.

As Thebes had been defiled with murder and incest, a plague descended on the city, leading the blind seer Teiresias to foretell that the city would be saved only if one of the Sparti give his life. Hearing this, Menoeceus, the father of Jocasta, threw himself from the walls of the city.

Still the plague raged, so Oedipus consulted Teiresias, who finally told the horrified king the truth. Jocasta hanged herself, and Oedipus put out his eyes with a pin taken from her garment. He then had Creon, Jocasta's brother, banish him. He was accompanied into exile at first by Antigone and was later joined by Ismene.

Oedipus found refuge at Colonos in Attica in a sacred grove of the Eumenides; there, under the protection of Theseus, Oedipus died. However, before dying Oedipus cursed his sons for their neglect, saying they should divide their inherited kingdom by the sword. To circumvent the curse, Eteocles and Polyneices agreed to rule in turn, but when the time came for Eteocles to abdicate he refused. Polyneices then sought the help of Adrastus, and the expedition of the Seven Against Thebes was mounted, thus fulfilling the curse.

See also: Jocasta; Seven Against Thebes; Sphinx

Oeneus

Greek

King of Pleuron and Calydon in Aetolia, he married Althaea and became the father of Tydeus, Meleager, Gorge, and Deianeira (who married Heracles). At one time Oeneus's realm was ravaged by a huge wild boar, but many of the heroes of the time came to his aid and partook in the hunt for the Calydonian Boar. The kingdom was later seized by his nephews, but his grandson, Diomedes, son of Tydeus, avenged him and put Andraemon, the husband of Gorge, on the throne. Oeneus then accompanied Diomedes to the Peloponnesos, where he was eventually killed by two nephews who had earlier escaped the wrath of Diomedes.

See also: Altmaea

Oenomaus

Greek

Son of Ares, king of Pisa in Elis, and father of Hippodameia. Oenomaus always challenged his daughter's suitors to a chariot race from Pisa to the isthmus of Corinth. However, he had an unfair advantage, as the horses that pulled his chariot had been a gift from his father; every suitor lost the races, and hence their lives as well, being transfixed on Oenomaus's infallible spear, another gift from Ares. When Pelops came to Pisa and wanted to marry Hippodameia, he too was challenged to the race. Pelops was better prepared for the contest, for he drove a winged chariot, a gift from Poseidon. Yet to guarantee victory Pelops bribed Myrtilus, Oenomaus's charioteer, with a promise of half the kingdom to replace a linchpin of Oenomaus's chariot with one of wax. It broke during the race, and Oenomaus was thrown out and killed; Pelops reneged on the deal and killed Myrtilus.

See also: Hippodameia; Pelops

Oenone
Greek

A nymph who lived on Mount Ida and loved Paris, either actually marrying him, or simply living with him. She was deserted when Paris was promised Helen by Aphrodite. Later, after Paris had been mortally wounded by Philoctetes he returned to Oenone and beseeched her to save him. She refused, Paris died, and she then hanged herself.

See also: Paris

Ogyges
Greek

According to some sources the name of the first king of Thebes during whose reign a destructive flood occurred. It is possible, due to the later foundation story of Thebes by Cadmos, that Ogyges ruled a city that once stood on the site of Thebes, which was then destroyed in the flood.

See also: Thebes

Ogygia
Greek

The island home of the nymph Calypso, who tenderly cared for Odysseus for eight years after he had been washed ashore following one of the great hero's many shipwrecks. Odysseus left only after Zeus, at Athene's request, sent Hermes to remind him of his duty.

See also: Calypso; Odysseus

Oileus
Greek

King of Locris and father of Ajax the Lesser.

Olympia
Greek

One of the most important cities and religious centers of ancient Greece. Situated in the ancient kingdom of Elis, in the west Peloponnesos, the city was home to quadrennial games held between 776 B.C. and 393 A.D. to honor Zeus. Traditionally founded by Heracles after his defeat of Augeias, these became known as the Olympic Games, the forerunner of the modern games. Buildings at Olympia included a temple to Zeus and Hera that housed the elaborately adorned statue of the god, one of the Seven Wonders of the World. Archaeological excavations at Olympia have unearthed other great temples, the celebrated statue of Hermes by Praxiteles, other buildings, and the stadium. Reportedly there was a hippodrome at Olympia, but no trace has been found.

See also: Heracles

Olympian
Greek

Title applied to a dweller in Olympus, hence the 12 great gods of classical Greece; also used to refer to the nine Muses.

Olympic Games
Greek

Quadrennial games traditionally founded by Heracles at Olympia in Elis and dedicated to Zeus. After his victory over Augeias, Heracles fetched the wild olive tree from the source of the Danube, its leaves crowning the games' victors. The games appear to have lapsed for a period, for Pelops was said to have revived them at one point. Historical records of the games stretch back to 776 B.C., and their four-year cycle was used as the basic dating system of the Greeks. The last ancient games took place in 393 A.D.; the modern Olympic Games were revived in Athens in 1896.

See also: Heracles

Olympus
Greek

The abode of the gods on the summit of a mountain symbolized by Mount Olympus, the highest mountain in Greece, at the eastern end of a range dividing Thessaly and Macedonia. Usually swathed in clouds, the mountain, which has seven peaks and rises to more than

2,740 meters (9,000 feet), became the ideal home of gods who lived in the pure upper air beyond a cloud gate that was guarded by the Horae. Collectively referred to as Olympians, each god or goddess had a palace, but they all repaired to Zeus's great hall to feast on ambrosia and drink nectar served by Hebe, the daughter of Hera and cupbearer of Olympus. A distinctive spur on the mountain is still known as the Throne of Zeus. Ancient Greeks dared not venture onto the mountain, and even today few are intrepid enough to tackle the long climb.

At one stage Mount Olympus was said to have been piled on Mount Ossa, and then Olympus and Ossa on top of Mount Pelion, by giants led by Briareus in an attempt to reach Heaven and destroy the gods. As punishment the giants were imprisoned by the gods under Mount Etna, where their fury is still said to make that mountain erupt.

There are other mountains within the Greek world known as Mount Olympus, notably one near Pursa (modern Ulu Dag above Bursa).

Omalos
Greek

Located in western Crete along the northern fringe of the Levk Mountains, this pancake-flat, mountain-ringed plain, whose name means "belly-button," was regarded, at least by some ancient Greeks, as the navel of the world.

Omphale
Greek

Widow of Tmolus and queen of Lydia. She purchased Heracles when he sold himself into slavery; he served her for either one or three years, during which she bore him a son, Lamus. Later writers said that during his enslavement Heracles lived effeminately, dressing in Omphale's clothes while she wore his lion's-skin armor. Others, however, say Heracles continued to perform heroic deeds while serving out his required time.

See also: Heracles

Omphalos
Greek

The navel stone of the world that stood in the temple of Apollo at Delphi. Cronos suppos-

edly swallowed this stone, thinking it the infant Zeus; he later disgorged it, and it fell at this spot. Others say the stone fell onto the similarly named Omalos Plain in western Crete.

Onocentaur
Greek

A class of centaur with the tail and legs of an ass rather than those of a horse.

Opheltes
Greek

The son of King Lycurgus of Nemaea. His father was warned by an oracle that the infant Opheltes must not be allowed to touch the ground until he had learned to walk. However, Hypsipyle, his nurse, put him down when the Seven Against Thebes came to Nemaea looking for freshwater. He was bitten by a snake and died. The Nemaean Games were founded in his honor under the new name of Archemorus—the "beginning of doom," for the expedition against Thebes was fated to fail. The games were later rededicated by Heracles to Zeus. His shrine has not been definitely identified but is thought to be the large, irregularly pentagonal heroön at the southwest corner of the sanctuary at Nemaea.

Ophiuchus
Greek

"The Serpent Bearer"; the name given to Asclepios after he had been translated to the heavens as the constellation that carries this name. The founder of medicine and ship's doctor to the Argonauts, Asclepios was so skillful that he once succeeded in bringing a man back to life. This power so worried Hades that he persuaded Zeus to place Asclepios among the stars out of the way. There he is depicted holding a serpent, his most famous attribute.

Astronomical: An ill-formed constellation that lies across the celestial equator between approximate right ascensions 16h00m and 18h45m, declination from +14° to –30°. To either side are two smaller constellations, Serpens Caput (Head of the Serpent) to the west, Serpens Cauda (Tail of the Serpent) to the east.

See also: Asclepios

Ops

Roman

An early goddess of plenty who was later identified with the Greek Rhea, thus sometimes regarded as the wife of Saturnus. She is, however, more usually thought of as the consort of Consus.

Oracle

Greco-Roman

In Greek, *manteion;* in Latin, *oraculum.* A holy place where inquirers obtained sacred responses to questions about their futures. The responses were usually ambivalent, so that the oracle was always proved right, whatever actual events transpired. The earliest Greek oracle was probably that of Zeus at Dodona, in Epirus, where the priests interpreted the rustling of the leaves in a sacred oak tree. The most celebrated was that of Apollo at Delphi, the aptly named Delphic Oracle. Here the priestess, known as the Pythia, sat on a tripod over a chasm, which exuded noxious fumes, and chewed laurel, thereby inducing a hypnotic trance. Her demented ravings were translated for the questioner by priests, often giving the oracle in hexameter verse. Other major Greek oracles were at Didyma and Claros, both of Apollo, and at Ephyra, the Oracle of the Dead.

Though the normal manner of consultation was to simply question the priest in attendance, other methods existed. One could cast lots or receive communication from the god by "incubation," whereby the inquirer would sleep in a holy area and receive the answer via dreams. Although the responses, in English, are also referred to as "oracles," the Greeks called then *chremos* (pl. *chremmoi*), the Romans *oraculum* (pl. *oracula*).

By the advent of the Christian era oracles were no longer given in verse, and they entered a steady decline. When Emperor Julian sent to the oracle at Delphi, he was told that it had ceased to operate. The oracle at Didyma was closed by the Christian Emperor

Theodosius in 395 A.D., when he abolished all pagan observances.

See also: Delphic Oracle

Orchomenus

Greek

The capital city of the Minyan people of Boeotia. At one time they extracted tribute from Thebes, but Heracles challenged this, led a successful campaign against them, and subsequently made Orchomenus a tributary of Thebes.

See also: Boeotia

Orcus

Roman

One of the names the Romans used in referring to the Underworld; an alternative was Dis. The name appears to have been applied to Pluto, the Roman equivalent of Hades, god of the Underworld.

Oread(es)

Greek

One of the many classes of nymphs said to inhabit the mountains and grottos. The Oreades also appeared to share the habitation of glens with the Napaeae, another class of nymphs.

Oreithyia

Greek

The daughter of Erichthonius, or Erechtheus, who was abducted by Boreas.

Orestes

Greek

Son of Agamemnon and Clytemnestra, brother of Electra and Iphigeneia. After the murder of his father by Clytemnestra and her lover, Aegisthus, Orestes fled to the court of Strophius, king of Phocis and Agamemnon's brother-in-law, and there became the inseparable companion of Strophius's son, Pylades, some sources hinting at a homosexual relationship. During Orestes' adolescence Electra wrote him many letters begging him to return to Argos to avenge the murder of their father.

Having reached manhood, Orestes consulted the Delphic Oracle, which instructed him to return to Argos and exact his revenge. He did exactly that, killing mother and lover; Aegisthus had by this time become his stepfather. Even though he had been guided by the Delphic Oracle, the Erinnyes pursued Orestes and drove him mad. He returned to Delphi for further advice, and the oracle sent him to Athens, where he embraced a statue of Athene in her temple on the Acropolis. She then summoned a special sitting of the Areopagus. At the hearing Orestes was defended by Apollo on the grounds that motherhood is less important than fatherhood. He was acquitted of the murder on the casting vote of Athene, who appeased the Erinnyes by giving them a sacred grotto in Athens and declaring that they should be known thenceforth as the Eumenides.

This, at least, is the traditional version of Orestes' cure. Others say that he drove away the Erinnyes by biting off one of his fingers at Megalopolis, or that the madness that had overcome him simply vanished while he was visiting Gythion. Euripides, in his *Orestes*, does not let Orestes off the hook quite so easily. Euripides has Orestes condemned to death by the Argives, after which Orestes and Pylades try to murder Helen because Menelaus refused to help them. The pair then holds Hermione hostage until Apollo appears and orders the banishment of Orestes. No other source follows this line, and this weird story appears to be the invention of the playwright.

Later tradition continues Orestes' madness after the trial at Athens, a cure for which may be found, so Apollo informs him, if he travels to Tauris and brings back the statue of Artemis. Arriving, still accompanied by Pylades, Orestes finds that his sister, Iphigeneia, is the priestess to Artemis (he thought she was sacrificed by their father at Aulis). Together they narrowly escape the murderous Taurians and flee to Athens with the statue, Orestes finally cured of his affliction. The statue was set up either in the temple of Artemis Orthia at Sparta or in Attica, Iphigeneia going on to become the priestess of Artemis at Brauron. Orestes, now fully sane again, was reunited with his other

sister, Electra; returning to Mycenae, he killed Aegisthus's son and became the king of Mycenae and Sparta.

However, Orestes now found that Hermione, to whom he had been betrothed by Tyndareus, had been awarded to Neoptolemus by Menelaus after the Trojan War. Orestes traveled to Delphi and either killed Neoptolemus or arranged for his death. He then married Hermione; Electra married Pylades. There the adventures of Orestes seem to end, for the next reference is to his death as an old man and his succession as king by Tisamenus. His bones, however, do not appear to have remained at Mycenae or Sparta, for Herodotus recounts how the Spartans were told they would conquer Tegea only if Orestes' bones were brought to Sparta. They were discovered in a forge at Tegea, and the Spartans brought them triumphantly home.

See also: Agamemnon; Clytemnestra; Erinnyes; Iphigeneia

Orion
Greek

A giant son of Poseidon, Zeus, and Hermes who was conceived when the three gods took an ox hide, urinated on it, and then buried it. Nine months later it produced the baby Urion, who was given to King Hyrieus; the child was renamed Orion. His remarkable conception was the answer to the prayers of Hyrieus.

Exceedingly handsome and an excellent hunter, his favorite prey being the hare, Orion fell in love with Merope, the daughter of Oenopion of Chios; the latter promised his daughter's hand if Orion freed the island of wild beasts. Orion completed this task with ease, but Oenopion failed to keep his promise. Orion then seduced Merope but was blinded by her father, helped in his task by his father, Dionysos.

An oracle told the giant that his sight would be restored if he traveled far to the east and exposed his eyes to the rays of the rising sun. As a son of Poseidon, Orion had the ability to walk on water, and in this mode he made it to Lemnos. There Hephaistos provided him with his servant, the boy Cedalion, as a guide. Sitting on Orion's shoulders, Cedalion gave him directions toward the sunrise. There his sight was restored by Helios and Eos, Helios's sister, who took him to Delos.

There he shared his great pleasure of hunting with Artemis, but she was also responsible for his death, though that event is variously described. Either he boasted of his prowess to Artemis, and Apollo, upon hearing this, was afraid that Artemis might fall in love with him and so contrived his death; or he tried to rape Artemis's attendant, Opis, and Ge sent a scorpion, Scorpius, to kill him; or Apollo killed him by accident with a discus; or Apollo challenged his sister to target practice while Orion was swimming, and she hit the unfortunate giant's head, not realizing what it was.

After his death, by whichever means, Orion was placed among the stars as the constellation that bears his name. Accompanied by his faithful hunting dog, Sirius, he eternally pursues the Pleiades, the seven daughters of Atlas (one of them also named Merope, who he is said to have pursued during his lifetime). The scorpion was also placed in the heavens as the constellation Scorpius, far enough away to cause Orion no further distress. At the feet of Orion is the constellation Lepus, "the Hare," an eternal reminder of his favorite animal at the hunt.

Astronomical: Straddling the celestial equator, Orion is one of the best known of all the constellations, with three stars making up his belt; one of the few constellations that can be imagined as intended. The constellation lies between approximate right ascensions 4h40m and 6h25m, declination from +22° to –11°. Between the legs of Orion lies the Great Nebula of Orion, one of the wonders of the night sky. Directly below Orion is the constellation Lepus; the three stars that make up his belt lead to Sirius the Dog Star, the brightest star in the night sky, within the constellation Canis Major to the side of Lepus. Among the stars that make up the constellation Orion is one named Bellatrix (α Ori), the name of an Amazon warrior, possibly one of Orion's paramours.

See also: Artemis; Pleiades

Orpheus
Greek

A legendary Thracian, pre-Homeric singer and poet, the son of Oeagrus and Calliope (or possibly another of the Muses). He received a lyre from Apollo, who some make his father, and was taught to play by the Muses so that his music had the power to enchant beasts, trees, and rocks to follow its sounds. He was an Argonaut, accompanying Jason on his voyage to Colchis, during which he introduced his fellow adventurers to the mysteries of Samothrace and was, according to some, responsible for charming to sleep with his music the sleepless dragon that guarded the Golden Fleece. On his return he married the beautiful Eurydice. However, she was killed when she was bitten by a snake while being pursued by Aristaeus.

Grief-stricken, Orpheus now undertook his famous journey to the Underworld. There he played his lyre for Hades and so enchanted the god that he allowed Eurydice to return to the land of the living. Hades set but one condition: that Orpheus should not look back at his wife until they had both safely emerged from the Underworld. Nearing the exit, Orpheus began to wonder if his wife really was following him; no longer able to contain himself, he glanced back. Eurydice was thus lost to him forever.

Now despairing with grief, Orpheus made the fatal mistake of neglecting to honor Dionysos, and as a result he was torn to pieces by Thracian Maenads during one of their orgiastic celebrations. The Muses collected together the pieces of his body and buried them at the foot of Mount Olympus, but his head, which had been thrown into the River Hebrus, was carried, still singing, down to the sea and then on to Lesbos, where his lyre also drifted. There they were buried, though the lyre was later placed in the heavens as the constellation Lyra at the intercession of Apollo and the Muses. The gift of Orpheus to the Lesbians was their skill in music.

The ancient Greeks considered Orpheus to be the greatest poet before Homer, and fragmentary poems have been variously ascribed to him. These poems would come to influence the theology of the Pythagoreans, in the sixth century B.C., as well as later cults. This so-called Orphic doctrine remains one of the most intractable puzzles in the history of Greek religion. The most plausible explanation is that the human Orpheus exhibited the powers of the shaman, a type of medicine man or ecstatic prophet that was familiar in Central Asia regions northeast of Greece, including Thrace. The Orphic religion was characterized by a sense of sin and the need for atonement, the concept of a suffering man-god (Orpheus), and an underlying belief in immortality. The religion had a great influence on philosophers such as Pythagoras and Plato and formed a link between the worship of Dionysos and Christianity for, like the Maenads, Orphic worshippers sought mystic unions with their gods.

See also: Eurydice; Jason

Orthr~os, ~us
Greek

Two-headed dog of Geryon, one of the monstrous offspring of Typhon and Echidne and father of the Sphinx, either by Echidne or the Chimaera. He was killed by Heracles, along with Eurytion, when Heracles was sent to steal the cattle of Geryon, which Orthros and Eurytion guarded.

Ortygia
Greek

1. The island where Leto reportedly gave birth to Artemis under a palm tree before traveling on to Delos, where Apollo was born. It may be that these islands were one and the same, for Ortygia is said by some to be an early name for Delos.

2. The place in Sicily where Arethusa fled to when she was pursued by the river god Alpheus, whose waters were thenceforth said to flow unmixed through the sea to merge with the fountain of Arethusa here.

Ossa
Greek

Mountain in northern Thessaly that features in two stories relating the attempts of giants to reach Heaven and destroy the gods. In the first, the giants, led by Briareus, piled Mount Olympus on Mount Ossa, and then those two atop Mount Pelion. When they failed they were imprisoned beneath Mount Etna, where their fury is still said to vent itself when the mountain erupts. In the second, the gigantic Aloeidae, Ephialtes, and Otus, aged just nine, vowed to outrage Hera and Artemis and so piled Mount Pelion on Mount Ossa in their attempt to reach Heaven. They were tricked into killing each other by Artemis on the island of Naxos, and they were consigned to Tartarus.

See also: Artemis; Briareus

Otrere
Greek

Mother, by Ares, of Penthesilea, who was the beautiful queen of the Amazons killed by Achilles during the Trojan War.

See also: Achilles

Otus
Greek

Gigantic twin brother of Ephialtes; the sons of Iphimedeia by Poseidon, they became known as the Aloeidae after their mother married Aloeus. At the age of nine the brothers captured and imprisoned Ares. They then vowed to outrage Hera and Artemis and so piled Mount Pelion on Mount Ossa in their attempt to reach Heaven. Artemis tricked them into going to Naxos in the hope of meeting her. There, disguised as a doe, she leaped between them, and they killed each other. Hermes then released Ares, and the Aloeidae were tied back-to-back with vipers to a pillar in Tartarus. The Aloeidae were regarded as the founders of Ascra at the foot of Mount Helicon.

See also: Artemis; Iphimedeia

P

Pactolus
Greek

The river that Midas was told to bathe in to rid himself of the power to turn everything he touched into gold. As he entered the waters of the river, the sands turned to gold, and the river has, since that time, been rich in gold.

See also: Midas

Pae~an, ~on
Greek

Originally a hymn specifically addressed to Apollo as healer or deliverer from evil, also a title subsequently applied to Apollo or an alternative name for the god. Paeans were later addressed to other gods and were sung to mark military victories. Later still they developed into artistic tributes to gods and mortals alike.

See also: Apollo

Paestum
Greco-Roman

Modern name for the Greek colony of Poseidonia situated on the Gulf of Salerno, southern Italy. Paestum boasts some of the best preserved temple ruins in the world. The temple of Athene was built c. 520 B.C.; that of Hera was erected c. 430 B.C. Both are Doric buildings, as is a second temple of Hera, built c. 440 B.C.

Palaemon
Greek

The name given to Melicertes, the son of Athamas and Ino, when he drowned and became a sea god. Melicertes was honored under this name as the presiding hero of the Isthmian Games held near Corinth, as Melicertes washed up and was buried on the isthmus.

Palamedes
Greek

Son of Nauplius, king of Euboea, and inventor, or coinventor, of the alphabet, dice, chess, weights and measures, and signal fires. His name seems to derive from *palamai*, "hands," implying dexterity or cleverness. Palamedes joined the Greek muster at Aulis prior to the Trojan War. As Agamemnon needed allies to join up before he sailed for Troy, he, Menelaus, and Palamedes went to Ithaca to persuade Odysseus to join them. There they found the great hero feigning madness, sowing his fields with salt. Palamedes, however, proved that Odysseus was not mad by placing Telemachus, Odysseus's son, in a furrow before the plough, though some sources say the child was Cypria. Odysseus then acted like the sanest of fathers and rescued his son.

Having sailed from Aulis, the Greek fleet anchored at Tenedos, from where Palamedes, Menelaus, and Odysseus went as envoys to Priam to request the peaceable return of Helen. They were refused. Odysseus later took his revenge on Palamedes for uncovering his attempt to escape and forcing him to fight at Troy. He planted a quantity of gold in Palamedes' tent along with a letter written in the name of Priam, though some say Odysseus bribed Palamedes' servant to help him. Odysseus then publicly accused Palamedes of treason, his tent was searched, and the entire Greek army stoned the unfortunate Palamedes to death. Another version simply says that he was murdered by Odysseus and Diomedes while fishing. His father, Nauplius, later took his revenge by lighting misleading signal fires that guided many of the ships returning from

Troy onto the dangerous promontory of Caphareus.

See also: Odysseus; Trojan War

Palatine Hill
Roman

One of the hills of Rome. Archaeological material excavated from this hill and the Forum suggests that this region of Rome was settled by a community very closely associated with Alba Longa, in contrast to remains from the Esquiline Hill, which are more characteristic of southern Latium. Legend states that Romulus stood on the Palatine Hill when he and his brother, Remus, who stood on the Aventine Hill, consulted the auguries to decide which of them should name the new city. Soon after Remus had reported the sighting of six vultures, Romulus reported seeing 12. A fight ensued, Remus was killed, and Romulus gave his name to the city. Later, Aeneas was said to have been greeted by Venus as he came down from the Palatine Hill, the goddess presenting him with armor made by Vulcan.

See also: Aeneas; Remus; Romulus

Pales
Roman

An early goddess of flocks.

Palinurus
Greco-Roman

The helmsman of Aeneas who fell asleep at the helm and was washed overboard during the final journey to Italy.

Palladium
Greco-Roman

A wooden image of Athene (Roman: Minerva) that was kept in the citadel at Troy. This statue had been made by Athene as a memorial to her friend, Pallas, whom she had killed, and was thus sometimes referred to as the Palladium of Pallas Athene. The statue was originally housed in Olympus; Zeus threw it out after Electra, the daughter of Atlas, tried to hide in it to avoid his lust. It landed in Troy, which could not be captured while the image remained; it was stolen during the war by Odysseus with the help of Diomedes. After the fall of Troy and the end of the Trojan War, it was supposedly brought to Italy by Diomedes. Others say it was given to Aeneas by Diomedes and that Aeneas brought it to Italy; some accounts suggest it was brought to Rome by Numa Pompilius.

See also: Troy

Pallas
Greek

1. One of the 24 Gigantes, the gigantic sons of Ge who had serpents' tails. Led by Alcyoneus, they tried to avenge the imprisonment of their brothers, the Titans, by attacking Olympus. Among the attackers were Porphyrion, Ephialtes, Mimas, Enceladus, Polybutes, Alcyoneus, and Pallas. After a terrible struggle on earth and in Olympus, the giants were defeated by the gods with the help of the mortal Heracles, who found a magical herb of invulnerability and always struck the giants their final blow. One version of the Gigantes revolt says that Pallas was dispatched by Athene, after which she used his flayed skin as a shield. This is just one version of how Athene also became known as Pallas.

2. "Maiden"; a title or name of Athene brought into Greece by the Achaeans. A young warrior-goddess, she originally bore the titles Core (Girl), Parthenos (Virgin), and Pallas and was, about 1700 B.C., identified with the older, pre-Hellenic Palace Goddess worshipped in Crete. The name Pallas appears to have been used both as a forename, Pallas Athene, or as a surname, Athene Pallas. The complex Pallas Athene thus was not only the patroness of women's arts, such as weaving, and protectress of agriculture and inventor of the plough, rake, and ox yoke, but also a warrior, a supreme tactician depicted fully armored and bearing on her aegis the head of Medusa. During the Trojan War she was the greatest protagonist of the Greeks. Legend said that Pallas was a companion of Athene whom the goddess accidentally killed, adopting her name as a title, then making the Palladium in her image. This image, which was thrown from Olympus and landed in Troy, meant that Troy could not be taken so long as it remained in the city.

3. The name of one of the Titans, according to some sources. He married Styx and was the father of Victory, Violence, and Emulation.

4. Nephew, or half-brother, of Aegeus, whose 50 sons were scattered by Theseus when they vied for succession to the throne of Athens.

Roman

Great friend and fighting companion of Aeneas who was slain by Turnus, the latter stripping the dead Pallas of the great gold belt he wore. Later, when Aeneas and Turnus were involved in single combat to settle their feud, Aeneas was about to spare Turnus when he noticed the belt that had belonged to his friend. Enraged, Aeneas dispatched Turnus with a single thrust of his sword.

See also: Aeneas; Athene; Titan

Pan

Greek

Guardian of flocks and shepherds and of woods and fields. A purely pastoral deity, Pan, whom the Romans called Faunus or Sylvanus, was believed by some to be coeval with Zeus, though most make him the misshapen son of Hermes by a doubtful mother, Dryope; the nymph Oeneis; Penelope, the wife of Odysseus; or the goat Amalthea. Living in rural Arcadia, where he hunted and danced with the nymphs, Pan was so ugly at birth that his mother rejected him. He is usually depicted as a man having the horns, tail, and feet of a goat and had the annoying habit of hiding among the trees, startling passing travelers with a sudden shout, possibly a hideous laugh, for laughter belongs to Pan and so fills them with fear that it became known as "panic." As a result, his cult was usually centered around sanctuaries that were remote from cities. When he did receive cult within the boundaries of a city it was not in a temple but rather in a grotto that represented the wild countryside. His ability to strike fear into the hearts of men appears to have been put to good use during the Battle of Marathon (479 B.C.). Pan met Pheidippides, who was running from Marathon to Athens to warn of the Persian invasion, on Mount Parnes and promised to help. This help led to the introduction of his cult into Athens.

Having fertility connections, like most pastoral deities, Pan was a determined seducer who claimed to have seduced all the Maenads. He loved many nymphs, including Syrinx, who fled in terror from his advances and was turned into a clump of reeds by the nymphs of the River Ladon. From these the god made the syrinx—"Pan's Pipe"—which he was said to have invented and is his most usual attribute. He was also said to have seduced Selene (Moon) by spreading out a beautiful white fleece to entice her. He also managed to father a daughter, Iynx, on the insubstantial nymph Echo. However, Pan's love objects were typically unfulfilled or sterile boys, and he had the dubious reputation of having invented masturbation.

Looked down upon by the Olympian gods, though at one time he did help Hermes to rescue Zeus during his struggle with Typhon, Pan was the only deity whose death was reported. To escape from Typhon, Pan leaped into the River Nile; midleap his head, still above the water, became that of a goat, whereas his hindquarters became the rear part of a fish. Thus was created the sea goat Capricornus, which was later placed in the heavens. His worship originated in Arcadia, the region to which his worship was chiefly restricted, and he was despised by the Greeks as being backwards, though he was often seen in the company of the Muses as well as Apollo, the latter being one of the most beloved Olympian deities (and to whom Pan was said to have taught the art of prophecy). As a result his cult did not reach Athens until as late as the fifth century B.C., the reason for the introduction itself being Pan's assistance to the Athenians at Marathon. He is unusual among the Greek deities in being the only one not approached in revered silence. Thus, Pan is most dangerous during the midday rest period when he, or his attendant nymphs, can seize a man and make him mad or strike him dumb.

In later Orphic theology Pan acquired a quite different significance, tied solely to the resemblance of his name to the word *pan*, "all." As a result he became a universal, high god, but this is simply the aberration of theologians at play.

See also: Faunus; Iynx; Syrinx

Panathen~aea, ~aic

Greek

A yearly festival in Athens that culminated every fourth year in the Great Panathenaic Games that were founded in 566 B.C. by Pesistratus, its magnificent procession being represented on the frieze of the Parthenon that is now in the British Museum. It was founded about the same time as the Dionysia in Athens.

Legend says that Androgeos, the son of Minos, won every contest in the Panathenaic but was slain at the instigation of Aegeus. Minos mounted an expedition against Athens in revenge and, having made Athens a tributary, extracted a yearly tribute of seven youths and seven maidens who were to be fed to the Minotaur.

See also: Androgeos; Minotaur; Theseus

Pandareus

Greek

A Cretan king who once owned the golden dog of Rhea, which he gave to Tantalus, later denying to Zeus that he had ever heard of it, let alone seen it. Pandareus and his wife were killed for so incensing Zeus, but Aphrodite rescued their daughters; Hera made them beautiful, and Athene taught them to weave. However, when Aphrodite went to arrange marriages for them, the Harpies snatched and gave them to the Erinnyes as servants.

Pandarus

Greek

A skilled archer from Lycia who fought on the side of Troy during the Trojan War and was killed by Diomedes. His part in the tragic love story of Troilus and Cressida—acting as a go-between for the lovers—belongs to medieval legend and has no part in classical tradition.

Pandion

Greek

Legendary king of Athens, the son of Erichthonius and father of Procne, Philomela, and Erechtheus, who succeeded him.

Pandora

Greek

The Eve of classical Greek mythology. Infuriated by the theft of fire from Heaven by Prometheus, Zeus ordered Hephaistos to make a lovely woman from clay who was endowed with baleful powers by the gods. She was given life by Athene, jewelry by the Graces and Peitho, flowers by the Horae, beauty by Aphrodite, and treachery by Hermes. Hermes led her to Epimetheus, who married her, after which she opened a box that the gods had given her. From it all the ills that plague mankind escaped, Hope alone remaining.

See also: Prometheus

Pandrosos

Greek

One of the daughters of Cecrops entrusted with the baby Erichthonius.

Panopeus

Greek

The father of Epeius, the cowardly carpenter who constructed the Wooden Horse.

Panthous

Greek

Father of Euphorbus, the Trojan soldier who wounded Patroclus while he was fighting in place of Achilles before he was finally finished off by Hector.

See also: Hector

Paphos

Greek

The name of two towns in Cyprus, one on the coast, the other inland, the latter being the site of the sanctuary of Aphrodite. Historical evidence seems to suggest that the worship of Aphrodite, though not known by that name, as a fertility goddess was taken from Paphos to Cythera by the Phoenicians. Hesiod reverses this, saying that Aphrodite rose from the ocean near Cythera and then made her way to Paphos.

See also: Aphrodite

Parcae

Roman

The three Fates of ancient Rome, the counterparts of the Greek Moirae. Nona, Decuma, and Morta were sometimes said to be the daughters of Jupiter and were thus direct equivalents of Clotho, Lachesis, and Atropos, the Greek Moirae, the daughters of Zeus.

See also: Atropos; Clotho; Lachesis

Parentalia

Roman

An important annual festival that was celebrated between 13 and 14 February in honor of dead parents whose *di manes* were feasted to ensure they maintained well-being and placidity.

See also: Manes, di

Paris

Greek

The second son of Priam and Hecuba of Troy, exposed by them at birth following a dream in which Hecuba saw herself giving birth to a firebrand that destroyed the city. The infant was suckled by a bear, rescued and raised by a shepherd, and given the name Alexander or Alexandros, which means "Protector" or "Defender," after the skills he showed in protecting the shepherd's flocks. Reaching adolescence, Paris returned to Troy to take part in the games that were being held to commemorate his death. He won all the events; he was either recognized by his sister, Cassandra, or showed the clothes in which he had been exposed. His family welcomed him back, calling him Paris for the first time, but he returned to the hills to continue his pastoral life.

There, on the slopes of Mount Ida, he became the lover of the nymph Oenone, or Denone, by whom, some sources say, Paris had a son. His life, however, changed beyond all recognition when he was commanded by Zeus to judge the concurrent claims of Hera, Athene, and Aphrodite to the golden Apple of Discord. Inscribed with the dedication, "To the fairest," the apple was thrown by Eris among the guests at the wedding of Peleus and Thetis in revenge for being omitted from the guest list.

Hermes led the three goddesses to Mount Ida. There each appeared naked before Paris, the most handsome man in the world, and each tried to bribe him. Hera offered him rule over Asia. Athene offered him wisdom and military supremacy. Aphrodite, however, offered him the love of the most beautiful woman in the world. Paris judged in favor of Aphrodite, thereby sowing the seeds of the oncoming Trojan War, and ensured Hera's relentless hostility to Troy.

Immediately deserting Oenone, Aphrodite guided Paris to Sparta, where Helen, the wife of Menelaus, lived. Welcomed by Menelaus, Paris waited until he had left Sparta, then eloped with Helen, who, some sources say, was in love with Paris as much as he with her. After spending their first night on the island of Cranae off the southern tip of Mani, the couple made straight for Troy. Menelaus, finding his wife gone, called upon the Greek heroes and leaders to keep their oath to defend his rights, and a massive Greek fleet first assembled at Aulis before sailing for Troy. Thus the Trojan War began.

During the ten years of battle, Paris excelled as an archer, his most famous exploit being to strike (with guiding help from Apollo) Achilles in his one vulnerable heel during a battle outside the Scaean Gate. Paris, however, was then mortally wounded by Philoctetes, the arrow being guided by Hermes. Leaving Troy for Mount Ida, Paris beseeched his previous lover, Oenone, to cure him of his wound. She refused, and Paris died. She then hanged herself in remorse.

See also: Achilles; Hecuba; Helen; Menelaus; Priam; Troy

Parnassus

Greek

A lofty, double-peaked mountain in central Greece, northwest of the Gulf of Corinth. Situated on its southern slope is the town of Delphi, above which the sacred spring of Castalia rises. The mountain was one of the chief seats of Apollo and the Muses and was also sacred to Dionysos due to the location of the Corycian Cave, which lies on a plateau between Delphi and the summit and was associated with Bacchanalia festivals.

Legend says that the ark of Deucalion and Pyrrha settled on Mount Parnassus after the nine days of the great flood. The mountain remains, perhaps, most famous for its connections with Apollo and the Delphic Oracle. Soon after his birth, Apollo sought out the she-dragon Python on Mount Parnassus and killed her, taking over the Oracle of Earth at Delphi. Here Apollo became known as the Pythian, or Loxias, "the Ambiguous." His priestess, the Pythoness, imparted his oracles in hexameter verse.

See also: Delphi; Deucalion

Parthenon

Greek

Popular name for the temple of Athene Parthenos (Virgin Athene) on the Acropolis at Athens. Created by the architects Ictinus and Callicrates and built between 447 B.C. and 438 B.C. under Pericles' administration, it was decorated with sculptures by Phidias or his school. The eastern gable depicted the birth of Athene; the western depicted the contest between Athene and Poseidon. The huge gold and ivory statue of Athene once housed in this temple was destroyed in ancient times, and its inner chambers and porticos were ruined by an explosion in 1687 during the Venetian attack on Athens. Most of the surviving sculptures were removed by Lord Elgin between 1801 and 1803, including the frieze that depicted the magnificent procession of the Panathenaea. The surviving outer structure and sculptural pediments testify to the perfection of the design.

See also: Acropolis

Parthenopaeus

Greek

The son of Meleager and Atalanta who participated in the fated expedition of the Seven Against Thebes, an expedition in which Parthenopaeus and all his companions perished, with the exception of Adrastus.

See also: Atalanta; Seven Against Thebes

Parthenos

Greek

"Virgin"; a name or title applied to the goddess Athene, usually in the form Athene Parthenos.

It was originally one of the titles, along with Core and Pallas, borne by the young warrior-goddess and brought into Greece by the Achaeans c. 1700 B.C. Athene was worshipped as Athene Parthenos within her temple, the Parthenon, on the Acropolis at Athens.

Pasiphaë

Greek

"All-brightest"; in classical tradition Pasiphaë was worshipped as a moon goddess in Laconia, the daughter of Helios and Perseis, wife of Minos, thus queen of Crete and mother of Ariadne (All-Holy), Phaedra (Shining), Androgeos, and Glaucus, as well as the Minotaur. Her daughters seem to represent the faded memories of Cretan goddesses.

Legend says that as Minos had not sacrificed the bull sent by Poseidon for that purpose, the god made Pasiphaë fall in love with the bull. She had Daedalus construct her a wooden cow in which she could lie to mate with the bull, the monstrous result of this union being the Minotaur. When this help was discovered by Minos, Daedalus and his son, Icarus, were imprisoned, but Pasiphaë released them, and they flew away from the island on the wings of wax and feathers that Daedalus had constructed. Icarus flew too close to the sun and plunged into the sea.

Astronomical: One of the smaller satellites of Jupiter, lying twelfth closest to the planet between the orbits of Carme and Sinope.

See also: Minos

Patrocl~es, ~us

Greek

Son of Menoetius and an uncertain mother, from Opus. Having killed a friend in a quarrel, he and his father fled to the court of Peleus, where Patroclus became the inseparable friend and lover of Achilles. They went to the Trojan War, Patroclus acting as Achilles' squire. When Achilles famously withdrew from the fighting following his argument with Agamemnon, Patroclus borrowed the great hero's armor and led the Myrmidones back into battle. Initially successful, Patroclus was wounded by Euphorbus and then killed by Hector, who stripped him of the borrowed armor.

His body was recovered by Menelaus and Ajax the Greater; after a period of extravagant mourning, Achilles rejoined the fray, killed Hector, and dishonored his body. Each day at dawn Achilles, still crazed with grief, would pull the corpse three times around the tomb of Patroclus until Priam, led by Hermes, came to ransom the body of Hector. Patroclus was translated, like Achilles after his death, to the White Island in the Black Sea.

See also: Achilles

Pavo

Greek

Argos, the builder of the ship *Argo Navis,* was turned into this peacock before being placed in the heavens as the constellation that bears this name.

Astronomical: A constellation of the southern celestial hemisphere that lies between approximate right ascensions 17h45m and 21h30m, declination from –56° to –75°.

Pax

Roman

The female personification of peace, the Roman counterpart of Irene. She was less honored in Rome than was Victoria (Victory) and became significant only during the reign of Emperor Augustus. It was not until 75 A.D., under Vespasian, that a temple was finally dedicated to her.

Pegasus

Greek

The fabulous white winged horse who was born, along with the warrior Chrysaor, from the severed neck of Medusa, though some say he was born when the Gorgon's blood mingled with the sea. Pegasus and Chrysaor were the offspring of Poseidon, and their conception was the reason that the beautiful maiden Medusa was turned into the hideous Gorgon by Athene. Perseus, who had killed Medusa and thus enabled Pegasus and Chrysaor to be born, captured the animal. Riding his back, Perseus turned Atlas into the mountain that carries his name and rescued Princess Andromeda from the sea monster Cetus, both

Atlas and Cetus being petrified when Perseus exposed the head of Medusa.

Released by Perseus, Pegasus wandered to Mount Helicon, where he struck the mountainside with his hoof. At that spot the sacred spring of the Muses named Hippocrene (Horse's Spring) arose, and as a result Pegasus became a favorite of theirs. He also caused the fountain of Pirene to rise on the Acropolis at Corinth, and beside it he was caught and tamed by the hero Bellerophon, who rode on his back above the fire-breathing Chimaera, enabling him to kill the monster.

Bellerophon later presumptuously attempted to fly up to the heavens on Pegasus, so Zeus sent a gadfly that stung Pegasus, who reared and threw Bellerophon back to earth. Pegasus, however, continued to Olympus, where he made his home, fathered a colt named Equuleus, and carried the thunderbolt of Zeus. On his death the fabulous horse was placed in the heavens as the constellation that bears his name, but only his front half remained, his rear end falling back to earth to begin the breed of politicians.

Astronomical: A constellation of the northern celestial hemisphere that lies between approximate right ascensions 21h05m and 0h10m, declination from +2° to +37°.

See also: Bellerophon; Medusa; Perseus

Peitho

Greek

The personification, and thus the goddess, of the rhetorical or amatory power of Persuasion.

Pelasgian

Greek

The Lycians became known as the Pelasgians after they emigrated to Lemnos; their eponym was Pelasgus, who probably led the emigration, even though the Pelasgians are usually considered the autochthonous inhabitants of Greece, from whom the Athenians, Argives, and Thessalanians all claimed descent.

Pelasgus

Greek

King of Arcadia, either the son of Zeus and Niobe, or autochthonously born from the

Arcadian soil. He was the father of Lycaon and eponym of the Pelasgians, the autochthonous inhabitants of Greece, the Athenians, Argives, and Thessalanians all claiming direct descent from him. He was revered as the inventor of huts and the habit of wearing sheepskin coats. He was also said to have introduced the Arcadian people to a superior diet consisting of acorns.

Peleus

Greek

Son of Aeacus, king of Aegina, brother of Telamon, and father of Achilles. Banished in his youth with Telamon for their murder of their half-brother, Phocus, Peleus came to Phthia and married Antigone, daughter of King Eurytion, whom he accidentally killed during the hunt for the Calydonian Boar; he fled to Iolcos. There he was purified by Acastus, but Acastus's wife, Astydamia, fell in love with Peleus and, having been spurned, falsely accused him of attempting to rape her. She also told Antigone that Peleus was about to marry Acastus's daughter, and Antigone killed herself.

Unwilling to dispose of Peleus himself, Acastus took him hunting on Mount Pelion, where he abandoned him while he slept, hiding his sword and leaving him to the mercy of the centaurs. He was rescued by Cheiron, and they enlisted the help of Jason and the Argonauts to take vengeance on Acastus by killing Astydamia, cutting her body in half, and marching his army between the halves.

Peleus now returned to Phthia, where he became king of the Myrmidones and it was decided by Zeus that he should marry the Nereid Thetis. Cheiron advised him how he might capture the sea nymph. Peleus surprised her while she slept on the beach at Sepias, and even though she transformed herself into fire, then water, then a lion, then a snake, and finally a tree, Peleus held onto her and thus won the right to marry her.

Their wedding was attended by the gods, who brought various gifts, and the Muses sang the wedding hymn. However, one goddess, Eris, had been omitted from the guest list and, in a fit of pique, threw the golden Apple of Discord—inscribed, "To the fairest"—among the guests. This act would eventually lead to the Trojan War, as possession of the prize was disputed by Hera, Athene, and Aphrodite.

Thetis became the mother of Achilles by Peleus and tried to make the infant invulnerable, either by dipping him in the River Styx or by immolating him in fire. Peleus caught her in the act and cried out, thus breaking the taboo that no mortal shall speak to his mermaid wife, and she immediately returned to her home, the sea. Peleus then gave up the infant Achilles to be raised by Cheiron.

In his old age Peleus was driven out of Phthia by the sons of Acastus, and when he died he at last joined Thetis in the ocean depths and became immortal.

See also: Achilles; Antigone; Thetis

Pelias

Greek

Son of Poseidon by Tyro and twin brother of Neleus. Exposed at birth, the boys were raised by a horseherd and later adopted by Cretheus, king of Iolcos, after he had married Tyro, who then bore Aeson. On Cretheus's death, Pelias imprisoned Aeson, expelled his brother, Neleus, and made himself king. Neleus went to Messenia, where he became king. Aeson's infant son, Jason, had been smuggled out of the city and was raised by Cheiron. Pelias's children included Acastus and Alcestis.

An oracle forewarned Pelias of the return of Jason, saying that he must beware of a man wearing but one sandal. Jason duly returned, having lost a sandal while helping an old woman across a fast-flowing river, so Pelias decided to rid himself of the troublesome young man who had fearlessly laid claim to his throne. Pelias swore to give up the throne if Jason would fetch the Golden Fleece that once belonged to the winged ram Aries, which had carried Phrixus to Colchis. Jason agreed, and so began the expedition of Jason and the Argonauts. Pelias thought that would be the last he heard of Jason.

Upon his return with Medeä, Jason found that Aeson had been forced to take his own life. Medeä then demonstrated a technique of rejuvenation by chopping up an old sheep and boiling the pieces in a cauldron. When she pulled a newborn lamb from the mixture Pelias's daughters, with the exception of Alcestis, agreed to do the same for their father. This time, of course, the magic did not work. Acastus, horrified by the murder, expelled Jason and Medeä from Iolcos and became king himself. He then celebrated funeral games for his father, which became legendary for their magnificence and the number of heroes who took part.

See also: Jason; Medeä; Neleus

Pelides

Greek

The son of Peleus, hence a name applied to Achilles.

Pelion

Greek

Wooded mountain in southeastern Thessaly, the home of the centaurs, the wisest of whom, Cheiron, lived in a cave on the path to the summit, where the temple of Zeus Actaeus stood.

At one time the Gigantes were said to have piled Mount Ossa on Mount Olympus, and then the two atop Mount Pelion, in their attempt to reach Heaven and destroy the gods in revenge for the imprisonment of the Titans; the war became known as the Titanomachia.

See also: Cheiron

Pelopia

Greek

Daughter of Thyestes who was ravaged, on the advice of the Delphic Oracle, by her father while she was a priestess at the court of Threspotus at Sicyon. Later Atreus visited Sicyon and married Pelopia, believing her to be the daughter of Threspotus, as his third wife. When she gave birth to Thyestes' son, whom she exposed, Atreus, believing Aegisthus to be his own, rescued him.

Peloponnes~os, ~us

Greek

A peninsula in southern Greece that is separated from central Greece by the Gulf of Corinth. The region included the ancient cities of Sparta, Argos, Corinth, and Megalopolis. The River Alpheus runs through the area; the island of Cythera, sacred to Aphrodite, lies just off the coast. The entire peninsula was involved in the Persian Wars (500–449 B.C.), and it was the site of many battles between Sparta and Athens during the Peloponnesian War (431–404 B.C.). The region fell to the Romans in 146 B.C.; they reduced it to a provincial state.

Legend derives the name of the peninsula from Pelops, who had so much power and wealth that the region was named the "Island of Pelops," or Peloponnesos.

See also: Pelops

Pelops

Greek

Son of Tantalus, thus grandson of Zeus, brother of Niobe and Broteas, and father of Atreus. He was the mythological founder of the Pelopid Dynasty of Mycenae. When his father served him up as a stew to test the divinity of the gods, only Demeter did not realize what she was eating and so consumed Pelops's shoulder. After punishing Tantalus, Zeus ordered Hermes to boil the remaining pieces of Pelops in a kettle, from which Clotho took him fully rejuvenated, save for the shoulder eaten by Demeter. To make amends, the goddess made Pelops a new shoulder from ivory. Thus Pelops was restored to life and was made king of Phrygia, receiving a winged chariot from Poseidon, who had fallen in love with him and had, for a time, taken him to live in Olympus.

Later, however, Pelops was expelled from his kingdom and came with his followers to Pisa in Elis. Here King Oenomaus, a son of Ares, challenged all who wished to marry his daughter, Hippodameia, to a chariot race. The victorious challenger would win the right to marry his daughter. Losers would be killed by his infallible spear, which, like his wind-begotten horses, was a gift from his father, Ares. Many suitors lost their lives in this way.

To ensure victory, even though he had his winged chariot, Pelops bribed Myrtilus, Oenomaus's charioteer, with a promise of half the kingdom to remove a linchpin from Oenomaus's chariot and replace it with one of wax. During the race Oenomaus was thrown out and killed when the wax linchpin broke, and Pelops married Hippodameia, thereby becoming the ruler of Pisa. His promise to Myrtilus was broken; to ensure silence, Pelops threw the treacherous charioteer into the sea. Myrtilus cursed Pelops and his descendants as he died.

The sons of Pelops included Atreus, Thyestes, Pleisthenes, and Sciron, the eponyms of many Peloponnesian cities. His illegitimate son, Chrysippus, who was also his favorite, was loved by Laius, who thus instituted pederasty on earth and brought a curse on his descendants. Atreus and Thyestes murdered Chrysippus, either with or without the help of Hippodameia, and so had to flee their home. His great wealth and power in the peninsula led to it becoming known as the Peloponnesos, or "Island of Pelops." His tomb at Olympia was one of the central objects of devotion, and here the Olympic Games were established by his great-grandson, Heracles. Bringing Pelops's bones to Troy was one of the conditions for the Greeks' winning the Trojan War.

See also: Atreus; Clotho; Demeter; Hippodameia; Tantalus

Pelorus

Greek

A giant, one of the Sparti, or "Sown Men," who sprang from dragon's teeth that were sown by Cadmos after he killed the dragon that guarded a spring of Ares. As soon as the Sparti sprang from the ground, fully armed, they started to fight among themselves until only five remained. These five—Pelorus, Echion, Udaeus, Chthonius, and Hyperenor—helped Cadmos to build the Cadmea and were later revered as the ancestors of Thebes from whom the Theban aristocracy claimed descent.

Penates

Roman

Early household gods who inhabited the family storage cupboard—the *penus*. Regarded as the providers of victuals, they were worshipped privately with images and offerings of food. Sometimes identified with the Dioscuri or Cabiri, the two Penates were later regarded as the guardians of the nation. Legend says that they were brought to Rome from Troy by Aeneas and were kept in the temple of Vesta, depicted as two seated soldiers armed with spears.

Penelope

Greek

Daughter of King Icarius of Sparta who is depicted as a woman of great beauty, fine character, and righteous conduct. When Odysseus wanted to marry her, her father had challenged the suitor to a footrace, promising Penelope as the prize. Odysseus won, but Icarius tried to persuade his daughter to stay with him. Odysseus told her that she could do as she pleased and, veiling her face so as to hide her blushes, she followed Odysseus back to Ithaca, where she bore him a son, Telemachus.

When Odysseus went off to fight in the Trojan War after one year of marriage, Penelope faithfully waited for her husband to return for 20 years, though some sources say that during this period she became the mother, by Hermes, of Pan. As Odysseus took ten years to return from Troy, many began to believe that he had perished, and Penelope found herself besieged by suitors, led by the unruly Antinous. To keep them at bay she promised to choose her new husband once she completed a piece of embroidery she was working on, but every night she undid that day's work. However, just about the time Odysseus returned secretly to Ithaca, her ruse was betrayed by her servants.

Telemachus, who had been reunited with his father at the hut of Eumaeus on the island, persuaded his mother to set a challenge: She would marry whoever could shoot the great bow of Eurytus, a weapon that none but Odysseus had been able to wield. None could even bend the bow, let alone shoot an arrow with it, until Odysseus, dressed as a beggar, did just that, shooting Antinous. Supported by Telemachus, he killed all the other suitors and was at last reunited with Penelope.

Later, according to one tradition, Telegonus, Odysseus's son by Circe, came to Ithaca in search of his father and was opposed by Odysseus and Telemachus. In the ensuing fight, Telegonus killed Odysseus without realizing who he was. He then took Penelope and Telemachus back to Aeaea, where Telemachus married Circe, and he married Penelope. The latter became the mother of Italus, the eponym of Italy, by him.

A local Arcadian legend says that Odysseus doubted Penelope's fidelity and divorced her. She returned to Sparta and from there went to Matinea. In this legend it was in Matinea that Penelope became the mother of Pan by Hermes.

See also: Antinous; Odysseus

Peneus
Greek

A son of Oceanos and Tethys, father of Daphne and Cyrene, and god of the River Peneus, the principal river of Thessaly.

Penthesilea
Greek

The daughter of Otrere and Ares and queen of the Amazons. She led a force of Amazon warriors to the Trojan War to fight for Troy after Hector had been killed. There she was killed by Achilles, but at the very moment he killed her their eyes met, and he fell passionately in love with her. As he mourned her death he was ridiculed by Thersites, the ugliest and most scurrilous of all the Greeks. In anger Achilles felled him with a single blow. Angered by the death of a kinsman over such a trivial matter, Diomedes threw the body of Penthesilea into the River Scamander, but Achilles rescued and honorably buried her body.

See also: Achilles; Hector

Pentheus
Greek

King of Thebes, the son of Agave and Echion, thus a grandson of Cadmos. When he tried to resist the introduction of the worship of Dionysos he was discovered watching the frenzied celebrations of the Maenads, who included his mother and her sisters, Autonoë

and Ino. In their frenzy they tore Pentheus limb from limb, thinking him to be a wild animal, his mother actually parading his head on a pole back into the city.

See also: Dionysos

Perdix
Greek

Also known as Talos, this nephew of Daedalus was credited with the invention of the saw, the chisel, and compasses. So jealous was Daedalus of his nephew that he threw Perdix from the temple of Athene on the Acropolis at Athens. Athene changed Perdix into the partridge (genus: *Perdix*); the Areopagus banished Daedalus, and he fled to Crete, where he was welcomed by Minos.

See also: Daedalus; Talos

Pergam~um, ~on
Greco-Roman

Seat of the Attalid kings of a powerful Hellenic state, situated on the River Caicus in Lydia (modern Asiatic Turkey). In the shadow of the Acropolis are extensive remains of an Asclepieion, a healing center associated with the worship of Asclepios. Most of what survives is from the Roman period, when the sanctuary was the most famous of the god. Surviving remains include those of a theater, springs, a temple of Zeus/Asclepios, and what has been described as a pump room.

Periclymen~os, ~us
Greek

The son of Neleus and brother of Nestor. Having the ability to assume whatever shape he chose, Periclymenos accompanied Jason as one of the Argonauts but was killed by Heracles.

See also: Heracles; Jason; Neleus

Periphetes
Greek

A monster found at Epidaurus that killed unsuspecting passers-by with an iron club. He was killed by Theseus with his own club.

Pero
Greek

The daughter of Neleus and Chloris, she became the wife of Bias.

Perse
Greek

Daughter of Oceanos, wife of Helios, by whom she became the mother of Aeëtes, Circe, Perses, and Pasiphaë.

Persephone
Greek

Fertility goddess and goddess of spring, daughter of Demeter and Zeus—though some say she was the daughter of Demeter following her rape by Poseidon and thus sister to Arion and Despoena. However, this rape was usually said to have occurred while Demeter was searching for her daughter, Persephone.

Also known as Core or Kore, "Maiden," and called Proserpina by the Romans, Hades sought Zeus's permission to marry her. Receiving neither refusal nor permission, Hades abducted the maiden while she was gathering flowers. Demeter, disconsolate with grief, wandered the earth looking for her, during which time nothing grew. Finally Helios, who had witnessed the abduction, told Demeter, but she continued to shun Olympus and stopped anything from growing on earth. Finally, Zeus told Demeter that Persephone could return from the Underworld provided she had not eaten anything there. Hermes was dispatched to lead her back, but she had eaten a seed from a pomegranate given to her by Hades. As a result it was decreed that she spend one-third of each year as Hades' queen, during which time the earth would bring forth no fruit; the remainder of the year she spent on earth with her mother.

Various accounts give different locations for the abduction of Persephone. Demeter's priests said it was Eleusis, whereas Latin poets said it was Enna in Sicily, where she had been gathering poppies. Some sources say Ascalaphus revealed that Persephone had eaten in the Underworld, and for this Demeter turned him into an owl.

Hades was not always faithful to Persephone, and on one occasion he changed the nymph Minthe, whom he was pursuing, into the mint plant. Persephone was joined in the Underworld by the mysterious, dread Hecate, who had at one stage helped Demeter search for her daughter.

The Eleusinian Mysteries in honor of Demeter and Persephone were probably fully established in Athens by Pesistratus at the end of the sixth century B.C. There was an annual procession from Eleusis to Athens, and those who spoke Greek could be initiated into the final rite of the mysteries. The myth of Persephone originates in the most primitive rites of seedtime and harvest, this during a time when only women practiced the agricultural arts. Persephone, who represents the vegetation dying down during the winter, had her counterpart in the primitive corn puppet that was buried in the winter, to be dug up again in the spring, sprouting.

See also: Demeter; Eleusis

Perses
Greek

Son of Helios and Persë, husband of Asteria, and father of Hecate.

Perseus
Greek

The son of Danaë and Zeus who appeared to her in the form of a shower of gold while she was imprisoned in a brazen tower after her father, Acrisius, had been warned by an oracle that he would be killed by a son born to Danaë. Not daring to kill his daughter, Acrisius set her and the baby adrift in a chest that floated to Seriphos, one of the Cyclades, where it was found by Dictys, who took Danaë and the young Perseus to King Polydectes, who received them hospitably.

However, when Perseus had grown to manhood, Polydectes wanted to marry Danaë, but she refused. Thinking that Perseus was the reason behind his rejection, Polydectes charged all his subjects to provide a horse as a bridal gift. As Perseus owned no horses, Polydectes sent him to fetch the head of the Gorgon Medusa, saying that this would suffice instead. A slight variation of this story says that Polydectes, having been rejected by Danaë, announced he would marry Hippodameia, and that all his subjects were charged with providing horses as her bridal gifts. Perseus, having no horses, offered to bring the head of Medusa instead. The former of the two versions is perhaps the better known and most widely accepted.

In his potentially fatal task, Perseus was helped by three deities. Athene, eager to help Perseus against her enemy, Medusa, provided a polished shield so he might view Medusa only in reflection and thus be saved from the petrifying power of her stare. Hades loaned him his helmet of invisibility. Hermes provided him with a sickle to behead the Gorgon and told him how he might procure the other needed items—a pair of winged sandals, though some say Hermes loaned these as well, and a special bag or wallet in which to carry the decapitated head.

Following Hermes' advice, Perseus visited the Graeae, sisters to the Gorgons, three old women who had been gray from birth and had only one tooth and one eye among them, which they passed among themselves as need be. Perseus found them on the slopes of Mount Atlas and, by snatching the tooth and eye while wearing Hades' helmet of invisibility, forced them to tell where he could find the remaining items he needed (as well as where the Gorgons lived). The Graeae first directed him to the Stygian nymphs, who provided him with the winged sandals and the wallet, called a *kibisis*. He then further followed the directions of the Graeae and flew, with the aid of the winged sandals, to the land of the Hyperboreans, where he found the Gorgons asleep, though some sources say the Gorgons lived either beyond the Western Ocean or in Scythia.

Using the magical weapons of Athene and Hermes, Perseus successfully decapitated Medusa but was astonished to see, springing fully grown from the severed neck, the winged horse Pegasus and the warrior Chrysaor. These were the children of Poseidon who had been conceived when the sea god lay with Medusa in a temple of Athene, the act that led to the Gorgons being transformed by the furious goddess from beautiful maidens into

hideous creatures with serpents as hair. Drops of blood from the wound that fell on the ground became the serpents that infest the Libyan desert, thus suggesting that the Gorgons in fact still lived in the country of their birth.

Although pursued by Stheno and Euryale, Medusa's sisters, Perseus escaped to the south by wearing Hades' helmet of invisibility, others saying that he caught and rode on the back of Pegasus. Pausing to rest in the land of the Hesperides, Perseus was rudely treated by Atlas, who had been told to expect that a son of Zeus would come to steal the golden apples of Hera, a prophecy that actually referred to Heracles. Flying over Atlas, he turned him into stone by showing him the head of the Gorgon before flying on toward Ethiopia. There he saw Princess Andromeda chained naked to a sea cliff and instantly fell in love with her. Learning the cause of her predicament from her parents, Cepheus and Cassiopeia, Perseus promptly offered to rescue the unfortunate maiden in return for her hand in marriage. Her parents quickly agreed, and Perseus flew over the sea monster Cetus, who had been sent to ravage Ethiopia after Cassiopeia's boast and to whom Andromeda was to be sacrificed. Once again exposing the head of Medusa, Cetus was turned to stone.

Though Perseus had kept his part of the bargain, Cepheus and Cassiopeia were reluctant to keep theirs, saying that Andromeda had already been contracted to Phineus, Cepheus's brother. Perseus, however, insisted, but at their wedding Phineus arrived with his followers and tried to carry off Andromeda. Perseus easily thwarted them, once more using the petrifying power of Medusa's severed head. Perseus and Andromeda then married, their son, Perses, inheriting the kingdom and becoming the ancestor and eponym of the Persians.

Leaving Ethiopia, Perseus and Andromeda traveled to Seriphos. There they found that his mother was still being pestered by Polydectes and that both Danaë and Dictys had been forced to seek refuge in the temple. Going to the palace, Perseus confronted Polydectes, who refused to believe that Perseus had been successful in his quest. Perseus simply answered that question by reaching into the wallet he carried and pulling out the head of Medusa. Once again, all those who looked directly at it were turned to stone. Perseus then installed Dictys as king of Seriphos before giving the head of Medusa to Athene, who installed it in the center of her aegis, the serpentine locks forming the border. Hermes retook possession of his items and returned those Perseus had borrowed from other sources to their owners.

Perseus, Andromeda, and Danaë now returned to Argos, but Acrisius, mindful of the oracle, left for Larissa. Shortly afterwards Perseus visited Larissa, where he took part in some public games and accidentally fulfilled the oracle when he killed Acrisius with a discus he had thrown. Grief-stricken by this mishap, Perseus arranged to exchange kingdoms with Megapenthes, the son of Proetus, who now moved to Argos; meanwhile Perseus went to Tiryns. He also founded Mycenae, which, like Tiryns, had massive fortifications that were built by the Cyclopes. Here Andromeda bore him a daughter, Gorgophone, and five sons, his grandson being Eurystheus, the king of Tiryns and Argos responsible for the 12 great labors of Heracles. After his death, Perseus was placed in the heavens along with his beloved Andromeda.

The mighty remains of both Mycenae and Tiryns have been investigated by Heinrich Schliemann and other archaeologists. They remain some of the most fascinating of all the antiquities of Greece.

Astronomical: The constellation Perseus is a rambling arrangement roughly in the shape of the letter *K*. It lies in the northern celestial hemisphere between approximate right ascensions 1h40m and 4h50m, declination from +31° to +58°. Perseus is supposedly still holding the head of Medusa, as the constellation contains Algol the Demon Star (ß Per), which blinks, varying in brightness between magnitudes 2.06 and 3.28 every 2.87 days.

See also: Acrisius; Aegis; Andromeda; Chrysaor; Danaë; Graeae; Medusa; Pegasus

Pesistratus
Greek

Tyrant of Athens who in 566 B.C. founded the Great Panathenaic, the four-year culmination

to the yearly Panathenaea. The magnificent procession of this festival is represented on the frieze of the Parthenon that is now in the British Museum. He also introduced new coinage, with the head of Athene on one side and the owl, her bird, on the other. At about the same time as he instigated the Panathenaic Games, Pesistratus also introduced the worship of Dionysos and founded the Dionysia.

Petasus
Greek

The low-crowned, wide-brimmed traveling hat, later adorned with wings, that was one of the attributes of Hermes, along with his *alipes*, winged-sandals, and *caduceus*, herald's staff.

Phaeacia
Greek

The mythical kingdom of Alcinous where the shipwrecked Odysseus was found by Nausicaa after he left the island home of Calypso. Alcinous and Nausicaa provide the audience for Odysseus's narrative of adventures, which makes up most of Homer's *Odyssey*. Alcinous provided the vessel that conveyed Odysseus in a magic sleep back to Ithaca, but Poseidon turned the returning vessel to stone. It has become identified with the islet of Pondikonisi.

Although the kingdom of Phaeacia itself was mythical, its location has often been identified with Corfu, the island with which Scherie was equated and where Phaeacia was said to be located.

See also: Alcinous; Nausicaa; Odysseus

Phaedra
Greek

"Shining"; the daughter of Minos and Pasiphaë, sister of Androgeos, Glaucus, and Ariadne. She married Theseus some time after he had deserted her sister, Ariadne, and bore him the sons Acamas and Demophoön. She, however, fell desperately in love with her stepson, Hippolytus, Theseus's son by either Antiope or Hippolyte. When the young man rejected her advances she hanged herself, leaving a letter falsely accusing Hippolytus. Furious, Theseus cursed his son, praying to Poseidon that he would die that very day. The sea god replied by sending either a sea monster or a great bull that terrified the horses of Hippolytus's chariot as he drove along the shore, which dragged him to his death.

See also: Minos; Theseus

Phaët(h)on
Greek

"Shining One"; a son of Helios by Clymene. Anxious to prove his paternity, Phaëthon visited his father, who promised him any boon he cared to name. The boy chose to drive Helios's fiery chariot across the sky; unable to dissuade him, Helios agreed. Phaëthon, however, proved unequal to the task, for the horses that hauled the chariot across the sky would not respond to the unfamiliar hand. First, the Milky Way was etched across the sky before the chariot began a headlong dive toward Earth, where it scorched the tropics, turning the land into desert and the people black. According to one source, however, Phaëthon took the chariot without Helios's permission; having saved Earth from further catastrophe, Zeus then let loose the Flood to quench the scorched planet.

To avoid further catastrophe, Zeus threw a thunderbolt at Phaëthon that hurled him from the chariot to fall to his death in the River Eridanus (Po). His sisters, the Heliades, gathered on the banks of the river and wept unceasingly until they were turned into poplar trees, their tears becoming amber that dripped into the river.

Phaist~ós, ~us
Greek

Also: Faistós, Phaestós

Located about 5 kilometers (3.2 miles) from the coast of Crete, on a knoll overlooking the verdant plain of Messara to the south of the island, this ancient site was possibly the home of Rhadamanthus, the brother of Minos. After Knossos, Phaistós is the greatest of the Minoan palaces, sharing many of the former's characteristics. Built originally c. 1900 B.C., Phaistós was, like the other Minoan palaces, destroyed

c. 1700 B.C. A new palace was then erected on the site.

Excavated by an Italian team led by Federico Halbherr and Luigi Pernier while Sir Arthur Evans was working Knossos, their results were not published until some time after Evans's and so caused less of a stir. The ruins, which are in fact extremely complex, seem at first blush simple and pure, for no reconstruction has been carried out, unlike at Knossos. Today, a great deal of the so-called Old Palace has been revealed through excavation, and the Old and New Palaces are uniquely interlaced. Obviously, enough of the Old Palace survived the disaster of c. 1700 B.C. to enable the builders to utilize its remains in building the New Palace.

See also: Knossos

Phalanthus
Greek

Mythical Spartan who supposedly founded Tarentum in Italy c. 700 B.C.

Phasis
Greek

The river that Jason and the Argonauts sailed upon first arriving in Colchis after completing their adventurous voyage from Iolcos to collect the Golden Fleece.

See also: Colchis; Jason

Pherae
Greek

An ancient town in Thessaly named after Pheres; the home of Admetus.

Pheres
Greek

Son of Cretheus and Tyro, father of Admetus and Lycurgus, and founder and eponym of Pherae in Thessaly.

Philemon
Greek

Old Bithynian peasant living in Phrygia who, along with his wife, Baucis, hospitably received the disguised Zeus and Hermes, unaware of their identities. Giving unstintingly of their meager provisions, they found that their food and wine were magically replenished. Realizing that their guests were gods, they were rewarded for their kindness; their hut was transformed into a temple, and they were made its keepers. They were also granted the boon that they should both die at the same time, and when that time came they were transformed into an oak tree and a linden tree that continued to grow, side by side, next to the temple.

Philoctetes

Greek

Son of Poeas, he kindled the fire on Mount Oeta; Heracles immolated himself upon its flames. In gratitude he received from that great hero his bow, quiver, and poisoned arrows. Renowned as an archer, Philoctetes, once a suitor for the hand of Helen, led a small force of seven ships to join the Greek forces at the Trojan War. However, just before the start of the war, while the Greek forces were on Tenedos, Philoctetes was bitten by a snake while sacrificing to Athene (though some say he was wounded in the foot by one of Heracles' poisoned arrows and that the incident occurred on the island of Chryse).

This wound began to fester, its smell becoming so offensive that Odysseus suggested that Philoctetes be left behind on the island of Lemnos, then uninhabited. There, for most of the Trojan War, Philoctetes, lame from his wound, supported himself by shooting down gulls and gathering what other food he could find.

In the last year of the war, when things were going badly for the Greeks, Helenus, the captured Trojan seer, revealed that Troy could only be taken if the bow and arrows of Heracles were brought to the siege. Odysseus and Diomedes (or Neoptolemus) were sent to bring Philoctetes to Troy, but he was reluctant to go, as he felt bitter toward the Greeks, especially Odysseus.

There are various accounts of how Philoctetes was finally persuaded to go to Troy. The most common says that Odysseus tried a trick by saying that he was to be taken back home but, once aboard, they sailed for Troy

instead. However, Neoptolemus, an honest young man, gave the plot away and determined to keep their promise. Philoctetes was finally persuaded when Heracles appeared to him in a vision and ordered him to go to Troy, saying that one of his arrows was destined to kill Paris, though Paris is sometimes said to have been dead by this stage of the war.

At Troy Philoctetes' wound was cured by one of the sons of Asclepios, either Machaon or Podalirius. He then challenged Paris to an archery contest and mortally wounded the Trojan prince. After the war Philoctetes was said to have settled in southern Italy, where he founded several towns, including Croton, and a sanctuary to Apollo where he dedicated his arrows.

See also: Heracles; Odysseus; Trojan War

Philomel(a)

Greek

Daughter of Pandion (king of Athens) and sister of Procne, who was married to Tereus, king of Thrace, or of the Thracians in Phocis. Tereus fell in love with her and, falsely telling her that Procne was dead, seduced her and then tore out her tongue to ensure her silence. Philomela wove a message to her sister in a robe, and Procne exacted her revenge on her husband by killing their son, Itys, and serving him to Tereus. When he realized what he was eating he chased the two sisters with an axe. The gods intervened and changed all three into birds, Tereus becoming a hawk or hoopoe, Procne a swallow, and Philomela a nightingale. Some writers, especially in the later Roman tradition, reverse the sisters' bird transformations.

See also: Tereus

Philyra

Greek

A daughter of Oceanos and Tethys, she was seduced by Zeus in the form of a stallion. The result of this union was the centaur Cheiron, horse from the waist down, man above, and a wise teacher. To cover Philyra's shame Zeus granted her the boon of being transformed into a linden tree.

See also: Cheiron

Phineus

Greek

Son of Agenor, brother of Europa and Cadmos, and ruler of Salmydessos in Thrace. A renowned seer, he was blinded by Zeus for revealing too much of the gods' plans for the human race, though this punishment is sometimes ascribed to Phineus's imprisonment of his sons by his first wife, Cleopatra, because of a false accusation by Idaea, their stepmother and his second wife. As further punishment Phineus was continually harassed by Harpies, who stole his food and befouled his table.

Phineus was saved, half-starved, from his torment when Jason and the Argonauts arrived in Thrace. Zetes and Calais, the brothers of Cleopatra and sons of Boreas, drove the Harpies to the Echinades Islands before returning to vindicate their nephews, Phineus's sons by Cleopatra. They were released, and in his gratitude Phineus explained how the Argonauts might negotiate the hazardous Symplegades. Idaea was then sent home to her father, who killed her.

See also: Agenor; Cadmos; Jason

Phintias

Greek

Also: Pythias

The great friend of Damon who, when Phintias had been condemned to death by Dionysus I, tyrant of Syracuse, in the fourth century B.C., pledged his life against Phintias's failure to return after the latter was granted bail to settle his affairs. Phintias returned at the eleventh hour on the very morning of his scheduled execution and so saved the life of his friend. Such loyalty so impressed Dionysus I that he pardoned Phintias and begged to be admitted to their special bond of friendship.

Phlegethon

Greek

River of Flames, one of the five rivers of the Underworld that the dead had to cross before coming to the realm of Hades himself, there to be judged on past life.

Phlegeus

Greek

King of Psophis who purified Alcmaeon of the matricide of Eriphyle when he fled to his kingdom, the Erinnyes in hot pursuit. Alcmaeon married Phlegeus's daughter, Arsinoë, and gave her the robe and necklace of Harmonia. However, he was soon forced to flee again by the Erinnyes. This time Alcmaeon was purified by the river god Achelous and married his daughter, Callirrhoë, who demanded the robe and necklace of Harmonia. Alcmaeon dared to return to Psophis and obtained the fabulous artifacts on the pretext that he was going to take them to Delphi. Phlegeus, however, discovered the ruse, ordered his sons to kill Alcmaeon, and then took the ill-fated treasures to Delphi himself.

See also: Alcmaeon; Erinnyes

Phobos

Greco-Roman

One of the horsemen of Ares whose name means "fear." His companion was Deimos.

Astronomical: The innermost of the two satellites of the planet Mars, having a diameter of approximately 23 kilometers (14.5 miles) and orbiting at a mean distance of 9,400 kilometers (5875 miles). Its period of revolution, just 7h39m, is so fast that Phobos rises in the west and sets in the east despite the planet's eastward rotation.

Phocaea

Greek

The northernmost Ionian city on the western coast of Asia Minor that became famous for colonizing Massalia, modern Marseilles.

Phocis

Greek

Ancient region of northern Greece centered around the Cephissus Valley and containing Mount Parnassus and the Delphic Oracle.

Phocus

Greek

1. "Seal"; the son of Aeacus (king of Aegina) and the nymph Psamanthe who was killed by his half-brothers, Peleus and Telamon, either by accident during a discus match or deliberately at the instigation of Endeis, their mother. His sons later settled in Phocis, a country that has as its eponym Phocus, who may be a later derivation of this Phocus.

2. A son of Poseidon who was regarded as the eponymous founder of Phocis. However, it seems that he may be the same as Phocus, the connection with Poseidon being made later by the inhabitants of Phocis to enhance their standing.

Phoebe

Greek

1. "Shining One"; a name applied to Artemis as a goddess of the moon, successor to Phoebus, Apollo as god of the sun.

2. A Titan, one of the children of Uranos and Ge who were imprisoned by their father.

Astronomical: One of the satellites of Saturn lying furthest from the planet, outside the orbit of Iapetus.

Phoebus

Greek

"Shining"; the name of Apollo as the sun personified at his Ionian shrine at Delos, where he was also known as Lycius. As Phoebus, Apollo was succeeded by his sister, Artemis, as Phoebe (Moon).

Phoenicia

Greek

An ancient region of western Asia along the eastern coast of the Mediterranean that included the great city-states of Tyre, Sidon, Tripoli, and Byblos. Greek tradition said that Phoenicia was the birthplace of Adonis, the beautiful youth who was loved by Aphrodite and killed by a wild boar. He was restored to life by Persephone, who also loved him, after which Zeus decreed that he should remain in the Underworld with Persephone for half the

year, spending the remainder of the year on earth with Aphrodite. Agenor, the father of Europa, was said to have once ruled the region, though the Greeks said the country was named after Phoenix, one of Agenor's sons.

Phoenicia was founded c. 1600 B.C., and by the twelfth century B.C. the country controlled the Mediterranean sea trade, as the Phoenicians were great traders and colonizers. During the sixth century B.C. Persia began to absorb Phoenicia, completing the process by Roman times, although they fought Alexander the Great to retain their autonomy. They originated an alphabet that was later developed by the Greeks and were famous for their Tyrian purple dye.

See also: Adonis

Phoenix

Greek

1. One of the sons of Agenor, king of Tyre, and brother of Cadmos and Europe. He was supposedly the eponymous founder of Phoenicia.

2. Son of Amyntor, king of Ormeniun on Mount Pelion. Persuaded by his mother to seduce Amyntor's concubine, he was subsequently cursed and blinded by his father. Fleeing to Phthia, Cheiron restored his sight after being befriended by Peleus, who made him king of the Dolopes and tutor to his son, Achilles, whom he later accompanied to Troy along with Patroclus. When Achilles withdrew from the fighting, Phoenix featured in the unsuccessful attempts to have him rejoin the fighting. He died a peaceful death on the way home from the war.

See also: Achilles; Cheiron

Pholus

Greek

Centaur who entertained Heracles—who was on his way to capture the Erymanthian Boar as his fourth labor—in his cave on Mount Pholus in Elis with a cask of sweet, strong wine given to him by Dionysos. When the cask was opened other centaurs besieged the cave but were repulsed by Heracles, who accidentally wounded his old friend, Cheiron, and struck Pholus with one of his poisoned arrows, killing his host.

See also: Cheiron; Heracles

Phorcys

Greek

An ancient sea god, son of Pontus and Ge who married Ceto and became the father of the Graeae, the Gorgons (Stheno, Euryale, and Medusa), Echidne, and the serpent Ladon.

Phoroneus

Greek

Son of Inachus and the nymph Melia. He was an early mythical king of Argos.

Phosphor~os, ~us

Greek

A demigod regarded as the light-bringer, a forerunner of Eos (Dawn). He is generally portrayed as the herald and harbinger of dawn, bearing a torch.

Phr~ixus, ~yxus

Greek

Son of Athamas and Nephele, sister of Helle. When Ino, Athamas's second wife, persuaded him to offer Phrixus as a sacrifice, Zeus, or Hermes, sent a winged ram, Aries, to save the boy and his sister from their stepmother's cruelty. Sources vary the location of this dramatic rescue. Some place it in Thebes, some in Iolcos, others in Orchomenus. Wherever they set off, the story remains the same. During their flight Helle slipped from the back of Aries, falling to her death in the stretch of water thenceforth known as the Hellespont. Phrixus, however, was safely conveyed to Colchis, where he sacrificed Aries and hung the fleece on an oak tree in a grove sacred to Ares. There it changed to gold—the Golden Fleece that was sought, and taken, by Jason and the Argonauts. Phrixus married a daughter of King Aeëtes of Colchis and had four sons by her, all of who left Colchis upon the arrival of Jason and the Argonauts.

See also: Aries; Colchis; Helle; Jason

Phrygia

Greek

An ancient region of central and northern Asia Minor where Cybele was worshipped and that roughly corresponds to modern central Turkey. The region was originally settled by Balkan peoples (Phrygians) about the thirteenth century B.C., being ruled by Lydia in the seventh century B.C. and by Persia in the sixth century B.C. The Greeks used the region as a source of slaves, as its inhabitants were progressively considered submissive and servile (although the characteristic conical Phrygian hat became identified as a cap of liberty).

Legend says that Zeus watched the fortunes of the Trojan War from Mount Ida, which lies within the region. It was also the scene of the rape of Ganymede and the home of Paris and Oenone before he deserted her for Helen. Legendary kings of the region included Midas and Tantalus, and the region was associated with many other legends, including those of Gordius and of Helle, as the region contains the Hellespont, the modern Dardanelles. The Roman goddess of war, Bellona, was worshipped in Phrygia and may have originated there.

See also: Ganymede; Midas; Paris; Tantalus; Trojan War

Phth~ia, ~iotis

Greek

The area of southwest Thessaly from whence Achilles came.

Phylachus

Greek

The father of Iphicles.

Phyleus

Greek

The son of Augeias who witnessed the agreement made between Heracles and his father: If Heracles could clean his father's stables in a single day, the task that Eurystheus set Heracles as his fifth labor, Augeias would reward him with one-tenth of the cattle he owned. However, after Heracles accomplished the mammoth task, Augeias discovered he had been acting on the orders of Eurystheus and so refused the payment; Phyleus remained loyal to the oath and was banished for his trouble.

See also: Eurystheus; Heracles

Picus

Roman

A son of Saturnus and father of Faunus. A youth having the gift of prophecy who was in love with Pomona, he was himself loved by Circe. He rejected her and was changed into a woodpecker.

Pieria

Greek

The southeastern coastal strip of Macedonia, lying to the north of Mount Olympus, that was inhabited by Thracian peoples who, in early times, worshipped the Muses, hence called Pierides. The cult of the Muses was probably carried to Mount Helicon from here.

Pierides

Greek

1. A name for the Muses that comes from their worship in Pieria.

2. The collective name for the nine daughters of Pierus, a king in Macedonia, possibly Pieria, named after the Muses. Legend says that they were turned into birds after being beaten in a contest with the Muses.

Pillars of Heracles

Greco-Roman

Also: Pillars of Hercules

Two promontories in the Mediterranean Sea on each side of the Strait of Gibraltar. The European of the two was known as Calpe and is usually identified with the Rock of Gibraltar, whereas the African was known as Abyla, or Ceuta, being identified with Mount Acho. According to some traditions they were positioned by Heracles to mark the western boundary of the known world, beyond it lying the fabled Atlantis. In others they were joined together until Heracles parted them and let the waters of the Atlantic Ocean mingle with those of the Mediterranean.

See also: Abyla; Calpe; Ceuta

Pimplea

Greek

A town in Pieria that was dedicated to the Pierides, the Muses.

Pinus

Roman

Said to be a son of Numa Pompilius and the legendary founder of the Pinarian family of ancient Rome.

Piraeus

Greek

The principal port of Athens, some five miles from the city, on the Saronic Gulf; capital of the modern Piraeus Department. The naval and maritime headquarters of ancient Athens, it was planned c. 490 B.C. by Themistocles and built c. 450 B.C. by Hippodamus of Miletus. It was connected to Athens by the Long Walls, which would enable supplies and the like to be moved between the port and the city during times of siege.

Pirene

Greek

A nymph originating from Corinth who was the mother, by Poseidon, of Leches and Cenchrias, who gave their names to the two gates of Corinth. Leches was accidentally killed by Artemis, and so copious were the tears shed by Pirene that she became a spring. There were, in fact, two springs having this name at Corinth, one in the elegant Roman fountain house in the lower town, the other on the Akrocorinth. Legend said that Bellerophon found and caught Pegasus at the latter fountain.

P(e)irithous

Greek

The son of Ixion and Dia, successor to Ixion as king of the Lapithae in Thessaly, and, later, a close friend of Theseus. During Peirithous's wedding to Hippodameia a drunken centaur attempted to carry off the bride, though some sources say a horde of centaurs attempted to make off with Hippodameia and a company of ladies. Theseus joined with the Lapithae in their famous fight with the centaurs.

Following the later death of Hippodameia, Theseus and Peirithous carried off the young Helen of Sparta, who fell, by lot, to Theseus. As Helen was too young to marry, they concealed her in the village of Aphidnae, where she was cared for by Theseus's mother, Aethra. Full of misgiving, Theseus then promised Peirithous that they would carry off another daughter of Zeus. To do this the pair traveled to the Underworld to carry away Persephone. They were caught by Hades, who chained them to a rock, where they languished until Heracles, who had come to the Underworld to fetch Cerberus, released Theseus. An earthquake dissuaded Heracles from releasing Peirithous, who remained chained in the Underworld and was never released.

See also: Ixion

Pisa

Greek

The capital of Pisatis in Elis, very near Olympia, its inhabitants constantly disputing the Eleans for sponsorship of the Olympic Games; they were finally overcome in 572 B.C. Pelops came to Elis with his followers after his expulsion from Phrygia. At this time Oenomaus, a son of Ares, was the king, but following an oracle who foretold that he would be killed by his son-in-law he challenged all suitors for the hand of Hippodameia to a chariot race, killing those who lost. Many suitors lost their lives before Pelops arrived. He, however, bribed Myrtilus to replace a linchpin on Oenomaus's chariot with one of wax. It broke during the race and Oenomaus was killed. Pelops then murdered Myrtilus and married Hippodameia.

See also: Pelops

Pisces

Greco-Roman

Based on an ancient Syrian legend, the fish of the constellation Pisces were, to the ancient Greeks, the goddess Aphrodite and her son, Eros. To the Romans they were Venus and Cupid. Greek legend recounts the story that Aphrodite and Eros leaped into the River Euphrates to escape the fire-breathing monster Typhon, transforming into fishes to swim out of danger. The Roman story says that the fish carried Venus and Cupid to safety.

Astronomical: An ill formed constellation lying abreast the celestial equator, Pisces is the twelfth constellation of the Zodiac, February 20–March 20. It lies between approximate right ascensions 22h45m and 2h00m, declination from −7° to +34°.

Pisces Austrinus

Greek

Based on the Syrian recognition of this faint constellation as the god Dagon; Greek lore simply identified it as a fish swimming in the River Eridanus, possibly being connected to the story of Aphrodite and Eros that gave rise to the identification of the constellation Pisces.

Astronomical: A faint constellation of the southern celestial hemisphere that lies between approximate right ascensions 21h25m and 23h05m, declination from −25° to −37°.

Pittheus

Greek

King of Troezen, son of Pelops, and father of Aethra, thus the grandfather of Theseus.

Pleiad

Greek

Any one of the seven daughters of Atlas and Pleione.

Pleiades

Greek

The seven beautiful daughters of Atlas and Pleione; virgin companions of Artemis who were chased by the giant hunter Orion in Boeotia and turned into doves to enable them to escape his unwanted attentions. After their death they were placed among the stars as a grouping of equal beauty, either to escape Orion, who still pursued them—and indeed still does in the heavens—or because they died of grief for their sisters, the Hyades, who themselves died weeping for Hyas.

The sisters were named Alcyone, who mated with Poseidon; Merope, who married Sisyphus and bore Glaucus; Celaeno, who mated with Poseidon and bore Lycus and Nycteus; Taygeta, who mated with Zeus and bore Lacedaemon; Sterope or Asterope, who coupled with Ares and bore Oenomaus; Electra, who mated with Zeus and bore Dardanos and Iasion; and Maia, who became the mother of Hermes by Zeus. As Merope managed to marry only a mortal, she became ashamed and tried to hide her light. As a result she is the dimmest of the stars in the Pleiades cluster.

Astronomical: One of the beautiful sights in the night sky, the Pleiades or Seven Sisters star cluster is found in the constellation Taurus. They lie in the northern celestial hemisphere at approximate celestial coordinates right ascension 3h45m, declination +24°. The group lies 541 light-years distant and is approximately 2° wide. Only six stars within the group are visible to the unaided eye; a small telescope shows more than 100. Both Atlas and Pleione are within the group.

See also: Alcyone; Asterope; Celaeno; Electra; Hyades; Maia; Merope; Orion

Ple(i)one
Greek
The mother of the Pleiades by Atlas.

Pl(e)isthenes
Greek
Son of Atreus who was killed by his father, who was tricked into the act by Thyestes.

Pluto
Greek
1. "The Wealth"; a euphemism for Hades the god, which the ancient Greeks preferred to use when talking about one so dreaded. The name Pluto was later adopted by the Romans to refer to the god of the Underworld, a hard and inexorable being who dwelled beneath the secret places of the earth in a gloomy palace among barren fields.

Astronomical: The outermost of the known planets of the solar system; discovered in 1930. The planet has a single satellite, Charon, and lies at an average distance of 5,966 million kilometers (3,728 million miles) from the sun and has an approximate equatorial diameter of 3,000 kilometers (1,875 miles).

2. A nymph, the mother of Tantalus by Zeus.

Pluton
Greek
An epithet applied to Hades the god; it means "the Wealthy One," a reference to his owner-ship of all the minerals, gems, and precious metals of the earth.

Plutus
Greek
The god of wealth, the meaning of his name, and the son of Demeter and Iasion. He is possibly a corruption of Pluto or Pluton brought into being, as it would have been hard to consider a god as dreaded as Hades as also being the provider of wealth. He was a largely symbolic figure, represented as a blind god with little or no discrimination in those he attaches to.

Pluvius
Roman
"The Rainmaker"; an aspect of Jupiter used at sacrifices during periods of drought.

Podalirius
Greek
Son of Asclepios, brother of Machaon. Like his father, both he and his brother were healers, one of them being responsible for finally curing the festering and highly offensive wound of Philoctetes.

See also: Asclepios

Podarces
Greek
1. Son of Laomedon and the only one not killed by Heracles when that hero sacked Troy in revenge for not being rewarded, as promised, for saving Hesione from a sea monster. Thus spared, Podarces changed his name to the better-known Priam.

2. Son of Iphicles, he led an army of Thessalanians against Troy during the Trojan War.

See also: Priam

Poeas
Greek
Father of Philoctetes.

Polites

Greek

One of the sons of Priam and Hecuba. At the end of the war, when Priam, Hecuba, and the remnants of their family had taken refuge before an altar of Zeus, Polites was slain before their eyes by Neoptolemus, who also butchered the frail Priam when he tried to intervene.

Pollux

Roman

The Roman name for Polydeuces, brother of Castor, and thus one of the Dioscuri. It is by his Latinized name that Pollux/Polydeuces is perhaps best known. Roman tradition simply changed his name, not his tradition.

Astronomical: The star Pollux is designated Beta Gemini (ß Gem) in the constellation Gemini, the Heavenly Twins, which forms the third constellation of the Zodiac, May 22–June 21. The constellation lies in the northern celestial hemisphere between approximate right ascensions 6h00m and 8h00m, declination from +10° to +35°. The star Pollux lies at approximate celestial coordinates right ascension 7h45m, declination +28°. It is approximately 36 light-years distant, type K0III, and has a magnitude of 1.15, thus making it slightly brighter that the brother-star, Castor.

Polybus

Greek

King of Corinth, a child was brought to him by one of his shepherds. Naming the infant Oedipus for his swollen feet (they had been bound together and pierced by a nail), Polybus raised him as his own son.

See also: Oedipus

Polybutes

Greek

One of the Gigantes, the 24 giant sons of Uranos and Ge with serpents' tails. He and his brothers, led by Alcyoneus and including Porphyrion, Ephialtes, Mimas, Pallas, and Enceladus, determined to avenge themselves on Olympus for the imprisonment of their brothers, the Titans. After a terrible struggle in Olympus and on earth the giants were defeated by the gods, who were helped by Heracles, appearing here before his apotheosis, who always lowered the final blow and had discovered a magic herb of invulnerability. Polybutes was interred under the mountain of Nisyrus, his imprisonment accounting for its volcanic nature.

See also: Alcyoneus

Polydectes

Greek

King of Seriphos; Dictys brought Danaë and the infant Perseus to him after the chest in which Acrisius had set them adrift had washed up on Seriphos. When Perseus had grown to manhood Polydectes sent him off on some pretext to fetch the head of the Gorgon Medusa, for he had designs on Perseus's mother, Danaë. When Perseus successfully returned from his quest he found Polydectes still harassing his mother, who had been forced, along with Dictys, to seek refuge in the temple. Perseus simply thwarted Polydectes' plans by exposing him and all his followers to the head of Medusa. They were instantly turned to stone.

See also: Danaë; Perseus

Polydeuces

Greek

Brother of Castor, hence one of the Dioscuri, Polydeuces was known as Pollux to the Romans, the name by which he is probably better known. The son of Leda by Zeus, who appeared to her in the form of a swan, Polydeuces was also the brother of Helen and Clytemnestra, though the relationships among Leda's four children are confused. Some sources say that Helen and Polydeuces where fathered by Zeus and born from an egg, whereas Castor and Clytemnestra were her children by her mortal husband, Tyndareus. Others say that only Clytemnestra was the child of Tyndareus or that Helen, Castor, and Polydeuces were born from an egg but that Helen and Polydeuces were fathered by Zeus and that Castor, mortal through this fact, was conceived on the same night but fathered by Tyndareus.

The brothers were inseparable and together took part in the voyage of Jason and the Argonauts, Polydeuces killing Amycus on the island of Bebrycos during this voyage. They also took part in the hunt for the Calydonian Boar and rescued Helen from the village Aphidnae, where Theseus hid her after abducting her. On this occasion they had help from Academus, who told them where Helen was hidden, and took Aethra, Theseus's mother, to be her slave.

Their devotion to each other was displayed when Castor was killed, possibly during a quarrel over the ownership of some cattle. Unable to live apart from his brother, Polydeuces refused his immortality, and Zeus placed the pair in the heavens as the constellation Gemini.

Astronomical: See Gemini and Pollux.

See also: Clytemnestra; Helen; Leda; Tyndareus

Polydorus
Greek

1. Son of Cadmos and Harmonia, brother to Autonoë, Ino, Semele, Agave, and Illyrius, and father of Labdacus.

2. Youngest son of Priam and Hecuba who was, according to Homer, killed by Achilles. Later accounts give a different version, though these may refer to a second son of the same name. In these, Priam entrusted Polydorus, along with a large quantity of gold, to Polymester, king of the Thracian Chersonesus. However, when Troy fell, Polymester killed Polydorus for the gold and threw the body into the sea. Hecuba, who had fallen to the share of Odysseus, was taken by the latter to the Thracian Chersonesus, where she discovered the body of her son. She contrived to kill Polymester and his two sons, then evaded the angry Thracians by turning herself into a bitch named Maera.

Poly(e)idus
Greek

An Argive seer, a descendant of Melampus who helped Bellerophon to capture the winged horse Pegasus. He also solved the riddle set by the Curetes to find the most apt analogy for Minos's cow, which changed color from white to red to black every day. He sug-gested the blackberry. He also discovered the body of Glaucus, who had drowned in a vat of honey. Unable to revive the boy, Polyeidus and Glaucus were entombed by Minos. There a serpent revealed to Polyeidus an herb that restored Glaucus to life, which the serpent had previously used to revive its dead mate, and both seer and boy were released.

See also: Bellerophon; Minos

Polymester
Greek

King of the Thracian Chersonesus whom Priam entrusted with his youngest son, Polydorus, and a large quantity of gold just before the fall of Troy. When the city fell, Polymester killed the boy for the gold and threw his body into the sea. There it was discovered by Hecuba, who, being brought to the Thracian Chersonesus by Odysseus, to whom she had been allotted, contrived the death of Polymester and his two sons, then escaped the angry Thracians by turning herself into a bitch named Maera.

See also: Maera; Odysseus; Priam

Poly(hy)mnia
Greek

One of the nine Muses, the daughters of Zeus and Mnemosyne. Her name is cognate with *hymnos*, "hymn," and she is associated especially with the sublime hymn, the lyre, pantomime, and geometry.

Polyn(e)ices
Greek

One of the four children, along with Eteocles, Antigone, and Ismene, of Oedipus and his own mother, Jocasta. Following the death of Oedipus, Polyneices and Eteocles decided to rule Thebes in turn, but when it came time for Eteocles to abdicate, he refused. Polyneices turned to Adrastus, son of Talaus and king of Argos, for help; he married Argia, Adrastus's daughter.

Adrastus agreed to help Polyneices gain the throne that was now rightfully his, but the seer Amphiaraus prophesied the death of all the leaders except Adrastus himself. Polyneices, following the advice of Tydeus, his brother-in-law, bribed Eriphyle, Adrastus's sister and wife of Amphiaraus, by giving her the necklace of Harmonia on the proviso that she convince her husband to join their cause. This she did.

Adrastus, Amphiaraus, Polyneices, and Tydeus were joined by Capaneus, Hippomedon, and Parthenopaeus, and these seven led their forces against Thebes, their ill-fated expedition becoming known as the Seven Against Thebes. As Amphiaraus had prophesied, six of the seven leaders died, Adrastus alone surviving. Polyneices was mortally wounded during single combat with his brother, Eteocles, who was also killed. Now Creon seized the throne of Thebes.

This new ruler refused to allow the burial of Polyneices. Antigone, Polyneices' sister, dared to disobey him and was immured in a cave for her trouble. There she hanged herself; upon discovering her body, Haemon, Creon's son, who had been betrothed to Antigone, committed suicide.

See also: Adrastus; Antigone; Eteocles; Jocasta; Oedipus; Seven Against Thebes

Polypemon
Greek

The forename of Procrustes, father of Sinis, the wild sow of Crommyum, famous for inviting travelers along the road between Eleusis and Athens to spend the night. If they did not exactly fit the bed, he would either stretch them or lop off their limbs as necessary. He was finished off by Theseus, who dished out his own treatment to him.

See also: Theseus

Polyphemus
Greek

One of the Cyclopes but, unlike the rest of the tribe, a son of Poseidon; described as a shepherd who tended his flocks on the shores of Sicily. He fell in love with the nymph Galatea, but she spurned him in favor of Acis. Furious, Polyphemus killed Acis, the rocks he hurled at him becoming the Isole Ciclopee off Acireale in Sicily.

Polyphemus also features in the story of Odysseus, who was said to have taken refuge in his cave along with 12 of his companions.

Polyphemus, here portrayed as a giant cannibal, ate two of Odysseus's companions when he returned to the cave with his flocks, blocking the entrance with a huge boulder. By next evening only six of Odysseus's companions remained alive, so Odysseus contrived to get Polyphemus drunk; while the cyclops slept, Odysseus put out his single eye. The following morning, as Polyphemus let out his flocks to graze, Odysseus and his men made good their escape by clinging to the underbellies of the sheep. Safely returning to their ship, they left Sicily but thenceforth had to endure the hostility of Poseidon. Some sources say that the Isole Ciclopee were the huge boulders Polyphemus flung desperately at the fleeing Odysseus and that he simply crushed Acis under a huge boulder.

See also: Acis; Galatea; Odysseus

Polyxena
Greek

A daughter of Priam and Hecuba whom Achilles reportedly fell for, his love being one of the reasons for his refusal to rejoin the fighting after his famous argument with Agamemnon. After the fall of Troy she was sacrificed by Neoptolemus, Achilles' son, as Achilles' ghost had demanded to ensure favorable winds. Some sources say that this sacrifice took place at Troy, others when the Greek fleet had reached Thrace.

See also: Achilles; Hecuba; Priam

Pomona
Roman

The youthful and beautiful goddess of fruit trees and their cultivation who was accorded a sacred area 19 kilometers (12 miles) from Rome. Her male counterpart, Vertumnus, fell in love with her. Rejected, he transformed himself through a variety of guises until he pleaded his case so eloquently while in the guise of an old woman that Pomona changed her mind.

Pompeii
Roman

A city of Campania now two miles inland. It was a seaside resort in 62 A.D., when it was hit by an earthquake, and in 79 A.D. it was buried under lava and ash from the erupting Vesuvius. Some buildings had not been totally repaired between the two disasters; these include the temple of Venus, the city's patroness, which now displays far less impressive remains than, for example, the temple of Jupiter. The city contained a variety of temples: two to Jupiter, one for the imperial cult to Fortuna Augusta, to Vespasian, to the *lares*, and to Apollo. Venus was highly regarded, and after General Sulla attributed his successes to her he had the city renamed Pompeii Veneris. There are many portrayals of Venus in Pompeii in mosaic and painting, though Minerva was most often placed in statue form to guard the city gates.

Pompo

Roman

Brother of Mamercus and Pinus, the legendary founder of the great Pomponian family, regarded as one of the sons of Numa Pompilius.

Pons Sublicius

Roman

A wooden bridge over the River Tiber that gave access to the heart of ancient Rome. Legend says that during the attacks led by Lars Porsenna the bridge was held by Publius Horatius Cocles, who for a time had the help of Spurius Lartius and Titius Herminius. The trio successfully held off the enemy while the bridge was destroyed, Spurius Lartius and Titius Herminius being sent back just before the bridge finally collapsed. Publius Horatius Cocles leaped fully armed into the River Tiber and swam to safety under a barrage of Etruscan missiles.

See also: Lars Porsenna

Pontus

Greek

The personification of the primeval sea who was parthenogenetically born of Ge along with Uranos. Pontus has no identity other than his name, no mythology other than his creation.

Poplicola, Publius Valerius

Roman

A witness, along with Lucius Junius Brutus, of the suicide of Lucretia, the daughter of Spurius Lucretius Tricipitinus and wife of Lucius Tarquinius Collatinus who had been raped by Sextus.

See also: Lucretia; Sextus

Porphyrion

Greek

One of the 24 Gigantes, the giant sons of Ge with serpents' tails. He participated in the attack on Olympus to avenge the imprisonment of their brothers, the Titans, in Tartarus. Others who took part are Alcyoneus, the leader, Ephialtes, Mimas, Pallas, Enceladus, and Polybutes. They failed in their attempt on Olympus and were punished by being imprisoned beneath various mountains, volcanic activities attributed to their confinement below.

Porsen(n)a, Lars

Roman

Legendary Etruscan leader hailing from Clusium who laid siege to Rome as the final attempt to reinstate the Tarquinians. His attempt on the Pons Sublicius, which would have led him into the heart of ancient Rome, was thwarted by the heroic stand of Publius Horatius Cocles. Nonetheless, he laid siege.

While his army was encamped nearby, one Gaius Mucius Scaevola entered the camp disguised as an Etruscan, intending to assassinate Lars Porsenna. However, ignorant of Porsenna's appearance, he killed the wrong man. Captured, he was brought before the man he had intended to kill, there placing his right hand into a pan of flaming coals, holding it without flinching. This aroused such admiration in Lars Porsenna that he freed him and returned his sword. Receiving this in his undamaged left hand, Gaius Mucius earned the cognomen Scaevola, "Left-handed."

Scaevola, moved by the unwarranted compassion of Lars Porsenna, warned him that there were 300 disguised Romans in his camp seeking to kill him. He further ventured that such a great leader as Lars Porsenna should be a friend to Rome rather than an enemy. Lars Porsenna agreed and called a truce, thus putting to an end any hope the Tarquinians had of returning to power.

Poseidon

Greek

The god of salt water and freshwater, invoked especially before sea voyages; the Romans equated him with Neptune. Poseidon seems to derive from a god worshipped by the earliest Aryan invaders of Greece, the Ionians and Minyans, who arrived c. 2000 B.C. They brought the mastery of horses and wheeled vehicles and a sky god whose thunder was equated with the sound of horses' hooves, an aspect clearly demonstrated in Poseidon's title Ennosigaios, "the Earthshaker," the god of earthquakes. His mate was an earth goddess who later developed into Demeter. Poseidon's position as the god of the heavens was superceded when the Achaeans entered Greece c. 1450 B.C., bringing with them Zeus. Poseidon now became principally a sea deity, for by this time the Minyans had become expert in navigation.

An Arcadian legend says that in order to save him from Cronos, Rhea gave the latter a foal to swallow in his stead; a Rhodian variant says he was reared by the Telchines on Rhodes. However, usual classical tradition makes Poseidon the eldest son of Cronos and Rhea who was swallowed by his father in Rhea's attempt to prevent his deposition by one of his sons. When this happened, and Zeus had made him disgorge his children, Cronos's three sons—Zeus, Hades, and Poseidon—cast lots to divide the universe. To Zeus fell the sky and the heavens, to Hades the Underworld, and to Poseidon the waters, both seas and rivers. The land remained common domain among the three, though Poseidon may have had special claim to the land as his domain through his name, which appears to mean "spouse of the land," a role especially alluded to in his title Phytalmios, "fruitful."

The Cyclopes gave him his trident, his most common attribute, which he wielded to shake the earth—yet another reference to his earlier origins as "the Earthshaker"—or subdue the waves and which became in Hellenic and Roman times a symbol of sea power, as it is today. With the trident he established himself as the master of the older sea deities such as Nereus, Proteus, and Phocus. Poseidon dwelled on Olympus with the other gods as well as in an underwater palace near Aegea in Euboea, where he kept his horses with brazen hooves and golden manes, the Hippocamps. When they drew his chariot over the sea, they caused the sea to becalm.

Though inferior in status to Zeus, Poseidon once joined with the other Olympian deities, led by Hera, in an attempt to put Zeus in chains. They were successful, and for a time Zeus was bound fast. However, after Zeus had been released by Thetis and Briareus—and Hera suitably punished—Apollo and Poseidon, the two main conspirators, were sent as bondsmen to King Laomedon and built for him the mighty fortifications of Troy, hence called Neptuniia Pergama. Laomedon made the mistake of attempting to refuse reward for the work carried out; Poseidon sent a sea monster. Laomedon's daughter, Hesione, would have been sacrificed to it if Heracles had not happened by, killed the sea monster, and saved the girl. Naturally, when the Trojan War broke out Poseidon sided with the Greeks.

Poseidon was the father of two giant sons by Iphimedeia, Otus and Ephialtes, collectively known as the Aloeidae after their stepfather, Aloeus. When aged just nine these boys decided to attack Olympus to outrage Hera and Artemis, first having captured and imprisoned Ares. They failed, their spirits being condemned to Tartarus.

The invention of the horse is attributed to Poseidon during his dispute with Athene for the possession of Athens; possession was given to the goddess when Cecrops judged that her gift of an olive tree was better than the spring given by Poseidon. Indeed, in many legends Poseidon assumes an equine form. He taught men how to bridle horses, and thus he became the protector of horse races. He again disputed territory with Athene, this time over Troezen, and Zeus judged that they should share it equally. When Briareus awarded him the Corinthian isthmus during another dispute—this time with Helios over Corinth—the quadrennial Isthmian Games were founded in his honor, games that notably featured horse and chariot races. When the river gods of Argos awarded that region to Hera in yet another dispute over earthly territory, Poseidon dried up the rivers in anger, restoring them only after his liason with Amymone, for whom he created the springs of Argos with a single blow of his trident.

Poseidon first sought to marry Thetis but was warned that any son born to her would be greater than the father. He therefore turned his attentions to Amphitrite, daughter of Nereus. She at first rejected him, and it was only after Delphinos had so eloquently pleaded his case that she changed her mind. Poseidon, in gratitude for Delphinos's help, placed him among the stars. Poseidon had three sons by Amphitrite, though just one, Triton, is named, and many other children by gods and mortals alike. During these trysts he used his powers of metamorphosis to great effect, giving the gift to Mestra and Periclymenus.

Both he and Apollo vied for the love of their sister, Hestia, but she swore by Zeus to remain a virgin. He was, of course, the father of the giants Otus and Ephialtes by Iphimedeia, as well as the giant Antaeus by Ge, perhaps also Orion. His son Halirrhothius was killed by Ares, a crime for which he was tried before the gods and acquitted, the place of the trial becoming known as the Areopagus. In the form of a stallion he raped his sister, Demeter, the offspring of this union being the horse Arion and the nymph Despoena. Some say that Persephone was also born as a result of this mating, but usually the rape of Demeter occurs while the goddess is wandering the earth in search of her lost daughter.

Another of his loves, Scylla, was so hateful toward Amphitrite that the latter turned her into a monster with six barking heads and 12 feet. Poseidon also loved Tyro, mother of his children Pelias and Neleus, and Aethra, the mother of his most famous son, Theseus, whose prayer he answered, sending a bull that either killed or helped cause the death of Theseus's son, Hippolytus. Theseus was also responsible for the final destruction of the Cretan Bull, a magnificent animal that Poseidon had sent to Crete to confirm the rule of Minos. That king substituted another, lesser animal, as the sacrifice, and in revenge Poseidon caused Minos's wife, Pasiphaë, to fall in love with the bull, mate with it, and so bear the Minotaur.

At one time Poseidon seduced the beautiful Medusa in a temple of Athene, an outrage for which Medusa was turned into the hideous serpent-haired Gorgon later slain by Perseus. When her head was severed by Perseus, the winged horse Pegasus and the warrior Chrysaor, Poseidon's children, sprang fully grown from the wound. Perseus later used the severed head to turn Cetus, the sea monster sent by Poseidon to ravage Aethiopia after Cassiopeia's boast, to stone.

Poseidon was also the father of the renowned bully named Amycus, king of Bebrycos, who challenged all strangers to a boxing match and killed them. When the Argonauts arrived on Bebrycos, Polydeuces met the challenge and killed Amycus. Agenor, king of Phoenicia and father of Europa, was another of Poseidon's famous offspring. Yet another was the giant, one-eyed Polyphemus, who was a shepherd on Sicily. During the epic journey of Odysseus back to Ithaca after the Trojan War, he and 12 of his companions took shelter in Polyphemus's cave. When the giant returned he rolled a huge stone across the entrance and ate two of Odysseus's companions. By the next evening only Odysseus and six of his men remained. After getting Polyphemus drunk they put out his single eye and escaped the following morning; when the giant let his flock out to graze, they clung to the underbellies of the animals. Making good their escape they had to contend with the vengeance of Polyphemus's father, Poseidon, who shipwrecked them on more than one occasion.

Poseidon was also the lover of Pelops and gave him the divine chariot in which he won his race with Oenomaus, though Pelops ensured victory by bribing Myrtilus, whom he later killed.

Sacrifices to Poseidon were usually black and white bulls, though horses were also offered to him. His attributes were the trident, the horse, and the dolphin, and he was usually represented as a mature, bearded man, naked from the waist up, accompanied by Amphitrite, Triton, Nereides, and dolphins and sometimes also a tunny fish. He had major temples in the Peloponnesos and

Arcadia as well as one of the most famous of all, at Sunium, though the main site of his worship was at Isthmia, near the isthmus of Corinth, which was, of course, one of his earthly territories.

See also: Amphitrite; Cyclopes; Demeter; Medusa; Minos; Minotaur; Odysseus; Pasiphaë; Thetis; Triton

Postumius, Aulus

Roman

Roman leader who led the forces at the legendary Battle of Lake Regillus, where Tarquinius Superbus or Sextus Tarquinius and an allied force of Latins were defeated with the help of the Dioscuri. To celebrate the victory, Aulus Postumius founded the temple of Castor and Pollux in the Forum and is also reputed to have founded the temple of Ceres.

Potina Theron

Greek

"Mistress of the Animals"; a title sometimes applied to Artemis in her capacity as goddess of wildlife. In modern usage it more commonly refers to the Minoan Earth Goddess, a deity derived from the Near Eastern mother goddess (for example, Cybele).

Priam(us)

Greek

The name (translatable as "redeemed") taken by Podarces after his father, Laomedon, and all his brothers were killed when Heracles and Telamon sacked Troy. His sister, Hesione, was given to Telamon by Heracles. Some years later Priam sent Antenor to demand that Telamon should return Hesione, and the Greeks' scornful refusal was one of the causes of the Trojan War, though by no means the main one. Responsibility for starting the ten-year war lies with one of Priam's sons, Paris.

Priam is credited with having 50 sons, 19 of them by his second wife, Hecuba or Hecabe, who bore him many famous children including Hector, Paris, Deiphobus, Polyxena, Polydorus, and the prophetic twins Helenus and Cassandra. Troilus, whom Priam apparently accepted as his own, may have been Hecuba's son by Apollo.

Nothing is heard of Priam until the Trojan War, when he is getting on in years. On one notable occasion, following the slaying of his son, Hector, by Achilles, Priam was led by Hermes to Achilles' tent under cover of darkness to plea for the return of his son's body for burial. Shortly before the end of the war, obviously growing weary of the continued carnage, Priam sent Agenor to Agamemnon to sue for peace, but Antenor, out of his hatred for Deiphobus, conspired with the Greek forces.

As Troy fell, Priam and Hecuba took refuge before the altar of Zeus Herkeios. There he witnessed the savage murder of his son, Polites, by Neoptolemus, and when Priam tried to intervene Neoptolemus mercilessly butchered the aged king as well.

See also: Hecuba; Paris; Trojan War

Priapus

Greco-Roman

Son of Dionysos and Aphrodite (Roman: Bacchus and Venus), a god of fruitfulness, of animal and vegetable fertility. Originating in Asia Minor, he was most generally represented in the form of a small, grotesque, and misshapen caricature of the human form, usually a pillar with a human torso and head with an enormous phallus, the latter reportedly given to him by Hera. He functioned as a territory marker, a guardian of gardens and orchards, and later one of herds. The ass was sacrificed in his honor, as it symbolized lechery and was associated with the god's potency. He was regarded less as a god to pray to than a comic garden gnome whose statue in the rock garden could raise a laugh and do no harm.

Pro~cne, ~gne

Greco-Roman

Daughter of Pandion, sister to Philomela, wife of Tereus, and mother by him of Itys. Tereus hid her among the slaves, for he had fallen in love with Philomela, whom he seduced after he told her that Procne was dead. Tereus then tore out Procne's tongue to keep their secret, but she wove a message to her sister in a robe. Philomela rescued her from her enslavement, and to avenge herself on Tereus she killed their son, Itys, and served her husband the boy's flesh. When Tereus realized what he was eating he pursued the sisters, but the gods intervened and changed all three into birds. Procne became a swallow, Philomela a nightingale, and Tereus either a hoopoe or hawk. Later versions of the story, particularly Roman ones, reverse the sisters' roles as well as their bird transformations.

See also: Pandion; Philomela; Tereus

Procris

Greek

Daughter of the second Erechtheus that become king of Athens and wife of Cephalos. She was seduced by Pteleon and then fled Cephalos to Crete, where she had a liason with King Minos, whom she cured of a strange and fearsome affliction. In gratitude Minos gave her an infallible spear and the hunting dog Laelaps. These she gave to Cephalos to appease his anger when she returned to Athens.

Procris, however, now had reason to become jealous, for Eos fell in love with Cephalos. Procris hid in a bush to spy on her husband when he went hunting on Mount Hymettus. Seeing movement in the bushes, Cephalos threw the infallible spear, killing his wife.

Procrustes

Greek

Also: Damastes

"Stretcher"; the surname given to the robber Polypemon. Living beside the road between Eleusis and Athens, Procrustes would appear hospitable, inviting travelers to spend the night. He would, however, adjust their bodies to exactly fit his bed, stretching them if they were too short or lopping off their limbs if they were too tall. Theseus put an end to this when he dished out the same treatment to Procrustes.

See also: Theseus

Proetus

Greek

Son of Abas, king of Argolis, he jointly inherited the kingdom with his twin brother, Acrisius. Expelled soon afterwards for seducing Acrisius's daughter, Danaë, he fled to Iobates, king of Lydia, where he married Iobates' daughter, Anteia, also called Stheneboea. Returning to Argolis, he forced his brother to divide the kingdom and so became the king of Tiryns, building its massive walls with the aid of the Cyclopes.

Bellerophon visited his court, and his wife, Anteia, fell in love with the youth. Rejected, she falsely accused him to her husband. Unwilling to kill a guest in his house, Proetus sent Bellerophon to Iobates with a letter asking that the bearer be put to death.

He was the father of Lysippe, Iphinoë, and Iphianassa, all of whom were sent mad—either by Hera or Dionysos—for neglecting his rites. They thought themselves cows and wandered throughout the Argolid, spreading their affliction, until they were cured by the seer Melampus.

See also: Abas; Acrisius; Danaë

Prometheus

Greek

A Titan, the son of Iapetus and Themis or an Oceanid, possibly Clymene, brother of Epimetheus, Atlas, and Menoetius, and father of Deucalion. His name means "Forethought," whereas that of his brother, Epimetheus, means "Afterthought." He created the race of men from clay, provided them with the power of reason, and thereafter championed their cause. His most precious gift to mankind was fire, which he stole from the gods, hiding it in a fennel stalk. He also established a custom in which only the poorer parts of sacrificed animals are offered to the gods. To do this he hid the lean meat in a pouch and covered the remaining bones and entrails with rich fat. Zeus was then offered the choice and chose the latter, thus leaving the best parts for mankind.

By thus tricking Zeus, Prometheus brought divine vengeance upon both himself and mankind. Hephaistos, at Zeus's command, made a lovely woman, Pandora, the Eve of Greek mythology, who was given a box and told never to open it. She was then sent to Epimetheus, who made her his wife. Before long, Pandora could contain her curiosity no more and opened the forbidden box. All the ills that plague mankind escaped, Hope alone remaining in the casket.

Prometheus had until now been favored by the gods. On one occasion, according to some, he actually helped Zeus by cleaving open the latter's skull to release the fully grown Athene. He even relieved the pain of Cheiron by receiving the centaur's immortality, thereby allowing the unfortunate Cheiron to finally die of the wound accidentally afflicted by Heracles.

However, as he had tricked Zeus and had stolen fire from the heavens, he was now punished. He was chained to a rock in the Caucasus where, all day long, an eagle or vulture tore at his liver, which grew whole again during the night, an interesting anatomical detail as the liver is the only human organ that renews itself. His torment lasted many generations until he was finally released, with the consent of Zeus, when Heracles shot the eagle or vulture and untied his bonds. In gratitude Prometheus, though some say Proteus, advised Heracles how he might trick Atlas into obtaining the Golden Apples of the Hesperides for him.

See also: Atlas; Deucalion; Epimetheus; Heracles; Pandora

Proserpin~a, ~e

Roman

The wife of Pluto and the queen of the Underworld; the Roman equivalent of Persephone. She too was supposed to have eaten the seeds of a pomegranate and was thus compelled to spend a portion of each year in the Underworld, the remainder on earth.

Protesilaus

Greek

"First-Leaper"; husband of Laodameia, uncle of Philoctetes, and the leader of a force from Phylace, in Thessaly, to Troy. When an oracle foretold that the first Greek to go ashore would be killed, and all others hesitated, Protesilaus defied fate and leaped ashore. After killing several Trojans the oracle was fulfilled when he was cut down. He was buried on the European side of the Hellespont and had a temple near Sestos. Later legend says that his

ghost could still be seen haunting Troad (an ancient region of northwest Asia Minor) with ghosts of other heroes during the third century A.D.

His wife, Laodameia, daughter of Acastus, was so desolate with grief that she begged the gods to allow her husband to return for just three hours. They relented and allowed Hermes to lead Protesilaus back from the Underworld. When he died the second time, after three hours had elapsed, Laodameia died as well.

See also: Laodameia

Proteus

Greek

1. Ancient sea deity, the son of Oceanos and Tethys who, like Nereus, had the ability to change his shape at will. He is depicted as a little, fish-tailed old man, later subject to Poseidon, whose flocks of seals he tended. Proteus possessed the gift of prophecy, a gift he could avoid using by utilizing his ability to metamorphose at will. In an instant he could become fire, flood, or wild beast. However, if a person held him fast, no matter what form he assumed, he would eventually return to his normal form and deliver the truth. He could usually be found at midday on the island of Pharos, as indeed Menelaus did, needing directions to return to Sparta after the fall of Troy. On the advice of the nymph Eidothea, Menelaus and his companions disguised themselves as seals, and when Proteus went down for his noon rest they seized him and held on as he turned himself into a lion, a snake, a leopard, a boar, water, and finally a tree. He then resumed his own form and told Menelaus what he needed to know.

2. The name of a human king of Egypt, husband of Psamanthe who, according to the Stesichorean version of the legend of the siege of Troy, looked after Helen during the Trojan War. He was succeeded, while Helen was still a guest, by his son, Theoclymenus.

Protogonus

Greek

"First Born"; a god who in the Orphic theogonies was born from the world egg created by

Time. A hermaphrodite, Protogonus had golden wings, bulls' heads on his flanks, and a serpent on his head, the latter possibly deriving from the uraeus serpent worn by the Egyptian pharaohs. He is also known as Phanes, "the bright god" or "he who makes manifest." Being a hermaphrodite, Protogonus copulated with himself, thereby performing the functions of Demiurge, or Creator, functions that were not carried out by the supreme god, Time. Thus were born the heavenly bodies, monsters, and the golden race of mankind. Although this theogony is incompatible with classical traditions, Zeus later came to be identified with Protogonus.

Psamanthe

Greek

An Argive princess who was seduced by Apollo and became the mother of Linus. Ashamed, she exposed the child, who was reared by shepherds but later torn to pieces by her father's dogs. Her grief revealed her predicament to her father, who condemned her to death. Furious, Apollo visited Argos with a plague that raged until the Argives propitiated Psamanthe and Linus with dirges called *linoi*.

Psyche

Greek

The personification of the soul, purified by suffering to enjoy true love. Usually represented in art with the wings of a butterfly, or as a butterfly itself, Psyche was a fairly late conception in Greek thought.

Originally a beautiful mortal, Psyche was warned by the Delphic Oracle that she would love no mortal. Her great beauty aroused the jealousy of Aphrodite, who commanded her son, Eros, to bring the maiden to a castle in the mountains, where she was to marry a demon. At night a secret lover came to her but forbade her from lighting the lamp. On the fourth night her curiosity overcame her and she lit the lamp as her lover lay sleeping to find out exactly what kind of demon was giving her such intense pleasure. It turned out to be the beautiful boy-god, Eros. In her excitement Psyche allowed a drop of hot oil to fall on Eros's shoulder. He awoke and flew away.

Furious when she found out exactly what had been happening, Aphrodite set Psyche a series of seemingly impossible tasks. First she presented the unfortunate girl with a huge heap of assorted grains, which she had to sort into separate piles. She was helped by ants and accomplished the task.

Aphrodite then required Psyche to bring her some wool from a flock of man-eating sheep. Psyche waited until the sheep were asleep, then collected the tufts of wool that had become caught on some thorn bushes. Next Aphrodite told Psyche to fetch her a jar of water from the River Styx, but Zeus's eagle saw her plight and fetched the water for her.

Finally, Psyche was told to fetch a box of Persephone's ointment from the Underworld. As she was preparing to throw herself from a high tower, always a quick way of reaching the Underworld, the tower spoke to her and told her how she might enter the Underworld at Taenarum, telling her to take two *obolos* for Charon and two honey cakes to placate Cerberus. Psyche successfully came to Persephone, who gave her a small box containing the required ointment. However, once back on earth Psyche could not contain her curiosity and so opened the box. Upon doing so a sleep of death wafted up from the box; Psyche was succumbing when Eros arrived and fanned away the noxious fumes. Psyche then delivered the box to Aphrodite while Eros beseeched either Aphrodite or Zeus, contending that Psyche had been punished more than enough. Aphrodite relented, and Eros married the girl, who was made immortal.

This story, which is related in the *Golden Ass* of Apuleius, is one of the most enchanting stories of antiquity and allegorizes the freeing of the soul after purification through suffering.

See also: Eros

Puppis

Greek

"The Poop"; the stern section of the *Argo Navis* that was placed in the heavens as the constellation Puppis. Below Puppis in the sky is Carina, the Keel; to the east is Vel, the Sail; and just beside Puppis, on the deck, is Pyxis, the Ship's Compass.

Astronomical: A constellation of the southern celestial hemisphere located between approximate right ascensions 6h05m and 8h25m, declination from –12° to –52°.

Pygmalion
1. Greek
King of Cyprus and a famous sculptor, though only Ovid tells the famous story of Pygmalion's loneliness through the lack of a wife. He carved an ivory statue of the most beautiful woman he could image and then, having fallen in love with it, prayed to Aphrodite for a wife just like her. The goddess brought the statue to life, and Pygmalion married her. Some sources, though not the classical authors, name the living statue as Galatea. She bore Pygmalion a daughter named either Paphos or Metharme.

2. Roman
King of Tyre who murdered his uncle, Sychaeus, or Sicharbus, the husband of his sister, Dido, and thus gained sole rule. Dido then fled and founded the city of Carthage.

See also: Dido; Galatea

Pylades
Greek
Son of Strophius, king of Phocis, and the inseparable companion of the exiled Orestes. Orestes received numerous pleas from his sister, Electra, to return to Mycenae to avenge the murder of their father, Agamemnon, which is exactly what Pylades and Orestes did when they had come of age; with Electra's help they killed both Clytemnestra and Aegisthus.

Seeking purification and release from the continued torment of the Erinnyes, Pylades accompanied Orestes to Tauris, where they were captured by the barbarous natives, who intended to sacrifice them to their goddess, Artemis, as they did to all strangers. However, Orestes was amazed to find that the priestess was none other than his sister, Iphigeneia, who he thought had been sacrificed to Artemis at Aulis by Agamemnon. Iphigeneia rescued Orestes and Pylades, and the three returned to Greece, bringing with them the statue of Artemis. There they were reunited with Electra and returned to Mycenae, where

Orestes killed Aegisthus's son and thus became king. He then married his cousin, Hermione, after disposing of his rival, Neoptolemus; Pylades married Electra.

See also: Iphigeneia; Orestes

Pylos
Greek
Port in Messenia, western Peloponnesos, the safest harbor in Greece, which the Athenians successfully held against the Spartans in 425 B.C. Tradition said that the young Hermes drove the cattle he had stolen from Apollo to Pylos. Later, Nestor was said to have ruled the city and led an army in his old age, in support of the Greeks, to the Trojan War, where his justice, wisdom, and eloquence were proverbial.

Pyramus
Greek
Although its origins remain unknown, the story of Pyramus and Thisbe, which first appears in Ovid's *Metamorphoses*, was immortalized in William Shakespeare's *A Midsummer Night's Dream.* It has been suggested that the story was invented to explain the names of two adjacent rivers, Pyramus and Thisbe, in Cilicia, Asia Minor. Living in Babylon, where their parents were neighbors, Pyramus and Thisbe fell in love, even though forbidden to associate with each other. To overcome this they whispered through a hole in the garden wall and decided to meet at Ninnus's tomb outside the city walls. Thisbe arrived first but was frightened by a lioness, who mauled the veil the fleeing girl dropped. When Pyramus arrived and found this he thought that Thisbe had been killed. Despondent, he stabbed himself and fell dying beneath a mulberry tree, its fruit, white until then, stained with his blood. Thisbe found his body, took her sword, and fell onto it. When their parents discovered their bodies they buried the ashes of the two lovers in a single urn.

See also: Thisbe

Pyriphlegethon
Greek
"Flaming with Fire"; the alternative name for the River Phlegethon, the river of flames

that is one of the five rivers of the Underworld.

Pyrrha
Greek

Daughter of Epimetheus, wife of Deucalion, and mother of Hellen, the mythical ancestor of the Hellenes. Warned by Prometheus, Deucalion's father, of the coming deluge, Deucalion and Pyrrha rode out the resulting flood in a vessel that finally came to rest on Mount Parnassus. Consulting the Oracle of Themis on how they might repopulate the earth, they were told to throw the bones of their mother behind them. Pyrrha determined that this meant the rocks of Mother Earth. Those thrown by Deucalion became men, whereas those thrown by Pyrrha became women.

See also: Deucalion; Prometheus

Pyrrh~os, ~us
Greek

An alternative name for Neoptolemus.

Pythia
Greek

The name given to the priestess of Apollo, his mystic bride, in his oracle at Delphi. The mouthpiece of the god, the Pythia was an old woman without education. She sat on a tripod where, in a hypnotic trance, she delivered inspired utterances, ravings that were then interpreted and put into hexameter verse by the priests of the oracle. The two most popular concepts regarding the Pythia—that she either chewed laurel leaves or inhaled noxious vapors from a nearby chasm below the temple in order to induce her trance—have been shown to have no basis in fact.

Pyth~ian, ~ius
Greek

Name applied to Apollo at his Dorian shrine at Delphi, where he was also known as Loxias, "the Ambiguous," near the spring named Castalia on Mount Parnassus; the shrine is better known as the Delphic Oracle.

Python
Greek

The huge she-serpent or dragon that emerged from the mud following the Flood and lived in the caves of Mount Parnassus, where it was regarded as the guardian of the Oracle of Earth at Delphi. Just four days old, Apollo came to Delphi, killed Python, and took over the oracle as his own, the Pythia or Pythoness then becoming the mouthpiece of his oracles. Zeus commanded Apollo to visit the Vale of Tempe for purification and to preside over the Pythian Games held in Python's honor. Python's name is explained in the Homeric *Hymn to Apollo* of c. 700 B.C. by a pun. Apollo simply left the dead creature in the sun to rot, for *pythein* means "rot."

This story is a simple mythological analogy of the truth. The invading Hellenes took over the oracle at Delphi in the name of their own god, Apollo, displacing the oracular serpent, then founded the Pythian Games to placate the original inhabitants.

See also: Apollo; Delphi

Pyxis
Greek

"The Ship's Compass"; the navigational device used by Jason aboard the *Argo Navis* on his voyage to and from Colchis, later placed in the heavens along with other parts of the ship.

Astronomical: A constellation of the southern celestial hemisphere located between approximate right ascensions 8h25m and 9h25m, declination from −17° to −37°.

Q

Quirinus

Roman

An ancient Roman deity, possibly of Sabine derivation, who was third in importance in Rome after Jupiter and Mars, sometimes associated with Ops. Before the beginning of the historical period, Quirinus had become a somewhat obscure deity, regarded mainly as an aspect of Mars, though Romulus was also identified with him. His Sabine roots seem to be established through his cult, which was centered on the Quirinal, the traditional settlement site of the Sabines. His festival, the Quirinalia, was celebrated on 17 February.

See also: Ops; Sabine

R

Regillus
Roman

A lake that was the site of a legendary battle where Aulus Postumius, aided by the Dioscuri, defeated the Latins, who had attacked Rome in allegiance with either Tarquinius Superbus or his son, Sextus Tarquinius.

Remus
Roman

Twin brother of Romulus, the sons of Mars by Rhea Silvia, the Vestal Virgin daughter of Numitor who had been forced into the service of Vesta by her uncle, Amulius, when he usurped the throne of Alba Longa from Numitor. Following the birth of the twins, Amulius had Rhea Silvia imprisoned and ordered that the children be drowned. However, the servants sent to carry out this task left the boys in a basket on the riverbank in the shade of the Ruminalis fig tree. There they were discovered and suckled by a she-wolf, whose strange behavior attracted the attention of the shepherd Faustulus. Finding the infants, he took them home, where they were cared for by his wife, Acca Larentia.

As the boys grew up they took to attacking bandits and relieving them of their ill-gotten gains, which they divided among the poor shepherds. The robbers retaliated by laying a trap during the Lupercal festival but only succeeded in taking Remus, whom they took to Amulius, complaining that he and his brother had been raiding the lands of the exiled Numitor. Amulius sent Remus to Numitor, who discovered the twins' identities. They then assassinated Amulius and restored Numitor to his rightful position.

As the population of Alba Longa had grown, the twins decided they should found a new settlement on the spot where they had been exposed and then given a home. However, they could not decide who should name the new city, so they consulted the auguries. Romulus stood on the Palatine Hill while Remus stood on the Aventine Hill, where he soon saw six vultures. No sooner had this been reported than Romulus saw 12. Each was acclaimed king, but a fight broke out, and Remus was killed.

A variant on this says that Remus mocked Romulus and sacrilegiously leaped over the half-built walls of his new city. Furious, Romulus killed him, swearing that the same fate awaited all those who dared leap his walls.

See also: Acca Larentia; Amulius; Faustulus; Romulus

Rhadamanth~us, ~ys
Greek

Son of Zeus and Europa, brother to Minos and Sarpedon. The three boys were later adopted by the king of Crete when he married Europa, and upon his death they divided the island among themselves. However, the brothers quarreled over Miletus, the son of Apollo. As Miletus preferred Sarpedon, they fled from Crete to Asia Minor. Now Crete was ruled jointly by Minos and Rhadamanthus, but Rhadamanthus was later banished, leaving Minos as the sole ruler of Crete.

Rhadamanthus came to Boeotia, where upon Amphitryon's death he married Alcmene. He was so just a ruler that after his death he was made one of the three judges of the Underworld, along with Minos and Aeacus.

See also: Aeacus; Minos

269

Rhea

Greek

A Titaness daughter of Uranos and Ge, sister to Cronos, Oceanos, Hyperion, Iapetus, Themis, Tethys, and Mnemosyne. She married her brother, Cronos, after the latter had successfully deposed Uranos and bore him Hestia, Hera, Demeter, Poseidon, and Hades, all of whom Cronos swallowed at birth, mindful of the curse of Uranos and Ge that he would also be deposed by his son.

However, when Zeus, the youngest, was born, Rhea gave Cronos a stone wrapped in swaddling to swallow instead and saved Zeus, who, according to Minoan tradition, was raised in the Dictaean Cave on Crete. Here Rhea's priests, the Curetes, clashed their weapons to drown the sound of the baby Zeus, and the she-goat Amalthea acted as his nurse. Hephaistos was also said to have made a golden dog for Rhea, which she set to watch over the baby's cradle. Grown to manhood, Zeus was helped by his mother to administer a potion to Cronos by having himself made cupbearer to Cronos. She then prescribed a drink that Zeus gave to his father; the potion made him disgorge the stone that had replaced Zeus, then his other children. They joined forces to depose Cronos, after which Zeus, Hades, and Poseidon cast lots for the three regions of the universe. Rhea, unlike the other Titans, retained her status as Mother of the Gods, in which capacity she was often identified with Cybele.

Astronomical: One of the satellites of the planet Saturn, being the seventh closest to the planet between the orbits of Dione and Titan. Rhea has a diameter of approximately 1,530 kilometers (956 miles) and lies at an average distance of 526,000 kilometers (328,700 miles) from the planet.

See also: Cronos; Uranos; Zeus

Rhea Silvia

Roman

The daughter of Numitor who, after her father had been deposed by his uncle, Amulius, was forced to become a Vestal Virgin. In her sleep she was raped by Mars, and as a result she gave birth to twin boys, Romulus and Remus, the legendary founders of Rome.

See also: Numitor; Remus; Romulus

Rhesus

Greek

A king of Thrace who was born to one of the Muses who had waded in the River Strymon, though Homer names his father as Eïoneus. Raised by nymphs and worshipped as an oracular spirit in Thrace, Rhesus brought an army to assist the Trojans during the tenth and final year of the Trojan War. His arrival was revealed to the Greeks by the spy Dolon shortly before he was killed. The Greeks killed Rhesus and captured his horses, for an oracle had declared that once they had drank from the water of the River Scamander, and had eaten the grass of the Trojan Plain, the city would never fall.

See also: Dolon; Trojan War

Rhod~e, ~os

Greek

Said to be a daughter of Poseidon, she married Helios and was the eponym of the island of Rhodes.

Rhodope

Greek

A lofty mountain range in Thrace that was sacred to Dionysos.

Romulus

Roman

Twin brother of Remus, the sons of Mars by Rhea Silvia, the Vestal Virgin daughter of Numitor who had been forced into the service of Vesta by her uncle, Amulius, when he usurped the throne of Alba Longa from Numitor. Following the birth of the twins, Amulius had Rhea Silvia imprisoned and ordered that the children be drowned. However, the servants sent to carry out this task left the boys in a basket on the riverbank in the shade of the Ruminalis fig tree. There the children were discovered and suckled by a she-wolf, whose strange behavior attracted the attention of the shepherd Faustulus. Finding the infants, he took them home, where they were cared for by his wife, Acca Larentia.

As the boys grew up they took to attacking bandits and relieving them of their ill-gotten gains, which they divided among the poor shepherds. The robbers retaliated by laying a trap during the Lupercal festival but succeeded only in taking Remus, whom they took to Amulius, complaining that he and his brother had been raiding the lands of the exiled Numitor. Amulius sent Remus to Numitor, who discovered the twins' identities. The brothers then assassinated Amulius and restored Numitor to his rightful position.

As the population of Alba Longa had grown, the twins decided they should found a new settlement on the spot where they had been exposed and then given a home. However, they could not decide who should name the new city, so they consulted the auguries. Romulus stood on the Palatine Hill while Remus stood on the Aventine Hill, where he soon saw six vultures. No sooner had this been reported than Romulus saw 12. Each was acclaimed king, but a fight broke out, and Remus was killed.

A variant on this story says that Remus mocked Romulus and sacrilegiously leaped over the half-built walls of his brother's new city. Furious, Romulus killed him, swearing that the same fate awaited all those who dared leap his walls. Having murdered his brother, Romulus reigned alone and created a sanctuary on the Capitoline Hill, where any fugitive might find refuge. This plan was so successful that it soon led to an imbalance between men and women, and even though Romulus sought marriage alliances with various neighboring states and cities, all his advances were rejected. Therefore, at the annual harvest festival in honor of Consus, when Sabine visitors flocked to Rome, he ordered that all the young women among them should be taken captive.

Furious, Titus Tatius, king of the Sabines, led an army against Rome and encircled the Capitoline Hill. There Tarpeia, daughter of the Roman garrison commander, looked down on the besieging forces and was impressed by the gold jewelry and other adornments they wore. She sent a secret message to Titus Tatius saying that she would let them into the citadel by night in return for all the Sabines wore on their left arms. This proposal being agreed upon, she carried out her half of the bargain, but when the time came for payment the Sabines hurled their shields at her, and she was killed, an episode that demonstrated the Sabines' feeling that a traitor should never be trusted or rewarded.

The Sabines now attacked Romulus under the leadership of their champion, Mettius Curtius, but he was overconfident, and his horse foundered in the swamps on the site of what later became the Forum. Distraught with grief at the continuing conflict, the Sabine wives of the Romans interposed between the two armies and won a truce. It was then agreed that the two peoples, Romans and Sabines, should unite under a single government led by Romulus and Titus Tatius. The latter died before Romulus, who then ruled alone. His rule came to an end during a storm when his father, Mars, descended and carried him off to the heavens. Thereafter he was worshipped as the god Quirinus, a member of the supreme triumvirate that includes Jupiter and Mars.

Later, in a story clearly invented to glorify the origins of the Julian family, it was said that Julius Proculus, a friend of Romulus, was out riding when he was confronted by Romulus's ghost wearing shining armor. When Julius Proculus asked why his friend had deserted Rome, Romulus explained that the gods had decided that those on earth who were of divine descent, like Julius Proculus and himself, should ultimately return to the heavens.

See also: Acca Larentia; Amulius; Numitor; Quirinus; Remus; Rhea Silvia; Sabine

Ruminalis fig tree

Roman

The tree under which the infant twins Romulus and Remus were left by the servants of Amulius who did not carry out the latter's instructions to drown the boys. There they were suckled by a she-wolf, whose strange behavior attracted the attention of the shepherd Faustulus. He found the children and took them home, where they were cared for and raised by his wife, Acca Larentia.

See also: Remus; Romulus

S

Sabine

Roman

Also: Sabini

The Sabines were an ancient people of central Italy who inhabited the Sabine Hills northeast of Rome; they made up a significant part of Rome's early population. After sporadic fighting the Sabines were finally conquered c. 290 B.C., and thereafter they were gradually Romanized.

The most famous legendary incident concerning the Sabines was the story of the rape of the Sabine women. As Romulus's policy of giving sanctuary to fugitives had led to an imbalance between men and women in the population of early Rome, he ordered that at the annual harvest festival to Consus, which was well attended by Sabines, the young women should be seized. This led to Rome being besieged by the Sabines, a truce between the two factions finally being called after the Sabine wives of the Romans intervened. A joint government was established, and the Sabine population thus combined with that of Rome.

See also: Romulus

Sagitta

Greek

1. The arrow that Eros shot into the heart of Apollo, causing the latter to fall in love with the nymph Daphne.

2. The arrow that Heracles shot to kill the eagle or vulture of Zeus that was eternally tormenting Prometheus by pecking out his liver by day, the organ restoring itself at night.

3. The arrow Apollo shot that killed one of the Cyclopes.

Astronomical: A faint but distinctive constellation of the northern celestial hemisphere that lies between approximate right ascensions 19h00m and 20h20m, declination from +16° to +22°.

Sagittarius

Greek

"The Archer"; usually identified with the centaur Cheiron after he had been translated to the heavens, his bow and arrow eternally pointed at Scorpius.

Astronomical: A constellation of the southern celestial hemisphere lying between approximate right ascensions 17h40m and 20h15m, declination from –12° to –46°.

See also: Cheiron

Salamis

Greek

An island on the southwest coast of Attica near the Piraeus that was a naval power until 620 B.C., when it was occupied by the Athenians under Solon. The Greek forces beat the Persians under Xerxes in a great naval battle off the island in 480 B.C. From 318 B.C. to 232 B.C. the island was in Macedonian hands before it returned to Greek control. Legend made it the home and realm of Telamon, whose son, Ajax the Greater, led a force to Troy to fight on the Greek side during the Trojan War.

See also: Telamon

Salmoneus

Greek

Son of Aeolus and brother of Sisyphus. He emigrated from Thessaly and founded the city of Salmone, where he imitated Zeus by ordering sacrifices for himself using faked thunder and lightning. For this presumption, Zeus struck him down with a genuine thunderbolt, which also destroyed his city.

See also: Aeolus

Salus
Roman
Goddess of public health and prosperity.

Samos
Greek
Politically and culturally important island off the west coast of Asia Minor that was colonized by Ionians some time before 1000 B.C., in classical times gradually yielding precedence to Rhodes. Legend said that Zeus and Hera spent their wedding night on the island, which became an important center, along with Argos, for the worship of the goddess. The temple of Hera was one of the Seven Wonders of the World. The foundations and single column that survive are of the late sixth century B.C. The remains measure 179 feet by 365 feet and would have had 155 columns had the temple been finished (it never was).

Samothrace
Greek
An idyllic island that was the religious center of northern Greece. Originally a sanctuary of a local earth/mother goddess known as the Mother of the Rocks and her consort, it was later the center of worship of Demeter and Hermes, along with the Dioscuri or Cabiri, the protectors of sailors. The extant remains include buildings that would have been connected with the Mysteries of Samothrace, which were celebrated here.

See also: Demeter; Dioscuri; Hermes

Sandon
Greek
The Greek name for the Anatolian god Santas when he had a cult at Tarsus.

Sappho
Greek
A historical poetess of Lesbos from the sixth century B.C. who is famous for her poems declaring love for the young girls of her matriarchal society. In later antiquity she was thought to have fallen hopelessly in love with a young man named Phaon, a ferryman who never returned her feelings. In her despair she traveled to Leukas, possibly taken there by Phaon, and threw herself off a rock, which then as now is known as Sappho's Leap.

Sarpedon
Greek
Son of Zeus and Europa, brother to Minos and Rhadamanthus. He fled from Crete with Miletus when he and his brothers quarreled over the youth, who made his preference for Sarpedon known. They settled in Asia Minor, where Miletus founded the kingdom that bore his name. Sarpedon, after helping Cilix, the eponymous king of Cilicia, against the Lycians, became king of the latter, married Bellerophon's daughter, and was permitted by Zeus to live for three generations. He led a force of Lycians to the Trojan War, where his father attempted to save him but was overruled by the other gods. When Patroclus killed Sarpedon, Zeus sent Apollo to rescue the body, which was then transported safely back to Lycia by Hypnos.

See also: Minos; Rhadamanthus

Saturn(us)
Roman
Ancient Italian god of time and agriculture and protector of harvests, ruler of the world in a Golden Age of infinite happiness, innocence, and plenty that he established in Latium. He was later equated with the Greek Cronos as the father of the gods. The husband of Lua, though later associated with Ops, Saturn was the father of Jupiter, Neptune, Pluto, Vesta, and Juno but, significantly, not of Ceres (the Greek Demeter), most of whose functions in Greek thought were passed over to Saturn himself. In Rome he became the keeper of the treasury and was particularly associated with money. His festival, the Saturnalia, started on 17 December and lasted for seven days. It was a time of popular merrymaking; gifts were exchanged and slaves were briefly treated as their masters' equals. This festival later influenced the festivals surrounding Christmas and the New Year.

Astronomical: The second largest of the planets of the solar system with an ornate and beautiful system of equatorial rings, which are just 100 meters (300 feet) thick. Saturn lies at an average distance of 1,427 million kilometers (892 million miles) from the sun and has an equatorial diameter of approximately 120,000 kilometers (75,000 miles). The planet is surrounded by numerous satellites, possibly as many as 21, ranging in size from exceptionally small planetoids within the ring system to Titan, which has a diameter of 5,800 kilometers (3,625 miles), larger than the planet Mercury. Other moons orbiting the planet include Mimas, Enceladus, Tethys, Dione, Rhea, Hyperion, Iapetus, and Phoebe.

See also: Cronos; Latium

Satyr

Greek

The wild men of the woods, one of a class of woodland spirits who were also associated with the fields and mountains and who embodied the fertile power of nature. They were imagined as human in form with ugly, snub-nosed features, pointed ears, two horns on the forehead, and horses' tails. Satyrs were regarded as the sons of Hermes, wore skins, and had crowns of vines, fir, or ivy. Later writers gave them goats' tails and sometimes goats' legs as well, possibly a mistaken identification with Fauns. Devoted to drink and sex, they are thus—under the leadership of Silenus, who was raised by Dionysos—closely associated with that god, forming a part of his retinue. Older satyrs were often referred to as Sileni or Silenoi. They belong to a world of anomie, characterized by the wild and frenzied worship of Dionysos. In art they are generally shown with uncontrollable erections, or masturbating, or raping nymphs.

See also: Dionysos

Scaean Gate

Greek

Gateway to Troy; nearby, Achilles was wounded in his vulnerable heel by an arrow shot by Paris and guided to its mark by Apollo.

See also: Achilles

Scaevola, Gaius Mucius

Roman

Roman soldier who, during the siege of Rome by the Etruscans under the leadership of Lars Porsenna, disguised himself as one of the enemy and entered their encampment fully intending to assassinate Lars Porsenna. However, ignorant of the Etruscan leader's appearance, he guessed wrongly.

Captured and brought before Lars Porsenna, Gaius Mucius, as he was then simply known, placed his right hand into a pan of flaming coals and held it there without flinching. Lars Porsenna was so impressed by this display that he ordered the release of Gaius Mucius and returned his sword, which he received in his undamaged left hand, thus earning him his cognomen Scaevola, "Left-handed."

With each party earning the respect and admiration of the other, Scaevola now warned Lars Porsenna that there were at least 300 more Romans under disguise in the Etruscan camp intending to kill Lars Porsenna. He even ventured to suggest that so great a leader as Lars Porsenna should be a friend rather than an enemy of Rome; such was Lars Porsenna's respect for Scaevola that he agreed to a truce.

See also: Lars Porsenna

Scamander

Greek

Emigrant from Crete who founded a colony in Phrygia and was deified when he jumped into the River Xanthus that flows across the Trojan Plain. Thereafter the river was known as the River Scamander. The nymph Idea bore him a son, Teucer, the first king of the Troad; hence the Trojans are called Teucri.

The River Scamander features in several episodes from the Trojan War, most notably that of Achilles and Penthesilea. After Diomedes had thrown Penthesilea's body into the river, from which it was safely recovered, Achilles blocked the course of the river with corpses. Furious, Scamander flooded the Trojan Plain, and Achilles fought him single-handedly until Hephaistos sent a fireball that dried up his waters.

See also: Achilles; Penthesilea

Scheria

Greek

The island realm of Alcinous. Odysseus washed up there after the ever-vengeful

Poseidon wrecked his raft, which he had sailed from the island home of Calypso. Helped to the island by Leucothea and Athene, Odysseus was discovered by Nausicaa, who took the naked sailor to her father's palace, where Odysseus recounted the epic stories that form the narrative of Homer's *Odyssey*.

See also: Alcinous; Odysseus

Sciapodes

Greek

A legendary race from either India or Ethiopia. Sciapodes used their single huge foot as a parasol to shade them from the sun while sleeping.

Sciron

Greek

A brigand who lived on the frontier between Megaris and Attica, the Megarian side of the isthmus of Corinth—modern Kaki Skala. After robbing travelers, he compelled them to wash his feet while he sat on the Scironian Rock. From this vantage point he kicked them off the cliff into the sea, where they were devoured by a giant turtle. Theseus turned the tables on him and kicked the robber off the cliff to meet the same fate.

See also: Theseus

Scorp~io, ~ius

Greek

"The Scorpion"; it stung and caused the death of the hunter Orion and also stung the horses of Phaëthon. To place him out of harm's way the gods placed him in the heavens, well away from Orion, where he forms the constellation that bears his name.

Astronomical: An irregular constellation of the southern celestial hemisphere lying between approximate right ascensions 15h45m and 18h00m, declination from $-8°$ to $-46°$. Scorpio is the eighth sign of the Zodiac, 24 October–23 November.

See also: Orion

Scylla

Greek

1. A female monster with six barking heads around her waist and 12 feet who lived in a cave on the Italian side of the Strait of Messina between Italy and Sicily. Opposite her lived Charybdis, a violent whirlpool. There are two versions of how Scylla came to be a monster. In the first she was the daughter of Phorcys and one of the various lovers of Poseidon; but she was so hateful toward Amphitrite that the latter turned her into the monster. The second says that she was a nymph whom Glaucus loved and was turned into the monster by the jealous Circe, who also loved Glaucus.

When Odysseus successfully negotiated the twin terrors of Scylla and Charybdis, following the advise of Circe, the great hero lost many of his seamen to the Scylla, whose six mouths snatched and devoured the sailors. Later legend substituted a dangerous rock for the monster.

2. The daughter of Nisus, king of Megara. She fell in love with Minos when the latter was besieging Nisa, the port of Megara, and killed her father by cutting off the purple lock of hair upon which his life depended. Even though Scylla let Minos into the city, her parricide so disgusted him that he would have nothing to do with her. When he left she swam after his ship until her father's soul, changed to a sea eagle, pounced on her, and she became the bird Ciris. A slight variation says that Minos simply drowned the girl and that she was turned into the fish Ciris. Her father was then transformed into an osprey.

See also: Amphitrite; Charybdis; Circe; Minos

Scyros

Greek

Island in the Aegean Sea that was the realm of Lycomedes. Achilles was sent to his court by his mother, Thetis, in her attempt to keep him from going to the Trojan War after an oracle had foretold of his death there. Theseus went to the same island after he had been unable to maintain control in Athens after returning from Tartarus; there he was treacherously murdered by Lycomedes.

See also: Achilles; Thetis

Scythia

Greek

Ancient region in southern European and Asiatic Russia, between the Carpathians and the River Dun, considered by the Greeks to be an ill-defined area to the north of the Euxine or Black Sea. The Scythians, who originally came from Siberia, occupied the area between the eighth and third centuries B.C. Herodotus maintained that Scythia was the home of the Amazons.

Segesta
Greco-Roman
Also: Egesta, Acesta

Town in Sicily legendarily founded by Acestes. It is the site of an outstanding, though never completed, Doric temple of the late fifth century B.C.

See also: Acestes

Selene
Greek

Goddess of the moon, the daughter of Hyperion and Theia, sister of Helios and Eos, and identified by the Romans as Luna. Each night after bathing she dressed in gleaming robes and drove her chariot across the sky, as her brother, Helios (Sun), did during the day. She was normally depicted with a long robe and veil, a crescent moon on her forehead. Mother of Pandion by Zeus, by whom she also had three daughters, she was seduced by Pan, but the love of her life remained Endymion, a shepherd and the most beautiful of mortal men. In later times she became more or less identified with Artemis, whose brother, Apollo, became more or less identified with her own brother, Helios.

See also: Endymion

Semele
Greek

Daughter of Cadmos and Harmonia and sister of Autonoë, Ino, Agave, Polydorus, and Illyrius. Loved by Zeus, who made her pregnant, the ever-jealous Hera, disguised as an old woman, persuaded Semele, who was six months' pregnant, to ask her mysterious lover to appear before her in his true form. Reluctantly Zeus complied, appearing to Semele as a thunderbolt; the unfortunate Semele was incinerated. From her ashes Zeus

recovered the unborn baby; he had it sewn up in his thigh, and it was delivered from there three months later. The baby, Dionysos, was then entrusted to the nymphs on Mount Nysa.

When Dionysos had been accepted into Olympus, replacing Hestia, he traveled to the Underworld and brought Semele back with him. She ascended with him to Olympus and was thereafter known as Thyone.

See also: Dionysos; Thyone

Semiramis
Greek

The Greek form of Sammu-Ramat (Shammu Is Exalted), legendary queen and founder of Babylon, daughter of the fish goddess Derceto (the Greek form of Ataryatis) of Ashkelon and the Assyrian god of wisdom, Oannes. She married Ninus, king of Assyria, and with him conquered large tracts of the Middle East. When her husband died she built him a huge mausoleum at Nineveh (sometimes called Ninusa, a city she was said to have founded) and a huge palace for herself near the River Euphrates. Consulting the Oracle of Ammon as to when she would die, she was told it would happen only when her son conspired against her. Before that event finally took place she conquered large areas of India and was, upon her death, transformed into a dove and ascended to Heaven, where she was deified.

Sequ~ana, ~ena
Romano-Celtic

Goddess who presided over the source of the River Seine, France, which takes its name from her. Her totem bird was the duck. In the latter days of the Roman Empire her cult appears to have spread beyond the River Seine, and she seems to have become a general goddess of rivers.

Serapis
Greco-Egyptian

A god invented and introduced into Egypt by Ptolemy I in a partial attempt to unite Greeks and Egyptians in common worship. He was revered as a healing divinity and combined the attributes of Zeus, Hades, and Asclepios with the Egyptian god Osiris. His finest temple was the Serapeum at Alexandria.

Seriphos
Greek

An island in the Cyclades. The chest in which Danaë and the infant Perseus drifted there after Acrisius had set them adrift from Argos. There the chest was found by Dictys, who took its occupants to Polydectes, who received them hospitably. Later, Polydectes, wanting Danaë for himself, sent Perseus off on the potentially fatal quest to obtain the head of the Gorgon Medusa. Perseus turned Polydectes to stone on his return and made Dictys his successor.

See also: Acrisius; Danaë; Perseus

Serpens
Greek

The serpent held by Asclepios, or Ophiuchus, that was placed in the sky to either side of the constellation Ophiuchus, with the head, Serpens Caput, to the west, and the tail, Serpens Cauda, to the east.

Astronomical: The two constellations that make up the serpent straddle the celestial equator. Serpens Caput, to the west of Ophiuchus, lies between approximate right ascensions 15h10m and 16h15m, declination from +26° to –4°. Serpens Cauda, to the east, lies between approximate right ascensions 17h15m and 18h50m, declination from +7° to –16°.

Servius Tullius
Roman

The legendary fifth king of Rome whose conception, birth, and childhood were marked by supernatural portents. Born to Ocresia, he was raised as a slave in the household of Tarquinius Priscus. Servius Tullius's succession to the throne was engineered by Tanaquil after her husband's assassination. He built the first wall around the complete city, established the cult of Diana on the Aventine Hill, and made important constitutional reforms. He was the father of Tullia, who married Arruns Tarquinius. She prompted her brother-in-law,

Tarquinius, to kill his brother, which he did. She then married Tarquinius, who threw the aged Servius Tullius down the steps of the senate, where he was murdered by hired henchmen, his corpse being run over by his daughter, Tullia, who was bathed from head to foot in his blood.

According to the Emperor Claudius, Servius Tullius originated as an Etruscan hero named Mastarna, who the Etruscans believed was a companion of Caeles Vibenna.

Sestos
Greek

Settlement on the European shore of the Hellespont at its narrowest point opposite Abydos. An important site for the worship of Aphrodite, Hero was a priestess here. Every night Leander, her lover, swam the channel from Abydos, but one night her guide lamp blew out in a storm, and Leander drowned. Hero threw herself into the sea in her grief.

See also: Abydos; Hero; Leander

Seven Against Thebes
Greek

The name given to the fated expedition by seven Argive champions who made war on Thebes in support of Polyneices' claim to the throne, denied by his brother, Eteocles, who was supposed to alternatively share it.

Exiled from Thebes, Polyneices came to Argos, where he married Adrastus's daughter, Argia. He asked his father-in-law to help him regain his rightful kingdom. Adrastus agreed and raised an army, but the seer Amphiaraus foresaw the failure of the expedition and the deaths of all the leaders save Adrastus. He was thus disinclined to join the expedition, but Polyneices bribed Amphiaraus's wife, Eriphyle, with the necklace of Harmonia, and she talked her husband into going.

Adrastus, Polyneices, and Amphiaraus were joined by Tydeus, who was also in exile at Argos and had married Adrastus's other daughter, Deiphyle. They were reinforced by Hippomedon, Parthenopaeus, and Capaneus. These seven then marched against Thebes. En route they halted at Nemaea to seek water. There Hypsipyle showed them a well, but in so doing she put down the baby Opheltes, whom she was nursing, and he was killed by a snakebite. The seven buried him and celebrated funeral games, which became the origin of the Nemaean Games. Opheltes was renamed Archemorus, "beginning of doom."

Reaching Thebes, each of the seven commanders led attacks against the city's seven gates. Capaneus scaled the walls but was struck down by the thunderbolt of Zeus. Tydeus, mortally wounded by Melanippus, might have been saved by Athene, who was preparing to give him a lifesaving elixir given to her by Zeus. However, Amphiaraus, who bore him a grudge, persuaded him to drink the brains of the dead Melanippus, and this so disgusted Athene that she left him to his fate. Hippomedon and Parthenopaeus were also killed in their assaults. Polyneices thus offered to settle the dispute in single combat with Eteocles, but both were mortally wounded. Seeing that all was lost, Amphiaraus fled in his chariot and was pursued by Periclymenus. Zeus made the earth open, and Amphiaraus disappeared down the chasm, chariot and all, reemerging at Oropus, where he became a healing hero. As the seer had foretold, only Adrastus remained alive.

Thebes, however, was not unscathed. With Eteocles and Polyneices both dead, Creon seized the throne and refused the burial of Polyneices, condemning him as a traitor. Polyneices' sister, Antigone, disobeyed the king and buried her brother; for her trouble Creon had her immured in a cave, where she took her own life. When her body was found by Haemon, Creon's son and Antigone's betrothed, he took his own life in despair.

The Seven Against Thebes were later avenged by their descendants, the Epigoni. They mounted a successful expedition against Thebes shortly before the start of the Trojan War.

See also: Adrastus; Amphiaraus; Capaneus; Creon; Eteocles; Hippomedon; Parthenopaeus; Polyneices; Thebes; Tydeus

Sextus (Tarquinius)
Roman
The son of Tarquinius Superbus who raped Lucretia, the wife of Lucius Tarquinius Col-

latinus. After the act she committed suicide in front of her husband and father and two other witnesses. This act led to the expulsion of the Tarquinians from Rome and the establishment of the Roman republic.

See also: Lucretia

Sibyl
Greco-Roman
The name of a prophetess, the daughter of Lamia most commonly associated with Ionia but perhaps actually located in Libya. By the late fourth century B.C. her name had become generic, mainly being used by the Romans to describe the priestesses who delivered oracles. A first-century B.C. list by Varro names ten sibyls: the Persian, Libyan, Delphic, Cimmerian, Erythraean, Samian, Cumaean, Hellespontic, Phrygian, and Tiburtine. They were also referred to at Delos, Claros, Colophon, Sardis, and Dodona. Many, of course, were the sites of earlier Greek oracles that were simply taken over by the invading and conquering Romans. The rock from which the Delphic Sibyl, whose name was Herophile, delivered her prophecies can still be seen today.

Sibylline prophecies, like the earlier Greek oracles, were made in an ecstatic trance, then interpreted and written down by her attendants. Those at Cumae were written on palm leaves. The Cumaean Sibyl, who is a priestess of Apollo and perhaps the best known of all the sibyls, once offered nine books of sibylline prophecies to Tarquinius Superbus of Rome. When he refused to pay the asking price she set fire to three of them, offering him the remaining six for the same price. He again refused, so she once more burned three books before offering him the last three, still at the same price. Tarquinius Superbus then realized just what he was missing, and duly paid the full asking price. The books were then housed in the temple of Jupiter on the Capitoline Hill, where they were consulted only in times of national emergency. It was the Sibyl of Cumae who advised Aeneas to arm himself with the Golden Bough from a wood near Lake Avernus before she led him into the Underworld to consult his dead father's spirit.

Nonetheless, nine books of sibylline prophecies were preserved at Rome until they were destroyed by a fire in 63 B.C. In the Christian period, 14 books of sibylline prophecies in hexameter verse were composed, many of which tell the history of Rome in prophetic form, among much other material.

See also: Oracle

Sicyon

Greek

City of Achaea to the northeast of Corinth that was an important center for the worship of Dionysos. Legend makes it the kingdom of Threspotus when Thyestes visited the city, on the advice of the Delphic Oracle, and ravished his daughter, Pelopia, who was a priestess there.

See also: Dionysos

Silen(o)i

Greek

Name given to older satyrs that seems to derive from Silenus, the aging satyr who raised Dionysos. They are scarcely to be distinguished from satyrs, though Sileni appear to be Attic-Ionic in origin, whereas satyrs seem to have originated in the Peloponnesos. Often older, fatter, and far drunker than the lusty satyrs, they are also, surprisingly, the purveyors of wisdom. Silenus appears to have had prophetic powers.

Silenus

Greek

An aged satyr, offspring of Pan or Hermes, father of the centaur Pholus. He seems to have given his name to the Sileni, the generic term used to refer to older satyrs. Silenus raised Dionysos and was, thereafter, his constant companion. He is usually depicted as a jovial, bald old satyr, usually drunk, who followed the deity while swaying drunkenly on the back of an ass. Silenus was also revered, for he had the gift of prophecy and had a great knowledge of past events. During the battle with the Titans, Silenus rode the Southern Ass, Asellus Australis, while Dionysos rode the Northern Ass, Asellus Borealis.

See also: Asellus Australis; Dionysos

Silvanus

Roman

An agricultural deity associated with the mysterious forces in woods, fields, and flocks. Like another agricultural god, Faunus, he is often represented as a countryman or even a peasant. His character gradually became merged with that of the similarly goatish Greek deity, Pan, and was generally worshipped in solitude at a particular tree or copse.

See also: Faunus; Pan

Silvius

Greco-Roman

The first king of Alba Longa, the son or half-brother of the city's founder, Ascanius; the father of Brutus, who accidentally killed him and was then exiled from Italy. As Brutus was the great-grandson of Aeneas, this would make Silvius the grandson of Aeneas.

See also: Aeneas; Ascanius

Si(n)nis

Greek

A brigand who lived on the isthmus of Corinth, where he waylaid victims, tying their arms between two pine trees bent double. When these were freed the unfortunate victim was torn apart. When Theseus passed his way, he dished out the same treatment to Sinis.

See also: Theseus

Sinon

Greek

A cousin of Dionysos and grandson of Autolycus who played an important part in the strategy surrounding the use of the Wooden Horse. He was the sole Greek left behind when the Greeks burned their camp and sailed for Tenedos, leaving the Wooden Horse on the shore. When the Trojans hauled the horse inside the city walls, Sinon allowed himself to be captured and explained that the horse was the Greeks' atonement for having stolen the Palladium. That night, however, as Troy slept, Sinon lit a beacon, which signaled Agamemnon to return to Troy. Some sources say that Sinon gave the word to the Greek warriors within the Wooden Horse that they should make their presence felt and that he opened the city gates to let in the Greek forces.

See also: Autolycus; Dionysos

Siren

Greek

Generic name for one of the daughters of a sea god, possibly Phorcys, and one of the Muses. Originally two, there were later three Sirens, or Sirenes, who were portrayed as a bird with a woman's head, sometimes called a sea nymph but more closely resembling a Harpy. Yet unlike that horrendous creature, the Sirens were blessed with the gift of enchantingly sweet song. The Sirens lived on a rocky island near the Strait of Messina near the homes of the monsters Scylla and Charybdis. Their beautiful singing was believed to lure sailors to their death on the rocks, and in later myths they were identified with mermaids and mermen. Odysseus managed to sail past them by blocking his sailors' ears with wax, then tying himself to the mast so that he might hear their song. The Argonauts managed to navigate the hazard they posed, as the singing of Orpheus surpassed that of the Sirens. Later legend had them participating in a musical contest with the Muses, which they lost.

See also: Charybdis; Orpheus; Scylla

Sirius

Greek

The faithful hunting dog of the great hunter Orion who was, after the hunter had been placed in the heavens, also placed there as the star that is now known as Sirius the Dog Star. The star was especially important to the Egyptians, who called it Sothis and observed it carefully, for about the date when it rose at dawn the Nile would flood the surrounding countryside.

Astronomical: Located within the constellation Canis Major and designated the alpha star of that constellation (a CMa). It is the brightest object in the sky except for the sun, moon, Venus, and Jupiter. Located in the southern celestial hemisphere at approximate right ascension 6h45m, declination -17°, Sirius is magnitude –1.45, spectral type A1V; at nine light-years distant it is the fifth closest star to the Earth.

See also: Orion

Sisyphus

Greek

Son of Aeolus, Sisyphus married Merope the Pleiad, who bore him Glaucus. He seduced Anticleia, the daughter of Autolycus and mother of Odysseus, a liason that led some to say that Sisyphus was really Odysseus's father. He founded Ephyra, later called Corinth. He outwitted Autolycus, who had the gift of making anything he touched invisible and who had been stealing his cattle. By marking the undersides of the cattles' hooves he discovered the theft and the identity of the thief.

Sisyphus was known as one of the great sinners in the Underworld, where he had been condemned to eternally roll a large stone up a hill. Just as he reached the top the stone would roll to the bottom again. There were various reasons for his condemnation. Some say that he told Asophus that Zeus had carried off Aegina, or that he tried to cheat Hades, or that he had seduced his brother Salmoneus's daughter, Tyro.

See also: Aeolus; Autolycus; Merope; Odysseus

Smintheus

Greek

Title applied to Apollo.

Snake

Greek

Though the snake never singularly received cult and was never directly personified, the animal is an important part of Greek lore. They were frequently regarded as the animal into which the soul of a dead hero or a chthonic deity passed, the connection between the dead and snakes possibly being made by the common observance of snakes around graves. The healing god Asclepios took the form of a snake when his cult was introduced to Athens, a city where the serpent has particular importance, as witnessed by the story of the infant Erichthonius.

Gradually snakes became, perhaps suprisingly, regarded as protectors of the household, a role that was carried over into later Roman belief.

Sol
Roman

The personification of the sun, the Roman equivalent of the Greek Helios.

Astronomical: The star at the center of our solar system. It has a diameter of 1,392,530 kilometers (870,331 miles), about 109 times the size of the Earth; it is about 150 million kilometers (96 million miles) distant. It has been shining for an estimated 4.5 billion years.

Somnus
Roman

The Roman equivalent of Hypnos. God of sleep, father of Morpheus, god of dreams, and brother of Death.

See also: Hypnos

Sophocles
Greek

Greek dramatist (c. 495–406 B.C.) who, along with Aeschylus and Euripides, is one of the three great tragedians. He modified the form of Greek tragedy by introducing a third actor and developing true stage scenery. During his lifetime Sophocles wrote some 120 plays, though only seven tragedies survive today: *Antigone* (c. 441 B.C.), *Oedipus Tyrannus,* his greatest work, *Electra, Ajax, Trachiniae, Philoctetes* (409 B.C.), and *Oedipus at Colonus* (401 B.C.).

Born in Colonus Hippus, a suburb of Athens, and living in the city at the time of Pericles, a period of great prosperity, Sophocles was a popular man and the friend of Herodotus. His tragedies portray the human will as greater than that of the gods, unlike those of Aeschylus, whom he beat in a dramatic contest in 468 B.C. He won first prize at the Great Dionysia a total of 18 times. His characters were generally heroic in stature. A large fragment of a strategic play named *Ichneutae,* a tragedy treated in a grotesquely comic fashion, also survives.

See also: Aeschylus; Euripides

Sparta
Greek

The ancient capital of Laconia, also called Lacedaemon, its inhabitants noted for the military organization of their state and for their rigorous discipline, simplicity, and courage. The modern town lies in the southwest Peloponnesos in southern Greece on the River Evrotes, just north of the ruins of the ancient city-state that was founded by the Dorians c. 1000 B.C. Today it is the modern capital of the Lakonia Department.

Ancient Spartan society consisted of three classes: the Spartiates, who were the ruling class; the *perioeci,* who were free inhabitants with no political power; and the helots, who were slaves. Lycurgus gave the city a viable constitution, after which it began its conquest of Arcadia, Argos, and Messenia (c. 734–716 B.C.). Sparta then flourished as an economic and cultural center. After a massive helot revolt in the late seventh century B.C., it changed into an armed camp, with all Spartiates trained as soldiers from an early age.

It was originally ruled by two kings, later by the *geronsie,* the assembly, or *apella,* and *ephors.* The Peloponnesian League was formed c. 500 B.C., with Sparta as the most powerful member. After the Persian Wars (500–449 B.C.), Athenian powers began to rival those of Sparta, thus leading to the Peloponnesian War (431–404 B.C.), which ended in the defeat of Athens. Sparta dominated Greece until 371 B.C., when it was defeated by Thebes at Leuctra and Messenia was freed. Prosperity was revived under the Romans, but Sparta was finally destroyed by the Visigoths in 396 A.D.

Legend gave Sparta some very famous rulers, among them: Tyndareus; Menelaus, the brother of Agamemnon and husband of Helen, who was stolen from him by Paris, thus leading to the Trojan War; and Orestes, who was also king of Argos and Mycenae. The city was also an important center of the worship of Athene; not surprisingly, it was also a cult center of Ares, god of war. Artemis was another deity worshipped in the city, her cult being particularly brutal, for young men and boys were scourged at her altar until they sprinkled it with their blood.

See also: Menelaus; Orestes; Tyndareus

Sparti(i)

Greek

The "Sown Men" who sprang, fully grown and fully armed, from the dragon's teeth sown by Cadmos. They immediately began to fight among themselves until just five remained. These five—Echion, Udaeus, Chthonius, Hyperenor, and Pelorus—became the ancestors of Thebes and helped Cadmos build the Cadmea. The descendants of these five autochthonous men were also known as Sparti, though they are more usually referred to as Spartoi to distinguish them.

A second group of "Sown Men" were subsequently "created" by Jason when he sowed the remaining dragon's teeth in Colchis. Like the earlier ones, they began to fight among themselves, but on this occasion none survived. However, only the earlier "Sown Men" of Cadmos are usually referred to as Sparti.

See also: Cadmos

Spartoi

Greek

A slight variation on Sparti that was used by the descendants of these "Sown Men" to distinguish them from their ancestors. The name was widely used by the leading families of Thebes, who claimed descent from the Sparti created by Cadmos.

Spes

Roman

The goddess of hope, the Roman equivalent of Elpis who was simply personified in Greece in a number of sculptures. She was later allocated a number of temples in Rome.

Sphinx

Greek

A winged lioness who had the head and breasts of a woman, said to be another of the monstrous offspring of Typhon and Echidne or of Orthros and the Chimaera. She descended on the city of Thebes, where, seated on a rock or a clifftop, she challenged each passerby to answer her riddle. Those who failed she either strangled or threw down the cliff.

When Oedipus came to Thebes the Sphinx posed him the riddle, "Which being, having only one voice, has sometimes two feet, sometimes three and sometimes four, and is weakest when it has most?" Some versions of the riddle put it more simply as, "What is it that goes on four legs in the morning, on two legs at midday, and on three legs at evening?" Oedipus correctly answered, saying that the being was man, who crawls in infancy (four legs) and supports himself with a staff in old age (three legs). Her riddle, which has become known as the riddle of the three ages of man, was thus correctly answered, and so the Sphinx flung herself to her own death.

As the Thebans had promised that the person who could rid the city of the Sphinx would be made king, Oedipus now succeeded his father, Laius, and married his own mother, Jocasta, by whom he had four children: Eteocles, Polyneices, Antigone, and Ismene.

See also: Oedipus; Thebes

Stentor

Greek

The Greek herald at the Trojan War who was noted for the strength of his voice, reported to be as loud as 50 others together.

See also: Trojan War

Stheneboea

Greek

Alternative name for Anteia, daughter of Iobates (king of Lycia), and wife of Proetus (king of Tiryns). She fell in love with Bellerophon when he fled to Tiryns after killing Bellerus. He shunned her advances, so she falsely accused him, to her husband, of trying to seduce her. Proetus, hesitant about killing a guest, sent him instead to his father-in-law, Iobates, with a letter requesting that the bearer, Bellerophon, be put to death.

See also: Anteia; Bellerophon; Proetus

Sthenelus

Greek

1. Son of Perseus and Andromeda and king of Mycenae. He married Nicippe, who bore him

Alcimoë, Eurystheus, and Medusa (not the Gorgon).

2. Son of Capaneus and Evadne, he became a firm friend with Diomedes, the son of Tydeus. Together they took part in the expedition of the Epigoni against Thebes to avenge the deaths of their fathers in the earlier, fated expedition known as the Seven Against Thebes. This time they were successful. Both then went to the Trojan War, taking along another of the Epigoni, Euryalus the Argonaut. Not much is heard of him during the ten years of the war, but Sthenelus is mentioned as one of the bravest Greeks, who were chosen to be hidden within the hollow belly of the Wooden Horse.

3. The father of Cycnus, the youth who was changed into a swan.

See also: Andromeda; Perseus; Seven Against Thebes

Stheno
Greek

One of the three daughters of Phorcys and Ceto, her sisters being Euryale and Medusa. Of the three, only Medusa was mortal. She and her sisters were better known as the hideous Gorgons with serpents for hair and a look that could turn the beholder to stone. Originally beautiful, they assumed this form after Medusa had been seduced by Poseidon in a temple of Athene. After Perseus beheaded Medusa, Stheno and Euryale pursued the fleeing hero, but he escaped their attentions by wearing Hades' helmet of invisibility.

See also: Euryale; Medusa

Strephon
Greek

A shepherd who lived in Arcadia and lamented the loss of his beloved Urania.

Strophius
Greek

King of Phocis, the husband of Agamemnon's sister, and by her the father of Pylades, the inseparable friend of Orestes, who came to his court after the murder of his father by Clytemnestra and Aegisthus.

Stymphalian birds
Greek

Man-eating birds with brazen beaks, wings, and claws; they were sacred to Ares. They inhabited the marshy lake of Stymphalia in Arcadia and used their razor-sharp feathers as arrows, which they fired at attackers. Heracles was set the task of ridding the area of these dangerous animals as the sixth labor established by Eurystheus. With the aid of Athene, Heracles frightened the birds into the air, where he either shot them down with his poisoned arrows or simply drove them off. In the latter case they were said to have gone to the island of Aretius in the Euxine, or Black, Sea, where they were later discovered by the Argonauts.

See also: Eurystheus; Heracles

Styx
Greek

One of the five rivers of the Underworld flowing in seven concentric circles around the Underworld; the river across which the surly ferryman Charon carried the souls of the dead, who were accompanied on their journey by Hermes, upon receipt of the correct fare, an *obolos*. The river was named after a nymph, the daughter of Oceanos and Tethys, because of the help she gave Zeus during his conflict with the Titans. On reaching the far shore, Cerberus, the watch dog of the Underworld, had to be passed; he was usually appeased with an offering of honey cakes, reportedly a particular favorite. Four other rivers had to be crossed before the souls of the newly dead were brought before the three judges: Minos, Rhadamanthus, and Aeacus. They were Acheron, the river of woe; Phlegethon or Pyriphlegethon, the river of flames; Cocytus, the river of wailing; and Lethe, the river of forgetfulness.

The river was also famous as the one Thetis dipped the infant Achilles into to make him invulnerable, holding him by the heel, which was thereafter his only vulnerable spot. Oaths sworn by the waters of the Styx could not be broken, even by the gods, though it remains unclear whether this means the Underworld river or the River Styx in Arcadia. The water of the Styx within the realm of Hades was said to be so poisonous that it corroded clay and metal containers and could only be carried in a horse's hoof.

See also: Acheron; Achilles; Cerberus; Charon; Cocytus; Lethe; Phlegethon

Suada

Roman

The personification of the powers of persuasion, known as Pitho to the Greeks.

Sun~ion, ~ium

Greek

A headland on the southernmost tip of Attica and the name of the town that maintained a temple to Athene, part of which is still visible today. Perhaps the town's temple of Poseidon, dramatically situated overlooking the sea on a clifftop, remains its more notable feature. It was built by Kallikrates in 444 B.C., and 12 Doric columns still stand.

Sychaeus

Greco-Roman

The husband of Dido who swore on his death never to remarry. She broke this vow when Aeneas came to the city of Carthage, which she founded after fleeing to Africa.

See also: Aeneas

Symplegades

Greek

"The Clashing Rocks"; two floating islands at the northern end of the Bosphorus that came together and crushed any ship that attempted to sail between them. Jason, following the advice of Phineus, released a dove, which flew between the islands. They clashed together, nipping the fleeing bird's tail feathers, and as

the islands recoiled Jason urged his oarsmen to pull as hard as they could, and the *Argo Navis* slipped through, Athene giving the ship a final push. Henceforth the islands never came together again.

See also: Argo (Navis); Jason

Syracuse

Greek

The most thriving town in Sicily, having the advantage of a marvelous harbor. It was founded from Corinth in 734 B.C. after civil upheaval became a tyranny under Gelon (485 B.C.) and Hieron (d. 467 B.C.); after that a new democracy showed its teeth, twice resisting Athenian invasions (424 B.C. and 413 B.C.), the latter culminating in the defeat of Demosthenes and Nicias and the total destruction of their fleets. However, danger from Carthaginian ambitions encouraged the acceptance of Dionysus I as tyrant in 406 B.C. From the third century B.C. the town was a shuttlecock in the struggle between Rome and Carthage, and by 212 B.C. it was a part of Roman Sicily. The city today houses the ruins of a temple to Apollo. Another temple, dedicated to Zeus, dates from the middle of the sixth century B.C. and is among the earliest in Sicily. A temple to Athene is now incorporated into the cathedral.

Syrinx

Greek

A nymph from Arcadia; Pan fell in love with her. He pursued her to the banks of the River Ladon, where her prayers to the gods were answered when they turned her into a clump of reeds. From these Pan fashioned the first set of pipes, a row of tuned reeds fastened together with wax. More correctly known by her name, the instrument is more commonly known as the panpipe or panpipes.

See also: Pan

T

Taenarum

Greek

A headland in Laconia where a temple dedicated to Poseidon offered absolute sanctuary. A cave in the cliffs was said to be the entrance to the Underworld. Through it Heracles made his return with Cerberus. A statue on the shore commemorated the spot where Arion was said to have been brought ashore by a dolphin.

Tages

Romano-Etruscan

A sage who was said to have been autochthonously born from a furrow in the ground. His head was gray, though he had the face of a child. He was reputed to have taught the Etruscans all the arts of divination.

Talaria

Greco-Roman

The winged sandals that were one of the attributes of Hermes, Iris, Mercurius, and others.

Talassio

Roman

The god of marriage, the equivalent of the Greek Hymenaeus.

Talaus

Greek

King of Argos who was succeeded by his son, Adrastus.

Talos

Greek

1. A bull-headed, bronze giant, made by Hephaistos, who ran around the coast of Crete constantly, destroying anybody who attempted to land on the island, thereby securing the realm of Minos. According to some sources he was menacing the Argonauts, on their return journey from Colchis with the Golden Fleece, when Medeä identified the giant's one weak spot, the ankle, where his single vein of ichor came close to the surface. She either caused Talos to graze the ankle, or simply removed the nail that plugged the vein, or instructed the archer Poeas to shoot Talos in the ankle; Talos collapsed.

2. Nephew of Daedalus, also known as Perdix, who invented the saw, chisel, and compasses. So jealous was his uncle of his craftsmanship, which he thought might surpass his, that he threw Talos headlong from Athene's temple on the Acropolis at Athens. The goddess changed Talos into a partridge, and the Areopagus banished Daedalus.

See also: Daedalus; Hephaistos; Medeä; Minos

Tanaquil

Roman

The wife of Tarquinius Priscis who is sometimes also known as Gaia Caecilia, the name depicting her as the traditional Roman matron. However, most stories made her a vigorous and domineering woman who engineered her husband's succession to the throne, then later did the same for her protégé Servius Tullius.

Tantalus

Greek

Son of Zeus and the nymph Pluto, father of Niobe, Broteas, and Pelops, and a wealthy king; unclear whether he hailed from Lydia (possibly Aipylos), Argos, Phrygia, or Corinth. Greatly favored by his father, Tantalus was even invited to banquets on Olympus, but he proved unworthy of these honors, for he constantly divulged Zeus's secrets and stole nectar and ambrosia. He was also said to have received as a gift from Pandareus the golden dog that Hephaistos made for Rhea, but he lied to his father, saying he had not seen or even heard of it.

His greatest crime, however, was the brutal murder of his son, Pelops, whom he cut into small pieces, cooked, and then served to the gods in a stew at a banquet in order to test their omniscience. All the gods immediately recognized what they had been served—all, that is, except Demeter, who, still grieving for her daughter, Persephone, absent-mindedly consumed the shoulder. Pelops was later restored to life, but Tantalus was condemned to Tartarus, where his punishment became proverbial.

Tortured with eternal thirst, he was placed in a lake, its waters receding whenever he attempted to drink from it. To add to his misery he was tortured with an eternal hunger, and above his head were boughs heavily laden with fruit; they sprang upwards whenever he reached for them. His final torment was to see a huge rock perched precariously above his head that threatened to fall at any moment and crush him.

See also: Pandareus; Pelops

Taphian
Greek

The Taphians were a legendary people who feature in the legend of Alcmene and Amphitryon. While Amphitryon was absent from Thebes fighting the Taphians, who had killed Alcmene's brothers, Zeus visited her in the guise of her husband, told her how he had been victorious, and consummated the marriage (something Alcmene refused to do until she had been revenged). Amphitryon returned the following night amid much confusion. By her double consummation, with Zeus and Amphitryon, Alcmene became the mother of Heracles and Iphicles.

See also: Alcmene; Amphitryon

Tarchetius
Roman

A wicked king of Alba Longa who on several consecutive days saw the vision of a phallus rising from the flames of his household hearth. Consulting the Oracle of Tethys, he was told that should a virgin give herself to the vision she would bear a splendid son. Tarchetius ordered his daughter to unite with the apparition, but she, feeling insulted, sent her servant girl instead. Tarchetius then imprisoned both of them, but Vesta prevented him from executing them. Twin boys were born to the servant girl. Tarchetius gave these children to Teratius with orders to kill them. He laid them on a riverbank, where they were fed by a wolf and birds until found by a cowherd, who raised the children as his own. Grown to manhood, the children returned to Alba Longa and assassinated Tarchetius.

Tarchon
Roman

An Etruscan ally of Aeneas in his fight with Turnus.

See also: Aeneas

Tarpeia
Roman

Daughter of the Roman garrison commander during the siege of Rome by the Sabines under the leadership of Titus Tatius. Wantonly desiring the gold ornaments worn by the besieging Sabines, Tarpeia sent a messenger to Titus Tatius suggesting that she would let them into the citadel by night in return for all that the Sabines wore on their left arms. This was agreed upon and the Sabines were let in, but they killed her when she came to collect her reward, demonstrating their feeling that such a treacherous act should not be rewarded.

See also: Sabine; Tatius, Titus

Tarquin~ii, ~(ian)s
Roman

The name used to collectively refer to two semilegendary kings of ancient Rome who were, perhaps, Etruscan in origin. They were Tarquinius Priscus and Tarquinius Superbus, expelled c. 510 B.C. after Sextus, the son of Tarquinius Superbus, had raped Lucretia, the wife of Lucius Tarquinius Collatinus, after which she took her own life. Following their expulsion from Rome the republic was formed and quickly established; there were, however, three abortive attempts to restore the hated monarchy.

See also: Lucretia; Sextus

Tarquinius, Arruns

Roman

The brother of Tarquinius Superbus who was murdered by his brother at the instigation of Tullia, the daughter of Servius Tullius. A second character of the same name appears later in the chronology of Rome, when the consul Brutus was killed in single combat with Arruns Tarquinius. Yet it seems likely that this is the same character; different tradition has him exiled from Rome by Tarquinius Superbus, not murdered.

See also: Romulus

Tarquinius Priscus

Roman

Originally an Etruscan named Lucumo, he later took the name Lucius Tarquinius Priscus and became the fourth successor to Romulus as king of Rome. He is one of the semi-legendary Tarquinii. According to some sources his father was a Greek refugee from Corinth named Demaratus. As king of Rome he started building the Capitoline Temple to Jupiter, Juno, and Minerva, a task completed by his successor, Tarquinius Superbus. Tarquinius Priscus was assassinated by the son of Ancus Marcius.

Tarquinius, Sextus

Roman

The notorious son of Tarquinius Superbus. While besieging the town of Gabii he asked his father how he might defeat the Gabians. Silently Tarquinius Superbus decapitated the tallest poppies in the garden. Taking the hint, Sextus killed the Gabian leaders, and his father successfully took the town.

Soon afterwards he, along with Lucius Junius Brutus, went to consult the Delphic Oracle to learn who would succeed Tarquinius Superbus. The oracle replied that it would be the first who kissed his mother; pretending to

stumble, Brutus fell to the ground and kissed the earth.

Meanwhile, Tarquinius Superbus's brutality was alienating his subjects. Rebellion was already in the air when Sextus brought the crisis to a head by raping Lucretia, the wife of Lucius Tarquinius Collatinus. She committed suicide, and so the people of Collatia, her husband's city, marched on Rome under the leadership of Lucius Junius Brutus and roused the people to shut the gates against Tarquinius Superbus and his son, who were away besieging Ardea. Thus the hated monarchy of Rome was driven out and the republic was founded; three abortive attempts to restore the monarchy followed.

See also: Lucretia

Tarquinius Superbus

Roman

Also known as Tarqin the Proud, one of the Tarquinii and the seventh and last semi-legendary king of Rome, the sixth successor after Romulus. Like Tarquinius Priscus, the other of the Tarquinii, he was probably Etruscan in origin, a despot who traditionally reigned from 534 B.C. to 510 B.C. He usurped the throne by killing his brother, Arruns Tarquinius, at the instigation of Tullia (his sister-in-law and daughter of King Servius Tullius, whom he also killed to secure the throne). He then married Tullia. His son, Sextus Tarquinius, raped Lucretia, the wife of Lucius Tarquinius Collatinus, an act that led to the ultimate expulsion of Tarquinius Superbus and his son—the death of the monarchy in Rome and the birth of the Roman republic. Three attempts were made to restore the monarchy, but each failed.

See also: Romulus; Tullia

Tartarus

Greek

The deepest, darkest, most infernal region of the Underworld, as far below the earth as the heavens were above it. It was the prison of the Gigantes and Titans, who were guarded by the Hecatoncheires, and at one time the Cyclopes were confined there. According to Homer, an anvil dropped from Olympus would fall for nine days before reaching Tartarus. The region had a ruler, also named Tartarus, a son of Chaos or Aether and Ge and father by Ge of the Gigantes, Typhon, and Echidne.

The region became the place of condemnation for the greatest sinners of Greek tradition, though it was also the region from where the Erinnyes were dispatched to punish unnatural crimes on earth. Early on, the Aloeidae were condemned to Tartarus, where they were tied back-to-back against a pillar with vipers. Tantalus was one of the most famous inmates, condemned for eternity to stand up to his chin in water that receded when he attempted to drink and under a fruit-laden tree that always remained just beyond his grasp.

See also: Cyclopes; Erinnyes; Hecatoncheires

Tatius, Titus
Roman

King of the Sabines who, to avenge the abduction of the Sabine women—commonly referred to as the rape of the Sabine women—led an army that laid siege to Rome. There Tarpeia, daughter of the Roman garrison commander, treacherously let the Sabines into the citadel at night; she was repaid for her treason, however, killed by the Sabines when she came to collect her reward.

Encouraged by their easy entry into Rome, the Sabines, led by their champion, Mettius Curtius, attacked Romulus, but Mettius Curtius's horse foundered in the swamps on the later site of the Forum. Distraught by the loss of life on both sides, the Sabine wives of the Romans interceded and thereby won a truce. It was decided that the two peoples should unite under a single government led by both Romulus and Titus Tatius.

Titus Tatius, who some said was the ancestor of the great Titurian and Vetian families of Rome, died before Romulus; he once more ruled alone until he ascended to Heaven, where he became revered as the god Quirinus.

See also: Sabine

Tauris
Greek

A name sometimes used to refer to the Crimea in ancient times, the name deriving from the earliest-known inhabitants of its southern coast, the Tauri. The goddess Artemis carried Iphigeneia to this area after snatching her from the altar at Aulis, where she was being offered as a sacrifice to the goddess by her father, Agamemnon, after the Greek fleet was becalmed while on its way to the start of the Trojan War.

Iphigeneia's brother, Orestes, accompanied by his friend, Pylades, later came to Tauris. They were captured by the barbarous inhabitants, who intended to sacrifice them, as was their custom with all strangers to their land. However, Orestes discovered that the priestess was none other than his own sister, and by her cunning the three managed to escape and return to Greece.

See also: Artemis; Iphigeneia

Taurus
Greek

The bull—Zeus in disguise—that carried off Europa, beautiful daughter of the king of Phoenicia, to Crete. The disguise that Zeus so successfully adopted was later placed in the heavens as the well-known constellation Taurus.

Astronomical: A constellation that lies mainly in the northern celestial hemisphere and forms the second constellation of the Zodiac, April 21–May 21. It lies between approximate right ascensions 3h20m and 5h55m, declination from –2° to +32°. Within its boundaries are the Pleiades, the Hyades, and the famous Crab Nebula.

See also: Europa; Pleiades

Tecmessa
Greek

The daughter of Teuthras, king of Teuthrania. She was taken captive by Ajax the Greater during one of the many raids made against Trojan allies during the first nine years of the Trojan War.

See also: Ajax (1)

T(e)iresias
Greek

A seer from Thebes who lived for a total of seven generations. As a youth he had seen two snakes mating, and upon killing the female serpent he was transformed into a woman. In a similar situation some seven or eight years later he killed the male and was transformed back into a man. This unique experience made him a useful arbiter when Zeus and Hera argued over whether a man or woman gained the greatest pleasure from sexual intercourse. Teiresias assured them that a woman gained nine times as much pleasure. Hera was furious, though why remains a mystery. She blinded Teiresias, but Zeus rewarded him with a long life and the gift of prophecy. Other versions say that he was blinded by Athene when he accidentally saw her bathing naked and that her nymph, Chariclo, gave him second sight. He reportedly received from Apollo the power to understand the language of birds.

He advised the people of Thebes that the only way to rid the city of the plague affecting their city following the incestuous marriage of Oedipus to Jocasta was for one of the Sparti to give his life. Hearing this, Menoeceus, father of Jocasta, leaped from the city walls to his death. Yet the plague raged, so Oedipus consulted him. Finally convinced that he was the cause of the troubles, and after Jocasta had hanged herself, Oedipus blinded himself with a brooch taken from her robe, then exiled himself or had Jocasta's brother, Creon, banish him. A short while later, after the city had suffered some further setbacks, Teiresias advised that a royal prince must sacrifice himself. A second named Menoeceus—a son of Creon—took his own life.

When Aegialeos was killed before the city walls during the attack on Thebes by the Epigoni, Teiresias foretold of the fall of the city and advised evacuation. He accompanied the populace but died the next morning, having drunk from the Well of Tilphussa. His daughter, Manto, was taken prisoner by the Argives and dedicated at Delphi. Though he was dead, his influence did not stop, for Circe advised Odysseus to consult with his spirit, which he did.

See also: Oedipus; Seven Against Thebes; Thebes

Telamon

Greek

Son of Aeacus and Endeis, brother of Peleus. Together he and Peleus killed their half-brother, Phocus, either accidentally with a discus or deliberately, after which they were banished from Aegina. Peleus went to Phthia, and Telamon married Glauce, the daughter of King Cychreus, whom he later succeeded to become king of Salamis. A companion of Heracles, Telamon was an Argonaut who took part in the voyage of the *Argo Navis;* he also participated in the hunt for the Calydonian Boar. He and Heracles then besieged Troy to punish Laomedon for breaking an earlier promise to reward Heracles for his labor.

Telamon then married Hesione, the daughter of Laomedon who bore him the son Teucer. By another wife—Eëriboea, or Periboea, or Athene—he became the father of Ajax the Greater. Telamon, however, plays no part in the legends of his children's generation.

See also: Aeacus; Heracles; Hesione; Peleus

Telchines

Greek

Either a mythical race or group, possibly of web-footed or fish-tailed *daemones,* living on Rhodes, described variously. Rhea was said to have entrusted the infant Poseidon to their care; they were great artisans, having the ability to work metal, and were supposedly the makers of the sickle of Cronos and the trident of Poseidon, though the trident's manufacture is usually attributed to the Cyclopes. They were also credited with the invention of sculpture, for which Hellenic Rhodes was famous. They were, however, also described as malevolent and destructive beings who interfered with the weather, thus earning the hostility of Apollo, who assumed the form of a wolf to destroy some of them, and of Zeus, who overwhelmed others with a flood.

Telegonus

Greek

Son of Odysseus by Circe. Searching for his father, he landed on Ithaca and began to plunder for food. When opposed by Odysseus and Telemachus, neither side recognized the other, and Telegonus killed his father with a spear tipped with the sting from a stingray. When all was revealed to him, he took Telemachus and Penelope back to Aeaea, where he married

Penelope; Telemachus married Telegonus's mother, Circe.

See also: Circe; Odysseus

Telemachus

Greek

The son of Odysseus and Penelope. While still a baby his father, feigning madness, was tricked into revealing his sanity when Palamedes placed the infant in front of the plough that Odysseus was using to sow salt into his fields. Thus Odysseus went to the Trojan War, and Telemachus was raised by Penelope alone, Mentor being his teacher and adviser during this period.

Following the end of the Trojan War, and when his father had not returned, Telemachus went in search of him. He visited both Menelaus and Nestor before returning to Ithaca, where he went to the hut of Eumaeus. There he found and was reunited with Odysseus; he told how Penelope was being besieged by suitors vying for her hand. Together father and son planned their revenge. Telemachus returned to Penelope and persuaded her to hold an archery contest; whoever was able to bend the great bow of Eurytus would win her as the prize.

None had been able to do it until Odysseus, disguised as a beggar, managed the feat and shot Antinous, the leader of the unruly suitors. Telemachus and his father then killed all the other suitors, and so after a separation of 20 years Odysseus and Penelope were reunited.

A later tradition adds to this story, saying that Telegonus, Odysseus's son by Circe, later came to Ithaca in search of his father. During a struggle Telegonus killed Odysseus, after which Telemachus and Penelope returned with him to Aeaea, where Telemachus married Circe and Telegonus married Penelope.

See also: Circe; Odysseus

Telephassa

Greek

Wife of Agenor, king of Phoenicia, and mother by him of Europa and Cadmos.

See also: Cadmos; Europa

Telephus

Greek

The son of Heracles and Auge, the priestess-daughter of Aleus, king of Tegea. Exposed at birth by Auge's father but found and raised by shepherds, Telephus upon reaching manhood questioned the Delphic Oracle about his parentage. The oracle told him to sail to King Teuthras of Teuthrania in Mysia. There he found Auge married to the king. He subsequently succeeded the king and was reputed to have married one of Priam's 50 daughters, possibly Laodice.

When the Greek fleet, en route to Troy, landed at Mysia, Telephus at first repelled them until Dionysos caused him to stumble over a vine, whereupon Achilles wounded him, a wound that refused to heal. Consulting an oracle, Telephus was told that only the inflictor could cure the wound, so Telephus visited the Greeks, who had likewise been advised by an oracle that Troy could not be taken without the help of Telephus. At first at a loss as to how to cure Telephus, they finally realized that the inflictor of the wound was not Achilles but rather the spear he had used. By scraping some rust from the spear into the wound, they healed it. In return Telephus told the Greeks exactly how they might reach Troy.

See also: Achilles; Auge; Heracles

Telepylos

Greek

The city of Lamus, king of the cannibalistic Laestrygones, where Odysseus lost all his ships but one, which he sailed to Aeaea, the island home of Circe.

See also: Laestrygones; Odysseus

Tellus (Mater)

Roman

The Roman goddess of the Earth, a fertility goddess whose Greek equivalent is Ge.

Tempe

Greek

A beautiful valley in Thessaly, between Mounts Olympus and Ossa, through which the River Peneus flows. Here Apollo pursued

Daphne, the daughter of the river god Peneus; it was also the place where he sought purification after killing the Python.

Tenedos
Greek
Island within sight of Troy; the realm of Tenes, son of Apollo or Cycnus. The Greek fleet first landed here as it approached the start of the Trojan War. Philoctetes received his festering, stinking wound here as well. The envoys Menelaus, Odysseus, and Palamedes were probably dispatched from Tenedos before the start of the Trojan War to request the return of Helen, a request that was refused. Ten years later the Greeks returned to the island, leaving behind the Wooden Horse on the Trojan Plain to await the signal of Sinon to return and sack the city.

Tenes
Greek
Son of Apollo or of Cycnus, the king of Colonae in Troas. His stepmother falsely accused him to Cycnus when she failed to seduce him. Cycnus then threw Tenes, along with his sister, Hemithea, into the sea in a chest, which eventually washed up on the shore of the island of Leucophrys, where the inhabitants made Tenes their king. The island was thenceforth known as Tenedos. Cycnus, having discovered the truth, sailed to Tenedos and there reconciled with his son. Both father and son, however, were killed by Achilles when the Greek fleet landed on Tenedos shortly before the start of the Trojan War.

Teratius
Roman
Servant or companion of Tarchetius, the tyrannical king of Alba Longa. When twin boys were born to the servant girl of Tarchetius's daughter following union with the apparition of a phallus that rose from the household hearth, Teratius was told to kill the infants, but instead he simply left them beside a river. There they were tended by a wolf and birds until found and raised by a cowherd. Grown to manhood, the boys returned to Alba Longa and killed Tarchetius.

See also: Alba Longa; Tarchetius

Tereus
Greek
A son of Ares and king of Daulia. He helped Pandion, king of Athens, and was rewarded with the hand of Pandion's daughter, Procne, in marriage. She bore him a son, Itys, but Tereus fell in love with Procne's sister, Philomela. Hiding his wife among the slaves, he told Philomela that her sister was dead and seduced her. He then tore out Procne's tongue to keep the secret safe, but she wove a message to her sister in a robe. Philomela then released Procne, who then avenged herself on Tereus by killing and cooking their son, Itys. When Tereus realized he had been eating his own son he chased the sisters with an axe, but the gods intervened and changed all three into birds. Procne became a swallow, Philomela a nightingale, and Tereus either a hoopoe or a hawk. Some sources, particularly later ones, reverse the sisters' roles and transformations.

See also: Itys; Pandion; Philomela; Procne

Terminus
Roman
The Roman god of boundaries whose milestones and boundary stones became occasional altars.

Terpsichore
Greco-Roman
One of the nine Muses, being that of choral song and dancing; often depicted wearing the long robe of a *citharode* and carrying a lyre and a plectrum. She was the mother of Linus, Hymenaeus, and the Sirens.

See also: Muses, the

Tethys
Greek
A sea deity, one of the Titan daughters of Uranos and Ge; wife of her brother, Oceanos, by whom she became the mother of the Oceanides, including Zeus's first wife, Metis,

and Proteus. As the foster mother of Hera, she refused to allow Callisto—who had been Zeus's concubine and was turned into the constellation Ursa Major—to ever enter her realm, the sea.

Astronomical: One of the satellites of the planet Saturn, lying fifth closest to the planet at an average distance of 295,000 kilometers (184,375miles), between the orbits of Enceladus and Dione.

See also: Metis; Oceanos

Teucer
Greek

1. The first king of the Troad (hence the reason the Trojans are called Teucri); the son of Scamander and the nymph Idea who was later succeeded by Dardanos, who some sources make his son but who is usually said to be the son of Zeus and Electra, one of the Pleiades.

2. The son of Telamon and Hesione. A skilled archer, he fought alongside his brother, Ajax the Greater, during the Trojan War, gaining recognition as the greatest archer to fight with the Greeks before the arrival of Philoctetes. When Ajax took his own life, Teucer upheld his brother's right to burial. However, Telamon subsequently expelled Teucer from Salamis on suspicion of complicity in the death of Ajax. On the instructions of the Delphic Oracle, Teucer traveled to Cyprus, where he founded a new Salamis, there marrying a daughter of Cinyras.

See also: Ajax (1); Hesione; Scamander; Telamon

Teucri
Greek

A name for the Trojans, after the first king of the Troad, Teucer, the son of Scamander and Idea.

Teuthras
Greek

King of Teuthrania in Mysia, husband of Auge (the mother of Telephus by Heracles and mother by Teuthras of Tecmessa). He was killed by Ajax the Greater, who took his daughter, Tecmessa, his successor being his stepson, Telephus.

See also: Ajax (1); Auge; Heracles

Thalia
Greek

1. One of the nine Muses, being that of comedy and pastoral poetry; depicted wearing or carrying a comic mask and holding a shepherd's staff or wearing a wreath of ivy. She was the mother of Corybantes.

2. One of the three Charites or Graces.

See also: Charites; Graces; Muses, the

Thamyris
Greek

A mythical bard hailing from Thrace. He fell in love with the beautiful youth Hyacinthos, reputedly the first man to love another of his own sex. Having entered and won a singing contest at Delphi, he became extremely arrogant and challenged the Muses to a contest. They won and blinded him for his vanity.

See also: Hyacinthos

Thanatos
Greek

"Death"; the brother of Hypnos (Sleep) and son of Night. He was equated by the Romans with Mars. Heracles was said to have wrestled Thanatos when he traveled to the Underworld to win back the dead Alcestis.

Thargelia
Greek

The annual festival of Apollo that was held in Athens.

Thasos
Greek

Island off the southern coast of Thrace that has remains of a Greek city containing sanctuaries to Dionysos, Heracles, Poseidon, and Pan as well as the city guardians. There is also a large altar to Hera and a temple dedicated to Athene, though only the foundations of the latter now survive. It was also the home of Theagenes and the site of a bronze statue erected in his honor, which fell on an enemy who nightly flogged the statue.

See also: Dionysos; Heracles; Pan; Poseidon

Theagenes

Greek

A great semilegendary athlete from Thasos who won the boxing competition at Olympia in 480 B.C., along with a great many other victories. When he died a bronze statue of him was erected. However, a rival came and flogged the statue every night until one night it fell on and killed the assailant. The dead man's son prosecuted the statue for murder; found guilty, it was thrown into the sea.

Thasos subsequently became barren, so the Delphic Oracle was consulted. They were advised to "take back the exiles," but restoring a number of men made no effect. A second consultation elicited the response, "You leave great Theagenes unremembered." At about that time a fishing boat brought up the statue of Theagenes in its nets. Restored to its rightful place, where it was rededicated and offered divine sacrifices, the land of Thasos once more bore fruit.

Theano

Greek

The wife of Antenor who was, along with her husband and children, spared when the Greeks sacked Troy. They sailed to the western coast of the Adriatic Sea, where they were said to have founded Venice and Padua.

See also: Antenor

Thebe

Greek

The wife of Zethus who gave her name to the city of Thebes.

See also: Zethus

Thebes

Greek

In Greek, Thivai, an ancient city in Boeotia that is the subject of many classical legends. Founded sometime before the six century B.C., it was, from the late sixth century B.C., the bitter rival of Athens and, after the Peloponnesian War, the rival of Sparta for the hegemony of Greece. Razed to the ground in 335 B.C. but subsequently rebuilt, the city survived Roman times before it was destroyed as late as 1311 A.D.

Legend says that Thebes was founded by Cadmos, son of Agenor and Telephassa and the brother of Europa, who was carried off by Zeus. Unable to find his sister, Cadmos consulted the Delphic Oracle, who advised him to give up the futile search and instead follow a cow and build a town where the animal finally sank down out of fatigue. Cadmos followed the cow from Phocis to Boeotia, and where she finally rested he started to build the Cadmea.

Sacrificing to Athene, Cadmos sent some of his men to fetch water from a spring that was sacred to Ares, not knowing that it was guarded by a dragon, which killed most of his men. Cadmos killed the dragon and then, on the advice of Athene, sowed the dead animal's teeth. The Sparti or "Sown Men" sprang up immediately, fully grown and fully armed, and began to fight each other until just five remained. These five—Echion, Udaeus, Chthonius, Hyperenor, and Pelorus—helped Cadmos finish the Cadmea and later became revered as the ancestors of Thebes.

Cadmos married Harmonia at a service attended by the Olympian deities. By her he became the father of Autonoë, Ino, Semele, Agave, Polydorus, and Illyrius. He reigned until old age, when he relinquished the throne to Pentheus, his grandson by Agave and Echion.

The fortifications of the city, below the site of the Cadmea, were built by Amphion and Zethus, who jointly ruled the city. Amphion married Niobe; Zethus married Thebe, who gave her name to the city.

Many other legends concern or involve the city of Thebes, including the legend of Oedipus and the expeditions of the Seven Against Thebes and the Epigoni.

See also: Boeotia; Cadmos; Harmonia; Oedipus; Seven Against Thebes; Sparti

Theia

Greek

One of the Titan daughters of Uranos and Ge, she was the mother of Helios, Eos, and Selene by Hyperion and of the Cercopes by Oceanos.

Themis
Greek

The personification of law, order, and justice; one of the Titan daughters of Uranos and Ge, she was the second wife of Zeus and by him became the mother of the Horae, the Moirae, Eunomia, Dike, Astraea, and Eirene, or Irene. Although a Titan, she was honored by the gods of Olympus for her wisdom and foresight.

She acted as the housekeeper to the gods and muse to Zeus, functioning also as midwife at the births of Apollo and Artemis. Until Apollo usurped her she held the position of oracle at Delphi, her most famous prophecy being that to Zeus: that any son born to Thetis would be greater than his father, a prophecy that quickly dissuaded Zeus from attempting to make Thetis his mistress. She also told Deucalion and Pyrrha how they might repopulate the earth after the Deluge sent by Zeus.

Themis was depicted as a stern woman bearing a pair of scales that were seen as weighing facts brought before her before permitting judgment to be passed. Her scales were passed to her daughter, Astraea, and were later placed in the sky as the constellation Libra.

See also: Astraea; Horae; Moirae

Theogony
Greek

A verse narrative of the origins of the gods. The only surviving one is that by Hesiod, giving the canonical succession of Uranos—Cronos—Zeus. Many other theogonies existed in antiquity, ascribed to Orpheus and others. These accounts, which essentially treated cosmology in mythical terms, are often conflicting. Orphic theogonies became the basis of mystery cults and later religious beliefs. The only true theogony from classical times, however, is that of Hesiod.

Thersander
Greek

Son of Polyneices who followed the example of his father in bribing Eriphyle, this time with the robe of Harmonia, when Alcmaeon, the son of Amphiaraus, showed a decided disin-terest in joining the expedition of the Epigoni against Thebes.

See also: Harmonia; Polyneices; Seven Against Thebes

Thersites
Greek

An ugly, common, scurrilous, and misshapen Greek soldier at the Trojan War. He provided a good laugh for the Greek forces when he was beaten by Odysseus for complaining of Agamemnon's seizure of Briseis. Later he derided Achilles while he mourned the death of the Amazon Queen Penthesilea. Achilles killed him with a single blow.

See also: Achilles

Theseus
Greek

The heroic son of Aegeus, king of Athens, and Aethra, daughter of King Pittheus of Troezen. Though Aethra was not Aegeus's wife, she made an agreement with him to provide an heir when he had come to Troezen. Poseidon lay with Aethra on the same night she conceived Theseus, so some sources say that Theseus is in fact a son of Poseidon rather than of Aegeus. As Aegeus left Troezen to return to Athens he hid a sword and sandals beneath a large rock. He told Aethra that when their son, whom she was to raise in secret, had reached manhood she was to show him the tokens; if he could lift the rock and retrieve them, she was to send him on to Athens.

Naturally enough the young Theseus succeeded in retrieving the tokens, and rather than going by sea he left for Athens via the Isthmus of Corinth. This journey provided his first adventures, for during the course of the trip he encountered, and dispatched, several notorious bandits. The first was Periphetes at Epidaurus, who had the annoying habit of cracking travelers over the head with his club. Theseus dispatched him by his own preferred method of killing. Next he came across Sinis, who tied victims by their arms between two double-bent pines then released the trees, thus tearing them apart. Theseus did the same to him. Next he encountered the wild sow of Crommyum, which Theseus simply speared.

Continuing on his journey, Theseus next faced Sciron, who made passers-by wash his feet then kicked them over the cliff to their deaths. Theseus did likewise to Sciron. At Eleusis he met Cercyon, who wrestled travelers to their deaths, but he met his end when Theseus duly beat him. Finally he came across Sinis's father, Polypemon (surname Procrustes), who invited victims to spend the night, stretching them or lopping their limbs as necessary to fit his bed. Theseus took care of him by fitting him to his own bed.

Having been purified of all these killings by some men he met at a shrine of Zeus Meilichius, Theseus finally made it to Athens, where he was greeted as a hero. However, Medeä, who had become Aegeus's consort and bore him the son Medus, recognized Theseus and plotted to get rid of him. At that time the Cretan Bull was terrorizing Marathon (the reason it became known as the Marathonian Bull), so Medeä persuaded Aegeus that a hero as great as Theseus should be sent to dispatch it. Theseus successfully captured the great bull and brought it back to Athens, where he offered it to Athene. At the celebratory banquet Medeä poisoned a drink and had Aegeus offer it to Theseus, but in the nick of time Aegeus saw the sword Theseus was carrying and, recognizing it as the token he had left under the rock all those years before, welcomed Theseus as his son. Medeä fled, taking Medus with her.

However, the time was fast approaching when Athens was due to send the tribute of seven maidens and seven youths to Minos on Crete, where they would be fed to the Minotaur. Theseus immediately volunteered to be one of the 14, fully intending to kill the Minotaur and thus put an end to the tribute. He rigged a ship with black sails, promising to change them to white should he return victorious.

During the voyage to Crete, Minos and Theseus quarreled, each casting doubt on the other's paternity. Minos called on his father, Zeus, to send thunder and lightning to prove his status. After this had been duly sent Minos flung his ring into the sea and challenged Theseus to fetch it back from the realm of his alleged father, Poseidon. Without hesitation Theseus dived in, was welcomed by Nereides, and was taken to the underwater palace of Amphitrite. There Thetis not only returned Minos's ring but also gave him the crown she had received from Aphrodite as a wedding gift. Theseus then returned to the ship and gave Minos his ring.

Having arrived in Crete, Theseus was seen by Ariadne, one of Minos's daughters. She fell immediately in love with the youth and was determined to help him. She first made Daedalus reveal to Theseus how the Cretan Labyrinth—where the Minotaur was housed—could be safely penetrated, then gave Theseus a spool of thread to unwind and thereby find his way out. Having cornered the Minotaur, Theseus wrestled it and tore off one of its horns, for the beast was vulnerable only to its own horns. With this horn Theseus stabbed the creature to death and then, following the thread he had unwound behind him, made his escape.

Quickly, Theseus and his companions escaped from Crete, taking Ariadne along with them. However, while she slept on the island of Naxos, or Dia, Theseus abandoned her and sailed off. There she was later found by Dionysos, who made her his bride. Theseus next stopped at Delos, where he instituted the festival of the Crane Dance around an altar consisting of twisting horns, the festival dance imitating the winding intricacies of the Cretan Labyrinth.

Unfortunately Theseus forgot to hoist the white sails as he had promised and so approached Athens with the black sails still in position. Aegeus, from his lookout on the Acropolis, saw the black sails. Thinking Theseus dead, he threw himself into the sea, which thereafter became known as the Aegean Sea.

Theseus was now proclaimed king of Athens and quickly made himself master over all Attica. He was later regarded, by fifth-century A.D. Athenians, as the founder of their democracy. He refounded the Isthmian Games and dedicated them to Poseidon. He then accompanied Heracles against the Amazons and he carried off their queen, Antiope, or Hippolyta, who bore him a son, Hippolytus. The Amazons tried to take their revenge by attacking Attica, but they were finally defeated by Theseus in the very heart of Athens. He then participated in the hunt for the Calydonian Boar and may even have been one of the Argonauts.

Theseus was with his Lapith friend, Peirithous, at his wedding to Hippodameia and joined in the famous fight between the Lapithae and the centaurs, when one of their drunken number tried to carry off the bride. Following the death of Hippodameia the two decided they would carry off a daughter of Zeus. They succeeded in abducting the young Helen from Sparta; she fell, by lot, to Theseus. However, as she was too young to marry, they left her in the village of Aphidnae with Theseus's mother, Aethra. They next decided to carry off Persephone for Peirithous. Descending to the Underworld, they were invited to sit down. The chairs on which they sat, however, bound them fast, and there they stayed until Heracles came to the Underworld during his last labor, to fetch Cerberus, and managed to release Theseus. Peirithous was not so lucky and remained in the Underworld for all time.

Theseus now married Phaedra, another of Minos's daughters, who bore him the sons Acamas and Demophoön. He and his family were, however, exiled from Athens for a year for killing the 50 sons of Pallas, the nephew of Aegeus who had tried to usurp his throne. They traveled to Troezen, where Phaedra fell in love with her stepson, Hippolytus. When the chaste youth rejected her advances she falsely accused him to Theseus of attempting to rape her. Theseus believed her and cursed his son, praying to his father, Poseidon, that Hippolytus should die that very day. As the youth fled in his chariot along the seashore, Poseidon sent a bull that frightened the horses and dragged Hippolytus to his death. Phaedra then hanged herself.

Upon returning to Athens, Theseus found that the hearts of the people had been turned against him by the Dioscuri, who had come during his absence and rescued Helen, taking Theseus's mother, Aethra, captive to act as Helen's slave. They had placed Menetheus on the throne, and as king he was proving immensely popular. Finding no place for himself in Athens, Theseus traveled to Scyros, where he died after accidentally falling off a cliff or being pushed by King Lycomedes, who

was jealous of Theseus's fame. He nevertheless returned in spirit, at least according to a later tradition, to help the Athenians at the Battle of Marathon. Though Menetheus had been made king in Theseus's absence, his sons were afterwards restored to the throne.

See also: Aegeus; Aethra; Ariadne; Crommyum; Daedalus; Helen; Heracles; Medeä; Minos; Minotaur; Periphetes; Phaedra; Procrustes; Sinis

Thesmaphoria
Greek

Annual festival in honor of Demeter that celebrates the foundation of laws, held in Athens and other parts of Greece.

See also: Demeter

Thespius
Greek

A ruler in the vicinity of Mount Cithaeron whose herds, along with those of his neighbor, Amphitryon, were being attacked by a huge lion. Heracles set out, when aged just 18, to kill the lion. The chase lasted for 50 days, during which time Heracles stayed with Thespius, who rewarded Heracles by giving his 50 daughters to him. He slept with a different maiden each night. Heracles killed the animal with a blow from his wild olive club and made himself a garment from the pelt and a helmet from the head, though most say that Heracles made these items later, after he had killed the Nemaean Lion.

Heracles' sons by the daughters of Thespius were later sent, under the leadership of Iolaus, to settle in Sardinia.

See also: Heracles

Thessaly
Greek

An ancient district of northern Greece that was divided from Macedonia by a mountain range. At the eastern end of the range rose Mount Olympus, and between it and Mount Ossa was the Vale of Tempe, a beautiful valley through which flowed the River Peneus. Modern Thessalía, the largest natural area in Greece, is an administrative district of north-central Greece. It was the center of an extensive

Neolithic settlement until c. 2500 B.C. and remained cut off from much of the culture and politics of classical Greece. Thessaly was taken by Macedonia in 325 B.C. and became a part of the province of Macedonia under Roman rule in 148 B.C. It later became a part of the Byzantine Empire with the decline of Roman rule, passing to the Turks in 1393. It was annexed to Greece in 1881.

Legend made it the site of the ten-year Titanomachia, the war between the Titans and the Olympian gods. It was also the homeland of the centaurs, the children of King Ixion who lived on the slopes of Mount Pelion. The Myrmidones, a warlike people, lived on the southern borders of Thessaly and were led to the Trojan War by Achilles, a Thessalanian prince who was the son of Peleus and Thetis.

See also: Ixion; Myrmidones; Titanomachia

Thetis

Greek

A daughter of Nereus and Doris, chief of the Nereides. When Hephaistos was thrown into the sea by Hera, Thetis and Eurynome looked after the unfortunate deity in an underwater grotto. She was loved by both Zeus and Poseidon. Helped by Briareus, she released Zeus on the occasion he was put in chains by the other Olympians. Upon being told by Themis, some say Prometheus, that any son born to her would be greater than his father, the gods decided that she should marry a mortal. That mortal was Peleus, king of the Myrmidones at Phthia in Thessaly. Having been advised what to do, he caught her while she slept on the shore at Sepias and held on while she transformed into many different shapes. He then made her his wife, their wedding being attended by all the immortals, who brought wonderful gifts. However, there was one omission from the guest list, the goddess Eris, who in a fit of pique threw among the guests a golden apple inscribed with the words, "To the fairest." Ownership of this apple, the Apple of Discord, was contested by Hera, Athene, and Aphrodite and would ultimately lead to the Trojan War.

Thetis and Peleus had a single son, Achilles, whom Thetis attempted to make invulnerable, either by dipping him in the waters of the River Styx—his ankle, where she held him, remaining his only vulnerable spot—or by immolating him on a fire. Peleus caught her in the act and shouted at her to stop, thus breaking the taboo that no mortal shall speak to his mermaid wife. She immediately returned to the sea but continued to watch over her son during his short but eventful life. She attempted to forestall the prophecy that Achilles would die at the Trojan War by hiding him among the daughters of King Lycomedes on the island of Scyros, but he was discovered and made to enlist along with his great friend, Patroclus.

Following the death of Patroclus, Thetis came to Achilles and gave him a new set of armor that had been made by Hephaistos. Wearing it he rejoined the fray and drove the terrified Trojans back to their city, killing Hector in the process. His return to the battle was short-lived, however, for a short time later he was killed by an arrow fired by Paris. Guided by Apollo, the arrow struck him in his one vulnerable spot, fulfilling the prophecy Thetis had attempted to circumvent.

See also: Achilles; Eris; Nereus; Peleus

Thisbe

Greco-Roman

Maiden from Babylon who was the lover of Pyramus. The couple was forbidden to marry or even to see each other, so they had to make do with conversing through a crack in the wall separating their houses. Through this they laid their plans to meet outside the city at the tomb of Ninus. Thisbe arrived first but fled from a lioness that had just killed an ox, dropping her cloak or her veil in the process, which the animal mauled and covered in blood. When Pyramus arrived and found the blood-stained clothing he thought Thisbe had been killed, and so he stabbed himself under a mulberry tree. Thisbe returned and found his body. Grief-stricken, she threw herself onto Pyramus's sword. Their parents buried the tragic couple in the same urn.

See also: Pyramus

Thoas

Greek

Son of Andraemon, king of Calydon, who sailed with 40 ships to join the Greek forces at Troy and was among those chosen to sneak into the city within the hollow belly of the Wooden Horse.

See also: Andraemon

Thrace
Greek
An ancient region of the eastern Balkan Peninsula that included Bulgaria and eastern Macedonia and was, from about 1300 B.C., peopled by savage cannibals. Today the area is split among Greece, Turkey, and Bulgaria. The Thracians had a rich and flourishing culture, passing on many important elements of religion, poetry, and music to the Greeks. Thrace came under Macedonian rule in 342 B.C., but it remained a warring and anarchic territory until it became a Roman province in 46 A.D. From the seventh century A.D. it was divided between the Byzantine Empire and the Bulgar kingdom, eventually falling to the Ottoman Turks in 1453. During the nineteenth century Russia tried to extend its influence over Thrace; the region was divided among its neighbors by treaties following World War I.

Threspotus
Greek
King of Sicyon to whom Pelopia, daughter of Thyestes, was priestess.

Thrinicia
Greek
Island where Helios maintained a herd of cattle. Against the warnings of both Teiresias and Circe, Odysseus's men slaughtered many of the beasts. When they put to sea again all save Odysseus were destroyed by Zeus.

See also: Odysseus

Thrugii
Greek
Town in Lucania where Herodotus was born.

Thule
Greco-Roman
The Greek and Roman name for the northernmost known land, Roman tradition saying that it was six days' sail from Britain. It was often applied to the Shetland Isles, the Orkneys, and Iceland, though later writers most commonly used it to refer to Scandinavia.

Thy(i)ades
Greek
The name given to the Attic votaries of the god Dionysos. Meaning "raging women," *thyades* is an apt description of the Bacchae. They were supposedly known by this name after Thyia, the first Attic woman to make sacrifice to the god.

See also: Dionysos

Thyestes
Greek
Son of Pelops and brother of Atreus. With the connivance of their mother they killed their half-brother, Chrysippus, and were compelled to flee to Mycenae, where they were hospitably received. However, following the death of King Eurystheus, Atreus seized the kingdom and banished his brother. Having already seduced Atreus's second wife, Aerope, Thyestes tricked Atreus into killing Pleisthenes, his son by his first wife, before leaving the city.

Atreus planned a grisly reprisal and lured his brother back to Mycenae on the false promise that he was ready to give him half the kingdom. Atreus then killed Thyestes' sons and served them to their father. When Thyestes realized what he had been eating he cursed his brother and fled once again. He now sought the advice of the Delphic Oracle, who told him to father a child on his own daughter. Going to Sicyon, where his daughter, Pelopia, was a priestess in the service of King Threspotus, he ravished her and fled.

Atreus subsequently visited Sicyon and, believing Pelopia to be the daughter of Threspotus, married her as his third wife. When she gave birth to Aegisthus, Thyestes' son, she exposed the child, but Atreus, believing the child to be his own, rescued him and reared him. Later Thyestes was captured and brought to Mycenae, where Atreus ordered Aegisthus to kill him. However, Thyestes disarmed the boy and, recognizing him as his own son, made himself known to Aegisthus, whom he then had kill Atreus. Thus, finally, Thyestes ruled Mycenae, though he was later routed by Agamemnon, Atreus's son, who had the help of Tyndareus. His son, Aegisthus, was later to become the lover of Clytemnestra, Agamemnon's wife, and with her connivance he killed Agamemnon and so avenged his father.

See also: Atreus; Pelops

Thyia
Greek

Reputedly the first Attic woman to sacrifice to Dionysos. As a result the Attic women who annually traveled to Parnassus to take part in the Dionysiac orgies became known as Thyiades, or Thyades. However, *thyades* means "raging women," an apt description of the Bacchae, which the Thyiades were another name for.

See also: Dionysos

Thyone
Greek

The deified name of Semele, mother of Dionysos, after her son had rescued her from the Underworld and taken her to live with him in Olympus.

See also: Dionysos; Semele

Thyrsus
Greek

A wand or rod wreathed with ivy and crowned with a fir cone; an attribute of the god Dionysos. It was also carried by his votaries, the Bacchae.

Tiber
Roman

The river that runs through Rome, personified in Father Tiber, the god of the river, possibly the deification of Tiberinus, who appeared to Aeneas as he sailed into the Tiber estuary following his journey to the Underworld. Father Tiber told Aeneas, in a dream, that Helenus's prophecy was about to be fulfilled. Forewarned, Aeneas set out next day and soon came upon the white sow and her 30 piglets at the future site of the city of Alba Longa, which would be founded by his son, Ascanius, some 30 years later.

Father Tiber also advised Aeneas to seek the help of Evander, the Greek king from Arcadia who now ruled the Palatine Hill. Aeneas followed the advice and was promised the help of the king, whose son, Pallas, joined the noble Trojan's forces.

See also: Aeneas; Ascanius

Tiberinus
Roman

Son of Janus and Camise who drowned in a river that was thenceforth known as the River Tiber.

Tilphussa
Greek

A well near Thebes where the seer Teiresias died when he drank the water; whether the water was actually poisonous remains unstated.

See also: Thebes

Timon
Greek

A legendary Athenian misanthrope, a hermit who hated mankind and thus would have nothing to do with it.

Tiryns
Greek

A town in the Argolis with massive fortifications built by Proetus, the king, with the aid of the Cyclopes. Proetus was succeeded by Megapenthes, who later exchanged his kingdom with his cousin, Perseus, who then became the king of Tiryns. Tiryns is, perhaps, most famous as being the home of King Eurystheus, who set Heracles his 12 Great Labors.

See also: Cyclopes; Heracles; Proetus

Tisamenus

Greek

The son of Orestes who inherited the kingdoms of Sparta and Argos. He was later overthrown by the Heracleidae and fled to the northern Peloponnesos; from there his bones were later returned to Sparta on the orders of the Delphic Oracle.

See also: Orestes

Tisiphone

Greek

1. The daughter of Alcmaeon and Manto, daughter of Teiresias; through her mother she appears to have inherited some of her grandfather's powers of prophecy.

2. One of the three winged, serpent-haired daughters of Ge who were known collectively as the Erinnyes or Furies; later they became known as the Eumenides. Her sisters were Alecto and Megaera. They were born from drops of blood that fell onto the earth, Ge, from the wound Cronos inflicted on Uranos. Living in Tartarus, the deepest, most infernal region of the Underworld, they were dispatched to avenge and punish unnatural crimes.

See also: Alcmaeon; Alecto; Erinnyes; Megaera

Titan

Greek

1. A generic term used to refer to any of the 12 giant children of Uranos and Ge whose names are variously given, the most common listing, that found in Hesiod's *Theogony*, being: Oceanos, Hyperion, Coeus, Crius, Iapetus, Cronos, Theia, Rhea, Themis, Mnemosyne, Phoebe, and Tethys. They were the primeval gods and goddesses who preceded the Olympian order led by Zeus, who overthrew them during the ten-year Titanomachia and condemned the male Titans to Tartarus, where they were guarded by the Hecatoncheires. After the battle Zeus burned incense at Ara, the altar of the centaur, in celebration of the victory. The Titans have a specific role in Orphic theogony, where they tore apart Zagreus, identified with Dionysos. Zeus swallowed his heart and gave birth to Dionysos for a second time with the aid of Semele. However, the Titans of this myth do not appear to be the pre-Olympian gods and goddesses but rather a race of primeval men and women.

2. A little-used generic term to refer to the second generation of gods born to several of the primeval gods and goddesses referred to as Titans, the original Titans. There were four second-generation Titans: Astraeus, Atlas, Epimetheus, and Prometheus. Technically, the Olympians were also second-generation Titans, and so they should be included in this generic grouping. Sometimes the term is applied to the Gigantes, the 24 giant sons of Ge with serpents' tails who attempted to avenge the imprisonment of their brothers, the original Titans.

Astronomical: The largest satellite in the solar system and the only one to have any atmosphere. With a mean diameter of 5,800 kilometers (3,625 miles), it is larger than the planet Mercury. It orbits Saturn at an average distance of 1,221,000 kilometers (764,000 miles), between the orbits of Rhea and Hyperion.

See also: Ara; Cronos; Dionysos; Oceanos; Prometheus

Titanomachia

Greek

The ten-year war waged in Thessaly between the new order of Olympian deities and the original primeval Titans, though the children of these Titans, the second-generation Titans, also seem to have played a part, for Atlas was said to have led the forces against Zeus and his companions. A second battle between the Olympian gods and giant sons of Ge, the Gigantes, was later fought; this battle sometimes has been referred to as the Titanomachia, or as at least a phase of it. Victorious Zeus condemned the original Titans to Tartarus, where they were guarded by the Hecatoncheires. In the second battle Zeus was again victorious, though he needed the help of Heracles; this time he consigned the conspirators to prisons below mountains, which thereafter were volcanic.

See also: Atlas; Tartarus

Tithon~es, ~us

Greek

Son of Laomedon and Strymon, the half-brother of Priam who was loved by Eos, the mother of his son, Memnon. Eos persuaded Zeus to grant him immortality but failed to ask for eternal youth. He lived as a shrunken old man, though some sources say he shrank away to become a cicada.

See also: Memnon

Tityus

Greek

The giant son of Zeus and the nymph Elara, though some sources make him another of the giant sons of Ge and Uranos. Hera, still implacable over Zeus's liason with Leto, sent Tityus to violate Leto as she came to Delphi with Artemis. Apollo and Artemis shot him, though some say Zeus struck him down with a thunderbolt, and he was condemned to the Underworld. There he was chained down, his body covering a total of two (or nine) acres. Two eagles (or vultures or snakes) constantly devoured his liver, which would renew itself according to the phases of the moon.

See also: Leto; Apollo; Artemis

Tlepolemus

Greek

A son of Heracles who, having killed his uncle, Licymnius, was forced to leave Argos and settle in Rhodes, where he became king and founded the cities of Lindos, Ialysos, and Camirus. From Rhodes he led nine ships to Troy, but his fate there is unknown.

See also: Heracles

Tmolus

Greek

King of Lydia and husband of Omphale. After his death Omphale famously purchased Heracles to serve as her slave for either one or three years.

Trachis

Greek

City or region from which Heracles invaded Oechalia and to where he sent Iole after he had killed Eurytus. Mount Oeta, atop which Heracles was immolated, was possibly located in Trachis.

Tricipitinus, Spurius Lucretius

Roman

Father of Lucretia who witnessed her suicide, along with her husband, Lucius Tarquinius Collatinus, and two others, Lucius Junius Brutus and Publius Valerius Poplicola, having first promised to avenge his daughter's rape by Sextus Tarquinius.

See also: Lucretia

Trident

Greco-Roman

The three-pronged spear or scepter that was an attribute of Poseidon, allegedly given to him by the Cyclopes; it later became the main attribute of Neptune.

Triptolemus

Greek

A son of Metaneira and Celeus (king of Eleusis). While the goddess Demeter was staying with his parents during her futile search for her daughter, Persephone, Demeter taught Triptolemus how to sow, tend, and reap grain, thus giving him a grounding in the arts of agriculture. As a result Triptolemus is credited with the invention of the plough. Demeter then sent him to travel the world and spread the knowledge she had given him. Arriving at Athens, he was said to have instituted the Thesmaphoria to honor Demeter. Following his death Triptolemus joined Aeacus, Minos, and Rhadamanthus as the fourth judge of the Underworld.

See also: Celeus; Demeter

Triton

Greek

1. The son of Poseidon and Amphitrite who is usually depicted in the form of a merman, half-man and half-fish, with a scaled body, sharp teeth, and a forked fish's tail. He had power over waves and possessed the gift of prophecy. He is usually shown blowing on a conch shell, a role in which he appears to be the personification of the wild sea. He gave his name to a class of lesser sea deities also known as Tritons and was said to have guided the Argonauts to the sea from Lake Triton.

2. One of a class of lesser sea gods, the Tritons, who take their name from the son of Poseidon, Triton. Like him they are half-man, half-fish and carry a shell trumpet, usually a conch, which they blow to soothe the waves, unlike Poseidon's son, who blows his conch to rouse the force of the sea. One legend says that Tritons once attacked the people of Tanagra, though they were normally perceived as neither malevolent nor benevolent.

Astronomical: The innermost and largest satellite of the planet Neptune, its orbit within that of Nereid. It is larger than the Moon that orbits the Earth.

See also: Amphitrite; Poseidon

Triton, Lake
Greek

In the company of Hermes, Zeus was walking along the shore of this inland lake when he suffered an agonizing headache. Fully realizing just what the cause was, Hermes quickly persuaded Hephaistos, some say Prometheus, to cleave open Zeus's skull. Doing this relieved the headache, for Athene sprang, fully grown and fully armed, from the wound. It was also the lake where the Argonauts had to enlist the help of Triton, the son of Poseidon, in order to navigate back to the sea.

See also: Athene

Troad
Greek

An ancient region of northwest Asia Minor; the ancient Troy was its chief city.

See also: Troy

Troezen
Greek

The birthplace of Theseus. Its ownership was once disputed by Athene and Poseidon; Zeus decreed they should share it equally.

Troilus
Greek

A son of Hecuba by either Priam or Apollo, he was killed by Achilles at the start of the Trojan War. The famous story of his love for the beautiful Cressida, the Greek Chryseis, and the actions of Pandarus, the lovers' go-between, has no place in classical legend. It was first described in the twelfth-century romance *Roman de Troie* by Benoît de Sainte-More and was later celebrated by both Geoffrey Chaucer and William Shakespeare. Shakespeare's five-act play *Troilus and Cressida* (1602) tells of Cressida falling in love with the Trojan Prince Troilus, but after he is killed—and she is exchanged for a Trojan prisoner of war—she transfers her attentions to Diomedes.

See also: Achilles; Cressida; Hecuba; Priam

Trojan Horse, the
Greek

Possibly better known as the Wooden Horse; the seemingly innocuous but treacherous gift left for Troy by the departing Greek forces. Within the hollow belly of the huge wooden animal were secreted more than 20 of the bravest Greek warriors. The horse was dragged within the city despite warnings by the priest Laocoön. While the city slept, the warriors descended from their hiding place, opened the city gates, and thereby enabled the Greek forces—which had feigned leaving and were awaiting the return signal—to enter and take Troy, thereby ending the ten-year Trojan War.

Trojan War
Greek

The greatest epic adventure of classical tradition concerns the abduction of the beautiful Helen by Paris and the resulting war. Traditionally thought to have been fought in 1184 B.C., the war probably took place earlier, if archaeological evidence of the destruction of the city can be accepted. Some people cite the refusal of Telamon to return Hesione to her father, Priam, as one of the causes of the Trojan War, but this is not the usual reason for the ten-year struggle.

The true cause lies with the Apple of Discord, which was thrown among the guests at the wedding of Peleus and Thetis by Eris, who was in a fit of pique at being omitted from the guest list. Inscribed with the words, "To the fairest," the apple was immediately claimed by Hera, Athene, and Aphrodite. To settle the dispute Zeus ordered that the three goddesses should be taken to Paris on Mount Ida and that he should award the apple as he saw fit. The three goddesses paraded naked before the hapless Paris, and each attempted to bribe him. Aphrodite promised that if she were awarded the apple she would enable him to carry off the most beautiful woman in the world; Paris decided in her favor.

The goddess accompanied Paris—who deserted his lover, Oenone, on Mount Ida—to Sparta, where he was warmly welcomed by Menelaus and his beautiful wife, Helen. While Menelaus was absent from Sparta, Paris and Helen eloped, taking a great deal of Spartan treasure with them, thus precipitating the Trojan War, now inevitable, as Helen's suitors had sworn an oath to defend her chosen husband.

Helen, the daughter of Zeus by Leda and sister of Castor, Polydeuces, and Clytemnestra, had been brought up in the court of Tyndareus, king of Sparta. Her beauty led to her abduction, while she was yet a young girl, by Theseus and Peirithous. She was later rescued from Attica by her brothers, the Dioscuri. All the noblest leaders vied for the hand of the beautiful maiden, and at the instigation of Tyndareus they swore to defend the rights of her chosen husband. She married Menelaus, brother of Agamemnon, who married her sister, Clytemnestra; when the Dioscuri were immortalized, Menelaus succeeded Tyndareus as king of Sparta.

Having fled with Paris, Helen left behind her husband and daughter Hermione. Menelaus thus called upon all those who had sworn the oath to make good. Agamemnon, the powerful king of Mycenae, was chosen commander in chief, and he gathered together the necessary forces. He was joined from the Peloponnesos by Nestor, the only one of Neleus's 12 sons who had been spared by Heracles. Diomedes, the son of Tydeus, had been one of the Epigoni, and he came from the same region, bringing along 80 ships as well as two fellow Epigoni—Sthenelus, the son of Capaneus, and Euryalus, the Argonaut. Tlepolemus, the son of Heracles, came from Rhodes and brought nine ships. Palamedes,

the son of Nauplius, joined the expedition from Euboea.

Although he had already assembled a mighty force, Agamemnon went to Ithaca along with Menelaus and Palamedes to attempt to persuade Odysseus to join them. When they arrived they found Odysseus, warned by an oracle not to go to Troy, ploughing a field with an ox and an ass, sowing it with salt. His pretence of insanity was uncovered when Palamedes placed Telemachus, Odysseus's infant son, in the furrow before the plough. Odysseus reacted as any sane father would, rescuing the child. Thus he was unable to avoid serving in the war.

Additional forces joined the huge fleet that Agamemnon was gathering. Ajax the Greater, the son of King Telamon, came from Salamis, bringing with him 12 ships as well as his half-brother, Teucer, the best archer in all Greece. Ajax the Lesser, the son of Oileus, came from Locris, bringing with him 40 ships. However, the Greek forces were incomplete, for an oracle had foretold that Troy would never be taken unless Achilles was among their number.

Thetis, Achilles' mother, had been warned by an oracle that her son would die if he went to Troy. She therefore sent him to the court of Lycomedes, king of Scyros, where he was hidden among the maidens of the court. Deidameia, one of Lycomedes' daughters, bore him a son, Neoptolemus. When Odysseus, Nestor, and Ajax the Greater visited Scyros to recruit forces for the coming war, Odysseus left a bundle of presents for the maidens, among them a shield and a spear. Achilles naturally chose these and so exposed himself. At the age of just 15, Achilles joined the Greek forces, taking with him his tutor, Phoenix, and his inseparable friend, Patroclus.

More forces came from Crete with King Idomeneos, who in the company of Meriones brought 100 ships. Having brought such a sizable force, he would share command with Agamemnon.

Assembling at Aulis, the huge fleet was fortunate to have along Anius, son and priest of Apollo in Delos; his three daughters had been dedicated to Dionysos. They had in return received the power to produce corn, oil, and wine at will, so the fleet would be amply provisioned.

Setting out from Aulis, the fleet mistakenly landed in and ravaged Mysia, the country of Telephus, the son of Heracles and Auge. When Telephus began to repel the invading Greeks, Dionysos caused him to stumble and fall over a vine, allowing Achilles to pounce on and wound him. This wound refused to heal, so Telephus consulted an oracle, who told him that only the inflictor of the wound could cure it. Telephus thus went to Achilles, who first was at a loss, for nothing he did cured the wound. Finally it dawned on him that he was not the true inflictor of the wound—the spear was. By scratching some rust from the weapon into the wound, Telephus was cured. The Greeks had been told they could not take Troy without the help of Telephus, and the grateful king showed them the correct route.

The fleet now reassembled at Aulis but was delayed by unfavorable winds after Agamemnon had angered the goddess Artemis by killing a hart. The seer Calchas foretold that only the sacrifice of Iphigeneia, Agamemnon's daughter, would appease the goddess. Reluctantly Agamemnon gave his permission, and the unfortunate girl was offered to Artemis. Different sources give varying outcomes of this phase of the story. Some say that the girl was indeed sacrificed, thus earning Agamemnon the enduring hatred of his wife, Clytemnestra. Others say that the goddess substituted a deer for the girl at the final moment, carrying Iphigeneia away to become her priestess in Tauris. Whatever the outcome, the winds changed in the Greeks' favor, and the fleet set sail.

Landing first on the island of Tenedos in sight of Troy, Achilles killed the king, Tenes, and his father, Cycnus. But Philoctetes, the famous archer-son of Poeas, suffered a festering wound, inflicted either by one of Heracles' poisoned arrows, which he now owned, or alternatively by a snakebite. The wound began to smell so offensively that Odysseus recommended they maroon Philoctetes on the island of Lemnos, which the Greeks quickly did.

Envoys were now sent to Priam to seek a peaceable solution to the forthcoming conflict. Menelaus, Odysseus, and Palamedes were hospitably received in Troy, where they were entertained by Antenor, who advised his people that Helen should be returned. The Trojans remained obdurate, so war became inevitable.

The Greeks attacked the mainland, though no one was eager to be the first to leap onto Trojan soil, for an oracle had forewarned that the first to do so would quickly die. Seeing his compatriots hesitate, Protesilaus of Thessaly leaped from his ship—even though he knew it meant certain death—and was soon cut down by the Trojans. Desolate with grief, his wife, Laodameia, the daughter of Acastus, pleaded the gods to let her husband return to her for just three hours. Zeus ordered Hermes to lead Protesilaus back from the Underworld, and when he died for the second time, Laodameia died with him.

The second to jump onto Trojan soil was Achilles, who soon distinguished himself as the greatest of all the Greek warriors. It was through him that Aeneas entered the war. Although he was the son of Priam's cousin, Anchises, he at first took no part; but Achilles raided his herds on Mount Ida, and he led his Dardanian forces against the Greeks. His mother, Aphrodite, frequently helped him and once carried him off after he had been wounded by Diomedes. He was even saved from Achilles by Poseidon, even though that god was normally hostile toward Troy.

For the first nine years of the war Troy remained impregnable, so the Greeks concentrated on raiding the surrounding countries, states, and cities that were allied with the enemy. In Thebes, in Cilicia, Achilles killed Eëtion, the father of Andromache, Hector's wife. Ajax the Greater raided the Thracian Chersonesus and, in Teuthrania, killed King Teuthras and abducted his daughter, Tecmessa.

In the tenth and final year of the war the Greeks at last concentrated solely on Troy, which was defended by Hector and Aeneas and many mighty allies, including Sarpedon, a son of Zeus, who was in command of the Lycian forces.

The Greeks were not hampered not only by the resistance of the Trojans but also by rivalries between their own chiefs. Odysseus first took his cruel revenge on Palamedes, who had uncovered his ruse on Ithaca. By bribing one of Palamedes' servants, Odysseus had a quantity of gold and a letter, written in Priam's name, hidden under Palamedes' bed. Odysseus then accused him of treason, his tent was searched, and the incriminating evidence was discovered. Palamedes was stoned to death by the entire Greek army as a traitor.

Next the famous quarrel between Achilles and Agamemnon broke out, and that is where Homer's *Iliad* opens. Agamemnon had been awarded Chryseis, the daughter of the Trojan priest Chryses, after she had been taken captive. Chryses came to ransom her but was roughly repulsed by Agamemnon, so he prayed to Apollo, who avenged him by sending a plague against the Greek forces. Calchas advised that only the return of Chryseis would free them of the terrible affliction, so Agamemnon unwillingly returned the girl to her father. He recompensed himself, however, by seizing Briseis, the concubine of Achilles. After losing his concubine Achilles sulked in his tent, obdurately refusing to take any further part in the fighting. Some sources, however, say that this was an attempt by Achilles to curry favor with Priam, for he had fallen deeply in love with Priam's daughter, Polyxena.

Things quickly turned in favor of the Trojans, so much so that Agamemnon was glad to grant a truce while Paris and Menelaus met in single combat in an attempt to settle the conflict. However, when Paris was on the point of losing the duel, Aphrodite carried him away, and the fighting once more broke out.

Diomedes wounded Aeneas and, amazingly, Aphrodite, then fought with Glaucus, a Lycian prince who was second in command to Sarpedon. However, when they remembered the friendship of their ancestors they gave up the fight and exchanged gifts. Hector and Ajax the Greater also fought in single combat until nightfall, when they too exchanged gifts, Hector giving Ajax a sword and receiving a purple baldric.

The hard-pushed Greeks were now forced to build a wall and trench, but when they were driven even farther back Agamemnon quickly offered to return Briseis to Achilles, still sulking in his tent. Achilles politely but firmly refused the offer. Odysseus and Diomedes then made a night raid on the Trojan lines, during which they killed the spy Dolon. They then killed Rhesus of Thrace and drove off his snow-white horses, for an oracle had foretold that once they drank from the River Scamander, and after they had eaten the grass of the Trojan Plain, Troy would not be taken.

The next day the Trojans once again took the upper hand and victoriously set fire to one of the Greek ships. Achilles, still refusing to return to the fray, loaned his armor to his friend Patroclus, who then led the Myrmidones back into the thick of things. At first successful, Patroclus killed Sarpedon, and his forces drove the Trojans back to their city walls. There Patroclus was wounded by Euphorbus, son of Panthous, and killed by Hector, who stripped him of his borrowed armor. Menelaus, who had killed Euphorbus, joined Ajax the Greater in rescuing Patroclus's body.

Prostrate with grief, Achilles finally made his peace with Agamemnon, who duly returned Briseis to him. Thetis then visited her son, bringing along new armor that had been made by Hephaistos. Wearing this Achilles rejoined the fighting and drove the terrified Trojans back to their city, Hector alone remaining outside to defend, even though Priam and Hecuba implored their son to return to the safety of Troy. Three times Achilles chased Hector around the walls of the city before he killed him, stripped him of his armor, and, tying him by the ankles, dragged him unceremoniously back to the Greek lines. Some sources vary these events, saying that Hector's body was dishonored after death by being dragged three times around the city walls with the purple baldric Ajax had given him.

Each morning, at dawn, still crazed with grief for Patroclus, Achilles would pull the corpse of Hector three times around the tomb of his great friend. Finally, Priam was led by Hermes, at night, to beg for the release of his son's body so that he could be honored with burial.

With Troy seeking reinforcements, the Amazons now came to its aid, led by their queen, the lovely Penthesilea, daughter of Ares and Otrere. She too was killed by Achilles, but as he struck the fateful blow he fell in love with her. Mourning over her, Achilles was ridiculed by Thersites, the most scurrilous and ugliest of all the Greeks. Achilles killed him with a single blow, angering Diomedes, a kinsman of Thersites. He threw Penthesilea's body into the Scamander, where it was then rescued and buried, some sources saying Achilles performed these tasks.

Memnon, the black-skinned son of Eos and Priam's half-brother, Tithones, king of Ethiopia, now came to reinforce the Trojans. He killed several Greeks, including Antilochus, the son of Nestor, before the vengeful Achilles faced him in single combat; Zeus weighed their fates in the balance, which tipped in Achilles' favor. Eos then persuaded Zeus to honor her dead son by causing birds, known as Memnonides, to rise from the flames of his funeral pyre and fly above it until they fell back into the fire as a sacrifice. These birds were said to visit Memnon's tomb on the Hellespont annually.

However, Achilles' own course had now run, and during a battle with Paris outside the Scaean Gate an arrow, fired by Paris but guided by Apollo, struck Achilles in his vulnerable heel. Ajax the Greater killed Glaucus, and he and Odysseus rescued the body of the fallen Achilles. They now quarreled violently over Achilles' armor. Two sources relate slightly different outcomes of this quarrel, but both say the armor was awarded to Odysseus. In the first, Odysseus simply killed Ajax; the second says that after the armor was awarded to Odysseus Ajax offended Athene and was sent mad, after which he killed the Greek sheep, believing them to be his enemies, then killed himself with the sword he had received from Hector.

Seeing so many heroes dead, the Greeks lost heart. In an attempt to bolster the Greek morale, Calchas said they must fetch to their ranks the bow and arrows of Heracles. As these were now in the possession of Philoctetes, Odysseus and Diomedes sailed to Lemnos to persuade the unfortunate archer to accompany them back to Troy. Having been marooned for nine years, he was at first reluctant to go but was eventually persuaded.

At Troy his festering wound was cured by either Machaon or Podalirius, sons of Asclepios, after which he challenged Paris to an archery contest. Mortally wounded, Paris returned to Mount Ida, where he sought out his former lover, Oenone, to cure him. She refused, but after relenting too late she took her own life.

With Paris dead, Helenus and Deiphobus quarreled over possession of Helen, now homesick for Sparta. When Deiphobus forcibly married her, Helenus fled to Mount Ida, where he either freely joined the Greek forces or was captured by Odysseus, for Calchas had foretold that only Helenus could reveal the secret oracles that protected Troy. Helenus freely gave the advice that the city would fall that summer if a bone of Pelops was brought to the Greeks, if Achilles' son, Neoptolemus, joined them, and if Athene's Palladium was stolen from the citadel of Troy.

Agamemnon immediately sent for the shoulder blade of Pelops; Odysseus, Phoenix, and Diomedes traveled to Scyros, where they persuaded Lycomedes to allow Neoptolemus to join their cause. Odysseus then gave Achilles' armor to Neoptolemus.

By this time the Trojans were also tired of the conflict, so Priam sent Antenor to Agamemnon to sue for peace. However, out of hatred for Deiphobus, Antenor plotted with the Greek leader as to how they might secure the Palladium and thus ensure the downfall of the city. They arranged for Odysseus, disguised as a filthy, runaway slave, to enter the city, which he did. Recognized by Helen, he gained much useful information from her, including the fact that she longed to return home. He then stole the Palladium, either on this occasion or on a later expedition in the company of Diomedes.

With the required talismans now secured, Odysseus is said to have devised the stratagem of the Wooden Horse, though some sources say the idea was put in his head by Athene. It is generally agreed that the goddess supervised the construction of the wooden animal by Epeius, the cowardly son of Panopeus, who inscribed on the horse a dedication to Athene. When it was completed, 23 or more of the bravest Greeks, including Neoptolemus, Odysseus, Thoas, and Sthenelus, climbed into its hollow belly and waited.

As night fell, Agamemnon ordered the Greek camp burned. They then sailed to the island of Tenedos, leaving behind just one man, Sinon, a cousin of Odysseus and grandson of Autolycus, whose cunning he appears to have inherited.

The following morning the jubilant Trojans discovered that the Greeks had gone, leaving the huge Wooden Horse on the shore. Believing it to be sacred to Athene, it was drawn, despite some opposition, up to the citadel. Cassandra rightly declared that the horse concealed Greek warriors. She was disbelieved, as usual. Laocoön, the son of Antenor and a priest to both Apollo and Poseidon, supported Cassandra, even going so far as to throw a spear at the horse's flank, causing a clatter of arms from within. This warning too was neglected, partly because of Sinon (he had allowed himself be taken prisoner, and he said the horse was the Greeks' atonement for having stolen the Palladium) and partly because of the misinterpretation of the fate that now befell Laocoön.

Being a priest of Apollo, he had sworn celibacy, but nevertheless he had married. To punish him the god sent two huge serpents, which crushed to death the priest and his two sons. Priam falsely interpreted this as punishment for smiting the Wooden Horse, and it was now welcomed within the city with much feasting and revelry. That evening, Helen and Deiphobus strolled around the horse. She, imitating the voices of the wives of each hidden warrior, called out to the heroes, but they managed to stifle their replies. As the city slept—having celebrated what they believed to be the end of the ten year war—Sinon lit a signal beacon, and Agamemnon and the Greek fleet sailed back from Tenedos. On the command of Antenor the warriors jumped down from inside the Wooden Horse, opened the gates, and razed the city.

Priam had been persuaded by his wife, Hecuba, to seek refuge along with she and her daughters before an altar sacred to Zeus. However, Neoptolemus slew their son, Polites, before their eyes, and when the frail king tried to intervene Neoptolemus mutilated him as well. Odysseus and Menelaus came across Deiphobus and Helen. Killing Deiphobus, Menelaus was about to kill Helen as well when he once again was overcome by her beauty, immediately pardoned her, and led her back to the safety of the Greek fleet.

Cassandra fled to the sanctuary of Athene but was forcibly dragged away by Ajax the Lesser and claimed as booty by Agamemnon. Her sister, Laodice, the wife of Helicaon, was swallowed up when the earth opened beneath her. Andromache, the widow of Hector, fell to the lot of Neoptolemus. The Greeks, eager to exterminate the entire family of Priam, went so far as to kill her infant son, Astyanax, by throwing him from the city walls, lest he should one day rise up to avenge his parents. Polyxena, whom Achilles had reportedly loved, was sacrificed to him, at his ghost's demand, by Neoptolemus to ensure favorable winds for the return voyage. Some sources say this happened at Troy, whereas others report Thrace, where the fleet had once again becalmed.

Hecuba, Priam's widow, fell to the share of Odysseus. He took her to the Thracian Chersonesus, where she avenged the death of one of her sons, Polydorus. According to Homer this boy, the youngest of Priam's sons, had been killed by Achilles, but later sources speak of another son of the same name. Shortly before the fall of Troy, Priam had entrusted him, along with a large quantity of gold, to Polymester, the king of the Thracian Chersonesus. When Troy fell Polymester murdered the youth, cast his body into the sea, and made off with the gold. Hecuba discovered the body and contrived to kill Polymester and his two sons. Having achieved her goal, she then turned herself into a bitch named Maera in order to evade the angry Thracians.

Few of the Trojans escaped slavery or death. The wise Antenor, his wife, Theano, and all their children were spared. They were reported to have sailed to the western coast of the Adriatic Sea, there founding Venice and Padua. Odysseus took ten years to return to his island realm of Ithaca, an epic journey related in Homer's *Odyssey*.

The tradition that Greek survivors of the Trojan War—notably Epeius, Diomedes, Philoctetes, and Odysseus—later emigrated to Italy was probably current sometime before 300 B.C. The origin of Aeneas's arrival remains unknown, though Homer's *Iliad* makes it clear that he escaped the final sack of the city. Carrying his blind father, Anchises, on his back and leading his son, Ascanius, he was given safe conduct through the Dardanian

Gate, some saying that he was afforded safe passage because he had betrayed Troy out of his hatred for Paris. Later Roman tradition says that he also took with him the Penates of Troy as well as the Palladium, the Palladium stolen by Odysseus having been only a copy. After a total of seven years of wandering he reached Italy, there becoming the founding father of the Roman nation. The epic cycle of the Trojan War remains, to this day, one of the most remarkable pseudo-historical accounts of a great classic battle and forms the most essential core of research for any student of the classical period in Greece.

See also: Achilles; Aeneas; Agamemnon; Ajax (1) and (2); Anchises; Aphrodite; Apple of Discord; Athene; Briseis; Calchas; Cassandra; Chryseis; Diomedes; Hector; Helen; Hera; Hermione; Memnon; Menelaus; Nestor; Odysseus; Palamedes; Palladium; Paris; Patrocles; Peleus; Penthesilea; Priam; Sparta; Telephus; Tenedos; Thetis; Tlepolemus; Wooden Horse.

Trophonius
Greek

Son of Erginus (king of Orchomenus in Boeotia) and brother of Agamedes. The brothers are credited with building many early temples and other religious buildings, including Alcmene's burial chamber at Thebes. They were also said to have built the first temple of Apollo at Delphi, but its beauty was such that all those who saw it pined away, so the gods destroyed it.

They also built a treasury for Hyrieus, king of nearby Hyria, but left a secret entrance, through which Agamedes removed a great deal of the treasure. Hyrieus caught Agamedes in a trap, and, afraid that he too would be uncovered, Trophonius decapitated his brother so that the king would be unable to recognize the thief he had caught. Trophonius was not long to survive his brother, for he was swallowed by the earth at Lebadeia, the gulf where he vanished becoming the site of an oracle. This oracle was first discovered by Saon, who was led there by a swarm of bees. There Trophonius instructed him in all the procedures of the oracle.

A simpler version of the deaths of the two brothers says that as a reward for building the temple of Apollo at Delphi they were allowed to live merrily within the sanctuary for six days and, on the seventh, die peacefully in their sleep.

See also: Agamedes

Tros
Greek

King of Phrygia, grandson of Dardanos, father of Ilus and Ganymede, the latter of whom he gave to Zeus as his cupbearer in return for some magnificent white horses. Tros is certainly the eponymous founder of Troy, but archaeological evidence suggests the amalgamation of three small towns: Dardania, founded by his grandfather, Dardanos; Tros; and Ilium, founded by his son, Ilus, the name later used by the Romans.

See also: Dardanos; Ganymede

Troy
Greek

Once thought of as a purely legendary city, the historicity of Troy was established between 1871 and 1873 when the German eccentric Heinrich Schliemann, putting his faith in the descriptions of Homer, excavated a site on the coast of Asia Minor near modern Hissarlik, close to the mouth of the Dardanelles. He unearthed the foundations of not only one but seven Troys, his most remarkable find being a hoard of exquisite gold ornaments. Since then two further layers of foundations have been uncovered, mainly through the work of Wilhelm Dörpfeld, who worked on the site during the 1890s.

Current thinking says that Bronze Age Troy was an important trading center on the main tin route between Europe and Asia. Frequently attacked—and subsequently rebuilt many times, as Schliemann's multiple foundations would seem to suggest—the Greeks, Cretans, and Phrygians all claimed to have had a hand in founding the city. In Homer's time, when the sixth or seventh Troy would have been standing, it probably had already absorbed three smaller towns: Dardania, Tros (Troy), and Ilium, each names being represented in the early legends of the city's foundation.

The three towns of Dardania, Tros, and Ilium were reportedly founded by Dardanos, Tros, and Ilus respectively. Dardanos was the son of Zeus by Electra the Pleiad. He received a piece of land from Teucer, the son of Idea and Scamander (formerly Xanthus), and on this land he founded the town of Dardania. His grandson was Tros, founder of the town by the same name and the father of Ganymede, who became cupbearer to Zeus, and Ilus, who founded Ilium. His son was Laomedon, who seems to have combined the three smaller towns into the larger conglomerate that became Troy.

Zeus assigned Apollo and Poseidon to Laomedon as laborers to build the city walls, but Laomedon refused to make them any payment. Poseidon in return sent a sea monster to which Hesione, Laomedon's daughter, was to be sacrificed, but the monster was killed by Heracles. Again Laomedon refused to reward Heracles, and the great hero later returned with Telamon to sack the city, killing Laomedon and all his sons but one, Podarces, who subsequently changed his name to Priam. Hesione was given to Telamon.

Priam was, of course, the king of Troy during the Trojan War, a war in which he lost his life during the final struggle and one that resulted in the destruction of the city. Recent research appears to suggest that this was the seventh city to stand on the site, designated Troy VIIa, and was sacked and burned c. 1250 B.C. Abandoned c. 1100 B.C., it was succeeded by a shantytown that itself seems to have been sacked c. 780 B.C. The final settlement on the site seems to have lasted until c. 400 A.D.

See also: Homer; Priam; Trojan War

Tullia

Roman

Daughter of King Servius Tullius, wife of Arruns Tarquinius, and thus sister-in-law to Tarquinius Superbus. She prompted her brother-in-law to murder her husband, then married Tarquinius Superbus. Tarquinius Superbus then threw the aging Servius Tullius down the senate steps, where he was killed by hired assassins and where his corpse was run over by Tullia as she returned from proclaiming Tarquinius Superbus's usurpation. She was, reportedly, covered from head to toe in the old man's blood.

Tullius, Servius

Roman

See Servius Tullius.

Tullus Hostilius

Roman

The third legendary king of Rome, second successor to Romulus. Reputed to have built the Curia Hostilia (Senate House) and to have captured Alba Longa, Tullus Hostilius seems, unlike his two predecessors, to have some historicity, though the stories associated with him are imaginary.

See also: Romulus

Turnus

Roman

Prince of Ardea in Rutulia. When Latinus agreed to the marriage of his daughter, Lavinia, to Aeneas after an oracle had told him that she would marry a foreigner, Juno incited Turnus to lay claim to the girl, saying that since he was of Mycenaean ancestry the oracle clearly referred to him, a view supported by Amata, Latinus's wife. When Ascanius, Aeneas's son, accidentally shot a pet stag, war was inevitable between the two factions.

Aeneas sought and gained the support of Evander, whose son, Pallas, joined Aeneas's forces. Turnus opened the hostilities by setting fire to Aeneas's ships. During the battle many great heroes were killed including Pallas, who was slain by Turnus, who stripped the body of a golden belt his victim always wore. To settle the conflict Aeneas and Turnus agreed to meet in single combat, though both Latinus and Amata tried to convince their son of his folly.

Jupiter pacified Juno by saying that the Trojan and Latin peoples should unite to form a single nation, thus swinging the balance in favor of Aeneas. As Turnus entered the combat his mother, believing him already dead, hanged herself. Aeneas mortally wounded Turnus, who asked that his father be allowed to have his body. Aeneas was about to concede this point when he noticed that Turnus was wearing the belt of his dead friend, Pallas. With a single thrust of his sword he dispatched Turnus.

See also: Aeneas; Amata

Tyche

Greek

Also: Tuche

Goddess of fortune whom the Romans equated with Fors Fortuna. Said to be a daughter of Zeus, she was considerably more popular with the Romans than she was with the Greeks. As goddess of luck she conferred or denied gifts with an air of abject irresponsibility. Tyche became a popular object of cult in the fourth century B.C. and later. She was regularly considered the presiding deity of a city in later times, most notably at Antioch, where the Tyche of Antioch, a statue portraying the goddess, was one of the most famous works of antiquity and was used on the city's coinage. She was portrayed juggling a ball that represented the instability of fortune, sometimes with a rudder seen as guiding men's affairs, with Amalthea's horn, or accompanied by Plutus, whose wealth she distributed willy-nilly.

Tydeus

Greek

Son of Oeneus, the king of Calydon. Banished for killing either an uncle or a brother, Tydeus fled to Argos, where he married Deiphyle, daughter of Adrastus, their son being Diomedes. Tydeus then joined his father-in-law and brother-in-law, Polyneices, who had married Adrastus's daughter, Argia, as one of the Seven Against Thebes. The other leaders of this ill-fated expedition were Capaneus, Hippomedon, Parthenopaeus, and Amphiaraus, who had married Adrastus's daughter, Eriphyle, and who was persuaded to join the expedition by his wife, who had been bribed by Polyneices with the necklace of Harmonia on the advice of Tydeus.

During the assault against Thebes, Tydeus killed Melanippus but was mortally wounded in the fight. Amphiaraus, who held a grudge against Tydeus for the bribing of Eriphyle, persuaded him to drink the brains of the dead Melanippus. Athene, who was fond of Tydeus, had been about to give him an elixir that would have conferred him with immortality. However, when she saw Tydeus drinking the brains of Melanippus she was so disgusted that she left him to die. In later portrayals of this tragic scene, immortality takes the form of the maiden Athanasia.

See also: Adrastus; Deiphyle; Diomedes; Oeneus; Seven Against Thebes

Tyndareus

Greek

King of Sparta, possibly the son of Perseus's daughter, Gorgophone. His brothers or half-brothers were Aphareus, Leucippus, Hippocoön, and Icarius, the latter two expelling Tyndareus from Sparta and claiming the throne. Tyndareus was later restored to his rightful position by Heracles, whose descendants later claimed Sparta as theirs.

Tyndareus married Leda, daughter of Thestius of Aetolia, and became the father by her of Clytemnestra. Her other children—Helen, Castor, and Polydeuces—were the result of her union with Zeus. As Tyndareus had once forgotten to sacrifice to Aphrodite, she retaliated by making his daughters unfaithful to their husbands. When the Dioscuri were immortalized, Tyndareus was succeeded as king of Sparta by his son-in-law, Menelaus, husband of Helen.

See also: Leda; Menelaus; Sparta

Typho~n, ~eus

Greek

A son of Tartarus and Ge, a gigantic monster who had 100 snakes' heads or dragons' heads for arms, wings on his back, thighs covered with vipers, and eyes of flame. He once tried to usurp Zeus's position by cutting the tendons out of Zeus's legs and hiding them in a bearskin. They were discovered by Hermes and Pan, who gave them back to Zeus. Typhon fled to Mount Nysa to gain strength from the magical fruits that grew there. Zeus pursued him, and as they ran they hurled mountains at each other. One of them became so covered in Typhon's blood that it later became known as Mount Haemus (from *haima*, "blood"). Finally Zeus crushed Typhon under the island of Sicily, where his fiery breath is the source of Mount Etna's constant smoke and flame.

Before being finally vanquished by Zeus, Typhon fathered many terrible beings on Echidne, among them the Chimaera, the

Nemaean Lion, the Hydra, Orthros, Ladon, and the Sphinx.

See also: Echidne; Etna

Tyro
Greek
Mother of the twins Pelias and Neleus by Poseidon. She exposed the children at birth, but they were found and raised by a horseherd. When Tyro later married Cretheus, founder and king of Iolcos, he adopted the boys as his own. Tyro then became the mother of Aeson by Cretheus, but upon Cretheus's death Pelias imprisoned Aeson and banished Neleus.

See also: Neleus; Pelias

Tyrrhenus
Romano-Etruscan
The mythical founder of the Etruscan people; no mythology remains of this character.

U

Udaeus
Greek
One of the five surviving Sparti, or "Sown Men," who sprang, fully grown and fully armed, from the ground when Cadmos sowed dragon's teeth at Thebes. These warriors started to fight among themselves until just five remained: Udaeus, Echion, Chthonius, Hyperenor, and Pelorus. They helped Cadmos build the Cadmea and became revered as the ancestors of Thebes.

See also: Cadmos; Sparti

Ulysses
Roman
The Roman form of Odysseus who retained all his earlier Greek attributes and adventures.

Underworld
Greco-Roman
The realm of Hades in Greek tradition that later became the realm of Pluto following Roman absorption. The world of the dead was not, as it usually is in modern religious beliefs, a singularly dread realm where only sinners went after death as Heaven was the sole domain of the gods and no mortal, unless specially blessed by the gods themselves, could ever aspire to reach its lofty heights. Instead the Underworld was considered to contain three very distinct regions: the Elysian Fields, where righteous and blessed souls were consigned to live a life of eternal bliss; Asphodel, where the indifferent remained for all eternity; and Tartarus, where the wicked were sent to join the likes of Tantalus, Ixion, and Sisyphus. This lowest region, the nearest equivalent to Hell, was also the home of the Erinnyes or Furies. They were dispatched to hound those

who rightly belonged within its confines but had yet to die.

To decide which region best suited each new soul entering the Underworld, Hermes brought them before three judges: Aeacus, Minos, and Rhadamanthus. En route they crossed five rivers: Styx, Acheron, Cocytus, Lethe, and Phlegethon, or Pyriphlegethon. They encountered the ferryman Charon, who ferried them across the Styx upon receipt of an *obolos*, and the two-headed guard dog of the Underworld, Cerberus.

See also: Hades; Pluto

Urania
1. Greco-Roman
One of the nine Muses, being that of astronomy and the sciences. Her name simply means "heavenly," and she is usually depicted with a staff pointing to a globe. She was loved by Strephon, a shepherd of Arcadia, who lamented her when she was lost to him.

2. Greek
A title given to Aphrodite to imply her "heavenly" countenance, especially in Oriental countries; also applied variously to other non-Greek goddesses.

See also: Muses, the

Uran~os, ~us
Greek
The personification and god of the sky and the heavens, the most ancient of all the Greek gods and the first ruler of the universe in the very earliest Greek cosmology. He was the parthenogenetic son of Ge and brother of Pontus, who was similarly created. By his mother, Ge, Uranos became the father of the Hecatoncheires, or Centimani (Cottus, Briareus, also

called Aegaeon, and Gyas, or Gyges), the one-eyed Cyclopes (Brontes, Steropes, and Arges), and the 12 Titans.

Having first quelled a rebellion by the Cyclopes, whom he consigned to Tartarus, Uranos now had to deal with the uprising of the Titans instigated by his mother, Ge, though one of them, Oceanos, refused to take part in the rebellion. Cronos, the youngest of the Titans, was given a flint sickle by his mother, which he used to castrate Uranos. Drops of blood from the wound fell onto Mother Earth (Ge), and she bore the Gigantes, Meliae, and the three Erinnyes (Alecto, Tisiphone, and Megaera). From the drops of blood that fell onto Pontus (Sea), Aphrodite was born.

With Uranos deposed a new order took his place. The Titans freed the Cyclopes, but Cronos, now supreme, quickly consigned them back to Tartarus, where they were guarded by the Hecatoncheires.

Astronomical: Discovered by chance in 1781 by Sir William Herschel, Uranus is a gas giant that has its axis tilted over to almost 90°; as such it might be considered to roll around its orbit on its polar axis rather than spin around it, as is the case with all other planets in the solar system. It is slightly larger in size than Neptune, having an approximate equatorial diameter of 50,800 kilometers (31,750 miles), and lies at an average distance of 2,869 million kilometers (1,794 million miles) from the sun. The planet has at least five known satellites: Miranda, Ariel, Umbriel, Titania, and Oberon.

See also: Cronos; Ge; Pontus

V

Valerii

Roman

One of the five powerful families that seem to have dominated the Roman republic toward the end of the fifth century B.C. The other four families were the Aemilii, Claudii, Cornelii, and Manlii. Each decisively affected the myths and legends of the Roman era, tampering with content to enhance the status of their own family.

Vegoia

Romano-Etruscan

Also: Begoe

Ancient Etruscan goddess who is believed to be the root of the Roman goddess Egeria.

Veii

Roman

Ancient Etruscan city some 12 miles from Rome that controlled the crossing of the River Tiber at Fidenae and thus exerted a powerful influence over the entire area to the south, including a vital salt route. It also rivaled neighboring Caere as the most Hellenized of the early Etruscan cities.

At the turn of the fifth and fourth centuries B.C. the Romans attacked Veii, a fact that is not disputed in history. However, the later belief that the city withstood the Romans for ten years surely owes more than a little to the stories of the siege of Troy. The city finally fell to Rome in 396 B.C., when Marcus Furius Camillus was appointed dictator, having been sole governor of Rome for the duration of the war.

Surviving legend tells very little about the siege of Veii other than how at one point the Romans captured a Veientine soothsayer who revealed that the city would only fall when the Alban Lake was drained. When this story was confirmed by the Delphic Oracle, Camillus ordered the lake to be drained, then ordered his troops to tunnel beneath the city. Having reached a point directly below the temple they heard the Veientine king about to sacrifice to Juno, saying that whosoever made the sacrifice should win the war. Quickly bursting through the floor the Romans offered the sacrifice and then stormed the city. The Veientine Juno was then carried to Rome in triumph.

It is not hard to see the parallel between the tunnel under the city—which gave the Romans a secret entrance to the city—and the earlier Greek stratagem of the Wooden Horse.

Vela

Greek

The sail of the *Argo Navis* that was placed in the heavens along with three other parts of the ship: Carina, the Keel; Puppis, the Poop; and Pyxis, the Ship's Compass.

Astronomical: A constellation of the southern celestial hemisphere that is located between approximate right ascensions 8h00m and 11h00m, declination from –36° to –57°.

Venus

Roman

An ancient Italian goddess of unknown origin who was originally associated with springtime, gardens, and cultivation but also with the ideas of charm, grace, and beauty. She was later identified by the Romans with Aphrodite when her cult was introduced to Rome from Mount Eryx toward the end of the third century B.C., though legend suggests that Aeneas, her son, brought her cult with him when he landed in Italy to found the Roman race. Thus she also personified love and fertility and became the mother of the cherubic, impish Cupid. She was the patroness of Julius Caesar and Augustus as well as the city of Pompeii, where remains of many Venus representations have been recovered. Her Sicilian name was Cythera, which was used as her surname.

Astronomical: The second-closest planet to the sun, lying between the orbits of Mercury and the Earth. Venus is, at times, the brightest object in the night sky except the Moon and has become well known as the Morning or Evening Star. The planet has an equatorial diameter of 12,102 kilometers (7,594 miles) and lies at an average distance of 108 million kilometers (68 million miles) from the sun. Venus has no satellites and is roughly the same size as the Earth.

See also: Aeneas; Aphrodite

Vergilia
Roman
The wife of Coriolanus who, with his two young sons and his mother, Volumnia, pleaded with him to withdraw his men, who were besieging Rome after he had sided with the Volscians.

Vertumnus
Roman
An ancient Etruscan deity who was absorbed into the Roman tradition as the god associated with the ripening of fruit and hence with the seasons of the years. Having the ability to change shape, he used this power to great effect after he had fallen in love with, and been rejected by, Pomona. Changing himself into an old woman, he pleaded his cause so eloquently that Pomona changed her mind. At his festival, held on August 13 to coincide with the ripening of fruit, people made offerings of the first fruits of harvest, a definite forerunner of the modern harvest festival.

See also: Pomona

Vesta
Roman
Identified with the Greek Hestia, Vesta was the goddess of the hearth and household, fire, and purity and was the patroness of bakers. The daughter of Saturn, she was supreme in the conduct of religious ceremonies and prepared the food of the gods. As goddess of the household hearth, regarded as the center of every home, she in effect had an altar in every home. However, her sanctuary on the Forum in Rome became of paramount importance, for so long as the eternal flame burned within, Rome would not fall. Entry to her sanctuary was permitted only to the Vestal Virgins, servants who tended the sacred flame. As she was regarded as the national guardian of the Roman republic, Vesta's festival, the Vestalia (7–15 June), became one of the most important events of the religious calendar.

Astronomical: One of the larger asteroids, having an approximate diameter of 550 kilometers (344 miles).

See also: Hestia

Vestal Virgin
Roman
Priestess or priestesses of the cult of Vesta who tended the sacred flame that eternally burned in her temples and who officiated at ceremonies in honor of the goddess. For some rather vague reason, the Vestal Virgins became subject to the most intense and jealous discipline. They entered her service at the age of six or seven and took a vow of chastity, which was absolute for the 30-year period they remained in the goddess's service. Any girl who broke this vow would, in the early years of the cult, be whipped to death. In later years the punishment consisted of being whipped and then walled in a tomb alive. Due to the national importance of the cult of Vesta, the Vestal Virgins enjoyed a position of unrivaled high prestige within the social order of Rome.

Victoria
Roman
An ancient agricultural deity who became increasingly associated with Roman military successes. As the personification of victory she was associated with both Mars and Jupiter.

Vilvanus
Roman
A god of the woods who had some attributes in common with Faunus, perhaps being simply an aspect of the latter.

Virgil
Roman

Full name Publius Verilius Maro Virgil (70–19 B.C.). Roman poet born in Andes near Mantua in Cisalpine Gaul, where his father was a small-scale farmer. Educated at Cremona and Mediolanum (Milan), he arrived in Rome at the age of 16 to study rhetoric and philosophy before returning to his father's farm shortly before it was confiscated. Virgil, however, was amply compensated and returned to Rome, where he became a court poet. In 37 B.C. his *Eclogues,* a series of ten pastoral poems that he had started some six years before while still on his farm, were received with great enthusiasm. Shortly afterwards he left Rome and moved to Campania, though he still retained the patronage of Maecenas, a Roman statesman and trusted counselor of Augustus whose name has become a synonym for a patron of letters.

Having acquired a considerable degree of affluence under Maecenas, Virgil was able to boast a villa at Naples and a country house near Nola. His *Georgics* or *The Art of Husbandry,* a series of four books dealing with the various arts of farming, appeared in 30 B.C. and confirmed him as the foremost poet of his age. The remaining 11 years of his life were devoted to his masterpiece, *Aeneid,* considered the most important poem in Latin literature and a great influence of later European works. The work was almost complete by 19 B.C., when Virgil left Italy to travel Asia and Greece. He landed in Athens, returning home simply to die. At his own wish he was buried in Naples, for many hundreds of years his tomb being revered as a sacred place.

The supremacy of Virgil in Latin poetry was immediate and almost unquestioned. His books had become classics in his own lifetime and had, soon after his death, become textbooks throughout western Europe. By the third century A.D. they ranked as sacred works and were regularly used for divination purposes.

Virgo
Greco-Roman

"The Maiden"; said to be Astraea, goddess of justice and the daughter of Zeus and Themis. After her death she was placed in the heavens as the constellation Virgo, with her scales of justice, given to her by her mother, next to her in the sky as the constellation Libra. To the Romans the constellation represented Ceres, goddess of the harvest, holding a spike of wheat.

Astronomical: A large constellation straddling the celestial equator and forming the sixth sign of the Zodiac (August 24–September 23). Virgo lies between approximate right ascensions 11h40m and 14h10m, declination from +14° to –22°. The star Spica (a Vir), which the Romans took to represent the spike of wheat held by Ceres, is an eclipsing variable of magnitude 0.91–1.01, spectral type B1V, at a distance of 260 light-years.

See also: Astraea; Ceres; Libra

Virtus
Roman

The personification of manly valor, represented as a victorious, armed, virginal youth.

Volscian
Roman

The Volscians were an ancient people who inhabited the town of Corioli (modern Monte Giove). The town was captured in 493 B.C. by Cnaeus Marcius, after which he received his cognomen Coriolanus. He, however, sided with the Volscians and attacked Rome.

Volumnia
Roman

The mother of Coriolanus who, with his wife, Vergilia, and their two young sons, came to plead with her son to withdraw his forces, then attacking Rome following his allegiance with the Volscians.

Vulcan(us)
Roman

An ancient Italian god—like Jupiter, a god of the sun—and the first god of the Tiber, he evolved to become the god of fire and patron of metalworkers, sometimes known as Mulciber, who was eventually identified with the Greek Hephaistos. Originally called

Volcanus as the god of volcanoes, he was born when a spark fell from the heavens onto a human girl. His temples were sensibly sited outside city walls. Often invoked to avert fires, he had associations with thunderbolts and the sun and was finally interpreted in terms of life-giving warmth. His main festival, the Volcanalia, was held on August 23.

Having become equated with Hephaistos, Vulcan naturally absorbed many of his attributes and qualities. His main legends concern his involvement with Aeneas, in the role taken earlier by Hephaistos. He supplied Aeneas with wonderful armor, which included a magnificent shield that depicted the future history of Rome, including the great victory of Augustus at the Battle of Actium. According to Evander in relating a story to Aeneas, his son, Cacus, was killed by Heracles on the Palatine Hill.

See also: Aeneas; Hephaistos; Jupiter

Vulci
Romano-Etruscan

One of the oldest and most powerful Etruscan cities that lay in close proximity to the somewhat more powerful Tarquinii, about 40 miles north of Rome.

⇒ W ⇐

Wandering Rocks

Greek

Sometimes confused with the Symplegades, these rocks were off the coast of Sicily, not in the Strait of Messina. Safe passage between them could be affected, as done by the Argonauts, with the help of the Nereides.

Werewolf

Greek

Though the concept of a man-wolf—a werewolf—might be considered modern, the idea was current during classical times. Indeed, at the feast of Zeus Lycaeus a cauldron of miscellaneous animal entrails and those of a man was stirred. Participants in the celebrations would eat the resulting mixture, and anyone who ate a human part would be instantly transformed into a wolf. The transformation of a man into a wolf frequently appears in classical mythology, notably the story of Lycaon.

See also: Lycaon

Wooden Horse

Greek

Also known as the Trojan Horse, the stratagem by which the besieging Greek forces finally managed to gain entry to, and thus sack, the city of Troy at the end of the ten-year Trojan War. Homer reports that the idea of the Wooden Horse was thought up by Odysseus, though the scheming Athene seems to have had more than a passing hand in its conception. It was built by the cowardly Epeius and had room within its hollow belly to hide upwards of 23 of the greatest Greek heroes, Odysseus among them. It was inscribed, "To Athene from the Greeks for their safe return," then left on the shore when the Greek fleet sailed to the island of Tenedos.

Alerted by Sinon, the only Greek that remained on Trojan soil, the warriors within the horse emerged while the city slept, its citizens having dragged the huge edifice within the confines of the city amid much celebrating. The warriors opened the gates to the city and allowed the returning Greek forces to enter and sack Troy.

See also: Trojan War; Troy

Xanthus

Greek

1. The original name of the River Scamander, the river running across the Trojan Plain; its name was changed when Scamander of Crete jumped into its waters.

2. One of the horses of Achilles along with Balius. They were the offspring of Zephyrus, the west wind, and Podarge, the Harpy. Given to Achilles' father, Peleus, at his wedding to Thetis, they passed into the ownership of Achilles, who took them to the Trojan War. They wept at the death of Patroclus, and Xanthus was briefly given the power of speech by Hera to warn Achilles of his approaching death.

See also: Achilles; Scamander

Xuthus

Greek

Son of Hellen and brother of Dorus and Aeolus, he was allotted the Peloponnesos when he and his brothers divided Greece among themselves. Instead he came to Athens, where he married Creusa, daughter of Erechtheus, the king. Their sons were Ion and Achaeus. Following the death of Erechtheus, Xuthus judged that Creusa's eldest brother, Cecrops, should succeed his father, a decision that led his other brothers-in-law to expel him from Athens. After that he settled in Achaea, though some sources say it was Xuthus rather than Cecrops who succeeded Erechtheus.

See also: Aeolus; Cecrops; Creusa; Dorus

⇛ Z ⇚

Zagreus

Greek

A son of Zeus according to a Cretan legend in which the Titans tore him to pieces and ate him alive, though Athene saved his heart. He was later identified with Dionysos when the ceremonies of his cult were designed to promote closer harmony and union with the god.

Zalmoxis

Greek

A Thracian deity who closely resembled Dionysos and provided his votaries with immortality after death. Petitions to the god were accompanied by the barbarous ritual of hurling a man onto the points of three spears. If he died it was a sign that the prayers had been heard. If he lived, they tried again.

See also: Dionysos

Zephyrus

Greek

The god, and thus the personification, of the west wind. One of the sons of Astraeus and Eos and the brother of Hesperus, Notus, the south wind, Eurus, the east wind, and Boreas, the north wind. He lived with the other three winds in a cave on the floating island of Aeolia, where they were released by Aeolus, either at his whim or at the command of the gods. Along with Apollo he loved the youth Hyacinthos, who was accidentally killed by a quoit thrown by Apollo. At first rough and forceful, Zephyrus was later tamed, perhaps through his marriage to Chloris.

See also: Aeolus; Astraeus; Boreas; Eurus; Notus

Zetes

Greek

The twin brother of Calais, the winged offspring of Boreas and Oreithyia, and brother of Cleopatra. The twins accompanied Jason on his quest for the Golden Fleece and were thus Argonauts. In Thrace they drove away the Harpies that were plaguing the blind prophet Phineus, Cleopatra's husband, and freed from prison the sons of Cleopatra, their cousins, whom Phineus had falsely suspected.

See also: Calais

Zethus

Greek

Twin brother of Amphion, the sons of Antiope by Zeus. Having given birth to the divinely conceived twins, Antiope was divorced by her husband, Lycus, king of Thebes, who then married Dirce, who treated Antiope cruelly. Meanwhile, Zethus and Amphion had been reared by cattleherds on Mount Cithaeron. When they had grown to manhood they were told the truth and returned to Thebes to exact their revenge. They killed Lycus and then disposed of Dirce, tying her to the horns of a wild bull, which threw her body into a well that henceforth bore her name. The twins then took possession of the city and built the lower fortifications below the Cadmea. Zethus married Thebe, who gave her name to the city; Amphion married Niobe. The twins then jointly ruled Thebes.

See also: Amphion; Lycus; Niobe; Thebe

Zeus

Greek

The supreme god of the Greek pantheon, later equated with the Roman Jupiter or Dis (Pater), omnipotent king of gods, god of the sky, weather, thunder, and lightning (hence called "the Thunderer"), ruler of mankind, gatherer of clouds, and especially associated with mountaintops, though his greatest temples, at Dodona, Olympia, and Nemea, all lie in peaceful valleys. Zeus was also revered as the god of home and hearth and dispenser of good and evil, of hospitality to strangers, and of oaths. He was identified with the snake-formed Meilichius, "the Placable," and Ktesios, the god of storerooms. His attributes were the scepter, thunderbolt, eagle, a figure of Victory in one hand, and his aegis, a sacred goatskin shield, representing the thundercloud. The oak, the eagle, and mountain summits were sacred to him, and his sacrifices were usually bulls, cows, and goats, the latter holding special significance through his legendary connection with the she-goat Amalthea. The Dodonean Zeus was usually portrayed wearing a wreath of oak leaves, whereas the Olympian Zeus was sometimes wearing one of olive leaves.

His origins appear to be the Achaeans, who entered Greece and introduced his worship c. 1450 B.C. together with his consort Dione, who some sources, including Homer, make the mother of Aphrodite by Zeus. However, her worship did not penetrate south of Epirus, where the earliest of Zeus's sanctuaries was located, at Dodona. Here the sacred rustling of oak leaves was interpreted as the oracle of the god. Oak trees are especially sacred to Zeus, for they were believed to be struck by lightning far more frequently than was any other species of tree. He was also worshipped at Olympia in Thessaly and at Olympia in Elis.

On Crete Zeus was a young god, the consort of the dominant Mother Goddess, though the more usual legend makes him the youngest son of Cronos and Rhea. He was replaced with a stone wrapped in swaddling when his father sought to swallow him, as he had his other children. Rhea, at least according to Minoan tradition on Crete, hid the baby Zeus in the Dictaean Cave, where her priests, the Curetes, clashed their weapons together in order to drown the baby's cries while the she-goat Amalthea acted as his nurse.

Having safely reached manhood, Zeus was first counseled by Metis, a daughter of Oceanos; upon her advice and with Rhea's help, she administered a potion to his father, Cronos, which made him vomit first the stone he had swallowed in place of Zeus and then his other children—Hestia, Demeter, Hera, Hades, and Poseidon. Together they made war against their father and the other Titans, who were led by Atlas, though the latter's brothers, Prometheus and Epimetheus, stood alongside Zeus.

This war, known as the Titanomachia, was waged in Thessaly and lasted for ten years until Ge promised Zeus victory if he would free her sons, the Hecatoncheires, and the Cyclopes from their imprisonment in Tartarus. The Cyclopes provided the three deities with divine weapons. To Zeus they gave his thunderbolt, to Hades his helmet of invisibility, and to Poseidon his trident. Thus armed, the three quickly overcame Cronos as the Hecatoncheires stoned the other Titans. Defeated, they were consigned to Tartarus, where they were guarded by the Hecatoncheires. As punishment Atlas, the leader of the Titans, was made to carry the sky on his shoulders for eternity. In this way the third generation of deities came to rule supreme.

Dividing the universe by lot, Hades became god of the Underworld, Poseidon god of the sea, and Zeus god of the sky; earth remained the common territory of all three. Zeus established his court on the lofty summit of Mount Olympus between Macedonia and Thessaly, and there he lived in a wondrous palace along with Poseidon, their sisters, Hestia, Hera, and Demeter, and seven other great deities: Aphrodite, Athene, Apollo, Artemis, Hephaistos, Ares, and Hermes. Hades also had a palace on Olympus but usually resided in the Underworld. Likewise Poseidon, who also had a palace beneath the sea. At a later date Hestia was replaced as one of the Olympian deities by Dionysos.

A post-Homeric story tells that Zeus had to put down a rebellion by the Gigantes, 24 giant sons of Ge with serpents' tails who tried to avenge the imprisonment of their brothers, the Titans, by attacking Olympus. This rebellion was led by Alcyoneus and included the likes of Porphyrion, Ephialtes, Mimas, Pallas, Enceladus, and Polybutes. A terrible struggle ensued on earth and in

Olympus, and victory was won only after the intervention of Heracles—appearing before his apotheosis and indicating the late origin of the myth—who provided the gods with a magic herb of invulnerability and always leveled the final blow. Enceladus was imprisoned beneath Mount Etna on Sicily and Polybutes under Mount Nisyrus, the interments being seen as the cause of the volcanic natures of the mountains.

Ge now brought forth the terrible monster Typhon to avenge the destruction of her sons. Fathered by Ge's own son, Tartarus, Typhon was the largest being ever created, his huge limbs ending in serpents' heads, his eyes breathing fire. As he approached Olympus the gods fled, disguised as animals, to Egypt. Zeus assumed the form of a ram, Apollo a crow, Dionysos a goat (his inclusion again indicating the late origin of the myth), Hera a white cow, Artemis a cat, Aphrodite a fish, Ares a boar, and Hermes an ibis. Athene alone remained undaunted and persuaded Zeus to attack Typhon. After a terrible battle—during which Zeus was temporarily incapacitated but rescued by Hermes and Pan—Zeus finally destroyed Typhon with his thunderbolt and buried him under Mount Etna, once more causing the volcanic nature of that mountain.

Unlike their brothers, the Titans, Prometheus and Epimetheus had not been imprisoned, for they had sided with Zeus in his epic struggle. Prometheus became regarded as the benefactor of mankind when he stole fire from Heaven, an act that brought about divine retribution. Prometheus was chained to a crag in the Caucasus, where an eagle or a vulture tore at his liver during the day, the organ regenerating each night. There he remained until Heracles, with Zeus's permission, shot the eagle and freed Prometheus. To punish mankind Zeus ordered Hephaistos to make the first woman, Pandora, who married Epimetheus. Having done so she opened a box she had been given, and from it all the ills that plague mankind escaped, Hope alone remaining at the bottom.

Luxuriating in the warmth of the fire stolen for them by Prometheus, mankind became impious, thus ensuring the anger of Zeus. He decided to wipe out mankind by releasing the great Flood. However, Prometheus overheard Zeus's plans and relayed them to his son, Deucalion, who built a wooden vessel in which he and his wife, Pyrrha, daughter of Epimetheus, would ride out the storm, which covered the face of the earth for nine days.

Reigning supreme in Heaven, Zeus first married Metis, an Oceanid, the daughter of Oceanos and Tethys. However, while she was pregnant with Athene an oracle foretold that any son born to Metis would be greater than his father. Mindful of how he had overthrown his own father, Zeus swallowed Metis. Sometime later he was walking on the shores of Lake Triton when he suffered an agonizing headache. Realizing the cause of the pain, Hermes persuaded either Hephaistos or Prometheus to cleave open Zeus's skull. From the wound sprang the fully grown and fully armed Athene.

Zeus then married Themis, a Titan daughter of Uranos and Ge. Their children were the Horae and the Moirae, though some sources say that the latter were the children of Erebos and Night and that even Zeus himself was subject to them. There followed a daylong marriage to Mnemosyne, during which the nine Muses were conceived. Zeus next married his reluctant sister, Hera, whom he sought out in the form of a cuckoo on the island of Crete, perhaps in Argos, their wedding night being spent on Samos. Zeus became the father by her of Ares, Hebe, and Hephaistos. The latter may have been the parthenogenous son of Hera, a situation that is more likely, as Hephaistos was apparently present at the birth of Athene, and if he had been the son of Zeus and Hera he would have attended the event before he himself was even born.

On one occasion Zeus's authority was challenged by his wife in collaboration with Poseidon and Apollo. This revolt was successful in putting Zeus in chains, but he was freed by Briareus and Thetis, and he punished Hera, hanging her by the wrists to the sky, an anvil on each ankle. Apollo and Poseidon were sent to serve King Laomedon as bondsmen, and there they built the great, unbreachable walls of Troy. Apollo later killed the Cyclopes after Zeus had killed his son, Asclepios. Zeus punished him by sending him to serve King Admetus of Thessaly.

Though oft-married, Zeus is perhaps most famous for his many extramarital liaisons. He became the father of numerous beings by these affairs, which his jealous wife was always trying to end or at least to hinder. He was the father of Persephone by his own sister, Demeter, and of the Charites or Graces by Eurynome. Four of the Olympian deities were sons of Zeus by mortal women. Apollo and Artemis by Leto; Hermes, his herald, by Maia; and Dionysos by Semele, whom he appeared before as a mortal. Hera persuaded the hapless Semele to ask her mysterious lover to appear in his true form. Zeus reluctantly agreed, and Semele was consumed by the fire from his thunderbolt. Zeus rescued the unborn child from the ashes and sewed him up in his thigh; Dionysos was thus delivered three months later. Zeus is also one of the possible fathers of Eros by Aphrodite, though both Hermes and Ares are also credited with his paternity.

Other mortals were pursued by Zeus. Danaë, imprisoned by her father, Acrisius, after an oracle had foretold that her son would kill him, bore Perseus to Zeus, who had appeared to her as a shower of gold. Perhaps his most famous son is Heracles, born to the mortal Alcmene after Zeus appeared to her in the guise of her absent husband, Amphitryon, who returned the following day amid much confusion and fathered Iphicles. The twins were born at the same time, though Heracles was in fact one night older than his half-brother. When Heracles finally died and was brought to Olympus, Zeus persuaded Hera to adopt him as her son, after which he married their daughter, Hebe.

In the form of a bull Zeus carried the beautiful Europa, daughter of Agenor, to Crete. There he fathered her three famous sons: Minos, Rhadamanthus, and Sarpedon. Other conquests, and mortal children, included the twins Amphion and Zethus to Antiope, to whom he appeared as a satyr; Dardanos, the son of Electra the Pleiad; Tantalus, the son of the nymph Pluto; Helen, Castor, and Polydeuces by Leda, to whom he appeared as a beautiful white swan; and Boötes, the son of Callisto, whom he turned into a she-bear as punishment for her lack of chastity. Io was approached by Zeus disguised as a cloud, but Hera saw through the deception and turned Io into a white heifer; she also sent a gadfly to sting it. Io fled to Egypt, where Zeus restored her human form and she bore their son, Epaphus. He wooed the nymph Aegina as a flame, later turning her into the island that bears her name, upon which he became a rock. Zeus also had a liking, though not displayed as often compared to other gods, for beautiful youths, his only real exhibition of any homosexual tendency being when he bartered for Ganymede and had the youth carried up to Olympus by an eagle to be made his cupbearer and catamite.

It is impossible to compile an accurate narrative concerning Zeus, for there are very few Greek myths that do not have some connection with the supreme deity. No other deity in any other culture became so entangled in virtually the entire mythology of that culture. Zeus remains the most powerful god of ancient civilization, yet strangely his mythology is merely concerned with the legends of other gods and mortals, save for his struggle to gain supremacy at the start of his life. Various festivals were connected with the worship of Zeus, notably the Pandia (the Festival of All-Zeus), the Diasia, which was celebrated at night and was connected with fertility rites, and the Dipolieia, in which events centered on the commission of a sacrificial act of murder.

Zeus was not normally thought of as having ever died, for that simple task would be impossible of an immortal. However, there was a Cretan belief that Zeus did indeed die and was buried on Mount Youktas, a peak approximately 15 kilometers south of Iráklion that from a certain angle has the uncanny look of a helmeted warrior.

Zeus was often depicted in art either seated on his throne or striding forward, usually clutching his thunderbolt and sometimes accompanied by an eagle. He was also often shown holding a small figure of Victory and wearing a wreath of oak or olive leaves. The most famous representation of Zeus in ancient art, regrettably no longer extant, was the massive statue by Phidias at Olympia. First erected c. 430 B.C., it was almost 12 meters tall, showed the god enthroned, holding a Victory figure and scepter, and was decorated with ebony, ivory, gold, and precious stones. Notable surviving representations are a bronze statuette from Dodona and a larger-than-life-size bronze figure from Cape Artemisium thought to represent either Zeus or his brother, Poseidon.

See also: Alcmene; Amalthea; Apollo; Artemis; Castor; Charites, the; Cronos; Danaë; Demeter; Deucalion; Dione; Dionysos; Dodona; Europa; Ganymede; Hades; Helen; Hera; Heracles; Hermes; Hestia; Io; Jupiter; Leda; Leto; Maia; Metis; Mnemosyne; Olympus; Pandora; Persephone; Polydeuces; Poseidon; Prometheus; Semele; Themis; Titanomachia

Bibliography

The following bibliography lists those books that have been used during the compilation of this volume, along with a multitude of other titles that might be considered useful or essential for further research. Although this bibliography is fairly exhaustive, it by no means covers all the volumes ever written on the subjects of Greek and Roman mythology, as these cultures are perhaps the best represented in literature of all the world cultures. This bibliography also goes further than solely concentrating on volumes connected with myth and legend, and as such includes many essential works on classical history, as from these it is able to determine the importance that the classical deities played on politics and everyday life.

Aldrington, Richard, and Delano Ames (trans.). *The Larousse Encyclopedia of Mythology*. London, 1959.

Anderson, J. K. *Xenophon*. London, 1974.

Andreae, B. *The Art of Rome*. New York, 1977.

Andrewes, A. *Greek Society*. Harmondsworth, 1975.

———. *The Greek Tyrants*. London, 1956.

Arias, P., M. Hirmer, and B. B. Shefton. *History of Greek Vases*. London, 1961.

Ashmole, B. *Architect and Sculptor in Ancient Greece*. London, 1972.

Ashmole, B., and N. Yalouris. *Olympia*. London, 1967.

Athanassiadi-Fowden, P. *Julian and Hellenism*. Oxford, 1981.

Austin, M. M. *The Hellenistic World from Alexander to the Roman Conquest*. Cambridge, 1981.

Austin, Norman. *Archery at the Dark of the Moon: Poetic Problems in Homer's Odyssey*. California and London, 1975.

Bagnall, R. S. and P. Derow. *Greek Historical Documents: The Hellenistic Period*. California, 1981.

Balsdon, J.P.V.D. *Romans and Aliens*. London, 1979.

———. *The Emperor Gaius (Caligula)*. Oxford, 1934.

Barnes, J. *Aristotle*. Oxford, 1982.

Barsby, John. *Bacchides*. Warminster, 1986.

Bassett, S. E. *The Poetry of Homer*. California, 1938.

Beard, M., and M. H. Crawford. *Rome in the Late Republic*. London, 1984.

Behr, C. A. *Aelius Aristides and the Sacred Tales*. Amsterdam, 1981.

Bell, H. I. *Cults and Creeds in Graeco-Roman Egypt*. Liverpool, 1953.

Bell, Robert E. *Dictionary of Classical Mythology: Symbols, Attributes, and Associations*. California and Oxford, 1982.

Bellingham, David. *An Introduction to Greek Mythology*. London, 1996.

Berlitz, C. *Atlantis: The Lost Continent Revealed*. London, 1984.

Bernal, M. *Black Athena II*. London, 1991.

Bespalof, Rachel (trans. Mary McCarthy). *On The Iliad*. New York, 1947.

Beye, Charles R. The Iliad, The Odyssey, *and the Epic Tradition*. New York and London, 1966.

Bieber, M. *The Sculpture of the Hellenistic Age*. New York, 1961.

Blake Tyrrell, W., and Frieda Brown. *Athenian Myths and Institutions*. Oxford, 1991.

Bloch, Raymond. *The Origins of Rome*. London, 1960.

Bloom, Harold (ed.). *Homer's* Odyssey. New York, 1996.

Boardman, J. *The Greeks Overseas*. Harmondsworth, 1964.

———. *Greek Art*. London, 1985.

———. *Greek Sculpture: Archaic Period*. London, 1978.

———. *Greek Sculpture: Classical Period*. London, 1985.

———. *Athenian Black Figure Vases*. London, 1974.

———. *Athenian Red Figure Vases: Archaic Period*. London, 1975.

———. *Greek Gems and Finger Rings*. London, 1971.

Boardman, J. and D. Finn. *The Parthenon and Its Sculptures*. London, 1985.

Boardman, J., J. Griffin, and O. Murray. (eds.). *The Oxford History of the Classical World*. Oxford and New York, 1986.

Boethius, A. *Etruscan and Early Roman Architecture*. Harmondsworth, 1978.

Bonner, S. F. *The Literary Treatises of Dionysius of Halicarnassus*. Cambridge, 1939.

Boulanger, A. *Aelius Aristide*. Paris, 1923.

Bowra, C. M. *Early Greek Elegists*. Cambridge, Mass., 1935.

———. *Pindar*. Oxford, 1964.

———.(ed.). *Oxford Book of Greek Verse*. Oxford, 1930.

Bremmer, J. *The Early Greek Concept of the Soul.* Princeton, 1983.

———.(ed.). *Interpretations of Greek Mythology.* London, 1987.

Brendel, O. J. *Etruscan Art.* Harmondsworth, 1978.

Brewer, E. C. *Dictionary of Phrase and Fable.* London, 1970.

Bright, David F. *Haec Mihi Fingebam: Tibullus in His World.* Leiden, 1978.

Brown, N. O. *Hermes the Thief.* New York, 1969.

Brueton, Diana. *Many Moons.* New York, 1991.

Buckler, J. *The Theban Hegemony, 371–362 B.C.* Harvard, 1980.

Buitron, Diana, and Beth Cohan (eds.). The Odyssey *and Ancient Art: An Epic in Word and Image.* New York, 1992.

Bulfinch, Thomas. *The Golden Age of Myth and Legend.* Ware, 1993.

Burford, A. *Craftsmen in Greek and Roman Society.* London, 1972.

Burkert, W. *Structure and History in Greek Mythology and Ritual.* California, 1979.

———.(trans. W. Raffan). *Greek Religion.* Oxford, 1985.

Burn, A. R. *The Lyric Age of Greece.* London, 1960.

———. *Persia and the Greeks.* London, 1962.

———. *The World of Hesiod.* London, 1936.

Burnet, J. *Early Greek Philosophy.* London, 1908.

Burnett, A. P. *The Art of Bacchylides.* Cambridge, Mass., and London, 1985.

———. *Three Archaic Poets: Archilochus, Alcaeus, and Sappho.* London, 1983.

Cairns, Francis. *Tibullus.* Cambridge, 1979.

Campbell, D. A. *Greek Lyric Poetry.* London, 1967.

Camps, W. A. *An Introduction to Virgil's* Aeneid. Oxford, 1969.

———. *An Introduction to Homer.* Oxford, 1980.

Carne-Ross, D. S. *Pindar.* New Haven, 1985.

Carpenter, R. *Discontinuity in Greek Civilization.* Cambridge, 1966.

———. *Folk Tale, Fiction, and Saga in the Homeric Epics.* California, 1946.

Carpenter, T. H. *Art and Myth in Ancient Greece.* London, 1991.

Carter, Jane B., and Sarah P. Morris (eds.). *The Age of Homer: A Tribute to Emily Townsend Vermeule.* Texas, 1995.

Cartledge, P. A. *Sparta and Laconia.* London, 1979.

Cary, M. *A History of the Greek World from 323 to 146 B.C.* London, 1963.

Cawkwell, G. L. *Philip of Macedon.* London, 1978.

Chadwick, John. *The Mycenaean World.* London and New York, 1976.

Chapman, J. J. *Lucian, Plato, and Greek Morals.* Boston, Mass., 1931.

Charbonneaux, J., R. Martin, and F. Villard. *Hellenistic Art.* London and New York, 1973.

Clarke, Howard. *Homer's Readers: A Historical Introduction to* The Iliad *and* The Odyssey. Delaware, 1981.

Clay, Jenny Strauss. *The Wrath of Athena: Gods and Men in* The Odyssey. Princeton, 1983.

Cohen, Beth (ed.) *The Distaff Side: Representing the Female in Homer's* Odyssey. New York and London, 1995.

Coleman, Robert (trans.). *Eclogues.* Cambridge, 1977.

Comte, Fernand. *Les grandes figures des mythologies.* Paris, 1988.

Connor, W. R. *Theopompus and Fifth Century Athens.* Washington, D.C., 1968.

Cook, A. B. *Zeus.* Cambridge, 1940.

Cook, R. M. *Greek Painted Pottery.* London, 1972.

Cornell, T. and J. Matthews. *Atlas of the Roman World.* Oxford, 1982.

Cottrell, L. *The Bull of Minos.* London, 1955.

Crawford, M. H. *The Roman Republic.* London, 1978.

Daniel, G. *The First Civilizations.* Harmondsworth, 1971.

Davies, J. K. *Democracy and Classical Greece.* London, 1978.

de Camp, L. S. *Lost Continents.* New York, 1970.

de Franciscis, A. *The Buried Cities: Pompeii and Herculaneum.* London, 1978.

de Romilly, J. *L'évolution du pathétique d'Eschyle à Euripide.* Paris, 1980.

———. *Thucydides and Athenian Imperialism.* Oxford, 1963.

de Saint Croix, G.E.M. *The Origins of the Peloponnesian War.* London, 1972.

de Sélincourt, A. (trans.). *Herodotus: The Histories.* Harmondsworth, 1954.

Deiss, J. J. *Herculaneum: A City Returns to the Sun.* London, 1968.

Den Boer, W. *Laconian Studies.* Amsterdam, 1954.

Desborough, V.R.D'A. *The Greek Dark Ages.* London, 1972.

Detienne, M. *Les Jardins d'Adonis.* Paris, 1972.

———.(trans. J. Lloyd). *The Gardens of Adonis.* Hassocks, 1977.

Dickinson, O. *The Aegean Bronze Age.* Cambridge, 1994.

Dicks, D. R. *Early Greek Astronomy to Aristotle.* London, 1970.

Dinsmoor, W. B. *The Architecture of Ancient Greece.* London, 1952.

Dodds, E. R. *The Greeks and the Irrational.* California, 1968.

Donaldson, I. *The Rapes of Lucretia: A Myth and Its Transformations.* Oxford, 1982.

Donnelly, I. *Atlantis: The Antediluvian World.* New York, 1882.

Dover, K. J. *Greek Popular Morality in the Time of Plato and Aristotle.* Oxford, 1974.

———. *Greek Homosexuality.* London, 1978.

Dowden, K. *Religion and the Romans.* London, 1992.

Drews, R. *The End of the Bronze Age.* Princeton, 1993.

———. *The Greek Accounts of Eastern History.* Harvard, 1973.

Duckworth, George E. *The Nature of Roman Comedy.* Princeton, 1952.

Dunbabin, T. J. *The Western Greeks.* Oxford, 1948.

Easterling, P. E. and J. V. Muir (eds.). *Greek Religion and Society.* Cambridge, 1985.

Ebon, M. *Atlantis: The New Evidence.* New York, 1977.

Edelstein, E. J., and L. Edelstein. *Asclepius.* Baltimore, 1945.

Edmonds, J. M. (ed.). *Lyra Graeca* (3 vols.) Cambridge, Mass., and London, 1922–1927.

———. *Greek Elegy and Iambus.* Cambridge, Mass., and London, 1931.

Edwards, Mark W. *Homer: Poet of* The Iliad. Baltimore and London, 1987.

Ehrenberg, V. *The People of Aristophanes.* London, 1951.

Errington, R. M. *The Dawn of Empire: Rome's Rise to World Power.* Ithaca, New York, 1972.

———. *Philopoemen.* Oxford, 1969.

Evelyn-White, H. G. *Hesiod, the Homeric Hymns, and Homerica.* Harvard, 1914.

Fagles, Robert (trans.). *The Iliad.* New York, 1990.

———.(trans.). *The Odyssey.* New York, 1996.

Farnell, L. R. *The Cults of the Greek States* (5 vols.) Oxford, 1896–1909.

———. *Greek Hero Cults and Ideas of Immortality.* Oxford, 1921.

Farquharson, A.S.L. *The Meditations of the Emperor Marcus Antoninus.* Oxford, 1944.

Fenik, B. *Typical Battle Scenes in* The Iliad: *Studies in the Narrative Techniques of Homeric Battle Description.* Wiesbaden, 1968.

———. *Studies in* The Odyssey. Wiesbaden, 1974.

Ferguson, J. *Utopias of the Classical World.* London, 1975.

Ferguson, W. S. *Hellenistic Athens.* London, 1911.

Festugière, A.-J. *Personal Religion Among the Greeks.* California, 1954.

Finley, John H. Jr. *Homer's* Odyssey. Cambridge, Mass., and London, 1978.

Finley, Sir M. I. *The World of Odysseus.* Cambridge, 1954.

———. *Politics in the Ancient World.* Cambridge, 1983.

Fitzgerald, Robert (trans.). *The Aeneid.* Harmondsworth, 1985.

Ford, Andrew. *Homer: The Poetry of the Past.* London, 1992.

Fornara, C. W. *Archaic Times to the End of the Peloponnesian War.* Cambridge, 1983.

Forrest, W. G. *The Emergence of Greek Democracy.* London, 1966.

———. *A History of Sparta.* London, 1980.

Forsdyke, J. *Greece Before Homer.* New York, 1957.

Foxhall, L., and J. K. Davies (eds.). *The Trojan War.* Bristol, 1984.

Fraenkel, Eduard. *Plautinisches im Plautus.* Berlin, 1922.

———. *Horace.* Oxford, 1957.

Fränkel, H. *Early Greek Poetry and Philosophy.* Oxford, 1975.

Frazer, Sir James G. *The Golden Bough.* London and New York, 1922.

———.(ed. and trans.). *Pausanias's Description of Greece.* London, 1898.

———.(trans.). *Apollodorus: The Library.* Harvard University Press, 1921.

Friedländer, P. *Plato: An Introduction.* London, 1958.

Friedrich, P. *The Meaning of Aphrodite.* Chicago, 1978.

Galanopoulos, A. G., and E. Bacon. *Atlantis: The Truth Behind the Legend.* London, 1969.

Gantz, T. *Early Greek Myths.* Baltimore, 1993.

Garzetti, A. (trans. J. R. Foster). *From Tiberius to the Antonines.* London, 1974.

Gibbon, Edward. *Decline and Fall of the Roman Empire.* London, 1776–1788.

Goold, G. P. *Catullus.* London, 1983.

Gordon, R. L. (ed.). *Myth, Religion, and Society.* Cambridge, 1981.

Goring, Rosemary (ed.). *Dictionary of Beliefs and Religions.* Ware, 1995.

Gransden, K. W. *Virgil: The Aeneid.* Cambridge, 1990.

Grant, F. C. *Hellenistic Religions.* Indianapolis, 1953.

Grant, M. *Cities of Vesuvius: Pompeii and Herculaneum.* London, 1971.

Grant, Michael. *Myths of the Greeks and Romans.* London, 1962.

———. *The Roman World.* London, 1960.

Graves, Robert. *The Greek Myths* (2 vols.) Harmondsworth, 1960.

———. *The White Goddess.* London, 1948.

Griffin, J. *Homer.* Oxford, 1980.

———. *Homer on Life and Death.* Oxford, 1980.

———. *Virgil.* Oxford, 1986.

———. *Homer: The Odyssey.* Cambridge, 1987.

Griffin, Miriam. *Nero: The End of a Dynasty.* London, 1984.

Grimal, P., et al. *Hellenism and the Rise of Rome.* London, 1968.

Gruen, E. S. *The Hellenistic World and the Coming of Rome.* California, 1984.

———. *The Last Generation of the Roman Republic.* California, 1974.

Guerber, H. A. *Greece and Rome—Myths and Legends.* London, 1994.

Guiley, Rosemary Ellen. *Moonscapes: A Celebration of Lunar Astronomy, Magic, Legend, and Lore.* New York, 1991.

Guthrie, W.K.C. *The Greeks and Their Gods*. London, 1949.

———. *Orpheus and Greek Religion*. London, 1935.

Hainsworth, J. B. *The Flexibility of the Homeric Formula*. Oxford, 1968.

Hamilton, J. R. *Alexander the Great*. London, 1973.

Hammond, Martin. *The Iliad*. Harmondsworth and New York, 1987.

Hanfmann, G.M.A. *Roman Art*. London and New York, 1964.

Harding, P. *From the End of the Peloponnesian War to the Battle of Ipsus*. Cambridge, 1985.

Harris, H. A. *Greek Athletes and Athletics*. London, 1964.

———. *Sport in Greece and Rome*. London, 1972.

Harris, W. V. *War and Imperialism in Republican Rome, 327–370 B.C.* Oxford, 1979.

———.(ed.). *The Imperialism of the Roman Republic*. Rome, 1984.

Harrison, J. E. *Themis*. Cambridge, 1927.

Harvey, Sir Paul. *Oxford Classical Dictionary*. Oxford, 1948.

Haspels, C.V.E. *The Highlands of Phrygia: Sites and Monuments*. Princeton, 1971.

Havelock, C. M. *Hellenistic Art*. London, 1971.

Havelock, E. A. *The Literate Revolution in Greece and Its Cultural Consequences*. Princeton, 1982.

Hawkes, J. *Atlas of Ancient Archaeology*. New York, 1974.

Hazlitt, William. *The Classical Gazetteer*. London, 1851.

Henderson, B. W. *The Life and Principate of the Emperor Nero*. London, 1903.

Henle, Jane. *Greek Myths: A Vase Painter's Notebook*. Indiana, 1973.

Henig, M. (ed.). *A Handbook of Roman Art*. Oxford, 1983.

Hexter, Ralph. *A Guide to* The Odyssey: *A Commentary on the English Translation of Robert Fitzgerald*. New York, 1993.

Higgins, R. A. *Greek and Roman Jewellery*. London, 1961.

———. *Greek Terracottas*. London, 1963.

Higham, T. F., and C. M. Bowra (eds.). *Oxford Book of Greek Verse in Translation*. Oxford, 1938.

Hignett, C. *History of the Athenian Constitution*. Oxford, 1952.

Hill, G. F. (rev. R. Meiggs and A. Andrewes). *Sources for Greek History, 478–431 B.C.* Oxford, 1951.

Hogan, James C. *A Guide to* The Iliad: *Based on the Translation by Robert Fitzgerald*. New York, 1979.

Hooker, J. T. *Mycenaean Greece*. London, 1976.

Hopkins, K. *Conquerors and Slaves*. Cambridge, 1978.

Hornblower, Jane. *Hieronymus of Cardia*. Oxford, 1981.

Hornblower, S. *The Greek World, 479–323 B.C.* London and New York, 1991.

Hubbard, Margaret. *Propertius*. London, 1974.

Hunter, R. L. *The New Comedy of Greece and Rome*. Cambridge, 1985.

Hutchinson, R. W. *Prehistoric Crete*. Harmondsworth, 1962.

Ions, Veronica. *The World's Mythology in Color*. New Jersey, 1974.

Isager, S. and M. H. Hansen. *Aspects of Athenian Society in the Fourth Century B.C.* Odense, 1975.

Jacoby, F. *Atthis*. Oxford, 1949.

———. *Die Fragmente der griechischen Historiker* (14 vols.). Leiden, 1923–1958.

Jaeger, W. *The Theology of the Early Greek Philosophers*. Oxford, 1947.

James, Peter. *The Sunken Kingdom: The Atlantis Mystery Solved*. London, 1995.

Jay, Peter (ed.). *The Greek Anthology*. London, 1973.

Jeffery, L. H. *Archaic Greece*. London, 1976.

Jenkyns, R.H.A. *Three Classical Poets*. London, 1982.

Jones, A.H.M. *Athenian Democracy*. Oxford, 1957.

———. *The Greek City from Alexander to Justinian*. Oxford, 1966.

Jones, C. P. *Plutarch and Rome*. Oxford, 1971.

———. *The Roman World of Dio Chrysostom*. Cambridge, Mass., 1978.

Jones, Peter V. *Homer's* Odyssey: *A Companion to the Translation of Richard Lattimore*. Bristol, 1988.

Jowett, B. *The Dialogues of Plato*. Oxford, 1892.

Katz, Marylin A. *Penelope's Renown: Meaning and Indeterminacy in* The Odyssey. Princeton, 1991.

Kerényi, C. *The Heroes of the Greeks*. London, 1959.

———. *The Gods of the Greeks*. London, 1974.

King, Katherine Callen. *Achilles: Paradigms of the War Hero from Homer to the Middle Ages*. California and London, 1987.

Kirk, G. S. *The Nature of Greek Myths*. Harmondsworth, 1974.

———. *The Songs of Homer*. Cambridge, 1962.

———. *Homer and the Epic*. Cambridge, 1965.

———. *Myth: Its Meaning and Functions in Ancient and Other Cultures*. California, 1970.

Kirkwood, G. M. *Early Greek Monody*. Cornell, 1974.

Kraut, R. (ed.). *The Cambridge Companion to Plato*. Cambridge, 1992.

Kraay, C. M., and M. Hirmer. *Greek Coins*. London, 1966.

Kurtz, D. C., and J. Boardman. *Greek Burial Customs*. London, 1971.

Lacey, W. K. *The Family in Classical Greece*. London, 1968.

Laistner, M.L.W. *The Greater Roman Historians*. California, 1963.

Lamberton, Robert. *Homer the Theologian: Neoplatonist Allegorical Reading and the Growth of the Epic Tradition*. California and London, 1986.

Lane Fox, R. *Alexander the Great*. London, 1973.

———. *The Search for Alexander*. Boston, Mass., 1980.

Lattimore, Richmond. *The Poetry of Greek Tragedy.* Baltimore, 1958.

———. *Story Patterns in Greek Tragedy.* London, 1964.

Lawrence, A. W. *Greek Architecture.* Harmondsworth, 1957.

———. *Greek and Roman Sculpture.* London, 1972.

Lawrence, T. E. (trans.). *Homer: The Odyssey.* New York, 1932.

Leaf, W. *Homer and History.* London, 1915.

———.(ed.). *The Iliad* (2 vols.). London, 1902.

Lee, Guy (trans.). *Eclogues.* Liverpool, 1980.

Lee, H.D.P. (trans.). *Plato: The Republic.* Harmondsworth, 1955.

———.(trans.). *Plato: Timaeus and Critias.* Harmondsworth, 1971.

Leeman, A. D. *Orationis Ratio.* Amsterdam, 1963.

Lefkowitz, M. *Women in Greek Myth.* London, 1986.

Lesky, A. *Greek Tragic Poetry.* Yale, 1983.

———. (trans. J. Willis and C. de Heer). *History of Greek Literature.* London, 1966.

Lévi-Strauss, C. *Anthropologie structurale.* Paris, 1958.

———. *Introduction to a Science of Mythology* (4 vols.). London, 1964–1981.

Levick, B. M. *Tiberius the Politician.* London, 1976.

Liebeschuetz, J.H.W.G. *Continuity and Change in Roman Religion.* Oxford, 1979.

Linforth, I. M. *The Arts of Orpheus.* California, 1941.

Lloyd-Jones, Sir Hugh. *The Justice of Zeus.* California, 1984.

———.(trans.). *Oresteia.* London, 1979.

Luce, J. V. *The End of Atlantis.* London, 1969.

Lullies, R., and M. Hirmer. *Greek Sculpture.* London, 1960.

Lyne, R.O.A.M. *Further Voices in Virgil's* Aeneid. Oxford, 1987.

MacCulloch, John A., and Louis H. Gray. *The Mythology of All Races* (13 vols.) New York, 1922.

Macdowell, D. M. *The Law of Classical Athens.* London, 1978.

Mackenzie, Donald A. *Crete and Pre-Hellenic Myths and Legends.* London, 1995.

Magie, D. *Roman Rule in Asia Minor.* Princeton, 1950.

Marrou, H. I. *History of Education in Antiquity.* New York, 1956.

Martin, R. *Tacitus.* London, 1981.

Mavor, J. W. *Voyage to Atlantis.* London, 1969.

McLeish, Kenneth. *Myth: Myths and Legends of the World Explored.* London, 1996.

———. *Theatre of Aristophanes.* London, 1980.

Meiggs, R. *The Athenian Empire.* Oxford, 1972.

———. *Trees and Timber in the Ancient Mediterranean World.* Oxford, 1982.

Mikalson, J. D. *Athenian Popular Religion.* North Carolina, 1983.

Millar, F. *The Emperor in the Roman World.* London, 1977.

———. *A Study of Cassius Dio.* Oxford, 1974.

Millar, F., and E. Segal (eds.). *Caesar Augustus.* Oxford, 1984.

Momigliano, A. (trans. W. D. Hogarth). *Claudius: The Emperor and His Achievement.* Cambridge, 1961.

———. *The Conflict Between Paganism and Christianity in the Fourth Century.* Oxford, 1963.

Monro, D. B., and T. W. Allen (eds.). *Homeri Opera.* London, 1920.

Morford, Mark, and Robert Lenardon. *Classical Mythology.* New York, 1991.

Morrow, G. R. *Plato's Cretan City.* Princeton, 1960.

Moulton, Carroll. *Similes in the Homeric Poems.* Göttingen, 1977.

Muck, O. *The Secret of Atlantis.* London, 1979.

Mueller, Martin (ed. Claude Rawson). *The Iliad.* London, 1984.

Murnaghan, Sheila. *Disguise and Recognition in* The Odyssey. Princeton, 1987.

Murray, Gilbert. *Euripides and His Age.* Oxford, 1965.

———. *Greek Studies.* Oxford, 1946.

Murray, O. *Early Greece.* Harmondsworth, 1980.

Mylonas, G. E. *Eleusis and the Eleusinian Mysteries.* London, 1962.

Myrsiades, Kostas (ed.). *Approaches to Teaching Homer's* Iliad *and* Odyssey. New York, 1987.

Nagler, Michael. *Spontaneity and Tradition: A Study in the Oral Art of Homer.* California and London, 1974.

Nagy, Gregory. *The Best of the Achaeans: Concepts of the Hero in Archaic Greek Poetry.* Baltimore and London, 1979.

Nilsson, M. P. *The Mycenaean Origin of Greek Mythology.* California, 1932.

———. *Greek Popular Religion.* Columbia, 1940.

———. *Homer and Mycenae.* London, 1933.

Nock, A. D. *Conversion.* Oxford, 1933.

Norden, E. *Die antike Kunstprosa.* Leipzig, 1915.

Ogilvie, R. M. *Early Rome and the Etruscans.* London, 1976.

———. *The Romans and the Gods.* London, 1969.

Olsen, S. Douglas. *Blood and Iron: Stories and Storytelling in Homer's* Odyssey. Leiden, New York, and Köln, 1995.

Otto, W. F. (trans. M. Hadas). *The Homeric Gods.* London, 1955.

Page, D. L. *Sappho and Alcaeus.* Oxford, 1955.

———. *Further Greek Epigrams.* Cambridge, 1981.

Parke, H. W. *Greek Oracles.* London, 1967.

———. *Festivals of the Athenians.* London, 1977.

Parke, H. W., and D.E.W. Wormell. *The Delphic Oracle.* Oxford, 1956.

Parker, Robert. *Miasma: Pollution and Purification in Early Greek Religion.* Oxford, 1983.

Parry, Adam M. *The Language of Achilles and Other Papers.* Oxford, 1989.

Parry, Milman (ed. Adam Parry). *The Making of Homeric Verse: The Collected Papers of Milman Parry.* Oxford, 1971.

Pearson, L. *Early Ionian Historians.* Oxford, 1939.

———. *The Lost Histories of Alexander the Great.* New York, 1960.

Pellegrino, C. *Unearthing Atlantis.* New York, 1991.

Peradotto, John. *Man in the Middle Voice: Name and Narration in* The Odyssey. Princeton, 1990.

Perowne, S. *Roman Mythology.* Twickenham, 1983.

Perry, B. E. *The Ancient Romances.* California, 1967.

Pinsent, John. *Greek Mythology.* London, 1969.

Platner, S. B. and Ashby, T. *Topographical Dictionary of Ancient Rome.* Oxford, 1929.

Podlecki, A. J. *The Early Greek Poets and Their Themes.* Vancouver, 1984.

Pollitt, J. J. *Art in the Hellenistic Age.* Cambridge, 1986.

———. *Art of Rome.* Cambridge, 1983.

Pomeroy, Sarah B. *Goddesses, Whores, Wives, and Slaves.* New York, 1975.

Pritchard, J. B. (ed.). *Ancient Near Eastern Texts Relating to the Old Testament.* Princeton, 1968.

Ramage, E. S. (ed.). *Atlantis: Fact or Fiction?.* Bloomington, 1978.

Rawson, E. *The Spartan Tradition in European Thought.* Oxford, 1969.

Reardon, B. P. *Courants Littéraires grecs des IIe at IIIe siècles.* Paris, 1971.

Redfield, J. M. *Nature and Culture in* The Iliad: *The Tragedy of Hector.* Chicago, 1975.

Reinhardt, Karl. *Sophocles.* Oxford, 1978.

Rice Holmes, T. *The Roman Republic* (3 vols.). Oxford, 1923.

———. *The Architect of the Roman Empire* (2 vols.). Oxford, 1928–1931.

Richter, G.M.A. *Handbook of Greek Art.* London, 1974.

———. *Sculpture and Sculptors of the Greeks.* Oxford, 1971.

———. *Portraits of the Greeks.* Oxford, 1984.

Rieu, E. V. (trans.). *The Iliad.* Harmondsworth, 1950.

Robertson, D. S. *A Handbook of Greek and Roman Architecture.* Cambridge, 1943.

Robertson, M. *A History of Greek Art.* Cambridge, 1975.

———. *Shorter History of Greek Art.* Cambridge, 1981.

Rohde, E. (trans. W. B. Hillis). *Psyche.* London, 1925.

———. *Der griechische Roman.* Leipzig, 1876.

Rose, H. J. *A Handbook of Greek Mythology.* London, 1928.

———. *Ancient Roman Religion.* London, 1949.

Rossi, L. *Trajan's Column and the Dacian Wars.* London and New York, 1971.

Rostovtzeff, M. I. *The Social and Economic History of the Hellenistic World* (3 vols.). Oxford, 1941.

Rubens, Beaty, and Oliver Taplin. *An Odyssey Round Odysseus: The Man and His Story Traced Through Time and Place.* London, 1989.

Russell, D. A. *Plutarch.* London, 1972.

Saccon, A. *Corpus delle Iscrizioni Vascolari in Lineare B.* Rome, 1974.

Sacks, K. *Polybius and the Writing of History.* California, 1981.

Sakellariou, M. P. *La Migration grecque en Ionie.* Athens, 1958.

Salmon, E. T. *Roman Colonisation.* London, 1969.

Salmon, J. B. *Wealthy Corinth.* Oxford, 1984.

Sandbach, F. H. *The Comic Theatre of Greece and Rome.* London, 1977.

Saunders, T. J. (trans.). *Plato: The Laws.* Harmondsworth, 1970.

Schaps, David M. *Economic Rights of Women in Ancient Greece.* Edinburgh, 1979.

Schefold, K. *Myth and Legend in Early Greek Art.* London, 1966.

Schein, S. L. *The Mortal Hero: An Introduction to Homer's* Iliad. California and London, 1984.

———. (ed.). *Reading* The Odyssey: *Selected Interpretive Essays.* Princeton, 1995.

Schmidt, E. *The Great Altar of Pergamon.* London, 1965.

Scott, John A. *The Unity of Homer.* California, 1921.

Scott-Kilvert, I. (trans.). *The Rise and Fall of Athens: Nine Greek Lives by Plutarch.* Harmondsworth, 1960.

Scramuzza, V. M. *The Emperor Claudius.* Cambridge, Mass., 1940.

Scullard, H. H. *History of the Roman World 753–146 B.C.* London, 1981.

———. *From the Gracchi to Nero.* London, 1982.

———. *Festivals and Ceremonies of the Roman Republic.* London, 1981.

Seaford, R. *Pompeii.* London, 1978.

Seager, R. *Tiberius.* London, 1972.

Segal, C. *The Theme of the Mutilation of the Corpse in* The Iliad. Leiden, 1971.

Sellar, W. Y. *Virgil.* Oxford, 1877.

Sergent, B. *Homosexuality in Greek Myth.* London, 1987.

Settegast, M. *Plato Prehistorian.* New York, 1990.

Seznec, J. *The Survival of the Pagan Gods: The Mythological Tradition and Its Place in Renaissance Humanism and Art.* New York, 1961.

Shewring, Walter. *The Odyssey.* Oxford, 1980.

Shive, David M. *Naming Achilles.* New York, 1987.

Silk, Michael. *The Iliad.* Cambridge, 1987.

Simpson, R. Hope. *Mycenaean Greece.* New Jersey, 1981.

Singh, M. *The Sun in Myth and Art.* London, 1993.

Slatkin, Maura M. *The Power of Thetis: Allusion and Interpretation in* The Iliad. California and London, 1991.

Snell, Bruno. *The Discovery of the Mind.* Harvard, 1953.

Snodgrass, A. M. *The Dark Age of Greece.* Edinburgh, 1971.

———. *Archaic Greece.* London, 1980.

Spence, L. *The Problem of Atlantis.* New York, 1924.

———. *Introduction to Mythology.* London, 1994.

Stadter, P. A. *Arrian of Nicomedia.* Chapel Hill, 1980.

Stanford, W. B. *The Ulysses Theme: A Study in the Adaptability of a Traditional Hero.* Oxford, 1983.

Staveley, E. S. *Greek and Roman Voting and Elections.* London, 1972.

Stewart, J. A. *The Myths of Plato.* London, 1905.

Strong, D. *Greek and Roman Gold and Silver Plate.* London, 1966.

Syme, Sir Ronald. *The Roman Revolution.* Oxford, 1939.

———. *Tacitus* (2 vols.). Oxford, 1958.

———. *History of Ovid.* Oxford, 1978.

Taplin, O. *The Stagecraft of Aeschylus.* Oxford, 1977.

———. *Greek Tragedy in Action.* London, 1978.

———. *Homeric Soundings: The Shaping of* The Iliad. New York and London, 1992.

Tarn, W. W., and G. T. Griffith. *Hellenistic Civilisation.* London, 1952.

Taylor, L. R. *The Divinity of the Roman Emperor.* Middletown, 1931.

Tomlinson, R. A. *Argos and the Argolid.* London, 1972.

Toynbee, J.M.C. *Art of the Romans.* London and New York, 1965.

Tracy, Stephen V. *The Story of* The Odyssey. Princeton, 1990.

Trendall, A. D., and T.B.L. Webster. *Illustrations of Greek Drama.* London, 1971.

Trypanis, C. A. (ed.). *Penguin Book of Greek Verse.* Harmondsworth, 1971.

Vermeule, Emily T. *Greece in the Bronze Age.* Chicago and London, 1964.

Vernant, J.-P. (trans. Janet Lloyd). *Myth and Thought Among the Greeks.* New York, 1990.

Versnel, H. S. (ed.). *Faith, Hope, and Worship: Aspects of Religious Mentality in the Ancient World.* Leiden, 1981.

Vickers, Brian. *Towards Greek Tragedy.* London, 1973.

Wace, A.J.B., and F. H. Stubbings (eds.). *A Companion to Homer.* London, 1962.

Wade-Gery, H. T. *The Poet of* The Iliad. Cambridge, 1952.

Walbank, F. W. *The Hellenistic World.* London, 1981.

———. *Polybius.* California, 1972.

———. *Philip V of Macedon.* Hamden, Conn., 1967.

Walcot, P. *Hesiod and the Near East.* Cardiff, 1966.

Wardman, A. *Religion and Statecraft at Rome.* London, 1982.

Warmington, B. H. *Nero, Reality, and Legend.* London, 1969.

Warner, Rex. *Men and Gods.* Harmondsworth, 1952.

Webster, T.B.L. *Athenian Culture and Society.* London, 1973.

———. *Hellenistic Art.* London, 1967.

Weil, Simone (trans. M. McCarthy). *L'Iliade ou le poème de la force.* New York, 1940.

Welles, C. B. *Alexander and the Hellenistic World.* Toronto, 1970.

Wellesley, K. *The Long Year: A.D. 69.* London, 1975.

Wells, Robert (trans.). Georgics. Manchester, 1982.

West, D. *The Imagery and Poetry of Lucretius.* Edinburgh, 1969.

———. *Reading Horace.* Edinburgh, 1967.

West, M. L. (trans.). Theogony. Oxford, 1966.

———. *Works and Days.* Oxford, 1978.

———. *Studies in Greek Elegy and Iambus.* Berlin, 1974.

Westlake, H. D. *Thessaly in the Fourth Century* B.C. London, 1935.

Wheeler, A. L. *Catullus and the Traditions of Ancient Poetry.* California, 1934.

Whitman, Cedric H. *Homer and the Heroic Tradition.* Cambridge, Mass., and London, 1958.

Wilkinson, L. P. *Ovid Recalled.* Cambridge, 1955.

———. *Ovid Surveyed.* Cambridge, 1962.

———. *The Georgics of Virgil.* Cambridge, 1969.

———. Georgics. Harmondsworth, 1982.

Willcock, M. M. *A Companion to* The Iliad: *Based on the Translation by Richard Lattimore.* Chicago and London, 1976.

———.(ed.). The Iliad *of Homer* (2 vols.). London, 1978–1984.

Willetts, R. F. *Aristocratic Society in Ancient Crete.* London, 1955.

Willis, Roy (ed.). *World Mythology: The Illustrated Guide.* London, 1993.

Winnington-Ingram, R. P. *Sophocles: An Interpretation.* Cambridge, 1980.

Wiseman, T. P. *Catullus and His World.* Cambridge, 1985.

Wood, Robert. *An Essay on the Original Genius and Writings of Homer.* London, 1769 (reprint Philadelphia, 1976).

Woodhouse, W. J. *The Composition of Homer's Odyssey.* Oxford, 1930.

Wright, John. *Essays on* The Iliad: *Selected Modern Criticism.* Bloomington and London, 1978.

Zuntz, G. *Persephone.* Oxford, 1971.

One of the best paperback sources for the classical texts is the Penguin Classics series. The following volumes are essential core materials for any student of the classical Greek and Roman cultures. All are available within the Penguin Classics paperback series.

Aeschylus (trans. Robert Fagles). *The Oresteia.*

———. (trans. Philip Vellacott). *The Oresteian Trilogy.*

———. (trans. Philip Vellacott). *Prometheus Bound and Other Plays.*

Aesop (trans. S. A. Handford). *Fables.*

Ammanius (ed. William R. Hamilton). *The Later Roman Empire (A.D. 354–378).*

Apollonius of Rhodes (trans. E. V. Rieu). *The Voyage of Argo.*

Apuleius (trans. Robert Graves; rev. Michael Grant). *The Golden Ass.*

Aristophanes (trans. David Barrett and Alan Sommerstein). *Birds/Wealth/Knights/Peace/The Assembly Women.*

———. (trans. Alan Sommerstein). *Lysistrata/The Acharnians/The Clouds.*

———. (trans. David Barrett). *Wasps/The Poet and the Women/The Frogs.*

Aristotle (trans. Hugh Lawson-Tancred). *The Art of Rhetoric.*

———. (trans. P. J. Rhodes). *The Athenian Constitution.*

———. (trans. Hugh Lawson-Tancred). *De Anima (On the Soul).*

———. (trans. J.A.K. Thomson; rev. Hugh Tredennick). *The Ethics: The Nicomachean Ethics.*

———. (trans. T. A. Sinclair; rev. Trevor J. Saunders). *The Politics.*

Arrian (trans. Aubrey de Selincourt; rev. J. R. Hamilton). *The Campaigns of Alexander.*

Caesar (trans. Jane F. Gardner). *The Civil War.*

———. (trans. S. A. Handford). *The Conquest of Gaul.*

Cassius Dio (trans. Ian Scott-Kilvert). *The Roman History.*

Catullus (trans. Peter Whigham). *The Poems of Catullus.*

Cicero (ed. Michael Grant). *Murder Trials.*

———. (trans. Horace C. P. McGregor). *The Nature of the Gods.*

———. (trans. Michael Grant). *On Government.*

———. (trans. Michael Grant). *On the Good Life.*

———. (trans. D. R. Shackleton Bailey). *Selected Letters.*

———. (trans. Michael Grant). *Selected Works.*

Euripides (trans. Philip Vellacott). *Alcestis/Iphegenia in Tauris/Hippolytus.*

———. (trans. Philip Vellacott). *The Bacchae/Ion/The Women of Troy/Helen.*

———. (trans. Philip Vellacott). *Medeä/Hecabe/Electra/Heracles.*

———. (trans. Philip Vellacott). *Orestes and Other Plays.*

Herodotus (trans. Aubrey de Selincourt; rev. A. R. Burn). *The Histories.*

Hesiod and Theognis (trans. Dorothea Wender). *Theogony/Works and Dyas/Elegies.*

Hippocrates (ed. G.E.R. Lloyd; trans. J. Chadwick, et al.). *Hippocratic Writings.*

Homer (trans. Robert Fagles). *The Iliad.*

———. (trans. Martin Hammond). *The Iliad.*

———. (trans. E. V. Rieu). *The Iliad.*

———. (trans. E. V. Rieu; rev. Dominic Rieu). *The Odyssey.*

Horace (trans. W. G. Shepherd). *The Complete Odes and Epodes.*

Horace and Persius (trans. Niall Rudd). *The Satires.*

Justinian (trans. Colin Kolbert). *The Digest of Roman War.*

Juvenal (trans. Peter Green). *The Sixteen Satires.*

Livy (trans. Aubrey de Selincourt). *The Early History of Rome.*

———. (trans. Betty Radice). *Rome and Italy.*

———. (trans. Henry Bettenson). *Rome and the Mediterranean.*

———. (trans. Aubrey de Selincourt). *The War with Hannibal.*

Longus (trans. Paul Turner). *Daphnis and Chloe.*

Lucretius (trans. R. E. Latham). *On the Nature of the Universe.*

Martial (trans. James Michie). *The Epigrams.*

Menander (trans. Norma P. Miller). *Plays and Fragments.*

Ovid (trans. Peter Green). *The Erotic Poems.*

———. (trans. Peter Green). *The Poems of Exile.*

———. (trans. Harold Isbell). *Heroides.*

———. (trans. Mary M. Innes). *The Metamorphoses.*

Pausanius (trans. Peter Levi). *Guide to Greece* (2 vols.).

Petronius and Seneca (trans. J. P. Sullivan). *The Satyricon/Apocolocyntosis.*

Pindar (trans. C. M. Bowra). *The Odes.*

Plato (ed. Trevor J. Saunders; trans. T. J. Saunders, et al.). *Early Socratic Dialogues.*

———. (trans. Walter Hamilton). *Gorgias.*

———. (trans. Hugh Tredennick). *The Last Days of Socrates.*

———. (trans. Trevor J. Saunders). *The Laws.*

———. (trans. Walter Hamilton). *Phaedrus and Letters VII and VIII.*

———. (trans. Robin A.H. Waterfield). *Philebus.*

———. (trans. W.K.C. Guthrie). *Protagoras/Meno.*

———. (trans. Desmond Lee). *The Republic.*

———. (trans. Walter Hamilton). *The Symposium.*

———. (trans. Robin Waterfield). *Theaetutus.*

———. (trans. Desmond Lee). *Timaeus and Critias.*

Plautus (trans. E. F. Watling). *The Pot of Gold and Other Plays.*

———. (trans. E. F. Watling). *The Rope and Other Plays.*

Pliny the Elder (trans. John F. Healy). *Natural History.*

Pliny the Younger (trans. Betty Radice). *The Letters of the Younger Pliny.*

Plutarch (trans. Ian Scott-Kilvert). *The Age of Alexander.*

———. (ed. Ian Kidd; trans. Robin Waterfield). *Essays.*

———. (trans. Rex Warner). *The Fall of the Roman Republic.*

———. (trans. Ian Scott-Kilvert). *The Makers of Rome.*

———. (trans. Richard J.A. Talbert). *Plutarch on Sparta.*

———. (trans. C.B.R. Pelling). *The Rise and Crisis of Rome.*

———. (trans. Ian Scott-Kilvert). *The Rise and Fall of Athens.*

Polybius (trans. Ian Scott-Kilvert). *The Rise of the Roman Empire.*

Propertius (trans. W. G. Shepard). *The Poems.*

Quintus Curtis Rufus (trans. John Yardley). *The History of Alexander.*

Seneca (trans. E. F. Watling). *Four Tragedies and Octavia.*

———. (trans. Robin Campbell). *Letters from a Stoic.*

Sophocles (trans. E. F. Watling). *Electra and Other Plays.*

———. (trans. Robert Fagles). *The Three Theban Plays.*

———. (trans. E. F. Watling). *The Theban Plays.*

Suetonius (trans. Robert Graves; rev. Michael Grant). *The Twelve Caesars.*

Tacitus (trans. H. Mattingley; rev. S. A. Handford). *The Agricola/The Germania.*

———. (trans. Michael Grant). *The Annals of Imperial Rome.*

———. (trans. Kenneth Wellesley). *The Histories.*

Theocritus (trans. Robert Wells). *The Idylls.*

Thucydides (trans. Rex Warner). *History of the Peloponnesian War.*

Virgil (trans. W. F. Jackson Knight). *The Aeneid.*

———. (trans. Robert Fitzgerald). *The Aeneid.*

———. (trans. David West). *The Aeneid.*

———. (trans. Guy Lee). *The Eclogues.*

———. (trans. L. P. Wilkinson). *The Georgics.*

Xenophon (trans. Hugh Tredennick and Robin Waterfield). *Conversations of Socrates.*

———. (trans. Rex Warner). *History of My Times.*

———. (trans. Rex Warner). *The Persian Expedition.*

Other Penguin Classics that are of interest and use to the classical student are as follows.

Barnes, Jonathan (trans. and ed.). *Early Greek Philosophy.*

Birley, Anthony (trans.). *Lives of the Later Caesars.*

Dorsch, T. S. (trans.). *Classical Literary Criticism.*

Gibbon, Edward (ed. Dero A. Saunders). *The Decline and Fall of the Roman Empire* (abridged version).

Stoneman, Richard (trans.). *The Greek Alexander Romance.*

Sullivan, John, and Anthony Boyle (eds.). *Roman Poets of the Early Empire.*

Appendix 1: Chronologies for Ancient Greece and Rome

Ancient Greece Chronology

c. 1600–1200 B.C. The first Greek civilization, known as Mycenaean, owed much to the Minoan civilization of Crete and may have been produced by the intermarriage of Greek-speaking invaders with the original inhabitants.

c. 1300 B.C. A new wave of invasions began. The Achaeans overran Greece and Crete, destroying the Minoan and Mycenaean civilizations and penetrating Asia Minor.

1000 B.C. Aeolians, Ionians, and Dorians had settled in the area that is now Greece. Many independent city-states, such as Sparta and Athens, had developed.

c. 800–500 B.C. During the Archaic period, Ionian Greeks led the development of philosophy, science, and lyric poetry. The Greeks became great sea traders and founded colonies around the coasts of the Mediterranean Sea and the Black Sea, from Asia Minor in the east to Spain in the west.

776 B.C. The first Olympic games held.

594 B.C. The laws of Solon took the first step toward a more democtratic society.

c. 560–510 B.C. The so-called tyranny of the Pisistratids in Athens was typical of a predemocratic stage that many Greek cities passed through after overturning aristocratic rule.

545 B.C. From this date the Ionian cities in Asia Minor fell under the dominion of the Persian Empire.

507 B.C. Cleisthenes, ruler of Athens, is credited with the establishment of democracy. Other cities followed this lead, but Sparta remained unique, a state in which a ruling race, organized on military lines, dominated the surrounding population.

500–338 B.C. The classical period in ancient Greece.

499–494 B.C. The Ionian cities, aided by Athens, revolted unsuccessfully against the Persians.

490 B.C. Darius of Persia invaded Greece, only to be defeated by the Athenians at Marathon and forced to withdraw.

480 B.C. Another invasion by the Persian Emperor Xerxes, after being delayed by the heroic defence of Thermopylae by 300 Spartans, was defeated at sea off Salamis.

479 B.C. The Persians defeated on land at Plataea.

478 B.C. The Ionian cities, now liberated, formed a naval alliance with Athens, the Delian League.

455–429 B.C. Under Pericles, the democratic leader of Athens, Greek drama, sculpture, and architecture were at their peak.

433 B.C. The Parthenon in Athens was completed.

431–404 B.C. The Peloponnesian War destroyed the political power of Athens, but Athenian thought and culture remained influential. Sparta became the leading Greek power.

370 B.C. The philosopher Plato opened his Academy in Athens.

338 B.C. Phillip II of Macedon (359–336 B.C.) took advantage of the wars between the city-states and conquered Greece.

336–323 B.C. Rule of Phillip's son, Alexander the Great. Alexander overthrew the Persian Empire, conquered Syria and Egypt, and invaded the Punjab. After his death, his empire was divided among his generals, but his conquests had spread Greek culture across the known world.

280 B.C. Achaean League of 12 Greek city-states formed in an attempt to maintain independence against Macedon, Egypt, and Rome.

146 B.C. Greece became part of the Roman Empire. Under Roman rule Greece remained a cultural center and Hellenic culture remained influential.

Ancient Rome Chronology

753 B.C. According to tradition, Rome was founded.

510 B.C. The Etruscan dynasty of the Tarquins was expelled and a republic established, with power concentrated in patrician hands.

450 B.C. Publication of the law code contained in the Twelve Tables.

396 B.C. Capture of Etruscan Veii, 15 kilometers (9 miles) north of Rome.

387 B.C. Rome sacked by Gauls.

Index

345